Theology of Wagner's *Ring* Cycle I

Theology of Wagner's *Ring* Cycle I

The Genesis and Development of the Tetralogy and the Appropriation of Sources, Artists, Philosophers, and Theologians

Richard H. Bell

James Clarke & Co

For Jack

JAMES CLARKE & CO

P.O. Box 60
Cambridge
CB1 2NT
United Kingdom

www.jamesclarke.co
publishing@jamesclarke.co

Paperback ISBN: 978 0 227 17747 1
PDF ISBN: 978 0 227 90746 7

British Library Cataloguing in Publication Data
A record is available from the British Library

First published by James Clarke & Co, 2021

Copyright © Richard H. Bell, 2020

Published by arrangement
with Cascade Books

All rights reserved. No part of this edition may be reproduced, stored electronically or in any retrieval system, or transmitted in any form or by any means, electronic, mechanical, photocopying, recording, or otherwise, without prior written permission from the Publisher (permissions@jamesclarke.co).

Contents

List of Figures | vi
Preface | vii
Acknowledgements | ix
Abbreviations | xi

1 Introduction | 1
2 Genesis and Development of the *Ring* | 10
3 Wagner's Use of Germanic and Norse Sources | 46
4 The *Ring* and the Greeks | 100
5 The *Ring*, Drama, Poetry, and Literature | 129
6 The *Ring* and German Idealism | 173
7 Wagner and the New Testament | 252

Bibliography | 263
Index of Authors | 291
Index of Biblical Texts | 297
Index of Wagner's Works | 301
Index of Subjects and Names | 305

Figures

Figure 3.1: Rheingold! Reines Gold! | 95

Figure 4.1: Diagram for Theodor Uhlig (German) | 113

Figure 4.2: Diagram for Theodor Uhlig (English) | 114

Figure 5.1: Diagram for Theodor Uhlig (German) | 139

Figure 5.2: Diagram for Theodor Uhlig (English) | 140

Figure 6.1: Wagner and German Idealism | 174

Preface

I first worked systematically through Wagner's *Ring* cycle between finishing my final exams in Physics and Chemistry at University College London and awaiting the results. I borrowed the vocal scores from the Senate House Library and the vinyl recording of Karl Böhm (Bayreuth 1967) from my good friend Adrian Bury. I still remember vividly those weeks of being lost in the world of the *Ring* or, to be more precise, being lost for successive periods of half an hour, having to return to anxiety about degree results as I changed the record.

Over the next four years when I was working on a PhD in theoretical Physics I became more and more obsessed with this artwork and became an "evangelist" for the *Ring* cycle, which had so captivated me. I invited individual friends from the Department of Physics and Astronomy to my home to experience edited highlights from the *Ring* but I am unsure how many lasting converts I won. It was fitting that when I left the department to pursue the study of theology (with the intention of becoming a minister in the Church of England) I received the kind gift of Karl Böhm's *Die Walküre* recording.

The *Ring* has been part of my life ever since, but when my teaching and research interests turned to Wagner and Christian theology I was drawn first to the work that appears most clearly to address theological issues, Wagner's final stage work, *Parsifal*. My 2013 book was a theological appreciation of *Parsifal* in the light of the composer's intellectual development; I then decided to do the same sort of thing for the *Ring*. Moving from *Parsifal* back to the *Ring* does involve a change in perspective; e.g., being an earlier work means that the late theoretical essays such as *Religion and Art* (1880) are not so central and Hegel rather than Schopenhauer is the dominating philosopher in the artwork. Further, we appear to be in a somewhat different world—the tough world of the *Ring*, in many ways rather "Old Testament" in its outlook, contrasts with the atmosphere of compassion ("Mitleid") of *Parsifal*. Whether there is such a radical difference will be considered in the pages that follow and it may be that there are more continuities throughout the composer's creative years than has generally been acknowledged.

My work will not only consider the theological and ethical issues presented in the *Ring* cycle but also how Wagner presents them, looking at his theological method. Unearthing this will involve delving into his theoretical writings and whilst his gifts are most certainly in composing poetry and music and not in essay prose, the essays are nevertheless fundamental in understanding his artistic and theological project.

My work on the theology of the *Ring* cycle comes in two volumes. Just as an individual opera of the *Ring* can be appreciated on its own, so I have written each volume such that it is a complete entity (with its own bibliography and indices); but just as one gets a greater appreciation of an individual opera of the *Ring* in the light of the whole cycle, one will gain most benefit by reading both my volumes. This first volume studies the genesis and development of the *Ring* cycle together with Wagner's appropriation of sources (Germanic and Norse), artists, philosophers, and theologians. How Wagner appropriates his sources and the ideas of those who have gone before him (together with his contemporaries) is of general interest to the study of the *Ring* and will prove to be particularly important when we come to discern his theological interests. The second volume will then look at the various theological and ethical themes of the *Ring*, such as nature, power and love, law and sexual ethics, death and immortality, freedom and necessity, sin, incarnation, and redemption, together with questions of authority, gender, and human psychology. These themes will be prefaced by a chapter on Wagner's sketches *Jesus of Nazareth*, which, I claim, unlocks many theological secrets of the *Ring*, and a chapter on the question of "God" and the "Gods."

Acknowledgements

These volumes were written during my time of a being a holder of a Leverhulme Major Research Fellowship at the University of Nottingham. I am extremely grateful to the Leverhulme Trust not only for freeing me from undergraduate teaching and administration (and financing my excellent replacement Dr Sara Parks) but also for funding me to visit the libraries of Oxford and Cambridge and the archives in Bayreuth. The staff of the University Library, Cambridge, have been helpful in locating books in their vast collection. The staff of the Bodleian library, Oxford, have with kindness and good humor helped me access some rare books across the disciplines of music, theology, philosophy, and German literature. My annual visits to the Nationalarchiv der Richard Wagner-Stiftung/Richard Wagner Gedenkstätte have been invaluable and I record my special thanks to Frau Kristine Unger for her assistance and chats about some details of the works I have consulted in the archives. The library at the University of Nottingham has kindly allowed me to borrow a large number of books (I understand I have broken a University record) and it has always been a pleasure to chat with the dedicated staff, many of whom have taken an interest in my project.

The ideas for these volumes were partly developed in University teaching at Undergraduate and Masters level when I taught a module "Wagner's *The Valkyrie*" for a small but highly dedicated group of students. I have also given seminars in Nottingham (Department of Theology and Religious Studies), Oxford (Centre for the Reception History of the Bible; Centre for Theology and Modern European Thought), St Andrews (Institute for Theology, Imagination and the Arts), and Glasgow (School of Critical Studies), together with public lectures at Westminster College, Cambridge (Vacation Term in Biblical Studies), Nottingham Lakeside Arts (for the Opera North *Ring* production, 2016), St Mary the Virgin, Nottingham, Rutland Theological Society, Hull Theological Society, and the Nottingham Viking Open Day (2018). Public interest in the project has been enhanced by the work of Michael Timmins (who produced the website Wagner and Theology: www.nottingham.ac.uk/go/wagnertheology) and the encouragement of Keith Elliott, Peter Watts, Anna Walas, Carly Crouch, and Tom O'Loughlin. Launching this project was greatly helped by the encouragement of Chris Rowland, George Pattison, and Barry Millington. In addition to those who have read and discussed my work with me (see below) I have learned much through conversations (via e-mail or face to face) with Roger Allen, Lionel Friend, Barry Millington, Derrick Everett, Mark Berry, Barbara Eichner, Kevin Hilliard, Luke Murphy, Carolyne Larrington, Bennett Zon, Kerstin Bußmann, Roland Bauer, Ryan Häcker, Joanne Cormac, Laura Goede, and Alan Sommerstein. Writing these volumes has involved working across various disciplines, some of which have been fairly new to me, and I have been enormously helped by those who have given their time and effort to read through sections or whole chapters and to make corrections and suggestions for improvement (and I mention those who have read material from either volume or in some case both): Stephen Houlgate, Maike Oergel, Philip Goodchild, John Deathridge, Laura Tunbridge, Judith Jesch, Christina Lee, Dennis Vanden Auweele, Charlotte Alderwick, Jem Bloomfield, Stephen McClatchie, Oliver Thomas, Stephen Hodkinson, and Bob Morgan.

The staff of Wipf & Stock have been wonderfully efficient in bringing this work to publication, always answering my questions promptly and I thank especially Robin Parry, Calvin Jaffarian, and Savanah Landerholm. I should highlight that Robin, as well as working through the text at the copy-editing stage, was always on hand to offer advice, and Calvin has done magnificent work at the type-setting stage on a manuscript that was not always entirely straightforward. I am grateful to Matt Davies and Joe Bell for introducing me to the means of producing musical examples and diagrams and to Jeremie Cauchois for help with computer problems. I thank my Oxford friends who offered practical help when I was using the Bodleian library: Bob and Pru Morgan gave me hospitality and much intellectual stimulation; Bruce Kinsey gave me splendid facilities to use at Balliol College; David and Anita Wright gave me wonderful hospitality on many occasions; and Wycliffe Hall offered parking facilities. Finally, I thank those who have cared for me in my annual visits to Bayreuth: Joachim Korb (sadly no longer with us), Eva Graf, Reinhard and Ulrike Feldmeier, Eva Deyerling, Marie-Luise and Jörg Rasch, and my favorite "Mädel von Fürth," Diemut Meiners.

Abbreviations

Abbreviations follow the SBL Handbook of Style. References to Wagner's stage works are made by the German title (abbreviated if necessary), Act and bar (e.g., Act I bars 1–7 is expressed as I.1–7) or to the page number in *Sämtliche Werke* (*SW*) or the libretto given in the translation of Stuart Spencer (*WagRS*). Unless otherwise indicated, all Bible quotations in English are taken from the *New Revised Standard Version* (*NRSV*). Quotations of the German of Wagner's prose works are usually taken from *Gesammelte Schriften und Dichtungen* (*GSD*) and for the English I have generally used *Richard Wagner's Prose Works* (*PW*), translated by William Ashton Ellis.

Unless otherwise stated, all emphasis is that given in the source.

AA	*Kant's gesammelte Werke (Akademie-Ausgabe)*. 29 vols. Berlin: Georg Reimer (later Walter de Gruyter), 1900–1997.
ASSW	*Arthur Schopenhauer Sämtliche Werke, textkritisch bearbeitet von Wolfgang Frhr. von Löhneysen*. 5 vols. 1968. Reprint. Darmstadt: Wissenschaftliche Buchgesellschaft, 2004.
BBH-K	*Bremer Biblische Hand-Konkordanz*. Stuttgart: Anker/Christlichen Verlagshaus, 1979.
BBl	Hans von Wolzogen, ed., *Bayreuther Blätter*. Chemnitz: Ernst Schmeitzner, 1878–1938.
Braunes Buch	Joachim Bergfeld, ed., *Richard Wagner, Das Braune Buch: Tagebuchaufzeichnungen 1865–1882*. Zurich/Freiburg in Breisgau: Atlantis, 1975.
Brown Book	Joachim Bergfeld, *The Diary of Richard Wagner 1865–1882: The Brown Book*. Translated by George Bird. London: Victor Gollanz, 1980.
BSELK	*Bekenntnisschriften der evangelisch-lutherischen Kirche*. 10th ed. Göttingen: Vandenhoeck & Ruprecht, 1986.
BWL	*Briefwechsel zwischen Wagner und Liszt*. 2 vols. Leipzig: Breitkopf und Härtel, 1887.

CEWIK	Paul Guyer and Allen W. Wood, eds., *Cambridge Edition of the Works of Immanuel Kant*. Cambridge: Cambridge University Press, 1992–.
CD	Martin Gregor-Dellin and Dietrich Mack, eds., *Cosima Wagner's Diaries*. 2 vols. Translated by Geoffrey Skelton. London: Harcourt Brace, 1978–80.
CT	Martin Gregor-Dellin and Dietrich Mack, eds., *Cosima Wagner: Die Tagebücher*. 2 vols. Munich/Zurich: R. Piper, 1976.
CWE	Nicholas Vazsonyi, ed., *The Cambridge Wagner Encyclopedia*. Cambridge: Cambridge University Press, 2013.
CWL	*Correspondence of Wagner and Liszt*. Translated by Francis Hueffer. 2 vols. New York: Haskell, 1969.
DBE^2	*Deutsche Biographische Enzyklopädie*. 2nd ed. Munich: K. G. Saur, 2005–8.
DCT	Alan Richardson, ed., *A Dictionary of Christian Theology*. London: SCM, 1969.
DEBRN	Werner Breig and Hartmut Fladt, eds., *Dokumente zur Entstehungsgeschichte des Bühnenfestspiels Der Ring des Nibelungen*. SW 29,I. Mainz: B. Schott, 1976.
$DL\text{-}L^3$	*Deutsches Literatur-Lexikon*. 3rd ed. Vols. 1–28: Zurich/Munich: K. G. Saur; vols. 29–38: Berlin: Walter de Gruyter, 1968–2019.
$DL\text{-}LE^3$	*Deutsches Literatur-Lexikon, Ergängungsbände*. 6 vols. Zurich/Munich: K. G. Saur, 1994–99.
DTB	Isolde Vetter and Egon Voss, eds., *Dokumente und Texte zu unvollendeten Bühnenwerken*. SW 31. Mainz: B. Schott, 2005.
DTMN	Isolde Vetter and Egon Voss, eds., *Dokumente und Texte zu "Die Meistersinger von Nürnberg"*. SW 28. Mainz: B. Schott, 2005.
FBSW	Franz Hoffmann and Julius Humberger, eds., *Franz Xaver von Baader: Sämtliche Werke*. 16 vols. 1851–60. Reprint. Aalen: Scientia, 1987.
FHSWB	Michael Knaupp, ed., *Friedrich Hölderlin: Sämtliche Werke und Briefe*. 3 vols. Darmstadt: Wissenschaftliche Buchgesellschaft, 1998.
FNKSA	Giorgio Colli and Mazzino Montinari, eds., *Friedrich Nietzsche, Sämtliche Werke: Kritische Studienausgabe*. 15 vols. Berlin: Walter de Gruyter, 1999.
FSSW	Gerhard Fricke and Herbert G. Göpfert, eds., *Friedrich Schiller: Sämtliche Werke*. 5 vols. Darmstadt: Wissenschaftliche Buchgesellschaft, 1980.
FW	Immanuel Hermann Fichte, ed., *Fichtes Werke*. 8 vols. 1845–46. Reprint. Berlin: Walter de Gruyter, 1971.
GELW	Herbert G. Göpfert, ed., *Gotthold Ephraim Lessing: Werke*. 8 vols. Darmstadt: Wissenschaftliche Buchgesellschaft, 1996.

ABBREVIATIONS

GSD	*Gesammelte Schriften und Dichtungen von Richard Wagner*. 10 vols. 3rd ed. Leipzig: E. W. Fritzsch, 1897.
GWJA	Friedmar Apel et al., eds., *Goethe Werke: Jubiläumsasugabe*. 6 vols. Darmstadt: Wissenschaftliche Buchgesellschaft, 1998.
HHW	*G. W. F. Hegel: Hauptwerke in sechs Bänden*. Hamburg: Felix Meiner, 1999.
JGFAW	Fritz Medicus, ed., *Johann Gottlieb Fichte; Ausgewählte Werke in sechs Bänden*. 6 vols. Darmstadt: Lambert Schneider, 2013.
KB	Otto Strobel, ed., *König Ludwig II. und Richard Wagner: Briefwechsel*. 5 vols. Karlsruhe: G. Braun, 1936.
KFSA	Ernst Behler, ed., *Kritische Friedrich-Schlegel-Ausgabe*. 35 vols. Munich: Ferdinand Schöningh/Zurich: Thomas-Verlag, 1963–95.
KGB	Giorgio Colli and Mazzino Montinari, eds., *Friedrich Nietzsche Briefwechsel: Kritische Gesamtausgabe*. 25 vols. Berlin: Walter de Gruyter, 1975–2004.
KGW	Giorgio Colli and Mazzino Montinari, eds., *Friedrich Nietzsche Werke: Kritische Gesamtausgabe*. 24 vols. Berlin: Walter de Gruyter, 1967–2006.
LchI	Engelbert Kirschbaum, ed., *Lexikon der christlichen Ikonographie*. 5 vols. Rome: Herder 1968.
LFW	Erich Thies, ed., *Ludwig Feuerbach: Werke in sechs Bänden*. 6 vols. Frankfurt am Main: Suhrkamp, 1975.
LW	J. Pelikan and H. T. Lehmann, eds., *Luther Works*. 55 vols. Philadelphia: Fortress Press, 1943–86.
MECW	*Karl Marx/Friedrich Engels: Collected Works*. 50 vols. London: Lawrence & Wishart, 1975–2004.
MEGA	*Karl Marx/Friedrich Engels: Gesamtausgabe*. Berlin: Akademie, 1972ff.
MEW	*Karl Marx/Friedrich Engels: Werke*. Institut für Marxismus-Leninismus. 41 vols. Berlin: Dietz, 1966–70.
MGG²	Ludwig Finscher, ed., *Musik in Geschichte und Gegenwart*. 29 vols. 2nd ed. Stuttgart: J. B. Metler/Kassel: Bärenreiter, 1994–2008.
Mein Leben	Richard Wagner, *Mein Leben*. 2 vols. 1963. Reprint. Edited by Martin Gregor-Dellin. Munich: Paul List, 1969.
My Life	Richard Wagner, *My Life*. Translated by Andrew Gray. Edited by Mary Whittall. Cambridge: Cambridge University Press, 1983.
NDCT	Alan Richardson and John Bowden, eds., *A New Dictionary of Christian Theology*. London: SCM, 1983.
NibE	*The Nibelungenlied: The Lay of the Nibelungs*. Translated with an Introduction and Notes by Cyril Edwards. Oxford: Oxford University Press, 2010.

NibR	*Das Nibelungenlied: Song of the Nibelungs.* Translated from the Middle High German by Burton Raffel. Foreword by Michael Dirda. Introduction by Edward R. Haymes. New Haven: Yale University Press, 2006.
NibS	*Das Nibelungenlied, Mittelhochdeutsch und Neuhochdeutsch. Auf Grund der Übersetzung von Karl Simrock bearbeitet von Prof. Dr. Andreas Heusler.* Die Tempel-Klassiker. Wiesbaden: Emil Vollmer, n.d.
NPNF1	Philip Schaff, ed., *Nicene and Post-Nicene Fathers: First Series.* 14 vols. 1890–1900. Reprint. Peabody, MA: Hendrickson 1994.
NRSV	*The Holy Bible containing the Old and New Testaments with the Apocryphal/Deuterocanonical Books: New Revised Standard Version.* Edited by Martin H. Manser, John Barton, and Bruce M. Metzger. Oxford: Oxford University Press, 2003.
NWSEB	Dieter Borchmeyer and Jörg Salaquarda, eds., *Nietzsche und Wagner: Stationen einer epochalen Begegnung.* 2 vols. Frankfurt am M.: Insel, 1994.
OCD³	Simon Hornblower and Antony Spawforth, eds., *The Oxford Classical Dictionary.* 3rd ed. Oxford: Oxford University Press, 1996.
OCP	Ted Honderich, ed., *The Oxford Companion to Philosophy.* Oxford: Oxford University Press, 1995.
OD	Klaus Kropfinger, ed., *Richard Wagner: Oper und Drama.* 1984. Reprint. Stuttgart: Philipp Reclam, 2000.
PP	Arthur Schopenhauer, *Parerga and Paralipomena.* 2 vols. 1974. Reprint. Translated by E. F. J. Payne. Oxford: Clarendon, 2000.
PW	*Richard Wagner's Prose Works.* Translated by William Ashton Ellis. 8 vols. 1892–99. Reprint. New York: Broude Brothers, 1966.
RWWSB	Sven Friedrich, ed., *Richard Wagner: Werke, Schriften und Briefe.* Berlin, 2004 (CD-ROM).
SB	*Richard Wagner: Sämtliche Briefe.* Edited by Gertrud Strobel and Werner Wolf (vols. 1–5), Hans-Joachim Bauer and Johannes Forner (vols. 6–8), Klaus Burmeister and Johannes Forner (vol. 9), Andreas Mielke and Isabel Kraft (vols. 10, 14–15, 18), Martin Dürrer and Isabel Kraft (vols. 11–13, 16–17), Margret Jestremski (vol. 19), Andreas Mielke (vols. 21, 23), Martin Dürrer (vol. 22), Martin Dürrer and Hans Gebhardt (vol. 24), Angela Steinsiek (vol. 25). Leipzig: Deutscher Verlag für Musik, 1967–2000 (vols. 1–9); Wiesbaden: Breitkopf & Härtel, 2000–2017 (vols. 10–25).
SL	*Selected Letters of Richard Wagner.* Translated and edited by Stewart Spencer and Barry Millington. New York: W. W. Norton, 1987.

SSD	*Richard Wagner: Sämtliche Schriften und Dichtungen,* Volks-Ausgabe. 16 vols. Leipzig: Breitkopf & Härtel and C. F. W. Siegel (R. Linnemann), 1911 (vols. 1–12) 1914 (vols. 13–16).
SW	*Richard Wagner: Sämtliche Werke* 31 vols (projected). Mainz: B. Schott, 1970–.
SWMJ	Manfred Schröter, ed., *Schellings Werke, Münchner Jubiläumsdruck.* 12 vols. Munich: C. H. Beck, 1965.
SWNA	Julius Petersen et al., eds., *Schillers Werke: Nationalausgabe.* 43 vols. Weimar: Hermann Böhlaus, 1943–.
TBRN1	Gabriele E. Meyer, ed., *Texte zum Bühnenfestspiel "Der Ring des Nibelungen" 1 (1848–1853).* SW 29,IIA. Mainz: B. Schott, 2012.
TBRN2	Gabriele E. Meyer, ed., *Texte zum Bühnenfestspiel "Der Ring des Nibelungen" 2 (1853–1876).* SW 29,IIB. Mainz: B. Schott, 2018.
WA	*D. Martin Luthers Werke, kritische Gesamtausgabe.* Weimar: Hermann Böhlaus, 1883–.
WBV	Werner Breig, Martin Dürrer, and Andreas Mielke, eds., *Wagner Briefe Verzeichnis: Chronologisches Verzeichnis der Briefe von Richard Wagner.* Wiesbaden: Breitkopf & Härtel, 1998.
WagMB	Peter Branscombe, "Libretto." In *Die Meistersinger von Nürnberg: Overture Opera Guides,* 81–323. London: Alma Classics, 2015.
WagPS	Lionel Salter, "Libretto." In *Parsifal: Overture Opera Guides,* 105–237. London: Oneworld Classics, 2011.
WagRS	Stewart Spencer, "The Ring of the Nibelung." In *Wagner's Ring of the Nibelung: A Companion,* edited by Stewart Spencer and Barry Millington, 53–372. 1993. Reprint. London: Thames & Hudson, 2010.
WagTS	*Libretto for Richard Wagner's Tristan and Isolde.* Translated by Lionel Salter. Booklet accompanying the Compact Disk recording, conducted by Leonard Bernstein, Philips, 1993.
WDS	*Wagner: A Documentary Study.* Compiled and edited by Herbert Barth, Dietrich Mack, and Egon Voss. Preface by Pierre Boulez. Translated by P. R. J. Ford and Mary Whittall. London: Thames and Hudson, 1975.
WWR	Arthur Schopenhauer, *World as Will and Representation.* 2 vols. 1958. Reprint. Translated by E. F. J. Payne. New York: Dover, 1966.
WWV	John Deathridge, Martin Geck, and Egon Voss, eds., *Wagner-Werk-Verzeichnis: Verzeichnis der musikalischen Werke Richard Wagners und ihrer Quellen.* Mainz: B. Schott, 1986–87.

1

Introduction

Scope and Significance of the *Ring*

Dawson-Bowling is not alone in making this sort of comment on Wagner's *Der Ring des Nibelungen* (*The Ring of the Nibelung*):[1] "[i]n its scope and its reach, in its grandeur of conception and abundance of episode, in its universal relevance and its richness of suggestion [. . .] it has no near rival anywhere in art."[2] Even if one does not share such an assessment of the tetralogy one can make the simple point that of works regularly performed, the *Ring* is the longest work of Western classical music,[3] lasting around fourteen to fifteen hours. Derek Cooke writes that the poem of the *Ring* "still stands as the most prodigious 'opera libretto' ever written."[4] He continues: "It compresses into thirty-seven scenes, with the most decisive dramatic clarity and point, a story of phenomenal intricacy, involving thirty-four characters, sixteen of them main ones, each of whom has a sharply defined individuality [. . .]."[5] This poem is then "married" to highly complex music,[6] the orchestration alone being the most sophisticated up until that time.[7] Even if one does not like Wagner's *Ring* (and there are great musicians who do *not* like it) its creation must nevertheless be considered a consummate achievement.

My own view is that the *Ring* is one of the greatest of all artworks of Western civilization and is certainly one of the most comprehensive in what it attempts to achieve. It addresses the fundamental concerns that have faced humanity down the

---

1. Subsequently referred to as *Ring*.
2. Dawson-Bowling, *Experience*, 2:147.
3. Cf. Deathridge, "Beginnings," 7.
4. Cooke, *End*, 74.
5. Cooke, *End*, 74.

6. As we shall see in the discussion of sexuality and gender in volume 2, Wagner considered the "masculine" poet to "fertilise" the "feminine" music in his marriage of word and tone.

7. The size of the "base" orchestra (excluding any extra players on stage or say the addition of the organ for the Prelude to *Rheingold*) is 107: sixty-four strings; fifteen woodwind, seventeen brass, five percussion, and six harps (*SW* 10.I.1: X). A number of these players double on other instruments such that the orchestral size is even greater in terms of the instruments.

millennia, such as power and violence, love and death, freedom and fate. The work, despite being set in what sometimes appears to be medieval times,[8] is remarkably modern and has the capacity to address a whole gamut of issues from capitalism and the ecological crisis through to issues of gender and sexual ethics. It is understandable that Wagner took great pride in his *Ring*, presenting as it does a vast canvas of mythicized world history. He began work on the libretto in Autumn 1848 and when it was completed at the end of 1852 he had fifty copies privately published, one of which he sent to Franz Liszt on 11 February 1853, enclosing a letter in which he wrote: "Mark my new poem—it contains the world's beginning and its end!"[9] Three months earlier he wrote in a letter to Uhlig (18 November 1852), as he was completing the libretto: "The whole thing will then be—out with it! I am shameless enough to admit it!—the greatest poem I have ever written."[10] He then had the Herculean task of setting this to music, this being completed as late as November 1874.

Studying the Theology of the *Ring*

The artwork of four operas *Das Rheingold* (*The Rhinegold*), *Die Walküre* (*The Valkyrie*), *Siegfried,* and *Götterdämmerung* (*Twilight of the Gods*) is based on Norse and Germanic mythology and epic which has been radically modified in the light of Greek epic, lyric, and tragedy, and a case can be made that Wagner appropriated this Greek tradition through the lens of Hegel.[11] In the *Ring* we appear to be dealing with inner worldly events, beginning as it does with a remarkable representation of the evolution of the natural order, moving then to the birth of consciousness, then to the "fall" of humankind through the theft of the Rhinegold.[12] The cycle finally culminates in the death of the heroic couple Siegfried and Brünnhilde which is followed by the death of the gods as their heavenly abode, Valhalla, is engulfed in flames. But although the work appears to be dealing with "inner-worldly events," it is, as in all myth, attempting to point beyond this world. As Bultmann wrote: "Mythology is the use of imagery to express the other worldly in terms of this world and the divine in terms of human life, the other side in terms of this side."[13]

To some extent my interests in this work parallel what I attempted in my 2013 study *Parsifal*, which involved a theological appreciation of the artwork in the light of the composer's intellectual development.[14] However, the *Ring* will pose some special

---

8. As we shall see, Wagner often strips figures such as Siegfried of his medieval courtly background.
9. *SL* 281; *SB* 5:189.
10. *SL* 275; *SB* 5:118.
11. See chapters 4 and 6 below.
12. Also in *Götterdämmerung* we learn of the devastation of nature by Wotan, the chief god (*WagRS* 281).
13. Bultmann, "Mythology," 10 n. 2.
14. Bell, *Parsifal*, 2013.

challenges for Christian theology since it lacks the clear Christian symbolism found in *Parsifal* (e.g., the "holy grail" and "holy spear") and it could be legitimately asked whether seeking any Christian theology in the work is a fruitless exercise. There is the added problem that whereas Wagner on a number of occasions affirmed that *Parsifal* was a Christian work,[15] we have no such unambiguous utterance for the *Ring*. However, even if Wagner did not set out to present Christian theology in the *Ring* (and this can be debated) the power and mystery of Wagner's creation was such that even he himself felt he stood before his work "as though before some puzzle."[16] In short, we are presented with an artwork whose avenues of self-disclosure are incalculable and whose interpretation is inexhaustible.

If one avenue of interpreting the *Ring* is as Christian theology, how can this be discerned? The first way is by studying Wagner's appropriation and development of myth and saga, whether that be Norse, Germanic, Greek, or that found in literary sources. In my enquiry I will employ the sort of methods of "tradition history" employed by "biblical theology." Here we are not concerned with an abstract, timeless sense of revelation[17] but rather with a dynamic process occurring within the Testaments, Old and New, or across them. One approach is to seek "revelation" in the mutations (and even contradictions) that are perceived in this development.[18] For the *Ring* I will be concerned with two sorts of tradition and mutations within that tradition. First, there is Wagner's highly creative appropriation of a vast range of sources and here special attention will be paid to how, for example, Prünhilt of the *Nibelungenlied* and Brynhild of the Norse sources "mutate" into his Brünnhilde. The second set of traditions and mutations is the development of the *Ring* itself. As he worked on the libretto from 1848 to 1852 significant changes occurred, seen for example in the changing roles and character of Wotan, Siegfried, and Brünnhilde.

A second way of discerning Wagner's theology is by studying his whole world of thought fashioned by the many philosophical and literary giants in which he immersed himself, either by his reading their work or by simply breathing the intellectual air in which he found himself. Two such figures to consider are Goethe and Hegel. He clearly knew Goethe's *Faust*, a serious work of theology, very well, perhaps even knowing sections by heart. He may not have read so much Hegel, but even if he had never read a single work, the philosopher was in the very air he breathed. Wagner may not always be very good at acknowledging his debt to Hegel, and his debt may

---

15. Bell, *Parsifal*, 224–27.
16. Letter to August Röckel, 23 August 1856 (*SL* 356–57; *SB* 8:152).
17. Cf. Knight, "Revelation through Tradition," 180.
18. A stark example to consider is the way the idea of "life after death" developed in the Psalms: it is denied in Psalm 88 but then affirmed in Psalms 49 and 73 (cf. Gese, "Schriftverständnis," 17). An example across the Testaments is how the sacrifices of the Old are mutated into the sacrifice of Jesus Christ in the New.

not always be intentional, but I will argue that the philosopher has influenced the very fabric of the *Ring*.[19]

A third way of discerning Wagner's theology is in his use of allegory. This could answer an obvious objection to the current enterprise that if there is any theology it is primarily Norse and Germanic polytheism. By considering "allegory" (and "myth") it may be that a Christian theology can be found not *despite* the pagan background but *through* it. So one of my central contentions is that Brünnhilde in various respects is a figure who points *beyond* herself to the redeemer figure of Christian theology.

Fourthly, theological themes could be found in the way the composer portrays various ideas through music and specifically through his use of leitmotifs, many of which are related to each through some family resemblance (e.g., the various nature motifs). Further these motifs mutate as when the "Rheingold" motif, first heard in its unforgettable joy and orchestration of *Rheingold* Scene 1 (bars 540–41-42; 556–57) in C major, and repeated in E♭ major in *Götterdämmerung* as Siegfried journeys down the Rhine (bars 843–44), mutates into a darkened and sinister form as the interlude comes to an end (bars 883–84), indicating "that the rest of the journey will be ill-fated."[20] Such transformations of motifs are able to indicate not only the dramatic action or atmosphere but also theological ideas; the same is true when motifs are combined to present a canvas of related ideas as in the Prelude to *Siegfried* Act III. In addition, the music can have certain associations as when Brünnhilde approaches to announce to Siegmund his death and his hope of immortality; the music is reminiscent of solemn Church music and the orchestration resembles the "Posaunenchor," popular to this day in German Churches.[21]

Fifthly, Wagner can be found to do his theology through the very form of his poetry. As he started work on the libretto of the *Ring* in 1848 with *Siegfried's Tod*[22] (later renamed *Götterdämmerung*) he had moved from a style of verse writing we find in *Lohengrin* with its characteristic end-rhyme to one of alliteration.[23] The term he used for such alliterative verse was "Stabreim," probably adopting the term from Ettmüller, whose *Die Lieder der Edda von den Nibelungen; Stabreimende Verdeutschung* he had borrowed from the Dresden Royal library.[24] This interest in Stabreim

---

19. It may also be worth adding that the debt of "biblical theology" to Hegel is also often unintentional (and hence often unacknowledged), a clear exception being Vatke, *Biblische Theologie* (Bultmann, "Vatke").

20. Holloway, "Motif," 19.

21. Cf. Bell, *Parsifal*, 98 n. 66.

22. Throughout I will, according to Wagner's own orthography, use the apostrophe in *Siegfried's Tod* (*Siegfried's Death*).

23. Note that any rhyming in the first version appears to be accidental. See the very opening: Third Norn "Was wandest du im Western"; Second Norn "Was wobest du im Osten" (Haymes, *Ring of 1848*, 66, 68).

24. He borrowed this work 21 October 1848 to 29 January 1849 and he started using the term "Stabreim" in his 1849 essay *Artwork of the Future* (PW 1:132; GSD 3:102).

was to intensify as he worked further on the *Ring* in that in revisions to *Siegfried's Tod* further Stabreim was introduced and he argued that this form of poetry was demanded by the subject matter[25] and in the later stages of writing the libretto we find examples of intense and sophisticated Stabreim.[26] The expression in his poetry, which can actually stand alone as a work of art, is then able to be intensified by the way he combines it with the music.

A sixth way in which his theology (together with ethics) is discerned is through his politics which he believed was mediated by his art. Wagner's theology was the very opposite of a pietist quietism.[27] His political convictions were inextricably woven into his art and whatever moral censure one may make of the composer one can at least acknowledge that he was concerned to make the world a better place through his art; he genuinely believed that through his *Ring* Germany could be remolded and indeed transformed. It is no accident that as Wagner started work on the *Ring* he was very much bound up with political action, and that of a revolutionary nature.[28]

Through these various means I claim that Wagner, intentionally or unintentionally, expresses his views on a whole range of issues such as death and immortality, sin and redemption, power and love, freedom and necessity, nature and creation, law and sexual ethics, and sexuality and gender. In order to discern these views we can, in addition to considering the above six points related to the *Ring* itself, consider the vast array of sketches (prose, poetic, musical) not only of the *Ring* but of other works, together with essays, diaries, and letters where, among other things, the composer reflects on his own creative process as well as his theological and philosophical views. All this material can be invaluable in discerning the theology of the *Ring* and I consider three examples. First, as he started work on the *Ring* he wrote *Die Wibelungen* (*The Wibelungs*), which functions as a preliminary study for his *Ring* cycle. One of the striking aspects of this "World-History as Told in Saga" ("Weltgeschichte aus der Saga") is that the composer appears to make no clear distinction between history and myth and this raises various questions for the *Ring* in relation to myth and history. Secondly, around the same time, he composed prose sketches for an opera *Jesus of Nazareth* and although the work was never completed the material was not wasted since much of it ends up on the stage of the *Ring*.[29] Thirdly, he wrote essays on aesthetics such

---

25. See chapter 3 below.

26. See Siegmund's "Winterstürme wichen / dem Wonnemond [. . .]" (*Walküre* Act 1 Scene 3 (*WagRS* 134), discussed volume 2 chapter 3).

27. I will return in volume 2 to how Wagner's approach to theology and politics parallels that of Ernst Käsemann.

28. This concern with politics continued throughout Wagner's life although his views changed to some extent. Political concerns, often of a rather odious nature, are also propagated in the *Bayreuther Blätter*, a journal which ran from 1878 to 1938 under the editorship of Hans von Wolzogen, and Wagnerians are often prone to employ the composer to further their political aims (see the example of Enoch Powell, discussed in Bell, "Redemption," 73 n. 8).

29. See chapter 7 below and volume 2 chapter 2

as *Opera and Drama* where, among other things, he discusses his "total art-work" ("Gesamtkunstwerk") as a combination of music, drama, and "dance."

Wagner's *Ring*, I will argue, not only coheres with much Christian theology but also presents many challenges. To illustrate this I consider how Wagner's theology relates to the towering figure of St Paul. Sometimes we find a similar message in both Paul and in Wagner's *Ring*. Both stress the need for redemption through sacrifice: for Paul the sacrifice is that of God's own Son, Jesus Christ (Rom 8:32); for Wagner, the sacrifice is that of Siegfried and Brünnhilde.[30] But there are also differences, and the example of the law is a good one to consider. Paul and Wagner share common elements in that both understand the law to have a condemning function and relate law to sin, something that I will explore in detail in volume 2. But their ethics are rather different. It is the case that when Paul discusses ethical issues he rarely appeals explicitly to Old Testament law[31] and in 1 Corinthians 5–6 where he discusses ethical issues, including sexual ethics, he does not appeal to Old Testament law when he could have done so.[32] However, Paul alludes to a number of Old Testament texts and his argument is guided to some extent by the Old Testament law.[33] One such case regards his negative teaching on homosexuality, which has caused so much controversy both within and without the Church, and a theme I will discuss in volume 2. In 1 Cor 6:9 the very word *arsenokoitai* (men who have sexual relations with men)[34] is formed from Lev 18:22.[35] Further in Rom 1:26–27, where Paul again condemns same-sex practices, he is guided by Old Testament views on homosexuality, even perhaps appealing to Lev 20:13 in Rom 1:32,[36] something which conservative Christians may need to consider in their utterances on the authority of scripture.[37] So although Paul was in many respects a radical theologian and radically reinterpreted the Old Testament with reference to justification by faith, we see clear elements of his past life as a Pharisee in his discussion of ethics. Wagner, by contrast, is much more iconoclastic (and incidentally may help the Church in its current controversies). Not only does he hold to the Lutheran view of justification by faith and that salvation is not ultimately dependent on "works" but he is in many respects against the Jewish law in matters of ethics. This does to

---

30. See volume 2 chapter 11.

31. For rare cases where he does quote the Old Testament to make a theological point, see Rom 13:8–10; 1 Cor 9:9; 14:34–35; Eph 6:2. The Pauline authorship of the last two texts has been questioned.

32. In fact, his argument may sound a little strange. E.g., he argues you cannot be one flesh with a prostitute since you are one flesh with Christ (1 Cor 6:15–17).

33. The actual extent of this influence is hotly disputed. Rosner, *Ethics*, 3–13, gives an excellent overview of the debate. Rosner's own view (which actually focuses on 1 Cor 5–7) is that Paul was very much guided by Old Testament scripture and his approach contrasts to that of Harnack, "Briefen," Lindemann, "Toragebote," and others.

34. On the translation, see Schrage, *I Korinther I*, 432.

35. Lev 18:22: "You shall not lie (*koitēn*) with a male (*meta arsenos*) as with a woman."

36. See Loader, "Romans 1," 145.

37. Lev 20:13 declares the death penalty for a man who "lies with a male as with a woman."

INTRODUCTION

some extent reflect his anti-Judaism[38] and we see how he confronts a religion of law in both his *Jesus* sketches and in the *Ring*. The sketches present the fundamental opposition of "law" and "love." Jesus "slays the law"[39] (cf. Siegfried's destruction of Wotan's spear in *Siegfried* Act III Scene 2) and sets forth "love," which is the "law of life for all creation" ("das gesetz des lebens für alles erschaffene").[40] This opposition of "law" and "love" is acted out in *Walküre*. The love of Siegmund and Sieglinde is opposed by Hunding who calls upon the "law," embodied in the goddess Fricka, to defend his "rights." In Act II Scene 1 Fricka is appalled to discover that her husband Wotan, who is supposed to uphold law through his "contracts," advocates what one could call "situation ethics," the view that whatever one does should be guided not by "law" or "rules," but by "love." As Wagner's mouthpiece, the god points out that "those two are in love" and Fricka should "bestow that blessing on Siegmund's and Sieglinde's bond." It is not surprising that the stage direction accompanying Fricka's following entry is "breaking out in the most violent indignation."[41] This opposition of "law" and "love" that we find in the sketches of *Jesus of Nazareth* and in the *Ring* is reflected in the discussions today about sexual morality; and it does not take much imagination to guess where the composer would stand if he were here today.

I suggest that although regarding salvation one could hold to the Reformation view of *sola scriptura*, this is simply naïve in regard to ethics. An ethics based solely on the Bible would lead to a catalogue of positions that few (fortunately) would hold to today: capital punishment, beating children with sticks, regarding the institution of slavery as morally acceptable. Ethical issues have to be addressed not only by considering the biblical traditions (which I and countless others value) but also the traditions of the Enlightenment and those in artworks such as the *Ring* cycle; indeed such traditions can enable one to read the Bible from a new perspective.[42]

As well as challenging biblical ethics Wagner challenges Christian theology by raising issues that can be fundamental for Christian experience but which the New Testament witnesses simply do not address. I take the example of Brünnhilde calling Siegmund to Valhalla in Act II of *Walküre*. When he discovers that his beloved, Sieglinde, cannot follow him to Valhalla, he rejects immortality. He puts his love of Sieglinde first. It is in a way an expression of the decision many have taken regarding whether to put their love for a human being before their religious beliefs.[43] When

---

38. I use the term "anti-Judaism" for a negative view of the Jewish *religion* and "antisemitism" (deliberately not hyphenated) for a negative view of the Jewish *people*.

39. *PW* 8:300; *DTB* 249.

40. *PW* 8:301; *DTB* 249.

41. *WagRS* 142.

42. It is worth emphasizing here that among the many reasons for abolishing slavery in the late eighteenth and early nineteenth century were Enlightenment values, which in turn enabled a new reading of scripture (e.g., Phlm 15–16). One also wonders whether the movement to ordain women in the Church of England would ever have happened without the earlier rise of feminism.

43. If I may give an example from my personal experience, a single woman in a Church in which

Siegmund rejects this offer of immortality and life in Valhalla we hear the leitmotif that has been described as "Siegmund's Rebellion."[44] This recurs at Siegmund's death and in Brunnhilde's dialogue with Wotan in Act III Scene 3.[45] It was a decade and a half after composing this scene that Wagner was to relate it to the story of Radbod: "He tells of Radbod, the Prince of Frisia, who, with one foot already in the font, leaped back when he heard that he would not meet his heathen father in Heaven (Siegmund!)"[46] So Siegmund decides that he will choose "Hella" rather than be separated from his beloved. Wagner is not, of course, unique among dramatists and novelists in addressing such situations, although the way he does so is unique by his combination of drama, music, and "dance."

Sources and the Study of Wagner

In Wagner's later life we often know exactly what he was reading and when thanks to Cosima's diaries.[47] Such detail may not be available for the key years of the genesis and development of the *Ring* but we still have so many sources available in the form of letters, diaries, essays, and sketches. Further, we have his Dresden library, which now contains 408 volumes, and his Wahnfried library of 2,301 volumes,[48] although we are often in the dark as to what he read and possessed in the years between leaving Dresden (May 1849) and his more settled existence after 1864 when he was "rescued" by King Ludwig II. In comparison with St Paul's writing his letters, something I have researched for a number of years, we have so much more material for the composition of the *Ring*. But there is also a distinct disadvantage in researching Wagner: he was very good at covering his tracks. This is seen in a number of ways. First, he was very good at drawing a veil over his indebtedness to other composers, most notably Berlioz and Mendelssohn. His obscuring of his debt to Berlioz will be discussed in chapter 5 in relation to his *Faust Overture*. In relation to Mendelssohn, a good example is his probable debt to Mendelssohn's Overture *Die Märchen von der schönen Melusine*,

---

I worked had some years previously fallen in love with a non-Christian but decided not to marry him largely because St Paul enjoined Christians not to be "mismatched with unbelievers" (2 Cor 6:14). Putting her faith before her love had led to much distress and unhappiness in her life. Paul provided the principle but did not address (at least in his extant writings) the serious existential issues that arise from it.

44. Sabor, *Walküre*, 113. See Act II bar 1619 (in subsequent references to bars I will use the nomenclature II.1619). The motif then recurs at II.1621ff.

45. *Walküre* II.2001, 2003; III.1019–25. See the discussion of this scene in volume 2 chapter 11.

46. *CD* 21 July 1871.

47. I found this extremely helpful in studying his use of Gfrörer's *Geschichte des Urchristenthums* in relation to *Parsifal* (see Bell, *Parsifal*, 212–15).

48. I am grateful to Frau Kristina Unger of the Richard-Wagner-Museum for providing me with these precise figures. A number of volumes are missing from the Dresden library (see the list of twenty-nine titles given in Westernhagen, *Bibliothek*, 111–13) and, as I will argue in chapter 5 below, fourteen volumes now in the library were added after Wagner fled the city in May 1849.

where the arpeggios remind one immediately of the accompaniment to the Rheinmaidens in *Rheingold* Scene 1.[49] He does elsewhere refer to the myth of Melusine[50] but nowhere is there any extant reference to Mendelssohn's Overture. Secondly, in addition to his silence on such issues he even went to the point of falsifying his life history and artistic development not only in his *Autobiographic Sketch* and autobiography *My Life* but also in his rewriting of his *Annals*. We will see an example of this in the next chapter as we consider the development of the *Ring*.

---

49. This similarity was brought to my attention by Roger Allen. It is also discussed briefly in Nattiez, *Androgyne*, 285.

50. See "Annalen 1866–1868" (*KB* 2:3): "Melusine; fontaine de soif." He had "christened" a stream near Triebschen "Fontaine de Soif" (*CD* 23 September 1870) from the legend of Melusine. Cf. letter to Cosima 17 April 1866 (*SB* 18:122; Bauer, *Briefe*, 444). See also *CD* 27 July 1871; 23 June 1872; 13 June 1873.

— 2 —

Genesis and Development of the *Ring*

Questions concerning the Genesis and Development of the *Ring*

Studying the genesis and development of the *Ring* may appear to be a cumbersome addition to understanding an artwork that is complicated enough. Would it not be better simply to study the "final form" since this after all this is what we experience in the theatre? One could compare the *Ring* to certain books of the Bible that have evolved over time, some over a long period, such as Isaiah or the Pentateuch (the first five books of the Old Testament), others over a shorter time, such as John's Gospel. Some theologians have maintained we should concern ourselves only with the final form (or more precisely the final *forms*) of the biblical canon and ignore the successive sedimentary layers in the work of biblical theology.[1] Other have, rightly in my view, stressed that in order to understand the theology of these works it is essential to try to discover something of the way the books and individual ideas within the books developed. Research on the *Ring* has likewise taken an interest in how it was "forged,"[2] and whereas in biblical studies one often has to engage in much inspired (or not so inspired) guesswork in trying to discern how the Pentateuch or John's Gospel evolved, with the *Ring* we have, as I indicated in the previous chapter, much material at our disposal. In my own endeavour to study the "forging" of the *Ring* I will to some extent draw on the insights developed in biblical theology.[3] Applying such methods to the *Ring*, focussing on the mutations in the tradition, will bring out facets of the work that could otherwise be missed. Goethe's words to the composer,

---

1. See Anderson, "Tradition and Scripture," 12–14, points to Barth as a leading advocate of this approach.

2. See, e.g., Westernhagen's *Die Entstehung des "Ring,"* the English translation bearing the title *The Forging of the "Ring."* Note that the English translation has corrected some of the mistakes. Deathridge, "Sketches," 385–89, raises serious questions about Westernhagen's monograph, which attempts to analyze the "forging" of the whole cycle. There are also many studies on the genesis and development of particular sections of the *Ring*. Deathridge points to the fine study by Brinkmann, "Wanderer-Szene" on *Siegfried* Act II Scene 2. In volume 2 I will make use of Darcy, "Genesis," on the Prelude to *Rheingold*.

3. See chapter 1 above.

conductor, and music teacher Carl Friedrich Zelter in a letter of August 1803 could well be applied to his *Faust* and to the *Ring*: "We do not get to know works of nature and art as end-products; we must grasp them as they develop (im Entstehen) if we are to gain some understanding of them."[4]

A comparison of the development of the *Ring* and *Faust* is instructive. It took Goethe around sixty-one years (on and off) to complete his *Faust*.[5] If we date Wagner's first work on the *Ring* as the Autumn of 1848 with his sketches of *Der Nibelungen-Mythus* and the libretto for *Siegfried's Tod* and its ending with the musical composition of the final bars of *Götterdämmerung*[6] in November 1874 then we have a period of twenty-six years for his work (again on and off) on the *Ring*. However, this figure of twenty-six years fails to take account of two factors. First, he had clearly given some preliminary thought to the project, certainly for months and possibly for a few years. As external evidence we can turn to Eduard Devrient's diary for 1 April 1848, which tells that at 5 pm that day Wagner had picked him up to go for a walk during which he told him of "a new plan for an opera based on the Siegfried legend."[7] This coheres with Wagner's *Communication to My Friends* (1851) where he writes that even during the time of the musical composition of *Lohengrin* (completed 28 April 1848) two subjects which seemed "as one" had "usurped my poetic fancy": "Siegfried" and "Friedrich Barbarossa."[8] His *Friedrich I* had in fact been first sketched back in 1846 and, as I will argue, this work and his "Siegfried" were in fact intimately connected. How far we can push back the conception of his *Ring* is unclear since in that passage in *Communication* all he tells us is that when he first wrote the ideas for the work he had been considering the project "for some time previously."[9] The second factor regarding the period of composition of the *Ring* is that it did not finish in November 1874 since in a sense it was only completed with the first performance of the complete cycle in August 1876. He had to oversee the completion of his theatre in Bayreuth, choose his artists, sort out costumes and stages designs, oversee the rehearsals (during which details were introduced as to how the work should be performed),[10] and direct the performance. This second factor highlights the limitations in comparing the *Ring* to *Faust* for whereas bringing the *Ring* to performance was essential for Wagner, Goethe

---

4. Quoted in Luke, *Faust: Part Two*, xix.

5. This is assuming he began work on *Faust* around 1770. Part I was published in 1808 and Part II completed in 1831.

6. It was in a letter of 22 June 1856 to Franz Müller that we hear that Wagner changed the name of *Siegfried's Tod* (*Siegfried's Death*) to *Götterdämmerung* (*Twilight of the Gods*) and that *Der junge Siegfried* (*The Young Siegfried*) was to be simply *Siegfried* (*SB* 8:90). See Wagner's hand-written changes in his 1853 *Ring* (*TBRN2* 588).

7. Devrient, *Tagebüchern*, 1:427.

8. *PW* 1:357; *GSD* 4:311.

9. Deathridge, "Beginnings," 7. See *PW* 1:357; *GSD* 4:311.

10. An important resource here is Porges, *Rehearing the Ring*.

showed relatively little interest in having his *Faust* performed; indeed Part II was not even intended to be performed.[11]

Vischer and Otto: Clues to the Genesis of the *Ring*?

Back in 1844, the writer and philosopher Friedrich Vischer (1807–87), based in Tübingen,[12] had suggested in an influential essay that the Nibelung saga should be made into a "grand heroic opera."[13] It is unclear whether Wagner knew of this and he never refers to it and in fact rarely refers to Vischer anyway.[14] Some think he knew it on the basis of his knowledge of the plans of Louise Otto (1819–95) for a Nibelung opera. She published three articles "The Nibelungs as Opera" ("Die Nibelungen als Oper") in the *Neue Zeitschrift für Musik* in 1845[15] and at the end of the year the libretto for the first act.[16] She explains that she was motivated to write the libretto by Vischer's publication.[17] Newman argues that since Wagner read the journal he must have known of Otto's work and if he had not already known Vischer, then this would have drawn him to it.[18] Hence, "[t]he conclusion that he had read Vischer seems inescapable."[19] It has been suggested that a libretto sent to Wagner by Gustav Klemm, a Dresden Court official, with the request he set it to music was that of Louise Otto's *Die Nibelungen*.[20] This may at first seem probable since Wagner in his reply of 20 June 1845[21] refers to "the honoured poetess" (die verehrte Dichterin")[22] and female librettists were rare at this time. He declined the request, explaining that

---

11. On Wagner's debt to Goethe, see chapter 5 below.

12. Vischer studied theology, philosophy, and philology at the Tübinger Stift and came to take a keen interest in Hegel's philosophy. He taught in Tübingen first as "Privatdozent" in aesthetics and German literature 1835–37, then as extraordinary professor 1837–44, and then appointed full professor in 1844. However, because of his outspoken inaugural lecture, considered subversive by the University authorities, he was suspended for two years.

13. *DEBRN* 19. Vischer's essay, "Vorschlag zu einer Oper," appeared in his *Kritische Gänge* Volume 2.

14. For the rare references see *CD* 27 September 1870 and 10 June 1875. In the latter the couple discuss Vischer on Strauss' *Old and New Faith*, an article which appeared in *Kritische Gänge* Volume 2 (Neue Folge) in 1873. None of Vischer's works are in Wagner's libraries.

15. This was in volume 23 numbers 13 (12 August 1845), 49–52; 33 (21 October 1845), 129–30; 43 (25 November 1845), 171–72 (note her use of and praise for Simrock's translation of the *Nibelungenlied*). Extracts are given in *DEBRN* 25–26.

16. See volume 23 numbers 44 (28 November 1845), 175–76, which gives Scene 1; 46 (5 December 1845), 181–83, which gives Scene 2 and 3.

17. *DEBRN* 25.

18. Newman, *Life*, 2:32. Note that Wagner does not appear to have subscribed to the journal (it is not in the Dresden Library).

19. Newman, *Life*, 2:32.

20. *DEBRN* 24.

21. *SB* 2:436–8. Part of this letter is given in *SL* 123–24.

22. *SB* 2:438.

he is "fully convinced that if anything of significance & validity for the history of art is to emerge from this particular genre (which I see as diametrically opposed to the 'opera industry' of the present day), this can only be so if the poet and musician are one & the same person."[23] He suggests that "the honoured poetess" should turn to Ferdinand Hiller, who was looking for a text to set to music.[24]

One problem in identifying "the honoured poetess" with Louise Otto is that her articles on "Die Nibelungen als Oper" first appeared in the *Neue Zeitschrift* on 12 August 1845[25] and it was only in November to December of that year that she published the first three scenes of her Nibelungen drama. However, there are a number of significant links between Wagner and Louise Otto that may or may not point to Wagner knowing of her libretto and hence knowing of Vischer's suggestion for a Nibelungen opera. First of all, she admired Wagner and knew *Rienzi*[26] and shared not only Wagner's view about the triviality of the majority of opera material[27] but also his revolutionary ideals.[28] They did in fact correspond, but first on 26 September 1853, where he thanks her for her letter and explains *he knew of her already* (but does not mention her Nibelungen libretto).[29] He adds that he knew of her article of 1852.[30] Secondly, he may have known of Otto in the mid-1840s via Niels Gade (1817–90), a Danish composer, whom Mendelssohn had appointed deputy conductor of the Leipzig Gewandhaus Orchestra, and who was a friend of Schumann. Otto relates that on publishing the first act of her libretto (1845) she had received "letters upon letters from German musicians," the last being from Gade. He had visited her in Meissen and then in Dresden in around 1845–46.[31] We do know Gade met Wagner in Dresden when he attended the rehearsals and performance of Beethoven's Ninth Symphony in April 1846[32] and one wonders whether Otto was also present. According to Gade, Wagner told him on this occasion about his own Nibelungen plan: "I must come to grips with the ancient Edda poems which are much more profound that our medieval

---

23. *SL* 123; *SB* 2:437.

24. *SB* 2:438 (cf. Wagner's letter to Hiller of 10 April 1845, *SB* 2:424–25).

25. The second and third appeared on 21 October and 21 November 1845.

26. See her first article in the *Neue Zeitschrift* (volume 23 number 13) and her "Musikalische Erinnerungen" (*DEBRN* 25–26).

27. *DEBRN* 26 ("Musikalische Erinnerungen," 229).

28. She was a friend of the revolutionary Robert Blum (1807–48).

29. Although completed in 1846, the libretto (*Die Nibelungen*) was not published until 1852.

30. *SB* 5:439. The article was "Die Kunst und unsere Zeit" which was discussed by Uhlig in *Neue Zeitschrift* 37 no 3 (16 July 1852) 26–27. He further corresponded with her in 1854 (*SB* 6:318; the letter is lost) and in 1859 (*SB* 11:57–58).

31. On her completion of the libretto in 1846 he composed several scenes and arias but never completed the opera. She sent the libretto to Schumann who had expressed an interest in the Nibelungen as an opera (*DEBRN* 26) but because of his failing health was not able to make progress on it.

32. *PW* 7:246.

poems (die sind viel tiefsinner als unsere mittelalterlichen)."³³ The third indication that Wagner knew of Otto's libretto is that in her third article she sets out some of the significant voices as follows: "Brunhilde" and "Chriemhilde" (Wagner's "Gutrune") as sopranos; Siegfried as tenor, Gunther as Baritone and Hagen as bass.³⁴ Wagner's voices correspond exactly to this. Fourthly, her Act I Scene 2 with the "choir of the vassals" is reminiscent of Wagner's *Siegfried's Tod/Götterdämmerung* Act II.³⁵

I think it is plausible that Wagner knew something of Otto's libretto even though, as Deathridge points out, there is "no concrete evidence that Wagner knew the work of either Vischer or Otto."³⁶ But nevertheless it is instructive to contrast the approaches of Vischer and Wagner, for much of what Vischer writes about the possibilities of an opera based on the Nibelung saga is contradicted by Wagner. So Vischer points to the ways such an opera could extol the virtues of German culture and the Germanness of the heroes as found in the *Nibelungenlied*.³⁷ He argues that a work such as Gluck's *Alceste* and *Iphigenie* may emphasize heroism but has the distinct disadvantage of being placed in a foreign land. Something indigenous, something national is required; and although Goethe's *Iphigenie* has breathed Germanness into the Greek tragedy, he nevertheless has separated it from the ground of the fatherland. Vischer argues that German material should lead in another direction other than that of the Greeks, even if Goethe has managed to bring German spirit into it.³⁸ In many ways Wagner's approach is quite the opposite to Vischer's. He has mixed the *Nibelungenlied* with Greek culture (epic and tragedy) and *on one level* has not produced anything that is particularly "German,"³⁹ composing a libretto where the words "deutsch" and "Deutschland" fail to appear!⁴⁰ This though needs to be tempered by the view that in the *Ring* Wagner was not so much *reflecting* German culture but *creating* Germany.⁴¹ This is a subject to which I will return.

---

33. *DEBRN* 26. Wagner also tells of this meeting but does not mention the discussion of the Nibelungen (see *GSD* 2:55; Mein Leben 1:345). Hiller was also present at this performance.

34. *Neue Zeitschrift* volume 23, number 43, 172.

35. On the remarkable person and work of Lousie Otto and her relation to Wagner, see McManus, "Louise Otto."

36. Deathridge, "Beginnings," 8.

37. *DEBRN* 20: "Dieser Stoff ist *national*, das ist das erste, was von ihm zu rühmen ist" (Vischer's emphasis). "Die Nibelungen-Helden sind echt deutsche Charaktertypen" (21).

38. *DEBRN* 20.

39. The only German element is that the action takes place in Germany (i.e., the river Rhine); also reference to forests may be to German forests and rocky background to Alpine landscape (Westernhagen, *Biography*, 96). See also Wapnewski, "Richard Wagner und sein 19. Jahrhundert," 355; Cooke, *End*, 264.

40. By contrast, the extract of Vischer's article as given in *DEBRN* 19–24 speaks frequently of many German characteristics such as "[d]ie deutsche Milde und der gefürchtete, anhaltende deutsche Zorn, die deutsche Gutmütigkeit und Treue, die sich am stärksten in der eisernen Folge der tragischen Bestrafung einer Untreue ausspricht" (21).

41. Oergel, *Nibelungen*, 210–99.

Another stark difference between the two is that whereas Vischer praises the *Nibelungelied* for not having the interaction of the gods,⁴² Wagner has introduced them. One could argue that had Wagner known Vischer's article then it is ironic that he has taken various cues from him but not in the sense that Vischer wished. So whereas in the "Edda" (*Prose Edda*)⁴³ Brünnhilde is a Valkyrie, in the proposed opera Vischer says she should become, as in the epic, a human woman (Wagner's Brünnhilde is divine but becomes human at the end of *Walküre*). Vischer in fact makes a number of comparisons between the *Nibelunglied* and the "Edda" which are instructive and could well have given Wagner various ideas. Another example is that Vischer discusses the way "the songs of the Edda" (*Elder Edda*) could inform the *Nibelungenlied*. He asks why Brünnhilde is so angry with Siegfried in *Nibelungenlied*. The answer lies in the *Elder Edda*. Here Siegfried was her fiancé but Kriemhild's mother (i.e., Gudrun's mother, Grimhild) gives him a love potion so he forgets Brünnhilde and burns in love for Gudrun! This then explains why Brünnhilde wants to plot against Siegfried, something not made clear in the *Nibelungenlied*. Further, there are some limited similarities between Wagner and Vischer in that Vischer highlights in the *Nibelungenlied* what Wagner has also stressed in his poem: the curse on the gold and the prophecy of the downfall of the Nibelungen through the "Meerweiber."⁴⁴

Friedrich I

A significant step in the genesis of the *Ring* are the sketches for a five-act work "Friedrich I," depicting his life "from the Roncalian Diet down to his entry on the Crusade."⁴⁵ This first brief sketch (Text I) is dated 31 October 1846, but two additions were made, the second of which was in the Winter of 1848–49.⁴⁶ Wagner's presentation of the composition of this work is not straightforward.⁴⁷ In the *Annals* he dates

---

42. *DEBRN* 21.

43. Vischer's references to the "Edda" are to the *Prose Edda* and "die Lieder der Edda" to the *Elder Edda* (*DEBRN* 23).

44. *DEBRN* 23.

45. *PW* 1:359 (*Communication to My Friends*); *GSD* 4:313. Wagner's source for this was Raumer, *Hohenstaufen*, which was in his Dresden library (Westernhagen, *Bibliothek*, 14–15). Of the six volumes, he possessed volumes 1, 2, and 4, volume 2 being concerned with Friedrich I (the fourth book, *Hohenstaufen*, 1–326, takes us from 1152–87, the period covered in Wagner's drama; the fifth book, *Hohenstaufen*, 327–519, overlaps in that it covers the period 1149–93, including Friedrich's crusade and death (1188–90)). Wagner gives an outline of his drama in *My Life* 376; *Mein Leben* 1:390, and the sketch itself is given in *DTB* 238–40.

46. See *WWV* 328–30; *DTB* 238–40. For the additions Text IIa is written in German script but Text IIb is in Latin script and, with the exception proper names and the beginning of sentences, uses lower case letters. Since Wagner changed to the Latin script together with use of the lower case in November/December 1848 (see his letter to Eduard Devrient, 18 December 1848, *SB* 2:628–29, the first extant evidence of this change), Text IIb must be dated accordingly. In using the Latin script and lower case letters, he was following the example of Jacob Grimm.

47. I am grateful to John Deathridge for advice on this matter.

the original composition to 1848, linking it to *Siegfried's Tod* and *Die Wibelungen*: "Sketched in my head Barbarossa in five acts. Passed on to Siegfried by way of a prose work on his historical significance: *Die Wibelungen*."[48] Similarly, *My Life* dates the composition to 1848.[49] However, this simply cannot be correct since, as we have seen, the original plan was dated 31 October 1846. We can definitely say that the *second* addition can be dated sometime after December 1848 and the first addition sometime before December 1848 (when he changed his style of writing). The question is why Wagner wishes to give the impression that it was composed 1848–49. The answer would seem to be that he wished to give to the public the idea that he was moving from grand opera to spoken drama to music drama and which would give the impression in the later phase that he was going back to the Urdeutsch and away from French Grand Opera.[50] So we have a double falsification: first in claiming the work was to be a spoken drama when it was meant to be a Grand Opera[51] and secondly dating the whole work on Friedrich to 1848–49. As he dictated *My Life* he must have had the sketches of *Friedrich* in front of him[52] and he does appear then to falsify the actual facts (as he has done in the *Annals*).[53]

As pointed out above, *Friedrich I* has some key connections to his Nibelungen project[54] and despite falsification of chronology what he writes in *Communication to My Friends*[55] does throw light on the relationship between *Friedrich* and the *Ring*. He writes that "[e]ven during the musical composition of *Lohengrin*, midst which I had always felt as though resting by an oasis in the desert, *both* these subjects had usurped my poetic fancy: they were 'Siegfried' and 'Frederic Barbarossa.'—Once again, and that the last time, did Myth and History stand before me with opposing claims."[56] But then he came to see that placing *Siegfried* and *Friedrich I* side by side, the latter appeared as "a historical rebirth of the old-pagan Siegfried."[57] He claims in *My Life* that he gave up

---

48. *Brown Book* 95; *Braunes Buch* 113.

49. *My Life* 376; *Mein Leben* 1:390.

50. John Deathridge, communication of 12 October 2017.

51. Deathridge, *Good and Evil*, 257 n 36; contrast Wilberg, *Mythische Welt*, 208–11, who argues it was intended as a spoken drama. Another possibility is that what was originally intended as a grand opera was later conceived as a spoken drama.

52. Again suggested to me by John Deathridge. Note the details Wagner gives of the work in *My Life* 376; *Mein Leben* 1:390.

53. Note that the Annals are a rewriting of his earlier diary, covering the period 1846–67 (*Brown Book* 93–124; *Braunes Buch* 111–47). Deathridge, *Good and Evil*, 7, explains: "At the point in the dictation of *Mein Leben* when, within its narrative, his health and finances really began to take a turn for the worse (Easter 1846), he sat down—in February 1868—to create a second diary out of the first." In the process of doing this, he clearly changed some of the "facts" so as to present the development from "Grand Opera" to "Spoken Drama" to "Music Drama."

54. DEBRN 26–28, 46–54. *My Life* 376; *Mein Leben* 1:390.

55. PW 1:357–66; GSD 4:311–20.

56. PW 1:357; GSD 4:311.

57. PW 1:359; GSD 4:313.

his Friedrich I for the *Ring* in 1848[58] and his rationale is expressed in *Communication to My Friends* in this way: "Had I chosen to comply with the imperative demands of History, then had my drama become an unsurveyable conglomerate of picture incidents (ein unübersehbares Konglomerat von dargestellten Vorfällen), entirely crowding out from view the real and only thing I wished to show."[59] He therefore felt himself pushed to engage in myth. "In order to make plainly understandable both my hero and the relations that with giant force he strives to master, only to be at last subdued by them, I should have felt compelled to adopt the method of Mythos, in the very teeth of the historic material."[60] This would then lead to a fundamental contradiction in that he wanted to treat Friedrich as a historical figure yet this would fail to get to the essence of the matter.[61] But if he were to complete *Friedrich* he argues that as a historical work it could only appear as a spoken drama: "it could only be dealt with as a spoken play, and by no manner of means as a drama set to music."[62] He adds: "In that period of my life when I conceived *Rienzi*, it might perhaps have struck me to regard the 'Rothbart,' also, as an opera subject: now, when it was no longer my purpose to write operas, but before all to give forth my poetic thoughts (meine dichterischen Anschauungen) in the most living of artistic forms, to wit in Drama, I had not the remotest idea of handling a historico-political subject otherwise than as a spoken play."[63] Although Wagner does not falsify the nature of *Jesus of Nazareth* as he does *Friedrich*, there are occasions when he is slightly ambiguous about the nature of the work.[64]

Die Wibelungen

As preparatory study for his *Ring* Wagner composed two works, *Die Wibelungen* and his *Nibelungen-Mythus*. The *Annals* suggest *Die Wibelungen* was written before his October sketch for the *Nibelungen-Mythus*.[65] However, although it is highly likely that he had started work on *Die Wibelungen* in 1848 in order to work out ideas for the *Nibelungen-Mythus* (see above), the writing on the same sort of green paper that he used for *Jesus of Nazareth* together with the use of Latin script and preference for small letters actually suggests a date of early 1849.[66]

58. *My Life* 376; *Mein Leben* 1:390.
59. *PW* 1:359; *GSD* 4:313.
60. *PW* 1:359; *GSD* 4:313.
61. *PW* 1:360; *GSD* 4:313–14. In a footnote he adds that in *Die Wibelungen* he has produced something that is not to be laid at the feet of "historico-juristic criticism."
62. *PW* 1:360; *GSD* 4:314.
63. *PW* 1:360–61; *GSD* 4:314–15.
64. In *My Life* 387; *Mein Leben* 1:400, he refers to the work as a "tragedy" and "drama," not specifying that it was intended as an opera (as it clearly was).
65. *Brown Book* 95; *Braunes Buch* 113.
66. *WWV* 329 date *Die Wibelungen* to February 1849, noting that Eduard Devrient's records that Wagner read *Die Wibelungen* to a group in his home on 22 February 1849 (Devrient, *Tagebüchern*,

Die Wibelungen is highly significant in that Wagner expresses some of his fundamental ideas on the relation of myth to history.[67] Further, he associates the key figures of Siegfried, Friedrich Barbarossa, and Jesus and, perhaps more surprising, he relates the last two also to Wotan. This work is a key to understanding the theology of the *Ring* and hence I shall be looking at this somewhat neglected work in some detail.

In bringing together myth and history *Die Wibelungen* has an association with both the *Ring* (in that this is based on historical figures) and with the *Jesus of Nazareth* sketches,[68] but not with the *Friedrich I* sketches, which were meant to be purely historical.[69] In the short preface Wagner explains that he was "occupied with the reawakening of *Frederick the Red-beard*, so longed for by so many, and strove with added zeal to satisfy an earlier wish to use my feeble breath to breathe poetic life into the hero-Kaiser for our acting stage."[70]

The first section concerns "The Ur-Kinghood" ("Das Urkönigthum"),[71] whose origin is preserved in sagas. The idea of the kingly power restricted "to one favoured race" ("bei einem bestimmten Geschlechte") lies deep in the people's consciousness, resting on the memory of the "Asiatic ur-home" of the "ur-folk" whose Stem-father was "sprung from the Gods."[72] With the "Sint-Fluth" or "Great Deluge" the "largest island" of the "northern world-sea" was "the highest mountain-range of Asia, the so called Indian Caucasus,"[73] which is the "cradle" of both the present Asiatic peoples and those who wandered into Europe. "Here is the ancestral seat of all religions, of every tongue, of all these nations' Kinghood."[74] We find here therefore the view, current at that time, that the European peoples had wandered into Europe from the "Indian Caucasus," the highest point of the earth, which survived the Great Deluge that had covered the Northern hemisphere.[75] The roots of this idea come from the Göttingen school of history, the relevant figures being the historian Christoph Meiners (1747–1810)[76] and the professor

---

470) and that it was the composer's custom to read his works shortly after completion.

67. Spencer, "Romantic Operas," 72, suggests that it was the "medieval German studies" (*Brown Book* 95; *Braunes Buch* 112) that "alerted him to the mythological interpretation of history" and in the writings of Mone, Lachmann, and Grimm that he found the "blurring of the borders between history and myth that characterizes *The Wibelungs*."

68. But in "the contradictory nature of the subject-matter" (*PW* 1:380; *GSD* 4:332) did he have in mind that Jesus was a historical figure?

69. Note that Hegel, *Philosophy of History*, 388, emphasized the importance of Friedrich Barbarossa and this may well have contributed to Wagner's ideas in *Die Wibelungen* (see chapter 6 below). However, Wagner has a much more important role for myth and legend.

70. *PW* 7:258; *GSD* 2:115. I will return to the reawakening of Friedrich I in volume 2, chapter 5.

71. *Die Wibelungen* is full of words compounded with "Ur-."

72. *PW* 7:259; *GSD* 2:115.

73. *PW* 7:259–60; *GSD* 2:116.

74. *PW* 7:260; *GSD* 2:116.

75. *PW* 7:259–60; *GSD* 2:115–16.

76. Meiners, *Grundriss* (1785), introduced the word "Caucasian" in its wider racial sense.

of anatomy and comparative zoology Johann Friedrich Blumenbach (1752–1840),[77] whose ideas on epigenesis influenced Kant[78] and Herder.[79] Other roots of Wagner's idea are the discovery that Sanskrit is related to European languages[80] and the Friedrich Schlegel's suggestion that the locus of the proto-Indo-European homeland had been in India.[81] Schlegel influenced Schelling,[82] who in turn influenced Max Müller,[83] who in the 1850s suggested a western and eastern Aryan race. Wagner stood in this line of thought and this can be found in his late essay *Religion and Art* (1880).[84]

Wagner then explains that once the waters retreated the population moved westwards into Europe.[85] Wagner then traces the Frankish royal race (who first appeared as the "Merovingians") back to their origins. The Saga of the Nibelungen "is the birthright of the Frankish stem"[86] and suggests a "mythical identity of the Frankish royal family with those Nibelungen of the saga."[87] In this saga Siegfried "as God of Light or Sun-god" is the winner of the Nibelung hoard.[88] "This Hoard, and the might in it residing, becomes the immovable centre around which all further shaping of the saga now revolves" and "he who owns it, who governs by it, either is or becomes a Nibelung."[89] His then clarifies why Siegfried is termed a "Nibelung" although in Wagner's *Ring* Siegfried does not own nor is governed by the hoard itself.

---

77. He argued that the biblical account of human origins was essentially correct in that there was fundamentally just one species ("Gattung"), all being descended from Adam (*Handbuch der Naturgeschichte* (1779), second edition 1882, 59). See also Blumenbach, *The Institutions of physiology* (1817), and *Über den Bildungstrieb* (1781, new edition 1789).

78. See Guyer and Matthews, *Critique of the power of judgment*, 292 (AA 5:424); Irrlitz, *Kant Handbuch*, 92, 376. See also Look, "Blumenbach and Kant."

79. Herder, *Ideen*, 963–64, 988–89.

80. On 2 February 1786 William Jones presented his landmark paper "On the Hindu's" to the Asiatic Society of Bengal ("Third Anniversary Lecture," *Works*, 1:19–34).

81. See Schlegel, "Über die Sprache und Weisheit der Indier" (*KFSA* 8:105–433); "Vorlesungen über Universalgeschichte" (*KFSA* 14:18–31); "Über den Anfang unserer Geschichte" (*KFSA* 8:474–528). See the further discussion in chapter 5 below.

82. Eichner, *Schlegel*, 105.

83. Stone, *Essential Max Müller*, 11.

84. *PW* 6:227; *GSD* 10:226: "At the first dawning of history we believe we find the aborigines of the present Indian peninsula in the cooler valleys of the Himalayan highlands." *PW* 6:228–29; *GSD* 10:226–27: "[I]n the selfsame valleys of the Indus we think we see at work that cleavage which parted cognate races from those returning southwards to their ancient home, and drove them westwards to the broad expanse of hither-Asia, where in course of time we find them as conquerors and founders of mighty dynasties, erecting ever more explicit monuments to History." He goes on to speak about the degeneration of humankind and of language: "Speech [. . .] shews a progressive degeneration from Sanskrit to the newest European amalgam" (*PW* 6:244; *GSD* 10:244).

85. *PW* 7:260; *GSD* 2:117.

86. *PW* 7:262–63; *GSD* 2:119.

87. *PW* 7:263; *GSD* 2:120.

88. *PW* 7:263; *GSD* 2:119. Later we will see how in the *Ring* Siegfried is portrayed as Sun-god.

89. *PW* 7:263; *GSD* 2:119.

One of Wagner's etymological feats was to trace the name of "Wibelungen" to the "Nibelungen" rather than to "Waiblingen,"[90] Friedrich Barbarossa's birthplace.[91] So for Wagner the "Wibelingen" or "Wibelungen" are equivalent to the "Nibelungen" and are in opposition to the "Welfen."[92] (Note that others have presented the opposition as the Welfs and the Ghibellines.[93]) In the process of doing this he offers some of his key insights into "history" ("Geschichte"). He argues that the "highly significant names" Wibelingen and Welfen cannot be explained by "bare History" ("nackte Geschichte") and we must turn to "Religion and Saga."[94] "Religion and Saga are the pregnant products of the people's insight into the nature of things and men. [. . .] The Gods and Heroes of its religion and saga are the concrete personalities in which the Spirit and the Folk portrays its essence to itself."[95] He then contrasts two types of history. First there is "our dry-as-dust chronicles" ("unsere trockene Chronikengeschichte"),[96] the history of "Lords and Princes" ("Herren- und Fürstengeschichte") represented by Otto von Freisingen. Secondly, a "Folk-history" ("Volksgeschichte"),[97] which will enable "an exact and intimate understand of this race's wonderous strivings and ambitions."[98] By such a process one can discern that the "Wibelungen" are indeed the "Nibelungen" and are identified with "the ur-old Frankish dynasty" and will give insight "into the mainsprings of one of the most eventful periods of world-historic evolution (weltgeschichtlicher Entwickelung)."[99] Hence we must turn to "that mighty Nibelungen-saga" and "the popular mind of the Middle Ages," in particular the Hohenstaufen period "where we may plainly distinguish in the Christian-chivalrous poems (in den christlich ritterlichen Dichtungen) the Welfian element become at last a churchly one, in the

---

90. Köhler, *Titans*, 651 n. 30, thinks Wagner may have got this from Göttling, *Nibelungen und Gibelinen*, 29: "Nibelungen ist unstreitig die ältere Form für Waiblingen oder Gibelinen." Magee, *Nibelungs*, 53, 90–91, 105–6, 214, considers it probable that Wagner read this work and that it influenced both *Die Wibelungen* and the *Ring*.

91. He ascribes the derivation from "Waiblingen" to bishop Otto von Freisingen (*PW* 7:268; *GSD* 2:124).

92. *PW* 7:266–67; *GSD* 2:122–23. For a convenient genealogical table of the Welfs, Staufen (and Babenbergs), see Munz, *Barbarossa*, 400. A good overview of the empire under the Hohenstaufen is given by Heer, *Empire*, 65–93.

93. Friedrich, *Aura*, 124, notes that Meyerbeer's *Hugenotten* was performed as *Die Welfen und die Ghibellinen* in Vienna (1839); the title and content was changed so avoid offence in this catholic country.

94. *PW* 7:266; *GSD* 2:123.
95. *PW* 7:266; *GSD* 2:123.
96. *PW* 7:268; *GSD* 2:125.
97. *PW* 7:267–68; *GSD* 2:124–25.
98. *PW* 7:268; *GSD* 2:125.

99. *PW* 7:268; *GSD* 2:125. Note the Hegelian echo here and in the sub-title of the work: "Weltgeschichte aus der Saga" ("World History as told in Saga."). On Wagner's debt to Hegel, see chapter 6 below.

newly-furbished Nibelungenlieder that utterly contrasting Wibelingian principle with its often still ur-pagan (urheidnisch) cut."[100]

It is worth pausing at this point to make what I consider to be fundamental points about the related *Ring* cycle. First, if one asks where the *Ring* is set, the answer on one level has to be in "Germany" in the medieval period of the Hohenstaufens. But at the same time the work has links to the earlier centuries, particularly the sixth century, and the historical figures of Sigibert and Brunichild.[101] The striking thing about this history is that it is rooted in the early history of the Franks, Sigibert being more "French" than "German," although Brunichild is a "West Gothic king's daughter."[102] Secondly, Wagner has a view of history ("Geschichte") that is sophisticated. One cannot understand the world by looking at a dispassionate ("dry-as-dust") chronicle. Saga and religion are essential. Many influences are no doubt coming to bear on the composer, one of whom is no doubt Herder.[103] But I wonder if one of the key root figures is Martin Luther and his understanding of reality, which could be termed "mythical." Just as for Luther "the word of God" is a "Deed-word" of creative power,[104] so for Wagner the sagas and myths of the medieval period *create* a reality into which the folk are embedded. Can it be accidental that Wagner, as we shall see, placed so much emphasis on Faust's translation of John 1:1 as "In the beginning was the deed"?[105]

Wagner considers the "[o]rigin and evolution of the Nibelungen-myth" to be rooted in "Nature" and "Creation." Thanks and worship were first given to "*Light, the Day, the Sun*," which triumphs over "Darkness, Night."[106] "[T]his earliest nature-impression must be regarded as the common basis of all Religions of every people."[107] "[T]he Frank stem-saga shews the individualised Light or Sun-god, who conquers and lays low the monster of ur-Chaotic night:—this is the original meaning of *Siegfried's fight with the Dragon*, a fight like that Apollo fought against the dragon Python." But Siegfried too must succumb to Night as Summer yields to Winter. Siegfried is slain and "so the god became man, and as a mortal man he fills our soul with fresh and stronger sympathy." The "quintessence" of the "constant motion" of "ceaseless sway from life to

---

100. *PW* 7:268–69; *GSD* 2:125.

101. Wagner would have read of this earlier history in, e.g., Loebell, *Gregor von Tours*, 27–29, a work in his Dresden library (DB 83). See the further discussion in chapter 3 below.

102. Loebell, *Gregor von Tours*, 27.

103. On Herder's view of myth and history, see Rogerson, *Myth*, 11–15. On Wagner's debt to Herder, see chapter 5 below.

104. See Ebeling, "Luthers Wirklichkeitsverständnis," 418. He makes the fundamental points that for Luther the idea of accommodation (i.e., Calvin's view) for relation of the word of God to human language is inadequate. "Das Wort Gottes hingegen ist als solches Tatwort, von schöpferischer Macht und unfehlbarer Verläßlichkeit." Note, however, that Wagner's use of myth is very much related to allegory, as will be discussed in volume 2, chapter 12.

105. See chapter 5 below.

106. *PW* 7:274; *GSD* 2:131. Wagner does not mention Gen 1:1–3 but the allusion seems fairly clear.

107. *PW* 7:274; *GSD* 2:131.

death" finds its expression in "'*Wuotan*' (Zeus) [. . .] as the chiefest God, the Father and Pervader of the All. Though his nature marked him as the highest god, and as such he needs must take the place of father to the other deities, yet was he nowise an historically older god, but sprang into existence from man's later, higher consciousness of self."[108] He is therefore "more abstract than the older Nature-god."[109]

Wagner then passes to the question of the "hoard," which gives the Franks' race "its quite specific physiognomy."[110] He explains that "Nifelheim" of the Scandinavia myth is the subterranean home of the "Schwarzalben," "Black-elves," who burrow the earth and "find out its inner treasures, smelt and smith its ore" and are in opposition to the "Asen" (Æsir) and "Lichtalben" (light-elves). "When Light vanquished Darkness, when Siegfried slew the Nibelungen-dragon, he further won as victor's spoil the Nibelungen-hoard it guarded" but this in turn leads to his death "for the dragon's heir now plots to win it back."[111] The identity of the "dragon's heir" is unclear. In the *Nibelungenlied* this figure (as in *Siegfried's Tod*) is Hagen, but he is not named here in *Die Wibelungen*.[112] The reference may be, as Magee suggests, to "the powers of darkness"; or it may be to some individual mythological figure?[113] "This heir despatches him by stealth, as night follows day, and drags him down into the gloomy realm of Death: *Siegfried thus becomes himself a Nibelung.*"[114] Each generation seeks to seize the hoard though doomed to death by its acquisition. "For in the Hoard there lies withal the secret of all earthly might."[115]

Wagner then switches to a more historical discussion of Karl the Great, the Romans and the Franks. Both the Romans and the Franks come from Troy,[116] the Ro-

---

108. *PW* 7:275; *GSD* 2:131–32.

109. *PW* 7:275; *GSD* 2:132. This older Nature-god is presumably Wuotan/Odin as god of thunder or as an equivalent to Mercury and Mars. Tacitus, *Germania* 9 (*Tacitus I*, 142–45), likens the chief god of the Germans to Mercury in view of the cultic similarities. Grimm, *Mythologie*, 1:108–10; *Mythologie*, 1:120, suggests that Tacitus' omission of Jupiter is because his cult in the people Tacitus knew stood close to that of Mercury. Also if Tacitus was writing from a Gallic perspective, we may have the Gallic binding of Mercury with Mars. *Germania* was included in Wagner's Tacitus edition in his Dresden library (Tacitus, *Werke*, 4:161–212).

110. *PW* 7:275; *GSD* 2:132. The precise way in which the hoard has influenced the Franks' physiognomy is not entirely clear!

111. *PW* 7:276; *GSD* 2:133.

112. However, the end of *Die Wibelungen* in describing how the hoard was "sunk into an old God's-hill" may allude to Hagen sinking treasure in the Rhine in the *Nibelungenlied* (*PW* 7:298; *GSD* 2:155. Cf. *NibE* 106).

113. Note that Wagner speaks of a single heir ("der Erbe des Drachen"; *GSD* 2:133; *PW* 7:276); Magee, *Nibelungs*, 143, reads "dragon's heirs."

114. *PW* 7:276; *GSD* 2:133.

115. *PW* 7:276; *GSD* 2:133.

116. Note that the *Prose Edda* (*Gylfaginning* 9) calls Asgard "Troy" (Faulkes, *Edda*, 13). On the link between Odin and Troy, see the Prologue (Faulkes, *Edda*, 3–4). Wagner also refers to Asgard in *Die Wibelungen* just before he discusses Troy (*PW* 7:282; *GSD* 2:139).

mans via Aeneas, who took the Palladium, and the Franks from Priam.[117] They came together again when the Pontifex maximus was approached by "the full-blooded representative of Ur-world-Kinghood, *Karl the Great*: the bearers of the oldest Kinghood and the oldest Priesthood, dissevered since the razing of that cradle city (according to the Trojan saga, the *royal Priamos* and the *pious Æneas*) met after centuries of parting, and touched as body and spirit of mankind."[118]

In the next section of *Die Wibelungen* he explains that "[i]n its earliest form, the stem-saga (Stammsaga) of the Nibelungen went back to the memory of a divine Urfather, not only of the Franks, but perhaps of all the nations issued from the Asiatic home."[119] This divine Ur-father is then identified with "[t]he abstract Highest God of the Germans, Wuotan" who "did not really need to yield to the God of the Christians" but rather could be "completely identified with him."[120] The "God of the Christians" is Christ himself and this identification may be alluding to Odin being hung on a tree.[121] And so Wagner writes (referring to Odin/Wotan): "But that one native Stem-god, from whom the races all immediately derived their earthly being, was certainly the last to be given up: for in him was found the striking likeness to Christ himself, the Son of God, that he too died, was mourned and avenged,—as we still avenge Christ on the Jews of to-day. Fidelity and attachment were transferred to Christus [sic] all the easier, as one recognised in him the Stem-god once again; and if Christ, as Son of God, was father (at least the spiritual) of *all* men, that harmonised the better and more conclusively with the divine Stem-father of the Franks, who thought themselves indeed the oldest race and parent of all others."[122]

After identifying Christ with Wotan, something that we shall soon see has resonances with the *Jesus of Nazareth* sketches, Wagner identifies Christ with Siegfried: "In the German Folk survives the oldest lawful race of Kings in all the world: it issues from a son of God, called by his nearest kinsmen *Siegfried*, but *Christ* by the remaining nations of the earth; for the welfare of his race, and the peoples of the earth, derived therefrom, he wrought a deed most glorious, and for that deed's sake suffered death."[123]

There follows a section on Friedrich I[124] and his crusade: "But *Palestine* sent forth to him the cry to save the Holy Tomb.—To the land of morning Friedrich turned his gaze: a force resistless drew him on toward Asia, to the cradle of the nations, to

---

117. *PW* 7:280; *GSD* 2:137.
118. *PW* 7:284; *GSD* 2:141.
119. *PW* 7:286; *GSD* 2:144.
120. *PW* 7:287; *GSD* 2:144.
121. See *Hávamál* 138 (Dronke, *Edda III*, 30), discussed in volume 2, chapter 3.
122. *PW* 7:287; *GSD* 2:144–45.
123. *PW* 7:289; *GSD* 2:146.
124. He was here no doubt influenced by Hegel, *Philosophie der Geschichte*, 466; *Philosophy of History*, 388 (see chapter 6 below).

the place where God begat the father of all Men."[125] He is referring to Christ here, who is also "father."[126] He now introduces the Holy Grail. "Wondrous legends had he heard of a lordly country deep in Asia, in farthest India,—of an ur-divine Priest-King (urgöttlicher Priesterkönig) who governed there a pure and happy people, immortal through the nurture of a wonder-working relic called '*the Holy Grail.*'—Might he there regain the lost Sight-of-God, now garbled by ambitious priests in Rome according to their pleasure?—"[127] He then tells of Friedrich's crusade, marching through Greece, breaking the power of the Saracens (in Asia Minor),[128] and then, in his impatience to urge Eastwards, dying in the river.[129] He explains that there was a legend that "once the *Keeper of the Grail* (der *Hüter des Grales*) had brought the holy relic (Heiligthum) to the Occident; great wonders had he here performed: in the Netherlands, the Nibelungen's ancient seat, a Knight of the Grail had appeared, but vanished when asked forbidden tidings of his origin;—then was the Grail conducted back by its old guardian to the distant morning-land;—in a castle on a lofty mount in India it now was kept once more."[130] The "Knight of the Grail" is Lohengrin, eponymous hero of the opera he completed in 1848.

Wagner argues that the Grail was making its entry on the world

> at the very time when the Kaiserhood attained its more ideal direction, and the Nibelung's Hoard accordingly was losing more and more in material worth, to yield to a higher spiritual content. The spiritual ascension of the Hoard into the Grail was accomplished in the German conscience, and the Grail, at least in the meaning lent it by German poets, must rank as the Ideal representative or follower of the Nibelungen-Hoard; it, too, had sprung from Asia, from the ur-home (Urheimath) of mankind; God had guided it to men as paragon of holiness.[131]

125. *PW* 7:293; *GSD* 2:150. Note the allusion to the theory of Schlegel and others (discussed above).

126. Compare Wagner's unorthodox trinitarianism in the *Jesus of Nazareth* sketches (*PW* 8:300; *DTB* 249): "God is the Father and the Son and the Holy Ghost: for the father begetteth the son throughout all ages, and the son begetteth again the father of the son to all eternity: this is Life and Love, this is the Holy Spirit."

127. *PW* 7:293; *GSD* 2:150. This "ur-divine Priest-King" is presumably Titurel, although his status in Wagner's *Parsifal* as "pious hero" (*WagPS* 122–23) is somewhat more modest.

128. *PW* 7:293; *GSD* 2:150.

129. Wagner, against the historical details, writes that "on horse he plunged into the stream (zu Roß sprang er in den Fluß): none saw him in this life again" (*PW* 7:293; *GSD* 2:151). Cf Brünnhilde's immolation. Friedrich actually drowned by bathing in the river Saleph; he did not "disappear" but rather his body was dragged to the bank. Attempts were made to preserve the body in vinegar with the intention of taking him to Jerusalem for burial. According to tradition, his flesh was interred in St Peter's Church, Antioch, his bones in the cathedral in Tyre, and his heart and inner organs in Tarsus. By including the story of Friedrich's rapture Wagner clearly wishes to preserve the Kyffhäuser legend of Friedrich asleep in the mountain.

130. *PW* 7:293; *GSD* 2:151.

131. *PW* 7:293–94; *GSD* 2:151. Köhler, *Titans*, 651 n. 36, suggests Wagner could again have taken

The Keeper of the Grail was the Kaiser who was both priest and king alike, and this would appear to be Friedrich Barbarossa and his successors.[132]

> The quest (Streben) of the Grail henceforth replaces the struggle (das Ringen) for the Nibelungen-Hoard, and as the occidental world, unsatisfied within, reached out past Rome and Pope to find its place of healing in the tomb of the Redeemer at Jerusalem,—as, unsatisfied even there, it cast its yearning gaze, half spiritual, half physical, still farther toward the East to find the primal shrine of manhood,—so the Grail was said to have withdrawn from out the ribald West to the pure, chaste, reachless birth-land of all nations.[133]

Wagner then reflects on the growth and decay of the "ur-old Nibelungen-saga." It sprang "like a spiritual germ from an oldest race's earliest glance at Nature (*Naturanschauung*)"; with Karl the Great "it seems to thrust its knotty fibres deep into the actual earth" then finally with Friedrich I "we see this plant unfold its fairest flower to the light" but with him the flower faded. In Friedrich II (his grandson) "the highest mind of all the Kaisers, the wondrous perfume of the dying bloom spread like a lovely fairy-spell through all the world of West and East."[134] Then with Konrad, the grandson of Friedrich II, "the leafless withered stem was torn with all its roots and fibres from the ground, and stamped to dust."[135]

The final section is headed "Historic residue of the Material content of the Hoard is 'Real Property.'"[136] He writes of "[a] shriek of horror" ("Ein Todesschrei des Entsetzens") which rang through every country when Konrad fell in Naples to Charles d'Anjou.[137] Such violent acts of the Capets "were the pattern for the modern King- and Princehood: in no belief in ur-racial descent could it seek foundation for its claims." Violence was used to attain power and to keep it.[138] "With the foundering of the Wibelungen, humankind had been torn from the last fibre whereby it still hung, in a sense, to its racial-natural origin (geschlechtlich-natürlichen Herkunft). The Hoard of the Nibelungen had evaporated to the realm of Poetry and the Idea; merely an earthly precipitate remained

---

this idea from Göttling, who writes in *Nibelungen und Gibelinen*, 8: "the Holy Grail is the transfigured Nibelung hoard" ("der heilige Gral [ist] der verklärte Nibelungenhort").

132. Wagner writes of the "Master (Oberhaupt) of all Spiritual Knighthood, such as was introduced from the Orient in the twelfth century. So this Master was in truth none other than the Kaiser, from whom all Chivalry proceeded; and thus the real and ideal world-supremacy, the union of the highest kinghood and priesthood, seemed completely attained in the Kaiser" (*PW* 7:294; *GSD* 2:151). Note that after Henry IV (1050–1106) had added the title *Rex Romanorum*, Friedrich I (in 1157) added "Holy," "reflecting his ambition to dominate Italy and the papacy, as well as the areas north of the Alps" (Whaley, *Germany I*, 17).

133. *PW* 7:294; *GSD* 2:151–52.

134. *PW* 7:294; *GSD* 2:152.

135. *PW* 7:294–95; *GSD* 2:152.

136. *PW* 7:295; *GSD* 2:152.

137. *PW* 7:295; *GSD* 2:152.

138. *PW* 7:295; *GSD* 2:152–53.

as its dregs: *real property* (*der reale Besitz*)."¹³⁹ Wagner argues that in the Nibelungen-myth we see "an uncommonly clear idea of the *nature of property, of ownership* (*Wesen des Besitzes, des Eigenthumes*)."¹⁴⁰ The hoard originally was seen as positive, appearing as "the splendour of the Earth laid bare to all by daylight" and later "as the hero's might-conferring booty, won as guerdon of the bravest, most astounding deed from a vanquished odious adversary."¹⁴¹ But as it was passed on down the generations the hoard was associated with "blood, passion, love, hate, in short—both physically and spiritually—purely-human springs and motives at work in the winning of the Hoard."¹⁴² Wagner then criticizes hereditary possession and primogeniture.¹⁴³

Wagner concludes the work thus: "The '*poor Folk*' sang, read, and printed in time, the Nibelungenlieder, its only keepsake from the hoard: belief in it never wavered; only, one knew it was no longer in the world,—for it had been sunk into an old God's-hill again, a cave like that whence Siegfried once had won it from the Nibelungen. The great Kaiser himself had brought it back to that hill, to save it up for better times. There in the Kyffhäuser he sits, the old 'Redbeard Friedrich'; all round him the treasures of the Nibelungen, by his side the sharp sword that one-time slew the dreaded Dragon."¹⁴⁴ Rather than Hagen sinking the hoard into the Rhine as in *Nibelungenlied* 19,¹⁴⁵ Barbarossa had "sunk" it "into an old God's-hill again."

Die Wibelungen was published in 1850 and most readers have been puzzled ever since. However, Devrient, to whom Wagner read it on 22 February 1849, writes that this "historical-philosophical work" ("geschichtsphilosophische Arbeit") presents the true grandeur of Friedrich I and suggests that Wagner intended to work further on *Friedrich I*.¹⁴⁶ *Die Wibelungen* can be easily dismissed (and frequently is), but for Wagner it "was the root from which *Der Ring des Nibelungen* sprang."¹⁴⁷ To summarize, the key points in which *Die Wibelungen* can illumine the *Ring* are as follows:

1. *Die Wibelungen* establishes a parallel between Wotan and Christ as father of all.

2. The work establishes a parallel between Siegfried and Christ, and further connections with Apollo (the Sun-god who killed the Python) and Barbarossa (who will return to save German).

---

139. *PW* 7:295; *GSD* 2:153.
140. *PW* 7:295; *GSD* 2:153.
141. *PW* 7:295–96; *GSD* 2:153.
142. *PW* 7:296; *GSD* 2:153.
143. One wonders whether this has any connection with Wagner dying intestate.
144. *PW* 7:298; *GSD* 2:155.
145. *NibE* 106.
146. Devrient, *Tagebüchern*, 1:470: "Friedrich I. stieg als der gewaltigste Träger des ganzen Inhalts dieser Idee, von riesengroßer, wundervoller Schönheit auf. Er will ihn dramatisch behandeln."
147. Gregor-Dellin, *Life*, 156. The work has been unjustly neglected but, as Wilberg, *Mythische Welt*, has demonstrated, it is central to Wagner's understanding of myth. The importance of *Die Wibelungen* is suggested by the study of Köhler, *Titans*, 250–55.

3. It speaks of the relationship between the hoard and the Grail, and hence relates the *Ring* to both *Lohengrin* and *Parsifal*. But it also relates the gaining of the hoard to the dangers of "property."[148]

4. Elements in *Die Wibelungen* point to the possible "German" and "racial" aspects of the *Ring*, which could be otherwise overlooked.

5. *Die Wibelungen* highlights the important theme of blood, which also runs throughout the *Ring*: Fafner's blood, Hagen's corrupted blood, Siegfried's blood.[149]

6. *Die Wibelungen* points to the possible Old Testament views of kingship, which may also be present on the *Ring*. Note the king's role as priest ("the king soon lost his priestly office")[150] and the idea of the king incorporating the people: "Only to the person of the King and his immediate kinsmen, would the feeling of the stem still cleave: he was the visible point-of-union of all its members; in him they saw the successor to the Ur-father of the widely-branching fellowship, and in each member of his family the purest of that blood whence the whole Folk had sprung."[151] We also find Old Testament ideas of kingship being combined with Hegelian views of "Idea": "If in Karl the Great the drift of blood was still at height of its ancestral strength, in the Hohenstaufen *Friedrich I* we see almost nothing but the ideal stress: it had become at last the very soul of the Imperial entity, that could find less and less legitimation in its blood and real estate, and therefore sought it in the Idea."[152]

7. *Die Wibelungen* points to Wagner's archaizing style and the love of compounds formed with the prefix "ur-": "uralte" ("ur-old"),[153] "urälteste" ("ur-oldest"),[154] "Urberechtigung" ("ur-right"),[155] "urgöttlicher Berechtigung" ("divine ur-right"),[156] "Urbewußtsein" ("ur-conscience"),[157] "Urvölkerstadt" ("ur-people's city"),[158] "Urgeschlecht" ("primal race"),[159] "Urvölkerverhältnis" ("ur-folk

---

148. *PW* 7:295–96; *GSD* 2:153.
149. *WagRS* 242 (Siegfried sucks Fafner's blood from his fingers), 298 (blood brotherhood of Siegfried and Gunther, and Hagen's blood which "doesn't flow truly").
150. *PW* 7:261; *GSD* 2:117.
151. *PW* 7:261; *GSD* 2:118.
152. *PW* 7:288; *GSD* 2:145.
153. *PW* 7:287; *GSD* 2:144. *PW* 7:281; *GSD* 2:138. *PW* 7:279; *GSD* 2:136. *PW* 7:288; *GSD* 2:145. *PW* 7:294; *GSD* 2:152.
154. Cf. *PW* 7:282; *GSD* 139.
155. *PW* 7:280; *GSD* 2:137.
156. *PW* 7:297; *GSD* 2:155.
157. *PW* 7:263; *GSD* 2:119.
158. *PW* 7:280; *GSD* 2:137.
159. *PW* 7:280; *GSD* 2:137.

relationship"),[160] "Urvölkerheiligthum" ("ur-folk's sanctuary"),[161] "Urkönigthum" ("ur-Kinghood"),[162] "Urstadt" ("ur-city"),[163] "Urvater" ("ur-father"),[164] "urgöttlicher Priesterkönig" ("ur-divine Priest-King"),[165] "Urkönigthum" ("ur-kinghood"),[166] "Urheimath" ("ur-home"),[167] "urgeschlechtliche Herkunft" ("ur-racial descent").[168] The language of the *Ring* is also archaized and the use of the compound "Urgesetz" will prove to be significant.[169]

Der Nibelungen-Mythus

Although the title of the final artwork referred to just one Nibelung (*Der Ring des Nibelungen*), the genitive "des Nibelungen" referring to Alberich, his sketch employed the plural,[170] its full title being *Der Nibelungen-Mythus: Als Entwurf zu einem Drama*, which strictly should be translated *The Nibelungs Myth as a Sketch for a Drama*. This was completed on 4 October 1848[171] and the fair copy was produced on 8 October 1848. This contains most of the essential elements of what was to become the final *Ring* cycle.

Although it is often said that Wagner wrote the libretto for his *Ring* backwards, this sketch contains the essential elements that were to make the entire *Ring* cycle, although certain aspects that were important for the final work are missing. The figure of Loge is missing in the 1848 *Ring* and this can be explained to some extent by the fact that it was only later that he read the *Edda* poems, where Loki has an important

---

160. Cf. *PW* 7:259; *GSD* 2:116.
161. Cf. *PW* 7:280; *GSD* 2:137.
162. Cf. *PW* 7:284; *GSD* 2:141.
163. *PW* 7:282; *GSD* 2:139.
164. *PW* 7:286; *GSD* 2:144.
165. *PW* 7:293; *GSD* 2:150.
166. *PW* 7:259; *GSD* 2:116.
167. *PW* 7:259; *GSD* 2:116. *PW* 7:294; *GSD* 2:151.
168. *PW* 7:295; *GSD* 2:152.
169. See volume 2, chapter 7.

170. Note that had Wagner wished to entitle the work referring to just one Nibelung he could have written it as "Der Mythus des Nibelungen." However, he chose to write a compound noun "Nibelungen-Mythus," this form indicating a number of Nibelungs. Note also that the content of the myth tends to focus on the plurality of Nibelungs. It opens by describing their home and activity (Haymes, *Ring*, 44–45) and ends with their redemption ("Let the slavery of the Nibelungs be over; the ring shall no longer bind them") even though Alberich is the key Nibelung as indicated by how the text continues: "Alberich will not receive it. He shall no longer hold you as slaves. But he will now be free like you" (Haymes, *Ring*, 58–59). Note also that earlier versions of *Siegfried's Tod* emphasized the plurality of Nibelungs. But the switch to the singular is indicated by Hagen's referring to the "Den Ring des Nibelungen" ("The Ring of the Nibelungs") in the 1848 version (Haymes, *Ring*, 140–41; *TBRN1* 90) and up until the *Viertschrift des Textbuches* (May 1850) but then changed to "Des Nibelungen Reif" in the 1853 *Ring* (*TBRN1* 187).

171. See Strobel, *Skizzen*, Insert I, for the final page of this.

role, and the key article by Weinhold, which only appeared in 1849.[172] Erda also is missing, her role being carried out by the Norns. Perhaps the two most striking missing elements (also missing in *Siegfried's Tod*) are the explicit descent of Siegfried and Brünnhilde from the gods and the "erotic," both of which were to be important for the final *Ring*. So Siegmund and Sieglinde are not children of Wotan and although Brünnhilde is described as a "divine virgin" there is no indication she is the daughter of Wotan. The only indication of any divine origin is when Wagner writes "[a] second heroic dynasty, which is also descended from the gods, is that of the Gibichungs on the Rhine."[173] On the erotic, Dreyfus writes: "Wagner drafts this self-consciously archaic text in a pseudo-mythic style within which any intrusion of a modern Romantic love would seem anachronistic."[174] So Alberich does not renounce love to form the ring as in the final libretto;[175] rather he "stole the clear and noble Rhine-gold, carried it away from the depths of the waters and forged from it with great cunning and art a ring that gave him the highest power over his whole race, the Nibelungs."[176] Further, the goddess Freia does not feature in that section of the *Mythus* that corresponds to what was to become *Rheingold*[177] and so the giants simply demand "the hoard of the Nibelungs."[178] The wish maidens do not provide sexual favors for the fallen heroes,[179] something that may be suggested by Brünnhilde's words to Siegmund: "Wotan's daughter / will lovingly hand you your drink."[180] Instead "they accompany those who have fallen in battle to Valhalla, where the heroes in Wotan's company continue a magnificent life with battle games."[181] Siegmund and Sieglinde simply "come together themselves (begatten sich)" "[i]n order to bring forth a true Volsung,"[182] again the eroticism of the later *Walküre* being absent. On Brünnhilde's awakening "[s]he recognizes Siegfried, the most magnificent hero of the Volsung dynasty, joyfully, and gives herself to him,"[183] again with none of the eroticism we find in *Siegfried* Act III. Before the immolation Brünnhilde announces "Let only One rule, All-father, lordly one."[184]

172. See chapter 3 below. However, Loge does feature in other works he had read such as Grimm, *Mythologie* (he may also have read Rußwurm, *Nordische Sagen*, 289–91, 256, on Loge, a work in his Dresden Library).

173. Haymes, *Ring*, 49.

174. Dreyfus, *Erotic Impulse*, 92.

175. WagRS 68–69.

176. Haymes, *Ring*, 45.

177. "Holda" though features in that by eating one of her apples an otherwise childless couple give birth to Siegmund and Sieglinde (Haymes, *Ring* 47; see below).

178. Haymes, *Ring*, 45.

179. Dreyfus, *Erotic Impulse*, 93.

180. WagRS 160: "Wotan's Tochter / reicht dir traulich den Trank."

181. Haymes, *Ring*, 47.

182. Haymes, *Ring*, 46–49.

183. Haymes, *Ring*, 49.

184. Haymes, *Ring*, 59.

As Dreyfus comments, this is "[a]ll a very far cry from a redemption through Love."[185] In my judgement the key introduction of the erotic into the *Ring* would appear to be in the writing of the "Prosa-Entwurf" of *Der junge Siegfried* (24 May–1 June 1851), where Siegfried tells Brünnhilde of the burning passion in his lips, veins, and limbs, which she alone can quench.[186]

The archaic style is captured by Ellis' translation of the very opening of *Der Nibelungen-Mythus*: "From the womb of Night and Death was spawned a race that dwells in Nibelheim (Nebelheim), i.e., in gloomy subterranean clefts and caverns: *Nibelungen* are they called; with restless nimbleness they burrow through the bowels of the earth, like worms in a dead body; they smelt and smith hard metals."[187] The sketch goes on to tell of how Alberich stole the gold from the river Rhine and made from it a ring "that gave him the highest power over his whole race."[188] Meanwhile Wotan had a fortress built by the giants who demanded payment with the Rhinegold. Wotan therefore steals the hoard of gold and the ring from Alberich who places a curse on it. Wotan gives the gold to the giants as payment but keeps the ring "to maintain his own supreme dominion." The giants demand it and Wotan gives in "following the advice of the Fates (Norns), who warn him of the doom of the gods themselves."[189] The sketch omits the killing of Fasolt by Fafner and Fafner's transformation into a dragon using the tarnhelm; indeed the giants are not named at all and we just read "the giants cause the ring to be protected on the Gnita- (envy-) heath by a monstrous dragon."[190] By this ring Alberich and the Nibelungs are subjugated, but the giants do not know how to use their power.[191] "In the glory of the new race of gods the giants pale and are paralyzed, powerless; the Nibelungs languish miserably and full of guile in useless activity. Alberich broods without rest over recovering the ring."[192]

The next paragraph outlines how the gods plan to resolve the situation and takes us through to what became the end of *Der junge Siegfried/Siegfried*. "In high-minded activity the gods ordered now the world, bound the elements through wise laws, and

---

185. Dreyfus, *Erotic Impulse*, 93.

186. Strobel, *Skizzen*, 94: "Mein auge weidet auf deinem mund: meine lippen doch brennen in heißem durst, der augen weide zu kosten! [. . .] durch die adern glüth mir ein sengender strom: das feuer erlosch, das dich umbrann, jetzt brennt es mir im gebein!—Ach selig Weib, lösche den brand: schweige die schäumende gluth."

187. PW 7:301. Cf. Haymes, *Ring*, 45: "Out of the womb of the night and of death rose a race that lives in Nibelheim (Mist-Home) i.e., in subterranean dark crevasses and caves: they are called Nibelungs; in irregular, restless activity they dig (like worms in a dead body) through the bowels of the earth; they melt, purify, and shape the hard metals."

188. Haymes, *Ring*, 45.

189. Haymes, *Ring*, 45. Fafner's abode is later changed from "Gnita- (Neid-) Haide" ("Gnita- (envy-) heath") to "Neidhöhle" (literally "Envy-cave"). The Norns, of course, were to be replaced by Erda in what was to become *Rheingold* Scene 4.

190. Haymes, *Ring*, 45.

191. Haymes, *Ring*, 45–47.

192. Haymes, *Ring*, 47.

devoted themselves to the most solicitous care of the race of men. Their power stands above everything."[193] But the peace (Friede) through which they have risen to power is not based on reconciliation (Versöhnung!) but on violence (Gewalt) and cunning (List). The aim of their ordering of the world is "moral consciousness (sittliches Bewußtsein)" but the "injustice they perpetuate [. . .] adheres to them."[194] Wotan cannot "erase the injustices"; only "a free will, independent of the gods, which is willing to take all of the guilt on itself, and to suffer for it, can break the spell, and the gods see in human beings the capability for such a will. They try to transfer their divinity to humanity, in order to raise its power to such a level that it [. . .] turns away from divine protection in order to do whatever occurs to it by its own free will."[195] Although "[m]ighty human races (Geschlechter)" are arising "the real hero has not yet been born." The sketch then is rather different to the final form known from *Walküre*. Among the Volsungs a childless marriage was brought to fruition by Wotan causing a couple to eat one of "Holda's apples." The twins born, Siegmund and Sieglinde, each take a spouse but their marriages are childless.[196] Siegmund here is *not* intended as the person to recover the ring since Wagner writes: "In order for a true Volsung, brother and sister come together themselves."[197] With Hunding's killing Siegmund and the disobedience of Brünnhilde, the "divine virgin" ("die göttlich Jungfrau"), the story then reverts largely to what we know in the final *Ring*. Some details are different (e.g., Hunding is killed by Siegfried before he kills the dragon)[198] and some of the key scenes we know are absent, e.g., the plea of Waltraute for Brünnhilde to return the ring. The most significant difference between this sketch and the final *Ring* is that the work ends not with the end of the gods but their ruling, their "injustice" having been erased. Brünnhilde tells the gods: "Thank him, the hero, who took your guilt upon himself." The slavery of the Nibelungs comes to an end and Wotan as "All-father" rules eternally.[199] It was this ending that fashioned the close of *Siegfried's Tod*.[200]

Siegfried's Tod

Wagner's first sketch for *Siegfried's Tod* was completed on 20 October 1848.[201] He showed it to Eduard Devrient on the very next day,[202] who noted that Wagner "had

193. Haymes, *Ring*, 47.
194. Haymes, *Ring*, 46–47. "Moral consciousness" is related to the key issue of "law."
195. Haymes, *Ring*, 47.
196. Haymes, *Ring*, 46–47.
197. Haymes, *Ring*, 46–49.
198. Haymes, *Ring*, 48–49.
199. Haymes, *Ring*, 59.
200. Haymes, *Ring*, 182–85.
201. For the text see Strobel, *Skizzen*, 38–55.
202. Devrient, *Tagebüchern*, 1:451. According to *My Life* 380 (*Mein Leben* 1:394) Wagner read it

again high-flown socialist ideas" ("hatte wieder große sozialistische Rosinen im Kopf") and that his concerns were not just with Germany but with Europe and with the unity of the human race.[203] Wagner visited him again on 27 October when Devrient expressed his reservation about the opera, critique that Wagner took on board.[204] Wagner's autobiography fills in the details, explaining that Devrient felt the opera plan presupposed too much: "He showed me, for example, that before Siegfried and Brünnhilde could be displayed in bitter hostility to one another, it would be necessary first to let the audience become acquainted with this couple in their true relationship of prior harmony."[205] Wagner therefore prefaced the three-act work with a prologue at the end of October: a scene with the Norns and a scene with Siegfried and Brünnhilde.[206] The "poem"[207] was then written between 12[208] and 28 November 1848 and in December (probably) he produced the "Reinschrift" (fair copy) which was the second writing of the first version ("Zweitschrift" of "Erste Fassung").[209] The first version bore the title "Siegfried's Tod: Eine große Heldenoper in drei Akten." A second version (this is the "Drittschrift") was written (probably early 1849) bearing the title "Siegfried's Tod: Eine Heldenoper in drei Akten."[210] Later when he had settled in Zurich he then made a clean copy of this producing his "Viertschrift."[211] Then in the end of November and beginning of December 1852 he reworked it again to give the "Fünftschrift," which is essentially the work we know as the fourth opera of the cycle and was to be renamed *Götterdämmerung*.[212]

Once he had produced the fair copy in December 1848 he applied himself to some projects that were related to what was to become the *Ring*. Before the uprising in May 1849 the key work was *Jesus of Nazareth*. As noted above, it must have been at this time that he committed to paper *Die Wibelungen*, written on the same sort of green paper used for *Jesus of Nazareth* and again using small letters. It may also be around this time that he wrote his "Ideas for an 'Achilles' in 3 Acts."[213]

---

aloud to him.

203. Devrient, *Tagebüchern*, 1:451.

204. Devrient, *Tagebüchern*, 1:451.

205. *My Life* 380–81; *Mein Leben* 1:394.

206. For the text of the new prologue see Strobel, *Skizzen*, 56–58.

207. Wagner referred to the libretto as a "poem" ("Dichtung") (see e.g., his letter to Minna of 19 May 1849, *SB* 2:677), which suggests he saw it as an artwork in itself. He uses the term for his libretti as early as 1833 (*SB* 1:34, referring to "Die Hochzeit").

208. See Strobel, *Skizzen*, Insert III, for the first page.

209. Strobel, *Skizzen*, 58. From this Nietzsche later produced a fair copy after Wagner had made various changes (see Strobel, *Skizzen*, insert V).

210. Strobel, *Skizzen*, 59 (see also insert VI).

211. Strobel, *Skizzen*, 59 (see also insert IV).

212. Strobel, *Skizzen*, 60. For details of the sketches and texts of *Siegfried's Tod* see *WWV* 393–95.

213. *Brown Book* 96; *Braunes Buch* 114 (*Annals* for 1849, suggesting a date of early 1849). For the very brief sketches see *DTB* 268. See the discussion on Achilles in chapter 4 below.

Jesus of Nazareth

In his autobiography he explains that his "last creative project" in Dresden was a "draft of a five-act drama *Jesus of Nazareth*."[214] The manuscript of twenty-eight written sides was at some point lent to Carolyne von Sayn-Wittgenstein, the partner of the composer Franz Liszt. Considering herself a conservative Catholic, she clearly felt that a drama based on the life of Jesus of Nazareth was highly inappropriate and, despite Wagner's various pleas to return the sketches, held on to them. The work was called "A poetic draft" ("Ein dichterischer Entwurf") when it was first published in 1887. The latest critical edition more accurately describes it as a "prose draft" ("Prosaentwurf")[215] and the title given by Wagner was simply "Jesus von Nazareth." The sketches can be divided into two main parts with the second being further subdivided. So part one is the outline of the drama. Part two section one (II.1) is theological commentary and part two section two (II.2) gives the texts of a whole series of passages from the New Testament which the composer felt were relevant for the drama.[216] In the English translation of Ellis the sketches amount to fifty-six pages, so we are dealing with something fairly substantial.[217]

Generally speaking, the drama follows the outline of the Gospels, Jesus making his first appearance with his disciples and bringing to life the daughter of Levi.[218] The earlier events in his life (birth, youth, baptism, sojourn in the wilderness) come in a "flashback" in Act II, which, had he completed the sparse elements in the sketches, would involve a recitative, and possibly a long one![219] The action ends with Jesus' crucifixion (which occurs off-stage) and Peter, being filled with the Holy Spirit and able to interpret the significance of Jesus' death, proclaims "the fulfilment of Jesus' promise," i.e., that his death is a redemptive death and that the Holy Spirit will then be given. Whoever hears Peter "presses forward to demand baptism (reception into the community)."[220]

In Jesus' teaching his principal target is the Pharisees, whom he views as legalistic oppressors of the people. Given Wagner's own negative assessment of "the Romans" (as opposed to "the Greeks"), it is noticeable that Jesus does not attack them in the dramatic outline (I)[221] and Pilate is portrayed in a positive light, doing whatever he can to save Jesus from crucifixion. Further, Jesus opposes Barabbas[222] and appears

214. *My Life* 389; Mein Leben 1:403.
215. *DTB* 241.
216. Bell, "Prose Sketches," 263–64, argues that he wrote these sections in the order II.2; I; II.1.
217. *PW* 8:283–340.
218. *PW* 8:286; *DTB* 241.
219. Wagner's operas have frequent flashbacks, as in Wotan's monologue in *Walküre* Act II.
220. *PW* 8:297; *DTB* 246.
221. However, in the commentary Wagner speaks of the possibility of Jesus ending "the execrable Roman rule of violence" (*PW* 8:298; *DTB* 248).
222. Note that Wagner follows Luther's spelling "Barrabas"; Ellis in his translation replaces this

(the text is dense) to support paying taxes to Caesar.²²³ This, together with the clear idea we have seen in the drama of Jesus as redeemer, must question the view that Wagner conceives of Jesus preaching a purely worldly religion of "commonality and communism," advocating "freedom from law and thus liberation from the shackles of the state."²²⁴ Wagner's Jesus is definitely not a political messiah, and "his kingdom" is "no earthly sovereignty."²²⁵ Nevertheless, one can say that Wagner presented Jesus as a "social revolutionary," this being particular clear in the commentary rather than in the drama itself.²²⁶ However, the view that Wagner presents Jesus "*purely* as a social revolutionary"²²⁷ has to be rejected; being a social revolutionary is just one aspect of Jesus' ministry and in the drama it is a minor aspect.

The sketches for what was intended as a five-act opera, to be performed in Paris, were never returned to Wagner. But the material was not to go to waste since many of the ideas end up on the stage of the *Ring*; indeed, we will see that they are fundamental for understanding its theology, issues that will be explored in volume two, but also to some extent in chapters 6 and 7 below.

Revolution

There is a fundamental discrepancy between the pacifism of the *Jesus* drama and Wagner's revolutionary fervor at the time of composing the sketches.²²⁸ In a letter of 1849 to his first wife Minna, Wagner claims to have become "a revolutionary, plain and simple"²²⁹ and his revolutionary zeal, although going back to at least 1830,²³⁰ seemed to have come to a head in 1848–49. On 14 June 1848 Wagner delivered his *Vaterlandsverein*

---

with the correct spelling "Barabbas."

223. See *PW* 8:286: "Barabbas catechises Jesus. (Cæsar's-pence.) Undeception of Barabbas" (*DTB* 242: "Barrabas sucht Jesus zu erforschen. (Der kaiserzins.) Enttäuschung des Barrabas"). Presumably Barabbas is disappointed because Jesus has failed to support his opposition to paying taxes. Note that in the Gospels it is the Pharisees who put the question (Mark 12:13–17; Matt 22:15–22; Luke 20:20–26).

224. Kienzle, "*Parsifal* and Religion," 84.

225. *PW* 8:291; *DTB* 244.

226. In the commentary Wagner shows clear sympathy for the views of Proudhon (i.e., property should be fairly distributed). For Wagner's debt to French socialism, especially Proudhon, see Kreckel, *Frühsozialisten*.

227. Gregor-Dellin, *Life*, 161 (my emphasis).

228. The very fact that he changed to using a Latin script with virtually no capital letters in December 1848 (note the lack of capitalized nouns in any German quotations I have included) *may* be a sign of his revolutionary mind set (*WDS*, 75) but "revolutionary" in the sense of an obsession with the archaic; as noted above he was following the example of Jacob Grimm (not exactly a revolutionary) in using this Latin script with virtually no capitals.

229. *SB* 2:653. The postmark is Weimar 14 May 1849 (p. 657 n. 3); after fleeing Dresden he reached Weimar on 13 May.

230. His *Autobiographical Sketch* (published in 1843) tells how the July 1830 Revolution in Paris had turned him into a revolutionary (*PW* 1:6).

(Fatherland Society) speech, published two days later in the *Dresdener Anzeiger*. In a passage in which he calls for the aristocracy to be abolished, he appeals to Jesus: "If a limb offend thee, cut it off and cast it from thee: for it is profitable for thee that one of thy members should perish, and not that thy whole body should be cast into hell."[231] His point appears to be that the yoke of the aristocrats must be thrown off for the benefit of the whole "Volk." A little later he argues that society "is maintained by the *activity of its members*, and not through any fancied agency of *money* [. . .] and like a hideous nightmare will this demoniac idea of Money vanish from us, with all its loathsome retinue of open and secret usury, paper-juggling, percentage and bankers' speculations. That will be the *full emancipation of the human race*; that will be the *fulfilment of Christ's pure teaching*, which enviously they hide from us behind parading dogmas, invented erst to bind the simple world of raw barbarians [. . .]."[232] Such ideas of the abolition of capital are not put forward in the dramatic outline of the *Jesus of Nazareth* sketches although they do appear in a less extreme form in the commentary.

In opposition to the *Jesus* sketches, the *Ring* in many ways is concerned with the destruction of "old regimes" and the starting afresh of a "new order"[233] and it is significant that one of his companions in the uprising was the anarchist Mikhail Bakunin.[234] He also become familiar with the thinking of Proudhon.[235] From about 1848 Wagner's aim was to overthrow the aristocracy (but not the monarchy)[236] and radically to reform the artistic life in Dresden. By April 1849 his views seem to have become more extreme. This can be seen in an anonymous article "Revolution," which, as Glasenapp notes, was written under the immediate impression of Beethoven's Ninth Symphony, performed on Palm Sunday;[237] the essay appeared just eight days later in the *Volksblätter* (Dresden 8 April 1849).[238] Wagner's interest in theology was

231. PW 4:137; SSD 12:221.
232. PW 4:139; SSD 12:223.
233. On "Wagner, Feuerbach and the Future," see Magee, *Wagner and Philosophy*, 48–67.
234. Bakunin was personally acquainted with Marx and Engels and it is highly likely that Wagner came to know of Marx's teaching through Bakunin (cf. Millington, *Wagner*, 37). Note also that Bakunin was in Paris in 1844 and here he met Marx and Proudhon (Carr, *Bakunin*, 128–31). George Bernard Shaw saw Bakunin as one of the inspirations for the figure of Siegfried (Laurence, *Shaw's Music III*, 457–58).
235. *Mein Leben* 1:387; *My Life* 373. Wagner explains the "strange transformation" (372) in his friend Röckel: "On the basis of the socialist theories of Proudhon and others pertaining to the annihilation of the power of capital by direct productive labor, he constructed a whole new moral order of things to which, by some of his more attractive assertions, he little by little converted me to the point where I began to rebuild upon it my hopes for the realization of my artistic ideals."
236. His speech delivered on 14 June and published in the *Dresdener Anzeiger* 16 June 1848 is entitled *How do Republican Endeavours Stand in Relation to the Monarchy?* (PW 4:136–45; SSD 12:220–29).
237. Glasenapp, *Leben*, 2:538. One can discern allusions to the text of the fourth movement in the article ("brothers", Millionen").
238. The text was originally printed in Dinger, *Entwickelung*, 233–40. This work (the second volume of which never appeared) was an expansion of his inaugural dissertation submitted to the

clearly linked to his interest in politics and revolution. E.g., when he was keeping watch at the top of the tower of the Kreuzkirche he tells of how he was engaged in conversations with Dr Wilhelm Berthold with whom he lost himself "in a serious philosophical discussion which extended to the remoter boundaries of religion."[239]

After the Revolution

After the uprising he again applied himself to a number of projects again related to the *Ring*. The key trilogy of theoretical essays are *Art and Revolution* (1949),[240] *Art-work of the Future* (1849),[241] and *Opera and Drama* (1850–51),[242] all of which will be discussed in the following chapters. Also important are *Judaism in Music* (1850) and *Communication to My Friends* (1851).[243] He also made sketches for a play *Wieland der Schmied*, which, as we will see, is relevant for the *Ring*, including the issue of androgyny.[244] The

---

Philosophy Faculty of Leipzig University. He writes in the preface to the dissertation: "Es ist daher des Verfassers Absicht, das vorgenommene Thema vorläufig in zwei räumlich getrennten Abteilungen zu behandeln" (*Weltanschuung*, X). He explains that the first volume will look at the development of the composer's thinking and the second (which never appeared) will deal with his relationship to Young Hegelian and Schopenhauerian philosophy. Dinger's portrayal of Wagner's revolutionary activities in *Entwickelung* was criticized by Glasenapp, *Leben*, 2:VII, but defended by Newman, *Life*, 2:60–61. Nevertheless Glasenapp, *Leben*, 2:538–42, followed Dinger in printing "Die Revolution" in an "Anhang") and an English translation given in *PW* 8:232–38. "I [Revolution] will destroy the domination of one over the other [. . .] of the material over the spiritual, I will shatter the power of the mighty, of the law and of property. Man's master shall be his *own* will, his *own* desire and his only law, his *own* strength his only property, *for only the free man is holy and there is naught higher than he.* Let there be an end to the wrong that gives one man power over millions [. . .] *and since all are equal I shall destroy all dominion of one over the other*" (*WDS*, 172, Wagner's emphasis; cf. *PW* 8:236).

239. *My Life* 399; *Mein Leben* 1:412. This must have been on Saturday 6 May 1849. The discussion appears to have gone on to the Sunday. Gregor-Dellin, *Life*, 173, identifies Berthold as "a schoolmaster from Döbeln" and adds: "Another eyewitness, Professor Thum of Reichenbach, recalled Wagner discoursing at length on the ancient and Christian philosophies of life, Dresden's royal orchestra, and the Leipzig concert hall, the Gewandhaus."

240. Published 1849.

241. Completed 4 November 1849 and published in 1850 (Otto Wigand, Leipzig).

242. Extracts were published in 1851 but not published as a whole until 1852 (by J. J. Weber, Leipzig).

243. This was published at the end of 1851 (but with the date 1852) by Breitkopf & Härtel, originally with the title *Drei Operndichtungen nebst einer Mittheilung an meine Freunde als Vorwort*. Wagner received his copies on 27 December 1851 (*SB* 3:239).

244. Nattiez, *Androgyne*, 43–52, points to how the sketches relate to a whole series of themes in the *Ring* (e.g., themes of forging, swords, forgetfulness, as well as the power of a ring itself). Many of the similarities between Wieland and the *Ring* are set out in *Communication* (*PW* 1:290–91; *GSD* 4:250–51). Wagner allegorizes on themes from Wieland in his theories of art; indeed the first appearance of Wieland occurs at the end of *Artwork of the Future* where Wieland comes to represents both the Volk and the poet. After outlining the story (*PW* 1:210–13; *GSD* 3:175–77) the essay concludes: "*O sole and glorious Folk! This is it, that thou thyself hast sung. Thou art thyself this Wieland! Weld thou thy wings, and soar on high*" (*PW* 1:213; *GSD* 3:177). On the issue of androgyny, see volume 2 chapter 5.

first sketches are found at the end of *Artwork* but then expanded;[245] but eventually Wagner lost interest in completing the work.[246]

Amid all this theoretical writing and sketches for dramas that were never completed, Wagner did eventually get around to composing musical sketches in the summer of 1850. He expressed his intention of composing back in June 1849,[247] but it was Liszt's willingness to perform *Lohengrin* in Weimar (this took place on 28 August 1850) that finally motivated him to compose music for *Siegfried's Tod*,[248] which he began on 12 August 1850. As Bailey points out, they are not only the first sketches for the *Ring* but also "constitute Wagner's only dramatic music between the completion of *Lohengrin* in the spring of 1848 and the beginning of work on *Das Rheingold* in the late autumn of 1853."[249] We have now both the "Composition Sketch"[250] and the "Orchestral Sketch."[251] Included in the sketches is the music for Act I Scene 3 where all the Valkyries, not just Waltraute as in later versions, plead with Brünnhilde to give up the ring. We have here the development of a melody that was then later to be the "ride of the Valkyries."[252] However, he did not make great progress, and perhaps felt that he must apply himself to the issues of opera and drama, to which he applied himself in the essay of that name.

Der junge Siegfried

It was three years after first working on *Siegfried's Tod* that he applied himself to the libretto of *Der junge Siegfried*; this was developed in 1851, the prose sketch being

---

245. The first prose sketch (*Erster Prosaentwurf*) was composed between 12 and 28 January 1850 (*DTB* 269) and the second was completed 11 March 1850 (*DTB* 278). For these texts see *DTB* 269–77; 279–302 (*PW* 1:215–65). The source was Simrock's *Amelungenlied* volume 1 (volume 4 of the *Heldenbuch*), 1–204, which was in his Dresden Library (Westernhagen, *Bibliothek*, 84; DB 3).

246. Wagner asked Liszt to set it to music (*SB* 3:470) and when Liszt was not forthcoming Wagner asked if Liszt would offer it to Berlioz (*SB* 4:459). Later he offered it to Röckel and then Wendelin (*WWV* 343). The work is numbered as WWV 82.

247. *SB* 3:82, letter to Liszt of 18 June 1849. See also *SB* 3:124 (to Uhlig, 16 September 1849; note the avoidance of capital letters), *SB* 3:136–37 (to Liszt, 14 October 1849) and *SB* 3:149 (to Ferdinand Heine, 19 November 1849).

248. See his letters to Liszt of around 20 July 1859 (*SB* 3:356; on the date of this letter see *SB* 3:358–59 n. 5).

249. Bailey, "Sketches," 460.

250. The very beginning can be found in Kapp, *Wagner*, photograph 44.

251. Bailey, "Sketches," 485–94, gives a sketch that is made up of the "Orchestral Sketch" for the Prologue (bars 1–166), beginning with the Norns and then running on to the scene with Brünnhilde and Siegfried ("Brunnhilde zu gedenken") but then adding material from the "Composition Sketch" and "supplying the text and a detail of the accompaniment in the last nine measures" (Bailey, "Sketches," 469), hence stopping at bars 190–92 ("Brünnhilde zu erwecken!") The whole section can be followed in the libretto given in Haymes, *Ring*, 66–72.

252. Bailey, "Sketches," 464–69.

written 3–10 May,²⁵³ the prose draft 24 May–1 June, and the verse draft 3–24 June.²⁵⁴ He described the work as a "heroic comedy" ("heroisches Lustspiel") to complement the tragedy of *Siegfried's Tod*.²⁵⁵ However, as many have perceived, there is a darker side to the "comedy" in that the work is related to Wagner's essay *Judaism in Music* written the previous year.²⁵⁶ Ideas from this essay entered *Der junge Siegfried* in the portrayal of Mime as "synagogue singer" and as "master in technology." Regarding the former he writes: "Who has not had occasion to convince himself of the travesty of a divine service of song, presented in a real Folk-synagogue? Who has not been seized with a feeling of the greatest revulsion, of horror mingled with the absurd, at hearing that sense-and-sound-confounding gurgle, jodel and cackle, which no intentional caricature can make more repugnant than as offered here in full, in naïve seriousness?"²⁵⁷ Not only does Mime sing in this fashion but he has problems relating his words to his music seen at its most obvious in *Siegfried* Act II Scene 3, where the "lullaby" music clashes with the words telling of Mime's intention to kill Siegfried.²⁵⁸ This brings us to Mime as "master in technology." Back in 1848 Wagner could have Mime (also called Reigin or Eugel)²⁵⁹ as a master in a positive sense: in the *Nibelungen-Mythus* ("Siegfried under Mime's instruction forges the sword")²⁶⁰ and in *Siegfried's Tod* Act III Siegfried tells: "As master Mime taught me to forge."²⁶¹ Perhaps at this stage Mime was not Jewish at all. However, it appears that Wagner's 1850 *Judaism in Music* was to color the subsequent development of his Mime, becoming a "master" whose craft corresponds to that of Mendelssohn. Wagner argues that this composer "has shewn us that a Jew may have the amplest store of specific talents, may own the finest and most varied culture, the highest and the tenderest sense of honour—yet without all these pre-eminences helping him, were it but one single time, to call forth in us that deep, that heart-searching effect which we await from Art because we know her capable thereof, because we have felt it many a time and oft, so soon as once a hero of

---

253. In a letter to Eduard Avenarius of 3 May 1851 he actually writes of his intention to compose music for *Siegfried's Tod* (SB 3:567: "Ich mache mich jetzt an die musikalische Ausführung meines Siegfried") but a letter written a week later to Uhlig (SB 4:43; 10 May 1851) reveals that instead he had been working out the outline of *Der junge Siegfried*.

254. See Strobel, *Skizzen*, 66–68, 69–96, and 99–196. In all cases Wagner avoids capital letters, using them only for the beginning of a sentence or for proper names.

255. *My Life* 465; *Mein Leben* 2:478.

256. Although *Judaism in Music* is a literal translation of the title *Das Judenthum in der Musik* (and will be used here), the contents of the work is focussed not on the religion of Jews but the Jews themselves and should strictly be referred to as *Jewry in Music* (cf. Conway, *Jewry*, 9).

257. PW 3:90–91; GSD 5:76. Cf. Adorno, *Wagner*, 13–14.

258. Deathridge, *Good and Evil*, 187; WagRS 248–51.

259. Haymes, *Ring*, 44–45. On Regin and Eugel, see chapter 3 below.

260. Haymes, *Ring*, 48–49.

261. GSD 2:218; Haymes, *Ring*, 164–65: "als Meister lehrte Mime mich schmieden." Cf. Deathridge, *Good and Evil*, 187.

our art has, so to say, but opened his mouth to speak to us."[262] So in the earliest sketch for *Der junge Siegfried* (3–10 May 1851) we see how ineffective Mime's craft really is[263] and this is further elaborated as he composed his "Prosa-Entwurf" (24 May–1 June 1851)[264] and the "Dichtung" (3–24 June 1851).[265] The contrast clearly emerges of a self-taught Siegfried who does not need to learn his craft from his step-father.

Rheingold and *Walküre*

After writing the libretto for *Siegfried's Tod* and *Der junge Siegfried* Wagner realized he had to depict events leading up to the drama in those two Siegfried works. He sets out his intentions in a letter to Liszt of 20 November 1851, around the time that he had written his *Erste Prosa-Skizze* for *Rheingold* (c. 3–11 November) and *Walküre* (11–20 November 1851): "This plan will now comprise three dramas: 1st, *The Valkyrie*. 2nd, *Young Siegfried*. 3rd, *Siegfried's Death*. In order to present everything complete, these three dramas must additionally be preceded by a great prelude: *The Rape of the Rhinegold*."[266] Wagner considers that this plan "lends itself uncommonly well to presentation on stage":[267] "Imagine the wonderously ill-starred love of Siegmund and Sieglinde; Wodan in his deeply mysterious relationship to the love; then the discord between him and Fricka, his furious self-mastery when—for the sake of custom—he decrees Siegmund's death; finally, the glorious Valkyrie, Brünnhilde, divining Wodan's innermost thought, defying the god and being punished by him."[268] Wotan does indeed come over as a very human figure. Although Wagner's words to Röckel that "he resembles *us* to a tee" ("er gleicht *uns* auf's Haar") only strictly apply after he has put Brünnhilde to sleep and become a Wanderer,[269] they nevertheless carry a great deal of truth for his earlier life. It must be stressed that he fathers children to achieve his own ends: Siegmund is to be "the other" and Brünnhilde as an expression of his will. But, as Skelton points out, "[t]he love he has come to feel for them as individual beings is an unforeseen complication."[270]

---

262. *PW* 3:93–94; *GSD* 5:79.

263. Strobel, *Skizzen*, 66.

264. Strobel, *Skizzen*, 69–96.

265. Strobel, *Skizzen*, 99–196.

266. *SL* 238; *SB* 4:187.

267. *SL* 237; *SB* 4:187.

268. *SL* 238; *SB* 4:187. A facsimile of this section is given opposite *SB* 4:160 (plate 3) and shows that Wagner here was using the Latin script but with the usual German capitalization. Note that Wagner preferred the form "Wodan" until around 1860 (see the letter to Schott of 7 July 1860, *SB* 12:215).

269. *SL* 308; *SB* 6:69. This letters of 25/26 January 1854, as has been widely acknowledged, is central to understanding aspects of the *Ring*.

270. Skelton, "Conflict", 8.

The first prose sketches of these two operas were composed in the periods 3–11 November 1851 (*Rheingold*)[271] and 11–20 November 1851 (*Walküre*).[272] The second prose sketch of *Rheingold* was 23–31 March[273] and for *Walküre* 17–26 May 1852.[274] He then went straight on to write the poem (*Erstschrift des Textbuches*) for *Walküre* (1 June-1 July 1852)[275] and then the poem for *Rheingold* was composed 15 September–3 November 1852.[276]

Poem Finalized

It then just remained for Wagner to make final changes to *Der junge Siegfried* and *Siegfried's Tod* (completed 15 December 1852) to complete the poem of which fifty copies were published in 1853 (not giving Wagner's name).[277] It is worth emphasizing that this was seen as a literary work in its own right and was not merely as a "libretto" that was there to fulfil an operatic purpose.[278] In this published poem, as in the later editions (e.g., the "Collected Writings and Poems"), no scene numbers were indicated, these being introduced for the musical score.[279] A second edition was published in 1863 ("First Public Issue") with a new preface. Here he sets out various ideas largely concerning the performance of the final work, proposing that a "provisional theatre" be erected "perchance of mere timber"[280] in "one of the smaller towns of Germany."[281] There were to be three sets of performances in the middle of summer, invitations being sent to "the German public," and to "all the friends of Art, both near and far."[282] He describes plans for an invisible orchestra and "an amphitheatric plan of auditorium."[283] The problem with opera houses, he writes, is that "through the inevitable sight of the mechanical movement of the band and its conductor, he is made an unwilling witness of technical

---

271. *TBRN1* 347–48.

272. *TBRN1* 423–25. Notes were added at the beginning of 1852 for *Rheingold* (*TBRN1* 348–49) and *Walküre* (*TBRN1* 425–27).

273. *TBRN1* 350–61.

274. *TBRN1* 428–43.

275. *TBRN1* 446–519.

276. *TBRN1* 364–422.

277. *WWV* 352–53 gives details of this edition. The preface is given in *SSD* 12:289–90.

278. Deathridge, *Ring*, xvii, points out that a study was made of the poem as early as 1862 (by Franz Müller); this pre-dated even the Munich first performances of *Rheingold* and *Walküre*. A study by Ernst Koch (1875) pre-dated the first full *Ring* performance of 1876.

279. See, e.g., *TBRN2* 589, which shows his hand-written insertion "Zweite Scene" into the 1853 *Ring* text for *Rheingold* (Wagner, *Ring* (1853), 8).

280. Note that the theatre build in Lauchstädt for Schiller's *Die Braut von Messina* was also made out of wood.

281. *PW* 3:274; *GSD* 6:273.

282. *PW* 3:275; *GSD* 6:273. I read this to imply that those outside Germany would also be invited.

283. *PW* 3:276; *GSD* 6:275.

evolutions which should be almost as carefully concealed from him as the cords, ropes, laths and scaffolding of the stage decorations."[284] Festival performances would be such that one can rid oneself "of the cares (Sorgen) of workaday existence."[285] Key to performances is the "deed": "Just as *Faust* ultimately proposes to replace the Evangelist's 'In the beginning was the *word*' by 'In the beginning was the *deed*,' so the valid solution of an artistic problem seems feasible upon no other path than this of Deed."[286]

In this festival Wagner says there is "the prospect of seeing the German Spirit's most characteristic excellences brought yearly forward in a new work." He suggests that "a German Prince" could help financially to this festival performances.[287] "Will this Prince be found?—'In the beginning was the Deed.'"[288] Wagner's words were strangely prophetic since at this time there was indeed a prince whose father, king Maximilian, was to die unexpectedly at the age of fifty-two the following year. As king Ludwig II this prince was to come to Wagner's "rescue."

Musical composition

Looking back at the composition of the music of *Rheingold*, Wagner writes:

> After five years' arrest (Unterbrechung) of my musical productiveness, it was with great alacrity that I set to work on the (musical) composition of my poem, in the winter of 1853–54. With the "Rheingold" I was starting on the new path, where I had first to find the plastic nature-motives which, in ever more individual evolution, were to shape themselves into exponents of the various forms of Passion in the many-membered Action and its characters.[289]

After getting the libretto in a fairly finished form in February 1853[290] Wagner completed the musical composition of *Rheingold* in 1854 (28 May) and of *Walküre* in 1856 (23 March). However, when it came to the third opera, *Siegfried*, he broke off the musical composition when he was working on *Siegfried* Act II. The frequently quoted passage from his letter to Liszt of 28 June 1857 suggests he broke off composition in the middle of Act II: "I have finally decided to abandon my obstinate attempts to complete my Nibelungs. I have led my young Siegfried into the beautiful forest solitude; there I have left him beneath a linden tree and have said farewell to him

---

284. *PW* 3:276–77; *GSD* 6:275.

285. *PW* 3:277; *GSD* 6:276. Cf. Pogner's word in *Meistersinger* Act I Scene 3 that on the festival of St John's Day the people can forget all their cares ("vergessen seiner Sorgen"; *WagMB* 122–23).

286. *PW* 3:278–79; *GSD* 6:277. See Goethe, *Faust I*, ll. 1224–37 (*GWJA* 3:48).

287. *PW* 3:281; *GSD* 6:280.

288. *PW* 3:282; *GSD* 6:281.

289. *PW* 3:266; *GSD* 6:266.

290. He had fifty copies made at his own expense; among those receiving copies were August Röckel and Arthur Schopenhauer.

with tears of heartfelt sorrow:—he is better there than anywhere else."²⁹¹ The actual point here at which Wagner seemingly abandoned the composition was at the words "Daß der mein Vater nicht ist" ("That he is not my father")²⁹² which is roughly in the middle of the Act. However, two weeks later he decided to return to work on Act II, completing the "Kompositionsskizze" (composition sketch) down to the end of the Act on 30 July and completing the "Orchesterskizze" (orchestra sketch) on 9 August 1857.²⁹³ But although he had completed the "Orchesterskizze" he had done no work on the full score. Note also that although he had completed the *Partiturerstschrift* of Act I (31 March 1857) he had not completed the *Partiturzweitschrift* (*Reinschrift*); this was only achieved at the end of December 1868. Nevertheless, one can say that the composition of the first two acts was effectively finished in 1857 after which he devoted his energies to *Tristan und Isolde*, which was completed on 6 August 1859, and then to *Meistersinger*.

Rescue

On 10 March 1864, on the death of his father, Ludwig inherited the Bavarian throne. Meanwhile Wagner, living in Vienna, fled the city to escape his creditors (23 March), travelling to Munich, Mariafeld, and finally Stuttgart. On 14 April Ludwig sent his Cabinet Secretary Hofrat von Pfistermeister to find Wagner and bring him to Munich, and following the composer's movements he did eventually find him in Stuttgart on 3 May and on the following day Wagner met Ludwig in Munich.²⁹⁴ This truly was a rescue²⁹⁵ and despite the many emotional upheavals that were still to follow, Wagner enjoyed financial security and relative emotional peace such that he was able to make substantial progress on composition.²⁹⁶ However, the *Ring* was not the focus of his attention until 1869 (hence it is often said he took a "twelve year break," 1857–69), since he was preoccupied with completing *Meistersinger* and the first performances of *Tristan* (1865) and *Meistersinger* (1868). But after Ludwig acceded to the throne in 1864, he was able to resume work on the final full score of *Siegfried* Act I ("Reinschrift")

---

291. *SL* 370; *SB* 8:354. Later in the letter he adds: "I had to wrench Siegfried away from my heart and place him under lock and key as though I were burying him alive. I shall leave him there, and no one shall have a glimpse of him as long as he has to remain locked away like this" (*SL* 372; *SB* 8:356).

292. *WagRS* 238. Newman, *Life*, 2:473, points to the two points in the act when Siegfried rests under the linden tree and argues that in view of the "Kompositionsskizze" 27 June 1857 it was the first of these when Wagner interrupted his work.

293. All these terms ("Orchesterskizze" etc) are taken from *WWV* 382–83.

294. *KB* 5:181.

295. His desperation is clear from the letters. See, e.g., that to Cornelius (8 April 1864): "*some good and truly helpful miracle must now befall me, otherwise it will all be over*" (*SL* 583).

296. On 5 May 1864 Ludwig tells him that he will compensate for past sufferings, see to all his everyday needs, and give him peace so that in the "pure aether" he may develop his "blissful art" undisturbed (*KB* 1:11).

on 27 September and on 22 December started work on the "Partiturerstschrift" of Act II, completing this on 2 December 1865. After further work on *Meistersinger*[297] at the end of December 1868 he completed the "Partiturzweitschrift" ("Reinschrift") for Act I of *Siegfried* and then on 23 February 1869 he completed the "Reinschrift" of Act II[298] and then turned to Act III. He worked on the "Kompositionsskizze" (1 March to 14 June), on the "Orchesterskizze" (25 June to 5 August) and on 25 August started work on the "Niederschrift."[299] After doing work on the "Vorspiel" and Act I of *Götterdämmerung* (2 October 1869–2 July 1870) he returned to *Siegfried* Act III, eventually finishing this on 5 February 1871. The score was then completed with the final orchestration of *Götterdämmerung* on 21 November 1874,[300] and what should have been a happy occasion turned out to be one of exhaustion and anger for the composer and tears of suffering for Cosima.[301]

First Performances

Rheingold was first performed 22 September 1869 in Munich. Among those attending were King Ludwig (who had initiated and in many respects planned the performance) and friends of Wagner, namely Judith Gautier, her husband Catulle Mendès, and the poet Philippe-Auguste Villiers de l'Isle-Adam. It was not considered a success. Very different though was the first performance of *Walküre* on 26 June 1870. Among the audience for *Walküre* were Brahms, Liszt, Saint-Saëns, Duparc, and Joachim. It is said that Liszt was moved to tears in the scene with Brünnhilde and Siegmund.[302] It was given again on 29 June and then in July both *Rheingold* and *Walküre* were given three times each in alternation.

The significant person not present at either *Rheingold* or *Walküre* was Wagner himself. It is sometimes said he boycotted the performances because he felt the works had to be performed in the context of the whole *Ring* cycle.[303] However, there are

---

297. The first prose sketch goes back to 1845 but he had been effectively working on this opera since 1861. It was completed on 24 October 1867 and first performed 21 June 1868.

298. See *CD* 23 February 1869. We have detailed knowledge of the chronology since Cosima started her diary on 1 January 1869.

299. In various ways, Wagner's method of composition changed when he worked on *Siegfried* (Westernhagen, *Forging*, 131; Millington, *Wagner*, 197).

300. For the detailed chronology see *DEBRN* 12–13.

301. *CD* 21 November 1874 tells of Wagner being "worn out" the previous day (Friday) and Cosima assumed he would not finish the work until Sunday. In the event, Wagner finished it on Saturday and he was angered that she showed more interest in a letter from her father than the fact that he had finished his work. Cosima's distress at what seems to be a misunderstanding is indicated not only by her entry for that day, celebrating the completion of the *Ring* "in suffering," but even more eloquently by the fact that there are no further entries until 3 December 1874 (Deathridge, *Good and Evil*, 6).

302. Gregor-Dellin, *Life*, 396. Cf. Wagner's letter to Liszt of 20 November 1851 discussed above.

303. In this 20 November 1851 letter to Liszt, Wagner writes: "I cannot contemplate a division of the constituent parts of this great whole within ruining my intention in advance. The whole complex

other reasons for boycotting it, the main one being that when Ludwig had *Rheingold* staged in 1869, Wagner insisted on certain things that Ludwig did not agree to. Because rehearsals were going badly Wagner (in Tribschen) requested that the premiere be postponed. This was granted and Wagner went to Munich (1 September) in order to supervise rehearsals or to thwart performances, but he "succeeded in neither."[304] Ludwig dismissed the conductor (Richter) and Wotan (Betz) resigned[305] and the work was conducted by Franz Wüllner. Wagner wrote: "I warn you, Sir—keep off my score, or the Devil take you!" The following year Wüllner laid his hands on *Walküre* and again Wagner refused to attend.[306]

The first "proper" performance was in 1876 in the three *Ring* cycles performed under the direction of Hans Richter.[307] Illustrious people numbered among those who experienced it.[308] The first cycle (13–17 August) did not go well. In fact, after *Rheingold* Wagner was so devastated that he shut himself up in his room in the Bayreuth theatre;[309] *Siegfried* had to be delayed by a day since Betz claimed he was "hoarse."[310] But after the first cycle, on 18 August, the performances of the three "day" works having gone well, a banquet was held and the mood was much improved.[311] Cosima records the speech of her husband who brought together a key constellation in the whole world of the *Ring*: *Faust*, politics, Wagner's ambitious programme of changing opera, and Liszt's support:

> R., quite without preparation, makes a wonderful speech, paraphrasing the final chorus from *Faust*—"All things transitory are sent but as symbols (Gleichnis)." The idea: "The eternally feminine leads us on." The Reichstag deputy chooses very unfortunate words: one could not know what posterity would

---

of dramas must be staged at the same time in rapid succession" (*SL* 239; *SB* 4:188).

304. Taylor, *Wagner*, 188.

305. Fifield, *Richter*, 36.

306. Musically *Rheingold* appears to have been at least acceptable. The big problem was the production (see Westernhagen, *Biography*, 2:417, appealing to Judith Gautier's report). However, Carl Brandt as "masters of machines" managed to work such "miracles" (Drüner, *Wagner*, 573) that "Wagner never lost touch with him thereafter" (Gregor-Dellin, *Life*, 392). *Walküre* was seen as a success all round (Drüner, *Wagner*, 576). On these first performances, see Kämper, "Uraufführung," who cites von Bülow's praising Wueller's industry but not his inspiration (71).

307. Fifield, *Richter*, gives details of the rehearsals (104–8) and performances (108–15).

308. E.g., in addition to the composers Bruckner, Tchaikovsky, Grieg, Saint Saëns, and, of course, Liszt, the eminent scientist Hermann Helmholtz was present (*CD* 17 August 1876).

309. See Richard Fricke, in Spencer, *Wagner Remembered*, 248: "In the evening, first performance of *Das Rheingold*. Many of the scene changes went wrong and I can truthfully say that none of these mistakes had been made at any of the rehearsals. For half an hour or more at the end, the audience went on calling for Wagner to come out on stage—but he didn't. He sat in his room, beside himself with fury, hurling abuse at all the performers with the exception of Hill and me, who were both with him. There was no consoling him."

310. *CD* 15 August 1876.

311. Kellermann in Spencer, *Wagner Remembered*, 249, estimates about 500 were present.

think of it all, but the *striving* was worthy of recognition! Following that, Count Apponyi splendidly compares R. with Siegfried; he has brought tragedy back to life, because he never learned the meaning of fear. Quite splendid. Then R. proposes a wonderful toast to my father, without whom, he says, no one would have known anything about him, R.—A very, very lovely evening![312]

Kellermann[313] records Wagner's words to Liszt:

> Everything that I am and that I have achieved I owe to one man, without whom not a single note of my music would be known, a dear friend who, when I was exiled from Germany, drew me back into the light with incomparable devotion and self-denial and who was the first to recognize me. It is this dear friend to whom the greatest honour is due. It is my august friend and master, Franz Liszt!!

Kellermann then continues:

> Both men fell into each other's arms, weeping. Total silence filled the vast hall and everyone was held in thrall by the solemnity of this moment, as our two greatest composers stood clasped in each other's arms. But finally endless cheering broke out. I almost felt like falling to me knees, so great and hallowed was the moment.[314]

There was a plan to perform the *Ring* in 1877 ("Next year we'll do it differently")[315] but it had to be aborted because of the deficit of 148,000 marks. It cannot be said that the 1876 performances were a financial success. However, this should not blind one to the fact that, as Carnegy puts it: "It was indeed perhaps the most stupendous, most improbable operatic achievement of the nineteenth century."[316]

---

312. *CD* 18 August 1876. The word "Gleichnis" is better translated as "parable" or even as "allegory." The "*striving*" ("*das Streben*") may allude to Faust's "striving."

313. Spencer, *Wagner Remembered*, 250. On Kellermann, see *CD* 28 September 1878.

314. Spencer, *Wagner Remembered*, 250–51.

315. Spencer, *Wagner Remembered*, 252, gives the source as Fricke, *Bayreuth*, 143. Similar views were expressed to Apponyi, *Memoirs*, 93, Fritz Brandt (*CD* 29 September 1878), and Reinhardt von Seydlitz ("Erinnerungen" (18 December 1931)). Note, that this is often quoted to justify productions which go again Wagner's original intentions. However, the changes Wagner proposed were modest and the quotation hardly justifies modern productions even though there are other grounds with which to justify them.

316. Carnegy, *Theatre*, 94.

3

Wagner's Use of Germanic and Norse Sources

Wagner's List

In a letter of 9 January 1856 to Franz Müller, a government official in Weimar, Wagner listed on a separate piece of paper what he considered to be his ten sources for the *Ring*.[1] The list, just as Wagner wrote it, is:

1. "Der Nibelunge Noth u. die Klage" herausgegeb. von *Lachmann*.
2. "Zu den Nibelungen etc." von Lachmann.
3. Grim͂'s Mythologie.
4. "Edda".
5. "Volsunga-Saga" (Übersetzt von Hagen—Breslau.)
6. "Wilkina- und Niflungasaga" (ebenso. –)
7. *Das deutsche Heldenbuch*—alte Ausgabe. auch erneuert von Hagen. —Bearbeitet in 6 Bänden von Simrock. –
8. "Die deutsche Heldensage" von Wilh. Grimm.
9. "Untersuchungen zur deutschen Heldensage" von Mone—(sehr wichtig.)
10. "Heimskringla"—übersetzt von Mohnike. (glaub' ich!) (*nicht* von Wachter—schlecht.)

He clearly wrote down the list in some haste[2] as can be seen in errors (source 1) and his extreme brevity (source 4).[3] He possessed most of these works in his private Dresden Library, but since he no longer had access to them he had to rely on his memory for any details he offers. In addition to books in his personal library, he

---

1. See *SB* 7:336–37; Ströbel, *Skizzen*, 20. For English translations, see Magee, *Nibelungs*, 18–19; Björnsson, *Volsungs*, 111.

2. A photograph of the list is available in Björnsson, *Volsungs*, 113 and Müller/Panagl, *Ring und Gral*, 62.

3. The editor corresponding to source 1 would appear to be Vollmer rather than Lachmann, and under source 4 ("Edda") a whole range of works are relevant.

borrowed works from the Dresden Royal Library for which we have records.[4] Wagner would be able to be advised by the librarian, Hofrat Dr Gräße, who was "an authority on Germanic myth and legend and a literary historian."[5]

The precise authors/editors, titles and dates of the works he consulted are now given.[6] In cases where Wagner possessed the work, I have indicated the number given by Westernhagen in his listing of Wagner's Dresden Library (DB = Dresdener Bibliothek);[7] in cases where the book is now missing from the collection but has been recorded by Minna Wagner, I have marked it accordingly (DB: Minna);[8] in cases where he borrowed a work from the Royal Dresden Library I have given the relevant dates.

1. A.J. Vollmer. *Der Nibelunge Nôt und diu Klage*, 1843 (DB 99).

Additionally Wagner used:

i. *Daz ist der Nibelunge Liet*, 1840 (DB 98).[9]

ii. Gustav Pfizer. *Der Nibelungen Noth*, 1843 (DB 100).

iii. Karl Simrock. *Nibelungenlied*, 3rd ed. 1843 (DB 101; vol 2 of 6 vol *Heldenbuch* (see below)).

iv. J. von Hinsberg. *Das Lied der Nibelungen*, 4th ed. 1838 (borrowed 11 January to 1 February 1845).

v. Karl Lachmann. *Der Nibelunge Not mit der Klage*, 1826, 2nd ed. 1841 (borrowed 1 February to 1 March 1845).[10]

It is also possible that he read one of von der Hagen's editions of the *Nibelungenlied*.[11]

---

4. The loan journals give the author, short title, name of borrower, and dates of loan and return (Magee, *Nibelungs*, 38). Although providing valuable information, the records do present two problems. First, since just short titles with no date of publication are given, the precise work cannot always be identified. Secondly, by giving just the surname of the borrower we cannot always be sure the work was borrowed by the composer (Wagner is a not an unusual name). However, the encouraging sign for scholarship is that "loans to 'Wagner' drop off remarkably after early May 1849" (when he fled the city) and "large quantities of Nibelung literature were being borrowed from June 1848 onwards, when Wagner's involvement with the *Ring* material was reaching its peak" (Magee, *Nibelungs*, 39).

5. Westernhagen, *Biography*, 1:94. Wagner possessed Gräße's *Gesta Romanorum* translation (1842) and when the librarian published his *Saga of the Knight Tannhäuser* (1846) he dedicated it to "his dear friend, the Royal Saxonian court conductor Richard Wagner" (Magee, *Nibelungs*, 38).

6. I have been guided in what follows by the notes in *SB* 7:337–38. To the expanded list given there I have added Ettmüller's *Vaulu-Spá*, clearly a key work for Wagner, and Simrock's *Edda*. See also Westernhagen, *Bibliothek*, 36.

7. Westernhagen, *Bibliothek*, 84–110.

8. Westernhagen, *Bibliothek*, 111–13.

9. No editor is given for this edition which gives the Middle High German. A translation was made the same year using the same illustrations and giving the translator as Gotthard Oswald Marbach.

10. On his borrowing Hinsberg and Lachmann, see Magee, *Nibelungs*, 40.

11. See Magee, *Nibelungs*, 41, and the discussion below.

2. Karl Lachmann. *Zu den Nibelungen und zur Klage*. Wörterbuch von Wilhelm Wackernagel, 1836 (DB 78).

3. Jacob Grimm. *Deutsche Mythologie*. Zweite Ausgabe, 2 vols, 1844 (DB 44).

4. "Edda" which presumably refers to the following works from his Dresden Library:

   i. Friedrich Heinrich von der Hagen. *Lieder der älteren oder Sämundischen Edda*, 1812 (DB 27).

   ii. Friedrich Majer. *Mythologische Dichtungen und Lieder der Skandinavier*, 1818 (DB 28).[12]

   iii. Friedrich Rühs. *Die Edda nebst einer Einleitung über nordische Poesie und Mythologie und einem Anhang über die historische Literatur der Isländer*, 1812 (DB 119).[13]

   iv. Jacob and Wilhelm Grimm. *Die Lieder der alten Edda*, 1815 (DB: Minna).

   v. Ludwig Ettmüller. *Vaulu-Spá. Das älteste Denkmal germanisch-nordischer Sprache, nebst einigen Gedanken über Nordens Wissen und Glauben und nordische Dichtkunst*, 1830 (DB 149).

   vi. Ludwig Ettmüller. *Die Lieder der Edda von den Nibelungen: Stabreimende Verdeutschung*, 1837 (borrowed 21 October 1848 to 29 January 1849).[14]

   vii. Karl Simrock. *Die Edda, die ältere und jüngere*, 1851.[15]

   viii. J.L. Studach. *Sämund's Edda des Weisen*, 1829 (borrowed 21 August to 2 October 1848).[16]

   ix. Gustav Thormod Legis. *Fundgruben des alten Nordens, zweiter Band, erste Abtheilung: Edda*, 1829 (borrowed 21 August to 2 October 1848).[17]

---

12. This contained the two main parts of the *Prose Edda* (*Gylfaginning* and *Skaldskaparmal* (referred to as "Braga's Erzählungen"; Majer, *Lieder*, 83)) and seven of the mythological poems. Majer was a pupil of Herder.

13. Rühs (1781–1820) became Professor in History in 1810 at the newly formed University of Berlin. Böldl, *Mythos*, 172, points to Rühs's grim assessment of the morality in this Nordic literature.

14. Magee, *Nibelungs*, 44, 46. Note that this contained only seventeen of the heroic poems, starting with "Das erste Lied von Sigurd, Fafnirstödter, oder Gripirs Weissagung" (Ettmüller, *Edda*, 1–8; Magee, *Nibelungs*, 217).

15. Magee, *Nibelungs*, 50–52, rightly argues that Wagner did read this edition. Since the work was published and distributed by the end of February it is likely Wagner read it before resuming work on the *Ring* in May 1851 (52).

16. This contained eight of the mythological poems. Each has an introduction together with detailed notes. Of the editions Wagner consulted, this, together with Legis' edition, would appear to be the most scholarly.

17. This contained six of the mythological poems with introductions and notes. According to the subtitle, this was the first time the work was published on the basis of the "Urschrift" ("Zum erstenmal aus der isländischen Urschrift übertragen [. . .]"). Volume 1 appeared also in 1829 but with a different Leipzig publisher. Legis' original name was Anton August Glückselig.

5. Friedrich Heinrich von der Hagen. *Völsunga Saga oder Sigurd der Fafnirstöter und die Niflungen. Nordische Heldenromane*, vol. 4. 1815 (borrowed 21 October 1848 to 29 January 1849).

6. Friedrich Heinrich von der Hagen. *Wilkina- und Niflunga saga, oder Dietrich von Bern und die Nibelungen. Nordische Heldenromane*, vols 1–3, 1814–15 (borrowed).

7. i. Karl Simrock *Das Heldenbuch*. Übertragung mittelhochdeutscher Epen. 6 vols, 1843–46. This comprises:

    a. *Gudrun* vol 1. 1843 (DB 76)

    b. *Nibelungenlied* 1843 vol. 2 (DB 101)

    c. *Das kleine Heldenbuch* 1844 vol. 3 (DB 59).

    d. *Amelungenlied* 1843–49 vols. 4–6 (DB 3).

    ii. Friedrich Heinrich von der Hagen. *Der Helden Buch*. Erster Band, 1811 (DB 58).

8. Wilhelm Grimm. *Die deutsche Heldensage*, 1829 (DB 47).

9. Franz Joseph Mone. *Untersuchungen zur Geschichte der teutschen Heldensage*, 1836 (DB 93).

10. i. Gottlieb Mohnike. *Heimskringla. Sagen der Könige Norwegens von Snorre Sturlason*. Aus dem Isländischen. Erster Band. 1837 (DB 133).

    ii. Ferdinand Wachter. *Snorre Sturluson's Weltkreis (Heimskringla)*. 2 vols, 1835–36 (DB 132).

The list Wagner gave Müller was not necessarily exhaustive (as noted it appears to have been written in a hurry). So, e.g., if he continued subscribing to the *Zeitschrift für deutsches Alterthum* into 1849 he would have access to Weinhold's essay on "Die Sagen von Loki."[18]

Although Wagner's *Ring* is very much associated with the *Nibelungenlied*, one could argue that the main sources were in fact Icelandic/Norse. Björnsson estimates that in the *Ring* about 80 percent of the derived motifs are drawn from Icelandic literature, 5 percent exclusively from German literature, and about 15 percent common to Icelandic and German literature.[19] This may be true, but one must bear in mind that the first impulse for Wagner's *Ring* was the *Nibelungenlied*. Much secondary literature is extremely helpful in showing from where Wagner drew his sources.[20] I will also

---

18. Magee, *Nibelungs*, 35–36. Note, however, that his 6 volume collection in his Dresden library only extends to 1848.

19. Björnsson, *Volsungs*, 7. This may be skewed a little towards the Icelandic.

20. See, e.g., Koch, *Ring*; Golther, *Grundlagen*; Weston, *Legends*; Cooke, *End*; Magee, *Nibelungs*; Björnsson, *Volsungs*. Golther and Björnsson (130–274) work systematically through the *Ring* libretto drawing attention to parallels in the Norse and Germanic primary sources, the latter doing so in some detail. Magee charts Wagner's use of the sources diachronically.

engage in this in teasing out Wagner's theological interests. But I also think that in addition to focusing on how Wagner has appropriated specific passages it is important to have a macroscopic perspective on the theology of the Norse and Germanic material. In the course of this chapter I will offer an introduction to the key works (and say something about the key scholars Wagner drew upon such as Grimm, Mone, and von der Hagen), but I will also offer a more detailed discussion of key sources within the limitations of space. I turn first to what Hatto described as "the world's best heroic epic, bar one"[21] and, as we shall see, issues of Wagner's appropriation of the *Nibelungenlied* are considerably more straightforward than his use of the Norse material.

Nibelungenlied

The title of the cycle, *Der Ring des Nibelungen*, may suggest that the key source was the *Nibelungenlied*, an epic composed around 1200 probably in Passau, Austria. In the second half of the eighteenth century three manuscripts were discovered and published, beginning with what Lachmann designated as manuscript C,[22] discovered in 1755, excerpts of which were published in 1757.[23] The first complete edition (based on MSS A and C) was published in 1782 by Christoph Heinrich Müller. The work was not immediately popular and Frederick the Great (to whom Müller had dedicated his edition) dismissed the work as "not worth a shot of gunpowder" ("nicht einen Schuss Pulver werth").[24] However, with the Napoleonic wars and the rise of German nationalism the work became popular and became especially attractive since with the Holy Roman Empire coming to an end in 1806, Germans were able to look back to the Middle Ages idealized in the work. The Schlegel brothers likened the work to Homer's *Iliad* and *Odyssey*.[25] But it is important to remember that other versions of the story of the Nibelungs were known. So from the sixteenth century we have *Das Lied vom Hürnen Seyfrid* and Hans Sachs, *Hürnen Seufrid*, a tragedy in seven acts.[26] Further, as we shall see, there were traditions of the Nibelung saga circulating in Iceland and Scandinavia.

The epic draws on stories that go back in the main to the fifth or sixth centuries when Germanic tribes wandered across northern Europe and the main characters

---

21. Raffel, *Nibelungenlied*, x. See below on how the work was seen in relation to Homer's *Iliad*.

22. Lachmann, *Überlieferung*, Vff, introduced the letters A, B, C, to designate the manuscripts (Heinzle, "Manuscripts," 105–6).

23. Bodmer, *Chriemhilden Rache, und die Klage*.

24. McConnell, "Introduction," 5–6.

25. A. W. Schlegel even considered that "no other nation's poetry possesses anything that is more similar in design to the Homeric epic" ("Nibelungen," 29, quoted in Oergel, *Nibelungen*, 108). The first to work on the similarities between the *Iliad* and *Nibelungenlied* were the Swiss literary critics J. J. Bodmer and J. J. Breitinger (Ehrismann, *Nibelungenlied*, 26–38).

26. Magee, *Nibelungs*, 2.

are based on historical figures.[27] There are four strands of history which are mutated and spun into the *Nibelungenlied*. First, the East Germanic tribe of the "Burgundians" crossed the Rhine around 411 and the tradition arose (for which there is no sound historical or archaeological evidence) that they established a kingdom at Worms. In 436 AD King Gundaharius and his Burgundian army of twenty thousand was defeated and destroyed by an army of Huns and Romans somewhere west of the Rhine.[28] Gundaharius corresponds to Gunther of the *Nibelungenlied* and Gunnar of the *Völsunga Saga*. In fact, the *Nibelungenlied* tells of three brothers who are kings, Gunther, Gernot, and Giselher, and all three may be identified with figures in the sixth-century *Lex Burgundionum*.[29] The defeat of the Burgundians led to their being resettled in western Switzerland and southern France in the region we now know as Burgundy.

The second element is the story of Attila who ruled the Huns from 434 until his death in 453. Although he was not involved in the battle with the Burgundians, his death became entangled with the Burgundian defeat. Within a hundred years there developed the legend that he had been killed by his wife Hilde for having killed her father.[30] Attila corresponds to Kriemhild's second husband, Etzel, in the *Nibelungenlied*.[31]

A third possible strand is the death of King Sigismund of Burgundy in 524, to which Sivrit's death could correspond. But much more important is the fourth strand, which comes from the history recorded by Gregory of Tours and from the "Chronicle of Fredegar." Wagner would know this history from Loebell's *Gregor von Tours*,[32] which tells of Sigibert who married the westgothic king's daughter Brunichild, "a woman of highly virile mind, full of spirit, power-hungry, and having a drive for action which could never be satisfied" ("ein Weib männlichen hohen Sinnes, voll Geist, Herrschlust und nie befriedigten Thätigkeitstriebes").[33] His brother Chilperich, seeing the advan-

---

27. These stories are relevant also for other works I discuss such as the *Völsunga Saga*.

28. See Göttling, *Ueber das Geschichtliche*, 16–17, a work Wagner happened to borrow from the Dresden Royal Library from 10 February to 19 June 1849 (Magee, *Nibelungs*, 46, 214). See also Edwards in *NibE* 215-16. Göttling notes the complete absence of Siegfried, Grimhild, and Brunnhild in Gundaharius' defeat (19).

29. In *De libertatibus servorum nostrorum* King Gundobad refers to his ancestors Gibica, Gundomaris, Gislaharius and Gundaharius (Salis, *Leges*, 43). Gibica corresponds to Gibich, Gunther's father. This is found in a fifteenth-century version of the *Nibelungenlied* (Gillespie, *Catalogue*, 51); cf. *Götterdämmerung*. In the original version, Dancrat is father of the three kings and Gibeche is a king of the Huns. Gundomaris may correspond to Gernot and Gislaharius corresponds to Giselher. See Edwards in *NibE* 215.

30. Much later the *Völsunga Saga* and *Elder Edda* say he was killed by his wife Gudrun, Gudrun being identified with Kriemhild of the *Nibelungenlied*.

31. The very second verse tells us that Kriemhild was a Burgundian.

32. This work was in his Dresden library (DB 83).

33. Loebell, *Gregor*, 27. Another of Wagner's sources, Göttling, *Ueber das Geschichtliche*, 20–21, quotes Gregory: "She was a delightful maiden having a beautiful countenance; in manners she was modest, chaste, and noble; she was intelligent and knew how to speak wisely" ("Sie war eine herrliche Jungfrau; schön von Antlitz; züchtig, keusch und hold von Sitten, von klugen Geist, und wußte wohl zu reden").

tage of such a union, decided then to marry Brunichild's older sister Galswintha.[34] But Fredegunda, his beloved, strangled her[35] leading to war between Sigibert/Brunichild and Chilperich.[36] Nine years before Chilperich died Sigibert was murdered on the orders of Fredegunda (575 AD).[37] Fredegunda died in 597 but her son Klothar II captured Brunichild and she was drawn and quartered in 613.[38]

All this history fed into the *Nibelungenlied*, a work consisting of thirty-nine "adventures"[39] and 2,379 stanzas. It can be divided into two parts, the first nineteen adventures dealing with events which lead up to the death of the hero Sivrit (who corresponds to Wagner's Siegfried). The second part (adventures 20–39) deals with his wife's revenge for his death and culminates in an appalling slaughter. Sivrit's wife is called Kriemhilt; she could be seen as corresponding to Wagner's Gutrune, but in fact her character is based on "Brunichild." She is in fact the key figure of the epic, appearing right at the beginning (which emphasizes her beauty) and the work closes with her murder by Hildebrant and the mourning of her death.[40] I offer a brief outline of the plot, focusing on aspects that are relevant for the *Ring*.

The first adventure tells of Kriemhilt, a beautiful Burgundian princess (daughter of Queen Uote), who is under the guardianship of her brothers, the three kings mentioned above, Gunther, Gernot, and Giselher. We are also introduced to Hagen of Tronege, vassal and advisor to the kings at the Burgundian court in Worms on the Rhine. The second adventure introduces Sivrit, Prince of the Netherlands, living in Xanten, who in the third adventure rides to Worms to win Kriemhilt. Sivrit is close to King Gunther, who, like his namesake in the *Ring*, is a weak figure. In this third adventure we also hear from Hagen of Sivrit's upbringing, his strength, his taking of the hoard of the Nibelungs (a race of heroes according to the *Nibelungenlied*), his slaying of the dragon and bathing in its blood in order to make his skin impregnable.[41] Sivrit, on his arrival, challenges Gunther, but their fight is avoided and Sivrit becomes a guest of the Burgundians.

---

34. Loebell, *Gregor*, 27.

35. Loebell, *Gregor*, 28–29.

36. Loebell, *Gregor*, 29. He tells of Brunichild's fury: "Brunichilds Seele ward erfüllt mit Rachlust, die das alte germanische Gefühl der Pflicht, für vergossenes Blut der Verwandten an dem Thäten das Vergeltungsrecht zu üben, noch schärfte."

37. Loebell, *Gregor*, 233. Sigibert and Brunichild had a son Childebert II, born in 570.

38. Murdoch, "Politics," 232; Haymes, "Introduction," XIV. This part of the story is not given by Loebell.

39. The references that follow point to the Adventure (Middle High German Âventiure) and will usually give the stanza and the page number in Edward's translation (e.g., Av 17 (1004); *NibE* 94).

40. Eichner, *Mighty Sounds*, 48, notes her mutation from a "meek sister of the Burgundian kings and Siegfried's loving bride, cruelly betrayed by her relatives" in the first part, to "a reckless avenger who does not rest until countless heroes have been slain for her personal revenge" in the second.

41. *NibE* 12–14. Note that he killed the "dragon" ("einen lintrachen sluoc des heldes hant" (*NibS* 34)) whose blood has the effect of hardening his skin; however, in the Norse tradition Sigurd kills a "serpent" whose blood enables him to understand birdsong (see below).

After fighting the Saxons (Av 4) Sivrit sees Kriemhilt and falls in love with her (Av 5). Then Gunther desires to marry Prünhilt, Queen of Iceland. Sivrit accompanies him to Iceland and in the contest with Prünhilt, Sivrit acts for Gunther using his cloak of invisibility (Av 7–8). Sivrit goes ahead to Worms (Av 9). Prünhilt is welcomed in Worms. There is a double wedding. Sivrit makes love to Kriemhilt but Prünhilt denies Gunther intercourse, binds him, and hangs him on a peg. Sivrit, disguised with the cloak of invisibility, breaks down her resistance and takes her ring and girdle (Av 10). Sivrit returns to the Netherlands with Kriemhilt (Av 11). Ten years later Sivrit and Kriemhilt accept Gunther's invitation to festivities in Worms.[42] But the two queens argue over the relative merits of their husbands (Av 14). Sivrit is betrayed (Av 15) and killed (Av 16).[43] His body is taken to Worms where he is given a royal funeral. Kriemhilt is reconciled with her brothers and agrees to bring the hoard from Xanten to Worms. Hagen steals the treasure and hides it in the Rhine (19).

The second part concerns Kriemhilt's revenge. She marries Etzel, King of the Huns and invites the Burgundians to the Huns (the name "Nibelungs" being transferred to the Burgundians as they make their fatal journey). On the journey Hagen is warned by three watersprites that no one except the chaplain will return alive (Hagen therefore attempts to kill him) (Av 25 (1574–80)). The epic ends with the slaughter of the Nibelungs, an absolute devastation deeply etched into nineteenth- and twentieth-century German consciousness;[44] in fact, sometimes the work is referred to not as the "Song of the Nibelungs" but the "Doom of the Nibelungs," these being the last three words of the epic: "der Nibelunge nôt" ("The Nibelungs' Doom").

The part of the *Ring* that is most indebted to the *Nibelungenlied* is *Siegfried's Tod*, which, as we have seen, was the first part to be composed.[45] There are also elements in the first three operas of the cycle that could allude to the epic, but these are all cases where the event has been narrated already in *Siegfried's Tod*. Further, it is notable that with one or two exceptions (e.g., the scene with the water sprites) Wagner has not drawn on the second half of the epic. It is clear that he was to move away from the *Nibelungenlied* and focus more on the Norse sources as he developed his tetralogy. Indeed, he was to become quite critical of the *Nibelungenlied* (as he was of many of his medieval sources).[46] However, this should not blind us to the importance of part one

---

42. Sivrit and Kriemhilt have a baby but leave him in the land of the Nibelungs (Av 13 (779); NibE 74).

43. Adventures 5–16 will be discussed in more detail in volume 2, chapter 8.

44. In a speech of 30 January 1943, the tenth anniversary of Hitler's rise to power, Göring likened the "heroic battle" of the German army at Stalingrad to what was the *slaughter* at the end of the *Nibelungenlied*. For the relevant section of his speech, and criticism of Göring's interpretation, see Hoffmann, "Reception," 148–49.

45. The libretto was composed in 1848 (with revisions up to 1852) and the musical sketches in 1850–52.

46. See, e.g., his criticisms of Wolfram von Eschenbach's *Parzival* (Bell, *Parsifal*, 49, 57–58, 62).

of the epic for his initial plan to write just one heroic opera, *Siegfried's Tod*, giving the essential shape from the arrival of Siegfried through to his death.[47]

Before summarizing what Wagner has appropriated from the epic, I outline six of the essential differences. First, there is nothing in the *Nibelungenlied* of gods, Valkyries, or Norns which we find in *Siegfried's Tod/Götterdämmerung*. Secondly, Wagner has changed the whole character of the "Nibelungs": in the *Nibelungenlied* "Nibelungs" is a dynastic name for the people of Nibelunc, the king and father of the young kings Schilbunc and Nibelunc. They become subject to Siegfried, who gains the hoard (Av 3), and the name "Nibelungs" is then later applied to the Burgundians. In the *Ring* Nibelungs are the race of dwarves that live in "Nibelheim" (cf. the Norse Niflheim).[48] Thirdly, if we focus on the name "Nibelungs," *Siegfried's Tod* actually ends not with the *doom* of the Nibelungs as in the *Nibelungenlied*, but with their *redemption* (this was to change with the opera's revisions). Fourthly, Wagner has changed radically the character and role of Prünhilt, transforming her into his Brünnhilde and making her death fundamental for the salvation of the Nibelungs (in *Siegfried's Tod*) or for the death of the gods and renewal of the cosmos (in the revised *Siegfried's Tod*, later renamed *Götterdämmerung*). Fifthly, Wagner transforms Sivrit of royal lineage (son of king Sigmunt), the "worthy knight" whose parents' order that he be "elegantly dressed,"[49] into his somewhat uncouth Siegfried.[50] Sixthly, Wagner omits the whole background of the medieval church that we find in the *Nibelungenlied*. The epic stresses that Kriemhilt seldom missed daily matins;[51] adventure 31 (part two) has a scene of going to Church and we have a chaplain accompanying the Nibelungs to Hungary (whom Hagen tried to kill); and one of the pivotal scenes of part one is when the two wives Kriemhilt and Prünhilt insult one another in front of the minster (Av 14).[52] This Christian framework is replaced by a pagan one of Norse and Germanic gods.[53] But what does remain, at least in *Siegfried's Tod/Götterdämmerung*, is the medieval context with chivalry, horse, weaponry, etc. Indeed, as was established in chapter 2, the medieval background was essential for the whole *Ring* cycle in view of his preparatory study *Die Wibelungen*.

---

47. As noted in chapter 2, the original *Siegfried's Tod* started with Act I and the Prologue was added a little later.

48. The slightly confusing element is that according to the *Nibelungenlied* in the land of the Nibelungs there is a "strong dwarf," Albrich, who, after Siegfried had subjugated the Nibelungs, "became chamberlain in charge of the treasure" (Av 3 (96–98); *NibE* 13–14).

49. Av 2 (21, 25); *NibE* 7. Cf. Deathridge, *Ring*, xxxi.

50. Many influences were to be involved in this transformation including the Sigurd of the Icelandic texts (see below).

51. See Av 17 (1004); *NibE* 94.

52. This scene actually influenced the confrontation of Elsa and Ortrud in *Lohengrin* Act II. Kriemhilt corresponds to Elsa and Prünhilt to Ortrud (*NibE* 79–80).

53. In case removing the Christian framework is thought to suggest a paganization of the epic, many of the Christian elements in the epic do not demonstrate the best in Christian practice and can entail a hypocrisy at work, and it was this that Wagner in his writings particularly abhorred. See, e.g., *Communication to My Friends* (*PW* 1:350; *GSD* 4:304).

The seventh difference is that Wagner almost goes "behind" the *Nibelungenlied* to the historical in moving Siegfried and Brünnhilde from the North to "Germany." So Siegfried does not come from the Netherlands (as does Sivrit) and even more strikingly Brünnhilde does not come from Iceland (as does Prünhilt); rather, their location corresponds more to what we find in Gregory of Tours, where they are located in "Germany." But he could also easily have located them in Germany from Norse influence since in *Brot af Sigurdarkvidu* they are located on the Rhine.[54]

As was his wont, Wagner was highly selective in appropriating the material of the *Nibelungenlied* and the elements he takes over are as follows.[55]

1. The key quadrilateral of relationships (Siegfried = Gutrune; Gunther = Brünnhilde) which drive the drama of *Siegfried's Tod/Götterdämmerung* has been adopted from the *Nibelungenlied* (Sivrit = Kriemhilt; Gunther = Prünhilt), the Norse equivalent being Sigurd = Gudrun; Gunnar = Brynhild. The details he takes over are:

    i. Sivrit is belligerent when he arrives at Gunther's court.[56] This is reflected in *Götterdämmerung* Act I Scene 2: "nun ficht mir mir, / oder sei mein Freund!" ("now fight with me, / or be my friend").[57]

    ii. He falls in love with Kriemhilt (but no potion is needed) and woos Brynhild for Gunther (but does not have to forget about her as in *Götterdämmerung*) if Gunther will grant him Kriemhilt.[58] His use of the cloak of invisibility resembles the tarnhelm.

    iii. Before leaving for Iceland Sivrit already knows of Prünhilt's strength and aggression and there is even a hint that he has previously been with her.[59] In *Götterdämmerung* of course he has previously been Brünnhilde's husband.

    iv. Sivrit says he will not make love to Prünhilt[60] but makes the mistake of taking her ring and girdle.[61] In *Götterdämmerung* Act I Scene 3 Siegfried makes his crucial mistake also in taking the ring from Brünnhilde.

    v. Sivrit takes an oath in an attempt to clear his name,[62] which is taken up in *Götterdämmerung* Act II.

---

54. Orchard, *Elder Edda*, 176; Andersson, *Brynhild*, 29.
55. Many of the parallels will be obvious.
56. Av 3 (106–110; *NibE* 14–15).
57. *WagRS* 293.
58. Av 6 (332; *NibE* 34).
59. Av 6 (329–30; *NibE* 34).
60. Av 10 (655–56; *NibE* 63).
61. Av 10 (679–80; *NibE* 65). According to Kriemhilt, Sivrit not only took Prünhilt's girdle (Av 14 (848); *NibE* 81) but also her "gold" (Av 14 (846); *NibE* 80) after allegedly lying with her.
62. Av 14 (856–59; *NibE* 81–82).

    vi. Prünhilt is portrayed as aggressive,[63] vain,[64] and cunning.[65] To some extent this may have influenced Wagner's portrayal of Brünnhilde in *Götterdämmerung* Act II, which some find problematic (and contrasts with her almost saintly character in *Walküre* and *Siegfried*). Note that in the *Nibelungenlied* Kriemhilt may be guilty of telling lies.[66]

    vii. Sivrit does not care for riches,[67] which reflects his attitude in both *Siegfried* and *Götterdämmerung*.[68]

2. Albrich is presented as a "strong dwarf" who has a cloak of invisibility. After serving Nibelunc and Schilbunc, who are killed by Sivrit, Albrich is subdued by Sivrit, serves him, and is entrusted with the hoard.[69] For Wagner, Alberich becomes the lecherous figure who becomes leader of the Nibelungs, having fashioned the ring.

3. Hagen (who is not related to Albrich in the *Nibelungenlied*) has many key roles in the epic that are appropriated in *Siegfried's Tod*/*Götterdämmerung*.

    i. Before Sivrit arrives in Worms, Hagen tells of his bravery, how he became leader of the Nibelungs, gained the hoard, was given a special sword, gained Albrich's cloak of invisibility, and killed the dragon.[70] Hagen's introduction of Siegfried in *Götterdämmerung* Act I Scene 1 (before his arrival) bears some similarities.

    ii. Hagen plots with Prünhilt to kill Sivrit, Kriemhilt giving away the secret away of Sivrit's vulnerable spot on his back.[71]

    iii. Hagen is described as "grim Hagen"[72] and he kills Sivrit.[73]

---

63. Av 6 (329–30; *NibE* 34).

64. Av 14 (*NibE* 78).

65. Av 12 (727; *NibE* 69).

66. The issue of telling the truth, we shall see, is a possible problem with Brünnhilde in *Götterdämmerung* (see volume 2 chapter 10).

67. Av 9 (557; *NibE* 54).

68. *Siegfried* Act II Scene 3 (*WagRS* 246–47); *Götterdämmerung* Act I Scene 2 (*WagRS* 294).

69. Av 3 (*NibE* 13–14). Av 8 (*NibE* 48–49) which also tells of Sivrit fighting Albrich seems to be another version of the earlier story (Lionarons, "Otherworld," 163). Wagner later related his Albrich to Andvari of the Norse sources.

70. Av 3 (*NibE* 13–14).

71. Av 15 (*NibE* 85). Cf. *Götterdämmerung* Act II Scene 3. Note that because Wagner does not adopt Sivrit's bathing in the dragon's blood, he makes no use of the idea that "a broad linden leaf fell landed between his shoulder-blades," making him vulnerable at that spot (Av 15 (902; *NibE* 85)).

72. Av 17 (1039; *NibE* 97); Av 39 (2347; *NibE* 211); Av 39 (2368; *NibE* 213). Cf. *Götterdämmerung* Act II Scene 2.

73. Av 16 (980; *NibE* 92). Cf. *Götterdämmerung* Act III Scene 2.

iv. From the second part, Hagen meeting the water sprites who prophesy death[74] inspired the scene (*Götterdämmerung* III.1) of Siegfried's meeting with the Rhinemaidens. Adventure 30, which tells of "Hagen's watch," may also have inspired *Götterdämmerung* Act I Scene 2.[75]

4. The end of the *Nibelungenlied* describes the deaths of Gunther and Hagen (but at the hands of Kriemhilt).[76]

As indicated, Wagner was quite critical of the work as he was of most epic (the exception being the *Iliad*). Wagner's critique of epic was quite involved but basically the problem is that it makes a less immediate effect and is too "intellectual." Whereas in epic the heroes' deeds are celebrated, in drama they are enacted,[77] and it was drama that Wagner aimed at. Epic was an excellent quarry but one had to do creative quarrying so to speak to discern the crucial myths therein.[78] One way in which Wagner appropriated epic was to see it through the lens of the Greeks, particularly as Hegel understood it, an idea I explore in the following chapter. But for now I note Hegel's own critique of the *Nibelungenlied*: "it ascribes the ultimate bloody issue of all deeds neither to Christian Providence nor to a heathen world of gods."[79] The work has "a stiff and undeveloped appearance, a tone of mourning, objective as it were and therefore extremely epical."[80] By contrast the work made an enormous impact on Friedrich Panzer (1870–1956), one of the greatest of Nibelungen scholars.[81] Despite Wagner's negative comments on the epic he did later change his mind, at least for the second part, which he had largely ignored for the purposes of his *Ring*. Cosima records a conversation of 1873: "The chapter about Rüdeger moves us into admitting that this second part of the *Nibelungenlied* is superior even to the *Iliad* with its tender depiction of a devotion to duty which, as one reads it, utterly breaks one's heart."[82]

As already noted Wagner possessed four different editions of the *Nibelungenlied*. As well as using these sources he may well have been helped on his way in composing his *Ring* by using Raupach's *Nibelungen-Hort* (1834), the one Nibelungen drama that appeared before the publication of the *Ring* libretto in 1853 that Wagner actually acknowledged.[83] Magee points out that the Prologue to Raupach's drama

---

74. Av 25 (1533–40; *NibE* 141).
75. Av 30 (1828; *NibE* 166).
76. Av 39 (2369–73; *NibE* 213). Cf. *Götterdämmerung* Act III Scene 3.
77. *Opera and Drama* (*GSD* 3:268; *PW* 2:60); Foster, *Greeks*, 53.
78. See chapter 4 below.
79. Hegel, *Aesthetics*, 2:1071–72.
80. Hegel, *Aesthetics*, 2:1072.
81. Panzer, *Entstehung*, 7: "das Buch ließ mich nicht los. Ich [. . .] las und las die unerhörte Mär bis zum traurigen Ende" (quoted in McConnell, "Introduction," 11).
82. *CD* 4 July 1873. Cosima presumably has in mind adventures 20 and 37.
83. *PW* 3:261; *GSD* 6:261. Wagner passes over Fouqué, *Held des Nordens* (1810), Hermann, *Nibelungen* (1819), Müller, *Chriemhilds Rache* (1822), and Wurm, *Nibelungen* (1839). Of these it may

was based on *Das Lied von Hürnen Seyfrid* and tells of dwarves and giants, employing for the latter the Norse names Hreidmar, Fafner, and Reigen.[84] One particular passage in which the dwarf Eugel tells Siegfried of his servitude to the giants is reminiscent of Mime's complaint to Wotan and Loge in *Rheingold* Scene 3 and includes Hreidmar being killed by his sons Fafner and Reigen to gain the Nibelung-hoard and Fafner turning into a dragon.[85]

As noted above, Wagner *may* have read one of von der Hagen's editions of the *Nibelungenlied*. The uncertainty arises because according to the Dresden Royal Library records Wagner had borrowed von der Hagen's "Nibelungen von Hagen" from 17 January to 18 February 1844. This could simply be one of his editions of the *Nibelungenlied* which were held in the library.[86] But this could also be his 1819 study in which he argued that the epic was "an essentially Christian manifestation of universal myth."[87] He views the work as "the original ancestral saga (die Ur- und Stamm-Sage) of the human race itself, of Paradise and the Fall of Man, how through the serpent (with the human head), through woman and through gold sin and death entered into the world [. . .]"[88] If this is the work Wagner read then it has possible interesting implications for a Christian interpretation of the *Ring*.

Norse and Germanic Mythology

It may have been through his uncle Adolf that the young Richard first discovered something of Norse mythology. The end of the eighteenth and beginning of the nineteenth century had seen a great interest in this mythology[89] and it was reflected in Fichte's understanding that the Scandinavians were "German."[90] It was one of Fichte's followers, the Prussian-born baron of French descent, Friedrich Baron de la Motte Fouqué, who was "the first person to have promoted Old Icelandic literature vigorously in Germany."[91] So in 1808 he began publication of a trilogy of plays (*Sigurd der Schlangentödter*, *Sigurds Rache*, and *Aslaug*) and in 1810 the whole trilogy was

---

be that he was only familiar with Fouqué (see below). He does acknowledge the "grand opera" by H. Dorn, *Die Nibelungen* (libretto by E. Gerber) which Liszt had premièred in Weimar in January 1854.

84. Magee, *Nibelungs*, 75. On *Das Lied von Hürnen Seyfrid* and its relationship to the *Nibelungenlied*, see Flood, "Dragon-Fight," 54–65. He comments that the Lied "is no work of art" but has interesting motifs. The main part focuses on Seyfrid's rescue of Krimhild, who has been abducted by a dragon, a story found in *Nibelungenlied* manuscript m.

85. Magee, *Nibelungs*, 75–76.

86. Magee, *Nibelungs*, 41 n. 9, names these editions of 1807, 1810, and two from 1820.

87. Magee, *Nibelungs*, 41.

88. Translation of Magee, *Nibelungs*, 41 (von der Hagen, *Die Nibelungen*, 66–67).

89. Björnsson, *Volsungs*, 87–93.

90. *JGFAW* 5:423 (*Reden an die deutsche Nation*, 1807–8, fourth speech).

91. Björnsson, *Volsungs*, 93.

published as *Der Held des Nordens* (*Hero of the North*) and dedicated to Fichte.[92] It became highly popular and was admired by Jean Paul[93] and E. T. A. Hoffmann. Wagner does not mention Fouqué, but according to Björnsson his works were in his uncle's library and he may well have read them in his youth;[94] further, Adolf was a friend of Fouqué.[95] Drews and Björnsson point to instances where Wagner may be influenced by Fouqué.[96]

It was in the Paris years (1839–42) that Wagner came to know medieval German literature and to this he added Norse literature during his time in Dresden (1842–49) and beyond. Fundamental for his appreciation of Germanic and Norse mythology was Jacob Grimm's *Deutsche Mythologie* to which I now turn.

Jacob Grimm

Of the sources listed above, the first work he read was Jacob Grimm's *German Mythology*.[97] On visiting Teplitz[98] on holiday in 1843 he took with him this work.[99] He states in his autobiography: "Whoever knows this work will understand how the inordinate wealth of its contents, gathered from all sides and really intended almost solely for scholars, had an immediately stimulating effect on me, who was looking everywhere for expressive and meaningful symbols." There he discovered "a confusing construction which at first sight appeared to me as a huge rocky crevice choked with underbush." But he found himself "in the power of its strange enchantment" and his

---

92. Fouqué argued in *Der Zauberring* (1813) that Sweden is the Northern country of our German brothers (44) and Old Icelandic is the "Urdeutsche Sprache" (18).

93. His review of the work was printed as a part of the foreword.

94. Björnsson, *Volsungs*, 112.

95. Drewes, *Ideengehalt*, 101.

96. Björnsson, *Volsungs*, 112, points to "the three Norns who chant over Brünnhilde's resting place on the Valkyrie Rock before the second appearance of Siegfried" and that their appearance in the prologue of *Götterdämmerung* is drawn from this scene at the beginning of the "second adventure" (Fouqué, *Held*, 60–63). Note, however, that since in Fouqué's scene the appearance of the Norns is followed by Sigurd coming to the castle and discovering and wakening the sleeping Brynhildis, the parallel would appear to be *Siegfried* Act III Scene 3. Note the use of what Wagner called "Stabreim" (i.e., alliteration) in the Norns' first entry as they speak in unison (*Held*, 60). Drewes, *Ideengehalt*, 102, also points to Fouqué's use of Stabreim in Reigen's first entry (see *Held*, 9–10).

97. He also read *Deutsche Sagen* of Jacob and Wilhelm Grimm (*My Life* 260; *Mein Leben* 1:273).

98. This is modern day Teplice in the Czech Republic. It may have been significant for Wagner that Beethoven had spent around six weeks in Teplitz to recover in the summer of 1811 (Matthews, *Beethoven*, 47–48; Cooper, "Calendar of Beethoven's Life," 21). Among composers who also visited the spa town were Chopin (Niecks, *Chopin II*, 109–10) and Liszt (Walker, *Liszt II*, 232).

99. *My Life* 259–60; *Mein Leben* 1:273. Westernhagen, *Biography*, 320, points out that this must have been the first edition since the second (which he had in his Dresden library) did not appear until 1844. The other possibility is that he read the second edition and has given the wrong year in his autobiography (cf. Magee, *Nibelungs*, 28). My references for the German will be to the second edition of 1844.

"entire sensibility was possessed by images suggesting ever more clearly the recapture of a long lost yet eagerly sought consciousness."[100]

The work is indeed incredibly erudite, can be quite daunting to read, and frustrating to use.[101] It is also written using small letters for the initial letter of nouns, capitals being used only at the beginning of sentences and for proper nouns, writing which, as we saw in chapter 2, was to influence Wagner's usage from December 1848 through into 1852. As far as content is concerned, Grimm claims that he based his *German mythology* on *Norse* mythology in the sense that he determined what was Norse and then excluded that to determine what was German. So his purpose was "to collect and set forth all that can now be known of German heathenism, and that exclusively of [i.e., by excluding] the complete system of Norse mythology (zwar mit ausschliessung des vollständigen systems der nordischen mythologie selbst)."[102] The next sentence confirms that Grimm meant "ausschliessung" and not "aufschliessung"[103] in that he speaks of the "einschränkung":[104] "By such limitation (einschränkung) I hope to gain clarity and space and to sharpen our vision for a criticism of the Old German faith, so far as it stands opposed to the Norse, or aloof from it so that we need only concern ourselves with that of inland Germany."[105] Hence, Cooke clarifies that Grimm took the Norse system for granted "without trying to extend our knowledge of it any further" using it "as a foundation on which to erect his reconstruction of the cognate German mythology."[106] We can see this process at work in chapter VII on "Wuotan."[107] He be-

---

100. *My Life* 260; *Mein Leben* 1:273.

101. One reason is that there is simply no key to the abbreviations he uses and when referring to the Eddas he gives no indication as to which poem or section he has in mind. The *Prose Edda* is referred to by Sn. with page number; the *Elder Edda* is referred to by, e.g., Sæm. 188a (Grimm, *Mythologie*, 1:131; *Mythology* 1:144). I am grateful to Judith Jesch for identifying these works as Rask, *Snorra-Edda* (1818) and Afzelius, *Edda Sæmundar* (1818). So Sæm. 188a refers to page 188 column 1, and the reference is to Fafnis-mal 15. Stallybrass, *Mythology*, 1:vii, envisaged "[a] full classified Bibliography and an accurate and detailed Index to the whole work" to accompany his translation thereby rendering "the English Edition as complete and serviceable as possible." To my knowledge this resource never materialised; he died in 1888, the year in which the final volume of his translation (volume 4) appeared.

102. Grimm, *Mythology*, 1:10; *Mythologie*, 1:9. The English, quoted in Cooke, *End*, 127, clarifies somewhat the German, which could, out of context, be understood to mean that in determining German mythology he was "*excluding* the complete system of Norse mythology." That he was not excluding it is clear from what follows, which includes eight points showing the "antiquity, originality and affinity of the German and Norse mythologies" (*Mythologie*, 1:9; *Mythology*, 1:10).

103. I simply put this question since Jacob Grimm wrote with great rapidity and hardly ever made corrections in what he wrote. He commented with wonder that his brother Wilhelm Grimm (1786–1859) read through his manuscript before submitting it to the press.

104. I am grateful to Carolyne Larrington clarifying this for me in a tweet (3 June 2018).

105. Grimm, *Mythology*, 1:10; *Mythologie*, 1:9: "Durch diese einschränkung hoffe ich licht und raum zu gewinnen und den blick zu schärfen für die critic des altdeutchen glaubens, insofern er dem nordischen entgegen oder zur seite steht."

106. Cooke, *End*, 127.

107. Grimm, *Mythologie*, 1:120–150; *Mythology*, 1:131–65 (cf. Cooke, *End*, 127–28).

gins with an exercise in philology[108] and then brings together anything there is available on the god (Wednesbury in Staffordshire even gets a mention).[109] Then towards the end of the chapter he sifts out what in the Old German tradition contradicts the Norse, noting that in the former Wuotan is likened to an upgraded Hermes/Mercury (and Donar to a downgraded Zeus/Jupiter).[110]

A further aspect of Grimm's critical work in determining Germanic mythology was that he believed many Old and Middle High German works had been tainted with Romance culture, since they were based on French sources such as Chrétien de Troyes rather than indigenous traditions. In the preface he writes: "We have never had an Edda come down to us, nor did any one of our early writers attempt to collect the remains of the heathen faith. Such of the christians as had sucked German milk were soon weaned under the Roman training from memories of home, and endeavoured not to preserve, but to efface the last impressions of detailed progress."[111] Lee explains that Grimm's attitude reflects two widely held views at the time: "one, that there had been an overarching Germanic culture in the past; and two, that this culture had subsequently been destroyed, first by conversion to Christianity, and second through the preference for 'foreign' literature, notably work of French origin, over native works."[112]

Thus, Grimm set out to reconstruct German mythology, which, according to Cooke, "in his own time was widely reckoned never to have existed."[113] This should be qualified in the sense that there had been a succession of scholars who had used the Eddas to construct a "German mythology," one of the earliest being the pastor Trogillius Arnkiel (1639–1712);[114] further, there was interest in the Norse mythology in the eighteenth century and early nineteenth century among German poets before Grimm's *Mythologie* first appeared in 1835.[115] However, Grimm was the first to estab-

---

108. Grimm, *Mythology*, 1:131 (*Mythologie*, 1:120), relates the name to the verb OHG "watan" ("to move," etc) and the ON "vada" and then the substantive "wuot" to "ôd" ("fury"). But he also brings Latin and Greek into his discussion with examples from classical literature and the New Testament.

109. Grimm, *Mythology*, 1:158 (*Mythologie*, 1:144).

110. Grimm, *Mythology*, 1:164–65 (*Mythologie*, 1:149–50).

111. Grimm, *Mythology*, 3:ix; *Mythologie*, 1:viii: "Auf uns ist keine edda gebracht worden und kein einziger schiftsteller unsrer vorzeit hat es versucht die überreste des heidnischen glaubens zu sammeln. Wer unter den Christen auch noch deutsche milch gesogen hatte, wurde in römischer schule bald den erinnerungen des vaterlandes abgewandt und trachtete die letzten eindrücke des verhassten heidenthums zu tilgen statt zu bewahren."

112. Lee, "Receptions," 109–10.

113. Cooke, *End*, 127. Also Deathridge, *Ring*, xxx, points to Golther, *Sagengeschichte*, 3, and *Grundlagen*, 9, who writing in 1888 and 1902 respectively, denied it ever existed. Such views are opposed by Grimm, *Mythology*, 3:vii; 1:9; *Mythologie*, 1:vii; 1:8.

114. Lee, "Receptions," 101.

115. Lee, "Receptions," 104, points to Herder, *Ideen*, 694 (published in 1784), who writes of "this remote treasure of German fables, which has been preserved or collected at the end of the inhabited world, in Iceland, and which has been obviously enriched through the sagas of the Northmen as well as by Christian scholars,—I mean the Nordic *Edda*."

lish the Norse-German equivalents in such detail and this is why Wagner's reading of his *Mythologie* was so significant.

Although Grimm thought that conversion to Christianity had destroyed the pagan culture of the past he also has a fundamental interest in Christian theology in his treatment of "German mythology." He sees this mythology as cruel (grausam) and overcome by "mild" Christianity.[116] Furthermore, he understands much of the mythology through the lens of Christian theology (and there are references to biblical texts and discussion of Christian theology on many of its pages) and argues that characteristics of Jesus Christ and of the God of the Judeo-Christian tradition were transferred to the pagan gods. For example, in the discussion of Donar (chapter VIII) he likens Donar's killing the Midgard serpent to Christ's victory (through his death) over the serpent[117] and he draws a comparison between the cross and Donar's hammer.[118] He also notes the link between Donar and Elijah and Mary (in Serbian songs) as bringers of rain.[119]

Grimm's linking "pagan" mythology to the Christian tradition is something he shared with his contemporaries. Like Novalis, Arnim, and Görres, he aimed at a purely pre-historic era ("eine außerhistorische reine 'Urzeit'")[120] when human beings were larger, more pure and holy, and the glory of the departed gods shone in and over them, such ideas being influenced by the biblical tradition found in the early chapters of Genesis.[121] In reflecting on Wagner's appropriation of Grimm's *Mythologie* (and that of other figures) one must therefore bear in mind this theological dimension.

Two further key scholars for Wagner, although not having the academic stature of Grimm, were von der Hagen and Mone, to whom I now turn.[122]

---

116. Grimm, *Mythology*, 1:5; *Mythologie*, 1:4: "Der sieg des christenthums war der einer milden, einfachen geistigen lehre über das sinnliche, grausame, verwildernde heidenthum".

117. Compare Faulkes, *Edda*, 54, on Ragnarök: "Thor will be victorious over the Midgard serpent and will step away from it nine paces. Then he will fall to the ground dead from the poison which the serpent will spits at him."

118. Grimm, *Mythology*, 1:182; *Mythologie*, 1:166.

119. Grimm, *Mythology*, 1:173; *Mythologie*, 1:158–59. See also volume 2 chapter 3.

120. Requadt, "Grimm, Jacob," 1877.

121. See Grimm's letter to Achim von Arnim, 20 May 1811 (Reuß, *Briefwechsel*, 59): "Die alten Menschen sind größer, reiner und heiliger gewesen, als wir, es hat in ihnen und über sie noch der Schein des göttlichen Ausgangs geleuchtet."

122. Magee, *Nibelungs*, 5, points to Schneider's distinction between "great scholars" ("grosse Forscher") and "muddleheads" ("Wirrköpfe") or between "the good and bad fairies" ("Wagner," 109) in German philology. Grimm and Lachmann are generally regarded as belonging to the former. "Among the bad fairies were Carl Götting, von der Hagen in his less restrained moments, and, by common consent of contemporaries and posterity alike, F. J. Mone" (Magee, *Nibelungs*, 5).

Von der Hagen

Friedrich von der Hagen was "the first career philologist."[123] He studied law and practised for a while but his love was the medieval texts. He and the Grimms "were embroiled in a kind of nineteenth-century 'space race' for the first edition and translation of eddic texts into German."[124] In 1812, with some haste, von der Hagen published the Eddic texts available to him.[125] Apart from the very first poem, all of them are from the second section of the Edda, the "Heroic poems" (see the table below for details).[126] This was an edition Wagner possessed. Some have assumed he could not use it since the texts are not translated; but even if he could not read the Icelandic (a point to which I return shortly) over half the work (130 pages) is a foreword (I–XII) and introduction (I-CXVIII) with ninety-eight pages of Icelandic text.[127] Von der Hagen gave up on Eddic work when the translation of the Grimms appeared in 1815, a work Wagner possessed in his Dresden library.

Franz Joseph Mone

Of the ten works Wagner listed for Müller, it is only Mone's book that is marked as "very important." In his *Annals* (1846–67) Wagner tells how he engaged in "Old German Studies" and "Edda: Mone's researches."[128] This is expanded in his autobiography where, referring to the period he was composing the music for *Lohengrin* (1847–48), he writes:

> In my efforts to master the German myths more thoroughly than had been possible from my previous perusal of the *Nibelungen* and the *Heldenbuch*, I became especially attracted to the unusually rich pages of Mone's investigations of these heroic legends [. . .]. This drew me irresistibly to the nordic sources of these myths, and to the extent that it was possible without fluent

---

123. Lee, "Receptions," 110.
124. Lee, "Receptions," 111.
125. The Grimms were highly critical of the work (Lee, "Receptions," 111; Schoof, *Briefe*, 144–45).
126. In fact, this first poem, *Fra Völundi* (*Völundarkvida*), looks forward to the heroic poems and some editors assume that the scribe of the Codex Regius made a mistake in not placing it as the first is that section (Orchard, *Elder Edda*, 305). Note that Hagen identifies Völund with Wieland (*Lieder*, II) and this would chime in with Wagner's special interest in Wieland der Schmied. Hagen, *Lieder*, III, points out that in *Wilkina-Saga* chapter 26 Völund is reminiscent of Vulcan, the biblical Tubelcain (Gen 4:22).
127. The publisher was extremely doubtful whether von der Hagen himself could understand the Icelandic he presented: "it would border on a miracle if the editor of the *Sæmundar Edda* was able to comprehend the here presented originals of the second part" ("Es müßte mit einem Wunder zugehen, wenn der Hr Herausgeber die hier mitgeteilten Originale aus dem 2ten Theil der Saemundischen Edda alle bereits verstehen sollte"). Quoted in Lee, "Receptions," 111.
128. *Brown Book* 95; *Braunes Buch* 113. The way he sets it out, these studies would appear to be sometime in the period between July and October 1848.

knowledge of the Scandinavian languages, I now tried to get to know the Eddas, as well as the prose fragments comprising the basis for large parts of these legends. Viewed in the light of Mone's comments, the *Wälsungasaga* exerted a decisive influence on the manner in which I began to form this material to my own purposes.[129]

This quotation raises the questions as to whether and to what degree Wagner could understand the Icelandic of his sources. As we have seen, von der Hagen's *Lieder der älteren oder Sämundischen Edda* gives the untranslated poems and Ettmüller's *Vaulu-Spá* gives both the original and German translation. Magee reasonably argues that Wagner could sample the original Icelandic in von der Hagen since, according to Westernhagen, there are signs that Wagner thumbed through his copy of Ettmüller[130] and would then have some idea of the Icelandic/German correspondence.[131]

Norse Literature

There is a vast array of Norse literature and much writing on Wagner tends to assume a little too much and can lead to some confusion. In order to achieve some clarity I set out and discuss the most important works.[132] This literature can be legitimately termed "Norse," even though three of Wagner's key sources—the *Prose Edda*, *Elder Edda*, and *Völsunga Saga*—were composed in Old Icelandic, since the much of the material is traditional and deriving from the Scandinavian homelands.[133]

One of the most significant factors for my investigations is that those writing of the Norse "pagan" gods and heroes were Christians. Iceland "converted" to Christianity

---

129. *My Life* 343; *Mein Leben* 1:356–57. Note that Mone added two volumes to Creuzer's four-volume *Symbolik und Mythologie der alten Völker*, one on the religion of the Finnish, Slavic, and Scandinavian peoples (volume 5) and one on the religion of the south Teutonic peoples and Celts (volume 6). Although Wagner knew the first four volumes of Creuzer (see chapter 4 below), it is unclear whether he read these additional volumes by Mone.

130. Magee, *Nibelungs*, 30, referring to Westernhagen, *Bibliothek*, 36. I have looked closely at Wagner's copy of Ettmüller's *Vaulu-Spá* and I can confirm that it does look well used. Perhaps future Wagner research will involve DNA testing to confirm the pages were thumbed through by Wagner himself (this would be useful also for determining the finger marks in works such as Hegel's *Philosophy of History*).

131. Hauer, "*Völospá*," 56, argues that Wagner "continued [Old Norse] studies in later years," drawing attention to the presence of Ettmüller, *Altnordisches Lesebuch* (1861) and Wimmer, *Altnordische Grammatik* (1871), in his Wahnfried library. The presence of these works does not necessarily mean he read them of course and one wonders how motivated he would be to study Old Norse long after he had completed the *Ring* libretto.

132. Cf. Weston, *Legends*, 16–52, who sets out the essential contents of the *Völsunga Saga*, *Thidrek's Saga*, and the *Nibelungenlied*.

133. Björnsson, *Volsungs*, 14, 16, argues that these three works should be termed "Icelandic literature" since they "were written down in Iceland, in Icelandic, by Icelandic authors in the thirteenth century, three centuries or more after Iceland was settled." He makes the point that to deny calling this literature Icelandic is like denying that Henry Longfellow and Mark Twain were American, having been born in the New World more than two centuries after the European conquest.

in 999–1000 AD in a peaceful transition.[134] There had in fact been Christians in Iceland among the very first inhabitants who had come from Ireland and Scotland and there were also Christians among the Norwegians who had colonized Iceland.[135] But the predominant religion in the first hundred years was the Æsir cult[136] and it was into this cult that the annual national assembly, the Althing, was founded in 930.

A Christian mission began in 981 led by the German Bishop Friedrich and the Icelander Thorvald, who had been converted by Friedrich. This was not particularly successful but prepared the way for a second missionary wave, which was supported by King Olaf Tryggvason of Norway (995–1000).[137] At a meeting of the Althing in 999 or 1000 there were roughly equal numbers of Christians and pagans and a collective decision was made in a political compromise to "convert" to the Christian faith. But the pagans were allowed to practice their religion, to eat horse meat, and (for a time) to expose their new born children.[138] There was then a gradual transition to the new faith whereby the old belief system faded over a period of a few decades.[139] But such old stories were treasured, as is witnessed in the literature that came into being in the thirteenth century.

In the following I will briefly introduce the most important sources to which Wagner had access: first the Icelandic works (*Prose Edda*, *Elder Edda*, *Völsunga Saga*, *Heimskringla*)[140] and then works that may not be Icelandic (*Thidrek's saga*). I will then mention some works that Wagner may not have read first hand but which he would have encountered in his reading of the secondary literature (Saxo Grammaticus)

---

134. Byock, *Prose Edda*, xi, contrasts this with the Norwegian conversion whereby the Christian missionary kings forcefully uprooted the belief in the old gods. For a more nuanced view see Montgomery, "Norwegen," 643.

135. Einarsson, "Island," 358. It appears that these Norwegians had come to faith on stopping over on the British Isles before travelling on to Iceland.

136. As will be explained, the key gods among the Æsir were Odin, Thor, and Frigg. They are to be distinguished from the Vanir: Niord, Freyr, and Freyja. Gaining an impression of the religion practised in Iceland is not straightforward (see the nuanced discussion of Jesch, *Diaspora*, 132–34).

137. Olaf Tryggvason was converted in England and made a start to evangelize Norway itself.

138. Einarsson, "Island," 359. On the details of exposing children and pagan and Christian attitudes to it, see Lawing, "Infant Abandonment," who raises the issue that such infants abandoned could include those with "severe physical impairment" (138). He concludes: "Christianity at the outset aimed to extirpate the practice of infant exposure and thereby it substantially improved the lot not only of the physically impaired but of other marginalized categories as well" (148).

139. One must also reckon with the fact that Church needed to be built, priests educated, and the new faith taught; in Iceland it is estimated it took around 300 years for the full Christianization of the country (Jesch, *Diaspora*, 139).

140. Old Icelandic is a branch of Old Norse (the language spoken throughout Scandinavia during the Viking period) that had changed little from the time Iceland was settled in the late 800s. Wagner does not refer to the works as "Icelandic"; in referring to Icelandic mythology and language he speaks of the "Skandinaven" (*GSD* 2:131, 132, 138) or "skandinavisch" (*SB* 3:360, 370) respectively. I have found no reference to "Island" (i.e., Iceland) in Wagner's writings, but Cosima does record two comments about the country (*CD* 13 February 1872; *CD* 27 November 1881).

together with the *Heldenbuch* of von der Hagen and Simrock. The range of works can be overwhelming and confusing and I attempt to clarify some of the issues.

Prose Edda

The fourth work on Wagner's list is "Edda," by which he clearly meant both the poetic and the prose Eddas. These Eddas are based on oral tradition that stemmed from the earlier Viking age, around 800–1100, when Scandinavian seafarers explored and settled lands, including Iceland. The *Prose Edda* contains "the most comprehensive and systematic account of Norse mythology and legend found anywhere in the Middle Ages."[141] There is space here only to give the essential framework of the work, the mythological content being discussed later.

The *Prose Edda* is to be dated around 1220–30. There are four main manuscripts (the original is lost): the oldest is Codex Upsaliensis (first quarter of fourteenth century) but the most important is Codex Regius (first half of fourteenth century) since it is the most complete and is considered closer to the original.[142] According to tradition, the *Prose Edda* was composed by the writer and statesman Snorri Sturluson (1178/79–1241)[143] and the work is often referred to as *Snorri's Edda* (Icelandic *Snorra Edda*). But although he is named as the *compiler* of the work, it may be that only the final section, the *List of Metres*, was *composed* by him.[144] Any reference to "Snorri" in the following discussion is no commitment to Snorri's authorship.[145] It is not known whether the original bore the title "Edda," the name first appearing in Codex Upsaliensis, and the meaning of the term is unclear.[146]

The *Prose Edda* consists of four sections and begins with a *Prologue,* which may be a later addition since the sentence structure, subject matter, and genealogies differ from the rest of the Edda. All the editions that Wagner consulted did not contain this

---

141. Faulkes, *Edda*, xi.

142. The other two main manuscripts are Codex Wormianus (mid-fourteenth century) and Codex Trajectinus, which although late (c. 1600) is a copy of a manuscript from the second half of the thirteenth century.

143. Faulkes, *Edda*, xii, notes that, unlike many early writers in Iceland, he was not a cleric.

144. See Byock, *Prose Edda*, xii, who quotes the earliest possible evidence found in Codex Upsaliensis of Snorri's link to the work: "This book is called *Edda*. Snorri Sturluson compiled [literally, assembled] it in the way that it is arranged here. First it tells about the Æsir [the gods] and Ymir [the primordial giant], then comes the poetic diction section with the poetic names of many things and lastly a poem called the *List of Meters* which Snorri composed about King Hakon and Duke Skuli." Byock points out that the other main manuscripts are also ambiguous about Snorri's role.

145. Just as in New Testament scholarship referring to "Paul" in any discussion of say Ephesians is no commitment to Pauline authorship.

146. In the thirteenth century "Edda" meant great-grandmother. In the fourteenth century manuscripts we find also "edduregla" and "eddulist," referring to the rules and art of poetry. One can then infer that Edda came to be associated with traditional verse, and Edda came to mean the authoritative handbook for training poets in traditional verse forms (Byock, *Prose Edda*, xii).

Prologue: so it is missing in the editions of Majer and Rühs, both of which Wagner possessed, and missing in Simrock's *Edda* (which he consulted in 1851).[147] I will therefore pass over this section here but return to it in volume 2, chapter 3 since it does raise some important theological issues, opening with a number of Old Testament themes (creation, Adam and Eve, Noah's flood).

The second major section is *Gylfaginning* (The Deluding of Gylfi).[148] We enter a very different world, which may appear to contradict much of the Prologue, although, as I will explain, the contradiction may be resolved. Gylfi travels to "Asgard" and enters "Valhalla" with the intention of finding out why the Æsir know so much and why everything goes according to their wishes. He has disguised himself as an old man and calls himself Gangleri.[149] He meets the three figures—"High," "Just-as-high," and "Third"[150]—and asks a series of questions beginning with "Who is the highest and most ancient of all gods?"[151] This is not a contest, as in *Vafthrúdnismál* where "the questioner must know the answer to his question."[152] In the course of the questions and answers Gylfi comes to a fairly comprehensive knowledge of matters from "creation" and through to Ragnarök and the rebirth of the cosmos together with knowledge of gods, goddesses, Valkyries, and giants.[153]

As far as resolving any contradictions within the text, it is important to understand that the hall of Valhalla is a visual illusion conjured up by the Æsir and the whole illusion is destroyed at the end as Gangleri finds himself alone on a level plain with no hall or fortress. "Then he went off on his way and came back to his kingdom and told of the events he had seen and heard about. And from his account these stories passed from one person to another."[154]

The close of *Gylfaginning*[155] then explains how the Æsir not only deceived Gylfi but also subsequent generations. The author therefore presents the gods as kings of great power, descended from King Priam, and migrating to Scandinavia in prehistoric times.[156] Hence, the nature of the deception of Gylfi has nothing to do with losing a battle of wits. The deception is partly that the three figures produce this visual illusion,

---

147. Note, however, that it was important for Trogillius Arnkiel. See Lee, "Receptions," 101.

148. This is where the three editions which Wagner used begin (Majer, *Edda*, 3; Rühs, *Edda*, 163; Simrock, *Edda*, 211).

149. Faulkes, *Edda*, 8.

150. Arnkiel's *Cimbrische Heyden-Religion* (1702) identified them with Thor, Odin, and Freyja (see the image in Krömmelbein, "Schimmelmann," 126).

151. Faulkes, *Edda*, 8.

152. Larrington, *Poetic Edda*, 36.

153. The actual content will be discussed at various points in my two volumes.

154. Faulkes, *Edda*, 57.

155. Because this final section (Byock terms it an "Epilogue") differs in style, sentence structure, word choice and subject matter, it is often understood as a secondary addition (Byock, *Prose Edda*, 148). Majer and Simrock both omit it.

156. Faulkes, *Edda*, xviii.

which disappears at the end,[157] and more profoundly that the whole mythology they portray is simply a deception. Gylfi leaves thinking that the gods exist little knowing that these three mortal figures have decided to spin this elaborate mythology (and assign the names of gods to themselves!).

The slightly confusing element in *Gylfaginning* is that the migrating Æsir are presented as worshipping gods, "those gods about whom they tell Gylfi stories, and whose names they eventually assumed."[158] The *Prologue* makes it plain that the pagan religion developed from worship of the earth and natural forces. According to Faulkes' interpretation, "the author makes it clear that his view of the pagan religion is that it was a rational but misguided groping towards the truth."[159]

Just as the end of the *Prologue* and ending of *Gylfaginning* have explained how these kings came to be honoured as gods, the beginning of the third section, *Skaldskaparmal*, likewise offers an explanation as to how historical events can give rise to myths. For convenience, *Skaldskaparmal* can be divided into two sections: the first concerns stories of gods and heroes[160] and the second concerns how to refer to gods but also contains stories of heroes.[161] Wagner's editions only have material from the first section.[162] The material in Rühs' and Majer's edition does not reach the end of Byock's first section.[163] But Simrock takes us to the end of this first section, giving two main sections: "Bragis Gespräche"[164] and "Aus der Skalda,"[165] and in the latter he inserts the poem Grottenlied.[166] The very ending of "Aus der Skalda"—which tells of the never-ending battle of the Hjadnings ("Hiadningawig (Kampf der Hedninge)")[167]—is significant in the translation of the term "Ragnarök," telling that in the songs the Hjadnings so continue fighting until "Götterdämmerung."[168] Could this have inspired Wagner to some extent to rename his *Siegfried's Tod* as *Götterdämmung* (in June 1856)

---

157. Faulkes, *Edda*, xvii, compares this to the deception of Thor by Utgarda-Loki in *Gylfaginning* 45–47 (Faulkes, *Edda*, 38–46).

158. Faulkes, *Edda*, xviii.

159. Faulkes, *Edda*, xviii.

160. Faulkes, *Edda*, 59–123; Byock, *Prose Edda*, 80–108.

161. Faulkes, *Edda*, 123–64; Byock, *Prose Edda*, 108–118 (note that this section is translated by Russell Poole and offers "an appreciable sampling" 108). This section includes a paragraph on "References to Christ" (Faulkes, *Edda*, 126; Byock, *Prose Edda*, 116).

162. The heading given is "Braga's Erzählungen" (Majer, *Edda*, 83); "Bragis Gespräche mit Aeger" (Rühs, *Edda*, 235). Simrock gives the headings "Bragis Gespräche" (*Edda*, 290) and "Aus der Skalda" (*Edda*, 295).

163. Rühs, *Edda*, 266, finishes with Byock, *Prose Edda*, 102, (King Jormunrek's Tragedy); Majer, *Edda*, 100 finishes at Byock, *Prose Edda*, 86, has a different order of material.

164. This corresponds to Byock, *Prose Edda*, 80–86 (sections 1–2).

165. This corresponds to Byock, *Prose Edda*, 86–108 (sections 3–10).

166. Simrock, *Edda*, 308–11. See the list of Eddic poems given below.

167. Simrock, *Edda*, 314; cf. Byock, *Prose Edda*, 107–8.

168. Simrock, *Edda*, 314: "Und in den Liedern heißt es, die Hiadninge würden so fortfahren bis zur Götterdämmerung."

and to introduce the idea of the death of the gods in May 1851,[169] precisely the time when, as I will suggest below, Wagner read Simrock's *Edda*?

Hattatal is the final section of the *Prose Edda* and concerns verse forms. It is not included in any of the editions Wagner used.[170]

Elder Edda

The "Elder Edda"[171] or "Poetic Edda" is a collection of poems found in what is called the Codex Regius. This vellum manuscript, written in Iceland around 1270 by an unknown scribe,[172] came into the possession of Bishop Brynjólfur of Skálholt. Added on the first page was a pair of intertwined Ls to signify *Lupus Loricatus* ("Armored Wolf"), a latinized form of his name Brynjólfur, together with the date 1643 (presumably when he acquired it) and the title "Edda."[173] The bishop was a collector of manuscripts for the king of Denmark, Frederick III, under whom Iceland was subject, and in 1662 it was presented to him, hence the name Codex Regius.[174] The bishop believed the author was the Icelandic scholar and priest Sæmundr Sigfússon (1056–1133), known as Sæmundr inn fróði ("the wise").[175] There are forty-five vellum leaves, but there is a lacuna of probably eight leaves after folio 32, leaving a gap in the narrative of Sigurd the Volsung.[176]

Codex Regius contains thirty-one items, twenty-nine poems sometimes peppered with prose, and two sections entirely in prose, which function as transitional passages (*Frá dauda Sinfjötla* (About Sinfjötli's death);[177] *Dráp Niflunga* (The killing of

---

169. See the first sketches for *Der junge Siegfried* (Strobel, *Skizzen*, 66).

170. It is included in Faulkes, *Edda*, 165–220, but not in Byock, *Prose Edda*.

171. It is named the "Elder Edda" because it was considered the older of the two Eddas; it is in fact the younger of the two. See Quinn, "Editing the Edda," 69–70.

172. We do not know where it was composed or whether it was written "at a monastery, or at one of the two bishops' sees, or at the home of a secular patron" (Dronke, *Edda I*, xii) but it has been associated with the Benedictine monastery of Thingeyrar in North Iceland, founded in 1133 (Orchard, *Elder Edda*, xvi).

173. Orchard, *Elder Edda*, xvi.

174. It carries the shelf mark of the Royal Library of Copenhagen where it was once held (GkS 2635 4to). It is to be distinguished from the afore-mentioned Codex Regius of the *Prose Edda* (GkS 2367 4to) (fifty-five vellum leaves, early fourteenth century) which was part of the same gift to Frederick III. The Codex Regius of the *Elder Edda* was returned to Iceland in 1971 by ship with a military escort; the *Prose Edda* was returned in 1985. Both are in the Árni Magnússon Institute for Icelandic Studies.

175. Von der Hagen, *Edda*, I, thinks that the collection was probably recorded and compiled by him.

176. The break means that the last part of *Sigrdrífumál* (being folios 31v–32v) is missing (Codex Regius breaks off in the middle of stanza 29 (Orchard, *Elder Edda*, 174)). The gap can be filled from post-medieval manuscripts but entire poems may also have been lost (Orchard, *Elder Edda*, 322). The next poem in Codex Regius, *Brot af Sigurdarkvidu*, begins in midstream (folios 33r–33v) (Orchard, *Elder Edda*, 324).

177. Orchard, *Elder Edda*, 145–46.

the Niflungs)).[178] The first eleven poems are mythological and are followed by eighteen "heroic" poems and the two transitional passages just mentioned. The poems and prose pieces are compiled from various places and periods, and look back to the pagan past, which at the time of writing in the thirteenth century[179] would appear somewhat remote since the country's "conversion" to Christianity took place in 999–1000 AD.

Editions of the "Edda" often include four further poems not in Codex Regius (e.g., Baldr's dreams) and Simrock has seven additional poems (giving a total of thirty-eight). Discussion of the poems can lead to some confusion and I set out the works (giving Icelandic and English titles) indicating which poems were in the various editions Wagner was using.[180] I have also, where necessary, given alternative names of the poems.[181] The abbreviations for Wagner's sources are as follows, and I have indicated where possible when Wagner may have read the respective works:

H = von der Hagen, *Lieder der älteren oder Sämundischen Edda* (1812).

M = Majer, *Mythologische Dichtungen* (1818) (most likely read by 1848).

Ev = Ettmüller, *Vaulu-Spá* (1830) (most likely read by 1848).[182]

G = Grimm, *Die Lieder der alten Edda* (1815) (borrowed from 10 June to 13 September 1848).[183]

St = Studach, *Sämund's Edda des Weisen* (1829) (borrowed from 21 August to 2 October 1848).[184]

L = Legis, *Fundgruben des alten Nordens II.1: Edda* (1829) (borrowed from 21 August to 2 October 1848).[185]

E = Ettmüller, *Die Lieder der Edda von den Nibelungen* (1937) (borrowed from 21 October 1848 to 29 January 1849).

Si = Simrock, *Die Edda, die ältere und jüngere* (1851) (read Spring 1851).

178. Orchard, *Elder Edda*, 195–96.

179. The manuscript of Codex Regius is dated around 1270, but there is evidence the compilation took place around 1200.

180. This is a modified table of that set out in Magee, *Nibelungs*, 216–17. Note that she omits *Vafthrúdnismál* in Majer's edition (*Dichtungen und Lieder*, 135–56); also *Grottasöngr*, omitted by Magee, is included in Simrock, *Edda*, 308–11 ("Grottenlied"), but is placed in "Aus der Skalda" rather than among the Eddic poems.

181. E.g., *Brot af Sigurdarkvidu* is sometimes known as *Brot af Brynhildarkvidu*; this is because Brynhild has been mistakenly taken as speaker in v. 2 (Grimm, *Edda*, 231, calls it *Zweiten Lied der Brynhildur*) rather than Gunnar (Simrock, *Edda*, 174, is correct).

182. We have no definitive proof that he had read Ettmüller and Majer by 1848 but it seems probable given that reading them would motivate him to borrow further works from the Dresden Royal Library beginning on 10 June 1848.

183. Note that the brothers Grimm present *Reginsmál* as two separate poems: "Von Reginn und Oturs Buße" (152–65) and "Von Hnikarr" (166–73).

184. Magee, *Nibelungs*, 43.

185. Magee, *Nibelungs*, 43.

A	Mythological poems in Codex Regius								
1	Völuspá	The seeress's prophecy	M	Ev	G	St	L	E	Si
2	Hávamál	The lay of the High One				St			Si
3	Vafthrúdnismál	The lay of Vafthrúdnir	M			St	L		Si
4	Grímnismál	The lay of Grimnir	M			St	L		Si
5	För Skírnis	Skírnir's journey	M				L		Si
6	Hárbardsljód	Grey-beard's poem				St	L		Si
7	Hymiskvida	The song of Hymir	M			St	L		Si
8	Lokasenna (Oegisdrecka)	Loki's home-truths							Si
9	Thrymskvida	The song of Thrym	M			St			Si
10	Völundarkvida	The song of Völund	H		G				Si
11	Alvíssmál	The lay of All-wise				St			Si
B	Heroic poems in Codex Regius								
1	Helgakvida Hundingsbana in fyrri	The first song of Helgi, the slayer of Hunding	H		G				Si
2	Helgakvida Hjörvardssonar	The song of Helgi Hjörvardsson	H		G				Si
3	Helgakvida Hundingsbana önnur (Frá Volsüngum)	The second song of Helgi, the slayer of Hunding	H		G				Si
4	Frá dauda Sinfjötla	About Sinfjötli's death	H		G				Si
5	Grípisspá (Sigurdarkvida Fafnisbana fyrsta (Si))	Grípir's prophecy			G			E	Si
6	Reginsmál (Sigurdarkvida Fafnisbana önnur (Si)) (Second song of Sigurd, part I. Concerning Sigurd and Regin)	Regin's lay			G			E	Si
7	Fáfnismál (Second song of Sigurd, part II. Concerning Fafnir's death (E))	Fáfnir's lay	H		G			E	Si
8	Sigrdrífumál (First song of Brynhild (E))	Sigrdrífa's lay			G			E	Si
9	Brot af Sigurdarkvidu (Brot af Brynhildarkvidu (Si)) (Second song of Brynhild (E))	A fragment of the song of Sigurd	H		G			E	Si

10	Gudrúnarkvida in fyrsta	The first song of Gudrún	H					E	Si
11	Sigurdarkvida in skamma (Sigurdarkvida Fafnisbana thridja (Si)) (Third song of Sigurd (E))	The short song of Sigurd	H		G			E	Si
12	Helreid Brynhildar	Brynhild's Hel-ride	H		G			E	Si
13	Dráp Niflunga	The killing of the Niflungs	H					E	Si
14	Gudrúnarkvida in forna	The ancient song of Gudrún	H					E	Si
15	Gudrúnarkvida in thridja	The third song of Gudrún	H					E	Si
16	Oddrúnargrátr	Oddrún's lament	H					E	Si
17	Atlakvida	Atli's song	H					E	Si
18	Atlamál in grœnlenzku	The Greenlandic lay of Atli	H					E	Si
19	Gudrúnarhvöt	Gudrún's reciting	H					E	Si
20	Hamdismál	Hamdir's lay	H					E	Si
C	**Eddic poems not in Codex Regius**								
1	Rígsthula	Ríg's list							Si
2	Baldrs draumar (Vegtamskvida (Si))	Baldr's dreams / The song of Way-tamer				M			Si
3	Hyndluljód	Hyndla's poem							Si
4	Grottasöngr	Grotti's chanting							Si
D	**Additional poems**								
1	Gunnars Harfenschlag	Gunnar's harp-playing						E	
2	Svipdagsmál (Grógaldr) (Fiölsvinnsmál)	Svipdag's lay							Si / Si
E	**Spurious**								
	Hrafnagaldr Odhins	Odin's raven-magic							Si

Of all these poems the one that stands out is the very first, *Völuspá*, and I take this as an example as to how Christian theology may have come to influence Wagner's *Ring* via this majestic and powerful poem.

Völuspá

There are three main sources for *Völuspá*: Codex Regius, the fourteenth-century Hauksbók (AM 544 4to), and Snorri's Edda.[186] In my initial discussion I follow the

---

186. In the second section, *Gylfaginning*, Snorri not only quotes over forty stanzas but follows the chronological course of *Völuspá*. On the issues of textual criticism of the poem see Quinn, "Editing

version in Codex Regius, where we have a poem of sixty-two verses[187] the basic structure of which is:

vv. 1–2 introduction of the seeress;

vv. 3–20 her telling of the establishment of the cosmos;

vv. 21–53 her telling of the events leading to Ragnarök, and of the end of the world itself and the death of the gods;

vv. 54–62 her telling of the renewal of the cosmos.

The poem is important for the cosmology of the *Ring* cycle and its broad structure corresponds to that of the *Ring*.[188] One of the key questions for this investigation is the extent of Christian influence in *Völuspá* and other Norse writings that are generally considered "pagan." There have been Christian additions so in Orchard's translation stanza 65, which is in the fourteenth-century Hauksbók but not in Codex Regius, is a later Christian addition: "Then there comes the mighty one down from above, / the strong one, who governs everything, to powerfulness."[189] But although it is a later addition, it does nevertheless underline "the Christian flavour that permeates the poem."[190] Orchard suggests that the poet was "on the very cusp of becoming Christian (but not yet having fully embraced it)". There are several reasons why this may be a plausible assessment of the poem. There seem to be clear Christian influences throughout the poem (e.g., the portrayal of Baldr's death seems modelled on that of Christ);[191] but on the other hand, the poem does have an "oddly nostalgic and deferential view of the pagan gods, even as their amoral behaviour and culpable role in their own downfall are emphasized."[192] Wagner, if he followed Ettmüller's edition, would also be aware of the Christian flavor of the poem even if one were to take into account that there are "Christian additions." Ettmüller explains that his edition was based on editions of Resenius

---

the Edda."

187. This is given by Dronke, *Edda II*, 7–24, and Larrington, *Poetic Edda*, 4–12. The content of their versions corresponds roughly to that of Ettmüller, *Vaulu-spá*, 1–21 (Icelandic), 22–36 (German translation).

188. Hauer, "*Völospá*," 60–61, divides the longer sixty-five stanza *Völuspá* into seven sections, but it is not clear whether the poem can be so clearly structured and one wonders whether he has imposed a Wagnerian structure on the work. His analysis is: 1. vv. 1–16 creation; 2. vv. 17–20 institution of man and the fates; 3. vv. 21–26 corruption through gold and world war; 4. vv. 27–30 the need of Odin and the gods; 5. vv. 31–35 death of Balder; 6. vv. 36–58 Ragnarök; 7. vv. 59–65 world's rebirth. Hauer, "*Völospá*," 61, notes that "this is almost exactly Wagner's pattern as well, though he inverts the order of numbers 2 and 3, the creation of man and the corruption through gold." Note, however, that in v. 21 "Gullveig" ("Gold Brew"; Ettmüller, *Vaulu-spá*, 26, has "Gullweig") most likely refers to Freyja (who had an association with gold). Also a division between events leading to Ragnarök and Ragnarök itself (which Hauer's structure suggests) does not seem clear in the poem.

189. Orchard, *Elder Edda*, 14.

190. Orchard, *Elder Edda*, 265.

191. This will be further investigated in volume 2 chapter 8.

192. Orchard, *Elder Edda*, 266.

(Peder Resen), Stephan Olafsen, and Gudmundur Andreae (Copenhagen, 1665)[193] and of Bartholin (Copenhagen, 1667),[194] and he claimed that Resenius in turn had used three manuscripts, Codex Regius, the most important, and two others "C.M." and that of "Chr. Noldius."[195] However, "C.M." in Resenius appears to be an error in printing for "C.N.", Codex Noldii, belonging to Christian Nold.[196]

Ettmüller suggests Christians have added two verses (each of four lines):[197]

Da kommt der Mächtige zum ewigen Gericht,	Then there comes the mighty one to eternal judgement,
Der Starke von Oben, der alles beräth;	the strong one from above, who governs everything;
Gerecht Er Zwist und Streite schlichtet;	Righteously he settles discord and conflict;
Schicksal bestimmt Er, das dauern wird.	He determines fate, which will continue.
Einen Saal sieht sie (die Vala) stehen, schöner als die Sonne	She (the Vala) sees a hall standing, More beautiful than the sun
Mit Golde bedeckt in Gimli;	Covered in gold in Gimle;
Da sollen treue Völker wohnen,	There will virtuous peoples live,
Und in Ewigkeit Freude geniessen.	And enjoy joy for ever.

Ettmüller explains that the first verse is found only in Afzelius and the second is found also in Resen and Bartholin.[198] Codex Regius itself (which Resen used) contains this second verse (v. 61)[199] and ends with a verse which Ettmüller places earlier (LVII):[200]

Da kommt der dunkle Drache, der fliegende	Then there comes the dark dragon flying,
Die Natter, niedenher von Nidafiöll,	The serpent, up from Dark-of-moon hills,
Er trägt sich auf Schwingen, fliegt über die Erde	He carries himself in pinions, flies over the earth
Nidhauggr (über) die Todten. – Nun muss sie sinken.	Malice-striker over dead bodies. Now she must sink.

---

193. Ettmüller, *Vaulu-spá*, LV. Resenius, *Edda Islandorum*, contained *Völuspá*, *Hávamál*, and the *Prose Edda*.

194. He must mean the work of 1689 (Thomas Bartholin's dates are 1659–90).

195. Ettmüller, *Vaulu-spá*, LV.

196. Faulkes, *Two Versions*, 2:82–83.

197. Ettmüller, *Vaulu-spá*, 35–36 (for the Icelandic, see 21).

198. Ettmüller, *Vaulu-spá*, 35.

199. Dronke, *Edda* II, 24; Larrington, *Poetic Edda*, 12.

200. Ettmüller, *Vaulu-spá*, 34. His placing of this rather grim stanza earlier and ending on the more optimistic note of Hœnir prophesying that the sons of the two brothers Höd and Baldr will set up their home "in the wide wind realm" (Dronke, *Edda* II, 24) may have implications for how one understands the end of the *Ring* (see volume 2, chapter 11).

There are two issues to clarify regarding this final verse. First, although Ettmüller translates "dreki" as "Drache" ("dragon") he notes in his concluding "Wörterbuch" that it can also mean "Schlange" ("snake");[201] and in the synonymous parallelism we see the use of "Natter"/"naþr" ("serpent") in the following line. However, the serpent has wings so one would also expect a dragon (We will see that Wagner is insistent that the creature in his *Ring* is a serpent ("Wurm")). The name of the serpent, according to Ettmüller, is "Nidhauggr"/"Níþhauggr" who lives under the World Ash Tree.[202] The second issue is that the one who "sinks" must be the Vala since the pronoun is feminine ("sie"/"hón") and this makes perfect sense if, as in Codex Regius, this is the final verse, the Vala having finished her prophecy.[203]

In his edition of *Völuspá* Ettmüller discusses the theology of the poem, making comparisons with Greek and Roman literature and with the Bible. He discusses issues such as life after death[204] and compares the ideas of the end of the world in Matt 24:6–7, 10, 12, 29 to *Völuspá* XLVI (45), LVIII (57–58).[205] Comparisons are also made between the four horses and their riders of Revelation and *Völuspá*.[206] The white horse is that of Odin (Rev 6:2); the red is that of Loki (6:4); the black is that of Surtr (6:5); the pale horse, whose rider is death and hell and which is associated with destruction by sword, famine, pestilence, and wild animals (6:8), relates to the destructive forces in *Völuspá*, especially those of Fenrir, Freki, Garmr, and Nithhauggr (XXXV (30); XLI (39); XLV (43); XLVIII (45); L (48); LVI (46); LVII (62); LVIII (55)).[207] Rev 6:12–14, with its sun turning black and stars falling to earth, he compares to LVIII (54) and Rev 9:17 with fire, smoke, and sulphur (Schwefeldunst) issuing from the horses mouths he compares to Sutr's consuming trees with fire (LII-LIII (50–51)).[208] Ettmüller argues that the themes of destruction through fire in *Völuspá* can also be compared to Deut 32:22 (he quotes 32:15–27 in full). He also compares the destruction by wild beasts (including "Schlangen" and "Natter"; Deut 32:24b) with *Völuspá* XXXV (30); XLIX (47).[209] *Völuspá* actually has two serpent figures: the Midgard serpent described as a "Wurm" (XLIX (47); LV (53)) and the serpent Nidhöggr/Nidhauggr who lives

---

201. Ettmüller, *Vaulu-spá*, 116.

202. Ettmüller, *Vaulu-spá*, 145. "Nidhauggr"/"Níþhauggr" also appears in XXXV (Ettmüller, *Vaulu-spá*, 13, 29). Dronke, *Edda II*, 24, gives the spelling as "Niðhöggr."

203. Ettmüller, *Vaulu-spá*, 19 (LVII): "nu mun hon sökvast." It is worth noting that the Vala in *Völuspá* "is the only Nordic Sibyl who expressly concerns herself with divine matters" (Dronke, *Edda II*, 93).

204. Ettmüller, *Vaulu-spá*, 84–86.

205. Ettmüller, *Vaulu-spá*, 89–90. His biblical references have been corrected. Here and in the following lines Roman numerals refer to Ettmüller and Arabic to Dronke's verse numbers.

206. Ettmüller, *Vaulu-spá*, 90.

207. Ettmüller, *Vaulu-spá*, 91, also refers to Hati and Skoll, wolves who will devour the moon and sun respectively (*Grímnismál* 39).

208. Ettmüller, *Vaulu-spá*, 91.

209. Ettmüller, *Vaulu-spá*, 93.

under the World Ash Tree and takes to the air (XXXV (38); LVII (62)). Such figures, especially the second, are related not only to Deuteronomy 32 but also to Revelation. Here the adversary of God and human beings is either termed a "dragon" (drakōn: Rev 12:3–17; 13:2, 4, 11; 16:13; 20:2) or "serpent" (ophis), a term that can either stand alone (12:14–15) or qualify the dragon as in "the dragon, the great serpent" (12:9) or "the dragon, the ancient serpent" (20:2).[210]

As well as *Völuspá* sharing these details with the biblical texts there are also elements that point to a distinctive Christian ambience such as ideas of fall, judgement, and redemption,[211] one of the most important being the death of Baldr to which I return towards the end of the chapter and discuss in more detail in volume 2.

Wagner's appropriation of Eddic material

One of the striking factors regarding Wagner's use of sources is that we find an intensification of Eddic material in the *Ring* librettos in the Zurich period. After working on *Siegfried's Tod* in the Autumn of 1848, Wagner had a break of almost two and a half years before returning to the work in May 1851 with *Der junge Siegfried*.[212] This new *Siegfried* drama seems to be influenced by *Vafthrúdnismál*[213] and *Alvíssmál*,[214] *Fáfnismál*,[215] *Vegtamskvida* (*Baldrs Draumar*),[216] *Svipdagsmál* (*Fiölsvinnsmál*),[217]

---

210. Rev 13:3 speaks of a "great red dragon with seven heads and ten horns," which Caird, *Revelation*, 149, understands as a combination of dragon, serpent, and many-headed Hydra. Note that in the Old Testament such creatures are usually seas monsters, not those that fly.

211. Although the creation myth differs from that of Genesis 1–2, the figures of Ash and Embla (*Völuspá* 17) may recall Adam and Eve (cf. Orchard, *Elder Edda*, 268).

212. Dates are 3–10 May (prose sketch), 21 May–1 June (prose draft) and 3–24 June (verse draft).

213. Here Odin outwits the giant Vafthrúdnir (Orchard, *Elder Edda*, 39–49). Note that Odin's life is at stake (cf. Wotan's meeting with Mime) as indicated by Frigg's concern: "Go in one piece; come back in one piece; / stay in one piece on your trip. / I hope your wit's up to it, Father of Men, / when you bandy words with that giant" (40, verse 4). Odin outwits him in the final unfair question (49, verses 54–55).

214. This concerns the test of wisdom between a dwarf "All-wise" (Alvíss) and Thor (Orchard, *Elder Edda*, 108–13). Alviss lives "under the earth" (3) and hence is "pale-nosed" (2) (Orchard, *Elder Edda*, 108). With the questioning Alviss "is detained past daybreak and presumably turns to stone, like the giantess Hrímgerd at the end of a ritual exchange of insults in [*Helgakvida Hjörvardsson*] 12–30" (Orchard, *Elder Edda*, 309).

215. This has many parallels with *Siegfried* Act II and concerns the death of Fáfnir including a long dialogue with Sigurd (1–22) and then tells of the dialogue of Sigurd and Regin (23–31), the warning of the nuthatch of Regin's devious plans (32–38), Sigurd's decision to kill Regin (39), the nuthatch telling Sigurd of the Valkyrie asleep on Hind's Fell "entirely fenced with flame" (40–44).

216. Here "Odin rides to the world of the dead to summon a wise-woman from her grave, and questions her about the fate of his favourite son, the god Baldr" (Cooke, *End*, 111).

217. This was not in Codex Regius and was first published by Simrock in 1851. This tells of how "a Siegfried-like figure argues his way past a giant warder to reach a maiden in a flame-surrounded castle" (Cooke, *End*, 111). But this poem, comprising two poems, *Grógaldr* and *Fiölsvinnsmál*, both having a common narrator Svipdagr (see "D: Additionals poems" in the table above) is found in

and *Sigrdrífumál*[218] (although one can find parallels already in the *Ring* of 1848). For *Rheingold*, we see the influence of the *Prose Edda* and the poems *Oegisdrecka* (*Locasenna*)[219] and *Reginsmál*. *Walküre* shows traces of *Grímnismál* and *Helgakvida Hjörvardssonar*. The development of *Siegfried's Tod* appears to be influenced by *Hrafnagaldr Odhins*.[220]

Such Eddic influence could be ascribed to Ettmüller. Wagner, as we have seen, knew his two editions from his final years in Dresden (*Vaulu-Spá* (1830); *Die Lieder der Edda von den Nibelungen* (1937)) but he got to know him personally in Zurich. According to his autobiography, Ettmüller was present at his reading of *Siegfried's Tod*[221] and it appears he got to know him either in the second half of 1849 or in 1850.[222] The other possibility of Eddic influence is Simrock's *Edda* edition, mentioned by Wagner in his *Epilogue to the Nibelung's Ring*,[223] which was a more complete edition than the others available at that time.[224] Magee argues that whatever Ettmüller's role may have been[225] "Wagner was reading Simrock's new Edda translation during the lead-up to his resumption of the Ring" and concludes he read it between March and May 1851.[226] Magee points out that some are reluctant to accept that Simrock's edition could have influenced Wagner's "Edda-filled scenes of *Der junge Siegfried*" because it was only published in 1851, the very year Wagner wrote his *Der junge Siegfried*.[227] However, Simrock's publisher wrote to him on 14 March 1851 to say that his book had been published and distributed by the end of February. Hence Wagner would have "a good two months to read and digest the new translation before resuming work on the *Ring* in May."[228] Further, there are signs of influence of three poems which were first published by Simrock in that edition: *Oegisdrecka* (otherwise known as *Lokasenna*),[229] *Svipdagsmál*, and *Hrafngaldr Odhins*.

---

several seventeenth-century manuscripts.

218. Orchard, *Elder Edda*, 169–75.

219. *Oegisdrecka* is the name given by Simrock.

220. This work was included in Edda editions but has since been rejected as spurious. Its influence is argued by Golther, *Grundlagen*, 97. An introduction to the work together with text and commentary is given by Lassen, *Hrafnagaldur Óðins*.

221. *My Life* 424–25; *Mein Leben* 1:437. Gregor-Dellin, *Chronik*, dates his reading as 29 May 1849, this presumably based on *My Life* 417; *Mein Leben* 1:430, but this was just the day after first arriving in Zurich. Newman, *Life*, 2:113, rightly suggests the reading was later.

222. A letter to Julie Ritter of around 20–21 July 1850 tells of her son Karl studying "skandinavisch": i.e., Icelandic, with Ettmüller (*SB* 3:360) as does the letter to Uhlig of 27 July 1850 (*SB* 3:360).

223. *PW* 3:263; *GSD* 6:262.

224. See my table above comparing various editions of the poetic Edda together with that of Magee, *Nibelungs*, 216–17.

225. On Ettmüller's role, see below on Stabreim.

226. Magee, *Nibelungs*, 52.

227. Magee, *Nibelungs*, 52.

228. Magee, *Nibelungs*, 52.

229. The late publishing of this "authentic" poem from Codex Regius may be due to the vulgar

Völsunga Saga

The *Völsunga Saga* was written down sometime in the period 1200–1270[230] in Icelandic by an unknown author and based on stories found in the older Norse poetry.[231] This was to prove to be the most important source for *Die Walküre* (and also throws light on the other works in the cycle). Having failed to find the work in bookshops, Wagner borrowed it from the Dresden Royal Library.[232] Magee argues that, contrary to what Wagner's autobiography may suggest (i.e., that he was reading it in the summer of 1847),[233] he only read it in late October 1848, as indicated by the loan journals of the Dresden library. Magee points out that this may receive some confirmation by a letter he wrote to Wilhelm Fischer of 3 November 1848, where he tells him that "owing to a windfall" ("durch einen eingetretenen Fall") he is anxious to have his mornings free.[234] The significant thing about the dating of his reading the work is that it was after his writing *Der Nibelungen-Mythus*[235] (but read before writing the poem of *Siegfried's Tod*). However, Björnsson questions this since there are so many parallels between the two works, and suggests that Wagner may have borrowed the work from a friend or consulted it in the reading room of the Royal Library.[236] The other possibility is that he could know a little (but only a bare outline) of the *Völsunga Saga* from Wilhelm Grimm's *Deutsche Heldensage*.[237]

One highly significant factor in this saga, and I am not sure it has been emphasized sufficiently in secondary literature, is that much of it is set in continental Europe,

---

language used. Although first appearing in 1851, Magee, *Nibelungs*, 197, notes that Weinhold, "Loki," had produced a paraphrase in his 1849 article.

230. Byock, *Volsungs*, 3.

231. Finch, *Volsungs*, xxxvi, writes that the saga "is largely a prose version of certain Eddaic lays preserved in the Codex Regius"; but the compiler's source was not the Codex Regius itself "but an earlier no longer extant MS of the relevant Eddaic lays" (xxxviii). Hence *Völsunga Saga* chapters 24–31 are actually employed to fill in the eight-page lacuna in the Sigurd cycle of the Edda.

232. Wagner used the 1815 translation by von der Hagen, *Völsunga Saga oder Sigurd der Fafnirstöter und die Niflungen*. See the letter of 12 November 1851 to Theodor Uhlig (*SL* 232), where he asks Uhlig to borrow the book for him. Wagner acknowledged receipt of the book on 3 December 1851 (*SB* 4:206) and on 24 December explained that having reread it that he "really had had no further need for it in the first place" (*SB* 4:236; *SL* 232 n. 4). Clearly his first reading in Dresden was sufficient for him.

233. *My Life* 343: "Viewed in the light of Mone's comments, the *Wälsungasaga* exerted a decisive influence on the manner in which I began to form this [Germanic and Norse] material to my own purposes" (*Mein Leben* 1:357).

234. *SB* 2:627–28. Magee, *Nibelungs*, 45, points to the discussion by Ellis, *Life*, 2:275 and n. Ellis argues that "[a]s the morning hours were those he devoted to creative or literary work, whenever possible, it looks very much as if he had just 'happened' on the Völsunga-Saga." Could a sign of such activity to some extent account for there being fewer letters being written in late 1848 (or so it would appear)?

235. Magee, *Nibelungs*, 60–61.

236. Björnsson, *Volsungs*, 126.

237. Magee, *Nibelungs*, 70, quotes the relevant section (W. Grimm, *Heldensage*, 337).

specifically "land of the Huns"[238] and Germany (and the same is true of the heroic poems of the *Poetic Edda* although geographical references are rare). It thus provides a crucial link to the world of the *Nibelungenlied*, including the figure we know as Attila the Hun. Although a whole series of parallels between *Walküre* and the *Völsunga Saga* are given by Sabor[239] there are significant differences,[240] of which I mention four that occur in the Saga's first nine chapters.[241] First, the *Völsunga Saga* has four generations between Odin and Sigmund whereas there is just one between Wotan and Siegmund. Second, Signy was forced into an unloving marriage with Siggeir (king of Gautland,)[242] but her motive for sleeping with Sigmund is so that she can bear a son to avenge Siggeir for killing her father, Volsung.[243] She had two sons by Siggeir but she considered both too weak to be useful for revenge and told Sigmund to kill them![244] Thirdly, on the issue of her incest with Sigmund, there are key differences to Wagner's *Die Walküre*. Signy asks a sorceress to change shape with her. The sorceress (looking like Signy) sleeps with Siggeir whilst Signy sleeps with Sigmund (who does not realize this is his twin sister).[245] She returns home and she and the sorceress assume their former shapes.[246] Signy bears Sinfjotli, who grows to be strong and handsome and is sent to Sigmund, who does not know this is his own son,[247] assuming the father is Siggeir.[248] Only just before she dies in the fire that consumes Siggeir and the retainers does she confess to Sigmund that she visited him in the guise of a sorceress and that he is the father of Sinfjotli.[249] Sigmund's response to this news is not given. A fourth difference is that in the *Völsunga Saga* after Signy's death Sigmund married Borghild and had a son Helgi who killed Hunding and married Sigrun (who had been promised to Hodbrodd, son of king Hogni, and whom Helgi had killed).[250]

---

238. In *Völsunga Saga* 1 we read that Sigi ruled over "the land of the Huns" (Finch, *Volungs*, 2) and in the *Prose Edda*, Prologue, Siggi's kingdom is identified with "what is now called France" (Faulkes, *Edda*, 4).

239. Sabor, *Ring*, 95, gives a list. See also Cooke, *End*, 282–316, to whom I will return in the discussion of love in volume 2.

240. See Finch, *Volsungs*, vii–viii. The fact that the very opening of this work discusses "The Volsungs and Wagner" testifies to the way the Saga has become so closely associated with the composer.

241. Again, see Cooke, *End*, 282–316.

242. Finch, *Volsungs*, 4. Gautland is "Götland" in the sense of southern Sweden.

243. Finch, *Volsungs*, 6–7.

244. Finch, *Volsungs*, 8–9.

245. Finch, *Volsungs*, 9.

246. Cooke, *End*, 287, n. 8, notes that the phrase "and they resumed their own shapes" is missing in von der Hagen's translation.

247. Finch, *Volsungs*, 9–10.

248. Finch, *Volsungs*, 10.

249. Finch, *Volsungs*, 13–14.

250. Finch, *Volsungs*, 14–15.

After these events the story relates in chapter 10 the death of Sinfjotli:[251] he desired a woman whom the brother of his step-mother (Borghild) also wished to have. Sinfjotli killed him and in turn Borghild poisoned Sinfjotli.[252] Sigmund drove her out and she died shortly after. Chapter 11 tells of how Sigmund then visited King Eylimi[253] because he wanted his daughter Hjordis. But King Lyngvi, son of King Hunding, also wanted her but she chose Sigmund. Sigmund married Hjordis and went back to his kingdom of Hunland together with his father-in-law Eylimi. But Lyngvi and his brothers gathered an army[254] and fought against Sigmund and despite being helped by his "norns"[255] when Odin[256] intervened, breaking Sigmund's sword in two with his spear, the battle turned and Sigmund and Eylimi died.[257]

In chapter 12 it I related how, before dying, Sigmund told Hjordis to guard the broken pieces of sword which will be made good, called Gram, and wielded by their son. Hjordis later married Alf son of King Hjalprek of Denmark.[258] Chapter 13 tells of how Hjordis gave birth and the child "was sprinkled with water and named Sigurd"[259] and he was brought up with Hjalprek, Alf, and Hjordis and had Regin as a foster father who taught him "chequers," runes, and languages.[260]

Sigurd on meeting Odin gained the horse Grani, descended from Sleipnir.[261] Regin tells Sigurd of the serpent Fafnir who guards the hoard of gold at Gnitaheid[262] and then relates in chapter 14 the story of the "Otter's Ransom," important for Wagner,[263]

---

251. Cf. *About Sinfjötli's death* in the *Elder Edda* (Orchard, *Elder Edda*, 145–46).

252. Finch, *Volsungs*, 18.

253. Eylimi is occasionally mentioned in the *Elder Edda* (e.g., *Grípisspá* prologue, 9) but otherwise nothing is known of him (Finch, *Volsungs*, 19 n. 2).

254. Finch, *Volsungs*, 19. This army is then referred to as "Vikings" (Finch, *Volsungs*, 20). The etymology of "Viking" is unclear: it could come from "vík" (creek), "Vík" (the Oslofjord), the Old English "wic" and Latin "vicus" (camp, dwelling place), or even the Old Norse verb víkja" (to turn aside) (Jesch, *Diaspora*, 4–8). Such etymology, although not determining the meaning, can indicate something of the word's history.

255. Finch, *Volsungs*, 20. "Spádísir" were akin to both "nornir" (personified expressions of fate) and "dísir" (supernatural female guardian spirits). See Finch, *Volsungs*, 20 n. 1, 91, 93. Note spá = prophecy.

256. Not named but described as having "a black cloak and a hat coming down low over his face." Further, "[h]e had but one eye and in his hand he held a spear" (Finch, *Volsungs*, 20).

257. Finch, *Volsungs*, 20.

258. Finch, *Volsungs*, 20–22.

259. Finch, *Volsungs*, 23. This pagan rite of sprinkling may have elements in common with Christian baptism and may have originated from contact between pagan Norse people and Christian Anglo-saxons (Finch, *Volsungs*, 92–93).

260. Finch, *Volsungs*, 23. What is translated as "chequers" ("tafl") refers to board games and not necessarily just "chess."

261. Finch, *Volsungs*, 23–24.

262. Finch, *Volsungs*, 24. The words for the serpent are "ormr" (but Finch translates this as "dragon") and "lyngorma" (appropriately translated "serpents").

263. This is also related in *Skaldskaparmal* (Faulkes, *Edda*, 99–100).

which runs as follows. Regin tells of his father Hreidmar, an important and wealthy man, who had three sons: Fafnir, "the biggest and fiercest," Otr, a great fisherman who during the day "assumed the shape of an otter," and then Regin, "the least gifted and made least of."[264] A dwarf, Andvari, in the shape of a pike, was catching fish in a waterfall as did Otr. Odin, Loki, and Hœnir came to the Andvari Falls and Loki killed the "otter" Otr. They skinned the otter and brought the catch to Hreidmar, who said that to compensate they must fill the skin with gold and cover the outside with "red gold."[265] Loki was sent to get the gold and this he did by forcing Andvari to get gold, thereby ransoming his head from Hel.[266] Loki handed over the gold, but kept back the ring. But a whisker of the otter remained uncovered so Odin drew the ring "Andvaranaut" from his arm to cover up the hair.[267] Later Fafnir killed his father, turned into a serpent and now lies over the hoard. Regin then tells that after losing his legacy he became the smith of the king (Hjalprek).[268]

In chapter 15 Sigurd tells Regin he will kill "this great dragon"[269] if he will make a sword. Regin agrees, has two attempts, but the swords breaks when Sigurd strikes the anvil with them. Sigurd then asks his mother for the sword fragments of his father and Regin refashions the sword, which is so strong it can slice right through the anvil.[270]

Chapter 16 tells of how Sigurd visited his uncle Gripir (Hjordis' brother) who foretells his future.[271] Sigurd agrees to kill Fafnir but insists on first avenging his father. So he sets out (chapter 17) to the kingdom of the sons of Hunding to kill King Lyngvi, his brother Hjorvard, and all other sons of Hunding with his sword Gram.[272]

In chapter 18 Sigurd kills Fafnir, who, before he dies, warns Sigurd that the gold he takes will be the cause of his death.[273] Chapter 19 tells of how Regin came, drank Fafnir's blood, and got Sigurd to roast Fafnir's heart, which Sigurd had cut out with the sword Ridill.[274] At the roasting some blood touched his tongue, which enabled him to understand the speech of birds.[275] Six birds offer advice (chapter 20): he should cut off Regin's head since he plans to betray him, he should take the gold and he should ride

---

264. Finch, *Volsungs*, 24–25.
265. Finch, *Volsungs*, 25. "Red gold" means pure gold and happens to occur also in Goethe *Faust I* (Studierzimmer II) l. 1679 (*GWJA* 3:61).
266. Finch, *Volsungs*, 25–26.
267. Finch, *Volsungs*, 26.
268. Finch, *Volsungs*, 26.
269. Finch, *Volsungs*, 26. Usually the term "serpent" ("orm") equivalent to Wagner's "Wurm" is used. Here the word "dreka" is actually used.
270. Finch, *Volsungs*, 27.
271. Finch, *Volsungs*, 28. Cf. *Grípisspá* (Orchard, *Elder Edda*, 146–54).
272. Finch, *Volsungs*, 28–30.
273. Finch, *Volsungs*, 30–32.
274. Finch, *Volsungs*, 33.
275. Finch, *Volsungs*, 33. Cf. *Fáfnismál* (Orchard, *Elder Edda*, 168).

to Hind Fell where Brynhild sleeps.[276] He follows their advice beheading Regin, takes the gold together with the "helm of terror,"[277] and in chapter 21 rides to Hind Fell. There he finds the fire and a man "asleep and lying fully armoured."[278] On removing a helmet he realizes it is a woman.[279]

Brynhild wakes not through a kiss but by Sigurd slicing through her armor.[280] She knows that this is Sigurd, son of Sigmund, and Sigurd says he has heard of her beauty and wisdom and knows that she is the daughter of a powerful king. Brynhild explains why she has slept so long: in the battle between two kings she struck down Hjalmgunnar whom Odin had promised victory and "in retaliation" he pricked her with the "sleep thorn."[281] He said she must marry but she "made a solemn vow to marry no one who knew the meaning of fear."[282] Sigurd asks her: "Give me good advice on things that matter."[283] She gives advice first in poetry (stanzas 6–20)[284] and then in prose (chapter 22), and they agree to marry.[285]

Chapter 23 describes Sigurd's appearance, stressing the image of the "dragon" on his shield. As well as describing his strength the narrator also emphasizes his wisdom and intelligence (contrasting somewhat with Wagner's Siegfried).[286]

So far the Saga has been well structured and coherent. However, there is clearly a problem from chapter 24 where we encounter a different Brynhild story, the author bringing together two different sources.[287] So it describes how Sigurd travelled to Hei-

---

276. Finch, *Volsungs*, 34.

277. Finch, *Volsungs*, 34. The parallel to *Siegfried* Act II is clear apart from the fact that Siegfried stabs Mime rather than beheading him.

278. Finch, *Volsungs*, 35.

279. Finch, *Volsungs*, 35. Again there are clear parallels in Wagner's *Siegfried*, this time Act III Scene 3.

280. The same and earlier tradition is preserved in *Sigrdrífumál* where Sigurd wakes Sigrdrifa by cutting through her corselet (Orchard, *Elder Edda*, 169).

281. This is clearly reminiscent of what we know as "sleeping beauty" ("Dornröschen"). Cf Grimm, *Hausmärchen*, 3:87 (1819–22): "Die Jungfrau, die in dem mit einem Dornenwall umgegeben Schloss schläft, bis sie der rechte Königssohn erlöst, ist die schlafende Brunhild . . . Die Spindel . . . ist der Schlafdorn, womit Othin die Brunhild sticht." In the original written version of 1810 Jacob noted (correctly) that the story was taken from Perrault's *La Belle au bois dormant* and would presumably not deserve to be included in the "German" collection. Wilhelm, on the other hand, saw something different: "The virgin who is sleeping in the castle surrounded by the wall of thorns until freed by the king's son is analogous to Brynhild who is surrounded by a wall of flames through which Sigurd penetrates" (Murphy, *Owl*, 136).

282. Finch, *Volsungs*, 35.

283. Finch, *Volsungs*, 35.

284. Finch, *Volsungs*, 35–39.

285. Finch, *Volsungs*, 39–40.

286. Finch, *Volsungs*, 40–41.

287. This is often found in the Old Testament. See, e.g., 1 Samuel, where two contradictory stories concerning Israel's demand for a king are placed side by side. In 1 Samuel 8 God is displeased with Israel's request for a king (continued in 10:17–25) but in 1 Samuel 9:1—10:16 he is positively disposed. There are clearly two different sources (Smith, *Samuel*, xviii).

mir, the brother-in-law and foster father of Brynhild. There is no indication that the two have agreed to marry or even that they have already met. But Brynhild knows of Sigurd since she has embroidered a tapestry with gold telling of Sigurd's great deeds.[288] Sigurd falls in love with this "shield maiden" but Brynhild tells him he will marry Gudrun, daughter of Gjuki.[289]

It is worth noting that this problem in the narrative of the *Völsunga Saga* is avoided in the *Elder Edda* since the Valkyrie Sigurd awakes is not Brynhild but Sigrdrifa. But this is also not without problems (although the *Edda* is not intended as a coherent narrative) since there are indications Brynhild and Sigrdrifa are the same person, as can be seen by comparing *Sigrdrifumal* with *Helreid Brynhildar* 8–9 (they vow never to marry a man who knows the meaning of fear).[290]

Chapter 26 then tells of Gudrun who travels to Brynhild to have a dream interpreted.[291] Her grim interpretation (chapter 27) is: "Sigurd, whom I chose as my husband, will come to you. Grimhild will give him drugged mead. This will bring great sorrow to us all. You will marry him and soon lose him. Then you will marry King Atli. You will lose your brothers and then kill Atli."[292] Apart from the role of Atli, we have here the essence of Wagner's *Götterdämmerung*.

In chapter 28 Sigurd then rides on Grani to the hall of King Gjuki (cf. *Götterdämmerung* Act I). Grimhild wishes Sigurd to marry her daughter Gudrun rather than Brynhild and so gives him the drink of forgetfulness (it is not in addition a love potion as in *Götterdämmerung*). Sigurd then swears a pact of brotherhood with Gunnar, Gudrun's brother, and marries Gudrun. They have a son Sigmund.[293]

Since Gunnar is unmarried Grimhild suggests he marries Brynhild. He rides with Sigurd and Hogni to King Budli then to Heimir. Both agree to the marriage provided Brynhild also agrees. Gunnar tries to approach Brynhild but cannot penetrate the flames that surround her hall. So he and Sigurd exchange appearances and Sigurd wins her for Gunnar.[294] But although he stayed with her for three nights and slept in the same bed he placed Gram unsheathed between them. He took from her the ring Andvaranaut (which we now learn he had previously given her), and gave her "another from Fafnir's inheritance."[295]

As in *Götterdämmerung* Sigurd and Gunnar exchange shapes back. Brynhild journeys to her foster father (Heimir) and expresses surprise that Gunnar could fight

---

288. Finch, *Volsungs*, 41–42.
289. Finch, *Volsungs*, 43.
290. See Orchard, *Elder Edda*, 322–23. Note that Sigrdrifa does not occur in the *Prose Edda* or the *Völsunga Saga*.
291. Finch, *Volsungs*, 45–46.
292. Finch, *Volsungs*, 46.
293. Finch, *Volsungs*, 46–48.
294. Finch, *Volsungs*, 48–49.
295. Finch, *Volsungs*, 50.

the flames. She refers to Sigurd as her "first lover" and we now learn they even have a child, Aslaug. There is then a marriage festival for Gunnar and Brynhild at the court of Gjutki.[296] Note the difference to *Götterdämmerung* though: "when [the feast] was over, Sigurd remembered all his vows to Brynhild, but he gave no sign."[297] The *Völsunga Saga* lacks the realistic drama of *Götterdämmerung* when we read at the end of chapter 29: "Brynhild and Gunnar sat enjoying themselves and drank good wine."[298]

Chapter 30 then tells of the dispute between Brynhild and Gudrun.[299] It is an argument about precedence and about the fact that Brynhild was previously married to Sigurd. This then leads to Guttorm (brother of Gunnar and Gudrun) killing Sigurd by his sword.[300] After Brynhild's prophecy to Gunnar about the disastrous events which will overcome him and Gudrun, we read of the lighting of the funeral pyre upon which was placed Sigurd, the body of his three-year-old son (whom Brynhild ordered to be killed), and the body of Guttorm. Brynhild then went on to the blazing pyre, taking her own life.[301] Her death is neither an atonement for her own misdoings (instigating Sigurd's murder)[302] nor for anyone else.

The ending of the saga tells of the doom of Brynhild's prophecy being played out. Gudrun is pressurised to marry Atli,[303] Gunnar, Hogni and others travel to Atli[304] but Hogni was killed and Gunnar died in the snake pit.[305] Gudrun gives Atli the hearts of his sons to eat and drink their blood[306] and Alti is killed by Gudrun and Niflung (Hogni's son). Gudrun marries King Jonakr and has sons Hamdir, Sorli, and Erp.[307] Svanhild, daughter of Sigurd and Gudrun, marries Jormunrek and she is killed.[308] Finally, the sons of Gudrun try to kill Jormunrek but instead the sons themselves are killed.[309]

As well as the similarities with Wagner's *Ring* there are, as already noted, significant differences, and one of these is precisely the significance of Bryhild's death to which, as we shall see, Wagner attaches great significance.

---

296. Finch, *Volsungs*, 50.

297. Finch, *Volsungs*, 50.

298. Finch, *Volsungs*, 50.

299. For will be further discussed in volume 2 chapter 10.

300. Finch, *Volsungs*, 57–58. This includes the theme of Brynhild's laughter in response to Gudrun's sobbing (Finch, *Volsungs*, 59); cf. Gutrune's words in *Götterdämmerung* Act III Scene 3: "Brünnhilde's laughter / woke me up" (*WagRS* 344).

301. Finch, *Volsungs*, 60–61.

302. Finch, *Volsungs*, xxiv–xxv.

303. Finch, *Volsungs*, 63–64.

304. Finch, *Volsungs*, 68–69.

305. Finch, *Volsungs*, 71.

306. Finch, *Volsungs*, 72–73.

307. Finch, *Volsungs*, 74.

308. Finch, *Volsungs*, 75–76.

309. Finch, *Volsungs*, 77–78.

Saga of Thidrek of Bern

This work is to be dated around 1250 (hence roughly contemporary with the *Völsunga Saga*) and may well have been written by a Norwegian cleric.[310] These are tales from North and West Germany concerning Thidrek or Dietrich of Bern who, after fleeing Bern (i.e., Verona), seeks refuge with Attila (Etzel of the *Nibelungenlied*). Thidrek is identified with Theodoric the Ostrogoth (471–526), who was actually born after Attila's death.

It is to be assumed that Wagner borrowed the work since it was not in his Dresden library but neither is there any record of his borrowing it from the Royal library.[311] *Thidrek's Saga* includes a vast range of material and there are sections that are especially important for Wagner's portrayal of Siegfried. On the one hand, the *saga* tells the tragedy of the death of Sigurd as in the *Nibelungenlied*,[312] which chimes in with *Götterdämmerung*. But, on the other hand, we have a portrayal of the "young Sigurd" that corresponds to Wagner's *Der junge Siegfried*: there is the poignant story of his mother (Queen Sisibe) dying shortly after his birth[313] but also there is the story of his violence towards his adoptive father "Mimir" and others[314] and his "comic" character.[315]

Towards the end of the saga we read that Thidrek and his world converted from Arianism to orthodox Catholicism: "During the later years of Thidrek's reign the heresy of Arianus was condemned by Christian men, and all those who had followed the heresy turned to the true faith."[316] Then at the end Thidrek disappears on a black horse and the saga closes thus: "The German men say that it has been revealed in dreams that King Thidrek was helped by God and Saint Mary because he remembered their names at his death. Here we end the telling of this saga."[317]

Heimskringla

This work, as noted above, was the tenth on Wagner's list and was so named (in the seventeenth century) because of the first two words of one of the manuscripts "Kringla heimsins" ("the circle of the world"). This was an Icelandic work by Snorri Sturluson composed around 1230 and consists of sixteen sagas about the Norwegian kings, beginning with the Swedish dynasty of the Ynglings and ending with the saga of Magnus

---

310. Haymes, *Thidrek*, xix.

311. Wagner refers to the work as "Wilkina- und Niflungasaga" indicating the edition of von Hagen (Breslau).

312. Haymes, *Thidrek*, 210–14. Note that Kriemhild (of the *Nibelungenlied*) is named Grimhild.

313. Haymes, *Thidrek*, 104–5.

314. Haymes, *Thidrek*, 106–8.

315. E.g., he kills the dragon not with a sword but with beam of wood (Haymes, *Thidrek*, 107).

316. Haymes, *Thidrek*, 253; cf. xxv.

317. Haymes, *Thidrek*, 269.

Erlingsson (died 1184).[318] Wagner possessed the translations of G. Mohnike and Ferdinand Wachter in his Dresden library,[319] preferring, as noted above, the readable translation of Mohnike to Wachter's literal rendering.[320] Both works only contain the first six sagas (they both finish with the saga of King Olaf Tryggvason) and although Mohnike has only one volume as opposed to Wachter's two, Mohnike actually contain more material in that he offers 123 chapters for Olaf Tryggvason whereas Wachter's offers only seventy-six chapters.

As Magee points out, the only relevant sections for Wagner's *Ring* are the opening chapters of the *Ynglinga Saga* and the *Hákonarmál*. The first ten chapters of *Ynglinga Saga* have some parallels with the Prologue of the *Prose Edda*. It tells of the giants, dwarves, and "amazingly large wild animals and dragons" that live in "Svíþjóð" (Sweden or Russia),[321] of Odin as a great warrior, of the war between the Æsir and Vanir, and of how belief in Odin arose among the Swedes after his death.[322] Then the skaldic poem *Hákonarmál* by the tenth-century Norwegian poet Eyvindr skáldaspillir is quoted in *Heimskringla* at the end of *Hákonar saga góða* (saga of Hakon the good) (chapter 31).[323] It is also quoted by Frauer,[324] whose monograph on the Valkyries, according to Minna, was in Wagner's Dresden Library.[325] This poem tells of two Valkyries, Gondul and Skogul, being sent to bring Hakon to Valhalla;[326] this could have influenced the "Annunciation of Death" in *Walküre* Act II Scene 4.[327]

---

318. The last event is the death of the pretender Eystein Meyla in 1177.

319. Mohnike, vol 1 (1837, only one volume exists) and Wachter, 2 vols (1835–36) (Westernhagen, *Bibliothek*, 104).

320. Wachter, *Heimskringla*, ccxiii–cclxxx discusses Mohnike's 1835 work (this was the first edition; Wagner possessed the 1837 edition). He writes that "diese Muster-Arbeit [ist] über alles Lob erhaben." Unfortunately, Mohnike, *Heimskringla*, xiv–xv (1837), is not able to return the compliment when he briefly discusses Wachter's 1835 translation. He quotes Wachter's "Probe in Foryrdalag" in *Ynglinga Saga* 35 (cf. Wachter, *Heimskringla*, 91–92) and then quotes Droysen's "Vorrede" to his Aeschylus with the intention of questioning literal translations. Wagner would be aware of the literal nature of Wachter's translation (see, e.g., the very opening, *Heimskringla*, 3), but his views were no doubt confirmed by Mohnike's observations.

321. Finlay/Faulkes, *Heimskringla I*, 6; cf. Hollander, *Heimskringla*, 6.

322. Finlay/Faulkes, *Heimskringla I*, 7–13; cf. Hollander, *Heimskringla*, 7–13.

323. Finlay/Faulkes, *Heimskringla I*, 115–19; cf. Hollander, *Heimskringla*, 125–27.

324. Frauer, *Walkyrien*, 8–11.

325. Westernhagen, *Bibliothek*, 112.

326. Magee *Nibelungs*, 164 refers Mohnike, *Heimskringla*, 1:148, where Hakon asks: "War ich, Walkyria, / Werth nicht des Sieges: / Warum entscheidest du so die Schlacht." Cf. Finlay/Faulkes, *Heimskringla I*, 118; Hollander, *Heimskringla*, 126.

327. Björsson, *Volsungs*, 172–74. See also Golther, *Grundlagen*, 13.

Saxo Grammaticus: Gesta Danorum

The Danish historian and theologian Saxo (c. 1160–1220) wrote a history of the Danes from its founder Dan I to around 1187, a work found in Wagner's Dresden library. The first nine books contain mythological material (e.g., concerning the warrior Baldr, aided by what appear to be Valkyries)[328] and include three digressions into matters of the heathen gods.[329] In the second he writes concerning Frigg: "This woman, unworthy of a deified consort, felt no scruples about pursuing unchastity, provided she could more speedily enjoy what she coveted!"[330] It is striking that Wagner's portrayal of Fricka contradicts what Saxo writes of Odin's consort. The third digression tells of the evils of pagan worship (Snorri is more subtle on this): "At one time certain individuals, initiated into the arts of sorcery, namely Thor, Odin, and a number of others, clouded the minds of simple men and began to appropriate the exalted rank of godhead. Norway, Sweden, and Denmark were ensnared in a groundless conviction, urged to a devoted worship of these frauds, and infected by the smirch of their gross imposture."[331] No doubt there are passages that would interest Wagner but the question is whether he could cope with the difficult Latin. In his autobiography he confesses: "With regard to the ancient languages I was [...] able to concentrate only as much as absolutely necessary to learn through them about subjects that stimulated me to reproduce their most characteristic aspects for myself."[332] He then adds that it was Greek that particularly attracted him, but even here we know that he struggled with this language and was later to rely mostly on translations.[333] Magee concludes that it is unlikely that Wagner read the work.[334] I judge that it is unlikely he read extensive passages from Saxo, but he could use it as a reference work especially since Jacob Grimm refers to it (with pages numbers) in his *Deutsche Mythologie*.[335]

Simrock's Amelungenlied

The *Amelungenlied* comprises volumes 4–6 of Simrock's *Heldenbuch*,[336] the first three volumes of which were *Gudrun*, the *Nibelungenlied*, and *Das kleine Heldenbuch*. For the

---

328. Ellis Davidson, *Gods*, 184.
329. See §§ 1.5.2–6; 1.7.1–3; 6.5.3–5.
330. Saxo Grammaticus, *Gesta Danorum*, 1:53.
331. Saxo Grammaticus, *Gesta Danorum*, 1:379–81.
332. *My Life* 14; *Mein Leben* 20.
333. See chapter 4 below for further discussion of Wagner's knowledge of the Greek language.
334. Magee, *Nibelungs*, 37.
335. E.g., Grimm, *Mythologie*, 1:132 n. refers to Saxo Grammaticus p. 142.
336. Westernhagen, *Bibliothek*, 84, gives these three volumes the number 3 in his list of works present in the collection. As noted above, Wagner also possessed volumes 1–3 of the series (DB 76, 101, 59). As Magee, *Nibelungs*, 32, points out, since Wagner had all six volumes of Simrock's *Heldenbuch*, naming it in the appendix of works that have been lost (Westernhagen, *Bibliothek*, 112) is a

Amelungenlied he did not follow his usual practice of updating the language of existing poems, but rather he wrote a new one with the intention of covering the remaining areas of German heroic saga. He believed that all heroic saga was originally in poetic form and in cases where originals were no longer extant they should be recreated.[337] The main source is *Thidrek's Saga* and concerns Dietrich von Bern and the Amelungs, the heroes at his court; but Simrock also worked into his work "existing 'Heldenlieder', fragments of Norse mythology, some folk saga and fairy-tale, and a sprinkling of folk wit."[338]

One problem in the assessing the influence of this work on Wagner's *Ring* is that volume 3 of the *Amelungenlied* (volume 6 of the *Heldenbuch*), which appeared in 1849, is a paperback in Wagner's library and is uncut with only certain pages available for reading. It seems therefore that Wagner did not get around to reading this volume and hence a question mark has to placed by all those references in the secondary literature to this final part.[339]

Although there are clear problems in discerning any dependence on volume 3 of Simrock's *Amelungenlied*, there are instances where the first two had a probable influence on his *Siegfried*: the forging scene with the filing of the sword to dust[340] and the splitting of the anvil,[341] the atmosphere of the forest murmurs,[342] the playing on the reed and then the horn,[343] and Siegfried waking Brünnhilde.[344]

Other works in the Heldenbuch

As will already be clear, the term *Heldenbuch* is somewhat fluid but Wagner in his list clarifies what he means by referring to the editions of von der Hagen and Simrock.

"mystery," or should one say simply a mistake.

337. Magee, *Nibelungs*, 31.

338. Magee, *Nibelungs*, 31.

339. So Magee, *Nibelungs*, 154–55, refers to Simrock, *Heldenbuch*, 6:213, to indicate that "[f]or Simrock 'Neiding' is tantamount to 'coward.'" This page is not accessible in Wagner's uncut volume. Magee, *Nibelungs*, 162–63, refers to *Heldenbuch*, 6:417, in relation to the story of Odin begetting Wolfdietrich. By sheer accident, this page can be read. Likewise, *Heldenbuch*, 6:160, which concerns the "blood-friendship ceremony between Etzel and Alpker" (Magee, *Nibelungs*, 95), is readable, but again this is a coincidence. Magee though rightly comments that Simrock's volume 6 appeared too late to have any influence on *Siegfried's Tod*.

340. Magee, *Nibelungs*, 116–17, quotes *Heldenbuch*, 4:57: "Wieland in der Schmiede nahm eine Feile gut; Damit war zerfeilet das Schwert zu eitel Staub." Cf. *WagRS* 221–22.

341. Magee, *Nibelungs*, 119, quotes *Heldenbuch*, 4:94. Cf. *WagRS* 228.

342. *Heldenbuch*, 4:99 (Golther, *Grundlagen*, 69–70; Magee, *Nibelungs*, 116). Cf. *WagRS* 238–39.

343. Magee, *Nibelungs*, 117, quoting *Heldenbuch*, 5:37: "Ein Horn lag auf dem Stuhle. Verstand ers Blasen auch? / Er nahm es von dem Polster und hob es an den Mund. / Da fing er an zu blasen ob er es gleich nicht verstund. / Er mocht es selber merken, dass ihm die Kunst noch fremd; / Doch wollt er sie erlernen. [. . .] Er aber blies, als wollt er Eber, Bär und Wolf / Aus dem Walde blasen." Cf. *WagRS* 238–39.

344. Magee, *Nibelungs*, 118 (noting that the Norse sources omit the kiss) points to *Heldenbuch*, 4:368–75 (Heime narrating "Wittich Wielands Sohn"). Cf. *WagRS* 267.

Hagen in volume one (the only one Wagner possessed) contains *Hörnen Siegfried, Etzels Hofhaltung, Das Rosengarten Lied, Alpharts Tod, Ecken Ausfahrt,* and *Riese Siegenot*. Simrock's *Das kleine Heldenbuch* contains *Walther und Hildegunde, Alphart, Der hörnene Siegfried, Der Rosengarten, Das Hildebrandtslied,* and *Ortnit*. We have already seen the importance of *Hörnen Siegfried* and of the other works *Ecken Ausfahrt* is to be singled out since there we read of a storm giant Fasold/Fasolt. From von der Hagen Wagner would know the extended version of the poem of 377 stanza (each stanza having 13 lines)[345] where Fasold (Wilhelm Grimm render Fasolt), with his brothers Eck and Ebenrot, makes his appearance in the second stanza:[346]

Drei Helde sassen in einem Saal,	Three heroes sat within a hall,
Sie redten Wunder ohne Zahl,	They spoke of miracles without number,
Die auserwählten Recken:	The chosen heroes:
Das ein' das war sich Herr Fasold,	One of them was lord Fasold,
Dem waren schönen Frauen hold.	He was a man for the fair ladies.

The significant thing about Fasold/Fasolt is that he along with his brothers is holding captive three queens/maidens in Köln on the Rhine and as noted had a special love for women. This clearly parallels how Wagner portrays Fasolt (and we even have a connection with the Rhine). Fasold, despite not being in the title of the poem, seems to feature more than his brother Eck, whose death at the hands of Dietrich von Bern (roughly half way through the poem) Fasold seeks to avenge but instead dies also at the hands of Dietrich.

Icelandic Sagas

Björnsson considers that Wagner may have used material from Icelandic Sagas such as *Egils Saga* and *Gísla Saga*. Brief sections and retelling of sixty-six sagas, fifty of them from Iceland, were published in German translation by Lachmann in 1816, a work Wagner possessed in his Dresden library.[347] Bjornsson compares Hunding's not killing Siegmund at night with *Egils Saga* (chapter 59), where King Eiríkr Blood-Axe and Queen Gunnhildr refrain from killing Egil at night "because night-killings are murders."[348] This story is included in Lachmann's selection so it is conceivable Wagner may have been influenced by this.[349] Bjornsson also suggests the blood

---

345. W. Grimm, *Heldensage*, 213, mentions versions of 284 and 311 stanzas.

346. Von der Hagen, *Heldenbuch* ("Ecken Ausfahrt," 4). Cf. W. Grimm, *Heldensage*, 214: "Drey Helden sassen in einem Sal / Sye redten von wunder one zal / Die auserwoelten Recke / Das ein das was sich Herr Fasolt / Dem waren die schoenen frawen hold." Part of this is quoted in Magee, *Nibelungs*, 195.

347. Lachmann, *Sagaenbibliothek* (DB 123). For *Egils saga* see 81–95, and for *Gísla saga* see 124–29.

348. Bjornsson, *Volsungs*, 160.

349. Lachmann, *Sagaenbibliothek*, 87: "Erich antwortet, er möge sich zum Tode bereiten, Königin

brotherhood scene in *Götterdämmerung* Act I has been influenced by *Gísla saga*, chapter 6.[350] Again this is conceivable since the beginning of Lachmann's summary tells of the blood brotherhood (Pflegbrüderschaft) sworn between Gisli, Thorkel, Thorgrim, and Vestein.[351]

Having considered the key sources Wagner employed, I turn now to his appropriation of the Icelandic style of poetry in his *Ring* libretto.

Stabreim

Spencer points out that although other dramatists had used alliteration (e.g., Fouqué, Rückert, Goethe, and Bürger), Wagner was the first to employ it in an operatic libretto. Further he suggests that "Wagner's decision to abandon Romantic prosody appears to have been taken in the light of Ludwig Ettmüller's *Die Lieder der Edda von den Nibelungen* (Zurich, 1837)."[352] Mertens writes that in this work Ettmüller "attempted to reproduce the verse form of the original Eddic strophe when translating these poems into German, and it was from Ettmüller that Wagner borrowed the meter and *Stabreim* that characterize his poem for the *Ring*."[353] Further, Mertens suggests it was discussions with "Eddamüller," following their meeting in Zurich in 1849,[354] which left their mark on the final form.[355] It is indeed in the Zurich writings that the composer first mentions Stabreim; further, his engagement with Stabreim intensified from 1849, this being witnessed in changes in the wording of *Siegfried's Tod*. Take the example of Hagen's words in Act II Scene 4:[356]

Merket wohl,	Pay close attention
was die Frau euch klagt!	To this woman's accusation!

Strabreim was later introduced thus:[357]

Gunhild forderte dieses sogleich. Aber Arinbiörn stellt dem Könige vor, daß es Meuchelmord sey, einen Mann bei Nacht zu erschlagen, und verlangt, daß Egils Strafe auf den nächsten Tag aufgeschoben wird."

350. Bjornsson, *Volsungs*, 235,
351. Lachmann, *Sagaenbibliothek*, 124.
352. Spencer, "Text and translation," 11. Hauer, "*Völospá*," 54, considered that "virtually everything that Wagner understood (or at times misunderstood) about Old Norse metrics comes from Ettmüller."
353. Mertens, "Middle Ages," 248. Note the subtitle of Ettmüller's work: *Stabreimende Verdeutschung*.
354. Newman, *Life*, 2:158, tells of his "especially intimate" relationship with Ettmüller. See also Wille, *Erinnerungen*, 27; Magee, *Nibelungs*, 50–52.
355. Mertens, "Middle Ages," 248.
356. Haymes, *Ring*, 126–27.
357. *WagRS* 320 (my emphasis). Cf. Björnsson, *Volsungs*, 109.

Jetzt merket *k*lug,	Mark closely now
was die Frau euch *k*lagt!	what the woman discloses!

However, Wagner may well have had some knowledge of Stabreim before reading Ettmüller's *Die Lieder der Edda*[358] and before meeting him (in 1849) and three books in his Dresden library are relevant here. The first is Ettmüller's edition of *Vaulu-Spá* (1830), which in addition to giving the "Nordic" text (1–21), German translation (22–36), notes on various themes in the poem (36–108), including theological themes (see below), and an Icelandic—German dictionary (109–68), includes a fairly lengthy introduction (III–LV), part of which is devoted to questions of "Anreim" (alliteration) and the forms of Eddic poetry (XIX–XXII), including works beyond *Völuspá*.[359] The second work is von der Hagen's *Lieder*, which, although it has been suggested by some that Wagner did not use this since the poems are in Icelandic (which he could not read), does include a discussion of "Alliterazion" and poetic forms of Eddic poetry.[360] The third is Rühs' *Edda*, which although providing a translation of the *Prose Edda* (161–266) also has a section on Nordic Poetry (61–120), where alliteration is discussed (62–63) and "Fornyrdalag" (86–90). In addition to these works he possessed, the 1829 translation of eight of the mythological Eddic poems by the Swedish minister Studach (which Wagner borrowed from the Dresden Royal Library) employs Stabreim.[361]

However, Ettmüller's *Die Lieder der Edda von den Nibelungen; Stabreimende Verdeutschung* offers more detail on the characteristics of Eddic poetry.[362] Appealing to Rasmus Rask, a Danish linguist and philologist, he points out that Nordic poetry, as opposed to Greek and Roman, is not concerned with the number of "feet" (e.g., hexameter). Rather, it is determined by firstly the number of long syllables (or, as Ettmüller corrects Rask, lifts "Hebungen"), secondly alliteration, and thirdly a structure of strophes. At first he considers that all the Eddic poems have been composed in "Fornyrdhalag"[363] (having varying strophe length), subdividing this into "Starkadharlag" (from "Starkadh der Alten," "Starkadhr hinn gamli") and "Lióðhahâttr" (= "Liederhaft").[364] Later, however, he writes of "Fornyrdalag" and "Liodhahattr."[365]

---

358. As already noted this was borrowed 21 October 1848 and returned it 29 January 1849.

359. Note the subtitle: "Das älteste Denkmal germanische-nordischer Sprache nebst einingen Gedanken über Nordens Wissen und Glauben und nordische Dichtkunst."

360. Von der Hagen, *Edda*, V–VI, VI–VIII.

361. One need only read the very first strophe of *Völuspá* (Studach's "Das Wolagesicht") to perceive this (Studach, *Edda*, 7). Ettmüller, in his preface to his *Lieder der Edda* (1837), VIII, considers Studach's translation to be the best Stabreim translation so far such that one can perceive the sound of the original.

362. Ettmüller, *Edda*, IX-XIV; cf. Hauer, "*Völospá*," 54.

363. Ettmüller, *Edda*, XIII, derives this from "fornyrdhi" ("Altrede") and "lag" ("Gesetz").

364. Ettmüller, *Edda*, XIII

365. Ettmüller, *Edda*, XIV.

Since for various reasons Ettmüller can be somewhat confusing here I present the analysis of Larrington.[366] So in fornyrdislag we have four line stanzas that fall into two half lines, each half line (corresponding the Ettmüller's full line) having two stresses. The third stressed syllable (the "head stave"; "Hauptstab")[367] will alliterate with one or more of the stressed syllables in the first half line, but the fourth does not alliterate.[368] A variation of fornyrdislag is malahattr as found in the *Greenlandic Lay of Atli,* where there are five stresses per line.[369] The other main category is ljodahattr, used for wisdom and dialogue poetry. Stanzas are divided into two halves, each having a long line with four stresses and two alliterative syllables and a shorter line with two stresses and two alliterative syllables.[370]

Although analysis of Eddic poems is made clearer by considering such long lines, all of Wagner's Eddic sources with the exception of the brothers Grimm (i.e., von der Hagen, Ettmüller, Studach, Legis, and Simrock) present short lines (Larrington's "half-lines"). One can also note that the *Nibelungenlied* deals also with long lines divided into two.[371] The early version of *Siegfried's Tod* actually has a preference for longer lines, which could reflect Old High German long lines[372] or reflect the way the brothers Grimm presented their Eddic poems. Later though Wagner had a distinct preference for shorter lines. A good example to consider is the whole section of Brünnhilde's first entry where each line in the early *Siegfried's Tod* is split into two shorter lines in the 1853 version.[373] I give just the opening of Brünnhilde's entry, first of *Siegfried's Tod* (1848):

Zu neuen Thaten, theurer Helde,	To new adventures, beloved hero,
wie liebt' ich dich—ließ' ich dich nicht?	what would my love be worth—if I did not let you go forth?

and then the corresponding lines of *Götterdämmerung/Siegfried's Tod* (1853):

---

366. E.g., whereas Ettmüller, *Edda,* X n. 3, analyses strophes consisting of eight lines, Larrington, *Poetic Edda,* xxviii–xxx, like other modern commentators, deals with strophes of four longer lines.

367. Ettmüller, *Edda,* X,

368. Larrington, *Poetic Edda,* xxviii, gives the example of the *Second poem of Helgi Hundingsbani,* 20.

369. Larrington, *Poetic Edda,* xxix; cf. Ettmüller, *Edda,* X.

370. Larrington, *Poetic Edda,* xxviii, gives the example of the Sayings of High One 21.

371. See, e.g., the very first line: "Und ist in alten mæren—wunders vil geseit." Note, incidentally, that the past participle "geseit" is closer to the Swiss-German that it is to High German "gesagt". Hence, Walton, *Zurich,* 50, makes the interesting point that Wagner living in Switzerland would have heard a German dialect close to the Middle High German and prompted him further to study medieval German texts.

372. Branscombe, "Dramatic Texts," 279.

373. Haymes, *Ring,* 70–73. Compare Wagner, *Ring* (1853), 124 (*TBRN2* 448). Cf. *WagRS* 284–85. Wagner made this line division at the end of 1852 as can be seen in the *Viertschrift* (*TBRN1* 143–44).

Zu neuen Thaten,	To new adventures,
theurer Helde	beloved hero,
wie liebt' ich dich—	what would my love be worth
ließ' ich dich nicht?	if I did not let you go forth?

Note, however, that there are still some long lines in the final *Ring* libretto. See, e.g., Brünnhilde's words to Wotan in *Walküre* Act III Scene 3: "that you punish that wrong in so shameful a way?" ("daß mein Verbrechen so schmählich du bestraf'st?")[374]

The most detailed examination of Wagner's alliteration that I have found is an early twentieth-century study by Schuler, who rightly comments that "when analogies and comparison of such works which Wagner used are pointed out, the result remains, that in its actual outcome his alliteration is a work of his own."[375] Hence Wagner was not slavishly following the rules of Eddic poetry. In composing his libretto he could in theory have decided to use a fixed system of stanzas but it would be an unnecessary restraint that would restrict his drama. Schuler engages in a fairly detailed analysis of the types of alliteration in the *Ring*, examining couplets, triplets, quadruplets, right through to cases where even seven lines are connected,[376] and concludes that Wagner has a multiplicity of forms and variations within these.[377] So, for examples, in couplets we find among other cases five alliterative words with two different alliterative syllables. There are $2^5 - 12 = 20$ [378] possible permutations of which we find ten in the *Ring*: aba ab; aa bba; aab ab; ab bab; ab baa; ab aab; aba ba; aaa bb; aab bb; ab bba.[379]

The composer's first mention of Stabreim is in *Artwork of the Future*,[380] which is followed by a fuller discussion in *Opera and Drama*.[381] Then in his *Communication to My Friends* Wagner writes that his "Siegfried" (i.e., *Siegfried's Tod*) could not be written "in modern verse" since such verse would hinder him.

> With the conception of "Siegfried," I had pressed forward to where I saw before me the Human Being in the most natural and blithest fulness of his physical life. No historic garment more, confined his limbs; no outwardly-imposed relation hemmed his movements, which, springing from the inner fount of Joy-in-life, so bore themselves in face of all encounter, that error and

---

374. Branscombe, "Dramatic Texts," 279 (eleven syllables in German); *WagRS* 183. This passage is discussed in volume 2, chapter 11 (Example 11.2).

375. Schuler, *Language*, 50.

376. Schuler, *Language*, 50–62.

377. Schuler, *Language*, 62.

378. The number 12 is subtracted to exclude the possibilities aaaaa, bbbbb, aaaab, aaaba, aabaa, abaaa, baaaa, bbbba, bbbab, bbabb, babbb, abbbb. The superscript 378 is not a mathematical power!

379. Schuler, *Language*, 53–54.

380. *PW* 1:133; *GSD* 3:102.

381. *PW* 2:227–30, 269–71; 274, 279, 291–92; 307; *GSD* 4:94–97, 131–33, 137, 140, 152–53, 166.

bewilderment, though nurtured on the wildest play of passions, might heap themselves around until they threatened to destroy him.³⁸²

It was "Elsa" who taught him to "unearth this man": "to me, he was the male-embodied spirit of perennial and sole creative Instinct ('Unwillkür'), of the doer of true Deeds, of *Manhood* in the utmost fullness of its inborn strength and proved loveworthiness."³⁸³ He then goes on to explain why end-rhyme is inadequate and why he must employ Stabreim for Siegfried:

> Just so as this Human Being moved, must his spoken utterance need to be. Here sufficed no more the merely *thought-out* verse, with its hazy, limbless body; the fantastic cheat of terminal Rhyme could no longer throw its cloak of seeming flesh above the total lack of living bony framework, above the viscid cartilage, here stretched capriciously and there compressed, that verse's hulk still holds within as makeshift. I must straightaway let my "Siegfried" go, could I have dressed it only in such verse. Thus I must needs bethink me of a Speech-melody quite other. And yet, in truth, I had not to bethink, but merely to resolve me; for at the primal mythic spring where I had found the fair young Siegfried-man, I also lit, led by his hand, upon the physically-perfect mode of utterance wherein alone that man could speak his feelings. This was the *alliterative* verse, bending itself in natural and lively rhythm to the actual accents of our speech, yielding itself so readily to every shade of manifold expression, —that *Stabreim* which the Folk itself once sang, when *it* was still both Poet and Myth-Maker.³⁸⁴

Turning to the mechanics of Stabreim, Ettmüller analyzed lines in terms of "Hebungen" (lifts, heavily accented) and "Senkungen" (dips, weakly stressed), noting that there were two, occasionally three lifts per line and a variable number of dips.³⁸⁵ Spencer shows how Wagner, in adopting this scheme, could have lines from two to nine syllables or more, and gives the example of the cry of the Rheinmaidens at the close of *Das Rheingold*³⁸⁶ (see Figure 3.1).

---

382. *PW* 1:375; *GSD* 4:328.

383. *PW* 1:375; *GSD* 4:328.

384. *PW* 1:375–76; *GSD* 4:328–29. Cf *DEBRN* 34 (nr 44) "Foreword to the 1850 planned publication of the poem Siegfried's Death": "Ueber manches Technische in meiner Dichtung—wie namentlich über den Stabreim und seinen mir klar gewordenen entscheidend gewichtigen Einfluß auf die innige Vermählung des Sprachverses mit der Tonweise—teile ich mich Euch an einem anderen Orte ausführlicher mit." This was not published in Wagner's lifetime; it was sent to Uhlig in a letter of 3 June 1850 (*SB* 3:304–5) with the request to ask Wigand to publish it.

385. Hence we have an analysis quite different to that of spondees, trochees, dactyls, etc (Spencer, "Strike at Me Now," 11).

386. *WagRS* 118. Spencer, "Strike at Me Now," 12. In the example which I here reproduce "lifts" are marked with an oblique stroke (/) and weakly stressed syllables by a cross (x).

Figure 3.1

```
   /         /
Rhein-     gold!

   /     x     /
Rein-   -es   Gold!

  x     /     x    x    /
  O    leuch- te-  te   noch

  x    x    /    x    x    /    x    /
  in   der  Tie- fe   dein laut'- -rer Tand!
```

The pattern of alliteration has been indicated here and I now consider further examples of Wagner's Stabreim. First, I consider Alberich's very first entry in *Rheingold* with its insistent use of "n" words:[387]

He he! Ihr *N*icker!	Ha ha! You nixies!
Wie seid ihr *n*iedlich,	How dainty you are,
*n*eidliches Volk!	you delectable creatures!
Aus *N*ibelheim's *N*acht	From Nibelheim's night
*n*aht' ich mich gern,	I'd gladly draw near
*n*eigtet ihr euch zu mir.	if only you'd look on me kindly.

In a number of cases there is a switch from one alliterative consonant to another by anticipating the change at the end of a line. We find this in one of the most striking cases of Stabreim:[388]

---

387. *WagRS* 58; ll. 20–25 (Huber, *Kommentar*, 5).

388. *Walküre* Act I Scene 3 (*WagRS* 134–35; ll. 2281–92 (Huber, *Kommentar*, 36)). Spencer's translation, which I have slightly modified, captures something of the Stabreim. This "spring song" may well have been influenced by Uhland (see chapter 5 below).

Winterstürme *w*ichen	Winter's storms have waned
dem *W*onnenmond,	at May's awakening;
in mildem *L*ichte	in gentle light
*l*euchtet der *L*enz;	Spring is aglow;
auf *l*inden *L*üften	on balmy breezes,
*l*eicht und *l*ieblich,	light and lovely,
*W*under *w*ebend	working wonders
er sich *w*iegt;	he wafts this way;
durch *W*ald und *A*uen	through woods and meadows
*w*eht sein *A*them,	blows his breath;
*w*eit geöffnet	wide open
*l*acht sein *A*ug'.	his eyes are laughing.

Another example to consider is Brünnhild's address to Sieglinde in *Walküre* Act III Scene 2 which Björnsson believes is reminiscent of the "eddic verse-form *ljóðaháttr* 'song-form'":[389]

Denn eines *w*iss'	Know this alone
und *w*ahr' es immer:	and ward it always:
den *h*ehrsten *H*elden der Welt	the world's noblest hero,
*h*eg'st du, o Weib,	o woman, you harbor
im *Sch*irmenden *Sch*ooß! –	within your sheltering womb! –

For an example of Stabreim in respect to vowels, see *Walküre* Act II Scene 1, where the two vowels of "*Unhei*lig" are reduplicated in the third line "*Unliebende ei*nt":[390]

*Unhei*lig	Unholy
*a*cht' ich den Eid,	I deem the vow
der *U*nliebende *ei*nt	that binds unloving hearts

Dahlhaus believes Wagner adopted Stabreim to restore the "purely human."[391] Also it adds a "complete lack of metrical regularity"[392] and destroys the regularity of the musical phrase. "In Wagner's musical syntax the classical norm has been suspended" and Dahlhaus gives the example of the beginning of Waltraute's narration: "the Stabreim is the poetic cause and justification of Wagner's decision to dispense with musical periodic regularity and, in consequence, with a regular pattern of strong accents."[393]

389. Björnsson, *Volsungs*, 109; *WagRS* 177.
390. *WagRS* 142. Discussed by Ellis in *PW* 1:132 n.
391. Dahlhaus, *Music Dramas*, 104–5.
392. Dahlhaus, *Music Dramas*, 105.
393. Dahlhaus, *Music Dramas*, 105.

Regarding the traditional end-rhyme Wagner writes in *Opera and Drama*: "In this End-rhyme lies the characteristic essence of the Christian melody, as whose verbal residue it is to be regarded. Its significance we may figure to ourselves at once, by calling to mind the *chorale* of the Church."[394]

Norse Mythology and Christian Theology

Not only was the Norse material recorded by Christians; but also many Christian writers have taken an interest in the Norse myths. We have already seen the work of figures such as Grimm and Simrock, but to this one can add those in the UK such as C. S. Lewis, J. R. R. Tolkein, and Roger Lancelyn Green.[395] There does seem to be some fundamental link between the Norse mythology and Christian theology and the best way I have found of understanding the relation is by likening it to that between the Old Testament and the New. In both cases we find at the same time a prefiguring of what was to come but also a radical discontinuity.

Those writing on Norse myth and Christianity have certainly drawn a sharp contrast between the two. Arnkiel writes that if according to St Paul we have been redeemed from paganism, we should know from what we have been redeemed.[396] The Old Testament may not be "paganism" (although a case could be made that without Jesus Christ the God of the Old Testament could be seen as a "pagan God"). But when one reads Grimm's contrast (noted above) of the victory of Christianity, with gentle, simple spiritual teaching, over the sensual, grim, and wild paganism[397] then one could be forgiven for having in mind the contrast between the Old and New Testaments. Yet Grimm, as well as drawing attention to this contrast, discusses how pagan traditions have been appropriated by Christians for understanding Christ, Mary, and the saints: "Here and there a heathen tradition or a superstitious custom lived on merely changing the names, and applying to Christ, Mary and the saints what had formerly been related and believed of idols."[398] A somewhat different ambivalence is typified by Thor, who can be seen as both an opponent of Christ[399] yet whose power and hammer (likened to a cross) was seen as a parallel to Christ.

---

394. *PW* 2:244; *GSD* 4:108.

395. Green's *Myths of the Norsemen* helped make Norse myths popular (e.g., Orchard, *Elder Edda*, vii, acknowledges this work as an early inspiration).

396. Arnkiel writes in paragraph V of the Vorbericht of *Außführliche Eröffnung*: "Wie kónten wir die edle Gabe der Gesundheit recht vernehmen, / wenn wir von keiner Kranckheit wústen?" Cf. Böldl, *Mythos*, 48.

397. Grimm, *Mythology*, 1:5; *Mythologie*, 1:4.

398. Grimm, *Mythology*, 1:5; *Mythologie*, 1:5: "Einzelne heidnische überlieferungen und abergläubische dauerten fort, indem sie bloss namen änderten, und auf Christus, Maria und die heiligen anwendeten, was vorher von den götzen erzählt und geglaubt wurde."

399. Ellis Davidson, *Gods*, 73.

How then has Wagner appropriated the Norse sources in a Christian direction? I consider here two examples and others will be considered elsewhere. First, one of the most notable aspects of "Christian theology" in the myths is the death of Odin's son, Baldr, widely seen as reflecting the death of Christ. *Völuspá* 31 speaks of his "blood-stained sacrifice"[400] and Loki's role parallels that of Judas.[401] The Christian parallels are again found in the view that in the renewed cosmos "Baldr will come" (*Völuspá* 59).[402] Wagner has modelled Siegfried's death on Baldr's death, Hagen's spear taking on the role of the mistletoe dart of Höd. In his portrayal of Siegfried's death he has not christianized the Norse myth since it has already been christianized by Snorri and others. But he has radically changed the scheme of redemption in that he makes Brünnhilde the decisive redeeming figure by her sacrifice.

This brings me to Wagner's portrayal of Valkyries. Wagner adopts very few of the Valkyrie names in the sources. We saw above the two Valkyries Gondul and Skogul, who are sent to Hakon in *Hákonarmál*. Others are named in *Völuspá* 30: "She saw valkyries / come from afar, / ready to ride / to the realm of the gods. / Skuld bore a shield, / and Skögul was with her, / Gunnr, Hildr, Göndul / and Spear-Skögul."[403] Thirteen names are given in *Grímnismál* 36: "Hrist and Mist / I wish to bring me a drinking-horn / Skeggjöld and Skögul, / Hildi and Thrúdi, / Hlökk and Herfjötur, / Göll and Geirölul, / Randgrid and Radgrid, / and Reginleif / they bring the elect fighters ale."[404] None of these names were employed and in fact the only ones he did use were Brynhild and Sigrun, the other seven Valkyries having names that Wagner himself concocted. I suggest he abandoned names such as Gondul, Skogul, Skuld, etc., because they sounded ugly and did not suitably represent the Valkyries he wished to portray.[405] Three of the Valkyries of the *Elder Edda* with names that do not sound harsh, namely Sváva, Sigrun, and Sigrdrífa, are also the Valkyries who are presented with some nobility. So first *Helgakvida Hjördvardssonar* tells that "[Helgi Hjördvardsson] sat on a burial-mound and saw nine valkyries ride by, and one of them [Sváva] was most majestic."[406] Helgi and Sváva are lovers and are later reborn[407] as Helgi Hundingsbani and Sigrún and *Helgakvida Hundingsbana önnur* retells the scene now with Helgi Hundingsbani seeing "nine Valkyries riding" but singling out Sigrún, who becomes his lover.[408] Then

---

400. Dronke, *Edda II*, 15 (see also the commentary, 139).

401. Dronke, *Edda II*, 94–95. Loki was also seen as a demonic figure; the portrayal of the binding of Loki in the Gosforth cross recalls the binding of Satan in Revelation 20:2 (Ellis Davidson, *Gods*, 179).

402. Dronke, *Edda II*, 23 (see also the commentary, 60).

403. Dronke, *Edda II*, 15.

404. Cf. Dronke, *Edda III*, 120.

405. There were some soft-sounding Valkyrie names he could have used (e.g., Sváva (*Helgakvida Hjörvardssonar*; Sigrdrífa (*Sigrdrífumál*)).

406. Orchard, *Elder Edda*, 128.

407. Orchard, *Elder Edda*, 134, 136.

408. Orchard, *Elder Edda*, 137–38.

Sigrdrífa is awoken by Sigurd who offers him advice including respect and care for the dead.[409] It is not clear whether Brynhild is a Valkyrie in the *Elder Edda* but she does so appear in the *Prose Edda,* although not as a sympathetic character.[410]

In volume 2, chapter 10 I will consider in detail Wagner's portrayal of Brünnhilde but for now I note simply that as far as Norse sources are concerned her closest parallels are figures such as Sváva, Sigrun, and Sigrdrífa. She is certainly removed from her namesakes Prünhilt of the *Nibelungenlied* and Brynhild of the Norse sources.

409. Orchard, *Elder Edda,* 169–75.
410. Faulkes, *Edda,* 102–4.

— 4 —

The *Ring* and the Greeks

Introduction

The Greeks were fundamental for Wagner's artistic and political project. It is worth noting at the outset that one reason he was so strongly drawn to Goethe, a subject for chapter 5, is that *Faust* Part II is filled with references to the Greeks. In particular, Wagner would no doubt appreciate Faust marrying Helen in his medieval (German) castle, which has been placed in ancient Greece,[1] for it represented both the marriage of the Germans and the Greeks and situating Germany in the soil of Greece. As Mephistopheles comments in the Classical Walpurgis Night, a scene we know Wagner especially valued:[2]

Hier dacht' ich lauter Unbekannte,	I thought they'd be all strangers here;
Und finde leider Nahverwandte;	But they're my family, I fear.
Es ist ein altes Buch zu blättern:	How old a book I'm browsing in!
Vom Harz bis Hellas immer Vettern!	German and Greek, they're kith and kin.

A further link between the "Germanic" and "Greek" traditions is their mythology and the way Wagner in both cases saw this related to, and not simply separated from, history. However, Wagner's appropriation of "the Greeks" is not entirely straightforward as we shall discover and to some extent this is related to the view of A. W. Schlegel that the classical world is not merely to be imitated in our day but needs to be reborn within us.[3] Hence, Wagner writes in *Art and Revolution*: "we do not wish to revert to Greekdom; for what the Greeks knew not, and, knowing not, came by their downfall: that know *we*."[4]

---

1. Note that this marriage of Part II is anticipated in Part I: "Du siehst, mit diesem Trank im Leibe, / Bald Helenen in jedem Weibe" (*GWJA* 3:93 (ll. 2603–4); Luke, *Faust I*, 81).
2. *GWJA* 3:265 (ll. 7740–43); Luke, *Faust II*, 100.
3. See chapter 5 below on A. W. Schlegel.
4. *PW* 1:54; *GSD* 3:30.

Wagner's Knowledge of Greek Language and Culture

For details of Wagner's knowledge of the Greek language and culture in his youth we are almost entirely dependent on his autobiography, a work he started to dictate to Cosima in 1865 when he was fifty-two years old and which is not always entirely trustworthy. He tells of his enthusiasm for the Greek language "because the stories from Greek mythology seized my imagination so strongly that I wanted to imagine their heroic figures speaking to me in their original tongue." He makes it clear that his interest was not in the language itself, which was actually "a tiresome obstacle," and that he was "never thorough with [. . .] language studies."[5] He claims that at the Kreuzschule in Dresden he was "destined to be a poet" and that his teacher Julius Sillig set him the task of writing a major epic poem on "The Battle of Parnassus" after Pausanias. He further claims that he began to write in hexameter but did not get beyond the first canto, "[b]eing not far enough advanced in my studies to master the Greek tragedians in their own language."[6] But he explains that it was Greek mythology, legend, and history that really interested him[7] and some years later in a letter to August Lewald he claims that at the Kreuschule he and his friend Schlesier had sworn themselves to Creuzer's *Symbolik und Mythologie*.[8] His autobiography then tells that at the age of fifteen (1828), when he transferred from the Kreuzschule in Dresden to the Nikolaischule in Leipzig, he was put back a year, this being especially hurtful since he had already "produced a written translation of twelve books" of Homer.[9] However, one only has to read a little further to see that he had not in fact mastered Greek.[10] But

---

5. *My Life* 14; *Mein Leben* 1:21.

6. *My Life* 15; *Mein Leben* 1:22.

7. *My Life* 16; *Mein Leben* 1:22.

8. *SB* 1:354. The letter is not dated but Glasenapp, *Leben*, 1:272 n. 2, dates it as 12 November 1838. This work of Creuzer (1771–1858), *Symbolik und Mythologie der alten Völker, besonders der Griechen*, went through three editions (1810–12; 1819–21; 1837), was not later to be found in his Dresden library but the second edition was in his Wahnfried library. Creuzer's first volume deals with issues of allegory and symbol, and discusses the religion of the Egyptians, Indians, Medes and Persians. Volume 2 turns to the religion of the Near and Middle East and only half way through does the discussion move on to the Pelasgians (302–416), Homer and Hesiod (417–63), and an overview of Greek gods (464–818). Volumes 3 and 4 continue with the Greeks (heroes, etc.) and includes a discussion of the relationship of "paganism" to the Christian religion. Creuzer's theory that the mythology of Homer and Hesiod came from an Eastern source via the Pelasgians upset the German Philhellenism of Winckelmann, Schiller, and Schelling. His views were criticized by Voss (Williamson, "Gods," 152–55) but he was praised by Hegel, who refers to the fourth volume in his *Philosophy of Right*, 194 (§203). On Müller's relation to Creuzer (often taken to be an opponent), see Blok, "Quest." Wagner valued Creuzer right through to his later years (*CD* 1 December 1880).

9. *My Life* 22; *Mein Leben* 1:29. This claim to have translated what amounts to half of the *Iliad* (15,600 lines) or *Odyssey* (12,000 lines) seems hardly credible (each contains twenty-four books).

10. See *My Life* 38; *Mein Leben* 1:45–46, where he explains that at the age of seventeen he took private lessons in Greek and read Sophocles with his tutor. Then he adds: "For a time, I hoped that this noble subject would reawaken my desire to learn the Greek language thoroughly; but it was all in vain. I hadn't found the right teacher; and besides, the living room in which we pursued our studies looked out upon a tannery, whose disgusting smell affected my nerves badly enough to spoil Sophocles and

although he struggled with the Greek language, there can be no doubt that already in his youth he loved the spirit of Greek tragedy. He writes that his uncle Adolf "was delighted to find in me a very willing listener for his reading of classical tragedies, having himself begotten a translation of *Oedipus the King*."[11]

The next significant engagement with the Greeks occurred in Wagner's Paris years (1839–42) when he got to know Samuel Lehrs, who renewed Wagner's interest in the Greeks. But he writes: "Lehrs dissuaded me from any efforts to study the Greek classics in the original, consoling me with the well-intentioned statement that, given the way I was and the music I had in me, I would find a way to extract knowledge from them even without grammar and dictionary; whereas Greek, if it were to be studied seriously, was no joke and could not be treated as a secondary matter."[12]

The general impression therefore is that Wagner never really mastered the Greek language[13] and he did in fact develop an ideological justification for this, claiming that it was Mendelssohn's very ability to read Greek that prevented him from composing appropriate music for Sophocles' *Antigone*![14]

Wagner's engagement with the *content* of Greek works intensified in his years in Dresden in the 1840s. In 1843, when Wagner had secured the position of *Hofkapellmeister* to the Saxon Court, he was able to build up his personal library. One of the first indications of his working on Greek tragedy was revising Gluck's *Iphigenie in Aulis*, which he started in 1845.[15] But it was the summer of 1847 that was to prove particularly fruitful for his appreciation of Greek tragedy[16] when he read Aeschylus in

---

Greek for me completely." Wagner says much the same about his enthusiasm for Greek in his *Open Letter to Friedrich Nietzsche* (PW 5:292; NWSEB 1:176), praising Sillig and explaining that he was thoroughly discouraged when he moved to the Nikolai- and Thomasschule in Leipzig.

11. *My Life* 23; *Mein Leben* 1:30. Adolf also wrote a work on "Die Alkestis des Euripides" (SB 1:19) as well on other literature (see chapter 5 below).

12. *My Life* 209–10; *Mein Leben* 1:221.

13. A picture of Wagner's Greek in his mature years can be gleaned from his Wahnfried library (he had to leave his Dresden library behind when he fled the city in 1849) which contained a range of Greek texts and some reference works. Apparently when he visited the Dannreuthers in London (1877) "in a playful way [he] tried to speak a little Greek" (Spencer, *Wagner Remembered*, 256). But although he did not have good Greek it was still of some use to him such that he could compare the translation of *Oedipus* with the original Greek (CD 18 November 1874).

14. See his *Open Letter to Friedrich Nietzsche* (PW 5:293; NWSEB 1:177): "while envying Mendelssohn his philologic fluency, I could but wonder at its not having prevented him from writing just his music for dramas of Sophocles, since, with all my ignorance, I still had more respect for the spirit of Antiquity than he here seemed to betray." Wagner then goes on to castigate "teachers of Greek" who have little of the "Antique Spirit" within them (PW 5:293; NWSEB 1:177–78), naming in particular Ulrich von Wilamowitz-Möllendorff (who had written a highly critical review of Nietzsche's *Birth of Tragedy* and was the main target of this letter).

15. See the discussion of Euripides below.

16. This has been widely discussed. See, e.g., Schadewaldt, "Griechen," 347–50; Lloyd-Jones, "Wagner," 128–29.

Droysen's translation[17] and it can be said that he made a breakthrough in regard to his understanding of Greek tragedy:

> For the first time I now mastered Aeschylus with mature feeling and understanding. Droysen's eloquent commentaries [*Didaskalien*] in particular helped to bring the intoxicating vision of Attic tragedy so clearly before me that I could see the *Oresteia* with my mind's eye as if actually being performed, and its impact on me was indescribable. There was nothing to equal the exalted emotion evoked in me by *Agamemnon*; and to the close of *The Eumenides* I remained in a state of transport from which I have never really returned to become fully reconciled with modern literature. My ideas about the significance of drama, and especially of the theatre itself, were decisively moulded by these impressions.[18]

This interest in Greek tragedy continued throughout the rest of his life.[19] In addition to Aeschylus he adored Sophocles (both counted as his "indispensables")[20] although he felt he did not match Aeschylus[21] and he claims he did not care much for Euripides.[22]

I now turn to consider his appropriation of Greek history, philosophy, and myth, epic, lyric, and tragedy in the *Ring* cycle.

Greek History

In chapter 2 I made the point that in the *Ring* Wagner was not so much *reflecting* German culture but was essentially *creating* Germany; one of the ways he was doing

---

17. In his Dresden library he had the 1832 edition. For other Greek tragedy he possessed Sophocles (2 vols, 1842) and Euripides (2 vols, 1841–45), both edited by J. J. C. Donner (Westernhagen, *Bibliothek*, 89, 104).

18. *My Life* 342–43; *Mein Leben* 1:356. On the *Didaskalien*, see below on "Tragedy and performance."

19. See especially *CD* 23 June 1880 where Cosima tells of her husband's reciting Aeschylus' *Agamemnon*: "no stage performance could have a more sublime effect than this recital". See also *CD* 24 June (on *Agamemnon*; *Suppliants*) and 25 June 1880 (on *Choephoroi*; *Eumenides*). Her comments on *Choephoroi* are particularly interesting in relation to her husband's own art: "Speaking of the first scene in *Choephoroi* with its surgings and its constantly returning flow, he says, 'I know something else like this: *Trist. and Isolde* in the 2nd act.'"

20. *CD* 4 June 1871. His Wahnfried library had the editions of Theolorus Bergk (Latin) and that of J. J. C. Donner

21. See the comparison he makes between *Electra* and *Choephoroi* (*CD* 1 November 1877).

22. Cosima tells us that "[t]he Euripidean Helen [. . .] does not much interest him—only the idea, not the execution" (*CD* 1 December 1878). Four years earlier she and her husband attempted *Iphigenia* but gave up and turned to Racine's version instead (*CD* 1 April 1874). They eventually finished Euripides on 3 April. Cosima comments: "even its moment of beauty, the raising of Iphigenia, does not touch us—all feeling in it is killed by speech and explanations. Oh, Shakespeare! . . ." On another occasion they read *Phoenissae* "with very little enjoyment" (*CD* 29 September 1877). On another occasion she herself thought *Bacchae* was "very distasteful" but she liked the scene of the parting of Achilles and Clytemnestra in *Iphigenia in Aulis* (*CD* 13 January 1872).

this was by modelling his vision of the future Germany on the ancient Greeks, especially the Dorians, and his source for this would be Karl Otfried Müller, whose three-volume (second edition) work on the history of Hellenic peoples and cities was in his Dresden Library,[23] together with Herodotus.[24] Müller was influenced by Herder's view that the physical and mental characteristics of a people are determined by their original environment and the view developed in the nineteenth century that the Dorians originated in Germany. The Dorian invasion, although rejected by many archaeologists today,[25] was much discussed in Wagner's day, and the link between the Germans and the Dorians became fundamental. Friedrich Schlegel distinguished "animal" non-inflected languages from "noble and spiritual" inflected ones, by which he meant primarily "Indisch," Greek, and German.[26] Herder also stressed that for a people to retain its character it had to preserve its linguistic and ethnic authenticity[27] and it can be no accident that Humboldt used blood metaphors in claiming that both the German and Greek languages were "pure" and "uncontaminated."[28] No doubt such views would appeal to Wagner[29] as would Müller's view of the "northern character" of the Doric dialect[30] and his "Protestant" portrayal of the Dorians.[31]

One of the significant aspects of Müller's work for Wagner is that Apollo was seen as the principal deity for the Dorians and it was in fact the transmission of the cult

---

23. Müller, *Geschichten*, 3 vols, 1844 (DB 96). The second and third volumes were devoted to the Dorians. I found no markings in the Dresden library copies and we only know of his reading Müller on the Dorians in 1869 (CD 21 March 1869).

24. Wagner possessed the German translation by Friedrich Lange (DB 62), an edition which divided the work into nine sections, each entitled with one of the nine muses. We only know of his reading Herodotus from as late as 1877; he provided Richard and Cosima with their evening reading (CD 27 August–6 October 1877). Herodotus discusses the Dorians in numerous places (e.g., I.56, 57, 139, 146, 171; II.178; III.56; V.68, 72, 76; VIII.73). Foster, *Greeks*, 271, believes that Wagner's knowledge of the battles of Marathon, Thermopylae, and Salamis from his school days (*My Life* 39; *Mein Leben* 1:46), suggests he knew Herodotus. On these battles see Lange, *Herodotus*, 2:113–36 (Marathon, 490 BC), 2:231–44 (Thermopylae, 480 BC), and 2:266–92 (Salamis, 480 BC).

25. Hall, *Ethnic Identity*, 121, who points out that many ancient historians "are insistent that the literary tradition cannot be jettisoned so easily."

26. Schlegel, *Sprache und Weisheit* (1808), 27–86; KFSA 1.8:136–90; Book I, chapters 3–6). Hall, *Ethnic Identity*, 8, writes that in the German imagination Greek and German were linked by the fact that "both used definite articles, a plethora of particles and prepositions, and were the languages of religious protest after the Reformation." For further discussion of Schlegel see chapter 5 below.

27. Hall, *Ethnic Identity*, 8.

28. Hall, *Ethnic Identity*, 8, appeals to Wittenburg, "Müller," 1031–34.

29. Herder's selected works in one large volume of almost 1,400 pages were in his Dresden library (DB 61). Herder's influence on the *Ring* will be further discussed in chapter 5.

30. Müller, *Doric Race*, 1:18; *Geschichten*, 2:16. The English edition was itself a revised edition of the first German edition of 1824. This was then used to produce the second German edition of 1844 which Wagner possessed. See Müller, *Geschichten*, 1:III–X.

31. Hall, *Ethnic Identity*, 8, appealing to Wittenburg, writes that "the character of Müller's Dorians is uncannily Protestant," noting that Müller's father was a Protestant military chaplain in Silesia. See Müller, *Geschichten*, 2:413.

of Apollo that was used to trace the migration of the Dorians.[32] As we have already discovered in the discussion of *Die Wiblungen,* there is an important link between Apollo and Siegfried as Sun-god who slays the Python.[33]

The other key writer on the Greeks for Wagner in his Dresden years was Droysen. He will be discussed in more detail below in the discussion of Greek tragedy but for now I focus on historical and political issues. Droysen's German nationalism would no doubt please Wagner and particularly his view that Aeschylus in the Oresteia "composed [. . .] a ceremony of expiation (Sühnefeier) for the blood-guilt still present in the land, and at the same time a reconciliation between the savage parties (eine Versöhnung zugleich zwischen den wilden Partheien) which threatened to destroy the state, those who all ought to be of one mind in order to ward off the enemy at hand."[34] For Droysen the "savage parties" were the "democratic and oligarchic factions that violently opposed the other and threatened to tear Athens apart from within" and the "enemy at hand" were the Persians.[35] Hence Germany corresponded to Athens and Prussian rule was seen as "the key to solving Germany's disorder."[36] Droysen's reading of the trilogy appealed to Wagner who "must have sometimes imagined the *Ring* as the new *Oresteia* and himself as the new Aeschylus come to save Germany from internal strife and external threat."[37]

Droysen's two-volume *History of Hellenism* (*Geschichte des Hellenismus,* 1836, 1843) was in Wagner's Dresden Library, a work that he later purchased again, this same edition being found in his Wahnfried library. We know he read this in his years in Tribschen and in Bayreuth (and praised it)[38] and his reading it in Dresden is evidenced by his frequent markings (around 150 in volume 1 and around 100 in volume 2). However, there is *no evidence* that Wagner possessed Droysen's *History of Alexander the Great* (*Geschichte Alexanders des Großen,* 1833) in his Dresden library although it is found in the Wahnfried library[39] and Cosima records her husband's pleasure in the work and he comments: "If I were locked up in prison, I should ask

---

32. Hall, *Ethnic identity,* 6; Müller, *Doric Race,* 1:227–384; *Geschichten,* 2:200–370.

33. See chapter 2 above. This will be further developed in the discussion of Siegfried (and Wotan) in volume 2.

34. Quoted in Ewans, *Aeschylus,* 31 (to which I have added some key German phrases from the original). This text is not in Wagner's 1832 edition but it is in the 1868 edition (Droysen, *Aischylos,* 564–65) which was in his Wahnfried library.

35. Foster, *Greeks,* 286.

36. Foster, *Greeks,* 286.

37. Foster, *Greeks,* 286.

38. *CD* 3 July 1869, 2 January 1879.

39. Note that the Alexander book did constitute volume one of a *three*-volume second edition of Droysen's history that appeared in 1877. To clarify once more, in Wagner's two-volume Dresden edition the first deals with the *successors* of Alexander (*Geschichte der Nachfolger Alexanders*) and then in volume 2 we have *Geschichte der Bildung des hellenistischen Staatensystemes* with an appendix "über die hellenistischen Städtegründungen."

only for Greek literature and things about Greece."⁴⁰ But the *Annals* of 1847 suggest he did read it⁴¹ and he may have borrowed a copy either from the Royal Library or from friends. But as was noted in chapter 2, the *Annals* of 1846–67 were re-written and certain things were falsified. Presumably it is on the basis of the *Annals* that some secondary literature may give the impression Wagner had read the Alexander book when he was in Dresden.⁴² Hence a sentence such as "The name of Alexander signifies the end of one world epoch, and the beginning of a new one"⁴³ may not have been read by Wagner when he was in Dresden. Rather in his copy of Droysen's *Geschichte des Hellenismus* he would only read of Alexander's death.⁴⁴ Wagner must therefore have had another source for Alexander⁴⁵ and in his Dresden years this may not have been detailed. In *Die Wibelungen* Wagner considered Alexander an "offspring of Achilles."⁴⁶ Many years later Wagner claimed to have sketched out a drama *Alexander*: "the first act was the murder of Clitus, the second the decision to withdraw from Asia, the third his death."⁴⁷ However, we do not know whether this was sketched before he worked on the *Ring* libretto. Perhaps one can say that Wagner saw in his Siegfried "the Teutonic successor to Alexander"⁴⁸ but we have no firm evidence that Wagner had worked on his Alexander before completing the libretto at the end of 1852.⁴⁹ We do though have more evidence that Wagner had worked on his opera for Achilles⁵⁰ and that this probably influenced his portrayal of Siegfried.⁵¹ On the same day he told Cosima about his Alexander sketches he said he had once "sketched the third act of an Achilles,"⁵² though we do actually possess these sketches,⁵³ which can be dated as early as the turn

---

40. *CD* 6 March 1870.

41. *Brown Book* 94; *Braunes Buch* 111.

42. I find Westernhagen, *Biography*, 127, insufficiently precise here.

43. Quoted in Foster, *Greeks*, 287 (Droysen, *Geschichte des Hellenismus I* (1877), 3: "Der Name Alexander bezeichnet das Ende einer Weltepoche, den Anfang einer neuen").

44. Droysen, *Geschichte des Hellenismus* (1836–43), 1:3–5.

45. As well as Wagner's general knowledge one source would be Hegel, *History*, 31, 103 (*Geschichte*, 47–48, 133); although there is little detail on Alexander's history he appears as "[a] World-historical individual" (*History*, 31; *Geschichte*, 49: "[e]in welthistoriches Individuum").

46. *PW* 7:283; *GSD* 2:140.

47. *CD* 1 April 1878.

48. Foster, *Greeks*, 287.

49. Foster, *Greeks*, 287, seems to assume Alexander was written before the libretto was completed.

50. *WWV* 340 argue it was intended as an opera, although in 1865 he claimed his Achilles and Friedrich Barbarossa were intended as "reine dramatische Dichtungen" (*KB* 1:183).

51. Wagner's first setting of anything to do with Achilles was in his reworking of Gluck's *Iphigénie*, where Achilles is a tenor.

52. *CD* 1 April 1878.

53. *DTB* 268 (*WWV* 81).

of the year 1848–49[54] but most likely in the first half of 1849[55] and possibly as late as the writing of his Zurich essays.[56]

Wagner continued with his interest on Greek (and Roman) history and later in life not only read Theodor Mommsen but also got to know him via Helmholtz.[57]

Greek Philosophy

Wagner admired Plato and this appears to be intensified after his engagement with Schopenhauer, who in the very first words of his first publication wrote of "[t]he divine Plato" ("Platon, der göttliche");[58] further, Wagner became increasingly interested in certain dialogues, especially *Symposium*.[59] He possessed Schleiermacher's translation of Plato in Dresden and at some point re-purchased this same edition, which is found in the Wahnfried library. Lamm comments: "Schleiermacher's translation of Plato's dialogues, along with his accompanying 'Introductions,' was a momentous event in the philosophical, philological, and literary world."[60] It is also worth adding that Schleiermacher was to prove to be highly influential in studies of Socrates and his view of the so-called "Socratic problem," set forward in an 1818 article, was to influence scholarship for over a century.[61]

Wagner does not often mention his debt to Aristotle but his *Poetics* were important for the composer (see below on tragedy) and he features in *Opera and Drama* as a commentator on Greek drama.[62] He also shared Aristotle's organic view

---

54. This is when he changed to a Latin script and the avoidance of capital letters (the Achilles sketches were so written).

55. We know he was concerned with the figure of Achilles at this time. See *Brown Book* 96: "Ideas for an 'Achilles' in 3 Acts" (*Braunes Buch* 114). One should bear in mind though that these Annals were re-written. In his autobiography he says that on 5 May 1849 as he strolled back home "through the barriers" he "worked out a drama on the subject of Achilles which I had been musing for some time" (*My Life* 396; *Mein Leben* 1:410). However, this must have been Friday 4 May (Gregor-Dellin, *Life*, 172) since on 5 May he spent the night in the tower of the Kreuzkirche.

56. See the mentions of his Achilles in letters from 1850: *SB* 3:242 (24 February), 331 (26–27 June), 364 (27 July). Not also that Göttling, *Ueber das Geschichtliche*, 28 (a work Wagner borrowed 10 February to 19 June 1849), comments that "Siegbert" (the Austrasier) was named by his contemporaries as the "second Achilles."

57. *CD* 25 April 1875.

58. Schopenhauer, *Fourfold Root*, 1; *ASSW* 3:11.

59. This was one of his "indispensables" (*CD* 4 June 1871).

60. Lamm, "Plato," 92. It was in fact Friedrich Schlegel who suggested to Schleiermacher in 1799 that they together translate Plato but he then dropped out, the project being solely in Schleiermacher's hands from 1803. Five volumes appeared in 1804–9, the sixth then much later in the year of his death, 1828. Volume 7 (which would have included Timaeus, Critias, and Laws) never appeared. Wagner possessed the first five volumes in a second edition (1.1: 1817; 1.2: 1818; 2.1: 1818; 2.2: 1824; 2.3: 1826) and the sixth (3.1) in its first edition (1828).

61. Dorion, "Socratic Problem," 2–6. Note that Wagner in his extant works never refers to Schleiermacher.

62. *PW* 2:105; 124, 132, 139 (*GSD* 3:311, 4:6, 13, 19), all related to the "rules" of Aristotle. In *Public*

of the world, a view he most likely appropriated via Hegel (and possibly Schelling)[63] or possibly through Weisse, his philosophy professor.[64] But he must have had first-hand knowledge of Aristotle, whose works, according to his first wife Minna, were in the Dresden library, but are missing from the collection we now have available in the Richard Wagner Museum.[65] The Wahnfried library contains a good selection of Aristotle's works.[66]

Epic

Despite some of Wagner's reservations about "epic"[67] he had immense admiration for Homer and counted him among his "indispensables."[68] He considered him a great poet[69] and he possessed the translations of the classicist and poet Johann Heinrich Voss (1751–1826) in both his Dresden[70] and Wahnfried libraries,[71] and despite some reservations it was a translation he admired.[72]

A number of Homeric influences on the *Ring* have been discerned by Schadewaldt. In his second of three lectures given in Bayreuth (see below) he points to the similarity between the opening of *Rheingold* Scene 2 and *Iliad* 14.347–50[73] and the similarities between the quarrel between Wotan and Fricka in *Walküre* Act 2 and that between Zeus and Hera in books 4 and 14 of the *Iliad*.[74]

Wagner's understanding of epic may help unlock some of the political aspects of the *Ring*. Works such as the *Iliad* or *Nibelungenlied* could be understood as summing

---

and *Popularity* he argues for the limitations of "Criticism" ("Kritik") but says Aristotle produced the best (*PW* 6:62; *GSD* 10:70).

63. See chapter 6 below on Hegel's teleology.

64. Wagner notes that "Weiß" had translated Aristotle's *Metaphysics* (*My Life* 54; *Mein Leben* 1:62).

65. Westernhagen, *Bibliothek*, 111. Minna simply gives the details Aristoteles, *Werke*. Stuttgart: Metzler, 1836–40.

66. There are works such as the *Metaphysics, Natural History of Animals, Parts of Animals, Poetics, On the Soul and the World, Nicomachean Ethics, Politics*.

67. See the discussion in the previous chapter in relation to the *Nibelungenlied*.

68. *CD* 4 June 1871.

69. Cosima's comment reveals much about her husband's views on poets (*CD* 18 January 1869): "R. pointed out to me that all the great poets—with the exception of Homer and Dante—were dramatists." Wagner discussed Homer as poet in his *On Poetry and Composition* (*PW* 6:137–41; *GSD* 10:142–46).

70. He possessed the works in one volume (DB 65, 1840), magnificently illustrated by Bonaventura Genelli (1798–1868) and an edition of the *Odyssey* (DB 64, 1843). According to Minna's list he also possessed his edition of the *Iliad* (1842). See Westernhagen, *Bibliothek*, 94, 112.

71. In Wahnfried he also had Greek and Latin editions.

72. *CD* 1 April 1878. Hegel in a draft of a letter to Voss of March 1805 went as far to write this of his Homer translation: "Luther made the Bible speak German, and you have done the same for Homer—the greatest gift that can be made to a people" (Butler, *Hegel: Letters*, 107).

73. Schadewaldt, "Griechen," 366.

74. Schadewaldt, "Griechen," 361.

up the nation's heritage and essence and, as Hegel observes, does this through situations of war.[75] It is striking that Hegel understood the *Iliad* as "the triumph of the West over the East"[76] whereby "the Greeks take the field against the Asiatics."[77] Wagner actually had an ambivalent view of Troy, since in *Die Wibelungen* it is the origin of both the Franks and the Romans, considered good and bad respectively.[78] But a case can be made that he, like Hegel, understood epic as dealing with enemies both without and within.[79] As Foster puts it, "Wagner sought less to create a German epic than to create Germany through epic."[80]

Wagner certainly believed that Greece had to be cleansed of "Asiatic" influences.[81] So in *Art and Revolution* he writes: "After it had overcome the raw religion of its Asiatic birth-place, built upon the nature-forces of the earth, and had set the *fair, strong manhood of freedom* upon the pinnacle of its religious convictions,—the Grecian spirit, at the flowering time of its art and polity, found its fullest expression in the god Apollo, the head and national deity of the Hellenic race."[82] Germany, like ancient Greece, also had enemies without (the French) and enemies within (the Jews), a view that Wagner further developed in *Meistersinger*. But in establishing the nation's heritage and identity, epic was not simply triumphalist. The Trojan war in the *Iliad* ends with many deaths (books 20–22) and the *Nibelungenlied*, seen as German epic in *Die Wibelungen*, ends with a veritable bloodbath. Wagner's *Ring* too has many casualties, although the number of survivors is significant, as we shall see. But despite the catastrophes at the end of epics, they are, as Hegel saw them, "the Bible of a people, and every great and important people has such absolutely earliest books which express for its own original spirit."[83]

Wagner, however, appeared to see limitations in "epic." In *Opera and Drama* he argues that epic has a less immediate effect: whereas in epic the heroes' deeds are celebrated, in drama they are enacted.[84] He singles out Virgil for his *Aeneid*, "an epos written for dumb reading" ("ein für die Lektüre geschrieben[es] Epos")[85] and in *Art-*

---

75. Foster, *Greeks*, 37 (Hegel, *Aesthetics*, 2:1059).

76. Hegel, *Aesthetics*, 2:1062.

77. Hegel, *Aesthetics*, 2:1061.

78. *PW* 7:280; *GSD* 2:137.

79. Droysen was a student of Hegel and both employed their knowledge of the Greeks to bolster their German nationalism.

80. Foster, *Greeks*, 64.

81. Such "Asiatic" influences would appear to refer to the nature-worshipping "Ur-Hellene" (Pelasgians). See Warner, "Artwork," 58; *PW* 1:157; *GSD* 3:124–25, discussed below.

82. *PW* 1:32; *GSD* 3:9–10.

83. Hegel, *Aesthetics*, 2:1045.

84. *PW* 2:60; *GSD* 3:268.

85. *PW* 2:119; *GSD* 4:1. He refers to Lessing, *Laokoon*, who compares the sculpture of Laokoon with *Aeneid* 199–224 (*GELW* 6:43; see also Brown, *Gesamtkunstwerk*, 92–95). Foster, *Greeks*, 53, adds that in Wagner's 1879 essay *Poetry and Composition* he questions the *ars poetica* of the Latins,

work of the Future writes an "aesthetic obituary for Greek epic";[86] it was to be replaced by tragedy: "*Thespis* had already slid his car to Athens, had set it up beside the palace walls, dressed out his *stage* and, stepping from the chorus of the Folk, had *trodden* its planks; *no longer did he shadow forth* the deeds of heroes, as in the Epos, but *in these heroes' guise enacted them.*"[87] So the epic was seen as "literary" for the elite whereas drama was for the "senses" and for the Volk.

In the light of this it is interesting to see how Wagner felt dissatisfied with his libretto for *Siegfried's Tod*. Writing to Uhlig (12 November 1851) he explains how he "sketched out the entire myth in its imposing overall context." The libretto for *Siegfried's Tod* was "an attempt [. . .] to present a crucial turning point in the myth by *hinting* at the overall context." However, on turning to the "musical execution" he writes: "I felt how incomplete was the product I had planned: all that remained of the vast overall context—which alone can give the characters their enormous, striking significance—was epic narration (epische erzählung) and a retelling of events on a purely conceptual context."[88] With the prefacing of *Der junge Siegfried* he felt "all I had done was to increase the need for a clearer presentation *to the senses* of the whole of the overall context."[89]

Wagner's way forward was to retain the important content of the *Ring*'s narratives but convert them into dramatic form. In a letter to Liszt of 20 November 1851 he writes: "I must therefore communicate my entire myth, in its deepest and widest significance, with total artistic clarity [. . .] every unbiased human feeling must be able to grasp *the whole* through its organs of artistic perception, because only then can it properly absorb the *least* detail."[90] Wagner tells Liszt he intended to discard "all the narration-like passages which are now so extensive" or compress them "into a number of much more concise moments."[91] We are then left with the problem that much narration is still left in the final libretto.

Three points can be made in response to this supposed problem. The first is that "drama," and specifically "tragedy" can contain "narration." This is found in its most straightforward form in Euripides' prologues or a report from a messenger,[92] and

---

mentioning epics written since the middle ages: Dante, Ariosto, Cervantes and Scott (*PW* 6:139; *GSD* 10:143). Note however that the composer had great regard for Dante, Cervantes and Scott.

86. Foster, *Greeks*, 54.

87. *PW* 1:135; *GSD* 3:104. Thespis was believed in antiquity to be the inventor of tragedy (Seaford, "Thespis," 1510). According to Horace, he took his plays around on a wagon (to which Wagner is alluding). Hieronymus Müller's introduction to *Aristophanes*, 1:1–97, a work in Wagner's Dresden library, covers Greek drama generally and includes a discussion of Thepsis.

88. *SL* 232; *SB* 4:174.

89. *SL* 232–33; *SB* 4:174.

90. *SL* 237; *SB* 4:186.

91. *SL* 238; *SB* 4:187–88.

92. E.g., in *Iphigeneia at Aulis* (the work of Euripides which Wagner knew best because of his work on the Gluck opera) we have the "prologue" so to speak (ll. 49–105) and the key action of Iphigeneia's

Schadewaldt compared such narration ("in charakteristisch euripideischer Form") to the "prologue" of the *Holländer*, the Rome-narration in Act III of *Tannhäuser*, and the grail narrative in Act III of *Lohengrin*.[93] One can also make a case that in the *Ring* Wagner employs epic narration rather as Aeschylus does,[94] a good example being the Norns' narration in the Prologue in *Götterdämmerung* (to which I will shortly return), which could be said to bear a certain similarity to the long opening chorus of *Agamemnon*.[95]

Second, although Wagner was critical of certain epic poets (see above on Virgil, etc.), he had great admiration for Homer. Foster says that whereas in his letter to Liszt he bemoans his "halb epische Darstellung" ("half-epic mode of presentation") what he saw in Homer and what he wanted to produce in the *Ring* was, as Foster puts it, a "voll epische Darstellung."[96] Later, in 1879, Wagner wrote that Homer was "seer and poet in one; wherefore also they represented him as blind, like Tiresias. [...] This poet, as 'seer,' saw not the actual (*das Wirkliche*), but the true (*das Wahrhaftige*), sublime above all actuality; and the fact of his being able to relate it so faithfully to hearkening men that to them it seemed as clear and tangible as anything their hands had ever seized—this turned the Seer to a Poet."[97] Foster comments that "[t]he truth [...] when expressed by a seer of Homer's stature, need not be expressed in a way that is actually tangible to the senses." And so for Wagner, despite narrative forms, "Homer's epics were as true and immediately graspable by the senses as drama was. They were, to borrow [...] the terminology of his letter to Liszt, full-fledged epic dramas."[98] Foster argues that the clue to how Wagner made his epic more dramatic is found again in his essay *On Poetry and Composition*. After Homer "we have to seek the genuine epic fount in tales and sagas of the Folk alone, where we find it still entirely undisturbed by art."[99] As Foster points out Wagner is probably referring not only to the Greek myths Homer employed but also the medieval sources Wagner was using for the *Ring*. Like Homer, Wagner felt he was both poet and priest, i.e., a seer.[100]

---

being rescued and taken up is narrated by the messenger (ll. 1540–1612).

93. Schadewaldt, "Griechen," 387. The grail narrative could also be likened to the dramatic use of narration when Oedipus reveals his history in *Oedipus Tyrannus* (ll. 771–833).

94. Cf. Schadewaldt, "Griechen," 387–88.

95. After the exit of the Watchman, the chorus runs from l. 40 until l. 257 after which Clytemnestra enters (Lloyd-Jones, *Oresteia*, 20, 30, argues she does not appear at l. 83 but at l. 258).

96. Foster, *Greeks*, 60.

97. PW 6:138; GSD 10:142. On the tradition that Homer was blind, see Graziosi, *Inventing Homer*, 125–63. One reason he was so portrayed was because "blindness was regularly associated with prophecy and poverty" and "[a] blind man was thought to be particularly close to the gods, while at the same time he remained completely dependent on the goodwill of others for his daily sustenance" (133). Homer is made a poet and seer in one in that his *Odyssey* features Demodocus, the bind bard of *Odyssey* 8, and the figure Wagner mentions, the blind seer Teiresias of *Odyssey* 10 and 11.

98. Foster, *Greeks*, 61.

99. PW 6:139; GSD 10:143.

100. Foster, *Greeks*, 62.

The third point to make in relation to this problem of narratives in the *Ring* (although this does not necessarily solve the "problem") is that in one way or another they function essentially as songs, seen for example in the Norns' "singing" in the Prologue to *Götterdämmerung*,[101] Siegfried's "song" in *Götterdämmerung* Act III,[102] and perhaps even in Wotan's monologue in *Walküre* Act II.[103] This then brings us to the question of "lyric."

Lyric

Wagner read of the Dorian lyric from Müller, who writes that "while all poetry which was necessarily attended with music was called lyric, that which was sung to accompany dances, frequently of large choruses, has been called the Doric lyric poetry."[104] Müller makes the case that lyric did not develop out of epic poetry.[105]

In *Artwork of the Future* Wagner discusses the emergence of the "purely human" ("rein menschliche") artwork in Greek history and it is here that lyric played an important role. Building upon Müller's work on the Dorian invasion he argues that the "Ur-hellene" (Pelasgians) were Asiatic peoples who worshipped nature deities. The "Ur-Hellene" bowed himself before "gods'-oak"[106] at Dodona, waiting for the oracle. But "the *Orpheist*" (identified with "the art-glad *Lyrist*") "beneath the shady thatch of leaves, and circled by the verdant pillars of the [*gods'-grove* . . .] raised his voice."[107] The voice was not to support this nature religion but rather to lead the worshipper from "gods'-grove" to "gods'-temple," which appears to be identified with the theatre of Greek tragedy (having "gods'-altar" as its central point).[108] Hence, the lyricist enables the transition from nature to the "purely human" artwork, not that nature is in any sense abolished but that it is "conquered" such that the human being is placed on the pinnacle of nature.[109]

---

101. As well as refrains on "spinning" and "singing" (*WagRS* 280–82) there are the refrains "do you know what will become of him/it?" (*WagRS* 281–83) which he adopted from *Völuspá* 27, 28, 33, 34, 38, 40, 49, 59, 60 (Dronke, *Edda II*, 14–24).

102. *WagRS* 340: "I'll sing you tales / about my boyhood days."

103. See Abbate, *Unsung Voices*, 201–2, who argues that it is a narrative song, the text itself being "*strophic*" and "*musical*" (175). Note, however, that Wotan "speaks" to Brünnhilde (*WagRS* 148–49).

104. Müller, *Doric Race*, 2:380–81; *Geschichten*, 3:362, who refers to Schlegel, *Geschichte der Poësie der Griechen und Römer*.

105. Müller, *Doric Race*, 2:385; *Geschichten*, 3:367–68.

106. Cf. Warner, "Artwork," 58. *PW* 1:157, fails to represent the German plural "Göttereiche" (and "Götterhain") (*GSD* 3:124–25) with "God's-oak" (and "God's-grove").

107. *PW* 1:157; *GSD* 3:124–25.

108. *PW* 1:157–58; *GSD* 3:124–25. A little later (*PW* 1:158; *GSD* 3:125) he identifies "the *Temples of the Gods*" ("*die Tempel der Götter*") with "the *Tragic theatres* of the Folk" ("die *Tragödientheater* des Volkes"). This section of Artwork is primarily concerned with architecture.

109. *PW* 1:157; *GSD* 3:124. Hence, the "purely human" contrasts not with the "divine" but with "nature."

THE *RING* AND THE GREEKS

Wagner returned to the matter of lyric in *Opera and Drama*. In section 2.6 he writes that "the *Lyric* is the beginning and end of Poetry." In parallel with lyric is "tone-speech" ("Tonsprache"), the beginning and end of "word-speech" ("Wortsprache"), and "myth" as the beginning and end of "history" ("Geschichte"). In each case the mediator is *"the Phantasy"*[110] and this whole process is illustrated with a diagram he drew for Uhlig (see figures 4.1 and 4.2).[111]

Figure 4.1

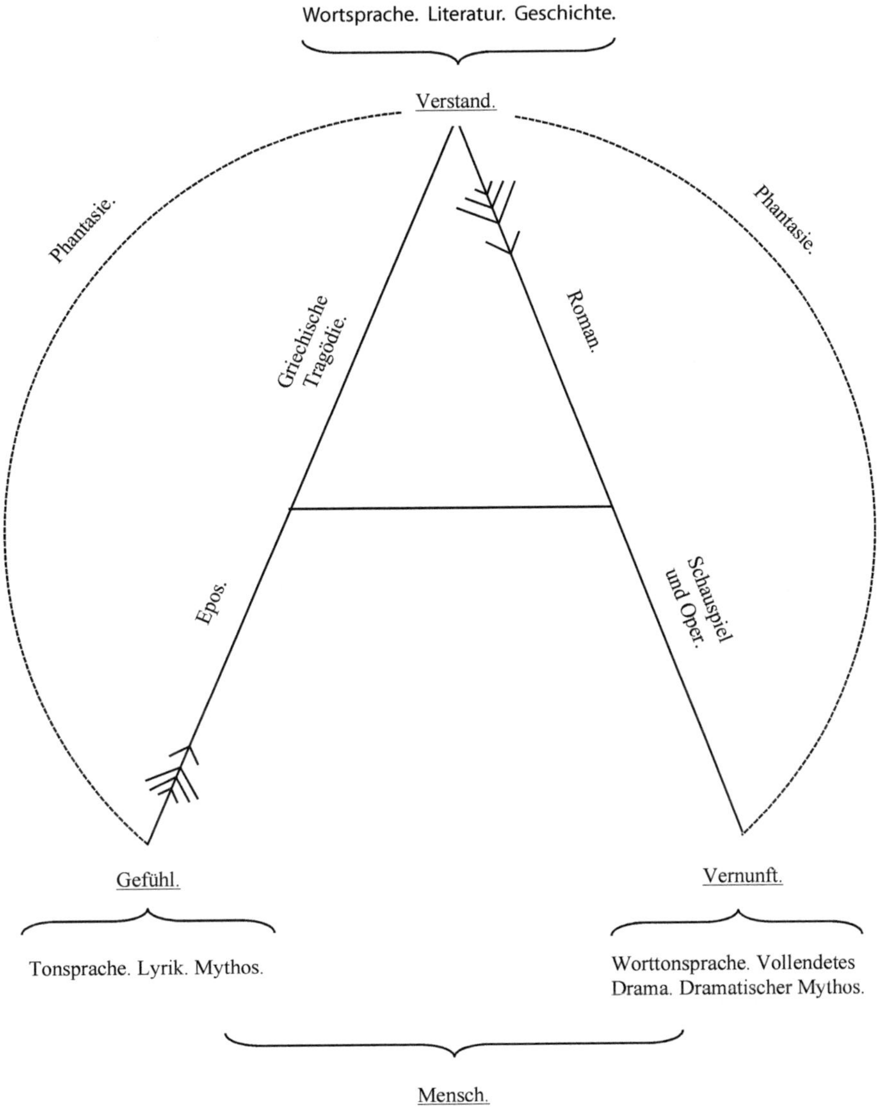

Wortsprache. Literatur. Geschichte.

Verstand.

Phantasie.   Phantasie.

Griechische Tragödie.   Roman.

Epos.   Schauspiel und Oper.

Gefühl.   Vernunft.

Tonsprache. Lyrik. Mythos.   Worttonsprache. Vollendetes Drama. Dramatischer Mythos.

Mensch.

110. *PW* 2:224; *GSD* 4:91.

111. *SB* 3:478 (and plate 7). The letter is undated but has been calculated as 12 December 1850 (*SB* 3:479 n. 4). A schematized version of diagram is also given in *SSD* 16:95 (see *WDS* 181) and *PW* 2:2 but there are errors in the directions of two of the arrows and with some minor misrepresentations.

Figure 4.2

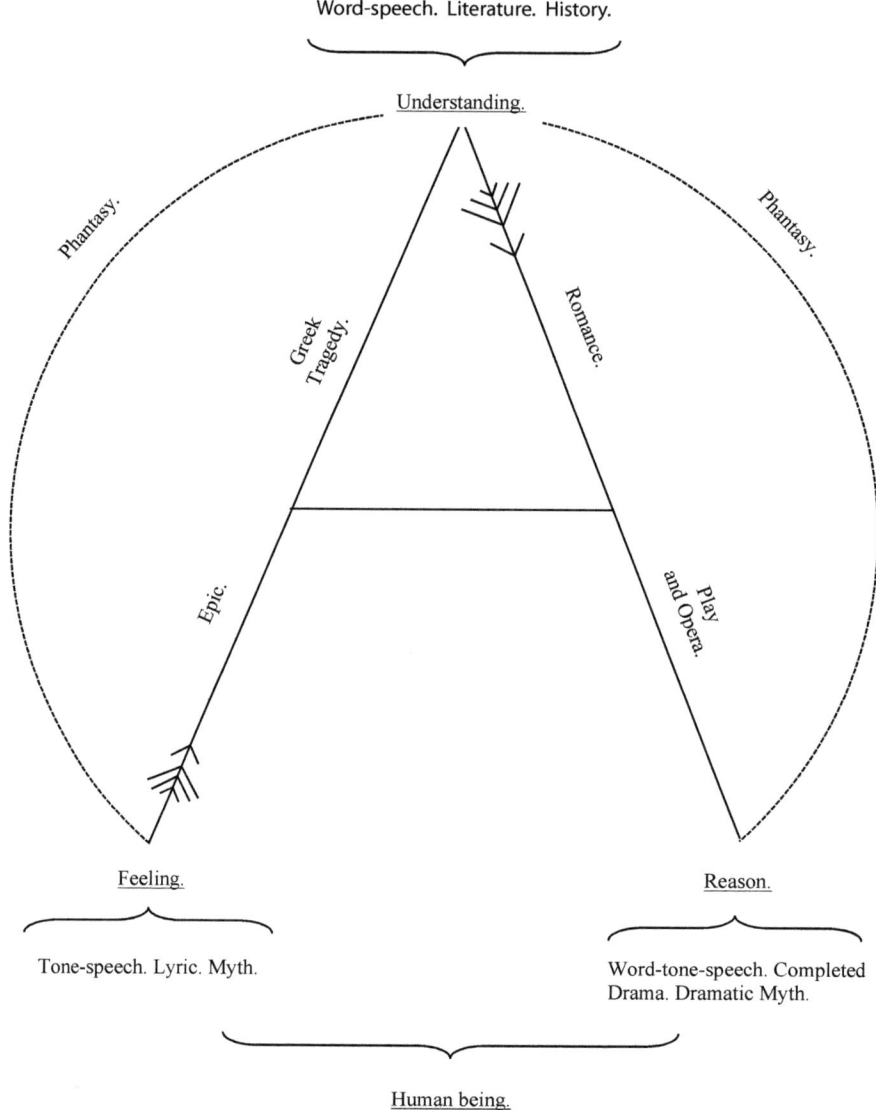

For now I consider the first part (left hand part of the diagram). Here we have an "evolution" from "tone-speech (Tonsprache)/lyric/myth" to "word-speech/literature/history" that involves a journey through "epic" and then "Greek tragedy," hence taking us from "feeling" ("Gefühl") to "understanding" ("Verstand"). "The march of this evolution ([d]er Gang dieser Entwickelung) is such, however, that it is no retrogression (Rückkehr), but a progress to the winning of the highest human faculty; and it is travelled, not merely by Mankind in general, but substantially by every social individual."[112] This movement from "feeling" to "understanding" is then taken up a little later where

---

112. *PW* 2:224; *GSD* 4:91.

he discusses the transition from Ur-melody to "Absolute Word-speech."[113] In "the oldest Lyric [...] the words and verse proceeded from the tones and melody."[114] "In the evolution of the human race, the more the instinctive faculty of Feeling ("das unwillkürliche Gefühlsvermögen") condensed itself to the arbitrary faculty of Understanding" ("zum willkürlichen Verstandesvermögen"); and the more, in consequence, the content of the Lyric departed from an Emotional-content (Gefühlsinhalt) to become an Intellectual-content (Verstandesinhalte)".[115] Hence there was a divorce of word and melody (which Wagner saw as his mission to reunite).

> The so exuberant Form of Greek speaking-Lyric, such as it has come down to *us*, and specifically the choruses of the Tragicists, we can never explain as necessarily conditioned by the *content* of these poems. The mostly didactic and philosophic content of these chants stands generally in so vivid a contrast with its sensuous expression, in the profusely changing Rhythmik of the verses, that we can only conceive this manifold investiture, not as having emanated from the Content of the poetic-aim, but as conditioned by the melody and obediently conforming to its immutable demands.[116]

This is especially interesting in view of the fact that the orchestra took over the role of the chorus for Wagner.

The key place lyric plays in Wagner's scheme is that it alloys with epic to create tragedy (see the left hand part of the diagram), and it to this that I now turn.

Greek Tragedy

Of the categories of Greek literature tragedy is by far the most important for understanding the *Ring*. As we saw in chapter 3, Wagner read Grimm's *Deutsche Mythologie* in 1843 and one question to address is why it was not until 1848 that he began to work on the *Ring*. One view is that it was his reading of Hegel's *Philosophy of History* and of the Greeks, especially tragedy, in 1847 that catapulted him into working on the *Ring*. There may be some truth in this and it could be that this motivated him to engage in his "Old German Studies" and "Mone's researches,"[117] hence renewing his interests of 1843. Therefore, Wagner may well be appropriating his Germanic and Norse sources through the lens of the Greeks, and in particular how Hegel understood the Greeks. His main source for Greek tragedy was Droysen (whom we have already encountered in relation to Greek history) and it is significant that he had been a student of Hegel in Berlin. Wagner's understanding of tragedy sometimes corresponds to Hegel's and it is

---

113. *PW* 2:281; *GSD* 4:143.
114. *PW* 2:281; *GSD* 4:143.
115. *PW* 2:281–82; *GSD* 4:143.
116. *PW* 2:282–83; *GSD* 4:144.
117. *Brown Book* 95; *Braunes Buch* 113.

striking that Hegel's favorites were also Wagner's: *Oresteia* of Aeschylus, and *Antigone*, *Oedipus at Colonus*, and *Oedipus Tyrannus* of Sophocles.[118] However, there are also significant differences between Wagner and Hegel, the most important being in relation to "conflict and collision," to which I return shortly.

Scholarly discussion concerning Wagner and Greek tragedy

That Wagner was fascinated with Greek tragedy is beyond doubt. But even though Wagner himself reflected on Greek tragedy in his theoretical writings, relating it to his own artistic project,[119] it is not always entirely clear how Greek tragedy influenced his art-works and the question is disputed to this day.

There were already discussions of the relationship of Wagner's art-works to Greek tragedy during his own lifetime, the writings of Nietzsche being the most significant. Then with a sense of "distance" to Wagner's operas, a series of works appeared after the composer's death that addressed more systematically the issue of Wagner and Greek tragedy.[120] But after the Second World War it was the three significant lectures given by Schadewaldt at the Bayreuth Festival (1962–65) that came to define the debate.[121] Following Schadewaldt there appeared in addition to studies in German a number in English such as that of the Greek classical scholar Lloyd-Jones (1982),[122] in many ways a response to Schadewaldt and, in the same year, the substantial study of Ewans.[123]

Tragedy and performance

The *Didaskalien* of Droysen's Aeschylus edition was fundamental for how Wagner developed his view of his theatre and performances.[124] In his essay *Art and Revo-*

---

118. Going forward to Shakespearean tragedy, one can also note that Hegel's view of Macbeth and the way tragedy functioned fits very well with Wagner's approach.

119. The most significant writings are *Art and Revolution* (Summer 1849), *The Art-work of the Future* (Autumn 1849), and *Opera and Drama* (1851),

120. The most significant studies before the Second World War were those by Petsch, "Tragödie" (1907); Braschowanoff, *Wagner und die Antike* (1910) (but this focusses on Homer, Plato, and Aristotle, rather than the tragedians themselves); Wilson, *Greek Tragedy* (1919); Drews, *Ideengehalt*, (1931). Sometimes Strobel, *Skizzen* (1930), has been wrongly cited as dealing with Wagner and the Greeks (e.g., Müller, "Wagner and Antiquity," 227). However, there is virtually nothing there on Wagner and the Greeks. I suspect a false inference has been drawn from Schadewaldt, "Griechen" (see below), who uses Strobel's work, but only in the sense that Strobel traces the evolution of the *Ring* (and its relation to *Siegfried's Tod*, etc.) in some detail.

121. They were published in 1970 and dedicated to the memory of Wieland Wagner. Schadewaldt's research actually influenced Wieland's productions of the *Ring* in Bayreuth during the years of those lectures. See, for example, the costumes worn by Hans Hotter (Wotan) and Martha Mödl (Brünnhilde) which suggest "Greek sculptures rather than Nordic gods" (Spotts, *Bayreuth*, 236).

122. Lloyd-Jones, "Wagner."

123. Ewans, *Aeschylus*.

124. Foster, *Greeks*, 350 n. 3, "can find no evidence" Wagner read this, although he thinks it a

lution Wagner found it highly significant that in Greek tragedy all elements of art come together and that performances should take place at a particular festival (that of Dionysus in Athens).[125] This religious aspect of Wagner's understanding was most likely informed by Droysen's understanding of the relation of Aeschylean tragedy to religion. It is also striking that Droysen emphasizes the joy involved in the religion of Greek tragedy (perhaps suggesting a lack of such joy in his Lutheran services).[126] It is also probable that Wagner's idea of the "total work of art" (Gesamtkunstwerk) owes something to Droysen's *Didaskalien*, although he could also just be thinking generally of the three essential elements in tragedy: dance, tone, and poetry.[127] Then Droysen's description of the layout of the theatre influenced Wagner, such as the arrangement of the stage and proscenium[128] and the layout of the auditorium.[129]

But Wagner was to make certain changes in his appropriation of tragedy, one of the most interesting being his orchestra taking on the role of the "chorus." In a performance of the *Oresteia* the parts were divided between three male actors and their dialogue would be punctuated by the chorus (of twelve members in Aeschylus' time and later increased to fifteen) who might "narrate past events relevant to the present situation, try to interpret that situation, or speculate about the future."[130] An example Wagner gave of the orchestra acting like such a chorus is Siegfried's Funeral March. Cosima records: "'I have composed a Greek chorus,' R. exclaims to me in the morning, 'but a chorus which will be sung, so to speak, by the orchestra; after Siegfried's death, while the scene is being changed, the Siegmund theme will be played, as if the chorus were saying: "This was his father"; then the sword motive; and finally his own theme.'"[131] Such a "chorus" could be compared to the "stasimon" of Attic tragedy,[132] a choral ode sung by a group, accompanied by music and dancing, and "usually made

---

reasonable assumption. But since it is part of Droysen's edition of Aeschylus, which we know he read, it seems highly likely he did read it.

125. See, for example, *PW* 1:47–48; *GSD* 3:23–24.

126. Droysen, *Werke*, 1:179: "Damals war die Andacht Freude und der Gottesdienst Genuß, damals die Kunst das Sakrament, in der die Gottheit die Gestalt ihrer Menschwerdung fand."

127. See *Artwork of the Future* (*PW* 1:95; *GSD* 3:67).

128. Droysen, *Werke*, 1:184: "Was von der Bühne vor diesem Vorhange liegt, ist das Proscenium, ein Vorbau, der in gleichen Höhe mit den untersten Sitzreihe gegenüber."

129. Droysen, *Werke*, 1:186: "in einem ringsaufsteigenden Halbkreise ordnet sich die Menge der Schauenden am natürlichsten."

130. Lloyd-Jones, *Oresteia*, v. The chorus in Greek tragedy fascinated Wagner and he felt "one could write a whole book about it" (*CD* 27 November 1879). Hieronymus Müller's introduction to *The Clouds* (*Die Wolken*) includes a discussion as to why the clouds function as the chorus (*Aristophanes*, 1:211), part of which Wagner underlines.

131. *CD* 29 September 1871. See also *CD* 16 January 1871: "The significance of the orchestra, its position as the ancient chorus, its huge advantage over the latter, which talks about the action in words, whereas the orchestra conveys to us the soul of this action—all this he explains to us in detail."

132. Borchmeyer, *Theatre*, 167. On the stasimon, see Stoeßl, "Stasimon," 342–43; Aristotle, *Poetics* 1452b 16 (Halliwell, *Aristotle XXIII*, 68–69).

up of one or more pairs of stanzas which have the same metrical form" known as the strophe and antistrophe ("turn" and "counterturn").[133]

Now in Greek tragedy the chorus and the dialogue could not operate simultaneously, but if the orchestra takes on the role of the chorus then a significant transformation is possible, as he explained in his *Prologue to a Reading of Götterdämmerung* (1873): "whilst Antique Tragedy had to confine its dramatic dialogue to separate sections strewn between the choruses delivered in the Orchestra—those chants in which Music gave to the drama its higher meaning—in the Modern Orchestra, the greatest artistic achievement of our age, this archetypal element goes hand in hand with the action itself, unsevered from the dialogue, and in a profounder sense may be said to embrace all the action's motives in its mother-womb."[134] In fact, he said something similar twenty years earlier in *Opera and Drama*:

> The *orchestra* thus plays an uninterrupted and, from every point of view, a leading and elucidatory role in the overall impression that the performer conveys both to the ear and to the eye; it is the teeming womb of music from which the unifying bond of expression grows.—*The chorus of Greek tragedy* has bequeathed to the *modern* orchestra the significance that is felt as being necessary to the drama, for only in the orchestra can it be developed, free from all constraint, and achieve so immeasurable varied an expression.[135]

Replacing the chorus with the orchestra also had visual as well as aural consequences: in Bayreuth the distance between audience and performers, which is partly introduced by having the orchestra, is fundamental, but in the Greek theatre the distance is virtually nil since it had no curtain, no double proscenium, and no "mystic gulf" ("mystischer Abgrund") from which the music sounds "rising from the holy womb of Gaia beneath the Pythia's tripod."[136] Further, this distancing of the audience from the performers has the effect of producing a sense of illusion that went against what the Greek theatre was attempting.[137]

Before leaving the issue of tragedy and performance, three further differences should be mentioned. First, the Greeks had three tragic plays followed by a satyr play[138] all performed on a single day[139] whereas Wagner's "Bühnenfestspiel" has four

---

133. Goldhill, "Language," 128. This pattern of strophe and antistrophe could possibly be discerned in Siegfried's Funeral March. See *Götterdämmerung* III.931–34/938–42 (Volsung motif) and 959–63/965–68 (Siegfried motif) where we have two sets of musical phrases which "answer" each other. However, it would be unwise to press such an argument.

134. *PW* 5:306; *GSD* 9:309.

135. Quoted in Müller, "Wagner and Antiquity," 230 (*GSD* 4:190–91; cf. *PW* 2:335–36).

136. *PW* 5:335; *GSD* 9:338.

137. Droysen, *Werke*, 1:181: "Die alte Bühne beabsichtigt nicht theatralische Täuschung, sie sucht nicht einen Schein von Wirklichkeit und äußere Wahrheit, die nur zu leicht unnatürlich, störend, selbst lächerlich wird."

138. Easterling, "Dionysus," 38.

139. Droysen, *Werke*, 1:188–89, writes that the performance "wenigstens bei Aischylos bis nach

"plays" performed over "three days and a preliminary evening." Secondly, Wagner has no satyr play although cases have been made that *Rheingold* should be so understood. The latest and most complete argument for this has been put forward by Sanson, who finds similarities between *Rheingold* and Droysen's reconstruction of *Proteus*,[140] the Satyr play for the *Oresteia*. Despite the fact that parallels can be found, *Rheingold* seems so removed from the genre of Satyr play, being "a bracingly austere tale about crime and deception that unfolds principally with the world of the gods,"[141] that I find this extremely unlikely.[142] The third difference is that whereas Wagner hardly saw his art-works as "entertainment", in Greek tragedy "[e]ntertainment was part of its function and an important part."[143]

Themes in Wagner's *Ring* from Greek tragedy

Although "any neat abstract definition [of tragedy] would mean nothing," nevertheless one knows well enough what "tragic drama" is.[144] In Wagner's *Ring* a number of Greek tragic themes can be discerned and I give two examples.

First, tragedy has a distinct view of conflict: "The first and most obvious quality of tragic conflict is its extremity: it does not ordinarily admit of compromise or mediation,"[145] one reason for this being the sense of a "hidden or malevolent God, blind fate, the solicitations of hell, or the brute fury of our animal blood."[146] Where reconciliation does occur it generally comes through divine intervention or it comes too late when the catastrophe has already occurred. This sense of conflict is found in most of the operas in the Wagnerian canon.[147] The conflict caused by the love between

---

Sonnenuntergang gespielt wurde."

140. Droysen, *Des Aischylos Werke*, 1:153–58.

141. Deathridge, *Ring*, xxii.

142. There is also the problem that it has been almost universally accepted that the Satyr play came last, a view assumed by Droysen and presumably by Wagner. Although Sansone may be right that "the surviving evidence no more guarantees that the satyr-play was last in the program than that it was first" ("Satyr Play," 7), the problem remains that Wagner would assume a final Satyr play. Sansone, "Satyr-Play," 6, actually finds parallels to *Proteus* not only in *Rheingold* but also in the closing scene of *Götterdämmerung*: "Brünnhilde is reunited with her (dead) husband Siegfried, whom she had wrongly thought to have betrayed her, just as Menelaus is reunited with the living Helen, whom he had mistakenly thought to have been unfaithful to him." This seems somewhat unconvincing given the "tragic" character of *Götterdämmerung*.

143. Lloyd-Jones, "Wagner," 137–38.

144. Steiner, *Tragedy*, 9.

145. Burian, "Myth," 181. He points out that conflict has been central to study of tragedy only since Hegel's *Aesthetics*.

146. Steiner, *Tragedy*, 9.

147. Consider these examples outside the *Ring*. 1: As the curtain rises in *Lohengrin*, we have an irresolvable conflict between Elsa and Telramund. Even though Lohengrin arrives as her supposed "redeemer," Elsa suffers a disastrous end. Wagner likened Elsa to Semele, who perished because she wanted Zeus to visit her as he visited Hera (*PW* 1:334; *GSD* 4:289). Aeschylus wrote a lost play about

Siegmund and Sieglinde, the Volsung twins who are fated to meet and fall in love, cannot be resolved and results in their death. Siegfried is fated to betray Brünnhilde and again reconciliation comes too late.[148]

One area where there is disagreement about the nature of this conflict and collision regards the moral standing of the conflicted parties. It was noted above that both Wagner and Hegel had a love for Sophocles' *Antigone*; but their interpretations were somewhat different. On Hegel's view, both Antigone and Creon had a principle they should hold to and the fact that neither was prepared to compromise meant that the drama was to end tragically for both parties. As Houlgate argues, "[t]he essence of original tragedy for Hegel [. . .] resides in a real contradiction."[149] So Antigone "lives under the political authority of Creon; she is herself the daughter of a King and the fiancée of Haemon, so that she ought to pay obedience to the royal command. But Creon too, as father and husband, should have respected the sacred tie of blood and not ordered anything against its pious observance."[150] Houlgate believes Hegel is right in showing that "contrary to A. W. Schlegel, *Antigone* presents a clash not between a tyrant and a heroine of 'the purest femininity,' but between two equally one-sided and blinkered tragic figures."[151] Wagner is clearly on the side of Schlegel and adds his own views about the fall of the state! So Antigone is most certainly the one in the right and Creon the one in the wrong. Whereas Creon was the "State personified"[152] in Antigone we see "the fullest flower of *pure Human-love.*"[153] But Creon is transformed at the end in that "at the sight of the dead body of the son who through Love perforce had cursed his father, the ruler became again a father" and "wounded deep within, *the State* fell crashing to the ground, to become in death a *Human Being*."[154] This raises the question whether there are any "villains" in the *Ring*. The clearest example is Hagen, but it is perhaps significant that his character

---

Semele, and Wagner would know the story from Droysen, *Aischylos*, 2:228–29. 2: It seems that Amfortas' sin was unavoidable and he is powerless to repent and reconciliation can only come through the divine intervention of the holy spear, which bleeds with the blood of Christ. 3: The love triangle of *Tristan* cannot be resolved and reconciliation does come but too late, as King Marke exclaims, "Todt denn Alles! Alles todt?" (*GSD* 7:78–79)

148. *WagRS* 347–48.

149. Houlgate, "Tragedy," 150.

150. Hegel, *Aesthetics*, 2:1217; *Vorlesungen über die Philosophie der Kunst* (1823), 95.

151. Houlgate, "Tragedy," 154, 172 n. 31, referring to Schlegel, *Über dramatische Kunst und Literatur*, 1:177, 186–87. Houlgate, "Tragedy," 154–55, also points out that a harmonization could have been achieved "by burying Polyneices far away from the city" but "both Antigone and Creon remain blind to—or refuse to countenance—this possibility." Houlgate refers to Nussbaum, *Fragility of Goodness*, 55, who could have some sympathy with such a position. But see also Bungay, *Beauty and Truth*, 168, who argues that Hegel's interpretation "makes better sense as a reading of the mythological material used rather than of [Sophocles'] play itself."

152. *PW* 2:190; *GSD* 4:63.

153. *PW* 2:189; *GSD* 4:63.

154. *PW* 2:190; *GSD* 4:63.

and form is largely drawn from the "epic" of the *Nibelungenlied*. Perhaps the most intriguing figure to consider regarding "conflict" is Fricka. Hegel's analysis would be that she has perfectly valid reasons for the position she takes regarding Siegmund and Hunding. Wagner also presents the complexity of the conflict between Fricka and Wotan and even makes her win the argument in *Walküre* Act II Scene 1. However, his portrayal is such that virtually every spectator comes to sympathize with Siegmund and Wotan and is antipathetic to Hunding and Fricka.

A second tragic theme in the *Ring* is tragic guilt and non-guilt. Schadewaldt gives the example of Oedipus, whom he considers is subjectively fully guiltless ("subjektiv völlig unschuldig") yet objectively he has murdered his father and married his mother.[155] One could doubt whether he is fully guiltless since, for example, he did kill someone in a fit of rage, although not realizing that the victim was his own father. But his character is portrayed positively,[156] and certainly more positively than Siegfried. But it could be said that in both cases there is "tragic guilt and non-guilt." At the end of *Götterdämmerung* Brünnhilde stresses the purity of Siegfried who betrayed her: "der Reinste war er, der mich verrieth!" ("the purest of men it was / who betrayed me!").[157] Siegfried is destroyed by powers beyond his control; yet he has his personal failings! Hence Aristotle may well be onto something when he argues that the protagonist "falls into adversity not through evil (kakia) and depravity (mochthēria), but through some kind of error (hamartia)."[158] Such a pattern is also found in Shakespeare's protagonists who fall through an "error" (Hamlet, Lear, Othello) in the way they respond to external circumstances although, unlike Oedipus and Siegfried, they are not destroyed primarily by powers beyond their control.

Religion and myth of Greek tragedy in the *Ring*

Lloyd-Jones argued that "[a]n understanding of the nature of Greek religion is the main requirement for an understanding of Greek tragedy"[159] and we know that Wagner took a keen interest in the religion of Greek tragedy. He felt that Aeschylus' choruses are "religion."[160] Further, he noted the link between holiness and nature, seeing this particularly in what he calls the "eagles' chorus" in *Agamemnon*.[161] He also speaks

---

155. Schadewaldt, "Griechen," 402.

156. See the discussion in Finglass, *Oedipus*, 70–73, who argues that regarding the killing of Laius, Oedipus would have been acquitted by an Athenian court "on the grounds of self-defence when his life was in danger."

157. *WagRS* 348.

158. *Poetics* 1453a9–10 (Halliwell, *Aristotle XXIII*, 70–71).

159. Lloyd-Jones, *Oresteia*, ii.

160. *CD* 24 November 1879.

161. *CD* 11 October 1879; 14 November 1879. This "eagles' chorus" (*Agamemnon* 104–59; Sommerstein, *Aeschylus II*, 15–19) comprises three stanzas within the long opening chorus, written in dactylic meters, interspersed with iambic passages (Lloyd-Jones, *Oresteia*, 21).

of "the sanctity and divinity of the curse-laden individual who is being punished on behalf of a whole generation. Oedipus is quite godlike in his harshness against Polynices, it could be Zeus himself speaking, which is why, when he lays aside his last mortal frailty, he is at once summoned to the gods. That appears to us harsh, for we do not share the religious feelings of the Greeks."[162]

Since Wagner took such an interest in the religious outlook of Greek tragedy, it comes as no surprise that this outlook is found in the stage works. But Wagner uses the religion of Greek tragedy in a highly creative and sophisticated manner. Central to this is the issue of myth, which Wagner considered "the basic material of Greek tragedy."[163] Wagner saw clear connections between the Greek and Germanic myths. For example, of both he writes this: "natural phenomena such as day and night, or the rising and setting of the sun, are transformed by an act of imagination into characters who act and who are worshipped or feared because of their actions, so that gods who are thought of as human finally become truly anthropomorphized heroes."[164] Such an idea of the numinous quality of nature is central to the *Ring* and Wagner's myth brings about a mixing of the human and the divine, the material and the spiritual. However, he faced some formidable problems in presenting his mythology to his nineteenth-century public.

The problem becomes apparent when we see that Greek tragedy drew on material from "a limited repertoire of legends."[165] The audiences of Aeschylus and Sophocles would therefore know something of the traditions, and tragedies partly functioned by introducing "mutations" into this tradition. The key was the "interaction between an ongoing series of tragic performances marked by sameness and difference and their reception by the 'interpretative community.'"[166] But if Wagner wished his *Ring* to function in the same way then he had a special problem: many in his audience would have little idea of the "tradition history." The Nordic gods and goddesses were alien to his audience and relatively few would know the *Nibelungenlied* and *Eddas*. He therefore had to present a new mythology. As Ewans points out, Wagner succeeds here by giving a full mythology in the final text of the *Ring* and "only very rarely makes the mistake of alluding to legends which are neither enacted nor expounded elsewhere in the trilogy."[167]

However, Wagner found another way of making his mythology more comprehensible; this was by alluding to what those in the audience may already know. So in *Rheingold* he unites his gods into one group headed by Wotan, "who like Zeus

---

162. CD 14 April 1870. See *Oedipus at Colonus* 1348–95 (Lloyd-Jones, *Sophocles II*, 556–59).
163. Ewans, *Aeschylus*, 41.
164. *PW* 2:161; *GSD* 4:38.
165. Burian, "Myth," 178; cf. Aristotle, *Poetics*, 1453a17–22 (Halliwell, *Aristotle XXIII*, 70–71).
166. Burian, "Myth," 179.
167. Ewans, *Aeschylus*, 58.

on Olympos is authoritative but not omnipotent."[168] In Wotan and Fricka (and their quarrels in *Rheingold* Scene 2 and *Walküre* Act II Scene 1) we find clear echoes of Zeus and Hera; in Loge we find echoes of Prometheus; in Freia, Aphrodite; in Erda, Gaia; in Siegfried, Heracles; in Brünnhilde, Athene.[169] Further, Wagner, like all myth-makers, "worked on" these earlier myths[170] and to gain a full appreciation of the artworks a thorough reading of his sources (whether they be Greek, German, or medieval) may be necessary so one can discern the "mutations" in the tradition, for therein lies the "message" he wishes to convey.

Aeschylus

As already noted, Wagner had particular admiration for the *Oresteia* of Aeschylus and many argue that this has influenced the *Ring*, although the precise nature of this influence has been disputed.[171] Although Wagner considered Aeschylus the greatest of the Greek tragedians, in the Romantic period admiration first came for Euripides and Sophocles and only later for Aeschylus,[172] and this largely thanks to Droysen (1808–84), who translated Aeschylus in 1832 and did so with remarkable success. Ewans believes that two "important biases" in Droysen's translation had "significant effects" on the composer. Although there is some basis for the second of these (which concerns "nationalism" and was discussed above), concerning the first, which concerns the moral aspect, I disagree. Ewans writes: "The principals of the *Oresteia* are in [Droysen's] version guilty of their actions, and suffer moral retribution for sin." So "*Hubris*" is translated as "guilt" and "*Dikē*" is simply "*Das Recht*, with all its implications of legal and moral rightness."[173] Ewans argues that Droysen misses a crucial aspect of Aeschylus: the tragedian renounces "the traditional motif of an assured, doom-laden house condemned by its distant past to inevitable self-destructive violence." This then in turn, according to Ewans, has led Wagner astray. Wagner, reflecting on the Oresteia in 1866, described *Agamemnon* as the play of "complete human error—crime—desire" and *Choephoroi* as "revenge-expiation-punishment." In 1880 he described Agamemnon's death as "expiation for his father's crimes." This then colored his conception of the *Ring* with Alberich's curse, Wotan's guilt, and Siegfried having to "throw off the doom of the Volsung race."[174]

Helpful though Ewans' work is in relating Aeschylus to the *Ring*, I cannot see how Droysen has misrepresented Aeschylus at this point and in turn cannot see how

---

168. Ewans, *Aeschylus*, 60.
169. Cf. Ewans, *Aeschylus*, 56–61.
170. Cf. Blumenberg, *Myth*.
171. For example, Ewans, *Aeschylus*, believes it has influenced details of the plot.
172. Ewans, *Aeschylus*, 25–26.
173. Ewans, *Aeschylus*, 29.
174. Ewans, *Aeschylus*, 30.

Wagner has been led astray. Consider these lines of Clytemnestra (*Agamemnon* 1497–1504) in response to the accusation of the chorus that she is the treacherous murderer of her husband: "You think this deed is mine? / <Do not suppose so,> nor reckon / that I am the spouse of Agamemnon: / no, the ancient, bitter avenging spirit / of Atreus, the furnisher of the cruel banquet, / has taken the likeness of this corpse's wife / and paid him out, / adding a full-grown sacrificial victim to the young ones."[175] Whatever the disagreement between Clytemnestra and the chorus may be regarding her own guilt, both agree that the curse of the "cruel banquet" (l. 1502) is at work. According to the chorus Clytemnestra is guilty yet at the same time asks (l. 1565): "Who can cast the seed of the curse (gonan araion) out of the house?"[176]

There has also been a long tradition of finding allusions to *Prometheus Bound* in the *Ring*.[177] One of the first to write on this was Schaefer (1899)[178] and there have been many subsequent studies.[179] Wagner used the reconstruction of Droysen, who assumed that the extant *Prometheus Bound* was the second play of the trilogy. Droysen thought the first concerned the theft of fire ("Feuerraub"), the second the binding of Prometheus ("Fesselung"), and the third (for which we have considerable fragments)[180] the freeing of Prometheus ("Befreiung"). I believe a good case can be made that Droyen's reconstruction corresponds well to the first three dramas of the *Ring*: originally *Rheingold* bore an alternative title "Der Raub" or "Der Raub des Rheingold" (the stealing the Rheingold);[181] *Walküre* concerns the binding of Brünnhilde;[182] *Siegfried* concerns the freeing of the bound Brünnhilde.[183] Further, as Wieland Wagner put it, "Jawohl, Brünnhilde ist Prometheus":[184] both are children of a knowing and warning earth goddess (Themis, Wala-Erda);[185] both are punished for their love to humankind;

175. Sommerstein, *Aeschylus II*, 182–83.

176. Sommerstein, *Aeschylus II*, 190–91. Note that Ewans, *Aeschylus*, 30, translates "gonan araion" as "seed of vengeance." I am grateful to Alan Sommerstein (private communication, 13 October 2015) for clarifying the issues.

177. Wagner described "Prometheus" as "the most pregnant of tragedies" (*PW* 1:34; *GSD* 3:11).

178. Schaefer, "Aischylos' Prometheus und Wagners Loge."

179. Petsch, "Tragödie"; "Drews, *Ideengehalt*, 141–45; Schadewaldt, "Griechen," 365–86. Note, however, the arguments against Promethean echoes by Ewans, *Aeschylus*, 256–60 (who believes the play is not by Aeschylus, a view now held by the majority of scholars; see Griffiths, *Authenticity*, and Sommerstein, *Aeschylus I*, 433). Nevertheless, Ewans believes Droysen's introduction (if not the play itself) has exerted some influence (159).

180. Sommerstein, *Aeschylus I*, 438.

181. *TBRN1* 348, 350.

182. See Brünnhilde's words to Waltraute in *Götterdämmerung* Act I Scene 3: "fesselte er mich auf den Fels" (*WagRS* 301). The fact that she was not literally chained to the rock does not exclude a clear allusion to *Prometheus Bound*. On the Brünnhild/Prmethus link see also volume 2, chapters 10 and 11.

183. Schadewaldt, "Griechen," 360–61.

184. Schadewaldt, "Griechen," 342.

185. Themis was daughter of Gaia and Ouranos (Hesiod, *Theogony*, l. 135) and identified with Gaia in Aeschylus, *Prometheus Bound*, ll. 208–12 (here Themis, like the Wala, prophecies).

both are "fastened" to the rock through the agency of a fire god (Hephaestus, Loge); both are eventually freed by a hero (Heracles, Siegfried) descended from a god and a dying woman (Io, Sieglinde) whom they have assisted. It is also worth noting that *Prometheus Bound* was beloved by revolutionaries.[186]

If these parallels fail to convince, one can consider Act I scene 3 of *Siegfried's Tod* where the influence of *Prometheus Bound* is unmistakable.[187] In the 1848 version the Valkyries come to Brünnhilde on her rock and there follows a lyrical-musical dialogue whereby the Valkyries ask and warn and Brünnhilde responds. This pattern very closely reflects *Prometheus Bound* 124–96 where Prometheus is visited by the chorus of nymphs, daughters of Oceanus.[188] Later Wagner was to replace the groups of Valkyries with Waltraute alone, and fresh allusions to *Prometheus Bound* were introduced, first in Brünnhilde's very opening words ("old-familiar sounds / steal to me ear from afar:—/ a winged horse is sweeping / this way at full gallop")[189] and then with the unmistakable allusion in Brünnhilde's reply to Siegfried: "an eagle came flying / to tear at my flesh."[190]

Sophocles

As we have seen, Sophocles' *Antigone* had an important role for Wagner's view on love and the state. In *Opera and Drama* she is, I believe, the figure who draws together so many of the threads of Part II from chapter 3 (where he discusses the Oedipus myth) right through to the end of Part II (chapter 6). I think she provides one clue to the difficult chapter 4 (which concerns issues of love and state) and in view of her parentage (Jocasta and Oedipus) she represents both feeling and understanding and can be said to be cast "as the patron saint of musical drama."[191] Oedipus himself is also fundamental for *Opera and Drama*[192] and it is widely recognized that in *Siegfried* Act III (and *Parsifal* Act II) the hero has a clear Oedipal rôle.[193]

---

186. Ruffell, *Prometheus Bound*, 105–30.

187. GSD 2:183–86; PW 8:15–17; Haymes, *Ring*, 96–101.

188. Schadewaldt, "Griechen," 375, even goes to the point of comparing Aeschylus' use of the anapaest (two unstressed syllables followed by a stressed) for Prometheus with the anapaestic shape ("anapästische Gebilde") Wagner uses for both Brünnhilde and the Valkyries.

189. WagRS 300; cf. *Prometheus Bound* 124–27 (Sommerstein, *Aeschylus I*, 458–59).

190. WagRS 307; cf. Aeschylus, *Prometheus Bound*, 1021–25 (Sommerstein, *Aeschylus I*, 556–57).

191. Borchmeyer, *Theatre*, 296. See volume 2 chapter 6.

192. See the discussion in *Opera and Drama* (PW 2:180–92; GSD 4:55–66).

193. Perhaps not so well known is that there is a further allusion to Sophocles in *Parsifal* Act II in that Kundry, playing the role of the sphinx, puts riddles to Parsifal, which he manages to "solve" and thereby he overcomes her. Wagner speaks of Kundry as sphinx-like and dog-like (SL 500). Compare *Oedipus Tyrannus* 390–400 (Lloyd-Jones, *Sophocles I*, 362–63), where Oedipus rebukes Tiresias for trying to throw out the very person who solved the riddle of the "versifying hound" (hē rhapsōdos kuōn).

Euripides

Wagner's study of Euripides was in relation to his re-working of Gluck's *Iphigénie en Aulide*.[194] In Euripides, Iphigenia, who has been called to Aulis on the pretext that she will marry Achilles,[195] disappears as she is about to be sacrificed, being replaced by a hind,[196] and Agamemnon interprets this as her having fellowship with the gods.[197] In Gluck's opera "Diana" grants the marriage. Wagner was clearly unhappy with this happy ending, and it is significant that he marked in his copy of Euripides these words of Agamemnon: "No man to the end is fortunate, / Happy is none; / For a lot unvexed never man yet won."[198] Indeed, Wagner's portrayal of the Greek general most probably colored the character of his Wotan.[199] Wagner's version ends with "Artemis," appearing as *dea ex machine*, and he inserted eight lines where she calls Iphigenia to serve her in her temple in Tauris and announces that her wrath is appeased ("versöhnt ist [...] mein Zorn") and the wind now blows for the journey of the Greeks to Troy.[200]

Conclusions on Greek tragedy

Although the above discussion demonstrates the way in which the *Ring* was influenced by Greek tragedy, the question remains whether it can be considered "tragedy" in this sense. Despite the influences and parallels I think the answer has to be "no."[201] The ending of *Götterdämmerung* is remarkably ambiguous; although it ends with the double sacrifice of Siegfried and Brünnhilde, it also offers a possible optimistic

---

194. He started on the reworking in 1845 and completed it in January or early February 1847 (*WWV* 333). It was performed on 24 February 1847 (reviews in Kirchmeyer, *Wagner-Bild III*, nos 752–59, 761–64, 812; see also Kirchmeyer, *Wagner-Bild I*, 717–30).

195. Way, *Euripides I*, 12–13, ll. 98–100.

196. Way, *Euripides I*, 146–47, ll. 1581–87.

197. Way, *Euripides I*, 148–49, l. 1622.

198. Way, *Euripides I*, 18–19, ll. 160–62; ll. 158–60 in J. J. C. Donner's edition of Euripides, used by Wagner. This marking was first noted by Westernhagen, *Bibliothek*, 22–23, and I have been able to verify it for myself.

199. Jost (*SW* 20.IV:IX) speaks of the "tormented king" of Act II "quarrelling both with the immortals and with himself, vacillating between his love for his daughter and his obligations to the soldiers" who "repeatedly changes his mind before finally becoming aware of the pitifulness of his desire for power." Further, she compares the "long pause" after his "nichts? nichts?" (*SW* 20.IV:80 (*Reinschrift*), 310 (bar 63)) with that noted by Porges, *Rehearsing the Ring*, 58, after Wotan's first "das Ende" in *Walküre* Act II (bar 944). Wagner praised Anton Mitterwurzer's role of Agamemnon (*My Life* 338; *Mein Leben* 1:351), whose singing was a model for his later Wotan (*SW* 20.IV:IX).

200. *SW* 20.IV:87 (*Reinschrift*), 401–3 (Nr. 30, bars 85–102). Wagner later explained that his ending was more faithful to Euripides than Gluck's (*SB* 5:88).

201. The opera that comes closest is *Lohengrin*, but even here there is an element of hope in that Gottfried is restored as "Herzog von Brabant" (*GSD* 2:114). *Tristan* is removed from the "tragic" for despite the deaths King Marke witnesses in the closing scene, Isolde's "Liebestod" is actually her "transfiguration" which Wagner understood in the light of the assumption of the Virgin Mary (*CD* 25 April 1882).

outlook for a renewed world order. All this raises the question whether Wagner "ever succeeded in writing a tragedy in the Greek spirit at all."[202] Schadewaldt equivocates in claiming that although Wagner was not interested in reviving Greek tragedy, he can nevertheless, as Deathridge puts it, "reach out and shake hands with Homer and Aeschylus over the ages after all."[203] Lloyd-Jones, by contrast, claims that "in the Ring in general we find something profoundly alien to the spirit of an ancient tragedy."[204] It is certainly the case, as Lloyd-Jones suggests, that Wagner's attachment to Christian theology prevented him from writing a truly tragic music drama. All the operas of the Wagnerian canon concern "redemption," which, for Wagner, had a distinctly Christian connotation. But Wagner was far from simply distancing himself from Greek tragedy. Two points can be made. First, tragedy does not have to end tragically, as Hegel noted in the case of *Eumenides*. This play I noted above was praised by Wagner, and one wonders whether Paul's speech on the Areopagus in Acts 17 was so important for Wagner[205] because the setting was precisely that of the close of the *Eumenides*. The second point is somewhat related to what I have just said, for a case can be made that Wagner was "baptizing" tragedy. I believe far too much emphasis has been placed on Wagner's opposition in *Opera and Drama* of Greek tragedy and Christian myth[206] and the overwhelming impression he gives in essays, letters, and diaries is that the two actually belong together. John's Gospel for him was a tragedy[207] as was his own sketch for *Jesus of Nazareth*.[208] Jesus of Nazareth must appear with Apollo.[209] Wagner was brought up in the world of Lutheran Protestantism and after his breakthrough with Greek tragedy in the 1840s, he was able to form a remarkable synthesis. Both Lutheranism and Greek tragedy share a pessimistic view of the human person;[210] and to this pessimism he added his distinctive idea of redemption through love.

Wagner's Later Reflections on *Ring* and Tragedy

Anticipating Nietzsche's *Birth of Tragedy* (1872), which famously discusses "the duality of the *Apolline* and the *Dionysiac*,"[211] Wagner wrote in *Destiny of Opera*

202. Deathridge, *Good and Evil*, 103.
203. Deathridge, *Good and Evil*, 104, discussing the end of Schadewaldt's first lecture ("Griechen," 364–65).
204. Lloyd-Jones, "Wagner," 141.
205. See chapter 7 below.
206. *PW* 2:159–60; *GSD* 4:37.
207. *CD* 11 February 1875.
208. *My Life* 387; *Mein Leben* 1:401.
209. See the ending of *Art and Revolution* (*PW* 1:65; *GSD* 3:41).
210. Hence I strongly disagree with Lloyd-Jones, "Wagner," 141, that Wagner believed in the "essential goodness of human feelings". This is hardly sustainable given his Lutheranism and the clear pessimistic anthropology found in both the stage works and writings.
211. Nietzsche, *Birth of Tragedy*, 14.

(1871): "The Tragedy of the Greeks having evolved from a compromise between the Apollinian and the Dionysian elements, upon the basis of a system of Lyrics wellnigh past our understanding, the didactic hymn of the old-Hellenian priests [i.e., "Apollinian"] could combine with the newer Dionysian dithyramb to produce that enthralling effect in which this artwork stands unrivalled."[212] He goes on to speak of Apollinian element of literature ("Word-speech") and contrasts "literary products" with Gluck's *Iphigenia* and Mozart's *Don Juan*:

> What so profoundly moved them in these last, must surely have been that here they found the drama transported by its music to the sphere of the Ideal, a sphere where the simplest feature of the plot was at once transfigured, and motive and emotion, fused in one direct expression, appealed to them with noblest stress. Here hushed all desire to seize a Tendence, for the Idea had realised itself before them as the sovereign call of Fellow-feeling.[213]

Wagner then quotes from the Prologue in Heaven of Goethe's *Faust* and from Schiller's *Braut von Messina*:[214]

> "Error attends man's ev'ry quest," or "Life is not the highest good," was here no longer to be clothed in words, for the inmost secret of the wisest apothegm itself stood bared to them in limpid Melody. Whilst that had said "it means," (das bedeutet) this said "it is!" (das ist) Here had the highest pathos come to be the very soul of Drama; as from a shining world of dreams, Life's picture stepped before us here with sympathetic verity.[215]

As in *Religion and Art,* Wagner applies Luther's view of communion ("das ist") to music and Zwingli's to other arts ("das bedeutet").[216]

---

212. *PW* 5:138–39; *GSD* 9:137–38.

213. *PW* 5:139–40; *GSD* 9:138–39.

214. See *GWJA* 3:19 (l. 317); Luke, *Faust I*, 11: "Es irrt der Mensch so lang' er strebt"; Schiller, *Braut von Messina*: "Das Leben ist der Güter höchstes nicht" (*FSSW* 2:912 (l. 2838)). The last two lines are: "Das Leben ist der Güter höchstes *nicht*/Der Übel größtes aber ist die *Schuld*."

215. *PW* 5:140; *GSD* 9:139.

216. For *Religion and Art*, see *PW* 6:224; *GSD* 10:222 (discussed in Bell, *Parsifal*, 305). No doubt Wagner's years in Zurich impressed upon him the dispute between Martin Luther and the reformer in Zurich, Huldrych Zwingli. As well as disagreeing on the Eucharist, they had diametrically opposing views on music. As Walton, *Richard Wagner's Zurich*, 9, comments: "It is an odd fact, but the greatest reformer of Zurich's musical life before Richard Wagner was the man who did away with it: Huldrych Zwingli (1484-1531)."

5

The *Ring*, Drama, Poetry, and Literature

Wagner, the Poet and Composer

In his autobiographical works Wagner presents his first calling as that of a "poet" and not a composer. Although he records his step-father Ludwig Geyer wondering, on hearing his step-son's piano playing a day before his death, "Has he perchance a talent for music?"[1] he confesses that he struggled with the piano and quotes his teacher, Cornelius Nepos, that "nothing would come of me" ("aus mir würde nichts").[2] Wagner added: "He was right; in my whole life I have never learnt to play the piano properly."[3] He records also that although he had a love for Weber's *Freischütz*,[4] and Mozart's *Zauberflöte*, his work with music was "quite a secondary matter" ("nur große Nebensache").[5] His main concerns were Greek, Latin, mythology, and ancient history. When he was eleven he "promptly determined to become a poet" after enjoying some success for a poem he wrote on the death of a fellow schoolboy[6] and he went on to sketch out "tragedies on the model of the Greeks" and to write a "Trauerspiel" *Leubald*.

Wagner can be described as a "late developer" regarding music, but the picture he goes on to paint of being a poor student who received only limited teaching (much of which he claims he disliked) is inaccurate and is probably so portrayed to emphasize that his musical gifts come from "inspiration"; in other words, he considered himself a musical "Siegfried" rather than a musical "Mime." He claims that his first desire to compose was for incidental music for *Leubald*[7] for which he needed "to first clear up a few

---

1. *PW* 1:3; *SB* 1:95: "Sollte er vielleicht Talent zur Musik haben?"
2. *PW* 1:4; *SB* 1:95.
3. *PW* 1:4; *SB* 1:95: "Er hatte recht, ich habe in meinem Leben nicht Klavierspielen gelernt." He also writes that his progress with the violin, for which he received lessons, was not particularly successful (*My Life* 36; *Mein Leben* 1:43).
4. *PW* 1:4; *SB* 1:95.
5. *PW* 1:4; *SB* 1:96.
6. *PW* 1:4; *SB* 1:96.
7. Deathridge, "Cataloguing Wagner," 189–91, accepts this as true, but rightly has serious doubts concerning Wagner's other claims to want to set the whole work to music.

of the general principles of thorough-bass" for which he borrowed Logier's *Thorough-Bass*.[8] His autobiography *My Life* does mention receiving "some lessons in harmony" from Christian Gottlieb Müller,[9] but this is not mentioned at all in his *Autobiographic Sketch*, remarkable given that he received from him three years of tuition.[10] Finally he received tuition from Theodor Weinlig.[11]

Just as his compositional gifts were to mature over the years in their remarkable way, so it was also with his poetic style and work as a dramatist. In *Communication to My Friends* he considered that it was only with *Holländer* that he came into his own: "From here begins my career as poet, and my farewell to the mere concoctor of opera texts"; but this was "no sudden leap."[12] The operas of the Wagnerian canon, especially the mature operas, can be remarkable for their libretti alone. Thomas Mann rightly uttered: "To have doubts of Wagner's gift as a poet has always seemed absurd to me. What could be more fine and profound, poetically speaking, than Wotan's relation to Siegfried: the paternally superior bantering of the god, his weakness for his destroyer, the surrender of the old power for love of the eternally young."[13] In addition, his use of metaphor in his prose works can be remarkable, especially in works such as *Opera and Drama*, where he writes of the role of music and the poet, even on occasions using Stabreim;[14] and when one speaks of his gifts as a "poet" this includes his work as a great dramatist. To highlight just one aspect of the dramatic genius of the *Ring*, no single element goes to waste, each being followed through in some way or another.[15]

Wagner's Literary Interests

Just as in his music he learned so much for those who had gone before him, so it was in literature, poetry, and drama. What is particularly interesting for the present enquiry is that among his literary sources were many who wrote on theology even if they are not generally classified as "theologians." The process of disentangling the various influences on Wagner will, it is hoped, help to identify theological themes that will be

---

8. *PW* 1:5; *SB* 1:97.

9. *My Life* 31–32; *Mein Leben* 1:38–39.

10. See his letter to Müller (probably to be dated 1830) given in Deathridge, "Lehrmeister," 74–75. Note also the range of compositions he produced as a pupil of Müller ("Lehrmeister," 72).

11. *PW* 1:7; *SB* 1:99. *My Life* 54–56; *Mein Leben* 1:62–64.

12. *PW* 1:308; *GSD* 4:266.

13. Mann, "Ring," 369.

14. *PW* 2:286; *GSD* 4:147. See volume 2, chapter 6.

15. Although Puccini's *Tosca* is a highly engaging drama, Scarpia's provoking Tosca to jealousy by suggesting Cavaradossi is romantically involved in the Marchesa Attavanti is simply followed through in the sense that Spoletta and his agents can follow her as she goes to confront Cavaradosssi and so they can find him and Angelotti. However, the drama does not function in the cumulative way that the *Ring* drama evolves.

followed through in volume 2. The sources are so rich that what I present will not be exhaustive, but I will deal with the major influences.[16]

A theme in Wagner's thinking, noted in the previous chapter, is that Greek art was married to the German, represented by the marriage of Faust and Helena in *Faust II*. Although for Wagner Goethe was the most important in linking the Greeks and the Germans, he was by no means the only one, as can be seen when Wagner writes:

> Hail Winckelmann and Lessing, ye who, beyond the centuries of native German majesty, found the German's ure-kinsmen in the divine Hellenes, and laid bare the pure ideal of human beauty to the powder-bleared eyes of French-civilised mankind! Hail to thee, Goethe, thou who hadst power to wed Helena to our Faust, the Greek ideal to the German spirit! Hail to thee, Schiller, thou who gavest to the reborn spirit the stature of the "German stripling" (des "deutschen Jünglings"), who stands disdainful of the pride of Britain, the sensuous wiles of Paris![17]

But Wagner's literary interests were by no means restricted to these German authors. Shakespeare was fundamental for him, although the English bard was seen as adopted into the German family of artists. Indeed, Wagner found the German translation superior to the English[18] and disliked reading Shakespeare in English, even though he had gone to some lengths to learn English with the sole intention of reading Shakespeare in the original.[19] Then outside this hallowed sphere he admired Dante, Calderon, and Cervantes,[20] and of these Dante is the one Wagner most often praises and who is most important for the development of the *Ring*.

Dante (1265–1321)

Wagner's love of Dante was fostered by his uncle Adolf Wagner, who was a serious student of Italian literature and had published works concerned with Dante,[21] one of

---

16. E.g., apart from passing references, I do not deal here with E. T. A. Hoffmann or Novalis. The biggest omission is Lessing, but he will be discussed in chapter 7 below.

17. *PW* 4:43; *GSD* 8:36.

18. See *CD* 14 November 1878 where he considers "Ruf" much finer than the "abstract and conventional" word "reputation" in the original of *Othello* (Cassio: "I have lost my reputation"; Act II Scene 3). *CD* 6 February 1881 tells of his praise of "Shakespeare's language, its dignity, in both wit and irony, and its majesty," but Cosima adds: "Yesterday we compared the English with the German and the German strikes us as much nobler."

19. See below.

20. In *Poetry and Composition* he speaks of Dante's "Seer's eye" also found to a lesser extent in Ariosto, Cervantes, and Scott (*PW* 6:139; *GSD* 10:143).

21. See *Zwei Epochen der modernen Poesie, dargestellt in Dante, Petrarca, Boccaccio, Goethe, Schiller and Wieland* (*SB* 1:19). Note also that he wrote *Theater und Publikum* (1826), which his nephew describes as giving an "overview on the development of drama of the European peoples (der europäischen Völker)" (*SB* 1:19).

which was an Italian edition of the *Divine Comedy* which Wagner had in his Dresden library.[22] In addition to this Wagner possessed two translations of the *Divine Comedy* in German.[23]

It was noted in chapter 2 that Wagner made much of the opposition between the Wibelungen/Nibelungen and the Welfs. He pointed out that the "Wibelingen" as the Kaiser party in opposition to the "Welfen" is especially frequent in Italy,[24] and goes on to speak of the terms used: Ghibelini and Guelphi.[25] This comment may possibly allude to Dante's *Comedia*, being conceived at a time of the opposition of the Ghibelline party (allied to the empire) to the Guelfs, who looked to the new power of the papacy.[26] Although Dante's family belonged to "a minor scion of an aristocratic Guelf clan" he came to detest many aspects of Guelf policy[27] and when in exile recognized "the intellectual merit of the culture promoted by Frederick II."[28]

Wagner was an admirer of Dante as a poet, considering the canzona of *La Vita nuova* in which Dante sees Beatrice lying dead as "the genesis of all poetry";[29] it was therefore entirely fitting that Liszt dedicated his *Dante Symphony* to him.[30] In a letter

22. This edition (*Il parnasso italiano*) also included three other key works (which would no doubt interest Wagner): *Le rime di Francesco Petrarca*; *L'Orlando Furioso di Lodovico Ariosto*; *La Gerusalemme liberata di Torquato Tasso* (DB 19). Adolf Wagner's name does not appear on the title page (perhaps a sign of his modesty) and the work is dedicated to Goethe (it was reviewed by Blanc in *Allgemeine Literatur-Zeitung* (1827) 857–64, 865–72). It is clear that the composer could read Italian: he conducted many Italian operas and we know he read Italian articles (e.g., *CD* 30 June 1870; *CD* 10 July 1870). According to his letter to Mathilde Wesendonck (around 20 December 1858) he spoke "pure Tuscan" (*SL* 433; *SB* 10:210) and no doubt his Italian improved over the years as he spent more and more time there. A search of "italien*" in *RWWSB* renders 2,288 items!

23. These translations (together with commentary) were by Karl Streckfuß (DB 17) and "Philalethes" the pseudonym for who was to become King Johann of Saxony in 1854 (DB 18). Volume 3 (*Das Paradies*) of Philalethes' edition is actually uncut from p. 77 to the end (p. 440) and is not nicely bound as in volumes 1–2. But this third volume only appeared in 1849, the year Wagner had to flee from Dresden.

24. *PW* 7:266; *GSD* 2:122–23.

25. *PW* 7:267–68; *GSD* 2:124.

26. Kirkpatrick, "Introduction," xix. Cf. *PW* 7:268. It is striking that Streckfuß devotes a large part of his introduction (*Komödie*, 1:1–54) to the question of the Ghibellinen/Guelfen (1–39). Also Philalethes has various notes on the relation of the two groups.

27. Kirkpatrick, "Introduction," xx. Streckfuß, *Komödie*, 1:16, explains the division of the Guelfen into the White and Black parties. Corso Donati, leader of the Blacks, claimed that Cerchi, leader of the Whites, wished to link with the Ghibellines. Dante sympathised with the White faction even though Corso's brother, Forese Donati, was his close friend (appearing as a redeemed sinnner in *Purgatorio* 23) whilst Corso's sister, Piccarda Donati, is among the blessed in *Paradiso* 3 (Kirkpatrick, "Introduction," xxi).

28. Kirkpatrick, "Introduction," xxiii.

29. *CD* 9 January 1870. As noted in the previous chapter, Wagner thought that all great poets were dramatists, although Homer and Dante were exceptions in not being dramatists but were nevertheless great poets (*CD* 18 January 1869). On a number of occasions Wagner mentions Dante as a consummate artist (e.g., *PW* 3:116; *GSD* 8:225).

30. See *BWL* 2:248 for the dedication. The work was premiered in the Hoftheater in Dresden on 7 November 1857. In a letter of 8 May 1859 Wagner thanks Liszt for sending a copy of the Symphony

to Liszt back in 7 June 1855 (as Liszt was working on the symphony), he argued that "the 'Inferno' and 'Purgatorio' will be a success I do not doubt for a moment: but I have misgivings about the 'Paradiso.'"[31] Instead of the "Paradiso" the first two lines of the *Magnificat* (together with "Hosanna!" and "Hallelujah!")[32] are set to women's (or boys') voices, and this does after all come to represent "Paradiso" as Wagner himself accepts in his late essay *Public in Time and Space* (1878).[33] He writes of Liszt's "creative act of redeeming genius, freeing Dante's unspeakably pregnant intention from the inferno of his superstition by the purifying fire of musical ideality, and setting it in the paradise of sure and blissful feeling. Here the soul of Dante's poem is shewn in purest radiance."[34] A disagreement he had with Liszt over the ending of the symphony reveals a key aspect of Wagner's theological outlook. Liszt played the work to Wagner in 1856, but he was shocked to hear that after the soft hint of paradise there was "a pompous plagal cadence" which Liszt explained was a reference to St Dominic. Wagner exclaimed: "Not that! Out with it! No majestic Lord God! (Keinen majästetischen Herrgott!) Let's stick with the fine soft shimmer."[35] Wagner is unlikely to be endeared to Dominic, portrayed by Bonaventura in Canto XII:100–102 of "Paradiso" as striking at the "shoots of heresy."[36] Further, Wagner throughout his life increasingly emphasized the suffering God, not the ruling, judging God; this, as we shall see, is reflected in the theology of the *Ring*. Liszt responded to Wagner's objection concerning the pompous ending: "I thought so too; the princess convinced me otherwise, but it shall be as you recommend." However, Wagner was to discover that Liszt failed to resist the wishes of Princess Carolyne von Wittgenstein.[37]

The central theme of love in the *Divine Comedy*[38] would no doubt attract Wagner and in particular he was clearly enchanted and moved by Dante's love of Beatrice[39] and that Beatrice is emancipated from "egoism" through love.[40] In *Paradiso* she appears as a "saviour" figure, taking over from Virgil as guide; this, together with the

---

(*SL* 455; *BWL* 2:252).

31. *SL* 343; *SB* 7:204.

32. The Magnificat does not actually feature in the *Comedy*.

33. The essay was inspired by Liszt's playing of Dante Symphony on the piano (Glasenapp, *Leben*, 6:146).

34. *PW* 6:92–93; *GSD* 10:100.

35. On this remarkable soft ending and the pleasure Liszt took in its harmonies, see Walker, *Liszt II*, 324.

36. Sisson, *Dante: Divine Comedy*, 403.

37. *My Life* 538; *Mein Leben* 2:551. The edition of the Franz Liszt-Stiftung (1920) gives the ending of which Wagner did not approve as a "Second conclusion" (*Symphonie zu Dantes Divina Commedia*, 140–45) which modern performances tend to omit.

38. Higgins, "Introduction," in Sisson, *Dante: Divine Comedy*, 13–14.

39. See above. Further, their love was not consummated which may parallel Wagner's relationship with Mathilde Wesendonck.

40. *SL* 344; *SB* 7:205.

role of the Virgin Mary in the final canto, is reminiscent of his central interest in the "eternal womanly"![41] But he had concerns that Beatrice "emerges from a car in a Church pageant" and "makes an ostentatious display of all the subtleties of Church scholasticism."[42] This reservation, expressed in the letter to Liszt, also re-emerges in his late essay *Religion and Art* (1880): "in his stupendous poem it is only where he can hold the visionary world aloof from dogma, that his true creative force is shewn, whereas he always handles the dogmatic concepts according to the Church's principle of literal credence; and thus these latter never leave that lowering artificiality to which we have already alluded, confronting us with horror, nay, absurdity, from the mouth of so great a poet."[43] This points to a recurring theme in Wagner's theological reflections: a suspicion of "stolid dogma."[44]

In another late essay, *Shall We Hope?* (1879), he praises the *Inferno* since it depicts "our world of life" in Schopenhauerian perspective,[45] one which to some extent was to color his *Ring* cycle.[46]

Shakespeare (1564–1616)

Cosima records in her diary for 21 January 1877: "R. not very well, finds his greatest pleasure in rereading *Faust*, tells us that Shakespeare, with Dante before him, and Goethe after him, forms a line shaped rather like this: _/‾_ , Shakespeare belonging to a culminating point in civilization; Goethe no less great, to a time of decadence."[47] Shakespeare was fundamental for Wagner throughout his creative life. He explains in his *Autobiographical Sketch* that at school he learnt English "merely to gain an accurate knowledge of Shakespeare" and translated Romeo's monologue metrically, and that he composed a tragedy *Leubald und Adelaïde*, "a medley of *Hamlet* and *King Lear*."[48] More detail is given his Autobiography: "I had put together a drama to which Shakespeare, principally through *Hamlet*, *Macbeth*, and *Lear*, and Goethe, through *Götz von Berlichingen*, had contributed."[49] He goes on to set forth the plot of *Leubald*[50] and explains how he has adapted the above-mentioned Shakespeare plays,

41. Sisson, *Dante: Divine Comedy*, 495–99 (Canto XXXIII). See below on Goethe's "Ewig-Weibliche."
42. *SL* 344; *SB* 7:205.
43. *PW* 6:221; *GSD* 10:122. In his 7 June 1855 letter to Liszt he criticizes the "Paradiso" from a Schopenhauerian perspective (*SL* 344–47; *SB* 7:205–9), even accusing Dante of being like "a childish Jesuit" (*SL* 347; *SB* 7:209).
44. *PW* 2:166; *GSD* 4:42 (*Opera and Drama*).
45. *PW* 6:117; *GSD* 10:219.
46. See chapter 6 below.
47. *CD* 21 January 1877.
48. *SB* 1:96; *PW* 1:4. He adds that the work occupied him for two years. The text is available in *DTB* 97–143.
49. *My Life* 25; *Mein Leben* 1:32.
50. *My Life* 25–27; *Mein Leben* 1:32–34.

adding ideas from *Henry IV Part I* (Leubald's character being a mixture of Hamlet and Hotspur) and *Richard III*.[51]

Shakespeare is central for his essay *Beethoven* (1870), a mature work on aesthetics. On Shakespeare he writes: "His dramas seem to be such a direct copy of the world (unmittelbares Abbild der Welt), that we cannot find in them any artistic mediation in their representation of the idea and more especially we cannot critically demonstrate this mediation, while our great poets, admiring them as the products of a superhuman genius, regarded them as natural wonders and found in them a means to study the laws of their own creation."[52] A similar view concerning the "picture of the world" was expressed the previous year. In a discussion of Henry IV and Prince Hal he comments: "in a genius such as Shakesp, the very incompleteness serves to impart a true picture of the world (ein treues Bild der Welt)."[53] Wagner makes a related and particularly arresting statement in his final complete written work (31 January 1883), his *Letter to Heinrich von Stein*: "His silence here has turned to revelation; and the world from which we are transported, that world to which we now have nothing more to say, appears redeemed in the great poet's smile. And this is of the essence of *Drama*, that is no form of poetry, but the likeness of the world reflected by our silent soul."[54]

When it comes to determining which editions of Shakespeare Wagner used when he was composing the libretto of the *Ring* there are a few problems. Westernhagen affirms that he possessed the translation of Schlegel and Tieck in his Dresden library in twelve volumes.[55] But there is one simple problem: these volumes cannot have been in his Dresden library since they are dated 1851–52 and the composer fled the city in May 1849. There is a further mystery. Westernhagen numbers the work 128 and the next one, an edition of sources for Shakespeare's dramas, is given the number 130. The missing work must be an English edition of Shakespeare that can be found in the Richard Wagner Museum, Bayreuth. But this is dated 1856! These works, numbers 128 and 129, were therefore *not* Wagner's but rather were purchased by Brockhaus after Wagner fled Dresden. One possible explanation for this anomaly is that Wagner did possess an earlier edition of Shakespeare in both English and in the Schlegel-Tieck translation,[56] they went missing (as had other works),[57] and Brockhaus replaced them with these later editions. There is only one other work in the collection with a date

---

51. *My Life* 26; *Mein Leben* 1:33.

52. Allen, *Beethoven*, 145.

53. *CD* 4 March 1869.

54. *PW* 6:327; *GSD* 10:319: "Hier ward [sein erhabenes Schweigen] zur Offenbarung, und die Welt, aus der wir jetzt entrückt sind, zu der wir kein Wort zu reden haben, sie dünkt uns im Lächeln des Dichters erlöst. Und dieß ist eben das Drama, welches keine Dichtungsart ist, sondern das aus unsrem schweigenden Innern zurückgeworfene Spiegelbild der Welt."

55. Westernhagen, *Bibliothek*, 103, gives details of the work and Shakespeare is discussed at a number of points in the main text.

56. The Schlegel-Tieck translation first appeared between 1825 and 1833.

57. See Minna's list in Westernhagen, *Bibliothek*, 111–13.

after 1849: de l'Ardeche, *Histoire de l'Empereur Napoléon*.[58] Perhaps again an earlier edition (the first edition appeared in 1839) had gone missing and Brockhaus again replaced it with a later one. There is also a further fact to note about the Dresden library. The books have glued in the back cover in the bottom right-hand corner a label "Bibliothek Heinrich Brockhaus" and above that another "Bibliothek Richard Wagner." The Brockhaus label was clearly pasted in first since there are cases where the Wagner label slightly overlaps the Brockhaus one;[59] further, the very positioning of the labels suggests Brockhaus' label came first. When they were inserted is unclear but it must have been after Wagner left Dresden and the books had been handed over to Brockhaus. Hence the existence of the label "Bibliothek Richard Wagner" is insufficient to prove that the book was in his possession.[60]

The one work we do have in the Dresden library in relation to Shakespeare is a three-volume work on the sources for his plays as found in novels, fairy tales, and sagas, edited by Theodor Echtermeyer, Ludwig Henschel, and Karl Simrock.[61] But in his Wahnfried library Shakespeare is very well represented: in addition to the sixth edition of the Schlegel-Tieck translation in twelve volumes (1863–65) he had a revised version by H. Ulrici, again in twelve volumes (1867–71), and a revised English version in nine volumes (by Dyce, 1866–67) together with various other versions.[62]

Giving Shakespeare an honorary German status is central to Wagner's understanding of the bard. In *German Art and German Policy* he writes that "while

---

58. This, like the Shakespeare English edition, is also missing in Westernhagen's list: it should appear as number 79 but again there is a jump in the numbering sequence, here from 78 (Lachmann and Wackernagel, *Zu den Nibelungen und zur Klage*) to 80 (*Le Sage. Histoire de Gil Blas de Santillane*). The work is available in the Richard Wagner Museum, Bayreuth. I suspect that numbers 79 and 129 were originally in Westernhagen's list but on realizing that the dates did not match Wagner's movements, deleted them at the last minute. Of course, he should have deleted 128 (Schlegel-Tieck translation) and perhaps he realized the problem with the dates; but since he had discussed Wagner's reading of Shakespeare in the main text, I imagine he felt it was best just to let it stay! On some aspects of Westernhagen's life and thought, see Dörte von Westernhagen, "Und was haben Sie vor 1945 gemacht?"

59. In the works I consulted I found only one instance where there were no labels: *Daz ist der Nibelunge Liet*. I found also an instance where the Brockhaus label was missing (Böttger (ed.), *Byron's sämmtliche Werke*).

60. It is worth adding that although in theory there is the possibility that Brockhaus rather than Wagner had the books re-bound, it must have been Wagner. "F. A. Brockhaus" writes in the "Vorbemerkung" of Westernhagen, *Bibliothek*, 7–8: "Die meisten Bücher der Dresdener Bibliothek sind in ihren vornehmen, zeitlosen Leinen- und Halbfranzbänden zweifellos nach dem Geschmack Richard Wagners einheitlich gebunden worden." But the proof that it must have been Wagner who had them re-bound is as follows. It was noted in chapter 3 above that Wagner's *Amelungenlied* in three volumes have the first two bound (these appeared in 1843 and 1846) but the third volume which appeared in 1849 was unbound (and uncut). Had Brockhaus had them re-bound after he took possession after May 1849 one would expect the whole series to be re-bound.

61. Simrock was the major contributor (he outlines how the work for the edition was distributed in *Quellen*, 3:287–88) and provided not only the prefaces for each volume but also wrote the notes (*Quellen*, 3:137–288).

62. He also had *Othello* (1867) and the Sonnets (1862) translated by Bodenstedt, the comedies in the 1623 version, and the poems edited by Simrock (1867).

Englishmen had turned the performances of their Shakespeare into circus-evolutions, the German spelled for himself the mysteries of human nature from this their miracle."[63] Further, after praising the Germanness of Bach and Goethe's "Götz," (a work inspired by Shakespeare's history plays)[64] he writes in *What is German?* "And beholding [Götz's] likeness, the German also know to shew himself, to shew the world, what Shakespeare is, whom his own people did not understand."[65]

Plays such as *Hamlet*, *Lear*, and *Macbeth* (which we saw fed into *Leubald*) were central for Wagner. He also had great love for *Romeo and Juliet* (we noted above his translating Romeo's monologue).[66] He admired Berlioz' "Romeo and Juliet" Symphony (although he also had certain reservations),[67] a work which was to influence *Tristan* and he sketched a funeral march for Romeo and Juliet (1868), a somber counterpart to the *Siegfried Idyll*.[68] *Henry IV Part 1*, also had a special place for him, as we have already seen.[69] And, of course, his second opera, *Das Liebesverbot*, was based on *Measure for Measure*.

One of the key things Wagner learned from Shakespeare was the sense of "drama," and the *Ring* is perhaps the work where Wagner more than anywhere else demonstrates what he has learned from the bard. Despite his admiration for Goethe, Wagner thought that Shakespeare was a superior dramatist.[70] Cosima records her husband complaining about "characters who talk endlessly in plays." He says: "In Shakespeare, speech, however detailed, is always action." After criticizing Schlegel and Tieck ("They knew all about the theater, but they couldn't write for it") she adds: "R. also blames

---

63. *PW* 4:86; *GSD* 8:76.

64. Wagner notes the connection in *Opera and Drama* Part II (*PW* 2:139; *GSD* 4:20).

65. *PW* 4:163; *GSD* 10:48. Could Shakespeare's "own people" ("sein eigenes Volk") not understanding him allude to Jesus not being received by his own people ("sein Eigenthum," John 1:11)?

66. Cosima tells of how her husband was in tears as he read excerpts from the play (*CD* 31 October 1882).

67. *PW* 3:249; *GSD* 5:193. This was to inspire his composition of his *Faust Overture* (see below).

68. *Brown Book* 147; *Braunes Buch* 175. Ten years later he commented "Perhaps I shall end up gobbling up the whole *Romeo and Juliet* march for Titurel!" (*CD* 19 October 1878). Cf. *CD* 21 October 1878 where he speaks of "music of mourning for the men who fell in the war."

69. In the context of discussing Act 2 Scene 4 and the "foolish hanging of thy nether lip" he told Cosima "Such a man comes once and never again" (*CD* 12 November 1878). Note also the allusion to this scene in *Public and Popularity* (*PW* 6:72; *GSD* 10:81).

70. Istel, "Wagner and Shakespeare," 505, makes the obvious but key point that "Shakespeare was first of all an actor and stage manager, and the fact that his most powerful dramas were evolved in response to the practical requirements of the stage [. . .] imparted to them a breath of robust life which [. . .] still suffices to elevate them over all the book-dramas written meanwhile."

Goethe to some extent for introducing this speechifying to the stage."[71] Nevertheless, he praises the Schlegel (Tieck) translation[72] as a "rebirth."[73]

The other significant thing about Wagner's debt to Shakespeare's sense of drama is that the external action is very much related to the internal psychology. Inwood rightly notes that in the *Oresteia* there is "very little of the complex and penetrating psychological insight into character which we find in Shakespeare and Wagner."[74] Further, whereas in the *Oresteia* tragedy develops out of external events, works such as the *Ring* and Shakespearean tragedies such as *King Lear* add psychological depth and have external fate growing out of the character of the protagonists. This relationship of fate to character is seen particularly in cases of Wotan and Brünnhilde.[75] Indeed, it is striking that whereas Siegfried seems to be more a tragic hero in the Greek sense,[76] Wotan and Brünnhilde are more Shakespearean. Wotan is responsible for the calamities that arise and receives just retribution for his deeds, even though there is a certain inevitability about his decisions and the events that arise from these decisions.[77] However, one should add that Brünnhilde is rather more complex in that she makes certain decisions (e.g., not returning the ring to the Rhinemaidens) that have tragic consequences but that ultimately lead to the redemption of the world and in this sense she transcends the Shakespearean sense of tragedy.[78]

In the previous chapter I discussed the left-hand part of the diagram Wagner sketched for Uhlig in his letter of 12 December 1850 where he traces the evolution from "feeling" to "understanding"[79] in order to elucidate a section of *Opera and Drama* (it is given again as Figures 5.1 and 5.2). The right-hand part deals with the evolution from "understanding" to "reason"; this is associated with the move from "word-speech/literature/history" to "word-tone-speech (Worttonsprache)/completed drama (vollendetes Drama)/dramatic myth (dramatischer Mythos)."[80]

---

71. *CD* 19 November 1878.

72. Note that most of the translation work was carried out by Schlegel and nearly all the plays which were important for Wagner were translated by Schlegel (the exceptions being *King Lear* and *Macbeth*).

73. *CD* 15 April 1880. The English translation of the diaries render "Wiedergeburt" as "reincarnation." This is a possible interpretation, but another possibility is simply "rebirth" as in Luther's use of "Wiedergeburt" in Matt 19:28 and Titus 3:5 and "wiedergeboren" in 1 Pet 1:3, 23.

74. Inwood, *Shakespeare*, 129.

75. Cf. Inwood, *Shakespeare*, 130.

76. In chapter 4 above I noted that Siegfried, like Oedipus, is destroyed not by personal failings but by circumstances beyond his control. We have a case here of Greek tragic guilt and non-guilt.

77. *CD* 2 July 1872 (it is not clear whether this is the thought process of Wagner or Cosima): "Which is greater, Wotan or Siegfried? Wotan the more tragic, since he recognizes the guilt of existence and is atoning for the error of creation."

78. This is where the New Testament becomes crucial, as we will discover in volume 2, chapter 2 and to some extent in the discussion of Wagner's debt to Hegel in chapter 6 below.

79. *SB* 3:478.

80. *PW* 2:224; *GSD* 4:91.

Figure 5.1

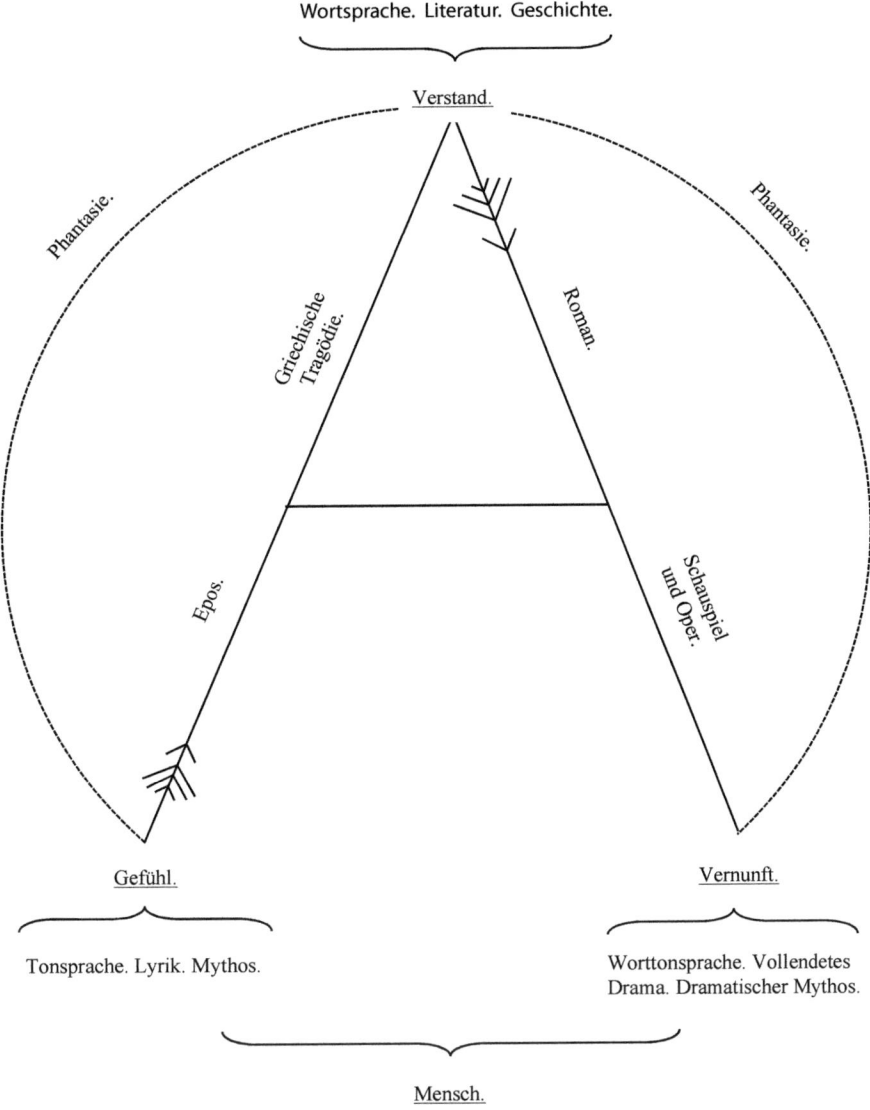

Figure 5.2

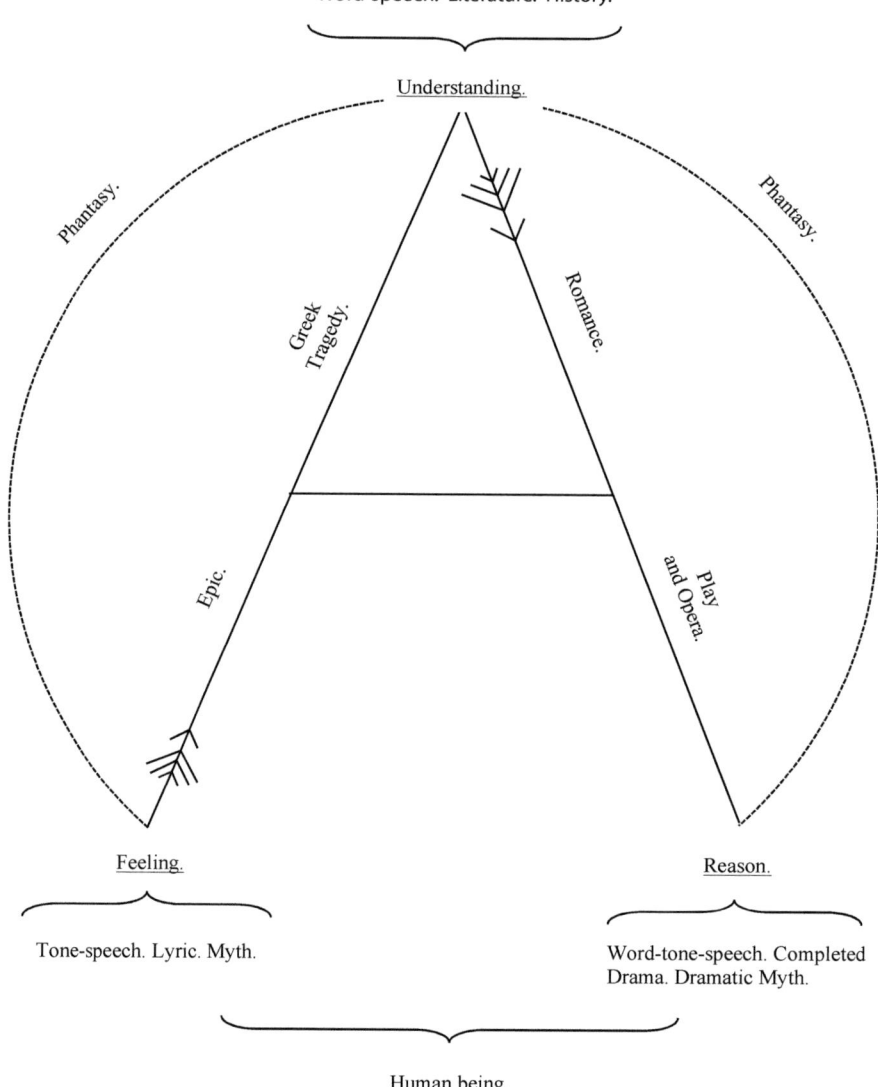

This takes us through the journey of "romance" ("Roman") and "play and opera" ("Schauspiel und Oper"). This second stage of evolution only seems to be discussed later on in the essay (section 3.5) and in fact concerns the role of the orchestra with its "word-tone-speech" rather than "romance" and "play and opera."[81] The work of the orchestra, he argues, is analogous to the of "dance-gesture" ("Tanzgebärde").[82] But what he wrote earlier about Shakespeare may elucidate the right-hand part of the diagram since he explicitly writes about "romance" and "play":

81. *PW* 2:319, 324; *GSD* 4:176, 180–81.
82. *PW* 2:319; *GSD* 4:176.

The real kernel of all our poesy may be found in the Romance (Der eigentliche Kern unserer Poesie liegt im Roman). In their endeavor to make this kernel as tasty as possible, our poets have repeatedly had recourse to a closer or more distant imitation of the Greek Drama.—The topmost flower of that Drama which sprang directly from Romance (Roman), we have in the plays of *Shakespeare*; in the farthest removal from this Drama we find its diametrical opposite in the "Tragédie" of *Racine*.[83]

Hence, if we refer to the diagram again, Shakespeare through "romance" and "play" presents for us the "completed drama" ("vollendetes Drama"). Wagner's further discussion of Shakespeare in this first section of Part II of *Opera and Drama*[84] would appear to support this interpretation with the discussion of romance becoming drama[85] and "phantasy."[86]

Rousseau (1712–78)

We do not know when Wagner first became acquainted with the thought of Rousseau. Although his complete works (eight volumes in French) are in his Wahnfried library, there is *no* Rousseau in Wagner's Dresden Library.[87] However, Rousseau's ideas were so embedded in German Idealism and Romanticism that Wagner would be naturally exposed to his thought and in his autobiography specifically mentions the inspiration Bakunin (whom he knew in Dresden) took from Rousseau.[88] In the extant sources Wagner mentions Rousseau on few occasions and when he does it can be in a negative light.[89] However, he praises Rousseau for his "sympathy with animals"[90] and Heinrich von Stein's article on Rousseau animated him to think about questions of "Erziehung" ("upbringing").[91] Despite this scarcity of references, there are some striking similarities between the thought of Wagner and Rousseau. One regards the origins of music and language.[92] Another possible influence, although this could be disputed, is

---

83. *PW* 2:124; *GSD* 4:6.

84. *PW* 2:124–51; *GSD* 4:6–29.

85. *PW* 2:126; *GSD* 4:8.

86. *PW* 2:129; *GSD* 4:11.

87. Bermbach, *Wahn*, 109 n. 85, claims they were in the Dresden library, but the works he possessed were those of Johann Baptist, not Jean Jacques Rousseau.

88. According to Wagner, Bakunin "had found the pressures of the most blinkered kind of military discipline so insufferable that, inspired by Rousseau's works, he fled to Germany under the pretext of going away on vacation" (*My Life* 385; *Mein Leben* 1:399).

89. *CD* 11 December 1870; 27 March 1882; 1 October 1882.

90. *CD* 11 January 1880.

91. *CD* 25 March 1882; letter to von Stein of 28 May 1882. The article appeared in *Bayreuther Blätter* 3 (December 1881).

92. See volume 2, chapter 4.

Rousseau's view that the decadence of human existence is not owing to "original sin" but rather to living in society.[93]

> That men are actually wicked, a sad and continual experience of them proves beyond doubt: but, all the same, I think I have shown that man is naturally good. What then can have depraved him to such an extent, except the changes that have happened to his constitution, the advances he has made, and the knowledge he has acquired? We may admire human society as much as we please; it will be none the less true that it necessarily leads men to hate each other in proportion as their interests clash, and to do one another apparent services, while they are really doing every imaginable mischief.[94]

Hence, provided one's needs are met, "savage man" can be "at peace with all nature, and the friend of all his fellow-creatures."[95] This idea may have influenced Wagner's portrayal of Siegfried as the free hero who "embodies that long-lost harmony between nature and human conduct."[96] Hence, Siegfried, being brought up in nature, is free and uncorrupted and his problems begin when he enters the society of the Gibichungs with its institutions and contracts.[97] Further, the decay that results from Wotan's exercise of power through law and contract would chime in with Rousseau's idea of social contract.[98] However, rarely can Wagner be neatly placed in any sort of box and I suggest that although Rousseau may well have influenced his portrayal of Siegfried in the earlier stages of the *Ring* (i.e., in *Siegfried's Tod* and *Der junge Siegfried*), there are also views of "original sin" in the *Ring* that he took from Luther and possibly from Schopenhauer. Further, when I discuss Hegel and Wagner's view of the "fall" I will argue that Wagner's views on the "goodness" or "wickedness" of humans beings defies the normal theological categories.

Herder (1744–1803)

Herder was one of the great polymaths of the Aufklärung.[99] Wagner's Dresden library contained Herder's selected works in one volume (1844), a massive collection of his key works including poems, hymns, cantatas, dramatic works, theoretical writings,

---

93. On Rousseau's view of original sin, see Welch, *Protestant Thought*, 1:40.
94. Rousseau, "Inequality," 222.
95. Rousseau, "Inequality," 223.
96. Millington, *Sorcerer*, 102.
97. Cf. Millington, *Sorcerer*, 105.
98. Borchmeyer, *Ahasvers*, 297, who calls this section of his discussion "Wotans Naturfrevel und Contrat social" (295).
99. Forster, *Herder: Philosophical Writings*, xxxv, notes that he has been insufficiently appreciated in Anglophone circles.

and sermons.[100] Wagner does not refer to Herder a great deal in the extant writings[101] but there are many reasons why this German nationalist (cultural rather than political) and admirer of the Reformation[102] would be attractive to the composer. One key reason he could be important for Wagner is that he believed that the earliest language "was meant to sound, not to depict"[103] and was primitive and a direct expression of human emotion, a view Wagner was to develop in relation to song in *Opera and Drama*.[104] This was all related to Herder's revolutionary idea about how language itself was to be understood: words are not simply referential, not simply describing the world, but "are also precipitates of an activity in which the human form of consciousness come to be."[105] Reflection ("Besonnenheit") can only be realized in embodied form, in a medium, and hence "[l]anguage is essential to thought."[106]

One of the few occasions where Herder is mentioned is in relation to a work of Goethe's in which Wagner took much interest: Diderot's *Rameau's Nephew*.[107] Cosima records: "R. observes that no other nation is as stupid as the French, he finds them more and more repellent." But she adds: "All the same, quotations in the *B. Blätter* from [Diderot's] *Le Neveu de Rameau* please him greatly, and the statement of Herder with which this article ends he also finds very striking."[108] This statement, which Ernst Ludwig in this article quotes, is from *Adrastea* (XXIII, 336), part of which is as follows:

> The course of the century will bring us to a man who, despising the cheap peddler's stock of wordless tones, saw the necessity of an intimate combination of purely human feeling, and of the plot itself, with his tones. [. . .] [P]erhaps there will soon be someone who [. . .] will tear down the entire claptrap of operatic jingle (die ganze Bude des zerschnittenen und zerfetzten Opern-Klingklanges umwirft) and erect an Odeum, one connected lyrical structure, in which poetry, music, action, and decoration are one.[109]

---

100. Note that this edition included one of his key works, *Ideen zur Philosophie der Geschichte der Menschheit*; it is named *Ideen zu Geschichte der Menschheit*, in Wagner's edition (*Werke*, 715–963).

101. Cf. *CD* 8 February 1881 tells that Wagner sings Herder's "Herr Oluf reitet spät und weit."

102. Wagner's edition of Herder's *Werke* contained the poems "An den Genius von Deutschland" (107–8), "Deutschlands Ehre" (115), "Luther" (110), "Auf Luthers Bild" (111), and "Reuchlin" (111–12).

103. Herder, "Origin," 91.

104. See *PW* 2:224–25; *GSD* 4:91–92, the discussion in the previous chapter, and that in volume 2, chapter 4 on nature.

105. Taylor, *Hegel*, 19.

106. Taylor, *Hegel*, 20, who points out how important this was to Hegel. Note that for Hegel's antipode, Schopenhauer, thought was more fundamental than language; he was here following Kant (Bell, *Evil*, 149–50).

107. This work of Diderot was first published in 1805 in German translation by Goethe. The original French was then lost but the German was translated back into French and published in 1821. Wagner's edition of Goethe's translation is quite heavily marked (Goethe, *Sämtliche Werke*, 29:206–316).

108. *CD* 23 February 1882.

109. Ludwig, "Neffe," 61–62. This translation is taken from Clark, *Herder*, 429, who thinks

For Wagner this would no doubt be just as prophetic as the words of the Bayreuth writer Jean Paul Richter. In the very year of the composer's birth he wrote in his foreword to E.T.A. Hoffmann's *Fantasiestücke* (in the form of a post-dated review): "for until now the Sun-god [Apollo] has given the gift of poetry with his right hand and that of music with his left to two so widely separated people that we are still waiting up until this moment for the man who can compose both the text and the music for the genuine opera."[110]

Schiller (1749–1805)

Introduction

Friedrich Schiller was not only a poet and playwright but also a philosopher (influenced by Kant), historian, and physician. He influenced Wagner on a whole range of issues, such as his love of the Greeks, his anti-Judaism and antisemitism, his view of the theatre, his aesthetics, and his understanding of nature and the state. There was a family connection in that Wagner's uncle Adolf had in fact met Schiller in Jena.[111] Wagner's Dresden library included Schiller's complete works in a twelve-volume edition (1838)[112] and an edition of the letter exchange with Goethe (1794–1805) in six volumes.[113]

The Greeks

Schiller's interests in the Greeks affected Wagner's views in many respects and here I mention just two: his view of nature and his understanding of tragedy. So first, Wagner, like Schiller, wished to see the re-mythicizing of nature as found in Schiller's poem *Die Götter Griechenlands*.[114] Secondly, he was clearly indebted to Schiller's understanding of the Greek tragedy. A work that was clearly central for Wagner was

---

"undoubtedly, Richard Wagner knew this passage" (430). I can confirm that he did, its quotation by Ludwig proving it. Note also that *Adrastea* was included in Wagner's Herder edition in his Dresden library (*Werke*, 964–1108).

110. *Hoffmann's gesammelte Schriften*, 7:10: "denn bisher warf immer der Sonnengott die Dichtgabe mit der Rechten, die Tongabe mit der Linken zwei so weit aus einander stehenden Menschen zu, daß wir noch bis auf diesen Augenblick auf den Mann harren, der eine ächte Oper zugleich dichtet und setzt." This work was not in Wagner's Dresden library but was in his Wahnfried library. It is interesting that neither Wagner nor anyone else marked this passage in this well used book.

111. *My Life* 9–10; *Mein Leben* 1:16.

112. Note though that volume 5 is missing.

113. Westernhagen, *Bibliothek*, 103. In his Wahnfried library there were a range of works including a 1862 edition of the twelve-volume set and his letter exchange with Goethe (1794–1805) (this was the second edition, 1856, in two volumes, presumably with smaller print; cf. the six-volume edition in Dresden).

114. *FSSW* 1:163–69 (1788); 169–73 (1800). For the way Schiller conceives such a re-mythicizing see *FSSW* 5:708–9 (discussed in Oergel, *Culture*, 36–37). See further volume 2, chapter 4.

Schiller's *Die Braut von Messina*, mentioned at the very beginning of *My Life*.[115] He also tells us that just before going to University he considered composing an overture for the work but abandoned the idea.[116] This drama is particularly significant since Schiller writes this "Trauerspiel" in the form of a Greek tragedy.[117] Wagner considered that the play "re-illumined in age and youth the study of the mighty Greeks"[118] and in this sense felt Schiller had gone beyond what Goethe achieved in *Iphigenia*.[119] Schiller also wrote a significant preface concerning the use of the chorus in the tragedy, a work that clearly influenced the composer.[120] As I discussed in the previous chapter, Wagner argued for the Orchestra having the role of the Greek chorus. In *Music of the Future* he writes that the interest of the Greek chorus "was more of a reflective kind" having "neither part nor lot in action or in motives." But the orchestra of the modern symphonist "will take so intimate an interest in the motives of the plot, that whilst, as embodied harmony, it alone confers on the melody its definite expression, on the other hand it will keep the melody in the requisite unceasing flow, and thus convincingly impress those motives on the Feeling."[121]

Germanness

Schiller's pride in his German heritage naturally attracted Wagner and he no doubt found it significant that Schiller shared his birthday, 10 November, with another German nationalist, Martin Luther.[122] In *German Art and German Policy*, after quoting Schiller's "Deutscher Genius" ("German, strive for Roman strength, for Grecian beauty! Both have sped thee; but never yet the Gallic spring!"),[123] he adds: "Thus Schiller

---

115. Wagner writes that his father, Friedrich, took Wagner's mother to see the first performance of the work in Lauchstädt "and pointed out Schiller and Goethe to her on the promenade" (*My Life* 3; *Mein Leben* 1:9).

116. *My Life* 53; *Mein Leben* 1:61. See also the mention of the work and theatre made out of wood (cf. Bayreuth) for its performance in Lauchstädt (*My Life* 86; *Mein Leben* 1:94).

117. *FSSW* 2:813–912. On this drama (and others of Schiller) as "Trauerspiel," see Benjamin, *Tragic Drama*, 122–23.

118. *PW* 4:107; *GSD* 8:96 (*German Art and German Policy*).

119. *PW* 2:146; *GSD* 4:26.

120. For Schiller's preface see *FSSW* 2:815–23. Borchmeyer, *Theatre*, 61, 167, points to its influence respectively on his understanding of tragedy in *Art and Revolution* and *Artwork of the Future* and the specific role of the chorus in *Prologue to a Reading of Götterdämmerung*.

121. *PW* 3:338; *GSD* 7:130.

122. See, e.g., *CD* 10 November 1878, where the couple toast Luther and Schiller with champagne and later discuss the two figures, Cosima adding that "they could not have been born anywhere except Germany."

123. *FSSW* 1:315: "Ringe, Deutscher, nach römischer Kraft, nach griechischer Schönheit, / Beides gelang dir, doch nie glückte der gallische Sprung." Note, however, that this is from a joint work, namely *Xenien von Schiller und Goethe* (*FSSW* 1:888).

invokes the German genius."¹²⁴ There then follows a discussion of Goethe and Schiller whose Weimar project was to have such influence on the composer.¹²⁵

Earlier in the same essay, when writing of the rebirth of German art, he again quotes Schiller, this time the first stanza of *Die deutsche Muse*: "No Augustan age's flower, / No Medici's bounteous power, / Smiled upon our German Art; / She was never nursed in lustre, / Opened wide her blossoms' cluster / Ne'er for royal Princes' mart."¹²⁶

Christianity superseding Judaism

Schiller gave "the fullest debunking of Moses," describing the Jews in their Egyptian exile "as a contemptible, degenerate, and probably leprous people,"¹²⁷ and he contributed significantly to the general atmosphere of anti-Judaism and antisemitism in Germany.¹²⁸ Schiller thought Christianity the noblest and highest religion, praised it for superseding the law¹²⁹ and the Kantian imperative, and considered it to be "the only *aesthetic* religion."¹³⁰

These views were shared by Wagner, and Schiller may well have had some influenced in this respect. In *Public and Popularity* (1878) Wagner relates his own denigration of Judaism and promotion of Christianity to Schiller's *The Maid of Orleans*, one of his favorite plays. He tells Cosima that he read it to his sister Rosalie when he was twelve¹³¹ and he is in tears after reading with Cosima through to the end of Act I: "As Goethe touches us through his objectivity, Schiller touches us through subjectivity."¹³² The logic in Wagner's essay is not entirely clear but it appears to run as follows. In the third chapter of *Public and Popularity* (published in August 1878) Wagner asks whether

---

124. *PW* 4:86; *GSD* 8:76.

125. *PW* 4:86–90; *GSD* 8:76–79. See below.

126. *PW* 4:40; *GSD* 8:33. Schiller's second strophe (the reference is to Frederick the Great) stresses the intrinsic value of German art: "Von dem größten deutschen Sohne, / Von des großen Friedrichs Throne / Ging sie schutzlos, ungeehrt. / Rühmend darfs der Deutsche sagen, / Höher darf das Herz ihm schlagen: / *Selbst* erschuf er sich den Wert" (*FSSW* 1:214). The third strophe takes a side swipe at French poetry rules!

127. Robertson, *Jewish Question*, 24.

128. See his 1790 lecture "Die Sendung Moses," in *FSSW* 4:783–804, where he argues that Moses as "a well-intentioned charlatan" learned monotheism from the Egyptians and hence the Jews must be considered "as a mean and unclean vessel in which something precious was preserved"; and once the truth of monotheism was brought to us the unclean vessel can then be broken (784). See further, Hartwich, *Die Sendung Moses*, 21–49.

129. He writes of the "supersession of the law" ("Aufhebung des Gesetzes") and he contrasts other monotheistic religions, clearly having Judaism in his sights.

130. See Schiller's letter to Goethe (17 August 1795), Seidel, *Briefwechsel I*, 94–95; cf, Boyle, *Goethe*, 2:268. Wagner marked this passage in his own copy (*Briefwechsel*, 1:194).

131. *CD* 9 January 1870. Note though the critical comments of *Maid of Orleans CD* 26 July 1878—but he remembers how it "moved him indescribably" in his youth.

132. *CD* 29 May 1870.

"the State's extravagant outlay on higher educational establishments can afford a single hope of beneficial influence on the Folk itself." The problem with theologians is that they have identified the "God of our Saviour" with "the tribal god of Israel"[133] and have been out of touch with the sort of people Jesus made himself known to, "poor Galilean shepherds and fisherman."[134] There are two types of critical mind and they can be represented by Voltaire's "filthy poem" *La Pucelle d'Orléans*[135] and Schiller's portrayal of the virgin. Voltaire, like the professional academic, employed "the historical documents of his day." Schiller, on the other hand, turned to "inspiration."

> This Jeanne d'Arc was virgin, and necessarily, because in her all natural instinct, miraculously reversed, had become the heroic bent to save her country. Behold the infant Christ on the arms of the Sistine Madonna. What our Schiller was given to recognise in the wondrous freer of her fatherland, had here been shewn to Raphael in the theologically defaced and travestied Redeemer of the world (für den theologisch entstellten und unkenntlich gewordenen Erlöser der Welt aufgegangen). See there the babe, with eyes that stream on you the sunrays of determinate and sorely-lacked redemption (den Sonnenblick des nun unerläßlich gewordenen Erlösungs-Entschlusses ausstrahlen); and far beyond you, to the world itself; and farther still, beyond all worlds yet known (über alle erkennbare Welt): then ask yourselves if this "*means*" or "*is*"?[136]

Hence Wagner implies that Voltaire corresponds to Zwingli ("es bedeutet") but Schiller corresponds to Luther ("es ist"). In the next paragraph the logic is that since science destroys the idea of the creator God,[137] theology should turn to Jesus alone. "Is it so utterly impossible to Theology, to take the great step that would grant to Science its irrefutable truths through surrender of Jehova, and to the Christian world its pure God revealed in Jesus the only [one]?"[138] He ends by again contrasting the rich and powerful with the poor, believing that with Christ's second advent "our Historical science [. . .] would also have come to end" and "Theology would by then have come to a final agreement with the Gospels, and the free understanding of Revelation be opened to us without Jehovaistic subtleties—for which the Saviour promised us his coming

---

133. *PW* 6:77; *GSD* 10:86.

134. *PW* 6:78; *GSD* 10:87.

135. This controversial poem was in volume 1 of Voltaire's collected works, which was in Wagner's Wahnfried library.

136. *PW* 6:79; *GSD* 10:88. Sistine Madonna is an altarpiece commissioned in 1512 by Pope Julius II for the church of San Sisto, Piacenza. It was moved to Dresden in 1754.

137. *PW* 6:77; *GSD* 10:86: "Science makes God the creator more impossible each day; but from the beginning of the Church the God revealed to us by Jesus has been converted by the Theologians from a most sublime reality into an ever less intelligible problem."

138. *PW* 6:79; *GSD* 10:88.

back (seine Wiederkehr)."[139] This "deepest Knowledge" corresponds to the "true Art" we find in Schiller's *Maid of Orleans*.[140]

Ode to Joy

Beethoven's *Ninth Symphony* was performed on the morning of the laying of the foundation stone for Wagner's Bayreuth theatre on his fifty-ninth birthday (22 May 1872)[141] and the work was again performed when the theatre reopened after the Second World War.[142] Reflecting on his 1876 *Ring* and the foundation ceremony he considered the work to be "the foundation-stone of my own artistic structure."[143]

This fascination with the symphony goes back to his teens when he produced a piano transcription for the work. The work then featured in his *Pilgrimage to Beethoven* where he has Beethoven speaking of "Schiller's beautiful hymn 'To Joy,'" "a noble and inspiring poem."[144] Then Wagner wrote a programme for the symphony's 1846 Dresden performance, using Goethe's *Faust* as a commentary (see below) and in 1873 published an essay on how to perform the work.[145]

The symphony can be understood as a key stage in the Hegelian development from "absolute music" to music drama; indeed, Wagner probably saw the Hegelian development within the symphony itself. In his 1846 programme notes for the final movement, he writes of how the recitative of the bass strings (and then the entry of the bass singer) breaks the bounds of "absolute music":[146] "It is wonderful how the master makes the arrival of Man's voice and tongue a positive necessity, by this awe-inspiring recitative of the bass-strings; almost breaking the bounds of absolute music already, it stems the tumult of the other instruments with its virile eloquence [. . .]"[147] The music of the opening of the fourth movement with its deliberately ugly opening and the instrumental recitative bears little resemblance to anything we hear in his next Opera, *Lohengrin*; however, it is certainly there in key passages in the *Ring*. Wagner clearly saw a special connection between Beethoven's *Ninth* and the *Ring*, both works being ultimately "optimistic"; although the *Ring* is a "tragedy" it is in fact an "optimistic

---

139. PW 6:80–81; GSD 10:89.

140. PW 6:81; GSD 10:89–90.

141. Bauer, *Bayreuther Festspiele*, 1:43–44.

142. It was also performed on 10 August 2001, the 125th anniversary of the festival and twentieth anniversary of "Neubayreuth" (Bauer, *Bayreuther Festspiele*, 2:526).

143. PW 6:98; GSD 10:104.

144. PW 7:42; GSD 1:111.

145. *The Rendering of Beethoven's Ninth Symphony*, PW 5:229–53; GSD 9:231–57.

146. Although the idea of "absolute music" had been around since the end of the eighteenth century the term was first coined by Wagner in these programme notes (Dahlhaus, *Absolute Music*, 18). He continued to use the term in essays and letters, often in the context of discussing Beethoven (see below).

147. PW 7:252; GSD 2:61.

tragedy," a view already seen in my discussion of Wagner and Greek tragedy and will again be seen when we look closely at Hegel's influence on the composer. Further, he described the symphony as "the *most complete Drama*" ("*das vollendetste Drama*"),[148] to which we can compare "Completed Drama" ("Vollendetes Drama") of the diagram he drew for Uhlig (see Figure 5.1, 5.2 above).

The importance of Beethoven's setting of Schiller's poem for the *Ring* can be discerned in *Opera and Drama* part III where he discusses the relation of the words of Schiller's poem to questions of the music. Beethoven's "patriarchal melody" is "for *fixing* the Feeling (zur *Bestimmung* des Gefühles)" and "did not arise *from out* the poem of Schiller, but rather was invented outside the word-verse and merely spread above it."[149] "This aim was a necessary one for Absolute Music, which does not stand on a basis of Poetry."[150] He then discusses the distinction between the "patriarchal melody" and "the melody which grows forth upon the word-verse through the working of the Poetic Aim."[151]

> Once that with this simple, straightened melody he feels the Poet's hand within his own, he strides towards the poem itself; and from out this poem—shaping after its spirit and its form—he passes forward to an even bolder and more manifold building of his tones: at last to set before us wonders such as we had never dreamt of, wonders such as the "*Seid umschlungen, Millionen!*," the "*Ahnest du den Schöpfer, Welt?*" and finally the un-misunderstandable combination of the "*Seid umschlungen*" and the "*Freude, schöner Götterfunken!*"—all arisen from the puissance of *poetic* (*dichtenden*) tone-speech.[152]

Wagner again returned to discuss Schiller's poem in his Beethoven essay (1870) with sentiments that cohere with the *Ring*, in particular his views on "nature" and "civilization": "In Schiller's poem, which he sets to the wonderful last movement of the Ninth Symphony, he above all recognized the joy of nature freed from the rule of fashion (die Freude der von der Herrschaft der 'Mode' befreiten Natur). Let us consider his remarkable conception of the poet's words: 'Your magic again binds together/ What fashion rigidly separated (Was die Mode streng getheilt).'"[153] Wagner notes the variants: "What the sword of fashion separated!"[154] which makes fashion "too loft and heroic" and then what "now we sing: 'What fashion *brazenly* (*frech*) separated!'"[155] This last reading he thinks reflects "*Luther* in his anger against the Pope!" and it is

---

148. Allen, *Beethoven*, 157; *GSD* 9:111; cf. *PW* 5:112.
149. *PW* 2:289; *GSD* 4:149–50.
150. *PW* 2:289; *GSD* 4:150.
151. *PW* 2:290; *GSD* 4:151.
152. *PW* 2:290; *GSD* 4:150.
153. Allen, *Beethoven*, 182–83. Cf. *GSD* 2:64.
154. This is the form in Schiller's poem: "Was der Mode Schwerd getheilt" (*SWNA* 1:169; *FSSW* 1:133); this was changed to "Was die Mode streng geteilt" (*SWNA* 2.IIA:147).
155. Allen, *Beethoven*, 184–85.

highly significant that he then goes on to discuss the renewal of "civilization" through being freed from the "bonds of fashion."[156]

There is though one aspect of Schiller's poem (which Beethoven used) that would later conflict with Wagner's theology: the creator God.[157] In view of Wagner's negative views on a creator God (see above), it is not surprising to see him distancing himself from the God of Schiller's poem in his New Year message for 1880, where he contrasts the God "above the starry tent" ("über'm Sternenzelt") of Schiller's poem with the "god within the human breast" who needs no heavenly home.[158] However, in his programme notes for the 1846 performance, there a positive appropriation of the creator God of Schiller's poem.[159] Further, he thinks that such an idea can only be grasped when set to music. Towards the end of *Religion and Art* he quotes "Ahnest du den Schöpfer, Welt?" ("Knowest thy Creator, world?") adding: "so cries the Poet, obliged to hazard an anthropomorphic metaphor for That which words can ne'er convey." In contrast "the Tone-poet seer reveals to us the Inexpressible."[160] This Tone-poet seer on one level could be Beethoven, setting (and selecting)[161] Schiller's words to music; but the obvious person is, of course, Wagner himself.

Theatre and state

As well as taking great pleasure in the plays,[162] Schiller was also important for Wagner's understanding of the theatre itself. Both had "a vision of the theatre as a potential engine of social amelioration"[163] and in particular Wagner was attracted to his ideas on art and the state. In *Shall we Hope?* first published in May 1879 in *Bayreuther*

---

156. Allen, *Beethoven*, 184–87.

157. It is interesting though that a half-verse of the "choir" (in the latter part of the poem which was not used by Beethoven) suggests a "creator God" whose divinity could be seen as down-played: "Brüder—überm Sternenzelt / Richtet Gott, wie wir gerichtet" (*FSSW* 1:135).

158. *PW* 6:34; *GSD* 10:30.

159. *PW* 7:254; *GSD* 2:64.

160. *PW* 6:250; *GSD* 10:250.

161. Schiller's poem (*FSSW* 1:133–36) consists of nine verses (of eight lines) each of which is followed by a chorus of four lines. Beethoven uses just the first three verses and the first, third, and fourth choruses. He also prefaced the poem with "O Freunde, nicht diese Töne! Sondern lasst uns angenehmere anstimmen, und freudenvollere!"

162. For example, *CD* 17–20, 29 January 1883 tells us that Richard and Cosima read and reflect upon *Don Carlos*. They both admired *Wallenstein* (*CD* 13–21 May 1869) and Cosima's own thoughts on the work are worth considering (*CD* 18 January 1869). In Wagner's Schiller collection *Wallenstein* stands out as being heavily marked. But these many minor markings in *Wallensteins Lager* and the first half of *Die Piccolomini* (together with a few in *Wallensteins Tod*) would appear to be made by another hand. One possibility is that the set of originally twelve volumes was lent out by Heinrich Brockhaus to someone who made these markings (possibly for a new *Wallenstein* edition) and later returned them but as an eleven volume set (volume 5 is missing).

163. Millington, "Gesamtkunstwerk," 48. Millington (47) quotes from Schiller's 1784 lecture *Wie kann eine gute stehende Schaubühne eigentlich wirken?* (*SWNA* 20.1:100).

Blätter, Wagner writes that he is not the first "who has declared our *State* incapable of promoting Art; rather does our great Schiller seem to me the first to have recognized and described our State-machinery as *barbaric* and utterly inimical to Art."[164] The text Wagner most likely has in mind is the Ninth Letter of Schiller's *Aesthetic Education*. Selections from *Aesthetic Education* were quoted in Glasenapp's contribution to the *Bayreuther Blätter* just two months earlier (March 1879), the most relevant being this: "All improvement in the political sphere is to proceed from the ennobling of character—but how under the influence of a barbarous constitution (unter den Einflüssen einer barbarischen Staatsverfassung) is character ever to become ennobled? To this end we should, presumably, have to seek out some instrument not provided by the State. [...] This instrument is Fine Art (die schöne Kunst); such living springs are opened up in its immortal examplars."[165] Although *Shall we Hope?* is a late essay there are clear parallels to the ideas of the Zurich essays.[166] A little later in this essay Wagner understands Schiller's "barbaric" in the light of Luther's translation of 1 Corinthians 14:11, a verse that concerns a tongue one does not understand. He discusses the Greek "barbaros," rendered by the Latin "barbarus" which, he argues, simply came to mean in that language "uncivilised and lawless foreign races." This translation is then followed by others (he gives the example of the French "barbare").[167] But Luther renders "barbaros" as "undeutsch" thereby giving "a milder, unaggressive aspect to our attitude towards the foreign." So the verse is translated: "If I know not the meaning (Deutung) of the voice, I shall be *undeutsch* to him that speaketh, and he that speaketh will be *undeutsch* to me." Wagner argues that Luther has given us the "inner meaning even more aptly than the original itself, for it sets 'Deutung' and 'Deutsch' in direct relation."[168] He then further develops this a few pages on: "neither Gideon, Samuel or Joshua, nor the God Zebaoth of the fiery bush, do we need to help us when we call awake the German Spirit in our bosoms, and strive our best to do its work. We simply have to prove all habits and opinions ruling us, and clear them of what is 'barbaric'—according to Schiller—according to Luther 'undeutsch'; for in 'German' alone can we be true to ourselves and sincere."[169]

Wagner had clearly gone beyond what Schiller intended by "barbarian" and was largely dependent on Glasenapp's selection. Glasenapp also quoted a passage from letter VIII which concerned the "barbarian."[170] But the key passage is a little earlier in

164. PW 6:116 (modified); GSD 10:121.

165. I quote from Wilkinson and Willoughby, *Aesthetic Education*, 54–55. Glasenapp, "Aus Schillers Briefen," 79–80, is translated by Ellis, PW 6:116 n. Note that Glasenapp has edited Schiller and adds emphasis (and there are typographical errors throughout the article).

166. Ellis in PW 6:116 n.

167. One can add that the King James Bible has "barbarian."

168. PW 6:123; GSD 10:128–29.

169. PW 6:126; GSD 10:132.

170. Glasenapp, "Aus Schillers Briefen," 79: "Die Philosophie selbst, welche uns zuerst von der *Natur* abtrünnig machte, ruft uns laut und dringend in ihren Schoss zurück—*wovon liegt es, dass*

letter IV and suggests that Schiller's understanding of the "barbarian" was more subtle than both Wagner (and Glasenapp) appreciated.

> But man can be at odds with himself in two ways: either as savage (Wilder), when feeling (Gefühl) predominates over principle; or as barbarian (Barbar), when principle destroys feeling. The savage despises Civilisation (Kunst), and acknowledges Nature as his sovereign mistress. The barbarian derides and dishonours Nature, but, more contemptible than the savage, as often as not continues to be the slave of his slave. The man of Culture (Der gebildete Mensch) makes a friend of Nature, and honours her freedom (Freiheit) whilst curbing only her caprice (Willkür).[171]

Hence, it is in *this* sense of destroying feeling (Gefühl) that the state is "barbarian." For Schiller the solution to the problem is in moral and aesthetic education. As Sturma writes: "One should make nature a friend and exert control only over its arbitrariness. Under the condition of a moral and aesthetic education it becomes possible to transform the state of need (Notstaat) into a state of freedom. [. . .] Following Rousseau, Schiller argues for the idea of a new community that overcomes the egoists' *Notstaat*."[172]

Wagner's idea of Bayreuth was indebted to the Weimar of Schiller and Goethe. He not only considered Goethe and Schiller "the two greatest German poets"[173] but also "saw himself as the direct, legitimate heir of Weimar Classicism."[174] He speaks of "the Weimar wonder" ("das Weimarische Wunder")[175] and came to see that for his own miracle he would, like Schiller, need an aesthetic nobility to support his cause. Borchmeyer, referring to *Über naïve und sentimentalische Dichtung*, writes: "Like Wagner, Schiller imagines a new kind of nobility: the aesthetic restoration of certain basic aristocratic values was, after all, an essential part of the social ideal of Weimar Classicism."[176] It was noted in chapter 2 that in his 1848 *Vaterlandsverein* (Fatherland Society) speech Wagner wished to abolish the aristocracy; but Schiller could show why it is necessary for a "revolutionary" to esteem "aristocratic values."[177]

---

wir noch immer Barbaren sind?" ("Philosophy itself, which first seduced us from our allegiance to Nature, is now in loud and urgent tones calling us back to her bosom. How is it, then, that we still remain barbarians?") I have corrected the typographical errors and included Glasenapp's emphasis. Cf. Wilkinson and Willoughby, *Aesthetic Education*, 48–51.

171. Wilkinson and Willoughby, *Aesthetic Education*, 20–21. Note Schiller's vocabulary is similar to that of Wagner's Zurich writings (e.g., Willkür).

172. Sturma, "Politics and the New Mythology," 316.

173. *PW* 3:301; *GSD* 7:94 (*Zukunftsmusik*).

174. Borchmeyer, *Theatre*, 81.

175. *PW* 4:45; *GSD* 8:38. Borchmeyer, "Liszt und Wagner," 72.

176. Borchmeyer, *Theatre*, 11. See *FSSW* 5:768. I will return to this work of Schiller in volume 2, chapter 12.

177. Although Schiller in principle supported the French revolution he was appalled by the subsequent atrocities. "The drive behind [the *Aesthetic Letters*] is [Schiller's] belief that any reform which

Goethe (1749–1832)

Wagner's knowledge of Goethe

In his famous "Morning confession" to Mathilde Wesendonck (7 April 1858) Wagner wrote: "Göthe for me is a gift of nature by means of which I learn to understand the world, and in this he is almost unique."[178] Goethe was indeed a fundamental influence on Wagner with respect to nature,[179] and a whole range of issues regarding theatre, drama, the Greeks, etc. In his Dresden Library he possessed a forty-volume edition (1840) of the complete collected works[180] and his Wahnfried library had a range of works including a new edition (1857–58) of the complete works in thirty-volumes, the Goethe-Schiller correspondence of 1794–1805,[181] and a German translation of George Lewes' book on Goethe's life and work.[182] Like Wagner, Goethe appropriated so many diverse literary traditions, had no tight philosophical system as such, and was concerned to relate art in its broadest sense to religion and philosophy.[183]

The composer's interests in Goethe go back to at least 1830. In *Die Rote Brieftasche* he notes that in that year he started his "Schäferoper,"[184] and in his autobiography[185] he says he was guided by Goethe's Schäferspiel (pastoral play) "Die Laune des Verliebten"[186] for which his sister Luise played Egle in the Leipzig Theatre.[187]

Of Goethe's works the most significant was *Faust*. Wagner's copy in the Dresden library is marked very little but he may have known the work by heart (or at least the

---

is to endure can only proceed from a change in man's whole way of thinking" (Wilkinson and Willoughby, *Aesthetic Education*, xx, referring to his letter to the Duke of Augustenburg, 13 July 1793).

178. *SL* 383; *SB* 9:230: "mir ist Goethe wie ein Naturgeschenck, durch welches ich die Welt erkennen lerne, wie durch wenig andere."

179. See volume 2, chapter 4, where I focus on nature.

180. Westernhagen, *Bibliothek*, 90.

181. See, e.g., *CD* 6 June 1870, where Cosima reads this out to her husband.

182. There is no evidence that Wagner read this. Cosima read it (*CD* 1, 2, 4, 6, 7, 16 April 1869) but considered it "wretched" despite the subject matter. The Wagners were later to meet Lewes (and George Eliot) in London (*CD* 7, 14, 17 May 1877).

183. A passage from *Dichtung und Wahrheit* is illuminating and could easily have appeared in Wagner's *My Life*: "When my friend [his guardian] saw that I got nothing at all from his dogmatic lectures, he was compelled to study the history of philosophy with me, and I actually found this very diverting, but only in the sense that all the teaching and opinions [. . .] seemed equal in value to me. What pleased me most about the oldest philosophers and schools was their amalgamation of poetry, religion, and philosophy, and I reiterated my original opinion the more vehemently when it was apparently borne out by the Book of Job, the Song of Solomon, the Proverbs, and also by Orphic and Hesiodic lays" (Saine/Sammons, *Poetry and Truth*, 171–72; *GWJA* 5:200–201).

184. *SB* 1:81.

185. *My Life* 33; *Mein Leben* 1:40.

186. "Guided by Goethe's *Die Laune des Verliebten* as far as form and content were concerned, I drafted little more than a synopsis of the text and began writing the poetry together with the music and its instrumentation one page at a time [. . .]."

187. Werner Wolf in the notes in *SB* 1:86 n. 19.

key passages of Part I). As we shall see there are innumerable references to this work throughout the composer's creative life and the way *Faust* became the very fabric of their lives together can be seen in the fact that allusions to *Faust* even enter when they have the builders at work on their villa.[188]

Compositions on *Faust*

In 1831 he produced his "Compositionen zu Faust,"[189] probably inspired by the first Leipzig performance of *Faust* (1831) in which his sister Rosalie played Gretchen.[190] He set to music seven "songs" from *Faust* Part I: "Lied der Soldaten" and "Bauer unter der Linde" from *Vor dem Tor*; "Branders Lied" and "Lied des Mephistopheles" ("Es war einmal ein König") from *Auerbachs Keller in Leipzig*; "Lied des Mephistopheles" ("Was machst du mir vor Liebchens Tür") from *Nacht* (*Straße vor Gretchens Türe*); "Gretchen am Spinnrade"; "Melodram" from *Zwinger*.[191] The last two scenes (Spinnrade; Zwinger) are theologically important since they present the guilt of Gretchen which forms the theological backdrop for the ending of *Faust* Part I.

When he was in Paris he composed his *Faust Overture*. Although he relates the composition to hearing Beethoven's *Ninth*,[192] and as we shall see he wrote a commentary on the symphony based on Goethe's *Faust*,[193] he was most likely inspired by Berlioz[194] and the work has musical associations not so much with Beethoven's *Ninth* but rather with the Overtures to Coriolanus and Freischütz.[195] In the text of the

---

188. *CD* 23 October 1878: "The weather is very wet; the *lemurs* are working here, that is to say, a canal is being dug around the house to dry it out; we think of *Faust*, the splendor of its poetry!" The Lemurs (ghosts of the dead) appear in *Faust* Part II Act V at the time of Faust's death (Luke, *Faust II*, 221–24).

189. *SB* 1:81.

190. Again, see Werner Wolf's comments in *SB* 1:86 n. 23.

191. The texts can be found in *GWJA* 3:38, 40, 75–76, 78–79, 132, 121–22, 129–30. See *WWV* 72–74 and Deathridge, "Kompositionen."

192. *My Life* 174–75; *Mein Leben* 1:185–86. He heard the rehearsals with the Orchestra de la Société des Concerts du Conservatoire under François Habeneck. See also "The Work and Mission of my Life" (1879), which was written by Wolzogen, but although Wagner felt compelled to sign it he considered it "very immature" (*CD* 1 May 1879).

193. See his programme for the Dresden performance of 1846 discussed below.

194. Deathridge, "Kompositionen," 92, 94. *My Life* 191–92 (*Mein Leben* 1:202) relates how Wagner was impressed by the Romeo and Juliet Symphony (together with *Harold en Italie*, *Symphonie fantastique* and *Grande symphonie funèbre et triomphale*) but fails to relate this to his Faust Overture. Deathridge, "Kompositionen," 94 points out that Wagner attended the first or second performance of *Romeo and Juliet* on 24 November or 1 December 1839 (there was a third performance on 15 December but Voss, *Faust-Ouvertüre*, 9, points to Wagner being unwell at that time). It is not insignificant that the first sketch for the *Faust Overture* was dated 13 December 1839 and the score 12 January 1840. Further, Deathridge, points out that the score uses French instrument names and has a typical orchestration used by Berlioz (e.g., four bassoons, but changed to three in the revised version).

195. Voss, *Faust-Ouvertüre*, 8–9.

first version ("1. Fassung") we find the title "Der einsame Faust. (oder: Faust in der Einsamkeit) / ein Tongedicht für das Orchester / von / Richard Wagner / (Paris im Jahre 1840)." This, however, was most likely added in 1852.[196] If the overture concerns Faust in his loneliness then he must have in mind Night (scene 4); Study (I) (scene 6), central though it was for Wagner with Faust's translating John 1:1, clearly does not fit. But for the score for the "2. Fassung" (second version) he turns to Study (II) and on the first page quotes from the end of Faust's speech (ll. 1544–71) where he despairs of his condition, alluding to the book of Job[197] (1566–71): "And though a god lives in my heart, / Though all my powers waken at his word, / Though he can move my every inmost part— / Yet nothing in the outer world is stirred. / Thus by existence tortured and oppressed / I crave for death, I long for rest."[198] There were many occasions when Wagner, despite his general optimistic outlook on life, would identify with Faust's bitter discontent and even despair.

Commentary on Beethoven's *Ninth*

On Palm Sunday (5 April) in 1846 Wagner conducted Beethoven's *Ninth* in Dresden and since the earlier performances in 1838 (27 August and 7 November), conducted by Carl Reissiger, had not gone well, and should the assumed obscure style of the late Beethoven take any blame,[199] it appears that Wagner felt that he should explicate the work and set about writing a commentary, making extensive use of *Faust*. He explains in the opening paragraph that Goethe's verses can provide a key since they "express so sublimely the higher human spiritual moods underlying the work."[200] Further one could add to this that just as *Faust* is remarkably "musical"[201] the *Ninth* for Wagner was, as he

---

196. See the letter to Liszt of 9 November 1852 (*SL* 272; *SB* 5:96) where he refers to the "Ouvertüre zu Faust" and "Faust in der Einsamkeit" ("Faust in Solitude"). See also his letter to Uhlig of 27 November 1852 (*SB* 5:122–23). These letters also indicate that Wagner intended a second movement to focus on Gretchen. See Deathridge, "Kompositionen," 98, who also gives the sketch (99).

197. Durrani, *Faust*, 68.

198. Luke, *Faust I*, 48. *GWJA* 3:58: "Der Gott, der mir im Busen wohnt, / Kann tief mein Innerstes erregen; / Der über allen meinen Kräften thront, / Er kann nach außen nichts bewegen; / Und so ist mir das Dasein eine Last, / Der Tod erwünscht, das Leben mir verhasst" (SW 18.III:1). Wagner quotes this "Motto" for the overture in his letter to Liszt 19 January 1855 (*BWL* 2:50; *SL* 325; *SB* 6:329).

199. Cf. Vazsonyi, *Self-Promotion*, 66–68.

200. Translation of Grey, "Program Notes, 481; *GSD* 2:56–57; cf. *PW* 7:247.

201. As well as the various "songs" there are liturgical elements as in the "Easter Hymn" ("Nacht") and "Dies Irae" ("Dom"). Note also "Tiefe Nacht" in *Faust II* Act V, where the stage direction reads "Lynkeus, der Türmer *auf der Schloßwarte, singend*" ("Lynceus the Watchman, on the castle tower, singing") (*GWJA* 3:379; Luke, *Faust II*, 214). Steiner, *Tragedy*, 200, points to Goethe's suggestion to Eckermann that the second half of Act III should be performed by singers.

later put it, "*the most complete drama.*"[202] Also, more importantly, both works were not only "spiritual" but specifically concerned redemption in their own way.[203]

For the first movement Wagner quotes two texts from "Studierzimmer II,"[204] for the second two texts from "Studierzimmer II,"[205] and "Auerbachs Keller,"[206] for the third two texs from "Nacht,"[207] and for the fourth from "Studierzimmer I"[208] and again "Nacht."[209] He then turns to discuss Schiller's poem (and Beethoven's own introductory couplet), but when he comes to discussing the instrumental canon (bars 431–542) he inserts a final reference to *Faust*, this time from Part II:[210] "Only that man earns freedom, merits life, / Who must reconquer both in constant daily strife." ("Nur der verdient sich Freiheit wie das Leben, / Der täglich sie erobern muß.") Then a few lines later (after l. 11586) Faust dies, the lemurs lay him on the ground, and Mephistopheles, echoing Luther's translation of John 19:30, assumes "All is fulfilled" ("es ist vollbracht").[211]

Goethe, Weimar, and Liszt

One of the many ways Liszt advanced Wagner's career was in conducting the first performance of *Lohengrin*. This had a double Goethe connection: it was performed in Weimar[212] on Goethe's birthday, 28 August 1850. Liszt shared Wagner's enthusiasm for Goethe,[213] composing a Symphonic Poem *Tasso*, based on Goethe's *Torquato Tasso*.[214] But his greatest work inspired by Goethe was the *Faust Symphony*, premiered for

---

202. Allen, *Beethoven*, 157 (cf. *PW* 9:112); *GSD* 9:111.

203. See Allen's "Introduction," in *Beethoven*, 22.

204. *GSD* 2:57; *GWJA* 3:58 (l. 1549); Luke, *Faust I*, 48. *GSD* 2:58; *GWJA* 3:58 (ll. 1554–65); Luke, *Faust I*, 48.

205. *GSD* 2:58; cf. Luke, *Faust I*, 54; *GWJA* 3:64 (ll. 1765–67). Luke, *Faust I*, 53; *GWJA* 3:63–64 (ll. 1750–59).

206. *GSD* 2:59; *GWJA* 3:76 (ll. 2161–63); Luke, *Faust I*, 65. Note that these words are found between two songs Wagner set to music: "Branders Lied" and "Lied des Mephistopheles."

207. *GSD* 2:59; *GWJA* 3:35 (ll. 771–74); Luke, *Faust I*, 26. *GSD* 2:59; *GWJA* 3:35 (ll. 775–78); Luke, *Faust I*, 26.

208. *GSD* 2:60. There is a slight change to *GWJA* 3:48 (ll. 1210–11); Luke, *Faust I*, 38.

209. *GSD* 2:60; *GWJA* 3:35; (ll. 782–84); Luke, *Faust I*, 26.

210. *GSD* 2:63; *GWJA* 3:388 (ll. 11575–76); Luke, *Faust II*, 223.

211. *GWJA* 3:388; Luke, *Faust II*, 223–24.

212. Liszt was appointed Hofkapellmeister in the Weimar court 1842 and lived there from 1848 to 1861 and, after his time in Rome, returned in 1869, where he remained (with breaks) until shortly before his death in 1886.

213. Both were concerned to found a "Goethestiftung." Liszt sent Wagner the proofs of his plans for the Stiftung, *De la Fondation Goethe à Weimar*, which was published by F. A. Brockhaus in February 1851. Wagner's detailed reply (8 May 1851; *SB* 4:42) was, with minor modifications, published in the *Neue Zeitschrift für Musik* 36.10 (5 March 1852). See *PW* 3:7–22.

214. This was first performed in Weimar for the celebration of the centenary of Goethe's birth, on 28 August 1849.

the dedication of the Goethe-Schiller Denkmal on 5 September 1857. Wagner greatly admired the work: "If anything had convinced me of the man's masterly and poetical powers of conception, it was the original ending (der ursprüngliche Schluß) of the *Faust* Symphony, in which the delicate fragrance of a last reminiscence of Gretchen overpowers everything, without arresting the attention by a violent disturbance."[215] Discounting the very first note (Ab) of the Symphony we have in bars 2–3 a series of four augmented broken triads 'mathematically' arranged such that each of the four drops down by a semitone on each successive occasion thereby tracing out the "Twelve Note Row": G B Eb / F# Bb D / F A C# / E G# C. Wagner alludes to this in each of the three acts of *Die Walküre*. It is in Act II (Scene 5) that the allusion to Liszt can be most clearly recognized, especially since the orchestration is similar.[216]

Theatre

Wagner considered Goethe the greatest German poet and among all dramatists his only rivals in Wagner's judgement were Aeschylus and Shakespeare. The "Prelude in the Theatre" from *Faust* part I was significant for the composer. Cosima records on 24 July 1872: "In a constant state of bliss at the thought of the completion of *Götterdämmerung*, I read Goethe's dedication (Zueignung) and then the two prologues [to *Faust*]; when I tell R. of my rapturous feelings regarding these, he says, 'Yes, all the art of the future (das ganze Kunstwerk der Zukunft) is connected with the Prologue on the Stage—it is all in there.'" There are various allusions to the "Prelude in the Theatre" in *On Actors and Singers*. For example, quoting the Director's lines, Wagner mocks opera houses "in which the audience feasts its eyes upon itself before all else, and where 'the ladies lend their dress and persons for an unpaid role.'"[217] And then quoting from the Director's final line he speaks of how the theatre could set the spectator "in a world of magic where the scene is changed before his eyes 'from heaven through earth with all due speed to hell.'"[218]

Faust, like the *Ring* cycle, was composed over extensive periods: for the *Ring* we are dealing with twenty-six years (1848–1874); for *Faust* we are dealing with around sixty-one years (c. 1770–1831). If the *Ring* is criticized for contradictions or lack of cohesion, compared to *Faust* it is remarkably internally consistent and cohesive. Commenting on *Faust*, Wagner told Cosima: "It is really just a sort of sketch [. . .] which Goethe himself looked upon in puzzlement, as a curiosity—he himself did not

---

215. *My Life* 537; *Mein Leben* 2:551. Note that Wagner here stresses Gretchen rather than the Mater gloriosa. Liszt in fact changed the ending in 1857, adding the Chorus Mysticus (marked Andante mistico) for tenor and male chorus (Walker, *Liszt II*, 334–35).

216. Liszt has muted violas and cellos; Wagner has muted violas.

217. *PW* 5:195; *GSD* 9:196 (cf. Luke, *Faust I*, 6 (ll. 119–20)).

218. *PW* 5:194; *GSD* 9:195 (cf. Luke, *Faust I*, 9 (l. 242)).

consider it a finished work of art"[219] But one fundamental difference between the two works is that whereas Wagner needed his tetralogy to be performed, Goethe appears not to be interested in having *Faust* staged, even though he was a director of the Weimar theatre. Although *Faust I* was published in 1808 it was not staged until 1829 when Goethe was over eighty and then it was severely cut. *Faust II* was not intended to be performed at all and indeed Goethe did not want it published until after his death (it was in fact completed just before he died).[220] The first performance of both parts had to wait until the Weimar production of 1876, the very year in which the *Ring* was staged in its entirety.

The marriage of Greece and Germany

Cosima records: "Talking of Goethe and whether he can be regarded as the sum total of the German spirit, R. says, 'I think he can, if one considers how he absorbed all the revivals and discoveries of the 18th century in this free manner; and in the ultimate things he was always full of prescience.'"[221] At the same time Goethe was a conduit for Wagner's knowledge and love of the Greeks. Goethe visited Rome in 1786–88, where, among other things, he studied classical art. This precipitated his intense interest in "the Greeks," which is manifest especially in the Classical Walpurgis Night, a scene that Wagner treasured, there being numerous references to it in Cosima's diaries.[222] Then, as noted in chapter 4 above, the marriage of Germany and Greece represented in *Faust* part II in the marriage of Faust and Helen was of central importance for Wagner, this taking place in Faust's medieval (German) castle followed by Faust's evocation of Arcadia.[223]

---

219. *CD* 19 February 1872.

220. It was in fact performed in 1854.

221. *CD* 8 April 1882.

222. E.g., *CD* 5 December 1878: "Speaking last night about the 'Classical Walpurgis Night' he said that it always seems to him to grow shorter, he had imagined Nereus and the Nereids to be much longer; the humor in it becomes ever more apparent." *CD* 8 April 1882: "he much admires Erichto's speech, but almost above all else the scene of Mephisto with the griffins and sphinxes, the Chiron—everything, in fact, in this most wonderful of conceptions". *CD* 20 June 1882 tells of how the couple "crown the evening with the 'Classical Walpurgis Night' from *Faust*." It is worth adding how the entry continues. Richard "delightfully recalled its popular style, reminded of it by the Biblical expression 'to kick against the pricks.'" Wagner rightly recalls that this occurs in St Paul's vision (Acts 26:14) and Cosima continues: "This quotation brings to mind the noble simplicity of the Gospels, and R. remarks sadly that there can be no help for a world to which these 'good tidings' mean nothing."

223. Luke, *Faust II*, 145–58. *GWJA* 3:308–22 (ll. 9127–573).

Faust, St John, Luther, and Theology

Goethe makes rich use of the Bible in *Faust*[224] and the "Studierzimmer (I)" scene was clearly important for Wagner, including the point at which Faust translates John 1:1. Faust's translating the New Testament alludes to his historical contemporary, Martin Luther. After moving through the various options of translating "Logos" in "In the beginning was the Logos" from "Word" ("Wort") to "Mind" ("Sinn") to "Force" ("Kraft") and finally to "Deed" ("Tat"),[225] Faust tells the stray poodle who has accosted him (who will shortly be revealed as Mephistopheles): "If we are to share this room in peace, / Poodle, this noise has got to cease, / This howling and barking has got to end!"[226] Luke comments: "As Faust restates his central positive principle, the dog (Mephistopheles as the antagonist of creation) howls in protest; the motif recalls the Devil's attempts to interrupt Luther as he worked on his translation of the Bible."[227]

The theological implication that Faust's translating of John 1:1 has rejected the Second Person of the Trinity[228] is one that Wagner may have perceived but is one he did *not* subscribe to, at least in his later years.[229] Wagner's main use of Faust's translation is in connection with the performance of the *Ring* cycle. In the middle of the *Preface to the "Ring" Poem* of 1863 he writes: "Just as *Faust* ultimately proposes to replace the Evangelist's 'In the beginning was the *word*' by 'In the beginning was the *deed*,' so the valid solution of an artistic problem seems feasible upon no other path than this of Deed."[230] He then returns to Faust's retranslation at the end of his preface. After wondering whether there is a "German Prince" who could fund his opera-house and asking "Will this Prince be found?"[231] he repeats "In the beginning was the Deed" and then explains: "In waiting for this Deed, the author feels constrained to make a faint beginning through the 'word'—and very literally through the word, without tone, nay, without sound, the word just merely given forth in type—inasmuch as he

---

224. Durrani, *Faust*, passim.

225. Luke, *Faust I*, 39 (1224–37).

226. Luke, *Faust I*, 39 (1238–40).

227. Luke, *Faust I*, 154 n. 27.

228. When he says "Is then the word so great and high a thing?" (Luke, *Faust I*, 39; *GWJA* 3:48 (l. 1226): "Ich kann das Wort so hoch unmöglich schätzen") Boyle, *Goethe*, 2:763, claims "he is not simply saying that he prefers action to talk; he is making a specifically theological assertion, rejecting the Logos, the Second Person of the Trinity, in favour of his own power of judgement." In moving from "In the beginning was the Word!" ("im Anfang was das Wort!") to "In the beginning was the Deed" ("im Anfang war die Tat!") "he unmistakably echoes the first principles of Fichte's philosophy." In an earlier work, Durrani, *Faust*, 57–62, pointed to how Goethe distances himself from Christian dogma in his translation of John 1:1, which, had it continued, would run "Im Anfang war die Tat, und die Tat war bei Gott, und Gott war die Tat."

229. *PW* 6:256; *GSD* 10:256 (*What Use Is This Knowledge?* published in *Bayreuther Blätter* December 1880). I will discuss this in volume 2, chapter 2.

230. *PW* 3:278–79; *GSD* 6:277.

231. This is strangely prophetic since the Prince was found the following year (May 1864).

resolves on handing over this poem, as such, to the larger public."[232] Faust's translation of John 1:1 and Wagner's interpretation of it here may also to some extent explain his description of his drama as "deeds of music made visible" ("ersichtlich gewordene Thaten der Musik").[233] This concern with *seeing* "deeds" is also reflected in the words of the director in the "Vorspiel auf dem Theater" ("Prelude on the stage"): "Come, that's enough of words! What I / Want now is [to see] deeds" ("Der Worte sind genung gewechselt, / Laßt mich auch endlich Taten sehn").[234]

Luther gets a mention in "Branders Lied," one of the songs from *Faust* Wagner set to music,[235] but of more theological weight is the presentation of sin in Gretchen's soliloquy from *Zwinger* (*Shrine inside the Town Wall*).[236] This last scene (Zwinger) is especially powerful in presenting Gretchen's experience of guilt, which I noted above forms the theological backdrop for the close of *Faust* I. The song from *Zwinger* is named "Melodram," having the soprano speak over the piano.[237] It is one of the most haunting scenes in *Faust I*,[238] where religion is shown to fail and oppresses Gretchen "by exacerbating her awareness of the burden of her guilt";[239] she has been exploited by Faust and Mephistopheles and it is as though all their sins have been placed upon Gretchen, making this scene particularly painful to experience. I quote the first half to show the key relationship between Gretchen and the Virgin Mary (which runs through much of *Faust I*, but which changes significantly in *Faust II*):[240]

---

232. *PW* 3:282; *GSD* 6:281.

233. *PW* 5:303; *GSD* 4:306 (*The Name Musikdrama*).

234. Luke, *Faust I*, 8; *GWJA* 3:15 (ll. 214–15).

235. Luke, *Faust I*, 64 (*GWJA* 3:75 (ll. 2128–29)): "It [rat] lived on butter and it got as fat / As Doctor Luther's belly" ("Hatte sich ein Ränzlein angemäs't, / Als wie der Doktor Luther").

236. *GWJA* 3:129–30. The music is available in Voss, *Klavierlieder*, 22–24.

237. Wagner would know of such "Melodrama" in the "Kerkerszene" in *Fidelio* and the "Wolfs-schluchtszene" in *Freischütz*. However, Wagner's song bears a stronger resemblance to Gertrude's "Melodrama und Lied" from Marschner's *Hans Heiling*.

238. Note that in one of the relatively rare cases where Wagner questions Goethe's art he says of "Wer fühlet, / wie wühlet," etc., from *Zwinger* that it is "[a] bit artificial" ("ein wenig künstlich"), comments made though fifty-one years after composing the songs (*CD* 7 March 1882).

239. Durrani, *Faust*, 111.

240. Luke, *Faust I*, 114; *GWJA* 3:129 (ll 3587–3601). Wagner replaces Goethe's "zu" with "nach" in l. 3592.

Ach neige,	O Virgin Mother, thou
Du Schmerzenreiche,	Who art full of sorrow, bow
Dein Antlitz gnädig meiner Not!	Thy face in mercy to my anguish now!
Das Schwert im Herzen,	O Lady standing by
Mit tausend Schmerzen	Thy Son to watch Him die,
Blickst auf nach (zu) deines Sohnes Tod.	Thy heart is pierced to hear His bitter cry.
Zum Vater blickst du,	Seeking the Father there
Und Seufzer schickst du	Thy sighs rise through the air
Hinauf um sein' und deine Not.	From his death-agony, from thy despair.
Wer fühlet,	Who else can know
Wie wühlet	The pain that so
Der Schmerz mir im Gebein?	Burns in my bones like fire from hell?
Was mein armes Herz hier banget,	How my wretched heart is bleeding,
Was es zittert, was verlanget,	What it's dreading, what it's needing,
Weißt nur du, nur du allein!	Lady, only you can tell!

To some extent something similar is happening with Sieglinde in *Walküre* Act II in that she places the sins of others upon herself; but her moral compass is clearly different and unlike Gretchen she does not have the Virgin Mary to whom she can confess and with whom she can share her suffering. She tells Siegmund:[241]

flieh' die Entweihte!	Flee one who's defiled!
Unheilig	Unhallowed
umfängt dich ihr Arm;	her arm enfolds you;
entehrt, geschändet	dishonored, disgraced,
schwand dieser Leib	this body is dead:
[. . .]	[. . .]
Lass' die Verfluchte,	Forsake the accursèd creature,
lass' sie dich flieh'n!	let her flee far away!
Verworfen bin ich,	Depraved am I
der Würde bar!	and devoid of all worth!

This, and Sieglinde's following hallucination, also reflects that of Gretchen in prison ("Kerker").[242] The very ending of *Faust I* is in my judgement one of the most powerful theatrical representations of the justification of the ungodly, and it has a biblical (and Lutheran) focus in that the accuser is the "devil."[243] Wagner to my knowledge does not

---

241. *WagRS* 157.
242. Luke, *Faust I*, 147.
243. For the key lines, see Luke, *Faust I*, 148; *GWJA* 3:164 (ll. 4611–12): Mephistopheles: "She is condemned!" ("Sie ist gerichtet!"); A voice: "She is redeemed!" ("Ist gerettet!"). For the biblical background for satan as the accuser, see Zech 3:1–5; Rev 12:10. This is a central theme for Luther found in

appeal to this scene but the final scene of *Faust II*, where Gretchen appears as Una Poenitentia, was central to him on the question of redemption.

Eternal Womanly

In *Opera and Drama* Wagner contrasts the "Eternal Womanly" ("ewig Weibliche") who has a redemptive role (and identified with "melody") with the "egoistic Man-ly" ("egoistische Männliche") (identified with the poet): "Only the poet [...] will feel driven so irresistibly to a heart-alliance with the 'eternal womanly' (mit dem 'ewig Weiblichen') of Tone-art, that in these nuptials he shall celebrate alike his own redemption."[244] The "ewig Weibliche" clearly alludes to the penultimate line of *Faust II*, the words of the chorus mysticus:[245]

Alles Vergängliche	All that must disappear
Ist nur ein Gleichnis;	Is but a parable;
Das Unzulängliche,	What lay beyond us, here
Hier wird's Ereignis;	All is made visible;
Das Unbeschreibliche,	Here deeds have understood
Hier ist's getan;	Words they were darkened by;
Das Ewig-Weibliche	Eternal Womanhood
Zieht uns hinan.	Draws us on high.

In this final scene we encounter four penitent women: Magna Peccatrix (Luke 7:36), Mulier Samaritana (John 4), Maria Aegyptiaca (*Acta Sanctorum*), and Una Poenitentium, Gretchen herself. They are greeted by the Virgin Mary, here called Mater gloriosa (contrast the epithet Mater dolorosa of Part I). In his 1867 essay *German Art and German Policy* Wagner praised Goethe as the greatest German poet who "closed his grandest poem with the beatific invocation of the *Mater gloriosa*, as the loftiest ideal of spotless purity."[246] But although here Wagner found Mater gloriosa the central key figure, in the close of his *Beethoven* essay, written three years later, Gretchen is clearly the redeeming figure: "Only *Gretchen* could redeem him; the untimely sacrificial victim, she who eternally lived on unnoticed in his innermost soul stretches out her hand to him from the world of the blessed."[247] He then relates these final lines of *Faust* to art:

---

writings and hymns such as *Ein' feste Burg ist unser Gott* (Wagner was in the habit of singing this to Cosima, *CD* 15 January 1869; *CD* 10 June 1871) and *Nun freuet euch, lieben Christen g'mein* (both are quoted in Kohls, *Luther*, 2:123; 1:103–5).

244. *PW* 2:285; *GSD* 4:146.
245. *GWJA* 3:404; (ll. 12114–21); Luke, *Faust II*, 239.
246. *PW* 4:112; *GSD* 8:101.
247. Allen, *Beethoven*, 191; *GSD* 9:125.

And if we now [. . .] draw analogies from philosophy and physiology to try to give meaning to this profound work, then we should by "All that is transitory is only an allegory"—understand the spirit of phenomenal art after which Goethe strove for so long and with such distinction. However, by "The Eternal Feminine draws us on" we should understand the spirit of music which arose from the poet's deepest consciousness and which now soars over him leading him on the path to redemption.[248]

Wagner's theological interpretation of *Faust* is underlined by words recorded by Cosima (12 November 1878): "[Richard] says as if to himself, 'Noble spirit, thou gavest me everything,' and then continues to reflect on the relationship of God to the world, how difficult it is to describe; mortals always think of it historically, in terms of time and space, and what emerges is something external. When I observe that Goethe expressed it best of all, he says, 'Yes, in Faust, Part Two; the curious form of that remarkable book makes it seem a kind of Gospel.'"[249]

Friedrich Schlegel (1772–1829)

As noted in the previous chapter, we have Schlegel to thank for suggesting to Schleiermacher that they together translate Plato, although Schlegel himself withdrew from the project.[250] I also noted his comments on the similarities between the "noble and spiritual" inflected languages, by which he meant primarily "Indisch," Greek, and German.[251] Originally Schlegel had a classical bent but then had a "romantic turn." His view of "romantic poetry" is set out in his *Athenaeum Fragments*: "Romantic poetry is a progressive universal poetry (Universalpoesie). Its goal is not merely to reunite all the separate forms of poetry, and to put poetry in contact with philosophy and rhetoric. It also wants to and should now mix, and then fuse, poetry and prose, inspiration and criticism, the poetry of art (Kunstpoesie) and that of nature (Naturpoesie)."[252]

Schlegel's thought coheres with many aspects of Wagner's[253] and in addition to the *Gesamtkunstwerk* hinted in the previous quotation, the most likely influences in

---

248. Allen, *Beethoven*, 190–91; *GSD* 9:125.

249. On Faust's speech beginning "Oh sublime Spirit" (Luke, *Faust I*, 102; *GWJA* 3:116 (l. 3217): "Erhabener Geist") see volume 2, chapter 4.

250. For an example of his interest in Plato see Nivala, *Romantic Idea*, 66–67, who points to the introduction he sketched out in 1800 (*KFSA* 2.18:5126–30).

251. Schlegel, *Sprache und Weisheit* (1808), 27–86; *KFSA* 1.8:136–90; Book I, chapters 3–6.

252. *KFSA* 1.2:182 (aphorism 116); Beiser, *Political Writings*, 116–17.

253. Daverio, *Ideology*, 155–81, has explored the *Ring* in terms of Schlegel's "Universalpoesie." Two further examples are Wagner's sharing Schlegel's organic view of nature (see the 1790s Fragments) and that Schlegel was the first to draw the attention of Germans to the Icelandic versions of the legends of Burgundians and Nibelungs (see his sixth and tenth lectures on *Geschichte der alten und neuen Literatur*; *KFSA* 1.6:159–67, 232–35).

relation to the *Ring* concern love and sex (and androgyny) as put forward in *Lucinde* and his "Indo-German" hypothesis.

Love and Sex

According to Gregor-Dellin, Wagner borrowed *Lucinde* from his uncle Adolf's library[254] and he dates this to early 1828.[255] However, I have found no evidence for this claim,[256] although one can image a young fifteen-year-old Wagner immersing himself in such a work. One of the key sections of *Lucinde* was "Idylle über den Müßiggang," ("Idyll of Idleness"),[257] the term Müßiggang ("idleness", "leisure") having an association with "Die Muße" ("leisure").[258] This section emphasizes the importance of passivity, which also has implications for the creative process: "Only calmly and gently, in the sacred transquillity of true passivity, can one remember one's whole ego and contemplate the word and life. How does any thinking and writing of poetry take place, if not by complete dedication and submission to some guardian genius?"[259]

It was in the winter and spring of 1798–99 that Schlegel wrote his novel *Lucinde*. Although its publication caused a scandal, the work is far from being pornographic; rather it celebrates the mutual love of Julius and Lucinde who clearly represent Schlegel and Dorothea Veit (she had left her husband to be with Schlegel). The love between Julius and Lucinde is so total, both spiritual and physical, that any religious or legal sanction and ceremony is superfluous. The penultimate section on "Yearning and Rest" ("Sehnsucht und Ruhe") and the lovers' longing for "night" anticipates what one finds in *Tristan*.[260] *Lucinde* may also have influenced Wagner in relation to androgyny.[261]

Indo-German hypothesis

No works of Schlegel are to be found in Wagner's Dresden library. His work on the Indo-German hypothesis, *On the Language and Wisdom of the Indians* (*Über*

---

254. Gregor-Dellin, *Leben*, 64. This is missing from the English translation, *Life*.

255. Gregor-Dellin, *Wagner-Chronik*, 14. He also claims he read Tieck and the Tannhäuser-Sage.

256. I can only assume Gregor-Dellin took this from the speculations in *SB* 1:27 ("Einleitung" by Werner Wolf). I quote this in full so readers are aware this is indeed *speculation*: "In diese Zeit [i.e., early 1828] könnte auch die Bekanntschaft mit Werken Ludwig Tiecks, vermutlich auch mit dem Tannhäuser-Stoff in der Novellensammlung 'Phantasus', und möglicherweise mit Friedrich Schlegels Romanfragment 'Lucinde' fallen."

257. Dischner, *Lucinde*, 60–65; Firchow, *Lucinde*, 63–68; KFSA 1.5:25–29.

258. This term is found fairly frequently in Wagner's letters (e.g., *SB* 7:38).

259. Dischner, *Lucinde*, 62; Firchow, *Lucinde*, 65–66.

260. *Tristan* is in fact closer to *Lucinde* than to Novalis in that in Novalis' work the lover has a longing for mythical reunion after he has lost his beloved (Eichner, *Schlegel*, 154–55).

261. See volume 2, chapter 6.

die Sprache und Weisheit der Indier), was later to find its way into the Wahnfried library[262] but Schlegel's view that the Germanic people originated in Asia can be detected at least as early as *Die Wibelungen* and it seems to be a view Wagner held for the rest of his life.[263]

In writing on Sanskrit and Indo-European[264] languages Schlegel put forward a view of human development, but employing biblical categories such as paradise, fall, and redemption. So the close of *Lectures on Universal History* (1805–6) clearly betrays such a biblical scheme, speaking of a paradise and period of innocence, degeneration, education (as in Old Testament times and classical Greece), Son of God, Antichrist, world judgement, and finally kingdom of God.[265] But Schlegel is skeptical about the historical value of the Pentateuch and stresses that adopting Judaism into Christianity was a serious mistake,[266] a view Wagner would share. He claimed the noble nations of Europe came from Asia, the original inhabitants of Europe possibly including the Celts who may have been the original inhabitants of the "large caves in Britain."[267] His influential *On the Language and Wisdom of the Indians* (1808)[268] sets out a similar scheme, using biblical categories, but, as the title suggests, including a fair amount of philology and speculation about the origin of languages (it was while writing this that he decided to converted to Catholicism). His narrative of German descent from India follows biblical ideas of the "original revelation" ("ursprüngliche Offenbarung")[269] and the degeneration of which we read in the early chapters of Genesis.[270] All this was interwoven with a history of the Indian people and their language. Schlegel thought Sanskrit the oldest language, the most approximate to the

---

262. He also possessed copies of *Geschichte der Poesie der Griechen und Römer*; *Die Griechen und Römer*; *Ueber die neuere Geschichte*.

263. According to Glasenapp, *Leben*, 6:602, some days after his birthday on 22 May 1882 he spoke to Herr von Bürkel of "unsere asiatische Urheimat."

264. Whereas Thomas Young introduced the term "Indo-European" in 1816, German speaking countries tended to speak of "Indo-Germanic," a term introduced by Klaproth in 1823.

265. "Vorlesungen über Universalgeschichte," *KFSA* 2.14:249–52. Note especially the theological terms employed in the table (252).

266. "Vorlesungen über Universalgeschichte," *KFSA* 2.14:11.

267. "Vorlesungen über Universalgeschichte," *KFSA* 2.14:17.

268. *Über die Sprache und Weisheit der Indier*. I will refer to the 1808 edition (which was in Wagner's Wahnfried library) and the critical edition (*KFSA* 1.8:105–433). Schlegel's interest in India was inspired by Herder's work from 1770 onwards (*KFSA* 1.6:CLXXXVII) and by figures such as the Welshman William Jones, mentioned right at the beginning of Schlegel's "Vorrede" (*Sprache und Weisheit*, III; *KFSA* 1.8:107). In his lecture of 1786, Jones suggested that Sanskrit, Latin and Greek (together with German and Celtic languages) all originated from a common source ("Third Anniversary Discourse," 25–27).

269. *Sprache und Weisheit*, 105; *KFSA* 1.8:207. It is worth noting that an analogous idea ("Ur-Offenbarung") was employed by the twentieth-century theologian Paul Althaus (Bell, *No one seeks for God*, 105–13).

270. *Sprache und Weisheit*, 197–98; *KFSA* 1.8:295.

lost "Ursprache,"[271] Latin, Greek, Persian, and German being derived from Indic.[272] These were set apart from Chinese, Hebrew, Arabic, and American Indian languages.[273] He speculates that the Germanic peoples on leaving India, were inspired to travel north by the saga of Mount Meru. The attraction of the "wonderful notion of the great dignity and splendor of the north (der hohen Würde und Herrlichkweit des Nordens)"[274] inspired them to travel to the Causcasus and from there they may even have travelled further north, by which he may be pointing to Scandinavia. He concludes this chapter by simply declaring that he will leave this very important question concerning the "history of our fatherland" to others to address.[275]

Schlegel in fact took up his own challenge in his *Beginning of Our History* (1819). Again he employed a biblical scheme, but here related it to J. G. Rhode's reconstruction of human origins based on the *Zend-Avesta*. Schlegel's attention moves from India (i.e., the area of the Ganges) to the mountains stretching from the Caucasus to the Himalayans, in particular "Aria" where the "Arier" used to live.[276] The Aryans were a warlike heroic people,[277] the forefathers of the German people,[278] whose "Aryan language" was closely related to Avestan (Zend) and to Sanskrit.[279] The Sanskrit "Ari" was related to the German "Ehre" (honour).[280]

Many years later Wagner was to allude to this "Ari"/"Ehre" word play in *Herodom and Christendom* (1881).[281] He may also have been influenced by the ideas of Julius Klaproth (1783–1835), who wrote of the antediluvian spread of tribes, some of which then, during the flood, took refuge on Mount Ararat (in the Armenian highlands) and in the mountains of India and America.[282] Indo-Germanic speakers migrated into Europe and southern Asia from two separate mountain chains, the Himalayas and the Caucasus. Ancient Indians had traveled South from the Himalayas and mixed with "brown or Negro-like natives." The Goths left the Himalayas for the North and entered Europe via Scandinavia. The other Germanic tribe (Medo-Germans) wandered from the Caucasus to the Caspian Sea, through Persia and into Europe from the south.[283] Such views may have influenced Wagner's *Die Wibelungen*, where he writes of the

271. *Sprache und Weisheit*, 62, 66; *KFSA* 1.8:167, 173.
272. *Sprache und Weisheit*, 16; *KFSA* 1.8:127.
273. *Sprache und Weisheit*, 44; *KFSA* 1.8:153.
274. *Sprache und Weisheit*, 194; *KFSA* 1.8:293. See Benes, "Indo-Germans," 170.
275. *Sprache und Weisheit*, 194; *KFSA* 1.8:293.
276. Schlegel, "Anfang," *KFSA* 1.8:518.
277. Schlegel, "Anfang," *KFSA* 1.8:519.
278. Schlegel, "Anfang," *KFSA* 1.8:520.
279. Schlegel, "Anfang," *KFSA* 1.8:519.
280. Schlegel, "Anfang," *KFSA* 1.8:520.
281. *PW* 6:278; *GSD* 10:278. See volume 2, chapter 10.
282. On Klaproth, see Bene, "Aryans," 173.
283. Klaproth, *Asia Polyglotta* (1823), 42.

"largest island of this northern world-sea" being the "Indian Caucasus [...] the cradle of the present Asiatic peoples."[284]

There can be no doubt that ideas of race that emanated from Schlegel and others influenced *Die Wibelungen*. Further, we find him using the term "Aryan" and its cognates later in his life.[285] The first reference we have is from 1872 where he writes that "the Aryans, returning from the mountains, found in the rich cradle of humanity people living almost like animals, while they, already developed, created Brahmanism as they dwelt in the rich valleys."[286] He then uses it in a letter to Ludwig (17 May 1881), telling the king of his experience of Angelo Neumann's Berlin production of the *Ring*:

> It is without doubt the Aryan's race's most characteristic work of art (das der arischen Race eigenthümlichste Kunstwerk): no nation on earth could be so clearly conscious of its origins and predisposition than this one tribe from Upper Asia, a tribe which was the last to enter European culture and which until that time had retained its purity better than all the other white races. One could well feel hope on witnessing the success of such a work in our midst![287]

Then the Aryan theme returns in 1882. In a discussion with Cosima on race he says "that it has been changed by women—for example, when an Aryan marries a Semite woman, the Creole race appears."[288] Then six months later he says that "in his Wotan he recognizes the true god of the Aryans."[289] In November the composer compares *Tristan and Isolde*, "[a] half-caste affair" with "a genuinely Aryan work like *Siegfried*."[290] Then just a few three weeks before his death he comments on the scene between Marquis Posa and Don Carlos in Act IV of *Don Carlos*. Responding to Cosima's comment that she believes these things will grow in people's estimation, he says: "'Of course. It is Aryan identity, and it is we who have produced it.' Then he plays the beginning of the 9th!" Perhaps he moved to the *Ninth* because of the Schiller connection. Other than these references we find discussions of race and Aryans in *Herodom and Christendom*.[291]

In view of Wagner's interests in human origins (*Die Wibelungen*) and the Aryans, comments made by Houston Stewart Chamberlain on Wagner and race seem curious.

284. *PW* 7:259–60; *GSD* 2:116. In a footnote in *GSD* Wagner points out that now he sees that this hypothesis does not really hold.

285. The Aryan hypothesis came to influence figures such as Ernst Renan and Joseph Arthur Comte de Gobineau, both of whom influenced Wagner in later life.

286. *CD* 7 June 1872. I have changed "Arians" to "Aryans" in this translation.

287. *SL* 914; *KB* 3:208.

288. *CD* 7 March 1882.

289. *CD* 5 September 1882, a comment made in the context of context Siegfried and Brünnhilde in *Siegfried* Act III Scene 3 acting "[l]ike two animals," and there "[h]ere there is no doubt, no sin." See volume 2, chapter 6.

290. *CD* 23 November 1882.

291. *GSD* 10:278 (three occurrences) where he likens Siegfried to Heracles and 10:281 where he speaks of the "earliest Aryan branches" (*PW* 6:281).

Pointing out that the term "Race" (Rasse) is absent in the *Wagner-Lexikon* of Glasenapp and Stein, he writes: "Wagner never in his whole life concerned himself with racial questions; he never devised thoughts or ideas and still less fundamental clauses on this matter."[292] Wagner's concern with race cannot be simply settled by doing a word search for "Rasse." Sometimes "Geschlecht" has a racial overtone[293] and one has to survey whole arguments rather than doing a word search or word study.[294]

August W. Schlegel (1767–1845)

Like his younger brother, A. W. Schlegel wrote on issues of Indology and in fact in 1819 he became the first professor in Sanskrit in continental Europe. His "On the Origin of the Hindous" (1834) argued that the Hindous came into being by white races coming down from the Indo-European homelands and conquering and mixing with the indigenous black "savages."[295]

Schlegel's views on race may have influenced Wagner but much more important was his influence in relation to literature.[296] As pointed out above, he must have possessed Schlegel's translation (with Tieck) of Shakespeare, even if, as I have argued, the edition now in the Richard Wagner Museum cannot have been his copy. In the Wahnfried library we have not only his editions of Shakespeare but also those of Calderon together with *Kritische Schriften*, *Vorlesungen über dramatische Kunst und Litteratur* and *Observations sur la langue et la littérature provençales*. His *Vorlesungen über dramatische Kunst und Literatur* became highly influential and could be particularly significant for the composer.[297] First of all, he criticized attempts to reproduce classicism, a view that, as we saw in chapter 4, Wagner also held to.[298] Secondly, he argued that whereas the classical mind-set was dominated by sensuality[299] the modern European consciousness with the strong Christian influence on redemption and future bliss has

---

292. Preface to the third edition of *Foundations* (*Grundlagen*, 1:xx). The translation is taken from Allen, "Weihe," 269–70 (translation by Roger Allen with the help of Stuart Spencer). Chamberlain accepts that *Herodom and Christendom* does address race, but claims he simply parrots Gobineau.

293. *PW* 7:295; *GSD* 2:152–53 (*Wibelungen*, discussed in chapter 2 above)

294. This, I hope, is a point that those working in biblical studies can accept.

295. Schlegel, "Origine," 469, 472–75.

296. The essays in Schlegel's two volume *Kritische Schriften* in Wagner's Wahnfried library dealt with issues of literature (e.g., Goethe, Shakespeare, Voss's translation of Homer).

297. Oergel, *Nibelungen*, 102–3.

298. Schlegel, *Kunst und Literatur* (ed. Amoretti), 1:7: "Bloße Nachahmung ist aber in den schönen Künsten immer fruchtlos: auch was wir von den andern entlehnen, muß in uns gleichsam wiedergeboren werden, wenn es poetisch hervorgehen soll." ("But mere imitation is always fruitless in the arts: even if we borrow something from others, it will have to be reborn within us, if it is to have a poetic existence." Translation of Oergel, *Nibelungen*, 104 n. 31.)

299. Schlegel, *Kunst und Literatur* (ed. Amoretti), 1:10 (quoted with a translation in Oergel, *Nibelungen* (ed. Amoretti), 104–5).

given rise to a poetry that yearns "for a lost past and a yet intangible future."[300] He then finds a certain correspondence between the Christian worldview and "the strict nature of the North" ("[d]ie strenge Natur des Nordens") such that their people readily embraced the Christian faith "so that it penetrated nowhere more deeply into the human soul" ("so daß es nirgends so tief ins Innere gedrungen ist").[301] In relation to this he earlier wrote of the "heroic mythology of the Middle Ages,"[302] taking a particular interest in the *Nibelungenlied* and the *Heldenbuch*.

Hölderlin (1770–1843)

It would appear that it was only in later life that Wagner came to know Hölderlin's work. Malwida von Meysenbug had given him the works of Hölderlin as a Christmas present in 1873[303] and on Christmas Eve he and Cosima read *Hyperion*.[304] Cosima records: "R. and I recognize with some concern the great influence this writer has had on Prof. Nietzsche; rhetorical extravagance, incorrect and clotted imagery (the north wind which scorches the blossoms, etc. (der Nordwind welcher die Blüten versengt u.s.w.)), but a fine noble intellect, though R. says he cannot really believe in such neo-Greeks (Neugriechen)."[305] Then in 1874 Nietzsche sent the composer a belated birthday greeting quoting the first three and last two verses of Hölderlin's "Gesang der Deutschen."[306]

Wagner's point about the "neo-Greeks" is revealing since it does highlight the fact that for Wagner, following A. W. Schlegel, the Greeks were not simply to be imitated but had to be reborn in Germany.[307] But despite Wagner's slight contempt for Hölderlin, it is worth bearing in mind that Hegel had been influenced by him, he, Hölderlin, and Schelling being students together at the Tübinger Stift (and indeed sharing a room).[308] In particular, Hölderlin fostered Hegel's love of the Greeks not only by saturating his poetry with Greek motifs but also in translating works into

---

300. Oergel, *Nibelungen*, 105, who quotes from Schlegel, *Kunst und Literatur* (ed. Amoretti), 1:13 (lecture 1).

301. Schlegel, *Kunst und Literatur* (ed. Amoretti), 1:11 (quoted with a translation in Oergel, *Nibelungen*, 106).

302. Oergel, *Nibelungen*, 107, quotes from Schlegel's *Geschichte der Romantischer Literatur: Kritische Schriften vol. 4*, 100.

303. This was edited by C. T. Schwab (1846).

304. See *FHSWB* 1:483–760.

305. *CD* 24 December 1873. Also in *CD* 13 January 1874 she records that "Hölderlin does not grip us." On assessing him as "mediocre" (also applied to Schumann!) see *CD* 29 March 1880. On Hölderlin as Nietzsche's favorite poet, see *CD* 6 April 1880. The reference to *Hyperion* is presumably 1. Band 1 Buch (Hyperion an Bellarmin): "Wie ein heulender Nordwind, fährt die Gegenwart über die Blüten unsers Geistes und versengt sie im Entstehen" (*FHSWB* 1:621).

306. *KB* 4:214 (letter of 24 May 1875). For the full poem see *FHSWB* 1:246–48.

307. Schlegel, *Kunst und Literatur* (ed. Amoretti), 1:7 (see above).

308. Pinkard, "Life," 19. See chapter 6 below.

German.[309] It is also worth bearing in mind the central role of Dionysus for Hölderlin and again we may have a link here with both Schelling and Hegel (and of course later with Nietzsche).

Ludwig Uhland (1787–1862)

Wagner possessed a copy of Ludwig Uhland's *Gedichte* in his Dresden library. When I consulted it in the Richard Wagner museum two things struck me immediately. First this well-used book naturally fell open at "Der Rosengarten" poem on pp. 268–69.[310] Secondly, although this particular poem was not marked, many were and, apart from his New Testament, this is one of the most heavily marked book in Wagner's possession that I have so far consulted. His practice with his copy of Uhland was to mark with a marginal vertical stroke the title of the poem together with the first one or two lines.[311] Two marked poems are reflected in Siegmund's greeting of spring in *Walküre* Act 1 Scene 3 ("Winterstürme wichen den Wonnenmond [. . .])"[312] and two others are reflected in Wotan's farewell.[313] Yet another poem may have influenced Wagner's development of *Die Meistersinger*.[314] Certain poems that one would expect to interest him are not marked.[315] Wagner clearly had an immense respect for this poet and

---

309. E.g., Sophocles, *Oedipus der Tyrann* and *Antigonae* (FHSWB 2:247–376), which became two of Hegel's favorite tragedies.

310. This "Rosengarten" poem spans pp. 268–70.

311. The marked poems are as follows: Uhland, *Gedichte*, 3, 6, 11, 16, 17, 20, 24, 27, 32, 33 (twice), 36, 41, 49 (twice), 50, 52, 54, 60, 66, 72, 79 (twice), 80, 81, 82, 83, 89, 91, 95, 97, 116, 121, 145, 146, 152, 157, 176, 177, 191 ("Glossen" is doubly marked), 237, 253, 257, 261, 283, 286, 287, 290, 300, 301 ("Der Rosengarten"), 305, 318, 330, 334, 336 ("Dante"), 350, 353, 367, 396, 401, 404, 418, 465, 469, 502, 513, 532.

312. Uhland, *Gedichte*, 49. See the phrases "O sanfter, süßer Hauch" ("Frühlingsahnung") and "O frische Duft, o neuer Klang" ("Frühlingsglaube"); cf. *WagRS* 135: "holde Düfte, / haucht er aus." See also "Die linden Lüfte sind erwacht, / Sie säuseln und weben Tag und Nacht" ("Frühlingsglaube," *Gedichte*, 49); cf. *WagRS* 135: "auf linden Lüften / leicht und lieblich, / Wunder webend."

313. Uhland, *Gedichte*, 79. See "Wanderlieder: 1. Lebewohl": "Lebe Wohl, lebe wohl, mein Lieb! / Muß noch heute scheiden. / Einen Kuß, einen Kuß mir gieb! / Muß dich ewig meiden." Cf. *WagRS* 190: "Leb' wohl [. . .] Muß ich dich meiden." See also "Wanderlieder: 2. Scheiden und Meiden" (*Gedichte*, 79): "So soll ich nur dich meiden, / Du meines Lebens Lust." Cf. *WagRS* 190: "du lachende Lust meines Auges."

314. Uhland, *Gedichte*, 283, "Des Goldschmieds Töchterlein." The daughter's name is given as Helene (and Wagner chose Eva presumably to make sense of Sachs' double reference to an "Eva" (English "Eve") in his song of Act II. Uhland's poem may have influenced Wagner in determining Bogler's/Pogner's profession as a goldsmith (first given in his 3. *Prosaentwurf* of 18 November 61, *DTMN* 127). See Uhland's second stanza: "Ein schmucker Ritter trat herein: / Willkommen, Mägdlein traut! / Willkommen, lieber Goldschmied mein! / Mach' mir ein köstlich Kränzchen / Für meine süße Braut!" Note also that Uhland's poem "Vom treuer Walther" (253) is marked.

315. See "Der Schmied" (Uhland, *Gedichte*, 43); "Jungfrau Sieglinde" (307); "Siegfried's Schwert" (402).

scholar[316] and later was to purchase and read Uhland's work on the history of poetry and saga.[317] It is also significant that Uhland had a particular interest in the *Volksbuch* of 1519, which narrates for stories concerning Friedrich Barbarossa's crusade and various conflicts with the pope.[318]

Novels

It is likely that novels did influence Wagner's *Ring*, although to argue this requires a little inspired guesswork.[319] Wagner had an ambivalent attitude to the novel, his problem being that the genre was individualistic rather than communal: "The Master of the House used to *read* to his family and guests from an expensive handwritten book; now, however, everyone can read silently to himself from the printed book and the *author* now writes for his readers."[320] He admired Goethe's *Wilhelm Meister*[321] and a range of novelists (e.g., Turgenev),[322] but two figures stand out for his praise: Sir Walter Scott (1771–1832) and Honoré de Balzac (1799–1850). He started taking a keen interest in the novels of Scott in 1856 when he took his water-cure in Mornex,[323] and his vast collection in his Wahnfried library witnesses to his admiration.[324] Scott's *The Pirate* (Waverley Novels 13) was highly influential in establishing the modern understanding of the term "Viking,"[325] although Wagner himself uses the term almost exclusively for a proper name, "König Wiking," in Wieland

---

316. See, e.g., *CD* 10 November 1871.

317. *CD* 25 June 1873 tells of Richard and Cosima starting on the eight-volume edition of *Uhlands Schriften zur Geschichte der Dichtung und Sage* that was in his Wahnfried library. This is followed by many references to the poet (e.g., reading of volume 6 on 1 October 1873).

318. Pfeiffer, "Volksbüchlein," 250–52. On the *Volksbuch* see the further discussion in volume 2, chapter 5.

319. See the discussion of Schlegel's *Lucinde* above and the discussion of this novel in volume 2, chapter 6.

320. Allen, *Beethoven*, 169.

321. Wagner considered that the conception of *Faust* and of *Wilhelm Meister*, this "gently flowing novel," "coincides with the first full flowering of Goethe's poetic genius" (Allen, *Beethoven*, 169). On the *Lehrjahre* as "Bildungsroman" and the omnipresence of journeying in the *Wanderjahre* see Swales, "Goethe's prose fiction," 140–46.

322. See his reading of *Virgin Soil* (*CD* 5 8 December 1878).

323. *Brown Book* 106–7; *Braunes Buch* 126–27. Borchmeyer, *Theatre*, 138 n. 14, detects a complimentary allusion to Scott's "Historical Romances" in *Opera and Drama* Part II (*PW* 2:144; *GSD* 4:24) where he describes "the Historical Romance" as "an art-form where we are not constrained by any outward consideration to disfigure the naked facts of history through a wilful sifting or compressing." There are frequent references to Scott in Cosima's diaries from 1870 onwards. See especially 25 January to 17 February and 14–17 March 1878, although this is obviously too late for any influence on the *Ring*.

324. He had a twenty-five volume edition of the *Waverley Novels* and a four-volume French translation.

325. Jesch, *Diaspora*, 6–7.

der Schmeid.³²⁶ If anything he praised Balzac even more. It would appear that he first took an interest in Balzac in 1865³²⁷ and praised him in chapter 11 of his *German Art and German Policy*, first published in 1867, for his portrayal of the evils of his society and "civilization."³²⁸ No doubt such pessimism attracted Wagner and he may have seen "a hidden correspondence between Balzac's cycle of novels and his own tetralogy."³²⁹ Cosima's diaries witness to his admiration for Balzac, including his gift "for identifying himself in such detail with some apparently insignificant character," in this respect Balzac being superior to Walter Scott.³³⁰

One significant thing the novel was able to achieve was to view drama from different perspectives.³³¹ Wagner can be said to achieve such viewing from all sides by means of his orchestra. As Borchmeyer argues, for Wagner "[i]t is [. . .] the omniscient orchestra which introduces into the musical drama that multifaceted modern spirit which is reflected in the novel."³³² Hence his *Ring* could be viewed as a "crypto-novel" or, as Wagner would have put it, as a "redeemed" novel.³³³

---

326. E.g., *PW* 1:218–19; *GSD* 3:179–80.

327. See the note for 25 February 1865 (*Brown Book* 120; *Braunes Buch* 143; *KB* 1:5) and the entry 26 October 1865 (*Brown Book* 79; *Braunes Buch* 92).

328. *PW* 4:102–3; *GSD* 8:91–92.

329. Borchmeyer, *Theatre*, 147. Balzac's *La Comédie humaine* (the title probably alluding to Dante's *Divine Comedy*) comprises ninety-one finished and forty-six unfinished works.

330. *CD* 26 July 1878; see also *CD* 30 December 1871, 11 April 1878, 27 July 1878, 7 December 1878.

331. This is something a traditional "play" could not achieve although there is the obvious exception of Greek tragedy with the special role of the chorus.

332. Borchmeyer, *Theatre*, 141.

333. Borchmeyer, *Theatre*, ix. See volume 2, chapter 12 for further discussion of this point.

— 6 —

The *Ring* and German Idealism

Introduction

Rüdiger Bubner writes in the "Introduction" to his anthology of key texts of German Idealistic philosophers: "There can be no doubt that throughout the long history of human thought, philosophy rarely climbed such heights as in the few decades around the year 1800. Probably only the flowering of ancient philosophy in the Athens of Plato and Aristotle would bear comparison."[1] In many ways this also reflects Wagner's own assessment of the history of philosophy. He could talk at length on the subject, one instance being recorded by Cosima on the eve of Siegfried's first birthday: "he spoke a long time about philosophy and said that from Plato to Kant there had been no real progress; that Spinoza, for instance, who had acknowledged the wickedness of the world, had still taken this world as it appears to us for the reality."[2] One reason he singles out Plato and Kant is that these were the two most important philosophers for Schopenhauer, whom Wagner, after 1854, most frequently cites.[3]

Wagner's comments to Cosima should not be taken to mean he wrote off all philosophy between Plato and Kant. Aristotle certainly had a role in that his *Poetics* was important for the issue of tragedy. Further, German Idealism itself is deeply indebted to Aristotle, especially in the case of Hegel. And it is worth pointing out that despite his dismissal of Spinoza mentioned above,[4] Spinoza's views on substance (e.g., "no substance can be produced or created by another thing")[5] and on nature as not being the result of God's free choice,[6] were key to Hegel[7] and cohere rather well with Wagner's

---

1. Bubner, *Idealist Philosophy*, ix.
2. *CD* 6 June 1870, Cosima referring to the previous evening's conversation.
3. His dissertation begins by speaking of "[t]he divine Plato and marvellous Kant" who "unite their firm and impressive voices in recommending a rule for the method of all philosophizing, indeed of all knowledge in general" (Schopenhauer, *Root*, 1; *ASSW* 3:11).
4. The only occurrence of Spinoza in Wagner's writings is in his *Beethoven* (*GSD* 9:90; Allen, *Beethoven*, 104–5) where he is simply mentioned in his role as a "glass grinder."
5. Curley, *Spinoza: Ethics*, 10 (Part I, Proposition 15, Scholium).
6. Curley, *Spinoza: Ethics*, 25–31 (Part I, Appendix).
7. Hegel though was to criticize Spinoza for his "acosmism," namely that "no actuality at all is

own views. Therefore, his dismissing of thinkers between Plato and Kant is somewhat disingenuous and also ignores the fact that there are a whole series of figures who made a philosophical contribution in this period without being labelled philosophers (e.g., German mystics such as Jakob Böhme, who had in fact influenced Wagner).

The figures in the time of German Idealism who exercised most influence on the *Ring* were Hegel, Feuerbach,[8] and Schopenhauer; the earlier figures of Idealism—Kant, Fichte, and Schelling—also left their mark on the artwork, although their ideas came to him largely indirectly. Wagner though was to make various disparaging remarks about Hegel, Fichte, and Schelling; these should be taken with a pinch of salt for all three were important to a greater of lesser extent for Wagner's thinking and artistry, directly or indirectly. In this chapter I will outline the key developments in German Idealism that are relevant to Wagner's *Ring* and endeavour to disentangle the various influences upon the composer. My understanding of the influences is given in figure 6.1.

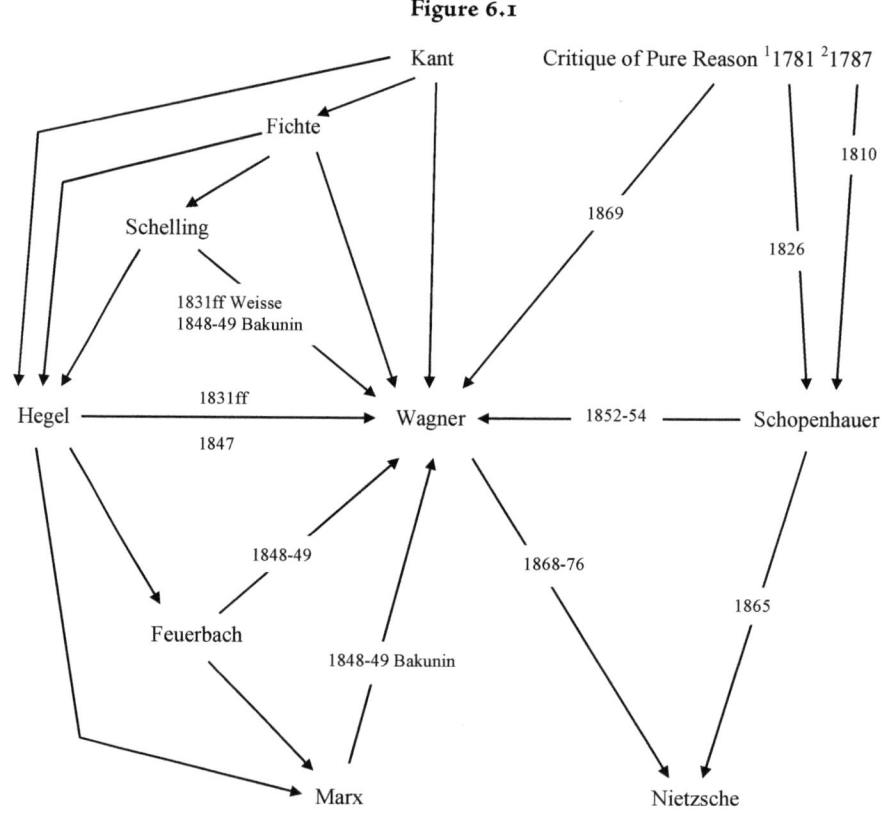

Figure 6.1

---

ascribed to individual things" (Hegel, *Philosophy of Religion*, 1:377; *Philosophie der Religion*, 1:274).

8. Feuerbach (and Nietzsche) were not "Idealists," but I include them in the discussion since both in their own way developed or reacted against Idealism.

The key date to bear in mind is the end of 1852, when Wagner had essentially completed the poem for the *Ring* cycle. Up until this point the key influences upon him were Hegel and Feuerbach. Most writers think that Wagner discovered Schopenhauer in Autumn 1854, which would be too late to influence the libretto (apart from the "Schopenhauer ending" of 1856). However, I will argue below that he had some knowledge already in 1852 and probably some earlier still. But nevertheless one can say that one of the most significant shifts in Wagner's relationship to Idealism is that he moved from an objective Idealism (Hegel) to a subjective Idealism (Schopenhauer, then Kant).[9] However, as I will later argue, Hegel's worldview always remained with him.

One reason it is important to assess how he appropriated each philosopher/theologian as the *Ring* developed is that this can give a clue to Wagner's theological intentions. Therefore, I am not just considering Wagner's finished artwork but also the "tradition history," considering various mutations in this history.[10] Further, in this chapter I hope to set out some of the key "mutations" as Idealism developed from Kant through to Hegel and Schopenhauer, one reason for doing this being because I am convinced that the study of philosophy is best pursued historically.

The process of disentangling the philosophical influences is not entirely straightforward and there is the added complication that much of this philosophical influence upon Wagner came via non-philosophical sources, the most important of these being German Romanticism, which, as we shall see, was bound up fundamentally with Idealism. The major Romantics were all influenced by Idealism, especially Schiller, Friedrich Schlegel, Novalis, and Hölderlin and they in their own way influenced its development, often by criticism;[11] the towering figure of Goethe though kept his distance. Conversely, many of the Idealist philosophers were interested in Romanticism: Kant was too early on the scene and Hegel had traits that were decidedly non-Romantic, but Schelling and Schopenhauer in particular had a keen interest in the art of Romanticism.

Kant (1724–1804)

German Idealism essentially started with the publication of Immanuel Kant's *Critique of Pure Reason*, the first edition appearing in 1781 and the second in 1787. As the work suggests, Kant placed strict limits on the use of what he called "pure reason" ("reine Vernunft"). In the preface to the second edition he explains that "even the *assumption* [. . .] of *God, freedom,* and *immortality* is not permissible unless at the same time speculative reason be deprived of its pretensions to transcendent insight."[12] He

---

9. On these two Idealisms, see Beiser, *Hegel*, 69.
10. See chapter 1 above, where I discuss the approach of "biblical theology" to tradition history.
11. See, e.g., Novalis, *Fichte Studies*.
12. Kant, *Critique of Pure Reason*, Bxxx; Kemp Smith, *Critique*, 29; Weischedel, *Werke*, 3:33.

limits knowledge "in order to make room for faith."[13] One of the key things to emerge from his approach is that reality is two-tiered or, to be more precise, finite things can be viewed from two different perspectives: as phenomena, objects of experience being subject to the conditions of cognition (space, time, and the categories) or as things in themselves (noumena). One way of appreciating the significance and revolutionary nature of Kant's "transcendental turn" is that he was moving from a position of compatibilism regarding human freedom to one of complete freedom,[14] a key concern of Fichte, Schelling, and Hegel.

Wagner's first references to Kant in his letters are in the context of his discovery of Schopenhauer, making the point that he is the greatest philosopher since Kant.[15] The first reference in the theoretical writings is from 1841, a passing reference to "adherents of Kant's 'Critique of pure Reason.'"[16] Kant does not make another appearance in these writings until 1869 where, in the "Appendix to Judaism in Music," he berates the Hegelian philosophy but praises Schiller's use of "Kant's great thought" "as basis for aesthetic views upon the Beautiful."[17] It is unclear how much of Kant the composer had studied by the time he started work on the *Ring*[18] but Kant's thought had implications, positive and negative, for virtually all areas the composer was interested in.[19] His interests in Kant were then to be very much tied to his love of Schopenhauer (whom he saw as Kant's most faithful disciple).[20] However, in later life he showed an increasing interest in Kant and possessed a twelve-volume edition of Kant in his Wahnfried library[21] together with an additional edition of the *Critique of Pure Reason*;[22] some of these volumes must have numbered among Wagner's gifts for Christmas 1869.[23]

---

13. Kant, *Critique of Pure Reason*, Bxxx; Kemp Smith, *Critique*, 29; Weischedel, *Werke*, 3:33: "Ich mußte also das *Wissen* aufheben, um zum *Glauben* Platz zu bekommen [...]".

14. Insole, *Freedom*, passim.

15. The first such extant letter is that to Gustav Schmidt of 9 December 1854 (*SB* 6:295): "[Schopenhauer] ist unbedingt der grösste Philosoph seit Kant." Cf. the letter to Liszt of 16(?) December 1954; *SL* 323; *SB* 6:298, discussed below.

16. "Der Freischütz" (1841), *PW* 7:175; *GSD* 1:213.

17. *PW* 3:113; *GSD* 8:251; Fischer, *Judentum*, 149.

18. In addition to anything he had read or learned from others, it may be significant that Bakunin, with whom he had contact in Dresden in 1848–49, had earlier taken a keen interest in the philosopher (Carr, *Bakunin*, 27).

19. So the first *Kritik* was important for the role of "pure reason," the second on "practical reason" is opposed in Wagner's views on ethics (i.e., he is anti-nomistic), and the third is important for the issue of aesthetics and teleology.

20. See, e.g., *What Use is This Knowledge?* where he refers to Schopenhauer as "Kant's continuator" (*PW* 6:256; *GSD* 10:257). But Schopenhauer was to depart from Kant in ways Wagner would no doubt approve of, such as opposing the categorical imperative.

21. Rosenkranz and Schubert, *Immanuel Kant's sämmtliche Werke*.

22. Hartenstein, *Immanuel Kant's Kritik der reinen Vernunft*.

23. *CD* 5 December 1869: "Arrival of Kant's works for R. at Christmas."

Fichte (1762–1814)

The person to develop Kant further (and to make Idealism more conducive to the world of the imagination) was Johann Gottlieb Fichte. He seems to have had little direct influence on the composer. In Wagner's extant writings we have only one reference to him and that is a negative one where he speaks of the "Fichte-Schelling-Hegelian nonsense and charlatanry"[24] and the two occurrences in Cosima's diaries are also critical.[25] No works of Fichte are in his Dresden library and the Wahnfried library has just one work, the *Orations to the German Nation*,[26] its nationalism no doubt appealing to Wagner.[27]

Any knowledge Wagner had of Fichte up to the time of his first work on the *Ring* in 1848 would come via his uncle Adolf who had attended Fichte's lectures in Jena. Another possible conduit is Bakunin. At the University of Moscow (1835–36) in the "circle of Stankevish" he immersed himself in some of the more accessible works of Fichte, such as *Guide to a Blessed Life* (*Die Anweisung zum seligen Leben*) and *On the Vocation of the Scholar* (*Über die Bestimmung des Gelehrten*, which he translated into Russian in 1836),[28] works which no doubt appealed to Bakunin who at that time stressed the "inner" rather than the "external life."[29] However, by the Autumn of 1836 he had become thoroughly disillusioned with Fichte.[30]

Fichte was to have a profound influence upon thinkers who in turn influenced Wagner and I first highlight two general points of his philosophy that could be relevant to our discussion. The first concerns the misrepresentation of Fichte over the years as a radical subjectivist. We find this from as early as 1794 when the *Wissenschaftslehre*

---

24. Letter to Röckel of 5 February 1855 (*SB* 6:347). He is no doubt reflecting the insults Schopenhauer cast on the three. In the preface to the second edition of his *World as Will and Representation* he writes of the "humbug" ("Windbeutelei") of Fichte and Schelling and "charlatanism" of Hegel (*WWR* 1:xxi; *ASSW* 1:18).

25. See *CD* 14 December 1874 (implied criticism) and 31 October 1879 where Wagner says "he can understand [Goethe's] dislike of Fichte and says with regard to ideality: 'It is exactly the same as with the valve trumpet—hardly was this facility discovered when all melodies were played with it. The same with ideality [Idealität]: hardly had Kant discovered it when everybody started making nonsense of it.'" Any other reference to "Fichte" in Cosima's diaries is to the tree!

26. This was the 1859 edition of Fichte's son, Immanuel Hermann Fichte.

27. See volume 2, chapter 5.

28. Carr, *Bakunin*, 31–32, 37.

29. "I am not made for external life or external happiness [Michael explains to Tatyana], and do not want it.... I live a purely inner life. I remain with my *I*, and am wholly buried in it, and only this *I* unites me with God" (quoted in Carr, *Bakunin*, 37). See also his remarkably pious letter to Tanyusha of 10 August 1836 (Lehning, *Bakunin*, 31–36).

30. Carr, *Bakunin*, 40–48, writes that a series of traumatic events led him to abandon Fichte. Nevertheless, later, on reading a life of Fichte, he "hailed his old master once more as a 'true hero of our age,' and praised his capacity for 'withdrawing himself from every incidental and external circumstance and from the opinion of the world in order to move steadily and unweariedly to his appointed goal'" (Carr, *Bakunin*, 74).

first appeared[31] right down to figures such as Bertrand Russell.[32] However, there has been a new appreciation of this unjustly neglected philosopher, whose *Wissenschaftslehre* has been described as "a theory of finite subjectivity."[33] His philosophy has been labelled "subjective Idealism," although now emphasis is rightly placed on this being an "Alleged Subjective, Psychological, One-Sided Idealism."[34] His "Original Insight," often overlooked both in the time of German Idealism and in subsequent times, has been well explicated by Dieter Henrich. He considers his "original insight" to be that expressed in the *Versuch einer neuen Darstellung der Wissenschaftslehre*, and the essential point is that every object comes to my consciousness on the condition that I am conscious of myself. But my own self-consciousness assumes that I am an object to myself—but such an object requires a new subject and we then have an infinite regression.[35] Hence, Fichte constantly stresses that the subject needs to be "posited."

The second point I want to emphasize concerns his view of God. Fichte wrote what was considered a provocative essay in 1798, *Concerning the Basis for Our Faith in a Divine World Power* (*Über den Grund unsers Glaubens an eine göttliche Weltregierung*).[36] He appeared simply to identify God with the moral order.[37] It is somewhat ironic that a work that ended by claiming that God is the most certain thing of all and indeed is the ground of all other certainty should have led to accusations of atheism and ultimately led to his dismissal from his post in Jena. In his response to the charge of atheism he said that God was neither one with world nor different from the world; he should not be thought of in connection with the world of the senses and "should not be thought at all, since this is impossible" ("überhaupt gar nicht gedacht werden, weil dies unmöglich ist").[38] It is probably unlikely that Wagner read this essay, but the work was so controversial that he may well have known something of the basic content with which I

---

31. See the letter of Schiller to Goethe, 28 October 1794, quoted in Pippin, "One-Sided Idealism," 147 (Seidel, *Briefwechsel I*, 34; NA 27:74).

32. He writes that Fichte "carried subjectivism to a point which seems almost to involve a kind of insanity" (Russell, *History*, 690). Breazeale, "Spirit," 177, discusses such misunderstandings of Fichte.

33. Breazeale, "Spirit," 109.

34. Pippin, "One-Sided Idealism." See also Breazeale, "Spirit," 192: "An *embodied* ego and a *social* self: this, not the 'absolute I,' is the real 'I' of the early *Wissenschaftslehre*."

35. "Versuch einer neuen Darstellung der Wissenschaftslehre" (1797), Fichte, *JGFAW*, 3:111: "jedes Objekt kommt zum Bewußtsein lediglich unter der Bedingung, daß ich auch meiner selbst, des bewußtseienden Subjekts, mir bewußt sei. Dieser Satz ist unwidersprechlich.—Aber in diesem Selbstbewußtsein meiner, wurde weiter behauptet, bin ich mir selbst Objekt, und es gilt von dem Subjekte zu diesem Objekte abermals, was von dem vorigen galt; es wird Objekt und bedarf eines neuen Subjektes, und so fort ins Unendliche." Cf. Henrich, "Insight."

36. It appeared in the *Philosophisches Journal*, volume 8, 1–20, entitled "Über den Grund unsers Glaubens an eine göttliche Weltregierung" (*JGFAW* 3:119–33).

37. *JGFAW* 3:130: "Jene lebendige und wirkende moralische Ordnung ist selbst Gott; wir bedürfen keines anderen Gottes, und können keinen anderen fassen."

38. *FW* 5:266. Cf. Jüngel, *Mystery*, 126–27; *Geheimnis*, 167.

am sure he would be in fundamental disagreement, since Fichte's God is simply identified with the moral order, no other God being necessary.[39]

Jüngel contrasts Kant and Fichte by saying that "[i]f Kant had limited *knowledge* ([h]atte Kant das *Wissen* aufgehoben) to make room for faith, but expressly asserted the thinkability (Denkbarkeit) of the God of faith and even postulated it in a moral sense, then Fichte had to limit *thought* (so mußte Fichte das *Denken* aufheben) in order to leave room for faith as immediate certainty"[40] and quotes the poem of Emanuel Geibel (whom Wagner knew):[41]

Studiere nur, und raste nie,	Only study and never rest,
Du kommst nicht weit mit deinen Schlüssen;	Thou dost not come far with thy conclusions;
Das ist das Ende der Philosophie:	Of philosophy it is the last and best
Zu wissen, daß wir glauben müssen.	To know that, after all, we must believe.

We do not know whether Wagner had any knowledge of Fichte's *The Characteristics of the Present Age* (*Gründzüge des gegenwärtigen Zeitalters*) but some of the views expressed there cohere with Wagner's. One of them is that Fichte "believes history, as a whole, is governed by purposeful necessity,"[42] a view also taken by Schelling and Hegel, and which Wagner held to.[43] Another regards myth as "the only extant remnant of the period of unconscious—tyrannical reason"[44] and that such myth precedes history and is repeated everywhere,[45] a perspective that chimes in with Wagner's view of the equivalences of myths across cultures.[46] On specific theological issues, Fichte took John to be the one authentic gospel, where, he claims, it remains wholly doubtful whether Jesus was of Jewish origin.[47] Wagner, as we shall see, also held John in special regard, but he did not discount the other Gospels. Perhaps the most significant difference is that Wagner did not consider Paul responsible for the "degeneration of Christianity" ("Ausartung des Christentums") as Fichte had argued and indeed admired Paul as a theologian.[48] Fichte argued that Christianity is not a religion of atonement ("Das

39. I think it is worth adding that when reading Fichte one sees the great strength of Hegel's approach to religion in that he takes seriously Christ and the Christ event.

40. Jüngel, *Mystery*, 140 (modified); *Geheimnis*, 185–86.

41. Geibel, *Juniuslieder*, 209 (Sprüche 4). I quote from the third edition (1848).

42. Oergel, *Nibelungen*, 64. See *JGFAW* 4:411 (second lecture); Smith, *Fichte*, 2:15.

43. See the discussion below on Hegel and providence.

44. Oergel, *Nibelungen*, 64. See *JGFAW* 4:532 (ninth lecture); Smith, *Fichte*, 2:142.

45. See *JGFAW* 4:532: "Myth [...] must be older than all History, since from the commencement of the historic period down to the time of Jesus there was none able even to *understand* (*verstehen*), much less *invent* (*erfinden*) it; and also I find the same Myth everywhere repeated, as the mythical beginning of the History of all nations" (Smith, *Fichte*, 2:142; I have added emphasis to Smith's translation to reflect Fichte's own emphasis).

46. See volume 2 chapters 3 and 12.

47. *JGFAW* 4:492–93 (seventh lecture); Smith, *Fichte*, 2:99–100. See Bell, *Irrevocable Call*, 356–57.

48. The denigration of Paul was characteristic of the German national religion as found in Paul

Christentum ist [. . .] kein Aussöhnungs- oder Entsündigungsmittel") and neither can human beings separate themselves from God ("der Mensch kann mit der Gottheit sich nie entzweien").[49] It is doubtful whether Wagner ever shared this view and in the *Jesus of Nazareth* sketches, *Parsifal*, and various other sources Jesus' death is seen as an atoning sacrifice (even though Wagner had no clear "theory of atonement"). But he did share Fichte's doubts as to whether Jesus was Jewish and Fichte's general anti-Semitic outlook.[50] So Wagner expressed doubts about Jesus' Jewishness in the *Jesus of Nazareth* sketches[51] and in his 1880 essay *Religion and Art* declared: "it is more than doubtful if Jesus himself was of Jewish extraction."[52] Further, Wagner may have shared to some extent Fichte's doubts about a creator God. In *Guide to a Blessed Life* (*Die Anweisung zum seligen Leben*), one of Fichte's works that Bakunin read, the idea of a creator God is seen as "the absolutely fundamental error of all metaphysics and all doctrine of religion, and especially the basic principle of Judaism and heathens."[53] Fichte credits John the Evangelist with denying a creator[54] and again sets John over again Paul, who propagates a half-Jewish form of Christianity.[55]

Fichte's position in the development of both philosophical and artistic thought was crucial. Schelling developed his "Naturphilosophie" very much as a reaction to Fichte (or how he perceived Fichte). Hegel's analysis of the difference between Fichte and Schelling was a significant stage in his philosophical development.[56] Then Fichte was crucial for Schiller's philosophical development and was central to Romantic writers such as Novalis. Friedrich Schlegel even went to the point of asserting: "The French revolution, Fichte's *Wissenschaftslehre*, and Goethe's *Meister* are the greatest tendencies of the age."[57]

Anton de Lagarde, Alfred Rosenberg, Oskar Michel, Artur Dinter, and others (Bell, *Irrevocable Call*, 357–61).

49. *JGFAW* 4:584 (thirteenth lecture); Smith, *Fichte*, 2:200.

50. *JGFAW* 4:493 (seventh lecture); Smith, *Fichte*, 2:99–100.

51. See the discussion in chapter 7 below and volume 2, chapter 2.

52. *PW* 6:233; *GSD* 10:232.

53. *JGFAW* 5:191 (sixth lecture). Translation taken from Laughland, *Schelling*, 31.

54. *JGFAW* 5:190–94 (sixth lecture).

55. *JGFAW* 5:188 (sixth lecture).

56. See Pinkard, *Hegel*, 153–60, on the *Differenzschrift*.

57. See *Athenæum Fragments*, aphorism 216, in Beiser, *Political Writings*, 118. Schlegel probably attended Fichte's *Wissenschaftslehre* nova methodo lecture in Jena starting in 1796.

Schelling (1775–1854)

Introduction

Schelling was a highly gifted student, entering the Tübingen Stift in 1790 at the age of fifteen,[58] and although five years younger than Hegel was breaking new ground in philosophy before him.[59] Schopenhauer considered him the most gifted of the "Charlatans" (Schelling, Fichte, and Hegel). However, it cannot be said he reached the heights of Hegel and the relative strengths of Schelling and Fichte could be debated.

In his early philosophy he was influenced by Spinoza and Fichte, being concerned principally with the freedom of the Absolute, identified with the I's power to act.[60] This was then to evolve into his "Nature Philosophy" and then his "Identity Philosophy," which finds expression in the *System of Transcendental Idealism* (1800).[61] But he was to shift quite radically in view of Hegel's critique of "Identity Philosophy" and of Baader's view of the fall.[62] He took Hegel's description in the preface to the *Phenomenology* (1807) of the "Absolute as the night in which [. . .] all cows are black"[63] as an attack on his "Identity Philosophy"[64] and his struggle with Hegel's philosophy enabled him to fashion his own distinctive view.[65]

When Schelling moved to Munich 1806 he came under the influence of Franz von Baader (1765–1841), a Roman Catholic who was concerned to relate theology to science and was interested in mysticism and radical evil. Beach points out that before knowing Baader, Schelling "had been inclined to treat the natural world as an incompletely developed, but otherwise intrinsically good, manifestation of God's perfection." Baader, however, maintained that "human nature is utterly fallen and that the entire natural world has been soiled as well."[66] Schelling only allowed himself to be influenced by Baader up to a certain point and their differences can be illustrated by the fact that whereas Schelling was happy to work within the *O felix culpa*, the view that the fall was within God's purposes (Schelling thought the fall made freedom

---

58. In the Tübinger Stift it was Schelling, not Hegel, who was the outstanding student; but Hegel's performance was affected to some extent by ill health (Harris, *Sunlight*, 65–70).

59. Harris, *Sunlight*, 186–90.

60. Laughland, *Schelling versus Hegel*, 40.

61. *SWMJ* 2:327–634.

62. Beach, *Potencies*, 75–82. See my discussion below.

63. Miller, *Phenomenology*, 9 (§16); *HHW* 2:17.

64. Schelling, *Transcendental Idealism*, 210, writes of the intelligence stepping out from "the absolute point of view," that is "out of the universal identity in which nothing can be distinguished" ("aus der allgemeinen Identität, in welcher sich nichts unterscheiden läßt"; *SWMJ* 2:602).

65. Laughland, *Schelling versus Hegel*, 59, claims that Schelling never criticized Hegel in public until after his death in 1831. However, Schelling was criticizing Hegel already in his Erlangen lectures and Hegel came to hear of this from Hinrichs in May 1821 (Pinkard, *Hegel*, 464).

66. Beach, *Potencies*, 79.

possible),⁶⁷ Baader rejected it.⁶⁸ Note also that Baader was concerned to hold to a clear distinction between God and the world, something which Schelling and Hegel did not always hold to. Wagner as far as we know possessed no works of Baader and I have found no references to him in his extant writings. However, Baader's views on androgyny are reflected in some of Wagner's views on this subject.⁶⁹ On the matter of *O felix culpa* however, Wagner held a position closer to Schelling.⁷⁰

In addition, Schelling was influenced by Jakob Böhme (1575–1624), perhaps even as early as his childhood,⁷¹ but the key influence occurred in Schelling's mature philosophy.⁷² Böhme "combined in his thought a deep Lutheran piety with abstruse theosophical ideas derived from several mystical traditions,"⁷³ and one such probable tradition was the Jewish Kabbala, teaching that had a pervasive effect in certain circles including the Tübinger Stift!⁷⁴ This Kabbala together with Böhme himself interested the Württemberg pietists and we know that Schelling had various links to leading pietists, such as Johann Michael Hahn (1758–1819), Friedrich Christoph Oetinger (1702–82), and Philipp Matthäus Hahn (1739–1790).⁷⁵ Wagner possessed Böhme's complete works in his Wahnfried library together with a 1675 edition of his theosophical writings.⁷⁶ Although we have only one reference to him, it indicates that Wagner had read Böhme. Discussing "Alles Vergängliches / Ist nur ein Gleichnis" ("All that must disappear / Is but a parable") from the end of *Faust II*, he says it is "in the tone of a mystical medieval saying, like something from Jakob Böhme."⁷⁷

In the only work we know Wagner consulted before working on the *Ring*, *System of Transcendental Idealism*, coming from his earlier period (1800), Schelling argued that nature is the unconscious product of subjectivity. But nature also has "an inherent bent to realize subjective life"⁷⁸ and there is a gradation from the inorganic through to life. The unconscious subjectivity in nature "strives to rejoin full subjectivity" and "reciprocally, conscious subjectivity tries to unite itself to its objective counterpart."⁷⁹

---

67. See *SWMJ* 4:571–720 (*Die Weltalter* (1813)). Cf. Schulze, "Verständnis," 587–88.
68. See Baader, *Bewegung* (*FBSW* 3:285).
69. See volume 2, chapter 6.
70. See below on "Schelling and the Fall."
71. Schulze, "Verständnis," 575–76. n. 10.
72. Brown, *Schelling*.
73. Beach, *Potencies*, 69.
74. Among those who studied in the Stift and who influenced Wagner (or whom he at least mentions) are Hegel, Schelling, Hölderlin, Vischer, Strauß, and Herwegh.
75. Schulze, "Vertständnis," 575–76.
76. *Sämtliche Werke*, 7 vols, 1831–47; *Optime de pietate & sapientia meriti*, 1675.
77. *CD* 16 June 1871. In a letter to Minna (11 July 1858) Wagner refers to Carl Tausig's father, Aloys, as "ein sehr ehrlicher Böhme, durchaus Christ" (*SB* 9:345). I assume the reference is to Jacob Böhme rather than the family Böhme or the music publisher "Böhme."
78. Taylor, *Hegel*, 41.
79. Taylor, *Hegel*, 41.

Although this unites necessity and freedom it does not incorporate consciousness and "[t]here must be a higher unity, where conscious subjectivity reaches out to incorporate nature, and this is attained in art."[80] Taylor points out that Schelling has taken up Schiller's vision of aesthetics recovering the unity between freedom and necessity but giving it an ontological foundation. "Subjectivity thus spawns two worlds, as it were, the unconscious world of nature, and the conscious one of moral action and history. Having the same foundation, these two strive to rejoin each other."[81]

Wagner's knowledge of Schelling

A key person in understanding Wagner's knowledge of Schelling (and Hegel) is Christian Hermann Weisse (1801–66), who was a philosopher, theologian, and New Testament scholar. Weisse was son of the historian and jurist Christian Ernst Weisse (1766–1832), who in turn was son of the librettist, hymn writer, and children's writer Christian Felix Weisse (1726–1804).[82] Christian Hermann Weisse married Christiana Elisabeth Weiss, daughter of the Leipzig theologian Christian Samuel Weiss (1738–1805). Weisse had studied under Schelling and Hegel and became Professor at Leipzig University. Wagner attended his lectures and in his autobiography writes: "Two or three times [. . .] I attended lectures on aesthetics given by one of the younger professors, a man named Weiss."[83] One wonders whether Wagner is underplaying the role of Weisse in his intellectual development by saying that he attended only two or three lectures and I even wonder whether the misspelling of his name is deliberate! It was noted in the previous chapter that he minimizes the influence of his music teachers Christian Gottlieb Müller and Theodor Weinlig, presenting himself as a largely self-taught "musical Siegfried," and shortly after discussing Weisse there is a further misspelling, and again one wonders whether this is deliberate: "Weinlich."[84] I return to Weisse in the discussion of Wagner's debt to Hegel below.

Later in his autobiography Wagner writes that his first attempts with philosophy "had been a complete failure." "None of the Leipzig professors had been able to hold my attention with their lectures on basic philosophy and logic." He continues: "I had later obtained Schelling's *System of Transcendental Idealism*, which had been recommended by Gustav Schlesinger, a friend of Laube, but upon reading even its first few pages had scratched my head in vain to make anything of it, and had always gone back

80. Taylor, *Hegel*, 41.
81. Taylor, *Hegel*, 42.
82. His work as librettist is discussed in Schuler, *Language*, 13–14.
83. *My Life* 54; *Mein Leben* 1:62.
84. *My Life* 54; *Mein Leben* 1:62. Elsewhere Wagner correctly spells "Weinlig" as in the *Autobiographical Sketch* (PW 1:7–8; GSD 1:8–9) and letters (SB 1:126–27, 150–51). The misspelling cannot be blamed on Cosima (the autobiography was dictated) since again she correctly spells his name elsewhere (CD 20 December 1878; 1, 3, January 1879; 4, 20 February 1879). On the other hand, there are a number of occasions when names in *My Life* are misspelt or confused with others (see below).

to my Ninth Symphony."[85] A letter to August Lewald (12 November 1838) suggests that Schelling was recommended not by a "Gustav Schlesinger"[86] but by Gustav Schlesier,[87] a writer and journalist, who worked on Laube's *Zeitung für die elegante Welt* and then for Lewald's weekly *Europa*. The testimony of *My Life* and his letter to Lewald suggests that his reading of Schelling took place around 1832–33.

It is not easy to assess the influence of Schelling on Wagner. There is no work of Schelling in his Dresden or Wahnfried library. However, he was in contact with those who had studied under Schelling. So Bakunin (1814–1876) was a conduit not only for Kant and Fichte but also of Schelling, having studied under him in Berlin 1841–42.[88] His uncle Adolf was another possible conduit: in 1798 he went to Jena for a year of study and, although, as we have noted above, he attended Fichte's lectures, we do not know whether he attended those of Schelling (in Jena 1798–1803).[89] But despite such uncertainties, Wagner does claim to have read Schelling's *System of Transcendental Idealism* and it is full of themes that were to concern him and, as we shall see, there are many parallels between the thought of Wagner and Schelling. We know he did come to know more of the philosopher but this was as late as 1880–81 and hence too late to have influence on the *Ring*. Constantin Frantz had written a substantial work of around 800 pages, *Schelling's Positive Philosophie*, which appeared in three parts in 1879–80 and was dedicated to Wagner. The work annoyed the composer, who, according to Cosima, complained: "As long as [Schelling] believes he has got hold of God Almighty, then everything is all right." She adds: "R. expresses his indignation with Schelling and reads to us a truly incredible passage, proving the existence of God by its impossibility!"[90] Wagner here had encountered a Schelling quite different

---

85. *My Life* 429; *Mein Leben* 1:442.

86. Wagner knew a Maurice (Moritz) Schlesinger in his time in Paris (1839–42) for whom Wagner wrote articles for the *Revue et gazette musicale*. Most of them can be found in *PW* 7:19–182 (a list of articles is given in *Wagner Handbook*, 639–40). Wagner writes, on and off, of his negative experiences with Schlesinger in *My Life* 185–208; *Mein Leben* 1:196–217.

87. Cf. the note in *My Life* 774. In fact, Wagner knew Schlesier, two year his elder, from his school days in the Kreuzschule (Dresden) and moved with Wagner to the Nicolaischule in Leipzig (Glasenapp, *Leben*, 1:173). In the letter to Lewald (12 November 1838) Wagner writes that he and Schlesier in their time at the Kreuzschule "im edlen Hofrath Böttigerschen Eifer Tod der Creutzer'schen Symbolik schwuren, wie ich philologische Epopöen, Tragödien anfing, wie uns später in Leipzig Schelling's transcendentaler Idealismus zwischen die Beine kam [. . .]" (*SB* 1:354). Schelling's work coming "between the legs" ("zwischen die Beine") suggests an uncomfortable encounter.

88. He attended lectures on "The Philosophy of Revelation" (Carr, *Bakunin*, 101) but is said to find him "interesting but insignificant" (Carr, *Bakunin*, 95). Nevertheless, he claims to have translated Schelling (Carr, *Bakunin*, 118).

89. Glasenapp, *Leben*, 1:21.

90. *CD* 24 November 1880. See also, e.g., 6 December 1880 (Schelling's transcendental philosophy treats God "more or less as a tumbler doll (Stehmännchen)"; 16 December 1880 (Wagner "talks with ever-mounting indignation about Schelling's revelation", referring to the subject of the third part of Frantz, *Schellings positive Philosophie*, concerned with *Philosophie der Offenbarung*; cf. *SWMJ* E6:1–530 (Books 1–2); *SWMJ* 6:389–726 (Book 3)); 18 December 1880 (Wagner "would sooner have spent his time reading the dreariest tract of a Protestant theologian than [Schelling's] nonsense").

to that of the 1800 *System*, his positive philosophy being a "Philosophy of Revelation" that "recognizes the God of Christianity—the 'Lord of Being'—as the 'fact' that alone explains human consciousness, the actuality of freedom and the created order."[91] Although Wagner had thirteen works of Frantz in his Wahnfried library, his work on Schelling was not numbered among them and one assumes that Wagner disposed of the work despite it being dedicated to him.

Schelling on history and the Absolute

Schelling was a fundamental figure in establishing the "foundational role of history for an understanding of humanity"[92] and in *System of Transcendental Idealism* wrote: "History as a whole is a progressive, gradually self-disclosing revelation of the absolute."[93] Zachhuber paraphrases that history "does not merely have meaning" but rather "has absolute meaning,"[94] Schelling arguing that "the primary characteristic of history" is that "it should exhibit a union of freedom (Freiheit) and necessity (Nothwendigkeit), and be possible through this union alone."[95] The terms "Freiheit" and "Nothwendigkeit" have an important role in Wagner's Zurich essays and in the *Ring* cycle itself.[96] Schelling argues that the tension between freedom (related to the spiritual) and necessity (related to nature) leads to the conclusion that "All my actions [. . .] proceed, as to their final goal, toward something that can be realized, not by the individual alone, but only be the entire species."[97] In the Zurich essays the term "species" ("Gattung") was to be important for Wagner, although, as we shall see, he borrowed it from Feuerbach rather than from Schelling.

Schelling on Nature

Schelling's *Ideas for a Philosophy of Nature* (*Ideen zu einer Philosophie der Natur*) was published in 1797.[98] He argued that only the organic concept of nature can resolve the outstanding aporia of transcendental philosophy. In his first main section, "On the Problems which a Philosophy of Nature Has to Solve,"[99] he asks about a basic prob-

---

91. Rasmussen, "Metaphysics," 21. This article offers an excellent and clear overview of the development of Schelling's metaphysics (16–22), indeed of the transformation of metaphysics during the long nineteenth century (11–34).

92. Zachhuber, "Historical Turn," 59.

93. Schelling, *System*, 211; *SWMJ* 2:603.

94. Zachhuber, "Historical Turn," 59.

95. Schelling, *System*, 203; *SWMJ* 2:593.

96. See volume 2 chapter 9.

97. Schelling, *System*, 205; *SWMJ* 2:596.

98. *SWMJ* 1:653–723.

99. Schelling, *Nature*, 9; *SWMJ* 1:662: "Ueber die Probleme, welche eine Philosophie der Natur zu lösen hat."

lem of transcendental philosophy: "How do ideas of external things arise in us? By this question we displace the things *outside* of ourselves, suppose them to be independent of our ideas. At the same time there ought to be connection between them and our ideas. But we are acquainted with no *real* connection between *different* things other than that of *cause* and *effect*. So the first endeavour of philosophy is to put object and idea into the relationship of cause and effect."[100] Such a view in relating object and representation as cause and effect is, as we shall come to see, disputed by Schopenhauer.

So if "Naturphilosophie" has a transcendental task, how do we make a correspondence between subjective and objective? This cannot be solved by his using Kant.[101] But Schelling argues that the bridge can be made if there is no distinction in kind between mental and physical, subjective and objective. The mental is simply the highest degree of organization and development of a single living force found throughout nature (and the body is the lowest degree of organization and development). So he concludes at the end of the Introduction to his treatise: "Nature should be Mind made visible, Mind the invisible Nature."[102] Therefore, we have to give an organism *constitutive* status not just a *regulative* status as in Kant.[103] Hence the dualism that had bedevilled Descartes (and Kant) can be overcome.

Fundamental for Schelling was his organic view of the world, something he would pass on to Hegel, and in turn both, especially Hegel, were to have an impact on organicism in the *Ring*.[104] The roots of Schelling's view go back to Leibniz and then ultimately back to Aristotle. According to Leibniz (1646–1716), the essence of matter was not in extension (Descartes' *res extensa*) but in living force.[105] Reviving Aristotle's organic view of the world and in particular his concept of entelechy[106] he wrote: "There is a world of creatures, living beings, animals, substantial forms [entelechies], souls in the very smallest part of matter. Each bit of matter can be thought of as a garden full of plants or as a pond full of fish—except that every branch of a plant, every part of an animal's body, every drop of the liquids they contain is in its turn another such garden or pond."[107] Leibniz's monads were not parts of matter but rather

---

100. Schelling, *Nature*, 12; *SWMJ* 1:665: "Wie entstehen Vorstellungen äußerer Dinge in uns? Durch diese Frage versetzen wir die Dinge *außer* uns, setzen sie voraus als unabhängig von unsern Vorstellungen. Gleichwohl soll zwischen ihnen und unsern Vorstellungen Zusammenhang seyn. Nun kennen wir aber keinen *realen* Zusammenhang *verschiedener* Dinge, als den von *Ursache* und *Wirkung*. Also ist auch der erste Versuch der Philosophie der: Gegenstand und Vorstellung ins Verhältniß der Ursache und Wirkung zu setzen."

101. Schelling, *Nature*, 13, 19–20; *SWMJ* 1:666, 675–76.

102. Schelling, *Nature*, 42; *SWMJ* 1:706: "Die Natur soll der sichtbare Geist, der Geist sie unsichtbare Natur seyn."

103. Guyer and Matthews, *Critique of the power of judgment*, 250–51.

104. This will be further developed in volume 2, chapter 4 and to some extent in the discussion concerning Hegel below.

105. On Leibniz' criticism of Descartes, see Jolley, *Leibniz*, 36–65.

106. See *De anima* II.1 412a (Hett, *Aristotle VIII*, 66–69).

107. *Monadology* §66, quoted in Ross, *Leibniz*, 95.

"requisites" of matter; monads "as principles of energy and life, were the perceivers on which material bodies ultimately depended."[108] Any difference between physical and mental is between different kinds of monads and thus could offer a means of linking the mental and physical.[109] Hence, by bridging the gap between the subjective and objective Leibniz became "the father of *Naturphilosophie*."[110] Thus, we find Schelling developing his own organic view of the world in his 1797 *Ideas for a Philosophy of Nature* (1797)[111] and *On the World Soul* (1799).[112]

Schelling on the fall

Although Schelling was already writing on the "fall" in his Master's dissertation of 1792 (*De malorum origine*)[113] and in *System of Transcendental Idealism* (see below), his views, as we have seen, were to change after his encounters with Franz von Baader. Previously he had viewed the natural world as an undeveloped but nevertheless good manifestation of God. But Baader stressed the complete fallenness of human nature and the consequent corruption of the natural world. Schelling argued that the presence of evil was actually necessary for the emergence of human freedom and saw evil as "dialectically necessary."[114] Schelling's new view of the metaphysics of evil was set out in his *Freedom* essay, where his idea of freedom consists in the human being's relationship to being and God rather than to himself.[115] The emphasis moves from one of reason to one of will.[116] We have no evidence that Wagner had read the *Freedom* essay before working on the *Ring* and any such ideas in the cycle that resemble Schelling's *Freedom* are more likely to come from Schopenhauer.[117]

Schelling on mythology

Schelling shared a number of Fichte's views on mythology, which were discussed above, but he had his own fundamental insights. He writes of an "Urwissen"[118] that is realized

---

108. Ross, *Leibniz*, 89.

109. Cf. Beiser, *Hegel*, 87: "The subjective or mental will be simply the highest degree of organization and development of living force, whereas the objective or physical will be simply its lowest degree of organization and development."

110. Beiser, *Hegel*, 87.

111. *SWMJ* 1:653–723.

112. *SWMJ* 1:413–651.

113. Knatz, *Mythos*, 115.

114. Beach, *Potencies*, 80.

115. Laughland, *Schelling*, 78.

116. Laughland, *Schelling*, 70.

117. See below.

118. See *Methode des akademischen Studiums* (1802; *SWMJ* 3:302). It was noted in chapter 2 that Wagner had a love for compounds with the "ur-" prefix, although I have not found his use of

as history progresses. The first evidence of such "Urwissen" is to be found in myth and in his *Introduction to the Philosophy of Mythology* wrote of the "dark foundry" ("dunkle Werkstätte") where mythology was first produced.[119] In his earlier *System of Transcendental Idealism*, the one work of Schelling's of which we know Wagner had some knowledge before working on the *Ring*, he writes: "Mythology has history begin with the first step out of the domain of instinct into the realm of freedom, with the loss of the Golden Age, or with the Fall, that is with the first expression of choice (Willkür)."[120] Wagner reflected and built upon these ideas in *Artwork of the Future*[121] and in the *Ring*.[122]

We have no evidence that he read the *Philosophy of Mythology* before completing the *Ring*,[123] and the lectures were from Schelling's later years, delivered in Berlin between 1842 and 1846, and published in 1842,[124] the year Wagner moved to Dresden. There are a number of ideas that find a parallel in Wagner but this may simply indicate a dependence on a common earlier source. The most interesting is the key role of Dionysus, who was to prove so important for Wagner.[125] Schelling's views regarding Dionysus and Urania as "one god"[126] coheres with some of the composer's views on "androgyny" and his ideas on the link between Dionysus and Christ again cohere with those of Wagner.[127] One of Schelling's most arresting ideas is that mythology was not allegorical but rather "tautegorical," a term he took from Coleridge.[128] This raises the

---

"Urwissen"; the closest is "Urbewußtsein" ("ur-conscience"), *PW* 7:263; *GSD* 2:119.

119. *SWMJ* 6:20.

120. Schelling, *System*, 200; *SWMJ* 2:589.

121. *PW* 1:69–70; *GSD* 3:42–43.

122. The idea of the "fall" in the *Ring* will be examined in volume 2, chapter 4.

123. *CD* 1 December 1880 indicates he knew of Schelling's philosophy of mythology (from the second part of Frantz's *Schellings positive Philosophie*) only after completing the *Ring* and is compared unfavorably with Creuzer.

124. Schröter's edition is somewhat confusing so I set out what is there given across the volumes. *Einleitung in die Philosophie der Mythologie, Erstes Buch* gives lectures 1–10 (*SWMJ* 6:1–254), and the *Zweites Buch* gives lectures 11–24 (*SWMJ* 5:437–754). Then the *Philosophie der Mythologie, Erstes Buch (Der Monotheismus)* gives lectures 1–6 (*SWMJ* 6:255–387), and the *Zweites Buch (Die Mythologie)* lectures 7–29 (*SWMJ* E5:1–540).

125. See Beach, *Potencies*, 209–20, who points to resonances with Nietzsche's *Birth of Tragedy* (213) and the psychological insights such as "identification with the aggressor" (218). See Lecture 13 (*SWMJ* E5:124–51).

126. He writes that the Arabs "verschmelzen [Urania und Dionysos] für das Bewußtsein zu Einem Gott; sie sind nicht zwei Götter, sondern die zwei Seiten derselben gemeinsamen Gottheit: Urania ist der Gott von der mütterlichen, Dionysos der Gott von der männlichen Seite" (*SWMJ* E5:140).

127. See Beach, *Potencies*, 211–12, comments that "the ultimate manifestation of this divine power [of Dionysus] would be none other than Christ himself—who, like his prototypes in mythology, would be born of a mortal woman, struggle against regressive values, sacrifice his life for the sake of humanity, and in the end be resurrected in his triumphant divinity. But, of course, the full significance of these events could only emerge in and through the revealed religion."

128. *SWMJ* 6:197–98. This is in the *Einleitung in die Philosophie der Mythologie* (lecture 8).

question whether mythology is always opposed to allegory; Wagner would appear to mix the two in that he writes of "mythic allegories."[129]

Schelling on art

Art has a fundamental role in Schelling's philosophy and the close of *System of Transcendental Idealism* present an exalted view of art that Wagner shared.[130] "Philosophy attains [. . .] to the highest, but it brings to this summit only, so to say, the fraction of a man. Art brings *the whole human being*, as he is, to that point, namely to a knowledge of the highest, and this is what underlies the eternal difference and the marvel of art."[131] He did not use the term *Gesamtkunstwerk*,[132] but its essence is found in his writings (and in those of Schiller and Friedrich Schlegel).[133] At the end of his *Philosophy of Art* he writes:

> [. . .] the most perfect composition of all the arts, the unification of poesy and music through song, of poesy and painting through dance, both in turn synthesized together, in the most complex theater manifestation, such as was the dream of antiquity. Only a caricature has remained for the *opera*, which in a higher and nobler style both from the side of poesy as well as from that of the other competing arts, might sooner guide us back to the performance of that ancient drama combined with music and song.[134]

Conclusions

There are a number of significant parallels between the thought of Schelling and Wagner. Schelling's fundamental interest in history and the "absolute," his organic view of nature, his view of the *O felix culpa*, and his understanding of mythology and art, all cohere with Wagner's thought. Such parallels do not, of course, necessarily mean direct influence. However, given his reading of *System of Transcendental Idealism* together with the time he spent with his uncle and Bakunin and the impressive figure of Weisse, it seems almost certain that Schelling exercised an influence, albeit often an indirect one.

Although, as we shall see, Hegel was the dominating philosophical figure when Wagner started work on the *Ring* there is clearly one point where he shared more with

---

129. See *Religion and Art* (*PW* 6:213–14; *GSD* 10:212), discussed in volume 2, chapter 12.
130. Schelling, *System*, 219–36; *SWMJ* 2:612–34.
131. Schelling, *System*, 233 (modified); *SWMJ* 2:630.
132. He does use the term "artwork" ("Kunstwerk") in *System*, 225; *SWMJ* 2:619.
133. Millington, "Gesamtkunstwerk," 47. On Schiller and Schlegel, see chapter 5 above.
134. Schelling, *Philosophy of Art*, 280. Brown, *Gesamtkunstwerk*, 40–41, and "Zurich Writings," 34–37, argues that Schelling anticipates Wagner's view in the Zurich writings, especially *Artwork of the Future*.

Schelling, namely the centrality of myth. Hegel "regarded mythical motifs as the products of a naïve and unreflective imagination. The philosopher's task was to translate religious symbols into purely conceptual terms."[135] For Schelling, Hegel's approach and those of Feuerbach and Strauß were inadequate.

Hegel (1770–1831)

Introduction

One sign of the genius of Hegel and Wagner is that both are open to so many different interpretations. In the case of Hegel, this is seen most clearly in the emergence of right and left Hegelians shortly after his death and to this day Hegel appeals to both conservatives and radicals, atheists and Christians, etc. Likewise, Wagner has been appealed to not only by different points on the political spectrum (e.g., G. B. Shaw and Ernst Bloch versus Houston Stewart Chamberlain and T. S. Elliot) but also, e.g., by differing views on sexuality.[136] I am not necessarily saying that all interpretations of Hegel and of Wagner are equally valid, although in many cases both sides of a debate may have an equal right to claim them as an ally.[137] But I think there is something intrinsic in Hegel's philosophy and in Wagner's art that defies a neat categorisation. It is the case that Wagner felt his art could be "perfectly understood" in some intuitive sense.[138] But at the same time he guarded against "an excessive eagerness to make things plain." Indeed, "to make one's intentions too obvious risks impairing a proper understanding of the work in question."[139]

Everyone accepts that Hegel did influence Wagner's *Ring*, but much secondary literature does not do justice to this. Either the focus is on Feuerbach (which could be called a "left-wing" approach) or Schopenhauer (a "right-wing" approach). Hegel often seems to fall between these two stools,[140] which I think has impoverished Wag-

---

135. Beach, *Potencies*, 2.

136. See the opposing views of Nattiez, *Androgyne*, passim, and Dreyfus, *Erotic Impulse*, 175–217 on the one hand and Scruton, *Truth*, 252, on the other.

137. Cf. Stern, *Phenomenology*, xiv, commenting on Hegel.

138. See his letter to Liszt of 20 November 1851: "In order to be perfectly understood, I must therefore communicate my entire myth, in its deepest and widest significance, with total artistic clarity; no part of it should have to be supplied by the audience's having to think about it or reflect on it; every unbiased human feeling must be able to grasp *the whole* through its organs of artistic perception, because only then can it properly absorb the *least detail*" (SL 237; SB 4:187).

139. Letter to Röckel of 25/26 January 1854 (SL 308; SB 6:68–69).

140. Two books devoted to Wagner and philosophy that are otherwise extremely helpful could offer a little more on Hegel (Young, *Wagner's Philosophies*; Magee, *Wagner and Philosophy*). Further, some writers go to the point of almost completely ignoring Hegel. E.g., Westernhagen, *Wagner: Sein Werk*, (certainly a "right-winger") has one reference in the index (510) (although Hegel is not mentioned on that page) and the biography of Wagner has just one sentence referring to Hegel (151). This reflects the sparse references to Hegel in his teacher, Glasenapp (on this relationship see D. von Westernhagen, "Westernhagen," 84–85).

ner scholarship. His philosophy is difficult and in view of this and the fact that he is so important for the *Ring* I will, after discussing Wagner's knowledge of Hegel, outline some of the crucial issues in Hegel's philosophy, relating him to his predecessors, Kant, Fichte, and Schelling. I will then outline some essential elements in absolute Idealism and his method of dialectic and then move on to themes that Wagner has adopted and adapted: organic worldview, spirit and love, idea, history, and providence, which will then run into questions of religion and in particular the death of God.

Wagner's knowledge of Hegel

Hegel was born in 1770, the same year as Beethoven, and one wonders whether this coincidence struck Wagner. He died in 1831 when Wagner was eighteen years old, and it was in this year that Wagner enrolled at the University of Leipzig. Hegel was the thinker everyone was talking about and, even if Wagner had never read a word of the most influential philosopher of that time, he would have imbibed much of Hegel's worldview. In discussing Wagner's philosophical development reference is often made to the influence of his uncle, Adolf Wagner (1774–1835). His uncle had studied at the Leipzig Thomana and then in 1792 registered in the theology faculty of the University, although his interests focussed on classics (C. D. Beck was teaching there) and philosophy, especially German philosophy. In 1798 he went to Jena for a year of study where he attended Fichte's lectures, but we do not know whether he attended Schelling's (in Jena 1798–1803).[141] Although he left before Hegel's arrival in Jena in January 1801 one can say that he was nevertheless "influenced above all by Hegel."[142] No doubt his enthusiasm for the philosopher spilled over to his nephew. Wagner may also have received Hegelian ideas from his uncle's friend, Christian Hermann Weisse, mentioned above. This much neglected philosopher/theologian had studied under Hegel and in 1829 two books appeared, one concerning the current state of philosophy in relation to Hegel's system and the other a translation of Aristotle "on the soul" (*de anima*) and "on the world" (*de mundo*, wrongly attributed to Aristotle).[143] Then in 1830 his *System of Aesthetics* appeared, which although holding to a Hegelian method did not entirely hold to the Hegelian teaching.[144] Wagner was justly enthralled with Weisse when he met him at his uncle's home and, no doubt, this encouraged him

---

141. Glasenapp, *Leben*, 1:21.

142. Köhler, *Titans*, 10, 638 n. 10. He rightly points to his "Hegelian German"; note, however, that the example he gives is taken from a point in Glasenapp, *Leben*, 1:490, where he is offering a free rendition. The original can be found in Adolf Wagner, *Zwei Epochen der modernen Posie*, 15.

143. Wagner appears to conflate these two works when he writes that Weisse "had just translated Aristotle's *Metaphysics* and had dedicated it, with a polemical intent, to Hegel, if I remember correctly" (*My Life* 54; *Mein Leben* 1:62).

144. Seydel, in the foreword to the 1872 edition of *System der Ästhetik*, IV, writes that Weisse did in fact lecture on aesthetics in the Winter Semester of 1831–32, hence corroborating Wagner's account I mentioned earlier about his attending Weisse's lectures.

later to study Hegel: "I had listened to a conversation between these two men about philosophy and philosophers, which impressed me very deeply."[145]

As far as we know it was about fifteen years later that Wagner started to read Hegel. First, he read the *Phenomenology of Spirit* (1807), sometime in the period 1846–47. Although he may well have had difficulty understanding this highly demanding work,[146] something even seasoned Hegelians experience,[147] I think the work did make a deep impression upon him.[148] As Shklar rightly observes, "[a] great part of the novelty of the Phenomenology is due to his use of the language of the emotions to discuss the work of reason."[149] Perhaps this influenced Wagner to some extent in his idea of "emotionalizing of the intellect."

Around the same time he read a much more accessible work, *Lectures on the Philosophy of History*.[150] Wagner used the second edition of 1840, the only work of modern philosophy in Wagner's personal library in Dresden, and he dates the first reading to 1847. In addition to these two works he may have read the *Aesthetics* and if he did not he must have learned about Hegel's ideas through some other means[151] since his Zurich essays so clearly reflect Hegel's *Aesthetics*,[152] not to mention the close correspondence between the two thinkers on Greek literature.[153] Wagner would be

---

145. *My Life* 54; *Mein Leben* 1:62.

146. See Pecht, *Aus meiner Zeit*, 1:294: "One day when I called on him I found him burning with passion for Hegel's Phenomenology, which he was just studying, and which, he told me with typical extravagance, was the best book ever printed. To prove it he read me a passage which had particularly impressed him. Since I did not entirely follow it, I asked him to read it again, upon which neither of us could understand it. He read it a third time and a fourth, until in the end we both looked at one another and burst out laughing. And that was the end of phenomenology" (*WDS* 167; German in Otto, *Wagner*, 90). This is found in the chapter 10 "Dresden 1846–47" (279–303), hence dating Wagner's reading of the *Phenomenology* in 1846–47.

147. E.g., Findlay, in Miller, *Phenomenology*, xxix, writes that "[t]he packed thought of §§803–4 [. . .] defies reproduction in terms other than its own, and one is quite unsure that one has got the full gist of it."

148. Corse, *Consciousness*, 19, even goes to the point of writing that Wagner "studied carefully" Hegel's *Phenomenology*.

149. Shklar, *Freedom*, 5.

150. This work is one of the more accessible of Hegel's because his account is concrete, dealing with specific historical events, and "provides an easy entrée to the more abstract parts of his philosophy" (Peter Singer, in Magee, *Great Philosophers*, 191).

151. The celebrated music theorist and critic A. B. Marx, editor of the Berlin *Allgemeine musikalische Zeitung*, whom Wagner knew, was a Hegelian (*Brown Book* 94; *Braunes Buch* 112, records his having dinner with him in 1847, Wagner having read Hegel's *Philosophy of History* earlier that year), and Schumann's influential *Neue Zeitschrift für Musik* devoted the greater part of ten successive issues (22 July to 23 August, 1842, the journal appeared twice weekly) to a critique by Eduard Krüger of Hegel's ideas on aesthetics (extracts in English translation are given by le Huray and Day, *Aesthetics*, 530–36).

152. See Bujić, *Music*, 51–52.

153. See Foster, *Greeks*, passim, and my discussion in chapter 4 above.

naturally drawn to Hegel on account of the exalted place he gives art,[154] but he clearly appropriates Hegel to suit his own artistic agenda.[155]

Hegel, Kant, and Fichte: categories and freedom

Hegel's first encounter with Kant's *Critique of Pure Reason* was in his second semester in Tübingen when he took J. F. Flatt's class on "Empirical Psychology and Kant's Critique."[156] Then in 1792–93 he became deeply interested in the practical and religious philosophy of Kant and Fichte.[157] Spurred on by Fichte, he eventually came to a position whereby he became critical of Kant's deduction of the categories (as in the first *Critique*):

> He criticized Kant [. . .] for not deriving his conception of the categories from a consideration of the free activity of thought *as such*, but simply reading them off from the structure of judgement [. . .] In Hegel's view—which is, of course, indebted to that of Fichte—Kant's failure in this regard meant that he was unable to demonstrate definitively which categories thought by its very nature should employ and how those categories are properly to be conceived.[158]

However, Hegel had a fundamental problem with Fichte's view of freedom. Fichte considered the self to have the *power* to make itself whatever it chooses to be. However, we do not have such power since we are subject to external causes and hence Fichte speaks of the struggle.[159] Hegel's solution can be seen as a way of bringing together Spinoza's determinism[160] with Fichte's view of freedom. Beiser sets out Hegel's argument thus:

> Fichte was indeed correct in placing self-consciousness at the center of all things, as the basis to explain nature, for self-consciousness is the purpose of nature, the highest degree of organisation and development of all its living

---

154. See, e.g., Hegel, *Aesthetics* 1:101: "Now, owing to its preoccupation with truth as the absolute object of consciousness, art too belongs to the absolute sphere of the spirit, and therefore, in its content, art stands on one and the same ground with religion (in the stricter sense of the word) and philosophy. For, after all, philosophy has no other object but God and so is essentially rational theology and, as the servant of truth, a continual divine service."

155. See Allen, *Beethoven*, 10–11, who quotes Bujić, *Music*, 52: "Instead of Hegel's closed categories, Wagner presents a fluctuating world in which the arts transform themselves. It is not a world of conceptual clarity, but one of fluctuating dynamic change, supported by the instinct and sensibility of an artist rather than the analytical thought of a philosopher."

156. Harris, *Sunlight*, 73, 83.

157. Harris, *Sunlight*, 107, explains that it was his fellow Stiftler, Schelling and Hölderlin, who encouraged him to study Kant. Fichte, whose *Critique of All Revelation* was published in 1792, visited Tübingen in 1793.

158. Houlgate, *Introduction to Hegel*, 31.

159. See, e.g., his "Review of Aenesidemus," in Breazeale, *Early Philosophical Writings*, 75–76.

160. On Spinoza's determinism see Hampshire in Curley, *Spinoza: Ethics*, xii.

powers. Where Fichte went astray, however, was in interpreting the *final* cause as the *first* cause. He had wrongly assumed that the ego is the fundamental ontological principle of nature when it is really only its purpose or end. The first cause is nothing less than Spinoza's substance, which does indeed act from the necessity of its own nature alone.[161]

Hegel therefore came to give human agency a greater role in the cosmos than anything imagined by Spinoza. Spinoza made humans into a mode of the single divine substance and thus they depended on God, God only being dependent on humans in the sense that substance cannot exist without finite modes of some kind. But for Hegel "God depends on human beings as much as they depend on God" and so "through human activity and self-awareness [. . .] the divine finally realizes itself."[162] Hence, Hegel does give some weight to Fichte's insight and sometimes even uses language reminiscent of Fichte.[163]

Freedom, we shall come to see, is central for Wagner, but before dealing with that there are some other key issues to discuss, namely Hegel's "absolute Idealism" and his views of "spirit," "love," and "idea."

Absolute Idealism

Although Hegel's philosophy is termed "absolute Idealism" the term is used only occasionally in his works[164] and has been variously interpreted.[165] In his autobiography Wagner says that when he read Hegel's *Philosophy of History* back in 1847 he was concerned "to get to the bottom of what was termed 'the absolute' and everything connected with it."[166] The "absolute" is Hegel's technical term for the subject matter of philosophy and he equates this with God: "this Idea (the Absolute, God) can be either more or less abstract" ("diese idee (das Absolute, Gott,) kann mehr oder weniger abstract seyn").[167] Schelling describes the absolute as "that which is in itself and through itself" ("welches von sich selbst und durch sich selbst ist") or "that whose existence is not determined through some other thing,"[168] sometimes calling it "the in-itself" ("das

---

161. Beiser, *Hegel*, 73.

162. Beiser, *Hegel*, 74.

163. Nisbet, *Reason*, 48: the spirit's freedom "does not consist in static being, but in a constant negation of all that threatens to destroy freedom."

164. Arndt, "Idealismus," 262.

165. E.g., Beiser, *Hegel*, 58, writes that "[a]bsolute idealism is first and foremost an idealism *about* the absolute" (my emphasis). This could be questioned on the basis that thought is not just *about* being but entails the unfolding *of* being itself (see below).

166. *My Life* 429–30; *Mein Leben* 1:442.

167. Hegel, *Encyclopaedia Logic* (Geraets, Suchting, Harris), 36 (HHW 6:52; §12).

168. *SWMJ* E2:78; *System der gesammten Philosophie* § 7 (1804).

An-sich").[169] Schelling's absolute is similar to Spinoza's idea of substance,[170] Schelling having converted to Spinoza in Jena,[171] even calling the absolute "die Substanz."[172] Like Schelling, Hegel had taken an interest in Spinoza in his student days but only seriously turned to his philosophy when he moved to Jena.[173] In his *Differenzschrift* of 1801 he sometimes refers to the absolute as substance[174] and as late as the 1820s expressed himself thus in the *Lectures on the History of Philosophy*: "When one begins to philosophize one must be first a Spinozist. The soul must first bathe itself in the aether of this single substance, in which everything one has held for true is submerged."[175] But against Spinoza he writes in the *Phenomenology*: "Of the Absolute it must be said that it is essentially a *result*, that only in the end is it what it truly is."[176]

However, although both Hegel and Schelling turned to Spinoza, the way they appropriated him was to be radically different. Spinoza argued for a monism whereby the mental and physical, the subjective and the objective, are ultimately different attributes of one and the same substance.[177] From this Schelling argued that the ideal and the real, the subjective and objective, are one and the same in the absolute.[178] But whereas Schelling sees the absolute as subject-object identity, Hegel argued in the *Differenzschrift* that the absolute is not only subject-object identity but the identity of subject-object identity and subject-object non-identity. But he does agree with Schelling that subject-object identity "is one important moment of the absolute."[179] So in the "Vorrede" he writes: "In the principle of the deduction of the categories Kant's philosophy is authentic idealism" ("In dem Princip der Deduktion der Kategorieen ist diese

---

169. SWMJ E2:78; *System der gesammten Philosophie* § 6.

170. Curley, *Spinoza: Ethics*, 1 (Part I, Definition 3): "By substance [*substantia*] I understand what is in itself and is conceived through itself: that is, that whose concept does not require the concept of another thing, from which it must be formed."

171. See his letter of 4 February 1895 to Hegel (Hegel, *Letters*, 32; Schelling, *Briefe 1*, 20): "For us as well [as for Lessing] the orthodox concepts of God are no more. My reply is that we get even *further* than a personal Being. I have in the interim become a Spinozist!"

172. SWMJ E2:128 (§41).

173. In the Tübinger Stift Hegel, Schelling, and Hölderlin became interested in the bitter dispute between Jacobi and Moses Mendelssohn concerning Spinoza (Harris, *Sunlight*, 98–101), entertaining the idea that Spinoza's view that the one substance which could be viewed as having mental and physical attributes could be combined with Kant's noumenal and phenomenal worlds (Pinkard, "Life," 21).

174. See Hegel, *Difference*, 80 (*HHW* 1:5) where in discussing Kant he refers to the "Absolute" as Spinoza's "substance."

175. Quoted in Beiser, "Introduction," 5.

176. Miller, *Phenomenology* 11 (§20); *HHW* 2:19. Cf. Beiser, *Hegel*, 59–60.

177. Spinoza, *Ethics* Part II, Propositions 1–7 (Curley, *Spinoza: Ethics*, 33–36).

178. SWJA 3:532 (*Ueber das Verhältnis der Naturphilosophie zur Philosophie überhaupt* (1802)).

179. Beiser, *Hegel*, 62. It should be added that "moment" in the English discussion of Hegel can be misleading since one must distinguish between "das Moment," which is like "impulse" (cf. momentum) and "der Moment," a point in time (cf. "Augenblick"). Beiser here means "das Moment." See further the discussion below on "Idea."

Philosophie ächter Idealismus, ...")[180] But in making reason an object of philosophical reflection, any identity of subject and object "vanishes from its home ground."[181] "Whereas intellect (Verstand) had previously been handled by Reason (Vernunft), it is now, by contrast, Reason that is handled by the intellect. This makes clear what a subordinate stage the identity of subject and object was grasped at."[182]

Hegel insists in the *Differenzschrift* that the difference between the subjective and objective must be not only ideal but also real, not only one in perspective but also one in the object itself. Therefore, "[i]f philosophy is to explain the opposition between subject and object in ordinary experience, then it must somehow show how the single universal substance, in which the subject and object are the same, divides itself and produces a distinction between subject and object."[183] Hegel's absolute Idealism is therefore a monism that is both anti-dualist, denying any substantial distinction between mental and physical, etc., and anti-pluralist in the sense that there is only one substance (although such "substance" takes the form of a multiplicity of different things).[184] He writes that "the Logical is to be sought in a system of thought-determinations in which the antithesis between subjective and objective (in its usual meaning) disappears. This meaning of thinking and of its determinations is more precisely expressed by the Ancients when they say that *nous* governs the world, or by our own saying that there is reason in the world, by which we mean that reason is the soul of the world, inhabits it, and is immanent in it, as its own, innermost nature, its universal."[185] Hence "thinking constitutes the substance of external things."[186] Just as Hegel's "universal" is Aristotelian rather than Platonic[187] so is his "idea" (to which I return below). His "idea" is not Plato's archetypes but rather Aristotle's formal-final cause. The formal cause is the essence or nature of a thing and the final is the goal of its development. Aristotle and Hegel join the two "because the purpose of a thing is to realize its essence or to develop its inherent form."[188] Kant calls this formal-final cause the "concept" (*Begriff*) of a thing[189] and Hegel calls it either "concept" or "idea" (which

---

180. Hegel, *Difference*, 79; *HHW* 1:5.
181. Hegel, *Difference*, 80; *HHW* 1:6.
182. Hegel, *Difference*, 80; *HHW* 1:6.
183. Beiser, *Hegel*, 65.
184. His *Philosophy of Nature* makes clear the difference between physical, chemical, and organic entities and that "each stage of nature 'has its own proper category' (ihre eigentümliche Kategorie), which is 'not also a category of a higher [stage] and is not to be carried over into the category of another stage'" (Houlgate, *Introduction to Hegel*, 119, quoting Hegel, *Naturphilosophie 1823/24*, 78, 93). Hence, Hegel excludes a reductive approach in the natural sciences.
185. Hegel, *Encyclopaedia Logic* (Geraets, Suchting, Harris), 56 (§24A1).
186. Hegel, *Encyclopaedia Logic* (Geraets, Suchting, Harris), 57 (§24A1).
187. See his discussion of the "universal" in Hegel, *Encyclopaedia Logic* (Geraets, Suchting, Harris), 56–57 (§24A1).
188. Beiser, *Hegel*, 67.
189. Guyer and Matthews, *Critique of Judgement*, 78 (*AA* 5:192; Weischedel, *Werke*, 8:267).

is a concept that has realized itself in and through objectivity).[190] Hegel's Aristotelian transformation of Spinoza's monism was that the single universal substance now becomes the single absolute idea, the formal-final cause of all things. This teleological dimension of absolute Idealism is seen in *Reason in History*:[191] "As history tells us, the Greek Anaxagoras was the first to declare that the world is governed by a 'nous', i.e., by reason or understanding in general."[192]

I return to the issue of history and reason below but now I want to take stock regarding the move from Kant to Hegel. A fundamental problem with Kant was what Hegel regarded as his subjective concept of reason: "reason is something imposed on the world by the activity of the subject, where the world prior to this activity is an unknowable thing-in-itself."[193] So subjective Idealists such as Kant consider the world to be rational because we make it so. Objective Idealists, on the other hand, argue that the rationality of the world is not something imposed on it by the subject, but is "something that inheres in the object itself, its concept or formal-final cause." Such objective Idealism is another way of saying that "reason governs the world."[194] Although historically Idealism moved from subjective to objective, Wagner, as I explained at the beginning of this chapter, could be seen as moving in the opposite direction throughout his creative life, from an objective Idealism (Hegel) to a subjective one (Kant, Schopenhauer). However, Hegel kept his grip on the composer. And one way of understanding this is that although for Hegel the absolute realizes itself in the realm of both subjectivity and objectivity, subjectivity is seen as "the highest manifestation, organization and development of the absolute."[195] One key in Hegel's objective Idealism is that it actually culminates in subjectivity.[196] As Robert Williams writes: "For Hegel God's care is focussed principally on the infinite value of human subjectivity: 'the [human] subject possesses absolute, infinite value on its own account, being conscious that it is the absolute object of the infinite love of God.'"[197] Hence, everything comes to a climax in self-consciousness, and this is seen clearly in the *Ring* in the figures of Wotan and Brünnhilde.[198]

---

190. On the "concept" ("Begriff") and "idea" see Hegel, *Logic*, 600–622, 755–844; *HHW* 4:32–70, 4:173–253.

191. This is to be distinguished from the *Lectures on the Philosophy of History*, which Wagner had read. See below for a discussion of the difference between the works.

192. Nisbet, *Reason*, 34.

193. Beiser, *Hegel*, 63.

194. Beiser, *Hegel*, 68.

195. Beiser, *Hegel*, 69–70.

196. Cf. Beiser, *Hegel*, 69–70.

197. Williams, *Tragedy*, 376, quoting Hegel, *Philosophy of Religion*, 1:352; *Philosophie der Religion*, 1:251.

198. Note, by contrast, that Wagner praises Siegfried's consciousness, not his self-consciousness (*LS* 309; *SB* 6:70).

Organic worldview

Kant argued that the idea of purpose is only regulative: "We are wholly unable to prove the impossibility of the production of organized natural products in accordance with the simple mechanism of nature."[199] As Beiser puts it, for Kant "the idea of an organism has only a *regulative* status, i.e., it has only a heuristic value in guiding enquiry into nature, so that [. . .] we have no right to assume that nature really *is* an organism."[200] By contrast Hegel thought nature really was an organism. Such views had been put forward by Friedrich Schlegel, Hölderlin, and Novalis, and given a systematic account by Schelling in *On the World Soul* (1798).[201] A number of factors influenced Hegel's views on an organic universe and one of the most obvious is that when Hegel entered the Tübinger Stift in 1788 he shared a room with Hölderlin and in 1790 they were joined by the Schelling.[202] An interest in botany no doubt contributed[203] as did mystical and religious thought,[204] and there is evidence that around 1800 Hegel came to see that "his holistic ideals are better served by metaphysics than mysticism."[205] Hegel's organic view of the world has similarities to Goethe's. Goethe writes of entelechy, the power of a body to realize its inherent form, an idea that, as we have seen, goes back to Leibniz.[206] Wagner very much shared this organic view of nature, and this will be discussed in detail in volume 2.

Spirit and love

As Beiser argues, organicism provides a necessary but not sufficient account of Hegel's understanding of spirit. The essential difference between Schelling and Hegel, both of

---

199. Meredith and Walker, *Critique of Judgement*, 216 (§71; AA 5:388; Weischedel, *Werke*, 8:502).

200. Beiser, *Hegel*, 98.

201. *SWJA* 1:413–651.

202. Pinkard, "Life," 19. Note, however, that it appears there were in all at least ten students sharing the room (Houlgate, "Life and Thought," 2).

203. Harris, *Sunlight*, 63, notes that in 1791–92 "Botany certainly interested Hegel more than theology."

204. Magee, "Mysticism," 255, argues that from 1793–1801 (Berne and Frankfurt periods) Hegel studied Böhme, Eckhart, Tauler, and von Baader, and that his interest in mysticism intensified in the Jena years (1801–7) through Schelling, who at that time had become fascinated with Böhme, Oetinger, and Swedenborg (256). Ideas from Böhme and Oetinger can be perceived in the Preface to the *Phenomenology* (272–76). Bielik-Robson, "God of Luria," 46, argues that in the close of the *Phenomenology* "Hegel openly resorts to the Lurianic image of the primordial creative 'self-emptying' (*Entäusserung*) and compares it to the kenotic passion of Christ." See below for my discussion of the close of the *Phenomenology*.

205. Beiser, *Hegel*, 89, points to a fragment (*Frühe Schriften*, 457–60) from 1799–1800 (discussed in Harris, *Sunlight*, 440–45).

206. Beiser, *Hegel*, 86.

whom as we have seen argued for an organic view of the world, was that Schelling had a philosophy of life whereas Hegel had a philosophy of spirit.[207]

For Hegel, spirit is not just life but self-consciousness of life. So Schelling understood the absolute identity with nature itself. Hegel, whilst still being interested in nature, then moved toward issues of "culture": ethics, politics, anthropology. Hegel criticized Schelling "for not admitting qualitative differences within the absolute standpoint."[208] In Hegel's 1802 "Natural Law" essay he declares that the realm of the spirit is higher than nature, because nature is only the externalization of the absolute, whereas spirit encompasses both its internalization and externalization.[209]

To understand spirit it is important to see how Hegel developed the idea by considering the meaning and structure of love. Many of the obscure aspects of Hegel's thought on spirit (e.g., the idea of the self going outside itself and returning within itself) suddenly make sense when seen in the light of his thoughts on love. In his Frankfurt period Hegel set out some important thoughts on love (fragments on religion and love, *The Spirit of Christianity and Its Fate*). For Hegel pure subject-object identity only exists in love. In love the self (subject) finds itself in the other (object). There is a mutual interpenetration of subject and object and a single structure of self-consciousness holding between the self and other. But love also involves a moment of identity and a moment of difference. Hegel distinguishes love and morality; in the latter the self attempts to dominate and control the other; here he is criticizing Fichte, who understood morality "as essentially a process of striving by which the self attempts to dominate and control the world."[210] Love, by contrast, gives and thereby becomes richer. As Hegel explains in his fragment on "love": "the giver does not make himself poorer; by giving to the other he has at the same time and to the same extent enhanced his own treasure (compare Juliet in *Romeo and Juliet* [ii.1.175–77: 'My bounty is as boundless as the sea, My love as deep;] the more I give to thee, The more I have')."[211] Likewise in *Spirit of Christianity* Hegel speaks of the whole process of self-surrender and self-discovery, of externalizing and internalizing, as spirit (Geist). He first uses "Geist" in a religious context when speaking of the spirit of Jesus as being the spirit of love, present at the Last Supper.[212] This is first objectified and externalized in the bread and wine and then

---

207. Hyppolite "Consciousness," 4: "Hegel is less concerned with life as a biological concept than as the life of mind as spirit."

208. Beiser, *Hegel*, 321 n. 7, points to Hegel's *Jenaer Systementwürfe II*, GW 7:15–16, which seems to oppose what Schelling wrote in his *Darstellung meines Systems der Philosophie* (1801). However, Schelling changed his view in *Bruno* (1802; *SWMJ* 3:109–228), where "he admitted that self-awareness, the realm of the ego, was the highest organisation and development of the organic powers of nature" (Beiser, *Hegel*, 112).

209. The essay "Ueber die wissenschaftlichen Behandlungsarten des Naturrechts" appeared in the "Kritisches Journal der Philosophie" which he started with Schelling in 1802 (*HHW* 1:417–64, 467–85).

210. Beiser, *Hegel*, 114.

211. Hegel, "Love," in *On Christianity*, 307.

212. Beiser, *Hegel*, 115. See Hegel, *On Christianity*, 248–53.

internalized through eating. "Not only is the wine blood but the blood is spirit. The common goblet, the common drinking, is the spirit of a new covenant, a spirit which permeates many, in which many drink life that they may rise above their sins. [. . .] All drink together; a like emotion is in them all; all are permeated by the like spirit of love."[213] These opposing movements in the experience of love (self-surrender and self-discovery) are related to what Hegel will later call dialectic.

Beiser points out that in his Jena years love slips into the background somewhat. "The legal and moral relations of ethical life rapidly gain favour over love, and eventually love is replaced by mutual recognition."[214] So already in his *System of Ethical Life* (1802–3) "Hegel states that the subject-object identity is realized not in love but in the mutual recognition between citizens in a community."[215] Such unity cannot be found in love since it is only a natural bond between the male and female.[216] In his 1805 *Philosophy of Spirit* love is confined to the family[217] and this development culminates in his 1821 *Philosophy of Right*: spirit actualizes itself in realm of ethical life (§156–57) and love within the family is the foundation for ethical life (§158).[218]

It is clear that it is the earlier philosophy on love that would appeal to Wagner rather than what could be considered the later "bourgeois" view of the *Philosophy of Right*. However, if he knew Hegel's section on "love" in the *Philosophy of Right* §158 I am sure he would offer his qualified assent.

Idea

Hegel's "idea' is teleological, i.e., it is concerned with the goal towards which the spirit is moving and one can sum up a fair amount of Hegel's thought with the phrase "the idea of spirit is freedom."[219] This constellation of idea, spirit, and freedom we will see also characterizes an essential aspect of Wagner's *Ring*.[220]

It is worth emphasizing at this point that when Wagner dictated to his second wife Cosima of the great impression Hegel's *Philosophy of History* made upon him,[221] he had come under the spell of Hegel's most vociferous opponent, Arthur Schopenhauer.[222] Wagner, as is well known, *did* criticise Hegel after his "discovery"

213. Hegel, *On Christianity*, 250.
214. Beiser, *Hegel*, 119.
215. Beiser, *Hegel*, 119–20.
216. Hegel, *System of Ethical Life*, 110.
217. Hegel, *System of Ethical Life*, 231–32.
218. *HHW* 5:148–49. Note especially the powerful additions to (§158) (Knox/Houlgate, *Philosophy of Right*, 162).
219. Cohen, *History*, 12.
220. This will be explored in volume 2; but see also the discussion below on the freedom Brünnhilde achieves.
221. The words are quoted below.
222. This dictation will have been sometime between October 1866 (when they had reached

of Schopenhauer around 1852–54,[223] but often this is just parroting Schopenhauer himself.[224] The absence of Hegel from the Wahnfried library may suggest that he had given up on Hegel, but Nietzsche I think rightly perceived that Wagner remained under Hegel's spell, specifically regarding the "idea":

> Let us remember that Wagner was young at the time when Hegel and Schelling were seducing people's minds; that he achieved, that he grasped in his hands, something only Germans took seriously—"the Idea," by which he meant something dark, uncertain, and full of vague presentiments; with Germans, clarity is an objection, logic is a refutation. . . . Let us keep morality out of this: Hegel is a *taste*. . . . And not just a German taste but a European one!—a taste that Wagner understood!—that he felt equal to! that he immortalized!—He just applied it to music—he invented a style that "meant the infinite,"—he became *Hegel's heir* . . . Music as "Idea"——[225]

This last comment corresponds exactly to Cosima's entry for 3 April 1870 (she is quoting her husband): "[Music] is not the representation of an idea (die Darstellung einer Idee), but the idea itself."[226]

So what is this "idea" for Wagner and, going back to his autobiography, what was it that Wagner discovered about "the absolute" in *Philosophy of History*? The "absolute," of course, is the world Spirit (Geist), the subject of world history. If the drama of the *Ring* can be seen in terms of the evolution of spirit,[227] what then is the "idea" when Wagner says "Music is not the representation of an idea, but the idea itself"? For Hegel the idea was the reason in being, nature, and history. It is the rationality immanent in the world itself,[228] and the world is a manifestation of the idea. So if Wagner considered music as the idea perhaps the ironic description he gave of his dramas as "deeds of music made visible" ("ersichtlich gewordene Thaten der Musik") is not so far off the mark.[229] A further aspect of the idea is that it is essentially teleological, i.e., it is working towards a certain goal (telos). So Houlgate writes, "in nature the idea is the logic that is immanent in and generated by space as such and that leads to the emergence of freely moving matter and eventually to life."[230] Hegel is therefore understanding his "idea" not

---

1839–40 (Gregor-Dellin in *Mein Leben* 2:796)) and 1872 when Part 2 (dealing with 1842–50) was published.

223. Wagner's knowledge of Schopenhauer is discussed below.
224. Again see *WWR* 1:xxi; *ASSW* 1:18.
225. In *The Case of Wagner* (Nietzsche, *Anti-Christ*, 252).
226. Note that later that year Wagner wrote his Beethoven essay, very much influenced by Schopenhauer. However, the comment Cosima records is clearly Hegelian, not Schopenhauerian (for whom music was the objectification of the "will," not the "ideas").
227. Cf. Perschmann, *Tragödie*, vii, who calls *Rheingold* "Die Historie des expansiven Geistes."
228. Houlgate, *Introduction to Hegel*, 25.
229. See *The Name Musikdrama* (PW 5:303; GSD 9:306).
230. Houlgate, *Introduction to Hegel*, 25.

in terms of Plato's forms but more with Aristotle's formal-final cause. Therefore, with this teleological sense it means that if everything is the appearance of an idea, "it strives to realize the absolute idea."[231] So for Wagner one could say the music provides the rationality for the development of the Spirit.[232]

This is particularly striking because Wagner's system of musical "leitmotifs" could be said to have a fundamentally "teleological" function above and beyond that of what could be music's general teleological function. The discussion could become somewhat muddied since Wagner did not use the term "leitmotif" but instead used a variety of other terms; but many of these point to a teleological function. First, one can point to "Motive," "musikalische Motiven," "plastische Natur-Motiven," and "thematische Motiven." As Grey argues, the English "motive" and "motif" are both included in the German "Motiv" so the terms just mentioned have a certain ambiguity and may include "motive," which is clearly teleological.[233] Secondly, the expression "melodische Momente"[234] is not referring to an instant *in time* (hence, I think the translation "melodic moments" can mislead) but rather with a movement *through time* and could be translated as "melodic impulses" and could likewise be understood as teleological. But whatever terms are used, it is clear that these melodic elements are employed for anticipation and recollection and, more fundamentally for our enquiry, mutate into other motifs.[235] I return to Wagner's teleology in volume 2, chapter 4 when I discuss in detail his views on "nature."

---

231. Beiser, *Hegel*, 67.

232. See Wagner's *Beethoven* essay, where music has an a priori function and where he writes of "this conscious representation of the idea of the world (Darstellung der Idee der Welt) in drama" being "preformed by those inner laws of music" (Allen, *Beethoven*, 144–45; cf. *PW* 5:106–7; *GSD* 9:106). *Beethoven* was written between 20 July and 7 September 1870 (Allen, *Beethoven*, 2), notes being made 3 to 20 July (ibid., 12), just three months after the entry from Cosima's diary quoted above.

233. Grey, *Prose*, 319–21.

234. This expression "melodische Momente" is used seven times in the collected writings (*GSD* 4:114; *PW* 2:251; *GSD* 4:200–202; *PW* 2:346–48). Since only the plural occurs there is an ambiguity as to whether Wagner is referring to "der Moment" (an instant in time) or "das Moment" (an aspect, factor, impulse). However, his use of "Moment" in the singular makes it clear we are concerned with the latter (I counted fifty-six instances in the works available in *RWWSB*). See, e.g., *GSD* 3:311: "Der Mensch, den die Musik herstellen wollte, war in Wirklichkeit aber nichts Anderes, als die Melodie, d.h. das Moment bestimmtester, überzeugendster Lebensäußerung des wirklich lebendigen, inneren Organismus der Musik." Ellis translates it thus; "But the man whom Music wished to erect, was really none other than *Melody*, i.e., the moment of most definite, most convincing utterance of her actual living, inner organism" (*PW* 2:106). It would be better to translate "Moment" here as "impulse."

235. See *Epilogue to the 'Nibelung's Ring'* (*GSD* 6:266; *PW* 3:266): "With the 'Rheingold' I was starting on the new path, where I had first to find the plastic nature-motives which, in ever more individual evolution, were to shape themselves into exponents of the various forms of Passion in the many-membered Action and its characters."

History

Collingwood writes that "[t]he culmination of the historical movement which began in 1784 with Herder came with Hegel."[236] One of the great strengths of Hegel is that he took history seriously, and more seriously than Kant. Although there have been some fine studies on Hegel's general understanding of history, Beiser notes that "[c]onsidering its historical importance and frequent use as an introduction to Hegel's philosophy, the dearth of solid secondary sources on Hegel's *Philosophy of History* is remarkable."[237]

In view of the confusion that can surround the editions of Hegel's *Philosophy of History* it is worth offering some words of clarification. The *Lectures on the Philosophy of History* was based on Hegel's notes and those of his students of the lectures he gave five times in Berlin, starting in the Winter Semester of 1822–23, and delivered every two years until the Winter Semester of 1830–31. He delivered four lectures a week. Eduard Gans edited the first edition of 1837 and this was updated by Karl Hegel (Hegel's son) for the second edition of 1840, the edition used by Wagner. This edition provides the basis for that of Eva Moldenhauer and Karl Markus Michel,[238] which corresponds to the English translation of J. Sibree.[239] The other work, *Introduction: Reason in History*, is a translation of Hoffmeister's *Vernunft in der Geschichte* (1955), which gives just Hegel's own "Introduction" to the lectures and has been translated by Nisbet (1975). Hoffmeister explains that over the years Hegel accumulated so much new empirical historical material that by the Winter Semester of 1830–31 he was no longer to cope with it and gave "The Philosophy of World History: Part One."[240]

One factor that drew Wagner to Hegel's philosophy was its relation to history. Wagner's *Annals* for 1847 tell of his interest in "Greek Antiquity" and for the history he mentions Gibbon, "classical historical works," Droysen's *Alexander* and *Hellenism*, and then adds "also Hegel's Philosophy of History."[241] His autobiography explains a little further the link between history and philosophy. He tells us: "I had always felt an inclination to try to fathom the depths of philosophy." After some rather bad starts he then writes of a much more detailed reading in the winter of 1848–49.

---

236. Collingwood, *History*, 113. But note that he considers the originality of *Philosophy of History* "less startling" when one considers his predecessors.

237. Beiser, *Hegel*, 335–36. Since then Hodgson, *Shapes*, appeared which focusses on the lectures of 1822–23. A very helpful introduction to Hegel on History is that of McCarney, *History*, but the focus of that work was actually the *Introduction* to the lectures.

238. *Vorlesungen über die Philosophie der Geschichte*. This is the edition quoted below, which I shall refer to simply as *Geschichte*. I will refer to Wagner's 1840 edition as *Geschichte* (RW).

239. *Lectures on the Philosophy of History*, first published in 1861. I will quote from the 1956 Dover edition.

240. Nisbet, *Reason*, 5. Hoffmeister used Hegel's text (printed in italics) together with students' notes in Roman type (Nisbet, *Reason*, 9).

241. *Brown Book* 94; *Braunes Buch* 111. But note that he may not have read Droysen's book on Alexander (see chapter 4 above).

> During the last period of my residence in Dresden I had nonetheless tried to do justice to this old, now newly awakened urge, and took as a point of departure the more searching historical studies which so greatly satisfied me at the time. For my introduction to the philosophy of Hegel I chose his *Philosophy of History*. Much of this impressed me, and it appeared as if I would gain admittance to the inner sanctum by this route. The more incomprehensible I found many of the most sweeping and speculative sentences of this tremendously famous intellect, who had been commended to me as the keystone of philosophic understanding, the more I felt impelled to get to the bottom of what was termed "the absolute" and everything connected with it. The revolution interrupted this effort.[242]

Although his comments in his *Brown Book* may suggest a rather cursory reading in 1847 ("*also* Hegel's Philosophy of History")[243] there is reason to believe that by 1848–49 he had imbibed much from this work as we shall see. In working through Wagner's copy I found only two marked passages. This may suggest that it was a cursory reading. But it must be stressed that Wagner rarely marked his books, and this applies to those we know he read.[244] The second marking regards animals,[245] and I will discuss this in volume 2 in the discussion of nature. The first passage marked is from the "Introduction" ("Einleitung"). Hegel has been writing of history as the "slaughter-bench (Schlachtbank) at which the happiness of peoples [...] have been victimized" and asks "to what final aim these enormous sacrifices have been offered."[246] He goes on to speak of the "*principle, aim, destiny,* or the nature and idea of Spirit"[247] and in this context we have the marking that includes Hegel's discussion of the human will and the consequences of the will,[248] which must have had an interest for Wagner already in 1847 (and well before his reading of Schopenhauer):

> Aims, principles, &c., have a place in our thoughts, in our subjective design only; but not yet in the sphere of reality. That which exists for itself only, is a possibility, a potentiality; but has not yet emerged into Existence. A *second*

---

242. *My Life* 429–30; *Mein Leben* 1:442. Note also that around this time that he had become associated with Mikael Bakunin (*My Life* 384–89; *Mein Leben* 1:398–402) for whom Hegel was central. See Carr, *Bakunin*, 59–72. Originally Bakunin belonged to the "Right Hegelians" (Carr, *Bakunin*, 75).

243. *Brown Book* 94; *Braunes Buch* 111 (my emphasis).

244. The marked passages are *Geschichte* (RW), 28–29, 391. There are in addition a number of pages (e.g., 30–61) where one can discern finger marks but these are not necessarily those of Wagner.

245. *Geschichte* (RW), 391. Cf. *Geschichte*, 389; Sibree, *History*, 321. On Hegel's understanding of "will" see Inwood, *Dictionary*, 311–14; Stederoth, "Wille," 494–96.

246. Sibree, *History*, 21; *Geschichte*, 35: "Aber auch indem wir die Geschichte als diese Schlachtbank betrachten, auf welcher das Glück der Völker, die Weisheit der Staaten und die Tugen der Individuen zum Opfer gebracht worden, so entsteht dem Gedanken notwendig auch die Frage, wem, welchem Endzwecke diese ungehersten Opfer gebracht worden sind."

247. Sibree, *History*, 22; *Geschichte*, 36.

248. On Hegel's understanding of "will" see Inwood, *Dictionary*, 311–14; Stederoth, "Wille," 494–96.

element must be introduced in order to produce actuality—viz. actuation, realization; and whose motive power is the Will—the activity of man in the widest sense. It is only by this activity that that Idea as well as abstract characteristics generally, are realised, actualised; for of themselves they are powerless. The motive power that puts them in operation, and gives them determinate existence, is the need, instinct, inclination, and passion of man. That some conception of mine should be developed into act and existence, is my earnest desire: I wish to assert my personality in connection with it: I wish to be satisfied by its execution. If I am to exert myself for any object, it must in some way or other be *my* object. In the accomplishment of such or such designs I must at the same time find *my* satisfaction; although the purpose for which I exert myself includes a complication of results, many of which have no interest for me. This is the absolute right of personal existence—to find *itself* satisfied in its activity and labor.[249]

The first trace of Wagner's appealing to Hegel's understanding of history I have found is his "Toast" given after a concert to mark the tercentenary of the "Royal Kapelle at Dresden" on 22 September 1848.[250] This speech, apparently given impromptu, reveals some interesting things about the composer and begins by alluding to Hegel's *Philosophy of History* (together with characteristic Hegelian vocabulary) and the Protestant character of the Kapelle.[251]

> The era spanned to-day by the existence of our Kapelle is of the most unwonted moment: the three centuries of life of this art-institute cover that period which historians call the Third in *World-History*, commencing with the epoch of the Reformation and continuing to the present day; it is the period of the human spirit's evolution to ever more distinct self-consciousness: in it that spirit has sought with surer tools to grasp is destiny, to probe the natural necessity of all

---

249. Sibree, *History*, 22 (the emphasis of "*my*" and "*itself*" is only in the English translation). The German as in *Geschichte*, 36–37, is: "Zwecke, Grundsätze usf. sind in unseren Gedanken, erst in unserer inneren Absicht, aber noch nicht in der Wirklichkeit. Was an sich ist, ist eine Möglichkeit, ein Vermögen, aber noch nicht aus seinem Inneren zur Existenz gekommen. Es muß ein *zweites* Moment für die Wirklichkeit hinzukommen, und dies ist die Betätigung, Verwirklichung, und deren Prinzip ist der Wille, die Tätigkeit des Menschen überhaupt. Es ist nur durch diese Tätigkeit, daß jener Begriff sowie die an sich seienden Bestimmungen realisiert, verwirklicht werden, denn sie gelten nicht unmittelbar durch sich selbst. Die Tätigkeit, welche sie ins Werk und Dasein setzt, ist des Menschen Bedürfnis, Trieb, Neigung und Leidenschaft. Daran, daß ich etwas zur Tat und zum Dasein bringe, ist mir viel gelegen; ich muß dabei sein, ich will durch die Vollführung befriedigt werden. Ein Zweck, für welchen ich tätig sein soll, muß auf irgendeine Weise auch mein Zweck sein; ich muß meinen Zweck zugleich dabei befriedigen, wenn der Zweck, für welchen ich tätig bin, auch noch viele andere Seiten hat, nach denen er mich nichts angeht. Dies ist das unendliche Recht des Subjekts, daß es sich selbst in seiner Tätigkeit und Arbeit befriedigt findet."

250. Hence, what is now known as the "Dresden Staatskapelle" can count as the oldest "orchestra" in Germany. The only contender is the Leipzig Gewandhaus Orchestra, founded in 1743 but with roots going back to 1479.

251. The founder in 1548 was Kurfürst Moritz of Saxony who, although brought up a catholic, converted to Lutheranism.

existing forms of being upon earth. An art-institute that has grown-up in and with this period, cannot have stayed a stranger to the spirit of that evolution: the influence of the era will have stamped and moulded it. And so we find: to the spirit of Protestant piety that seized all hearts 300 years ago, this institution owes its origin; a Prince who bore the sword in bold enterprise for Protestant independence, at like time founded at his Court the institute whereby that *spirit* was to find its art-expression.[252]

It is worth adding that despite this apparent eulogy to the "art-institute" Wagner was to put forward radical reforms for the "German National Theatre for the Kingdom of Saxony,"[253] including a musician's union.[254]

Providence

Hegel argues in *Philosophy of History* that "Reason directs the World," which is in the form "of the *religious truth*, that the world is not abandoned to chance and external contingent causes, but that a *Providence* (*Vorsehung*) controls it."[255] But such providence is not the simple optimism his opponents have credited him with.[256] Indeed, as we have seen, Hegel goes on to speak of history as a "slaughter bench" ("Schlachtbank").[257] But despite this Hegel nevertheless views history as a theodicy, a view he expressed in the final paragraph of *Philosophy of History*: "That the History of the World, with all the changing scenes which its annals present, is this process of development and the realization of Spirit,—this is the true *Theodicæa*, the justification of God in History. Only *this* insight can reconcile Spirit with the History of the World—viz., that what has happened, and is happening every day, is not only not 'without God,' but is essentially His Work."[258] Fundamental to this theodicy is that somehow the death of Christ is written into the very fabric of history, a point to which I will return.

---

252. *PW* 7:315 (the published version of *Toast on the Tercentenary of the Royal Kapelle at Dresden*; my emphasis); *GSD* 2:229-30. I have highlighted the Hegelian terms "World-History" ("Weltgeschichte") and "spirit" ("Geist"). Note that in the original the term translated here as "moment" is actually "Bedeutung".

253. See *PW* 7:319-60; *GSD* 2:232-73. Ellis (*PW* 7:314) notes that these reforms were drafted before his "Toast."

254. *PW* 7:356; *GSD* 2:270.

255. Hegel, *History*, 12-13; *Geschichte*, 25.

256. Houlgate, *Introduction to Hegel*, 18: Hegel is not "the naïve Enlightenment optimist caricatured by Nietzsche or Schopenhauer."

257. Hegel, *History*, 21; *Geschichte*, 35. This will be further explored in volume 2, chapter 9.

258. Hegel, *History*, 477. Hegel, *Geschichte*, 540: "Daß die Weltgeschichte dieser Entwicklungsgang und das wirkliche Werden des Geistes ist, unter dem wechselnden Schauspiele ihrer Geschichten— dies ist die wahrhafte *Theodizee*, die Rechtfertigung Gottes in der Geschichte. Nur *die* Einsicht kann den Geist mit der Weltgeschichte und der Wirklichkeit versöhnen, daß das, was geschehen ist und alle Tage geschieht, nicht nur nicht ohne Gott, sondern wesentliche das Werk seiner selbst ist."

Just as *Philosophy of History* deals with theodicy, so does the *Ring*. The world is recreated at the end of the drama and one of the purposes of the whole drama is that a woman (Brünnhilde) becomes wise, fully self-conscious, and hence free. This was only possible through her betrayal and the death of Siegfried: "it was I whom the purest man / had to betray, / that a woman might grow wise."[259] Freedom is the goal to which Hegel's spirit is directed and, as we have already seen, "the idea of spirit is freedom."[260] So Brünnhilde is free in that what she wants to do is exactly the right thing to do, i.e., sacrifice herself.[261] Desire and reason now finally coincide. We see this idea in these words from the final scene: "Alles, alles, / Alles weiß ich: / alles ward mir nun frei!" ("All things, / all things, all things I know: / all things became free to me").[262] The ideas behind "alles ward mir nun frei" I suggest are all things became free in relation to me such that I could find my own freedom in them or I am free from any misconceptions, misunderstandings or any other hindrances.

Wagner's letter to August Röckel of 25/26 January 1854, in prison in Waldheim, includes addressing an issue that was understandably close to Röckel's heart: freedom. What he writes could equally be a commentary on Brünnhilde's state of mind in that final scene of *Götterdämmerung*: "One thing counts above all else: freedom! But what is 'freedom'? is it—as our politicians believe—'licence?'—of course not! Freedom is: *integrity*. He who is true to himself, i.e., who acts in accord with his own being, and in perfect harmony with his own nature, is *free*."[263]

Absolute religion, thought and being, and the death of God

When one considers the theological scheme put forward by Kant and especially by Fichte who, in his *Critique of all Revelation*, considered that the only thing that could be revealed was the moral law, then Hegel's theological approach is so much richer. Full weight is given to history (including the life of Jesus), Trinity, and incarnation, and it is therefore understandable that Hegel considered Christianity the absolute religion.

Wagner found many of Hegel's theological ideas congenial. The works we know he read, *Philosophy of History* and *Phenomenology*, represent his mature thinking

259. WagRS 349.
260. Cohen, *History*, 12.
261. Her willingness to sacrifice herself contrasts rather starkly with Jesus' agony in Gethsemane as portrayed in the Synoptic Gospels (Matt 26:36–46; Mark 14:32–42; Luke 22:39–46). But Brünnhilde's willingness to die does find a parallel in Wagner's *Jesus of Nazareth* sketches. Although Wagner has a Gethsemane scene at the end of Act IV, there is, as in John's Gospel at this point (18:1), no agonizing prayer (PW 8:293; DTB 244–45). On John's influence on the sketches, see chapter 7 below.
262. Spencer's translation of the final phrase "alles ward mir nun frei!" as "all is clear to me now!" (*WagRS* 349) represents the usual translation found in English sources. A notable exception is that of Deathridge, *Ring*, 715: "All freedom has now become mine."
263. SL 301; SB 6:60. However, note that Hegel's has "an all-embracing theory of freedom" (Houlgate, *Introduction to Hegel*, 181), aspects of which Wagner would not embrace (e.g., regarding the state, economic life, and family life).

but we have no evidence he read the earlier works. These writings from his periods in Tübingen (1788–93) and Berne (1793–97) are considered critical of Christianity whereas those written in Frankfurt (1797–1800) are more sympathetic.[264] One significant shift in emphasis is that whereas in his *Life of Jesus* from the Berne years we find Jesus as a preacher of Kantian morality (although one has to add that Hegel is faithful to the Gospel of John by including his teaching on love),[265] in the Frankfurt years there is a much stronger emphasis on Jesus as a preacher of love,[266] a prominent theme in Wagner's *Jesus of Nazareth* sketches.

In the Jena years Hegel brings together theology and philosophy. In *Faith and Knowledge* (*Glauben und Wissen*, 1802) he criticizes Kant, Jacobi, and Fichte for their dualism between faith and reason. In the conclusion he makes two points which he was further to develop, and both I claim are central for Wagner. First, "[b]oth being and thought are one."[267] Hegel developed the view[268] that "thought" is not just *about* "being" but concerns "the self-determining and self-unfolding *of* being itself."[269] This coheres rather well with Wagner's understanding of music as "idea," which we saw is closely related to his understanding of teleology. Then in the mature Hegel we read these frequently quoted words from the *Philosophy of Right* (1821): "What is rational is actual and what is actual is rational."[270] Beiser comments: "Applying this dictum to the Church, the philosopher has to recognize that, though there is some rationality present in the Church, the Church will also have to change to realize the standards of reason."[271] On the second half of the dictum it must be stressed that Hegel in the *Enzyklopädie* (where the dictum is quoted) distinguished "actuality" ("Wirklichkeit") from "reality" ("Dasein") or "existence" ("Existenz").[272] So "not everything that exists qualifies as actual."[273]

---

264. Beiser, *Hegel*, 127.

265. See Hegel, *Leben Jesu*, 61–62; *Three Essays*, 154–55: "What I leave you is the commandment to love one another and the example of my love for you. Only through this mutual love are you to distinguish yourselves as my friends. [. . .] Love one another. Love all men as I have loved you. The life I give for the benefit of my friends is proof of my love." A detailed discussion of the Kantianism in *Leben Jesu* is given by Harris, *Sunlight*, 194–207. Hegel ends his account with the burial of Jesus (*Three Essays*, 165; *Leben Jesu*, 74).

266. See above.

267. Hegel, *Faith and Knowledge*, 190; HHW 1:413.

268. When it was developed is unclear but it is clearly expressed in the first edition (1812) of the *Science of Logic* (Gawoll/Hogemann, *Logik*, 17).

269. Houlgate, *Introduction to Hegel*, 45.

270. Knox/Houlgate, *Philosophy of Right*, 14. HHW 5:14: "Was vernünftig ist, das ist wirklich; und was wirklich ist, das ist vernünftig."

271. Beiser, *Hegel*, 140.

272. Beiser, *Hegel*, 222. Hegel, *Encyclopaedia Logic* (Geraets, Suchting, Harris), 29–30 (HHW 6:44–45, § 6).

273. Beiser, *Hegel*, 141.

THE *RING* AND GERMAN IDEALISM

The second key point Hegel presents in the conclusion concerns the "death of God": "Good Friday must be speculatively re-established in the whole truth and harshness of its God-forsakenness."[274] Hegel's point seems to be that up until his own time the death of God in Protestant religion and earlier philosophy had "only the rank of subjective grief, but not the harsh dignity of a grief of God. That God himself is dead was a feeling of subjectivity, but not a factor (Moment) of truth in God himself."[275] Hegel wishes to go beyond this and argues "the pure concept or infinity as the abyss of nothingness in which all being is engulfed, must signify the infinite grief [of the finite] purely as a moment of the supreme Idea, and no more than a moment."[276]

As Wagner worked on the libretto of the *Ring* it is highly significant that the focus moves from the hero Siegfried to the chief god Wotan, especially his downfall. In her Schlussgesang, Brünnhilde lulls Wotan to sleep in both the words "Rest now, rest now, you god!" "Ruhe! Ruhe, du Gott!")[277] and the "lullaby" music, a three-bar segment of the Valhalla theme which is similar to what we hear when Wotan puts Brünnhilde to sleep at the end of *Walküre*.[278] Just as this "lullaby" was a prelude to the flames of Loge, which were to dance around her rock, so here Wotan is lulled to sleep but in preparation for his destruction in the final conflagration that spreads to Valhalla. On one level then the God who dies in the *Ring* is Wotan together with his pantheon and everything is now in the hands of humanity. However, as is often the case with Wagner, he can turn things on their head. For the key god who dies is not Wotan, who, as we see in Brünnhilde's final speech, is guilty! Rather the god who dies is Brünnhilde herself.

She is the daughter of two gods, Wotan and Erda, and if "God is love" (1 John 4:8), something that we shall see was fundamental for Feuerbach (and for Wagner), then surely she is the true divine figure, not Wotan. At the end of *Walküre* she undergoes what can be legitimately called an incarnation. However, in distinction to the incarnation as represented in New Testament texts and in Hegel, she, according to Wotan, actually loses her divinity: "so he kisses your godhead away."[279] We have an emptying of her divinity, a "kenosis." This corresponds to Hegel's understanding of the incarnation: "the Divine Being is reconciled with its existence through an event,—the event of God's emptying Himself of His Divine Being (Entäusserung des göttlichen Wesens) through His factual Incarnation and His Death."[280]

However, when she appears in the final scene of *Götterdämmerung* there are signs that she is transfigured and is in the process of regaining her divinity. The stage

---

274. Hegel, *Faith and Knowledge*, 191; HHW 1:414.
275. Jüngel, *Mystery*, 74–75 (translation modified); *Geheimnis*, 99.
276. Hegel, *Faith and Knowledge*, 190; HHW 1:413–14.
277. WagRS 349.
278. Compare *Walküre* Act III (bars 1625–27) and *Götterdämmerung* Act III (bars 1357–60).
279. WagRS 191. This passage is discussed in volume 2 chapter 11.
280. I use here the translation of Baillie, *Phenomenology*, 780. HHW 2:418. I am not sure Miller, *Phenomenology*, 475 (§784), captures the sense, translating "Entäusserung" as "externalisation."

direction indicates that she enters "firmly and solemnly (feierlich)."[281] A little later "[h]er features grow increasingly transfigured."[282] So one gets the impression that Brünnhilde returns to her original godlike existence.[283] That she seems to recover her divinity in this final scene is highly significant theologically, for it means that the one who dies is not simply a human being but a divine figure. When she offers herself as a sacrifice at the end of *Götterdämmerung*, working "the deed that redeems the world,"[284] the entire cosmos is renewed. Because of Wagner's views on gender, redemption is achieved by the double sacrifice of Siegfried and Brünnhilde[285] and this is expressed musically right at the end as the Siegfried musical theme is followed by Brunnhilde's.

The death of Brünnhilde in *Götterdämmerung* resembles that of Christ in the *Jesus of Nazareth* sketches. After Jesus' death (which occurs off-stage), we read "John and the two Marys return from the crucifixion: 'He hath fulfilled.'—Peter feels himself inspired with the Holy Spirit: in high enthusiasm he proclaims the fulfilment of Jesus' promise: his words give strength and inspiration to all; he addresses the people,—whoever hears him, presses forward to demand baptism (reception into the community). The end."[286] The key element is that Jesus dies and then the Holy Spirit comes upon Peter and the Christian community. Such a telescoping of Good Friday and Pentecost is found in John's Gospel (see John 7:39; 19:30)[287] and it may well be that Hegel can throw some light on this. In *Philosophy of History* Hegel writes: "It has been already remarked that only after the death of Christ could the Spirit come upon his friends; that only then were they able to conceive the true idea of God (die wahrhafte Idee Gottes), viz., that in Christ man is redeemed and reconciled."[288] Hegel would know of Luther's view that in order to atone for sins God must die[289] and this was in fact central

---

281. *WagRS* 347.

282. *WagRS* 348.

283. Cf. Kienzle, "Brünnhilde," 101: "Im letzten Teil ihres Gesangs kehrt Brünnhilde selbst zu ihrer ursprünglichen Existenz zurück."

284. *WagRS* 258.

285. *SL* 307: "Not even Siegfried alone (man alone) is the complete 'human being': he is merely the half, only with *Brünnhilde* does he become the redeemer; *one* man alone cannot do everything; many are needed, and a suffering, self-immolating woman finally becomes the true, conscious redeemer: for it is love which is really 'the eternal feminine' itself" (*SB* 6:68). This letter to Röckel of 25/26 January 1854, will be discussed further in volume 2 in relation to a series of theological issues including that of gender.

286. *PW* 8:297; *DTB* 246.

287. See Brown, *John*, 1:324; 2:931.

288. *History*, 328; *Geschichte*, 396–97: 'Es ist schon bemerkt worden, daß erst nach dem Tode Christi der *Geist* über seine Freunde kommen konnte, daß sie da erst die wahrhafte Idee Gottes zu fassen vermochten, daß nämlich in Christus der Mensch erlöst und versöhnt ist.'

289. Jüngel, *Mystery*, 95–96; *Geheimnis* 125–26, refers to "Formula of Concord" (*BSELK* 1030–31) and a work by Karl Christian Flatt (brother of J. F. Flatt, Harris, *Sunlight*, 107) who had been Hegel's fellow student in Tübingen. Both works quote Luther's treatise *On Councils and Churches* which includes the phrase "if it cannot be said that God died for us, but only a man, we are lost" (*LW* 41:196).

to Hegel's understanding of the "Death of God." He refers to the second stanza of the passion hymn of Johann Rist "O Traurigkeit, O Herzeleid" (1641):

O grosse Not!	O Great woe!
Gott selbst liegt tot.	God himself lies dead.
Am Kreuz ist er gestorben;	On the cross he has died;
hat dadurch das Himmelreich	And thus he has gained for us
uns aus Lieb' erworben.	By love the kingdom of heaven.

The second line is quoted in Hegel's first discussion of the death of God I discussed above,[290] after which, to repeat: "Good Friday must be speculatively re-established in the whole truth and harshness of its God-forsakenness."[291] Jüngel points to one of the clearest explanations Hegel offers for the "death of God" in this aphorism: "God sacrifices himself, gives himself up to destruction. God himself is dead; the highest despair of complete forsakenness by God."[292] This, Jüngel argues, is the sense of the close of *Faith and Knowledge* where the pure concept ("der Begriff formeller Abstraction"), in designating the infinite grief of the metaphysic of subjectivity as a moment of the supreme idea ("höchste Idee"), must grant to "philosophy the Idea of absolute freedom along with the absolute passion, the speculative Good Friday."[293] Jüngel adds: "The idea of absolute freedom and absolute passion are linked together here because God gives himself up to destruction, and thus chooses suffering in absolute freedom."[294] Likewise, Brünnhilde gives herself up to destruction in the flames and does so in "absolute freedom." In fact, one of the striking aspects of the close of *Götterdämmerung* is that, as noted above, in Brünnhilde reason and desire coincide. For Hegel such a correspondence was exactly what freedom meant.

Christ's death is fundamental for Hegel, although, as we have seen, his interest is more in what he calls the speculative Good Friday rather than the Good Friday of the Gospels. Resurrection is seen in terms of the Spirit at work in the Christian community and the close of Wagner's *Jesus of Nazareth* corresponds to this. But for Hegel the death of God on Good Friday concerned not just this historical death but that "the abstraction of the divine essence" is changed. He writes in the *Phenomenology*:

> The death of the Mediator is the death not only of his *natural* aspect or of his particular being-for-self, not only of the already dead husk stripped of its essential Being, but also of the *abstraction* of the divine Being. [. . .] The death of this

---

290. Hegel, *Faith and Knowledge*, 190; *HHW* 1:414.

291. Hegel, *Faith and Knowledge*, 191; *HHW* 1:414.

292. Nicolin, *Aphorismen*, 16, quoted in Jüngel, *Mystery*, 74; *Geheimnis*, 98: "Gott opfert sich auf, gibt sich zur Vernichtung hin. Gott selbst ist todt; die höchste Verzweiflung der völligen Gottverlassenheit."

293. Hegel, *Faith and Knowledge*, 191; *HHW* 1:414.

294. Jüngel, *Mystery*, 74; *Geheimnis*, 98.

picture-thought (Vorstellung) contains, therefore, at the same time the death of the *abstraction of the divine Being* which is not posited as Self. That death is the painful feeling of the Unhappy Consciousness that *God himself is dead*.[295]

So "death becomes transfigured from its immediate meaning, viz. the non-being of this *particular* individual, into the *universality* of the Spirit who dwells in His community, dies in it every day, and is daily resurrected."[296] Note that the community undergoing daily death and resurrection is indebted to Luther's discussion of baptism in the *Shorter Catechism*: "[Baptizing with water] signifies that the old Adam in us is to be drowned by daily sorrow and repentance, and perish with all sins and evil lusts; and that the new man should daily come forth again and rise, who shall live before God in righteousness and purity forever."[297]

Hence, with Brünnhilde's death, the world is "reconciled"[298] and one can say the spirit of Brünnhilde runs through the re-created world. This is expressed musically by a motif wrongly called "redemption" or "redemption through love."[299] As Cosima explained on the authority of her husband to an inquirer in 1875, "the motive sung to Brünnhilde by Sieglinde [in Die *Walküre*] is the glorification of Brünnhilde which at the end of the work [*Götterdämmerung*] is taken up, so to speak, by the entirety ("das Motiv, welches Sieglinde der Brünnhildes zu-singt, die Verherrlichung Brünnhilden's ist, welche am Schluss des Werkes gleichsam von der Gesammtheit aufgenommen wird)."[300] Deathridge points out that by "taken up by the whole" Wagner meant "not only the silent chorus on stage, but also the audience and probably the entire world as well."[301] The final lines of the *Phenomenology*, which must be "one of the most famous endings in the philosophical literature,"[302] could also be said to apply to Brünnhilde. Hegel speaks of the "Spirit emptied out into Time" ("der an die Zeit entäusserte Geist")[303] and "Absolute Knowing, or Spirit that knows itself as Spirit" and the "recollection of the Spirits." Hegel concludes:

> [The Spirits'] preservation, regarded from the side of their free existence appearing in the form of contingency, is History; but regarded from the side

---

295. Miller, *Phenomenology*, 476 (§785); HHW 2:419. Note again the quotation of Rist's hymn.

296. Miller, *Phenomenology*, 475 (§784); HHW 2:418.

297. Schaff, *Creeds*, 3:86–87; BSELK 516. This connection between the two texts is discussed by Mattes, "Hegel's Lutheran Claim," 265.

298. I noted above Hegel's preferred term is "reconciliation" rather than "redemption."

299. Wolzogen, *Leitfaden*, 94, calls it "Liebeserlösung."

300. Given in Deathridge, "Reviews," 84. The identity of the inquirer is Eduard von Lippmann (1838–1919) of the Vienna Wagner Society (Geck, *Wagner*, 397 n. 52). If it were Edmund von Lippmann (1857–1940), as has been suggested, he would only be eighteen years old at the time. Although they both had a Vienna connection, Eduard being a professor at the university and Edmund being born there (and both being chemists), they were not related.

301. Deathridge, "Ring: an Introduction," 38.

302. Bloch, *Subjekt-Objekt*, 100.

303. Miller, *Phenomenology*, 492 (§808); HHW 2:433.

of their [philosophically] comprehended organisation, it is the Science of Knowing in the sphere of appearance: the two together, comprehended History, form alike the inwardizing and the Golgotha of absolute Spirit, the actuality, truth, and certainty of his throne, without which he would be lifeless and alone. Only "from the chalice of this realm of spirits / foams forth for Him his own infinitude."[304]

The final scene of *Götterdämmerung* suggests that Brünnhilde is not only "love personified" but also the absolute spirit personified;[305] she comes to a position of "Absolute Knowing" and through her there is the "inwardizing" ("Erinnerung") of the absolute Spirit and she represents the "Golgotha" of the absolute Spirit as she empties (entäussert) her spirit into the new created order.[306] As in Christian theology the crucified Christ's spirit fills the universe, so in the *Ring* it is Brünnhilde's that flows through the whole re-created order.

Heterodox Hegel?

Hegel's theological approach has been questioned and criticized from many angles and it could be said that his "heterodoxy"[307] is to some extent responsible for Wagner's unorthodox Christian faith. Hence, I conclude this section on Hegel by asking questions on his concept of God, salvation, atonement, and immortality, all of which were concerns of Wagner.

In the Introduction to the *Science of Logic* Hegel wrote that "logic is to be understood as the system of pure reason, as the realm of pure thought. *This realm is truth as it is without veil and in its own absolute nature*. It can therefore be said that this content is the *exposition of God as he is in his eternal essence before the creation of nature and a finite spirit* (die Darstellung Gottes ist, wie er in seinem ewigen Wesen vor der Erschaffung der Natur und eines endlichen Geistes ist)."[308] Therefore, a theological reading of the *Logic*[309] would imply that by arguing against any conception of the infinite that would separate it from the finite, Hegel has, by implication, argued "against any conception of

---

304. Miller, *Phenomenology*, 493; *HHW* 2:433–34. I have replaced Miller's "Calvary" with "Golgotha" (Schädelstätte); cf. Baillie, *Phenomenology*, 808. At the end Hegel quotes freely from Schiller's poem, *Die Freundschaft*, a poem that could have implications for Wagner's understanding of sexuality (see volume 2, chapter 6).

305. Cf. Corse, *Consciousness*, 21, who suggests that in the *Ring* "history is seen as a dialectic of progress, not of Hegelian spirit, but of Wagnerian love." I noted above that the early Hegel associated spirit very much with love but this was to change in his maturer works (Beiser, *Hegel*, 112–23).

306. Again compare Hegel's writing of "Spirit emptied out into Time" ("der an die Zeit entäusserte Geist") (Miller, *Phenomenology*, 492 (§808); *HHW* 2:433).

307. The title of this section is taken from O'Regan, *Heterodox Hegel*.

308. Hegel, *Science of Logic*, 50. I have followed Miller's translation but translated Geist as "spirit" rather than "mind" and added emphasis as in *HHW* 3:34.

309. On the "Hegelian Logic as Logica Divine" see O'Regan, *Heterodox Hegel*, 86–107.

the divine that would separate it from the world."[310] "If the infinite were conceived in opposition to the finite [...] then it would be finite itself, because it would be limited by the finite. There would then be *per impossibile* a greater reality than the infinite, namely, the unity of the infinite and the finite. The true infinite must therefore include the finite, so that the divine encompasses the entire universe."[311] So in the *Science of Logic*, Hegel argues that one must "distinguish the genuine Notion of infinity from spurious infinity, the infinite of reason (das Unendliche der Vernunft) from the infinite of understanding (d[as] Unendliche des Verstandes); yet the latter is the *finitized* infinite, and it will be found that in the very act of keeping the infinite pure and aloof from the finite, the infinite is only made finite" ("doch letzteres ist das *verendlichte* Unendliche, und es wird sich ergeben, daß eben indem das Unendliche vom Endlichen rein und entfernt gehalten werden soll, es nur verendlicht wird").[312] Although Hegel does not discuss it at this point, what he writes suggests that the concept of God cannot whatsoever be divorced from the idea of the incarnation of God in a finite human being. Hegel also goes a stage further and argues that God only becomes fully God as he comes to know himself in human beings: "God is God only in so far as he knows his own self; his self-knowledge is, moreover, a self-consciousness in man and man's knowledge *of* God, which proceeds to man's self-knowledge *in* God."[313]

A further key point to bear in mind with respect to God's infinity is that it is not only substance but also subject.[314] This entails that it reveals itself not only in nature but also in culture and history and that "it is not only organic but also spiritual, consisting not only in life but also the self-awareness of life."[315] Indeed, only if one holds to the subjectivity of the absolute can one have beliefs such as Trinity and incarnation.[316]

It is unclear how much of Hegel's concept of God Wagner had grasped. But he does hold to the view that one cannot hold God aloof from nature and indeed for him the incarnation is absolutely central. On the question as to whether Wagner identifies God with nature one has to proceed with caution for in his mythological scheme one is dealing with inner-worldly events and I reserve such a discussion for volume 2.[317]

The second issue to consider is whether Hegel was concerned with salvation. Beiser points to Hegel's critique of the "obsession with personal fate" in his early writings.[318] In the Berne Fragments Hegel extols Christ's moral teaching but attacks

---

310. Beiser, *Hegel*, 142.

311. Beiser, *Hegel*, 142–43.

312. Hegel, *Science of Logic*, 137; HHW 3:124.

313. Hegel, *Philosophy of Mind*, 263–64 (*Encyclopedia III* § 564); HHW 6:550. See the discussion in Houlgate, *Introduction to Hegel*, 252.

314. Beiser, *Hegel*, 144.

315. Beiser, *Hegel*, 145.

316. Beiser, *Hegel*, 145.

317. See chapter 3.

318. Beiser, *Hegel*, 146.

the apostolic teaching of faith in Christ and his expiatory death (both necessary for salvation) and the toiling of Catholics, Anglicans, and Protestants to "set up costly missions in faraway place."[319] Although Hegel's view of Christianity changed in the Frankfurt period, Beiser maintains that his critique of salvation remained and in fact resurfaces in the "Unhappy Consciousness" chapter of the Phenomenology.[320] However, the discussion of "Unhappy Consciousness" is full of deeply Christian insight, for it is a stage that one goes through: "true freedom and self-consciousness do not reside within actual, living, individual self-consciousness at all, but are to be found beyond the self in a being that Hegel (perhaps following St Augustine) calls the 'Unchangeable' (*Das Unwandelbare*)."[321]

Beiser argues that the mature Hegel never abandoned his critique of salvation.[322] He accepts that Hegel appears to support the Protestant view on salvation in the *Lectures on the Philosophy of Religion*,[323] but he argues: "Hegel accepts the Protestant doctrine only on a symbolic or metaphorical level. Christ's death and resurrection are a symbol for the dialectic of the spirit, for how each individual has to lose his individuality and to find himself in the universality of society and history."[324] Although Christ's resurrection is radically reinterpreted by Hegel, I wonder whether he really understands Christ's death as symbolic. In the *Phenomenology* (§724) he implies that Christ's death is a sacrifice when he writes of the cults of Ceres and Bacchus: "Spirit has not yet sacrificed itself as self-conscious Spirit to self-consciousness, and the mystery of bread and wine is not yet the mystery of flesh and blood."[325] O'Regan rightly argues that for Hegel "Dionysius is not a possible contender to the religious hegemony of Christ" but rather "is but a stepping stone."[326] Hence, Hegel writes: "This incarnation of the divine Being, or the fact that it essentially and directly has the shape of consciousness, is the simple content of the absolute religion."[327]

Assessing whether Wagner held to a symbolic or realistic view of salvation simply from his stage works is, by the very nature that we are dealing with artworks, virtually impossible. But it is clear from his essays and various utterances that he

---

319. Hegel, *Three Essays*, 90–92.

320. Beiser, *Hegel*, 136. The chapter in question is (B).IV.B entitled "Stoicism, Scepticism, and the Unhappy Consciousness (das unglückliche Bewußtsein)," Miller, *Phenomenology*, 119–38; HHW 2:129–61.

321. Houlgate, *Introduction to Hegel*, 75. See Miller, *Phenomenology*, 127.

322. Beiser, *Hegel*, 146, points to Hegel's *Proofs of the Existence of God* (1829), but the very nature of these lectures means that salvation as such is not a theme.

323. Hegel, *Philosophy of Religion*, 3:109–33; *Philosophie der Religion*, 3:45–69. Note the heading: "Redemption and Reconciliation: Christ" (109).

324. Beiser, *Hegel*, 146.

325. Miller, *Phenomenology*, 438.

326. O'Regan, *Heterodox Hegel*, 193. He notes that "Hegel recalls none of [Hölderlin's] equivocation." He points to "Brot und Wein" (see *FHSWB* 1:372–83).

327. Miller, *Phenomenology*, 459 (§759)

did believe Christ's death actually achieves salvation and that it was not simply symbolic,[328] and in this respect he parallels my interpretation of Hegel. But he did depart from Hegel in that "redemption" is central to virtually every one of his stage works whereas Hegel rarely writes of it, his focus being on "reconciliation" ("Versöhnung"), though in a very specific way.[329]

Perhaps the most searching question concerning Hegel's "orthodoxy" is his view on immortality. His whole philosophical system seems naturally to exclude immortality, one reason being the denial of the "thing in itself." McCarney writes that Hegel pays "lip-service" to personal immortality on the rare occasions he does discuss it but otherwise "in all his voluminous discussions of human destiny and divine providence" he is essentially silent.[330] So in referring to the salvation spoken of in 1 Tim 2:4, McCarney argues the emphasis is on the infinite value of subjectivity rather than salvation itself: "God wills that all men should be saved [1 Tim 2:4], and that means that subjectivity has an infinite value."[331]

It is the case that Hegel does not give prominence to an idea of immortality. However, on the issue of "infinite value" of subjectivity, it is worth considering another place where Hegel discusses it where immortality itself is stressed. He says that subjectivity

> is *capable* of having an infinite value, and this capacity or possibility is its positive absolute defining character. This character is the reason why immortality of the soul becomes a specific doctrine of the Christian religion: the soul or singular subjectivity has an infinite eternal vocation to be a citizen of the kingdom of God. This is a vocation, a life, that is removed from time and temporality, [existing] for itself, and since it [is] also opposed to temporality, this eternal vocation is defined as a future of immortality.[332]

Further, it should not be overlooked that in the *Philosophy of History* Hegel discusses and affirms texts that refer to a future life.[333] So he quotes Rom 8:18: "The sufferings of his present time are not worthy to be compared with that glory." In a footnote it is asserted (quite reasonably) that "the import of Matt. v. 12, is nearly the same" and he comments: "Here Christ says that outward sufferings, as such, are not to be feared or

---

328. See, e.g., Bell, *Parsifal*, 157–60. See also the indices (Jesus Christ, cross of, sacrifice of, suffering of).

329. E.g., Miller, *Phenomenology*, 408 (§670); HHW 2:361, where he writes of the "word of reconciliation" ("Wort der Versöhnung").

330. McCarney, *History*, 203, who points to McTaggert, *Hegelian Cosmology*, 5–7, who is discomforted by the fact that immortality appears to be of so little interest to Hegel.

331. Hegel, *Encyclopaedia Logic* (Geraets, Suchting, Harris), 223 (§ 147 Addition). See also *Philosophy of Religion*, 3:138; *Philosophie der Religion*, 3:73–74.

332. Hegel, *Philosophy of Religion*, 3:138; *Philosophie der Religion*, 3:73–74.

333. Hegel, *History*, 326–30.

fled from, for they are nothing as compared with that glory."³³⁴ This is then followed by a series of texts that refer to the *future* life.³³⁵ Hence, I question McCarney's argument that Hegel does not have an interest in the doctrine that "paves the way for acceptance of this vale of tears through the prospect of rewards for the righteous and punishment for the evil doers in another world."³³⁶

It therefore seems that Hegel's view on immortality is not unambiguous. The thrust though is not in the direction of the traditional view of immortality and this may reflect his Aristotelian bent.³³⁷ Hegel may be relevant to the question of immortality that arises in *Walküre* Act II concerning Siegmund's rejection of immortality, although a more immediate figure to consider is Feuerbach.³³⁸ And it to this somewhat neglected philosopher/theologian that I now turn.

Feuerbach

Introduction

Feuerbach is usually recognized as a figure who developed Hegel's philosophy radically, becoming a leading figure in the Hegelian left and a fundamental link between Hegel and Marx. While that may be true, there is so much more to this underrated figure and in order to start to appreciate Wagner's debt to him it is necessary to consider some key aspects of his philosophy and theology.

Feuerbach's theological studies did not get off to a particularly good start. Whereas Hegel had a thorough grounding in theology, Feuerbach's period of theological study was short. He went to Heidelberg with the intention of studying theology, but was there for just one year 1823–24 (his teachers were Daub and Paulus). He then moved to Berlin in order to hear Hegel lecturing (1824–26), but again studied theology for just one year before switching to the faculty of philosophy. Although Feuerbach became remarkably Lutheran in his approach,³³⁹ this being one reason Wagner was attracted to him, he initially had only had a vague knowledge of Luther and his brief study of theology partly explains why. So, as we will discover, in the first edition of his most famous work, *The Essence of Christianity*, there is virtually nothing of Luther.³⁴⁰ However, following an intense study of Luther in the early months of 1842,³⁴¹ he introduced many Luther quotations in the second edition.

---

334. Hegel, *History*, 327.
335. Matt 5:29–30; 6:25–26; 19:21 (Hegel, *History*, 327).
336. McCarney, *History*, 203.
337. Cf. Beiser, *Hegel*, 146.
338. See volume 2, chapters 6 and 8.
339. See especially Bayer, "Lutherrezeption."
340. Wallmann, "Feuerbach," 80–81.
341. Wallmann, "Feuerbach," 84, quoting Sass, "Feuerbach statt Marx," 113.

Wagner's knowledge of Feuerbach

Feuerbach (1804–72) was nine years older than Wagner (1813–83) and they had a similar lifespan.[342] All of Feuerbach's key works were written before Wagner started work on the *Ring* in 1848, these being *Thoughts on Death and Immortality* (1830), *Essence of Christianity* (1841, 1843, 1849), *Principles of the Philosophy of the Future* (1843), *The Essence of Faith according to Luther* (1844), and *Lectures on the Essence of Religion* (1846). Feuerbach reached his peak before 1848, being highly popular for Vormärz intellectuals[343] and losing his popularity after the defeats of the uprisings of 1848–49.[344]

To trace how and when Wagner become acquainted with Feuerbach I start with Wagner's autobiography. According to *My Life*, Wagner was recommended Feuerbach by Metzdorf (of Dresden), "a former student of theology, at the time a German-Catholic preacher and political agitator with a Calabrian hat."[345] This recommendation was most probably sometime in the period from March 1848 (when the political agitations in the German federation began) to the collapse of the Dresden uprising in May 1849 after which Wagner had to flee to Switzerland. Wagner gives no indication when he acted upon Metzdorf's suggestion and, as Windell points out, "it is not clear whether he did so before his escape to Switzerland."[346] So one could argue that it was only when he settled in Zürich in July 1949 that Wagner became acquainted with the works of Feuerbach. Wagner tells us that the piano teacher Wilhelm Baumgartner showed him Feuerbach's *Gedanken über Tod und Unsterblichkeit*.[347] He says that the "absorbing questions" there raised had occupied him ever since his "initial association with Lehrs in Paris."

Wagner continues in his autobiography to say he found *Thoughts on Immortality* "elevating and consoling to be assured that the sole authentic immortality adheres only to sublime deeds and inspired works of art."[348] A case could possibly

---

342. Feuerbach's dates are 28 July 1804 to 13 September 1872 (sixty-eight years two months); Wagner's were 22 May 1813 to 13 February 1883 (sixty-nine years nine months).

343. The term "Vormärz," often employed in the secondary literature but seldom explained, refers to "the time of political stirrings leading to the Berlin revolution of March 1848" (Robertson, "German Literature and Thought," 261).

344. Wallmann, "Feuerbach", 65 n. 43, who also points to the fact that there is more secondary literature about Feuerbach in the period 1840–48 than there is for the rest of the century.

345. *My Life* 430; *Mein Leben* 1:442. He is also mentioned earlier as Metzdorff in relation to the Dresden revolution (*My Life* 407; *Mein Leben* 1:420). Wagner was to encounter him years later in Lucerne (*CD* 19 August 1870).

346. Windell, "Hegel," 33.

347. *My Life* 430; *Mein Leben* 1:442. Walton, *Zurich*, 43, adds that Baumgartner's interest in Feuerbach was almost certainly due to the influence of Gottfried Keller. See the letter of Keller to Baumgartner (Ermatinger, *Briefe*, 184, quoted by Walton, *Zurich*, 43). If anyone is in any doubt whether Wagner had a sense of humor I recommend his letter to Baumgartner (19 February 1850; *SB* 3:232–35).

348. *My Life* 430; *Mein Leben* 1:442. One can say there is a fair amount in *Thoughts* on "sublime deeds" but very little on "inspired works of art." Wagner appears to be projecting his own interests into Feuerbach's work.

be made that this work from Feuerbach's early period (published 1830) is the only work of the philosopher Wagner really came to know.[349] However, on 4 November 1849 Wagner had completed a long essay, *The Artwork of the Future*,[350] which he dedicated to Feuerbach,[351] and the title itself, modelled on Feuerbach's *Principles of the Philosophy of the Future*, suggests he knew this work also. Feuerbach may even have influenced him already in *Art and Revolution* (*Kunst und Revolution*), which was written in a few days at the end of July 1849. This is suggested by the fact that in his preface to *Gesammelte Schriften* volumes 3–4 of 1872 (which opens with *Art and Revolution*) Wagner refers to his indebtedness to Feuerbach (although, as we shall see, it is severely qualified).[352]

He did later turn to *Essence of Christianity* but found it difficult to maintain an interest in it with its basic idea of "the interpretation of religion from a purely psychological standpoint."[353] But he continues: "Nonetheless, Feuerbach became for me the proponent of the ruthlessly radical liberation of the individual from the bondage of conceptions associated with the belief in traditional authority and the initiated will therefore understand why I prefaced my book *The Art-Work of the Future* with a dedication and an introduction addressed to him."[354] His *Artwork of the Future* was completed 4 November 1849 and around 21 November 1949 (we cannot be certain of the date) Wagner sent a copy to Feuerbach with an accompanying letter. A letter to Uhlig of 20 September 1850 indicates that Feuerbach had responded enthusiastically to Wagner's essay.[355] Wagner wrote a second letter to Feuerbach on 3 December 1851,[356] enclosing his long essay *Opera and Drama*, and inviting him (also in the name of the poet Herwegh)[357] to spend some time in Zurich, an invitation the philosopher never took up.

---

349. See his letter to Otto Wigand of 4 August 1849 (*SB* 3:105): "Leider ist es mir hier noch nicht möglich geworden, von Feuerbach's werken mehr als den dritten band mit den 'gedanken über tod und unsterblichkeit' zur kenntnis zu erhalten: wie wäre es wohl möglich mehr davon hierher zu bekommen?" The second half of the sentence (i.e., after the colon) is omitted in the citation in Chamberlain, *Wagner*, 188. Chamberlain, as we shall see, minimizes Feuerbach's influence on Wagner.

350. He refers to the writing of it in a letter to Uhlig of 26 October 1849 (*SB* 3:140) and sent him a copy of the completed but not yet published work 21/22 November 1849 (*SL* 181–82; *SB* 3:165–66).

351. Windell, "Hegel," 31–32. See *My Life* 430; *Mein Leben* 1:443. For the text see *SB* 3:163–64.

352. See the *Introduction to Art and Revolution* (*PW* 1:25). However, what he writes there applies not only to *Art and Revolution* but also to *Artwork of the Future* and *Opera and Drama* (*PW* 1:22; *GSD* 3:3), since this was actually the "Preface" to volumes 3 and 4 of the *Collect Writings* (*Gesammelte Schriften und Dichtungen*).

353. *My Life* 430; *Mein Leben* 1:443. His letter to Röckel of 8 June 1853 (*SB* 5:314) also suggests he knew the work.

354. *My Life* 430; *Mein Leben* 1:443.

355. *SB* 3:428.

356. *SB* 4:205–6.

357. Feuerbach had met Herwegh in Heidelberg and his thought can be discerned in Herwegh's poems (Kamenka, *Feuerbach*, 28).

In view of this one could then take the position that Wagner only came to know of Feuerbach once he had settled in Switzerland in July 1849. Westernhagen finds it highly significant that in Wagner's Dresden library Feuerbach's works are absent.[358] Therefore, while admitting Feuerbach's influence in *Art and Revolution*, he denies it in Wagner's articles written for Röckel's *Volksblätter* or in the *Jesus of Nazareth* sketches.[359]

Later I will argue that there are traces of Feuerbach's thought and vocabulary in the *Jesus of Nazareth* sketches and I think Köhler is correct to suggest that in his autobiography "Wagner refused to rule out the possibility that he had taken an interest in Feuerbach's theories during his first visit to Paris, even if at that date he knew nothing about their author."[360] But for now it is worth pointing to one significant factor in the discussion of Wagner and Feuerbach. Those who have attempted to minimize Wagner's indebtedness to the left-wing revolutionary Feuerbach are, understandably, "right wing" Wagnerian scholars:[361] Westernhagen, a Nazi party member as early as 1924,[362] and Houston Stewart Chamberlain.[363]

A different position is taken by Newman (perhaps Westernhagen has him in his sights), who thinks Wagner was reading Feuerbach as early as 1848–49.[364] I myself have not found a Feuerbachian style in the anonymous articles of Röckel's *Volksblätter* as Newman does (hence he thinks it likely they were written by Wagner).[365] Certainly the most famous of these, "Revolution," does not contain anything distinctively Feuerbachian. However, I think a good case can be made that *Jesus of Nazareth* does have a number of distinctive Feuerbachian elements (as do the Zurich essays). This is

---

358. The works also happen to be absent in Wahnfried library.

359. Westernhagen, *Wagner* (German edition), 151; *Biography*, 1:145; *Bibliothek*, 52. Windell, "Hegel," 34 n. 28, thinks Westernhagen is contradicting Lichtenberger, *Wagner*, 182–84, and Rawidowicz, *Feuerbach*, 399 n. 1, who described *Jesus of Nazareth* as "possibly the first Wagnerian work influenced by Feuerbach." On the issue of books not being mentioned by Wagner, one should perhaps consider these words of Cosima addressed to H. S. Chamberlain (letter of 26 March 1899): "wenn Sie aufstellen, dieses oder jenes Buch sei [von Richard Wagner] nicht gelesen worden, denn es komme in den 'Gesammelten Schriften' und in den Briefen nicht vor. Ich kann Sie versichern, daß manches Buch gelesen ward, welches nicht erwähnt wurde" (*Cosima Wagner und Chamberlain*, 560). This letter of Cosima was written after reading Chamberlain's lecture "Richard Wagners Philosophie" given to the Philosophical Society of the University of Vienna. As Allen, "Weihe," 261, notes, whereas Chamberlain's Wagner biography was generally uncritical, this lecture shows Chamberlain to be far from uncritical, depicting the composer "as a brilliant but essentially unsystematic dilettante."

360. Köhler, *Titans*, 260.

361. Cf. Newman, *Life*, 2:398 n. 8: "For some strange reason or other, Wahnfried and some of its partisans have always tried to minimize Wagner's obligations, as a philosopher, to Feuerbach."

362. Dörte von Westernhagen, "Westernhagen," 84.

363. Chamberlain, *Wagner*, 188: "Nicht [. . .] dem Philosophen Feuerbach vertraute sich Wagner an, sondern dem Gegner der abstrakten [. . .] Philosophie, dem Philosophen, dessen Streben dahin gerichtet ist, 'im Menschen aufzugehen'! Das Verhältnis Wagner's zu Feuerbach ist folglich vornehmlich ein moralisches; es ist die Sympathie für eine auf das rein Menschliche gewandte Geistesrichtung."

364. Newman, *Life*, 2:398 n. 8.

365. Newman, *Life*, 2:399 n. 8.

significant for our study of the *Ring* since many of the ideas in this uncompleted opera end up on the stage of the *Ring* cycle.

I now turn to the ways in which Feuerbach could have influenced Wagner's *Ring*.

God and Atheism

There is almost a consensus in the secondary literature on Wagner that Feuerbach in his publications from 1841 (that is beginning with *Essence of Christianity*) promoted an "atheism"[366] and many argue, like Wolf, that he moved the composer "to a materialist, atheistic worldview" ("zu einer materialistischen, atheistischen Weltanschauung").[367] To make his point, Wolf quotes from Wagner's *Art and Climate* (written February 1850), certainly a Feuerbachian writing.[368] Because this text is quite crucial I quote in full:

> There exists no higher *Power* than *Man's Community*; there is naught so *worthy Love* as the *Brotherhood of Man*. But only through the *highest power of Love* can we attain to *perfect Freedom*; for there exists no genuine Freedom but that in which *each Man hath share*. The mediator between Power and Freedom, the redeemer without whom Power remains but violence, and Freedom but caprice, is therefore—*Love*; yet not that revelation from above, imposed on us by precept and command,—and therefore never realised,—like the Christian's: but *that* Love which issues from the Power of true and undistorted human nature; which in its origin is nothing other than the liveliest utterance of this nature, that proclaims itself in pure delight at physical existence and, starting from marital love, strides forward through love for children, friends and brothers, right on to *love for Universal Man*.[369]

Two points need to be raised here. First, although there is criticism here of a Christian view of love that is commanded, Wagner in the *Jesus of Nazareth* sketches presents a Jesus who preaches love but opposes law; hence there *is* a Christian form of love Wagner would appear to support. Secondly, regarding the issue of "God," Feuerbach's thought is rather more subtle and complicated than is usually assumed. In the preface to the second edition of *Essence of Christianity* Feuerbach explains that he has not argued that "Religion is nothing, is an absurdity." He says that if that were his

---

366. In his earlier work of 1830 *Thoughts on Death and Immortality* Feuerbach merely argued that the mirror of human beings was not God himself but only a superficial understanding of God: "you should consider that God is the greatest of all conceivable mystics, that he is not a rationalist (but certainly not a pietist either), is not a superficial, barren, and stale essence, but is an infinitely profound essence" (*Thoughts*, 22; *LFW* 1:102).

367. Wolf in *SB* 3:13.

368. It closes by explaining that the climate which fundamentally conditions Art is "[t]he actual— and not the fancied—essence of the Human Race (Wesen der menschlichen Gattung)" (*PW* 1:265; *GSD* 3:221).

369. *PW* 1:263; *GSD* 3:218 (quoted by Wolf in *SB* 3:13–14).

argument it would be "an easy task."[370] Rather, "I by no means say [...] God is nothing, the Trinity is nothing, the Word of God is nothing, &c. I only show that they are not that which the illusions of theology make them,—not foreign, but native mysteries, the mysteries of human nature."[371] Further,

> The reproach that according to my book religion is an absurdity, a nullity, a pure illusion, would be well founded only if, according to it, that into which I resolve religion, [...] *man,–anthropology*, were an absurdity, a nullity, a pure illusion. But so far from giving a trivial or even a subordinate significance to anthropology,—a significance which is assigned to it only just so long as a theology stands above it and in opposition to it,—I, on the contrary, while reducing theology to anthropology, exalt anthropology into theology, very much as Christianity, while lowering God into man, made man into God.[372]

Feuerbach was not a crude materialist in reducing everything to matter,[373] although he did occasionally describe himself as an "atheist."[374] He writes in the preface to the second edition of *Essence of Christianity*:

> Religion is the dream of the human mind. But even in dreams we do not find ourselves in emptiness or in heaven, but on earth, in the realm of reality; we only see real things in the entrancing splendour of imagination and caprice, instead of in the simple daylight of reality and necessity. Hence I do nothing more to religion—and to speculative philosophy and theology also—than to open its eyes, or rather to turn its gaze from the internal towards the external, *i.e.*, I change the object as it is in the imagination into the object as it is in reality.[375]

Kamenka points out that Feuerbach (and Marx) object to the way Hegelian philosophy "reverses the relation of subject and predicate." "Instead of saying that man knows himself in God, it says that God knows himself in man; instead of saying reason is absolute, it says 'the Absolute is Reason'; instead of saying that man produces reason, it says that reason produces man."[376]

How then does our concept of God come into being? Feuerbach's argument is not rigorous, as many have suggested, but his view is that the human being objectifies

---

370. Feuerbach, *Essence*, xxxviii; *LFW* 5:406; Schuffenhauer, *Feuerbach: Wesen*, 19. Note that Feuerbach argues that part one is chiefly concerned with religion, part 2 chiefly concerned with theology (*Essence*, xxxvii; Schuffenhauer, *Feuerbach: Wesen*, 18–19).
371. Feuerbach, *Essence*, xxxviii; *LFW* 5:406; Schuffenhauer, *Feuerbach: Wesen*, 19.
372. Feuerbach, *Essence*, xxxviii; *LFW* 5:406–7; Schuffenhauer, *Feuerbach: Wesen*, 19–20.
373. Kamenka, *Feuerbach*, 36.
374. Feuerbach, *Lectures*, 35; *Vorlesungen*, 34.
375. Feuerbach, *Essence*, xxxix; *LFW* 5:407; Schuffenhauer, *Feuerbach: Wesen*, 20.
376. Kamenka, *Feuerbach*, 36–37 (see also 160 n. 2).

or, as George Eliot[377] translates it, "projects" all the good things in himself onto what he thinks is a divine being. "Man denies as to himself only what he attributes to God."[378] Rarely does Feuerbach actually use the term "Projektion" and the word he usually employs for this objectification is "vergegenständlichen" ("to objectify").[379] The reason therefore that God is "not nothing" is because we need to re-appropriate those good things that have been objectified in God; we need to internalize them. So Christianity as the absolute religion shows not what human beings *are* but rather what they *should be*.

In Feuerbach's theology, one of the key themes related to all this was the humanization of God and to establish this he often looked back to Martin Luther,[380] to whom I now turn.

Luther

We find the idea of the humanization of God right at the beginning of the *Principles*, written in the Winter of 1842–43:[381] "The task of the modern era was the realization and humanization of God—the transformation and dissolution of theology into anthropology. The religious or practical form of this humanization was Protestantism. The God who is man, the human God, namely, Christ—only this is the God of Protestantism."[382] I noted above that Feuerbach's time of theological study was short and it was only in 1842 that he truly discovered Luther.[383] Hence we find this appeal to the Reformation in *Principles*; also in his *Essence of Christianity*, which went through three editions (1841, 1843, 1849), we find a radical change between the first and second editions regarding citations of Luther.[384] The impulse to discover Luther was most probably the stinging review of Julius Müller of the first edition of *Essence of Christianity*, which castigated

---

377. Note that her translation, which appeared in 1854, is of the second edition (1843). When referring to the German I will generally use the edition of Erich Thies (*LFW* 5) but this is of the first edition of 1841. He does, however, provide the preface to the second edition (see the above footnotes). Schuffenhauer, *Feuerbach: Wesen*, to whom I occasionally refer, gives the readings from all three editions.

378. Feuerbach, *Essence*, 27; *LFW* 5:41.

379. The idea of this, but not the term, has its background in Hegel. Hegel, like Kant, prefers the derivatives of "Objekt" rather than "Gegenstand" (Inwood, *Dictionary*, 203).

380. Note, however, that the original source for ideas of divinization of the human and humanity of God was Christian mysticism, especially the "Stunden der Andacht" of Heinrich Zschokkes (which appeared 1808–16). See Wallmann, "Feuerbach," 75–79, and Feuerbach's pious letter to his mother and sister (74).

381. Winiger, *Feuerbach*, 346.

382. Feuerbach, *Principles*, 5 (§ 2–3); *LFW* 3:248.

383. Sass, "Feuerbach statt Marx," 113.

384. Wallmann, "Feuerbach," 80–81, points out that in the first edition there are only three Luther citations: one is a proverbial, one is from the *Book of Concord*, and one is from J. G. Walch's *Philosophical Lexikon*. By contrast, the second edition has ninety-one citations.

him for ignoring Luther. The substantial changes in the second edition, including the appeal to Luther and Protestantism, were noted by Feuerbach himself in a letter to his publisher, Wigand.[385] Feuerbach essentially came to see that Luther was "practical proof of his major thesis that theology was anthropology."[386]

This humanization of God was in fact a key aspect of the Lutheran doctrine of God. This is seen already in the first edition of *Essence of Christianity*, where Feuerbach quotes from the "Formula of Concord":[387] "When I believe that the human nature alone has suffered for me, Christ is a poor Saviour to me: in that case, he needs a Saviour himself."[388] Then Feuerbach adds: "And thus, out of the need for salvation is postulated something transcending human nature, a being different from man. But no sooner is this being postulated than there arises the yearning of man after himself, after his own nature, and man is immediately re-established." He then quotes again from the formula of concord: "Here is God, who is not man and never yet became man. But this is not a God for me. . . . That would be a miserable Christ to me, who . . . should be nothing but a purely separate God and divine person . . . without humanity. No, my friend; where thou givest me God, thou must give me humanity too."[389] Although Wagner's enthusiasm for Feuerbach was to diminish over the years, this Lutheran idea that divinity is focused in the person of Jesus (but note that it is just *one* aspect of Luther's doctrine of God) became a central concern for the rest of the composer's life.

Feuerbach's increasing interest in Luther can be discerned in a work written in the year following the publication of the second edition of the *Essence of Christianity*: *The Essence of Faith according to Luther* (*Das Wesen des Glaubens im Sinne Luthers*) and bearing the significant subtitle *A Supplement to the Essence of Christianity* (*Ein Beitrag zum "Wesen des Christentums"*). In many ways it is a remarkable and inspiring book and paying more attention to it than has often been the case throws a whole new light on Feuerbach and in turn on Wagner.

We do not know if Wagner read this but many of the ideas do cohere with what we find in the *Ring* cycle. Feuerbach argued that although Luther began with the utter contrast between God and human beings, he does not end there. For Luther ends up actually humanizing God. So in the early pages Feuerbach points to Luther's view that it is "impossible for man to be what God is" since "every affirmation in God presupposes

---

385. See *LFW* 5:428: "Die Schrift hat nicht nur formell, sondern auch materiell bedeutend gewonnen. [. . .] das dritte Kapitel, 'Gott als Verstandeswesen oder die Gottheit des Verstandes', ist ein höchst gewichtiger Zuwachs. Selbst schon durch die vielen Belegstellen aus Luther, durch die schließliche Deduktion der neuen Lehre als der Wahrheit des Protestantismus am Ende der Anmerkungen hat die Schrift eine neue Gestalt und Bedeutung bekommen." Note that for the second edition the Appendix was almost doubled (*LFW* 5:429). For the centrality of Luther at the end of the Appendix see Feuerbach, *Essence*, 336–39.

386. Harvey, *Feuerbach*, 150.

387. Feuerbach, *Essence*, 44–45; *LFW* 5:50–51; Schuffenhauer, *Feuerbach: Essence*, 90–91.

388. Cf. *BSELK* 1029.30–34; Tappert, *Book of Concord*, 598–99.

389. Cf. *BSELK* 1044.43–1045.13; Tappert, *Book of Concord*, 607.

a negation in man."³⁹⁰ For "if God is the Savior, the Redeemer, the Sanctifier, then man cannot be the redeemer of his own sins, his own savior."³⁹¹ Now Luther ascribes to God "virtue, beauty, sweetness, power, health, amiability" whereas "man is personified depravity, contrariness, hatefulness, worthlessness, and uselessness."³⁹² Then he makes this fundamental qualification: "Luther's doctrine [. . .] is only inhuman at its starting point, not as it develops; in its presuppositions, not in its consequences; in its means, not in its end."³⁹³ The Lutheran doctrine "places you in the condition of hunger [. . .] [b]ut places you in this inhuman condition only to encourage—by hunger—the enjoyment of food."³⁹⁴ So "[w]hat Luther takes away from you in your human condition, he replaces for you a hundredfold in God."³⁹⁵ Therefore: "Luther is inhuman towards man only because he has a humane God and because the humanity of God takes away man's own humanity from him."³⁹⁶ So all the good moral qualities are "projected" onto God and denied to the human being. Further, since God loves and cares for the human being, we do not have to love or care for ourselves. Feuerbach quotes these arresting words of Luther: "Go away, you loathsome Devil! You want to encourage me *to care for myself*, although God says everywhere, 'I will care for him Myself.'"³⁹⁷ Central for Luther was the *pro nobis* ("for us"). Feuerbach claims that Luther was concerned with the "God for us." He deals with Luther's *Deus absconditus* by saying that such a "God in himself" is no God; such a "God outside Christ" is, according to Luther, "a terrifying, fearful God."³⁹⁸ The basis for this belief in God's goodness is Jesus Christ. "But what gives us the certainty—the indubitable, irrefragable certainty—that God is actually a being for us, a good, a human-minded being? The appearance (Erscheinung) of God as a man in Christ, which was by no means a transitory appearance, for even today God is still a man in Christ. In Christ God has revealed himself; that is, he has shown and proved himself to be a human being. In the humanity of Christ the humanity of God is placed beyond all doubt. The chief sign that God is good is that he is a man."³⁹⁹ God is an object of the human senses: "Only a sensuous being (ein sinnliches Wesen) favors and satisfies man and can be a beneficent being. [. . .] And without certainty there is no beneficence."⁴⁰⁰ The word "sensuousness" (in the Luther book) means that one is sure that something exists and is real and is not the fruit of one's imagination (whereas

---

390. Feuerbach, *Luther*, 38; *LFW* 4:12.
391. Feuerbach, *Luther*, 39; *LFW* 4:12.
392. Feuerbach, *Luther*, 41; *LFW* 4:14.
393. Feuerbach, *Luther*, 41; *LFW* 4:14.
394. Feuerbach, *Luther*, 42; *LFW* 4:15.
395. Feuerbach, *Luther*, 43; *LFW* 4:15.
396. Feuerbach, *Luther*, 43; *LFW* 4:15–16.
397. Feuerbach, *Luther*, 44; *LFW* 4:16.
398. Feuerbach, *Luther*, 91–92; *LFW* 4:50–51.
399. Feuerbach, *Luther*, 63; *LFW* 4:30.
400. Feuerbach, *Luther*, 65–66; *LFW* 4:31–32.

in *Essence of Christianity* it has to do with need for images!). This corresponds to many of Wagner's utterances; so often he writes of the *historical* figure of Christ: for Wagner divinity was focused in the historical figure of Jesus. And it is worth emphasizing that although Wagner is a "receiver" and "creator" of myth, from around 1847 right up until his death he took a keen interest in history.

As in *Essence of Christianity* he ends the book by discussing faith and love but rather than contrasting faith and love by denigrating faith (faith is fanatical and separatist; love was tolerant and unifying) the Luther book has a much more profound and nuanced approach. For Luther the object of faith was love since "God is love." Love for whom? The human being! The human is therefore the object of faith *also*. Philanthropy, "love of the human being," is also the mystery of faith. "It [Philanthropy] is distinguished from love only in that *another* man is the object of love, whereas [in faith] *I myself* am the object of [love]. In love I love; in faith I am loved."[401] Love humbles us. But being loved by the supreme being exalts. "'Through faith,' says Luther, 'man becomes God'; 'In faith we are gods, but in love we are men.'"[402] Feuerbach would seem to be paraphrasing Luther's sermon for the Third Sunday after Epiphany.[403] Faith is about self-love. Loving ourselves entails concern for our salvation. Hence, faith is above love for Luther. But Feuerbach therefore concludes that for Luther self-love is above love for others. "This order of progression has a good and proper sense as well as a bad, egoistic one. For how will I make others happy if I myself am unhappy; how will I satisfy others if the worm of dissatisfaction gnaws at me?"[404]

Blessedness is central to self-love and the key to this is the resurrection. But this means transcending the limitations of our finitude. Feuerbach writes (and he is here asserting his *own* views): "To believe is but to change the 'There is a God and a Christ' into '*I am* a God and a Christ.' The mere belief 'There is a God' or 'God is God' is a moribund, vain, and empty belief. I only believe if I believe that God is my God. But if God is mine, then all divine attributes are my attributes. To believe is to make God a man and man a God."[405] Although I am doubtful Wagner had actually *read* Feuerbach when he wrote the *Jesus of Nazareth* sketches, this quotation is reflected in this seemingly heterodox sentiment in the commentary to the drama: "Jesus knows and practices God's-love through his teaching of it: in the consciousness of Cause and Effect

---

401. Feuerbach, *Luther*, 99; *LFW* 4:56.

402. Feuerbach, *Luther*, 100; *LFW* 4:56. See Harvey, *Feuerbach*, 157.

403. Luther, *Sermons*, 2:73–74: "Indeed, by faith we become gods and partakers of the divine nature and name, as is said in Psalm 82,6: 'I said, Ye are gods, and all of you sons of the Most High.' But through love we become equal to the poorest. According to faith we are in need of nothing, and have an abundance; according to love we are servants of all."

404. Feuerbach, *Luther*, 102; *LFW* 4:58.

405. Feuerbach, *Luther*, 106–7; *LFW* 4:61. The editor, Mervin Cherno, points out that the German in both 1844 and 1848 editions of the second phrase of the first sentence quoted above reads "I *am* a God and a Christian" ("Ich *bin* ein Gott, ein Christ"); i.e., they read "Christ," not "Christus". Changing it to "Christus" though renders a more satisfactory parallelism and better sense (106 n. 25).

he accordingly is God and Son of God; but every man is capable of like knowledge and like practice,—and if he attain thereto, he is like unto God and Jesus."[406]

Towards the end of his treatise he turns to questions of salvation. To sin you need others but you can be blessed on your own.

> In short, in blessedness I am not related to other beings, but only to myself. Blessedness is indissoluble and inseparable from myself, for it is only my ego itself, freed from all dependency, necessity, obligation, and ties. It is my deified ego. Blessedness is the supreme wish and the supreme essence of Christian (that is, supernatural) self-love; but blessedness is also the final goal—the essential object, or, rather, the supreme being—of the Christian faith. Thus the essence of faith, as distinguished from love and considered according to its ultimate aim, is simply the essence of self-love.[407]

And it is precisely this blessedness, this faith, this self-love which Siegmund rejects in *Walküre* Act II.[408]

Feuerbach's relationship to the Christian faith (and specifically to Lutheranism) is therefore much more ambiguous than usually considered.[409] In his notes on the *Essence of Christianity* Feuerbach asks: "Is the work *The Essence of Faith According to Luther* for or against Luther?" He answers: "It is just as much for as against Luther. But is this not a contradiction? Certainly; but a necessary contradiction, rooted in the nature of the object itself."[410]

Wagner's Appropriation of Feuerbach

Humanization of God

The most significant thing Wagner appropriated from Feuerbach was the humanization of God, which has just been discussed. In *Principles*, a work I suggested above that Wagner knew, Feuerbach writes of such humanization and that "[s]ensuous perception [. . .] is the essence of the Christian religion."[411] Likewise, in the *Luther* essay he writes: "Christ is the sensuous certainty (sinnliche Gewißheit) of God's love to humans. He

---

406. PW 8:301; DTB 249.
407. Feuerbach, *Luther*, 115–16; LFW 4:67.
408. See volume 2, chapter 8.
409. Note, incidentally, that Wallmann, "Feuerbach," 67 n. 51, is sharply critical of Bockmühl for totally ignoring Feuerbach's appeal to Luther and for viewing Feuerbach's criticism of religion as "aus der Froschperspektive" (Bockmühl, *Leiblichkeit*, 74). Wallmann, "Feuerbach," 60 n. 21; 67 n. 51, criticizes Bockmühl for what seems to be careless research.
410. Quoted by Cerno in the Introduction to Feuerbach, *Luther*, 13. LFW 4:219: "Ist die Schrift *Das Wesen des Glaubens im Sinne Luthers für* oder *gegen* Luther? Sie ist ebensoviel für als gegen Luther. Aber ist denn das kein Widerspruch? Gewiß; aber ein Widerspruch, der notwendig ist, der in der Natur des Gegenstandes liegt."
411. Feuerbach, *Principles* 57 (§40); LFW 3:304–5.

himself is the God who loves humans as a sensuous object, sensuous truth."[412] Further, he makes it clear that we have to give up our usual thoughts of who God is: "[W]hen God becomes a man, he ceases being what he is in your thoughts; namely, God, or an invisible, incomprehensible, unlimited, inhuman, nonobjective being."[413] Further, "if you do not bring the God in your mind out of yourself, a crucified God is just as laughable a contradiction as a thought corporeally punished with torture."[414] The only way one can make sense of a crucified God is "[b]y making the thought (den Gedanken) into a being perceptible and objective to others besides yourself; that is by making it into a sensuous being (sinnlichen Wesen)."[415] Whether Wagner knew this essay or not, his idea of God in the *Ring* almost exactly corresponds to this.

All the gods in the *Ring* are portrayed as very human, and we see this particularly in Wotan, the chief god; and psychologically he is the most complex of all the gods (indeed probably the most complex of all the characters in the *Ring*). But the theological humanization of God is found supremely in his daughter, Brünnhilde, who embodies the very nature of God of which Feuerbach writes in his chapter in *Essence of Christianity* on "The Mystery of Incarnation or God as Love," namely that "God is love" and is "for us."[416] Although we have the human Brünnhilde already in the *Ring* of 1848 her character was to be filled out and further humanized as he worked on *Walküre*, and this took place after reading Feuerbach. Hence, Feuerbach may have pushed Wagner to bring together a constellation of issues that we find in the *Ring*. First, the God we are concerned with is a God "for us." Feuerbach can be said to oppose the idea of a "Gott an sich,"[417] and held only to the "Gott für mich," this distinction corresponding to Luther's hidden God (*Deus absconditus*) and revealed God (*Deus revelatus*).[418] More precisely he wrote this: "How can you [...] distinguish in God a God in himself (*Gott an sich*) and a God for you (*Gott für dich*)? It is precisely God himself who removes the validity and possibility of this distinction."[419] He goes on to argue, building upon Luther, that the "terrifying, fearful God," the God in himself" ("Gott *an sich*"), is to be distinguished from the devil "only in imagination or name, but not in fact or in essence."[420] Early versions of *Siegfried's Tod* could be said to have a sort of "hidden

---

412. Feuerbach, *Luther*, 79 (modified); *LFW* 4:41.

413. Feuerbach, *Luther*, 75; *LFW* 4:38.

414. Feuerbach, *Luther*, 75; *LFW* 4:38.

415. Feuerbach, *Luther*, 76; *LFW* 4:39. I have modified the translation by rendering "sinnlich" as "sensuous" rather than "sensual." For discussion of "sinnlich" see volume 2 chapter 6.

416. Feuerbach, *Essence*, 50–58; *LFW* 5:56–66.

417. Feuerbach, *Principles*, 5 (*LFW* 3:248) argues Catholicism is concerned about the God in himself (§2) but although Protestantism claims not to be, it is "negated [...] only in a practical way; theoretically, it left him untouched" (§3). See also Bayer, "Lutherrezeption," 227.

418. See *On the Bondage of the Will* (*LW* 33:138–47; *WA* 18:684–90).

419. Feuerbach, *Luther*, 91; *LFW* 4:50. Bayer, "Lutherrezeption," 230, describes this as an "erstaunliche[r] Satz."

420. Feuerbach, *Luther*, 92; *LFW* 4:51.

God," although Wotan is "naughty" rather than "malicious" and so is quite different to the *Deus absconditus* of Luther's *On the Bondage of the Will*. Brünnhilde declares before her self-immolation: "Let only one rule: / All-father! Magnificent one!"[421] In the final *Ring* there is no such "ruling God" but a very human Wotan who is virtually comatosed before he is consumed in the final conflagration. It is therefore conceivable that Wagner's eliminating the idea of a "hidden God" as he developed the *Ring* after 1849 could be due to the influence of Feuerbach.[422] Secondly, there is the related point that Feuerbach emphasized, as does Wagner, that God is concerned for us and loves us. God is love; and such a God can only be perceived in the sensuous person of Jesus Christ. Feuerbach writes: "The fundamental proposition of Christianity—'God has revealed himself to man; that is, became man (for the Incarnation of God was indeed the Revelation of God)'—has no other meaning but that in Christianity God has become a sensuous being instead of a being in thought."[423] This is something Wagner affirms also. Feuerbach saw Christianity as the absolute religion,[424] but "whereas Hegel justified this evaluation on the grounds that Christianity taught the reconciliation of the Infinite with the finite, Feuerbach justified it on the grounds that it taught that God had renounced his divinity out of love for humanity."[425] Compare this summary of Feuerbach's thought with Wagner's comment that Brünnhilde "renounced her divinity for the sake of love. But she knows that love is uniquely divine."[426]

Divinization of human beings

Windell argues that one of the few influences of Feuerbach on the *Ring* is the elevation of human nature to the level of the divine. In *Essence of Christianity* Feuerbach argued that "the antithesis of the divine and human is altogether illusory, that it is nothing else than the antithesis between human nature in general and the human individual."[427] Windell suggests that this pushed Wagner to change the ending of *Siegfried's Tod*. No longer do "the shades of Siegfried and Brünnhilde arise from the ashes of the funeral pyre," Brünnhilde as a Valkyrie leading Siegfried to Valhalla where the gods continue to reign.[428] Rather, in the revised ending, implied in the earliest sketch for *Der junge*

---

421. Haymes, *Ring*, 182–83.

422. Note that although Hegel does not write of a *Deus absconditus* he does have a mysterious God who presides over the "Slaughterbench" ("Schlachtbank") of history (Sibree, *History*, 21; *Geschichte*, 35). See the discussion above on Hegel and history.

423. Feuerbach, *Luther*, 67 (modified); *LFW* 4:32–33.

424. Feuerbach, *Essence*, 145; *LFW* 5:172.

425. Harvey, *Feuerbach*, 121.

426. *SL* 309; *SB* 6:71.

427. Feuerbach, *Essence*, 12–13; cf. *LFW* 5:32. Cf. Windell, "Hegel," 34.

428. Haymes, *Ring*, 59, 183.

Siegfried of May 1851[429] and becoming definitive with the version of *Siegfried's Tod* of November and early December 1852, we have the gods consumed in a holocaust that originates from Siegfried's funeral pyre. "At the end the fate of the human race is for the first time totally under human control."[430]

However, Windell correctly points out that the changes in the libretto could be due to other influences. So the ending of *Götterdämmerung* could be based directly on the description of Ragnarök in the *Prose Edda*[431] or the final stanzas of the *Völuspá*, which tells of how the gods encounter their downfall.[432]

Egoism, death, and immortality

Feuerbach attacked egoism in *Thoughts* (1830)[433] and it comes to have a central role in *Essence of Christianity*.[434] For Feuerbach, egoism is opposed to love. So in a diary entry from the mid 1830s he writes: "There is only one evil—egoism; and only one good, it is love."[435] The discussion of egoism in the *Lectures on the Essence of Religion* is somewhat more nuanced and possibly confusing. He uses the term "to designate the ground and essence of religion."[436] He is not using it in a moral sense but in a metaphysical sense and it involves both self-love since "every love of an object or being is an indirect self-love."[437] Harvey suggests that the *Lectures* may be seen as the first budding of "Life Philosophy." Such Life-philosophers "regarded the human organism as a constellation of unconscious instincts and drives (will, will-to-power, libido), guided by consciousness to their proper satisfaction."[438]

---

429. In the sketch for Act III we read: "Wodan und die Wala: götterende" (Strobel, *Skizzen*, 66; *TBRN1* 211).

430. Windell, "Hegel," 35.

431. Faulkes, *Edda*, 52–57 (§§51–53).

432. Windell, "Hegel," 36–37 n. 38, writes that the gods are reborn after Ragnarök according to *Völuspá*; but this is based on a mistranslation of Hollander, *Poetic Edda*, which Windell quotes: "There will the gods all guiltless throne / and live forever in ease and bliss." However, the reference should be to the warriors, not the gods. See Dronke, *Edda II*, 24: "There shall the worthy warrior bands dwell / and all their days of life enjoy delight"; Orchard, *Elder Edda*, 14: "Virtuous folk shall live there, and enjoy the live-long day"; Larrington, *Poetic Edda*, 12, is similar.

433. Feuerbach, *Thoughts*, 30; *LFW* 1:109–10.

434. E.g., Feuerbach, *Essence*, 114–15 (*LFW* 5:136–37), where he attacks Jewish "monotheistic egoism" (*Essence*, 115; *LFW* 5:136).

435. Harvey, *Feuerbach*, 175.

436. Feuerbach, *Lectures*, 49; *Vorlesungen*, 60. Note that Feuerbach does not have a negative view of eternal life in the *Lectures*: "A God is essentially a being who fulfils man's desires. And the most heartfelt desire, at least of those men whose desires are not curtailed by natural necessity, is the desire not to die, to live forever; this is indeed man's highest and ultimate desire, the desire of all desires, just as life is the epitome of all blessing, and for that very reason" (*Lectures*, 269; *Vorlesungen*, 302).

437. Feuerbach, *Lectures*, 50; *Vorlesungen*, 61.

438. Harvey, *Feuerbach*, 177.

In the *Lectures* Feuerbach tried to distinguish between natural and unnatural egoism. Harvey explains:

> A natural egoism [. . .] is in conformity with human nature and reason and is the natural self-love that animates all creatures. It is the egoism which finds satisfaction in giving happiness to others. An unnatural egoism, by contrast, is manifest where persons act as if their own well-being could be realised in abstraction from the well-being of others. The good, then, "is merely what falls in with the egoism of all men, and evil is simply what falls in with the egoism of certain classes of men at the expense of others."[439]

A more satisfactory term than "egoism" and less confusing is "Glückseligkeitstrieb" ("drive-to-happiness"). This certainly includes natural self-love: "God—the object of Christian faith—is nothing but the satisfied urge towards happiness (Glückseligkeitstrieb), the satisfied self-love of the Christian man."[440] But it is also "fully realised only in interpersonal relationships."[441] Hence, Feuerbach can write that the Trinity "is the highest mystery and focal point of absolute philosophy and religion" and the "secret of communal and social life."[442]

Wagner's negative views on egoism relate to Feuerbach's works written before the *Lectures* (where it can have a positive as well as negative connotation). Wagner's attack on egoism can be discerned in the *Ring*, but the explicit attack occurs in the *Jesus of Nazareth* sketches (where "Egoismus" occurs thirty-eight times). First, we find egoism contrasted to love in the *Jesus* sketches: "The first act of surrender-of-oneself (entäusserung seiner selbst) is sexual love (geschlechtsliebe)."[443] Such ideas are also expressed in his letter to Röckel 25/26 1854. First, he relates the obliteration of egoism in language reminiscent of Feuerbach's I/thou:

> Egoism, in truth, ceases only when the "I" is subsumed by the "you": this "I" and "you," however, no longer show themselves as such the moment I align myself with the wholeness of the world: "I" and "the world" means nothing less than "I" alone; the world will not become a complete reality for me until it becomes "you," and this is something it can become only in the shape of the individual whom I love.[444]

---

439. Harvey, *Feuerbach*, 178–79, quoting Feuerbach, *Lectures*, 307; *Vorlesungen*, 345.
440. Feuerbach, *Luther*, 102; *LFW* 4:59.
441. Harvey, *Feuerbach*, 179.
442. Feuerbach, *Principles*, 72 (§63); *LFW* 3:321–22.
443. *PW* 8:315; *DTB* 255.
444. *SL* 304; *SB* 6:64: "In Wahrheit hört der Egoismus nur beim Aufgehen des 'Ich' in das 'Du' auf: dieses 'Ich' und 'Du' stellt sich aber nicht dar, sobald ich mich mit dem Ganzen der Welt zusammenstelle: 'ich' und die 'Welt' heisst nichts anderes, als 'ich' allein: volle Wirklichkeit wird mir die Welt erst, wenn sie mir zum 'Du' geworden ist, und diess wird sie nur in der Erscheinung des geliebten Individuums."

Then he moves on to the issue of love, arguing that the path to redemption and happiness is not for the individual on his own but rather for the "whole of humankind" and the goal is "to render love possible as the most perfect realization of reality—truth; not a conceptual, abstract, non-sensuous love (the only kind possible *now*) but the love of 'I' and 'you.'"[445]

The second contrast to egoism in the *Jesus* sketches is the wish for eternal life. So death is opposed to egoism, implying that the desire for eternal life is aligned with it: "The last ascension of the individual life into the life of the whole is Death, which is the last and most definite upheaval of egoism."[446] These issues of egoism as opposed to love and aligned to eternal life are reflected in Siegmund, who loves to the utmost intensity and this entails that he has to reject eternal life! Wagner's aligning egoism with the desire of eternal life does not correspond to Feuerbach's view; even in *Thoughts on Death and Immortality* when egoism is criticized it is done so on the basis of love;[447] further, as noted above, in the *Lectures*, Feuerbach has no problem with "Glückseligkeitstrieb" ("drive-to-happiness").

Finally, as in *Artwork of the Future*, and following Feuerbach, Wagner opposed egoism to communism: "for bearing there is a need for I and Thou, the passing over of Egoism into Communism" ("Zur Zeugung gehört das Ich und das Du, das Aufgehen des Egoismus in den Kommunismus").[448]

Love and eroticism

Although Wagner knew something of Feuerbach's thought before 1851[449] as one can see in *Artwork of the Future*, it was only when he extended his conception of *Siegfried's Tod* under Feuerbach's influence that we see those ideas entering the *Ring*. One such issue is the role of love, which is emphasized in the so-called "Feuerbach ending" composed towards the end of 1852. The significant words are:[450]

---

445. *SL* 305; *SB* 6:65: "die Ermöglichung der Liebe, als des vollsten Innewerdens der Wirklichkeit—Wahrheit; nicht aber der gedachten, abstrahirten, unsinnlichen (*jetzt* uns einzig nur möglichen) Liebe, sondern der Liebe des 'Ich' und 'Du.'"

446. *PW* 8:313; *DTB* 255. On this issue, see volume 2, chapter 8, where I discuss death and immortality.

447. Feuerbach, *Thoughts*, 30: "Know love and you have known God and everything. Thus only the genuine pantheist knows what love is; only he can love. Apart from pantheism everything is egoism [...]"; *LFW* 1:109-10.

448. *PW* 1:78; *GSD* 3:51 (cf. his introduction to the third and fourth volumes of his collected works, *PW* 1:27; *GSD* 3:5).

449. Dreyfus, *Erotic Impulse*, 93.

450. Wagner, *Ring* (1853), 158; *TBRN2* 482. Cf. *WagRS* 362-63. The whole ending was placed between the lines "in Walhall's prangende Burg" and "Grane, mein Roß." The words were not included in the final *Ring* but appeared as a footnote in *GSD* 6:254-55.

Nicht Gut, nicht Gold,	Not wealth, not gold,
noch göttliche Pracht;	nor godly pomp;
nicht Haus, nicht Hof,	not house, not garth,
noch herrischer Prunk;	nor lordly splendour;
nicht trüber Verträge	not troubled treaties'
trügender Bund,	treacherous bonds,
nicht heuchelnder Sitte	not smoothed-tongued custom's
hartes Gesetz:	stern decree:
selig in Lust und Leid	blessed in joy and sorrow
läßt—die *Liebe* nur sein. –	*love* alone can be.—

The emphasis on love could possibly come from Feuerbach, but the idea of being redeemed through love is, of course, central to the earlier operas. Further, one has to ask whether the highly charged eroticism of *Walküre* bears much relation to the philosopher, and for this one must, I will argue, look elsewhere for the inspiration.[451] But the significant contribution of Feuerbach to love is, I maintain, in its theological significance as discussed above and how Brünnhilde, as a divine figure, embodies love itself.

Species

The opening pages of *Essence of Christianity* speak of the importance of species. Humans, as opposed to animals, have consciousness, which "in the strictest sense is present only in a being to whom his species, his essential nature, is an object of thought."[452] The problem with Christianity is that it "cared nothing for the species, and had only the individual in its eye and mind."[453] Christians "sacrificed the species to the individual."

It is significant that Wagner's first use of the term "species" (Gattung) in a Feuerbachian sense is in *Artwork of the Future*, affirming that consciousness of the species is "the beginning and foundation of man's Thinking (der Anfang und Grund des menschlichen Denkens)."[454] Although he may have known something of Feuerbach before, use of his terminology suggest a reading between *Art and Revolution* and *Artwork of the Future*. Ellis points out that the terms "Nothwendigkeit" (necessity) and "Bedürfniß" (need) are employed richly in a Feuerbachian sense on the very first page of *Artwork*.[455] By contrast *Art and Revolution* does not employ the term

---

451. Discussed in volume 2, chapter 6. Wagner does indicate connections between passionate love and Feuerbach (*PW* 2:175; *GSD* 4:50) but such connections are not there in the philosopher's works themselves.

452. Feuerbach, *Essence*, 1; *LFW* 5:17.

453. Feuerbach, *Essence*, 151; *LFW* 5:179.

454. *PW* 1:82; *GSD* 3:55. See also *PW* 1:94, 96, 193 (*GSD* 3:66, 68, 159)

455. *PW* 1:xi, 69; *GSD* 3:42.

"Bedürfniß," and "Nothwendigkeit" is used three times in the sense of Greek fate. The term "species" also occurs (nine times) in *Art and Climate* (written February 1850)[456] and then again in *Opera and Drama*.[457]

It is not immediately clear what link there is between this focus on the species and the *Ring*. A case could be made that Siegmund's attitude is non-Feuerbachian. Does he not exalt the individual over species? He does, of course, rejoice in the blossoming of the Volsung blood,[458] but according to the general understanding of genetics this would not be good for the species!

I doubt whether Wagner would share Feuerbach's view that "Christ, as the consciousness of love, is the consciousness of the species"[459] such that Christians need to see through Christ to the species: "where there arises the consciousness of the species as a species, the idea of humanity as a whole, Christ disappears, without, however, his true nature disappearing; for he was the substitute for the consciousness of the species (der Stellvertreter des Bewußtseins der Gattung), the image under which it was made present to the people."[460] Rather, Wagner understands Christ as the representative of humanity as in Rom 5:15–21, and it is significant that in his New Testament he marked Rom 5:17–18, v. 18 being doubly marked and quoted in his *Jesus of Nazareth* sketches: "Now, as through the sin of one the condemnation came upon all, even so through the righteousness of one hath justification of life come to all."[461] According to these texts and according to Wagner's own understanding built upon them,[462] Christ is therefore the representative human being and humanity is incorporated into his death such that human beings become his fellow heirs.[463] It is also worth adding that the view of David Friedrich Strauß that *humanity* is to be seen as the union of two natures is alien to Wagner's understanding of both Christ and humanity.[464]

456. See, e.g., *PW* 1:260–61; *GSD* 3:216.

457. For a Feuerbachian sense, see e.g., *PW* 2:154; *GSD* 4:32: "All understanding comes to us through love alone, and man is urged the most instinctively towards the essence of his own species." Note also that love here has a cognitive function.

458. *WagRS* 139.

459. Feuerbach, *Essence*, 269; *LFW* 5:316.

460. Feuerbach, *Essence*, 269; cf. *LFW* 5:316.

461. *PW* 8:338 (modified); *DTB* 266: "Wie nun durch Eines sünde die verdamnis über alle menschen gekommen ist, also ist auch durch die gerechtigkeit die rechtfertigung des lebens über alle menschen gekommen." This is marked as relevant for Act IV (also for Act III) of his *Jesus* opera (see chapter 7 below and volume 2, chapter 2).

462. See chapter 7 below and volume 2, chapter 2.

463. Note that in his New Testament Wagner marked Rom 8:16–17 as relevant for Act IV and it was quoted in the sketches for Act IV (*PW* 8:338–39; *DTB* 266). Further, Rom 8:29 was marked IV, and he underlines "unter vielen Brudern" ("among many brother"), and this is also quoted in the sketches for Act IV (*PW* 8:339; *DTB* 266).

464. Strauss, *Life*, 780; *Leben*, 2:734–35: "In an individual, a God-man, the properties and functions which the church ascribes to Christ contradict themselves; in the idea of the race (in der Idee der Gattung), they perfectly agree. Humanity (Die Menschheit) is the union of the two natures—God become man, the infinite manifesting itself in the finite (der zur Endlichkeit entäusserte unendliche),

Words and the word

Finally, there are two further issues to consider in Wagner's appropriation of Feuerbach. First, it could be that the antitheses of the Zurich writings are based on Feuerbach's style.[465] Further, the style of the commentary section of *Jesus of Nazareth* (II.1) resembles parts of *Thoughts*.[466] Secondly, although Wagner was most likely not aware of this, Feuerbach shared Luther's view that language can effect a change in the world (thus anticipating "speech-act theory"),[467] something that figures such as Kant, Schleiermacher, and Hegel were unable to come to terms with.[468] Wagner's music could be understood to address the hearers rather as the word of God addresses humankind, enabling an existential change.[469]

Wagner's rejection of Feuerbach

After his initial enthusiasm for Feuerbach, Wagner was soon to reject him. "[A]fter only a short time it became impossible for me to return to his works, and I recall that one of his books appearing shortly afterwards entitled *On the Essence of Religion* scared me off by the monotony of its title alone to such an extent that, when Herwegh opened its pages in front of me, I closed the book with a bang before his very eyes."[470] Further, in 1855 "Hornstein noted that Wagner had nothing but disparagement now for Feuerbach."[471] If references to Feuerbach in Cosima's diaries are anything to go by, they would confirm that he had become remarkably cool towards the philosopher.[472] Further, although *Artwork of the Future* was originally dedicated to Feuerbach, when Wagner came to write an introduction to the 1872 edition of his works he relativizes his debt to the philosopher:

---

and the finite spirit remembering its infinitude (und der seiner Unendlichkeit sich erinnernde endliche Geist)."

465. Hence I give *qualified* support to Newman, *Life*, 2:399 n. 8.
466. See, e.g., Feuerbach, *Thoughts*, 40–41; *LFW* 1:121–22.
467. I actually prefer the use of "Speech-event" ("Sprachereignis"). See Fuchs, "Sprachereignis."
468. Bayer, "Lutherrezeption," 217–18.
469. See Bell, *Parsifal*, 290–91, 310, and the discussion in volume 2, chapter 12.
470. *My Life* 431; *Mein Leben* 1:443. His letter to Röckel of 8 June 1853 indicates that he had the work in his possession: he sent this copy to his friend then in prison.
471. Newman, *Life* 2:444 (referring to Robert von Hornstein, *Memoiren, herausgegeben von Ferdinand von Hornstein*, 1908).
472. We find a mention in *CT* 17 January 1874, where he speaks of two Feuerbach's (Ludwig and his nephew, Anselm, a painter); this is omitted in *CD* because of the "untranslatable wordplay." Then there are brief quotations from Feuerbach (about Goethe (*CD* 4 September 1874) and about the "abdomen" of men and women (*CD* 27 July 1880) and then the significant comment that the dedication to Feuerbach "never meant anything to me, or led me astray" (*CD* 3 June 1878). Further, in *CD* 22 February 1880, Cosima notes: "Yesterday R. spoke of the Empress's curious habit of persecuting people about whom she once raved, just like Nietzsche. He said, 'One can give up mistaken allegiances, as, for example, mine with Feuerbach, but one should not then abuse them.'"

Actively aroused by the perusal of some of *Ludwig Feuerbach's* essays, I had borrowed various terms of abstract nomenclature and applied them to artistic ideals with which they could not always closely harmonise. In thus doing, I gave myself up without critical deliberation to the guidance of a brilliant writer, who approached most nearly to my reigning frame of mind, in that he bade farewell to Philosophy (in which he fancied he detected naught but masked Theology) and took refuge in a conception of man's nature in which I thought I clearly recognised my own ideal of artistic manhood.[473]

Things absent in Feuerbach but important for Wagner

It is significant that even when Wagner was under Feuerbach's influence, there are a number of things absent in Feuerbach that were central for Wagner. First, the idea of the "death of God" appears to be absent in Feuerbach,[474] even though he does write of the "crucified god" in his Luther essay.[475] In the discussion of Hegel above, I argued that the death of God was fundamental for Wagner, and I will discuss this further in volume 2. Secondly, Feuerbach says little about the suffering of Christ. Again this was central for Wagner, especially so in his later years when composing *Parsifal*; but it is also important in the Zurich essays, written as he was still working on the libretto of the *Ring*. Thirdly, as discussed above, Wagner stresses the representative and inclusive role of Christ, who in his death incorporates humanity, something that contradicts Feuerbach's understanding of the person and work of Christ.

Feuerbach, Marx (1818–83), and Wagner

Engels said that Feuerbach came to realize that "the Hegelian pre-mundane existence of the 'absolute idea,' the 'pre-existence of the logical categories' before the world existed, is nothing more that the fantastic survival of the belief in the existence of an extra-mundane creator."[476] Feuerbach came to see that "[m]atter is not a product of mind, but mind itself is merely the highest product of matter. This is, of course, pure materialism."[477] However, he criticizes Feuerbach for not recognizing that this is indeed materialism. "[H]aving got so far, Feuerbach stops short. He cannot overcome the customary philosophical prejudice, prejudice not against the thing but against the name materialism."[478]

---

473. *PW* 1:25; *GSD* 3:3.
474. Jüngel, *Mystery*, 100; *Geheimnis*, 131.
475. Feuerbach, *Luther*, 75–76; *LFW* 4:38–39.
476. Engels, *Feuerbach*, 25.
477. Engels, *Feuerbach*, 25.
478. Engels, *Feuerbach*, 25.

There are no extant references to Marx in Wagner's writings. However, as noted in chapter 2, Bakunin was personally acquainted with Marx and Engels and it is highly likely that Wagner came to know of Marx's teaching through Bakunin. Bakunin became acquainted with Marx and Proudhon in Paris in 1844[479] and further links of Wagner to Marx come via Herwegh, who was also in Paris at that time. Both Marx and Bakunin were friends and admirers of Herwegh[480] and Herwegh wrote for the short-lived *Rheinische Zeitung*, edited by Marx.[481] Herwegh was also a friend of Feuerbach, including his ideas in his poems, even entitling one "Ludwig Feuerbach."[482] In view of these connections, any knowledge Wagner had of Marx would therefore be through Bakunin and Herwegh. He got to know Bakunin in Dresden in 1848–49, and Herwegh in Zurich in July 1851.[483] Hence, learning something of Marx via these sources was early enough to influence the *Ring* libretto, and it is significant that the opera that appears to have the most "Marxism" is one of the last to be developed, namely *Rheingold* (first sketched in November 1851), with its critique of "capitalism" and its portrayal of how work has become "alienating."[484] Marx himself was not too enamoured with Wagner. On his way to Karlsbad he decided to stop off at Nuremberg (14 August 1876), but on alighting his train and inquiring about accommodation at the nearby hotel, he discovered it was fully occupied. According to Marx, the hotelier explained that "the town was swamped (überschwemmt), partly as a result of a millers' and bakers' convention, partly by people from all over the world who were on their way to state musician Wagner's Festival of Fools (Narrenfest des Staatsmusikanten Wagner) at Bayreuth."[485]

Concluding remarks on Wagner and Feuerbach

Feuerbach then seems to have been responsible for modifying the "basic outlines"[486] of the *Ring*, which had been determined earlier, and the most important philosophical source for such basic outlines was, I maintain, Hegel. The main way Feuerbach

479. Carr, *Bakunin*, 128–31.

480. Their correspondence shows a fairly close working relationship. See Herwegh's letter to Marx of 17 February 1843 (*MEGA* 3.1:392) and Marx's letters to Herwegh on 27 July and 8 August and 26 October 1847 (*MECW* 38: 118–19; 119–21; 140–41).

481. On Herwegh's support for socialism see Büttner, "Der andere Herwegh."

482. Winiger, *Feuerbach*, 162–65.

483. See the letter to Benedikt Kietz of 2 July 1851 (*SB* 4:71). This was the first mention of Herwegh in Wagner's works. Daub, "Herwegh," 194, gives the first mention as January 1850 in a letter to Uhlig concerning Feuerbach. I assume he is thinking of the letter of 12 January 1850 (*SB* 3:207–11) but there is no mention here of Herwegh.

484. See volume 2, chapter 5.

485. *MECW* 45:135; *MEW* 34:23 (modified). In this letter to Engels (19 August 1876) he explains how he, accompanied by his youngest daughter Eleanor, could find no accommodation either in Nuremberg or Weiden and had to spend the night on the hard chairs at the Weiden railway station.

486. Windell, "Hegel," 37.

influenced the *Ring* was, I think, in the matter of the humanization of God (which was related to the Lutheranism of both figures) and certain aspects of the emphasis on love, particularly how it relates to God. The Feuerbachian influence could include the idea that religious mythology reveals profound truths, but truths applicable only to the human condition. But to argue that the *Ring* has *only* a message about the human person and has no Christian theological message is far too simplistic.[487]

Kamenka rightly remarks that Feuerbach did not attempt to "preach a systematic Feuerbachian philosophy"[488] and consequently he has appealed mainly "to those searching for insights and illumination rather than finished solutions or systems."[489] Wagner was one such person. And after his appropriation of Feuerbach he was then to continue his interests in Hegel and was to turn to a figure who, one could say, was Kant's authentic successor, Arthur Schopenhauer, whom I now consider.

Schopenhauer

Introduction

In the mainstream of German Idealism we have, building on Kant, the figures of Fichte, Schelling, and Hegel, who together with Feuerbach all essentially abolished the phenomenal/noumenal distinction that Kant had introduced. With Schopenhauer we leave this trajectory of Kant-Fichte-Schelling-Hegel-Feuerbach and go back to Kant himself. Schopenhauer was by no means an uncritical disciple of Kant, attacking the latter's idea of the categorical imperative, and introducing his own distinctive view of ethics. Further, since he felt that Kant had taken a step backwards in the second edition of the *Critique of Pure Reason* (1787) with its "Refutation of Idealism,"[490] he went back to the first edition (1781).

Wagner's knowledge of Schopenhauer

It is often assumed that Wagner's discovery of Schopenhauer was rather like the conversion of St Paul on the road to a Damascus[491] and it is generally argued that this took place in the Autumn of 1854. There are reasons for doubting both of these. First of all, as I will argue, there are indications that Wagner was thinking along "Schopenhauerian" lines long before his so-called "conversion." Secondly, there are indications

---

487. See, e.g., the theological reflections on the *Ring* of Hübner, *Erlösung*, 55–110.
488. Kamenka, *Feuerbach*, 149.
489. Kamenka, *Feuerbach*, 149.
490. Kant, *Critique of Pure Reason*, 244–52 (B274–87).
491. On Paul's conversion experience see Acts 9:3–19; 22:6–16; 26:12–18, together with 1 Cor 9:1; 15:8; 2 Cor 4:6; Gal 1:15–16.

he actually knew something of Schopenhauer long before Autumn 1854 and that his interest in the Frankfurt sage started in 1852.

The earliest link with Schopenhauer is that Wilhelm Wiesand, one of the witnesses of Wagner's baptism in the Leipzig Thomaskirche, was a friend of Schopenhauer and in 1818 represented him in his dealings with Brockhaus, who published his magnum opus, *The World as Will and Representation*. Further, Schopenhauer wrote the work when he lived in the Ostraallee in Dresden when the young "Richard Geyer" was growing up.[492] These two facts may not add up to much, but more significant is that two of Wagner's sisters, Luise and Ottilie, married into the Brockhaus family. Friedrich Arnold Brockhaus had three sons: Friedrich, Heinrich, and Hermann. In 1828 Luise married Friedrich and in 1836 Ottilie married Hermann.[493] Wagner had a series of dealings with the three brothers whose family ran F. A. Brockhaus,[494] which published not only the works of Arthur Schopenhauer but also those of Joanna and Adele, his mother and sister.[495] It would seem strange if Wagner had never heard of Schopenhauer even before his years in Dresden, although this does not necessarily mean he was familiar with his ideas still less that he read anything.

The standard view, and one I once held to myself, was that Wagner as a young Hegelian and disciple of Feuerbach became a fervent disciple of Schopenhauer in Autumn 1854 as he started work on the music of *Walküre*. The person who introduced him to Schopenhauer was the poet Georg Herwegh, who was also living in Zurich as a political refugee. The date of Autumn 1854 is based on four texts (the *Annals* (1846–1867), *My Life*, and letters to von Bülow and Liszt of 26 October and 16 December 1854 respectively) but there are some oddities in the first two. According to the *Annals* (1846–1867), his reading of *The World as Will and Representation* took place *before* finishing the fair copy of *Rheingold*: "First reading of Schopenhauer's 'The World as Will and Idea'. 26 September: complete fair copy of Rhinegold score."[496] Although the published additions give "First reading of Schopenhauer's 'The World as Will and Idea'" a careful examination of the original suggests a question mark at the end.[497] This question mark could mean he was not precisely sure about the order in which things took place. His autobiography, the second witness, would suggest that it was only *after* finishing *Rheingold* that he read Schopenhauer's *Will*: "I plunged deeply into my work, and on September 26th completed the exquisite fair copy of the score of *Rheingold*. In the tranquillity and stillness of my house I now also became acquainted

---

492. Köhler, *Titans*, 419.

493. Some mistakenly think Heinrich married into the family, but he married Pauline Campe (so he was only a "brother-in-law" to Wagner in the second degree).

494. For details, see Westernhagen, *Bibliothek*, 65–83.

495. Cartwright, *Schopenhauer*, 19 n 44.

496. Brown Book 104; Braunes Buch 123.

497. It so happens the precise original page is given in *Mein Leben* 2:809.

with a book, the study of which was to assume vast importance for me. This was Arthur Schopenhauer's *The World as Will and Idea.*"[498]

In assessing these records we have to be aware that *My Life* was dictated after 1865[499] and the *Annals (1846–67)* were rewritten in 1868. I noted in chapter 2 above that the composer was given to falsification of events in his life, particularly in the *Annals*,[500] and there is every possibility he is doing the same with his discovery of Schopenhauer. This brings me to the fact that various texts suggest he knew Schopenhauer's works already in 1852.

In a 1969 monograph Sans argues on the basis of the testimony of Eliza Wille and Mathilde Wesendonck that Wagner came to know Schopenhauer's work already in 1852.[501] Eliza Wille explains that Wagner visited her home in Mariafeld (near Zurich) first on a Sunday in May of 1852 ("an einem Sonntag im Mai des Jahres 1852"), being accompanied by Georg Herwegh.[502] She explained that Herwegh had brought the works of Schopenhauer to Mariafeld: these works were quite new to her husband François and to Wagner and they made the deepest impression on both of them. In fact, François was so taken by his philosophy that he wanted to get to know Schopenhauer personally and went every year to Frankfurt to meet him.[503] She writes that Wagner flew through the works rapidly and that he and Herwegh were amazed at the idea of renunciation of the world.[504] Then when Wagner and Herwegh visited frequently in the Autumn of 1852 they would discuss philosophy. She adds that Herwegh thought Calderon was more significant than Schiller since Schopenhauer's thought lived in Calderon's drama "Life is a Dream" ("denn Schopenhauers Gedanke lebte in seinem Drama 'Das Leben ein Traum.'")[505]

The other witness for Sans is Mathilde Wesendonck. Her testimony is quoted by Albert Heintz in an article of 1896, marking the thirteenth anniversary of the

---

498. *My Life* 508; *Mein Leben* 2:521.

499. Part III of *Mein Leben* was dictated around 1868–69.

500. See the discussion of *Friedrich I* in chapter 2 above.

501. Sans, *Wagner*, 18–20.

502. Wille, *Erinnerungen*, 29–30. Such a Sunday visit in May is corroborated by his letters to Eliza and François Wille (*SB* 4:366; 374) and would appear to be 30 May 1852 (*SB* 4:374 n. 1473).

503. Wille, *Erinnerungen*, 33. I have not been able to verify whether he went every year but we do know he went in 1855 and discussed the *Ring* (Cartwright, *Schopenhauer*, 531).

504. Wille, *Erinnerungen*, 33: "Wagner, mit unerhörter Schnelligkeit der Auffassung, hatte bald die Werke Schopenhauers durchflogen. Er und Herwegh staunten über das gelöste Welträtsel. Weltentsagung und Askese—dahin sollte die Menschheit gelangen! –Weltentsagung, Tugenden der Heiligen konnten doch nur ein leerer Schall für Männer sein, die die Welt brauchten zu ihrem Schaffen und Bestehen, während die Genüsse des Lebens weder zu verschmähen noch zu verachten gesonnen waren."

505. Wille, *Erinnerungen*, 36. Note that the same connection is made by Oxenford, "Iconoclasm," 406, who points out that Schopenhauer himself appeals to Calderon, quoting the couplet "Pues el delito mayor / Del hombre es haber nacido" ("For man's greatest offence / Is that he has been born"; *WWR* 1:254; *ASSW* 1:355).

composer's death. She is reported to have said: "In 1852 he introduced me to the philosophy of Arthur Schopenhauer. He was extremely concerned to make me aware of every significant appearance in literature and science. Either he read himself or he discussed the content with me."[506]

We must now ask whether these witnesses are entirely reliable. Eliza Wille's words (9 March 1804–23 December 93) were published in the *Deutschen Rundschau* for February and March 1887 when she was just turning eighty-three years old and she claims she wrote these lines when she was seventy-seven,[507] which would give a date of 1881.[508] The recollections of Mathilde Wesendonck (23 December 1828–31 August 1902) were conveyed to Albert Heintz after the publication of the first edition of Chamberlain's Wagner biography for which she offers some critical comments.[509] The book appeared around the time of her sixty-seventh birthday[510] and the recollections appeared in the *Allgemeine Musik-Zeitung* (14 February 1896). Regarding Wagner's life she can be remarkably precise (the composition sketches for *Walküre* being composed 28 June to 27 December 1854),[511] but on other issues she is out by over a year.[512] There is also a rather curious quotation that, if accurate, somewhat qualifies the nature of their "Platonic" relationship. At the time of the first performance of *Parsifal* she says: "Wagner complained to me: 'The old cudgel still hangs for him between the legs!'" ("Wagner mir klagte: 'Der alte Knüppel hänge ihm immer noch zwischen den Beinen!'")[513] As far as the date she gives of 1852 for his reading of Schopenhauer, I find no good reason to doubt. Glasenapp's suggestion that we should read "1854" and that "1852" is "a senseless writing or printing error" may be a case of changing the text

---

506. Heintz, "Gedenkblatt," 93: "Im Jahre 1852 führte er mich in die Philosophie Arthur Schopenhauers ein, war überhaupt darauf bedacht, mich auf jede bedeutende Erscheinung in Literatur und Wissenschaft aufmerksam zu machen. Entweder las er selbst, oder er besprach den Inhalt mit mir."

507. Wille, *Erinnerungen*, 106. Sans, *Wagner*, 19, incorrectly gives it as seventy-six.

508. Note that some secondary literature incorrectly give her date of birth as 1809 (e.g., *Wagner Compendium*, 34), this error perhaps coming from her correct date of birth of 9 March 1804.

509. Heintz, "Gedenkblatt," 91, 94. She particularly objects to Chamberlain's suggestion that neither her nor her husband appreciated the genius of Wagner but helped him "unerkannt und unverstanden" (94). Heintz (94) expressed the hope that her comments will be taken into account in Chamberlain's second edition. They appear not to be considered (see the 10th edition of 1940, 81). Later editions had minor revisions, but the preface to the second illustrated edition (1911) did discuss her; Chamberlain had by then met her and her correspondence with Wagner had been published (1908). Although he considers that "die Frau ist die geborene Antagonistin des Geistes" (XIII) he accepts that she had influence on the composer more often in her absence than in her presence (XIII-XIV)!

510. Although the work is dated 1896 the work had already appeared in Autumn 1895. So on 15 November 1895 Cosima wrote to Chamberlain thanking him for five copies of his book (*Cosima Wagner und Chamberlain*, 413). Mathilde was born 23 December 1828.

511. Heintz, "Gedenkblatt," 93.

512. Heintz, "Gedenkblatt," 92: "Im Sommer 1853 war die Komposition des 'Rheingold' vollendet." It was actually completed 26 September 1854.

513. Wesendonck, "Erinnerungen," 92.

in order to fit the theory.⁵¹⁴ Golther, in quoting from the "Erinnerung," also follows Glasenapp's reading "Im Jahre 1854 [...]."⁵¹⁵

Sans was not the first to argue for Wagner coming to know Schopenhauer in 1852, but he gives the fullest argument for this position. Back in 1895 Hébert dated his discovery of Schopenhauer to 1852⁵¹⁶ (he did not have access then to *Mein Leben*, first published in 1911, or to the *Annals*, both of which could have sown confusion in his mind!). He refers to Hausegger's 1892 monograph,⁵¹⁷ which dates Wagner's coming to know the philosopher in the same year he completed the poem for *Walküre* and *Rheingold*, i.e., 1852.⁵¹⁸

Another view is that of Koch, who writes in 1913 that Wagner read Schopenhauer in his first visit to Selisberg, which was in July 1854, and then again in the Autumn.⁵¹⁹ This may be correct in that it was indeed in this first visit to Selisberg that he read Schopenhauer, but this first visit was in May *1852*; note also that he also visited Selisberg with Herwegh in Autumn 1852, according to Eliza Wille.

If his reading of Schopenhauer does go back to 1852 how are we to interpret his letters to von Bülow and Liszt of Autumn 1854? His letter to von Bülow 26 October tells that a great gift ("Ein grosses Geschenk") has come his way through his acquaintance ("Bekanntschaft") of the works of the great philosopher Schopenhauer (who, he says, has been ignored for thirty-five years). He recommends his main works (implying that von Bülow should purchase them),⁵²⁰ namely "*Die Welt als Wille und Vorstellung*" (*The World as Will and Representation*) and "*Parerga und Parelipomena*" and gives the publishers (Brockhaus and A. W. Hayr).⁵²¹ I understand this to mean that although he had

---

514. Glasenapp, *Wagner*, 3:53 n 1.

515. Golther, *Wesendonk*, VIII. He quotes only passages from the second half of Heintz, namely "Gedenkblatt," 93–94, omitting any criticism of Chamberlain and the indelicacy of Wagner's "Knüppel."

516. Hébert, *Religious Experience*, 52. I have reviewed this English translation in *The Catholic Historical Review* (2017).

517. Hébert, *Religious Experience*, 52 n. 56.

518. Hausegger, *Wagner und Schopenhauer*, 4 n: "1882 [sic] wurde die Dichtung der 'Walküre' und des 'Rheingold' vollendet. In demselben Jahre lernte Wagner Schopenhauers Schriften kennen." 1882 is clearly a printing error and should read 1852.

519. Koch, *Wagner*, 2:334: "Bereits in die Zeit von Wagners erstem Aufenthalt im stillen Selisberg im Juli 1854, mehr noch in die Herbstmonate fällt Wagners eingehendere Beschäftigung mit Schopenhauer."

520. Bülow took up Wagner's suggestion, becoming a keen Schopenhauerian (Walker, *Bülow*, 20, 371).

521. *SB* 6:261 (*SL* 320–22 give the bulk of this letter but do not include the close where he refers to Schopenhauer). The correct title and publisher of the second work Wagner names is *Parerga und Paralipomena*, Hayn. This edition of 1851 is found in his Wahnfried library together with the third edition of 1874 of Brockhaus. The Wahnfried library only has the third edition of *Die Welt als Wille und Vorstellung* (Brockhaus, 1859). The work Wagner possessed in 1854 would be the second edition of 1844, an expansion (from one to two volumes) of the first of 1819. The work being ignored for thirty-five years is therefore calculated from the first edition in 1819 to Wagner's reading in 1854. On the development of this work through its three editions see Koßler/Morini, "Entwicklung."

knowledge of Schopenhauer he had now come in possession of the works (so "great gift" can also be understood literally) and is engaging in a more detailed study. Such a re-engagement and re-reading of Schopenhauer is how I also interpret the letter to Liszt of 16 December 1854. This letter shows the profound effect the philosopher was having on Wagner:[522] "I have now become exclusively preoccupied with a man who—albeit only in literary form—has entered my lonely life like a gift from heaven. It is *Arthur Schopenhauer*, the greatest philosopher since *Kant*, whose ideas—as he himself puts it—he is the first person to think through to their logical conclusion."[523] He notes that Schopenhauer, "to Germany's shame," had been rediscovered "by an English critic" and adds: "What charlatans all these Hegels etc. are beside him [Schopenhauer]!"[524] This "English critic" was John Oxenford.[525] It is certainly Oxenford who helped make Schopenhauer known. However, it should not be overlooked that Schopenhauer also had German "evangelists" and "apostles."[526]

Then Wagner writes something that requires careful reflection (the emphasis is my own): "His principal idea, the final denial of the will to live, is of terrible seriousness, but it is uniquely redeeming. *Of course, it did not strike me as anything new* (Mir kam er [sein Hauptgedanke] wahrlich nicht neu), and nobody can think such a thought if he has not already lived it. But it was this philosopher *who first awakened the idea in me with such clarity.*"[527] One way to understand his writing that the "principal idea" did not strike him "as anything new" is that he already knew something of the philosopher's thought going back to 1852. Another interpretation is that Wagner was thinking along these lines anyway. Further, in the second paragraph of his letter to Liszt he writes that he finds Schopenhauer's thoughts in Liszt's writings, pointing to his essay on *Der fliegende Holländer*:[528] "How strange that I have often found your own thoughts here: although

522. Cf. his earlier letter of 7 October 1854, discussed below.

523. *SL* 323; *SB* 6:298.

524. *SL* 323; *SB* 6:298.

525. The key article was Oxenford, "Iconoclasm", which appeared *Westminster Review* (1 April 1853), edited by George Eliot and G. H. Lewes. Exactly one year earlier (1 April 1852) Oxenford wrote a review of *Parerga and Paralipomena* (1851), included in his "Contemporary Literature of Germany," 677–81. As was the custom in the *Westminster Review*, both appeared anonymously. His article "Iconoclasm" was read by Schopenhauer's friend Ernst Otto Lindner (*PP* 1:xii) who arranged for a German translation in the *Vossische Zeitung* and published in June 1853 (this liberal journal was founded in 1721 but ceased publication in 1934 because of Nazi censorship (Hamann, *Winifred Wagner*, 170)). Schopenhauer was generally pleased with Oxenford's review even though he had been termed "this misanthropic sage of Frankfurt" ("Iconoclasm," 407).

526. See Cartwright, *Schopenhauer*, 504–13, 524. Schopenhauer reckoned he had eight "apostles": Friedrich Ludwig Andreas Dorguth (a court judge in Magdeburg), Julius Frauenstädt (Berlin Doctor of Philosophy and private scholar), Johann August Becker (a lawyer in Alzey), Adam Ludwig von Doß (a Munich lawyer), David Asher (a writer, Jewish activist and English teacher in Leipzig), J. Kormann (a Berlin doctor), August Gabriel Kilzer (Frankfurt bank employee), and Ernst Otto Linder (editor of the Berlin *Vossische Zeitung*). Note also the wider circle of followers (Fazio, "Schopenhauer-Schule").

527. *SL* 323; *SB* 6:298.

528. Millington and Spencer, *SL* 319 n. 1, point to the irony that although the essay was printed

you express them differently because you are religious, I nevertheless know that you think exactly the same thing. How profound you are! In your essay on the Dutchman you often struck me with the force of lightening. When I read Schoppenhauer [sic] I was mostly in your presence: you simply did not notice."529

The way Wagner expresses himself in these two letters is consistent with his earlier reading back in 1852, but with a more intensive reading in 1854 once he had come into possession of the works. I suggest that for various reasons he suppressed the idea of an earlier reading of Schopenhauer when he rewrote his *Annals* and dictated his *Mein Leben*. Although he was more honest in his debt to Schopenhauer than he was to say Mendelssohn and Berlioz we see the same pattern at work: Wagner wishing to credit himself with more originality than was actually the case.

This issue of dating raises the question whether Wagner later wrote of his first reading Schopenhauer in 1854 so as to suggest that his Schopenhauerian ideas in the *Ring* (see below on *Siegfried* Act III Scene 1) did not come from the philosopher. In response to Eiser's article on the *Ring*, which suggested Schopenhauerian ideas in the work, Wagner wrote: "As a curiosity I would remind you only that it was barely a year after completing the poem that I first became acquainted with Schopenhauer's philosophy (and, indeed, with philosophy in general), that it initially repelled me, and that only through a deeply tragic perception of the world—a view which I and Schopenhauer have in common—did I feel powerfully drawn to an understanding of it."530 Is he again trying to make out that he is a self-taught Siegfried, not only in the realm of music (see his downplaying of the musical tuition he received), but also in the realm of philosophy?

My conclusion therefore is that Wagner first read Schopenhauer in May 1852 and engaged in an intensive reading in Autumn 1854. Hence, when he writes that "Herwegh told me about this book"531 (i.e., *World as Will and Representation*) he is referring to events of 1852. The intensive reading in 1854 was enabled by some time of rest after finishing *Rheingold* (26 September) and precipitated by Oxenford's articles on Schopenhauer of 1852 and 1853 ("Iconocasm") together with the translation into German of "Iconoclasm" in 1853. This precipitation is reflected in his letter to Liszt mentioned above (16 December 1854), who alludes to Oxenford ("an English critic"). And although the earlier letter of 7 October does not refer to Oxenford, Wagner does speak in his own way of original sin, which Oxenford highlighted in his "Iconoclasm":532 "let us treat the world only with contempt; for it deserves no

---

under Liszt's name it was written partly, possibly predominantly, by his partner Carolyne von Sayn-Wittgenstein. Originally it was composed in French for the publication in the *Weymar'sche Offizielle Zeitung* in June 1854 and translated by Peter Cornelius for the *Neue Zeitschrift für Musik*.

529. SL 323; SB 6:298–99 (reading "als ich Schopenhauer las" as does BWL 2:46).
530. Letter of 29 October 1977 (SL 876).
531. *My Life* 508; *Mein Leben* 2:521.
532. "Iconoclasm," 406: "Thus every man brings his own depravity into the world with him, and this is the great doctrine of original sin, as set forth by Augustine, expounded by Luther and Calvin,

better [...] It is evil, *evil, fundamentally evil* [...] It belongs to Alberich: no one else!! Away with it!"[533]

Wagner's reading Schopenhauer was not a Damascene conversion; rather, as Sans argues, Schopenhauer found himself preaching to the converted.[534] Indeed, a trace of Schopenhauer's philosophy can be found in *A Happy Evening*, a work written as early as 12 May 1841:[535] "What music expresses is eternal, infinite, and ideal; she expresses not the passion, love, desire, of this or that individual in this or that condition, but Passion, Love, Desire itself, and in such infinitely varied phases as lie in her unique possession and are foreign and unknown in any other tongue."[536] This can be compared to these words of Schopenhauer: "Therefore music does not express this or that particular and definite pleasure, this or that affliction, pain, sorrow, horror, gaiety, merriment, peace of mind themselves, to a certain extent in the abstract, their essential nature, without any accessories, and so also without the motives for them."[537]

Schopenhauer in the *Ring*

So where do we see signs of Schopenhauer's philosophy in the *Ring*? One idea was that Schopenhauer confirmed Wagner's view of "original sin," seen in that letter to Liszt of 7 October 1854. Another example is Wotan's attitude in *Siegfried* Act III Scene 1:[538]

Um der Götter Ende	Fear of the end of the gods
grämt mich die Angst nicht,	no longer consumes me
seit mein Wunsch es—will!	now that my wish so wills it!
Was in des Zwiespalt's wildem Schmerze	What I once resolved in despair,
verzweifelnd einst ich beschloß,	in the searing smart of inner turmoil,
froh und freudig	I now perform freely
führe frei ich nun aus	in gladness and joy

The reference to once resolving "in despair" to give up his power is presumably to his words in *Walküre* Act II:[539]

---

and applauded by Schopenhauer, who, though a freethinker in the most complete sense of the word, is absolutely delighted with the fathers and reformers, when they bear witness of human degradation."

533. *SL* 319; *SB* 6:249.
534. Sans, *Wagner*, 263: "Schopenhauer prêchera à un converti."
535. Kühnel, "Prose Writings," 639. It was published in the *Revue et gazette musicale*, 24 October, 7 November 1841.
536. *PW* 7:81; *GSD* 1:148.
537. *WWR* 1:261 (§52); *ASSW* 1:364.
538. *WagRS* 257-8 (note the alliteration).
539. *WagRS* 153.

Fahre denn hin,	Farewell, then,
herrische Pracht,	imperious pomp!
göttlichen Prunkes	Godly show's
prahlende Schmach!	resplendent shame!
Zusammen breche	Let all I raised
was ich gebaut!	now fall in ruins!
Auf geb' ich mein Werk;	My work I abandon;
nur Eines will ich noch:	One thing alone do I want:
das Ende — —	the end — —
das Ende!—	the end!—

Magee[540] related these words of Act II to Wagner's comments to Cosima on 29 March 1878. But Wagner was actually referring to later events in the *Ring* and in fact in *Walküre* Act II we do *not* have a free denial of the will; rather, as the Wanderer in *Siegfried* Act III Scene 1 expresses it, "What I once resolved in despair, / in the searing smart of inner turmoil." Therefore, there is actually a contrast between the two passages. So here are Wagner's words to Cosima:

> "It does not say much for Schopenhauer that he did not pay more attention to my *Ring des Nibelungen*. I know no other work in which the breaking of a will (and what a will, which delighted in the creation of a world!) is shown as being accomplished through the individual strength of a proud nature *without the intervention of a higher grace*, as it is in Wotan. Almost obliterated by the separation from Brünnhilde, this will rears up once again, bursts into flame in the meeting with Siegfried, flickers in the dispatching of Waltraute, until he sees it entirely extinguished at the end in Valhalla." At supper he returns to this and says: "I am convinced Sch. would have been annoyed that I discovered this before I knew about his philosophy."[541]

If Wagner discovered Schopenhauer in May 1852 (as Eliza Wille suggest) then his philosophy could have influenced the libretto of *Der junge Siegfried* in its final stages. The *Prosaentwurf* (24 May to 1 June 1851)[542] and *Erstschrift des Textbuches* (3–24 June 1851)[543] do speak of Wotan not caring about the end of the gods since he wills it. We have what one could say is a toned down Schopenhauerian sentiment:[544]

---

540. Magee, *Wagner and Philosophy*, 179–80.
541. *CD* 29 March 1878.
542. Strobel, *Skizzen*, 89; *TBRN1* 229.
543. Strobel, *Skizzen*, 173; *TBRN1* 309.
544. Strobel, *Skizzen*, 173; *TBRN1* 309.

Der götter ende	The end of the gods
erkenn' auch ich:	I also perceive:
doch es sorgt mich nicht	yet I care not for it
seit ich es will!	because I intend it!

But as he re-worked the libretto in 1852 this Schopenhauerian sentiment is strengthened by adding the words "What I once resolved in despair, / in the searing smart of inner turmoil, / I now perform freely / in gladness and joy."[545] From his letters such a change was made towards the end of the year. His letter to Uhlig of 14 October explains that both his Siegfrieds require rigorous revision but has yet to do this and a letter to Liszt of 9 November explains that although he has started these revisions much work is still to be done. Then a letter to Uhlig of 20 November explains that he has almost completed revisions of *Der junge Siegfried*.[546] The fact that the changes to Wotan's words to Erda in Act III occurred after his visit to Eliza Wille in May (and also probably after the "Autumn" visits she mentions), where he learned of Schopenhauer, may be significant.

The most obvious example of Schopenhauer in the *Ring* is the "Schopenhauer ending" he wrote in May 1856 for the close of *Götterdämmerung*.[547] Although it was not used in the final *Ring* it appeared as a kind of footnote in the *Gesammelte Schriften und Dichtungen*.[548] This ending places in Brünnhilde's mouth a number of Schopenhauerian themes. First, the idea of renunciation ("I depart from the home of desire (Wunschheim)"); second, being freed from delusion ("I flee forever the home of delusion (Wahnheim)"); third, the idea of migration of souls and being freed from this ("redeemed from reincarnation"; "von Wiedergeburt erlös't");[549] fourth, the suffering of love ("Grieving love's / profoundest suffering / opened my eyes for me").[550]

Because Wagner's discovery of Schopenhauer is dated to after his composition of the libretto at the end of 1852 and after the composition of the music for *Rheingold*, Schopenhauerian influence on the *Ring* is often seen as somewhat limited. A very different view is put forward by Apponyi, who considers that "[t]his philosophical phase corresponds to his creation of the *Nibelungen*." He continues: "In that work, unbridled pursuit of worldly pleasures, greed, sensuality and, above all, lust for power, exhaust themselves in their mightiest incarnations and lead to self-destruction. It is the greatest dramatic expression of fatalistic pessimism, embodied in the most tremendous

---

545. *TBRN*1 341.

546. *DEBRN* 72–74 (no. 139, 144, 147).

547. *WagRS* 363, who point out that the versification was probably from 1871–72.

548. *GSD* 6:255–56.

549. Westernhagen, *Bibliothek*, 36–38, suggests that Wagner's idea here of re-birth (and of the ending discussed by Strobel, "Unbekannte Dokumente," 340) owes something also to Ettmüller, *Vaulu-Spá*, 73–75, where he discusses "Wiedergeburt."

550. *WagRS* 363.

music ever composed, and built on a foundation of wildest passion, yet at the close it sounds a note which heralds a different world."[551]

Problems with Schopenhauer

Philosophers have been critical of various aspects of Schopenhauer's philosophy[552] and Wagner himself in his late essay *Religion and Art* (1880) appeared to recognize a key problem in Schopenhauer's understanding of the denial of the will.[553] Further, Wagner was to make what he thought was a correction of Schopenhauer's view that redemption was *from* erotic love; rather, as he explains in a letter to Mathilde Wesendonck of 1 December 1858, redemption is *through* erotic love.[554] But perhaps one of the most serious problems in Schopenhauer's philosophy regards the subject-object correlation. Schopenhauer's view that there is always a certain subject-object correlation can be helpful in distinguishing say everyday experience (representation according to the principle of sufficient reason) from the aesthetic experience (representation not according to the principle of sufficient reason). However, he fails to explain why this should change. One can always, as I have done, say that this falls within the power of God. However, there is a problem here for philosophers. Gardner writes: "By affirming the necessary mutual implication of subject and object without having recourse to the kinds of complex arguments for transcendental idealism that Kant advanced in the Aesthetic, Analytic, and Antimony of his first *Critique*—that is, by advancing the principle as an apodictic or quasi-analytic truth—Schopenhauer effectively denied the need for and possibility of a philosophical theory of the relation of subject and object in the sense that Kant, and again the absolute idealists, sought to provide."[555]

However, this is something that did not appear to bother Wagner. Neither did it bother his philosopher friend Nietzsche—and it was to be their common love of Schopenhauer that brought them together.

Nietzsche

Although Nietzsche does not belong to German Idealism and although he had little influence on the *Ring*, it is nevertheless important to consider him here, albeit briefly. Once Wagner had completed the libretto of the *Ring* (December 1852) it was to be another almost sixteen years before he met Nietzsche, this being facilitated at the home of Hermann Brockhaus (married to Wagner's sister Ottilie) in Leipzig in November

---

551. Apponyi, *Memoirs*, 104.

552. E.g., see Young, *Schopenhauer*, 44–46, for sharp criticism of his view on concepts, reason, and perception.

553. See Bell, *Parsifal*, 171–72.

554. SL 432 (Golther, *Mathilde Wesendonk*, 79–80). This is discussed in volume 2, chapter 6.

555. Gardner, "Schopenhauer," 396.

1868.[556] The direction of influence was almost exclusively in one direction: from Wagner to Nietzsche. Nevertheless, the Wagner-Nietzsche relationship is important for an understanding of the theology of the *Ring* in that it highlights a number of key aspects and Nietzsche, for all his faults, could be extremely discerning.

First, I mention a constellation of four issues that link the two thinkers: "will to power," the "superman," the question of custom being elevated to morality, and the matter of "primeval law." All these issues will be discussed in volume 2, but very briefly one can now note the following: Nietzsche's idea of "will to power" reflects that craving found in both Alberich and Wotan; Nietzsche's "superman" ("Übermensch") is inspired by Wagner's Siegfried; Nietzsche's attack upon "Sittlichkeit," where morality is seen as based on social norms and conditioning, is anticipated in the *Ring*;[557] and his idea of "primeval law" ("Urgesetz") appears to be based on Wagner's own usage in the *Nibelungen-Mythus* and in the *Ring* libretto.[558]

Secondly, I consider issues that are rather more complex. Nietzsche appears to accuse Wagner of antisemitism, racism, and nationalism; but, I claim, Nietzsche is also not without guilt in this regard. These three issues went hand in hand in nineteenth-century Germany and Wagner subscribed to them all, although his views were often rather nuanced and contradict the popular image often given of the composer. Nietzsche objected to antisemitism for a range of reasons, among which were racism and nationalism,[559] but attacking Wagner on these grounds, as well as doing so with bitter irony, is ironic on another level and one wonders how aware Nietzsche was concerning this. A good example is "How I Broke away from Wagner" in *Nietzsche contra Wagner*: "In the summer of 1876, right in the middle of the first *Festspiel*, I took leave of Wagner. I cannot stand ambiguities: since coming to Germany, Wagner had acceded step by step to everything I hate—even to anti-Semitism. . . . At that time it was indeed high time *to take my leave*: and I immediately received a confirmation of the fact. Richard Wagner, seemingly the all-conquering, actually a decaying, despairing decadent, suddenly sank down helpless and shattered before the Christian cross . . . ."[560] These words do not reflect well on Nietzsche, as can be seen on examining his own attitude to the Jewish people. He considers the history of the Jewish people in three phases.[561] The first is the "Old Testament" period, by which he means the preexilic period. This "book of divine justice" ("Buch von der göttlichen Gerechtigkeit") is praised for "such grand style."[562] It contrast starkly with the second period, that of

---

556. See Nietzsche's letters to Erwin Rohde describing this first encounter (Benders, *Chronik*, 183–84).

557. These three issues are discussed by Berry, "Nietzsche," 13–19.

558. See volume 2, chapter 7.

559. Yovel, "Jews," 122; "Juden," 132.

560. Nietzsche, *Anti-Christ*, 276 (*FNKSA* 6:431; "Wie ich von Wagner loskam," §1).

561. Yovel, "Jews," 127–28; "Juden," 134.

562. Nietzsche, *Beyond Good and Evil*, 48 (*FNKSA* 5:72; §52).

the Second Temple and priests, where the "slave morality" revolution happened, out of which Christianity grew. Nietzsche writes: "The fact that this New Testament (which is a type of Rococo of taste in every respect) gets pasted together with the Old Testament to make a single book, a 'Bible,' a 'book in itself': this is probably the greatest piece of temerity and 'sin against the spirit' that literary Europe has on its conscience."[563] Then the third period is that of diaspora Jews: "the Jews are without doubt the strongest, toughest, and purest race (die stärkste, zäheste und reinste Rasse) living in Europe today."[564] So whatever he may say about the first and third periods (about which one could ponder) he attacks the Jews of the second, and in *Genealogy of Morals* singles out four of them: "consider to whom you bow down to Rome itself, today, as though to the embodiment of the highest values—and not just in Rome, but over nearly half the earth, everywhere where man has become tame or wants to become tame, to *three Jews*, as we know, and *one Jewess* (to Jesus of Nazareth, Peter the Fisherman, Paul the Carpet-Weaver and the mother of Jesus mentioned first, whose name was Mary)."[565] The Jews of this second period were still Jews so how can Nietzsche himself claim not to be antisemitic or indeed racist?

A second instance of Nietzsche's irony, this time a conscious irony, is that he attacks Wagner's German nationalism and sees this as hypocrisy in that Wagner's art appears by its very nature to be French! Alluding to his having to flee Germany to Paris in 1849 and his later positive reception by the French, he writes in *Ecce Homo* ("Why I am so Clever"):

> Wagner was a revolutionary—he ran away from the Germans.... As an artist, Paris is your only home in Europe. [...] Who was the first intelligent follower of Wagner? Charles Baudelaire, who was also the first to understand Delacroix, that typical decadent in whom a whole generation of artists recognized themselves—he might also have been the last.... What have I never forgiven Wagner for? That he condescended to the Germans,—that he became *reichsdeutsch*.... Wherever Germany extends it *spoils* culture.[566]

As well as attacking his antisemitism and nationalism Nietzsche objects to the "corporate" in Bayreuth. He explains in "How I Broke away from Wagner" (*Nietzsche contra Wagner*) that already in summer 1876, with the first Festspiel, he took his leave.[567] Then in "Where I Offer Objections" (*Nietzsche contra Wagner*) he elaborates:

> In Bayreuth, one is honest only as a mass; as an individual one lies, lies to oneself. One leaves oneself at home when one goes to Bayreuth; one relinquishes the right to one's own tongue and choice, to one's taste, even to one's courage as

---

563. Nietzsche, *Beyond Good and Evil*, 48–49 (*FNKSA* 5:72; §52).
564. Nietzsche, *Beyond Good and Evil*, 142 (*FNKSA* 5:193; §251).
565. Nietzsche, *Genealogy of Morals*, 34 §1.16 (*FNKSA* 5:287).
566. Nietzsche, *Anti-Christ*, 93; (*FNKSA* 6:289; "Warum ich so klug bin," §5).
567. Wagner," *Anti-Christ*, 276 (*FNKSA* 6:431; "Wie ich von Wagner loskam," §1).

one has it and exercises it within one's own four walls against God and world. ... In the theatre, one is people, herd, female, Pharisee, voting cattle, patron, idiot—*Wagnerian*: there, even the most personal conscience is vanquished at the levelling magic of the great number, there, the "neighbour" reigns; there, one *becomes* a neighbour . . . .[568]

One reason Wagner and Nietzsche were originally drawn together was their common admiration of Schopenhauer; but Nietzsche was to turn away from the philosopher and after their break up, around the time of the first Bayreuth festival, he attacked Wagner's dependence on Schopenhauer.[569] Wagner, he writes, found "the archetypal revolutionary in Siegfried," who declared war on morality and who "always followed his first impulses, he overthrew tradition, all respect, all *fear*. He strikes down whatever he does not like. He knocked down all the old deities without the least sign of respect. But his main project was the *emancipation of woman*—'the redemption of Brunnhilde'"[570] Possibly alluding to Tristan *and* Isolde[571] he writes of "Siegfried *and* Brunnhilde; the sacrament of free love; the dawn of the golden age; the twilight of the gods [. . .]."[572] But everything was to change. "For a long time, Wagner's ship ran blithely along this course. There is no doubt that this is where Wagner looked for *his* highest goal. What happened? An accident. The ship hit a reef; Wagner was stranded. The reef was Schopenhauer's philosophy; Wagner was stranded on a *contrary* worldview." He had set to music a "*reckless* optimism." His solution was to interpret the reef as his goal and "translated the *Ring* into Schopenhauerian." "Brünnhilde, who, according to the old conception, was to say goodbye with a song of honour of free love, leaving the world to the hope of a socialist utopia where 'all will be well', is now given something else to do. She has to study Schopenhauer first; she has to set the fourth book of the *World as Will and Representation* to verse."[573] It is in the fourth book that Schopenhauer puts forward his asceticism and which Wagner alluded to in his "Schopenhauer ending."

The biggest difference between the two was to be the issue of the Christian faith. It is frequently claimed that it was later in life that Wagner took an interest in Christianity with his composing of *Parsifal*. In fact, his first intensive work on the New Testament took place shortly after he started work on the *Ring*, and it is to this study that I turn in the next chapter.

---

568. Nietzsche, *Anti-Christ*, 267 ("Wo ich Einwände mache," *FNKSA* 6:419).

569. In fact, Wagner's appropriation of Schopenhauer was always qualified, even in *Tristan, Meistersinger*, and *Parsifal*, the works most clearly influenced by him.

570. Nietzsche, *Anti-Christ*, 239–40 (*FNKSA* 6:19–20; §4).

571. Isolde speaks of "this sweet little word (Wörtlein) 'and'" (*WagTS* 120; *GSD* 7:47).

572. Nietzsche, *Anti-Christ*, 240 (*FNKSA* 6:20; § 4).

573. Nietzsche, *Anti-Christ*, 240 (*FNKSA* 6:20–21; § 4). The quotation "all will be well" presumably comes from Julian of Norwich, *Revelations*, 22 (§13).

— 7 —

Wagner and the New Testament

Introduction

Already in the above chapters we have encountered many thinkers who were theologians either because this was one of their main areas (e.g., Herder, Hegel, Feuerbach) or because their work has significant implications for theology (e.g., Wilhelm and Jacob Grimm, Goethe, Schiller, A. W. and Friedrich Schlegel). In this chapter the focus moves specifically to the New Testament and this forms a bridge to the second volume where, in chapter 2, I focus particularly on the *Jesus of Nazareth* sketches. These sketches, I noted in chapter 2 above, were written just after Wagner had started on his *Ring* and since many of the key ideas he there expresses end up on the stage of the *Ring*, they will prove to be fundamental in discerning the theology of the artwork.

Wagner's Knowledge of New Testament Scholarship

A number of key figures with whom Wagner engaged took a keen interest in the New Testament and some of them contributed significantly to the field: Gotthold Ephraim Lessing (1729–81), Karl Lachmann (1793–1851), Christian Herrmann Weisse (1801–66), and David Friedrich Strauß (1808–74). The philologian Lachmann, whose edition of the *Nibelungenlied* and selections from Icelandic Sagas Wagner had used for his *Ring*[1] (and who had edited twelve volumes of Lessing, which Wagner possessed in Dresden), also applied his talents to the New Testament. In 1831 he produced the first edition of the New Testament to be based solely on ancient manuscripts[2] and in 1835 argued that Mark was earlier than Matthew and Luke, and Matthew was based on a collection of sayings that had been filled out by some Markan narrative.[3] Although

---

1. See chapter 3 above. He also used Lachmann's editions of Wolfram von Eschenbach and Walther von der Vogelweide which were in his Dresden Library (DB 154, 155, 163). On his edition of Lessing (DB 81) see below.

2. A later edition of 1842–50 included an extensive apparatus. He also explained the rationale for his text in an 1830 article "Rechenschaft." See Metzger, *Text*, 124–26.

3. See Lachmann, "De ordine narrationum"; Kümmel, *Investigation*, 147–48.

Wagner clearly valued Lachmann's work on medieval texts, we have no evidence that he knew of his work on the New Testament. More intriguing is Weisse, since Wagner had attended some of his lectures and had met him at his uncle's home. At this time (1831–32) Weisse was primarily involved in aesthetics,[4] but he was subsequently to turn his attention to the New Testament. He was impressed by Strauß's *Leben Jesu* (1835), which propelled him to the "reconstruction of the historical picture of Christ."[5] But he realized that in order to do this he must explain the relationship of the Synoptic Gospels to each other. This he did in his 1,157-page work *Die evangelische Geschichte* (1838), thereby coming to be the first to develop the now widely accepted two-source hypothesis.[6] The most significant thing about Weisse's portrayal of Jesus is that he is non-eschatological;[7] but again we have no evidence that Wagner knew Weisse's work on the Gospels.

Secondary literature often assumes that Wagner had a knowledge of David Friedrich Strauß. He did later possess the 1864 edition of Strauß's *Life of Jesus* in his Wahnfried library in Bayreuth[8] but we have no evidence of his reading of Strauß up to the time of his work on *Jesus of Nazareth*. In fact, Wagner's first mention of Strauß is as late as 1868, his *Annalen* for March of that year simply recording "David Strauss."[9] This refers no doubt to three ironical sonnets Wagner wrote "to David Strauss," which are critical of both his person and his theology.[10] To give an idea of his disdain for Strauß I cite the first verse of the first sonnet:[11]

O David! Held. Du sträusslichster der Strausse!	O David! Hero! Staussest of the Strausses!
Befreier aus des Wahnes schweren Ketten!	Deliverer from delusion's weighty chains!
So woll' uns stets von Irr' und Trug erretten,	May you ever redeem us from error and deception
wie du enthüllt der Evangelien Flausse!	as you expose humbug of the Gospels!

---

4. See chapter 6 above.

5. Kümmel, *Investigation*, 149.

6. Kümmel, *Investigation*, 149–51, quotes sections of this key work. See also the discussion below on source criticism.

7. Kümmel, *Investigation*, 149.

8. This was published in one volume (the first edition of 1835 was published as two volumes) and "[a]lthough ostensibly designed for more popular consumption [. . .] it was prefaced by a lengthy review of over 150 pages, dealing with the views of other scholars and outlining the critical theories underlying his approach" (Brown, *Jesus*, 200).

9. *KB* 2:8. However, one should not exclude the possibility that Wagner removed references to Strauß from his *Annals 1846–1867* in February 1868 (see volume 1, chapter 2).

10. *Brown Book* 125–26; *Braunes Buch* 149–50. One reason Wagner took a special dislike to Strauß was because he supported the conductor Franz Lachner, with whom Wagner had a bad relationship. Note also that Wagner supported Nietzsche's attack on Strauß in the first of his *Untimely Meditations* "David Strauss, the Confessor and the Writer," published in 1873 (Nietzsche, *Untimely Meditations*, 3–55).

11. *Brown Book* 125 (translation modified); *Braunes Buch* 149.

Wagner may, however, have learned something of Strauß from his fellow revolutionary in Dresden, Mikael Bakunin, who appears to have a reasonable knowledge of Strauß. Bakunin himself was negative about Christianity, believing that it was "the most impoverishing and enslaving religion of all,"[12] this contrasting with Wagner's portrayal of Jesus (and the various New Testament witnesses) as a proclaimer of freedom in the sketches. But on a positive note, Bakunin says that Strauß himself has established that Christ was an "actual historical figure" ("personage historique et reel") and represented a magnificent example of genius.[13]

Internal evidence in Wagner's *Jesus* sketches by no means establishes a knowledge of Strauß. One could argue that he shares with Strauß a denial of the "resurrection"; but, of course, Strauß was by no means the first to question it.[14] More to the point, the ending of Wagner's *Jesus of Nazareth* actually corresponds to Hegel's view that the "resurrection" is to be seen in terms of the Spirit at work in the Christian community.[15] Further, there are a number of points where Wagner's portrayal of Jesus contradicts that of Strauß:[16] Jesus is born in Bethlehem, continually prophesies his violent death and, most significant of all, Wagner's whole drama is colored by John's Gospel. Whether Wagner's view of myth corresponds to that of Strauß is disputed,[17] but there are so many other obvious sources that had shaped the composer's view of myth when he wrote his Jesus

---

12. McLaughlin. *Bakunin*, 137.

13. Bakounine, *Considérations*, 105. Arthur Lehning in the "Notes" (p. 123 n. 13) thinks Bakunin here refers to a brochure of Strauß, *Zwei friedliche Blätter: Vermehrter und verbesserter Abdruck der beiden Aüsätze: 'Über Justinus Kerner', und: 'Über Vergängliches und Bleibendes im Christentum'* (Altona, 1839). Bakunin is drawing on the thought of the second article (pp. 109–18). Bakunin briefly refers to the impression made by Strauß's *Das Leben Jesu* in his *Confession*, 35.

14. Over a hundred years before the publication of Strauss's *Das Leben Jesu* (1835), Thomas Woolston (1670–1733) had questioned the resurrection narratives in the sixth of his *Discourses on the Miracles of our Saviour* (1727–29) (Brown, *Jesus*, 40–42). Wagner would also no doubt be aware of Reimarus, whose "seventh fragment," *Von dem Zwecke Jesu und seiner Jünger*, was published by Lessing in 1778. But note that Wagner's edition of Lessing's collected works only included the "Vorrede," not the text of Reimarus.

15. See chapter 6 above, and volume 2, chapter 11. See also Bell, "Death of God," 42–45.

16. See Ellis, PW 8:xvii–xix.

17. Dinger, *Entwickelung*, 321 n. 3, suggested Wagner did take his idea of myth from Strauß. This is contradicted by Ellis, PW 8:xvii–xviii, who argues that Wagner's understanding of the "Christian myth" in *Opera and Drama* (written in the winter of 1850–51, with extracts published in 1851 and the final complete work appearing in 1852) is completely different. This can be seen in a key section of *Opera and Drama* (2.2) where he discusses the "Christian Mythos" (PW 2:157–61; GSD 4:35–38). One of his fundamental points is: "The enthralling power of the Christian myth consists in its portrayal of a *transfiguration through Death*" (PW 2:159; GSD 4:36). The most recent detailed work on the sketches, Giessel, *Jesus von Nazareth*, 78, argues that "Wagner's overall conception of the idea of myth does resemble Strauss's" (for Strauß's view of myth see Hartlich and Sachs, *Ursprung*, 121–47; Brown, *Jesus*, 187–96). I wonder though whether ultimately it makes much sense to compare Strauß and Wagner on myth since one is a biblical critic and the other a dramatist.

sketches.[18] All in all, if Wagner did know of Strauß's work, it does not appear to have influenced the sketches to any great extent.

Another figure who could have influenced Wagner's sketches is Wilhelm Weitling,[19] whose rather moralistic *Gospel of the Poor Sinner* (*Evangelium des armen Sünders*), published in 1845, presents a purely human Jesus who is a "communist" and "has no respect for property."[20] The impending publication of this work led to his arrest in Zurich in June 1843. The previous month the poet (and revolutionary) Georg Herwegh sent Weitling to Bakunin with a letter of recommendation. Bakunin wrote that in this "uneducated man" he found "wild fanaticism, noble pride, and faith in the liberation and future of the enslaved majority."[21] This encounter with Weitling proved to be "one of the capital events in [Bakunin's] life, completing his transformation from a speculative philosopher into a practical revolutionary."[22] The question is whether Weitling influenced Wagner's portrayal of Jesus via Bakunin when they met six years later. Weitling presents Jesus "as the first rebel and communist, 'the illegitimate child of a poor girl Mary'—in fact, as a prototype of Weitling himself."[23] However, Wagner's Jesus is not quite Weitling's "rebel and communist" even though his teaching regarding property and riches is radical.[24]

Given Wagner's keen interest in Lessing, noted in chapter 5 above, and the simple fact that the only works of what one would usually term "Christian theological scholarship" in Wagner's Dresden library were those of Lessing, it is rather surprising that secondary literature on Wagner's *Jesus of Nazareth* sketches has largely ignored Lessing's possible influence. Wagner possessed his "Complete Writings" in twelve volumes in his Dresden library[25] and he had an updated and expanded edition in his Wahnfried library.[26] Although Wagner's relation to Lessing has been discussed in Wagner scholarship on questions of "music and drama"[27] and the relationship of the arts to one

---

18. See, for examples, his study of Greek, Germanic, Norse mythology; his interests in medieval literature; his reading of Jacob and Wilhelm Grimm; his interests in the Romantics.

19. This was first discussed in some detail by Graap, *Jesus von Nazareth*, 59–66.

20. Weitling, *Poor Sinner's Gospel*, 117. On Weitling's book see Wittke, *Communist*, 72–78.

21. Bakunin, *Confession*, 38.

22. Carr, *Bakunin*, 123.

23. Carr, *Bakunin*, 123. Weitling was "the illegitimate child of a German girl of Magdeburg by a French officer quartered there after the Napoleonic campaign of 1806" (Carr, *Bakunin*, 122). On Jesus' illegitimacy see Weitling, *Gospel*, 87.

24. Note Wagner's reference to the whole of Rev 18 in section II.2 (*PW* 8:337; *DTB* 265) and the markings of vv. 3, 5–21, 23–24 in his New Testament.

25. These *Sämtliche Schriften* (1838–40) were edited by Karl Lachmann. Although there are some gaps it offers Lessing's main works.

26. This was Lachmann's edition, revised and extended by Wendelin von Maltzahn (12 vols.; Leipzig: Göschen, 1853–57).

27. Borchmeyer, *Theatre*, 160–61.

another,[28] and his dislike of Lessing's play *Nathan the Wise* (2:190–362),[29] the question of the relevance of his theological writings seems to have been largely overlooked. It seems highly likely that Wagner did read his edition of Lessing (although whether he read everything is another matter) in his Dresden years since Wagner's essay *Opera and Drama*, which engages with Lessing's aesthetics, was written within two years of leaving Dresden.[30] We know he read *Das Testament Johannis* (10:39–46) and *Anti-Goeze* (10:166–234) in his later years[31] and he may well have read these already in the Dresden years when he was composing the *Jesus of Nazareth* sketches. Although we do find Wagner disagreeing with Lessing, it is clear that he remained a key figure in the composer's thinking and he went as far as to place him in the inner sanctuary of figures who gave birth and formed the "new German spirit."[32] In addition to the works already mentioned, there are a whole series of writings scattered throughout Lessing's collected works that would no doubt interest him,[33] including theological works. Of the theological works there are three possible areas that would interest Wagner: writings on the resurrection, on the relationship of history to theology, and on the nature of the Gospels, especially John. So first, Lessing discusses the resurrection in his critical response to the fifth fragment he published of Reimarus in 1777 (10:30–32), "Eine Duplik" (10:46–121), which includes a discussion of ten contradictions in the resurrection narratives, and in his "Vorrede" to Reimarus' formidable seventh fragment (1778; 10:234–38). Secondly, the relationship of history to theology is a central concerns of Lessing, and here the key work is *Ueber den Beweis des Geistes und der Kraft* (1777; 10:33–39), where he argues that "accidental truths of history can never become the proof of necessary truths of reason."[34] Thirdly, the relation of the Gospels to one another features in *Theses aus der Kirchengeschichte* (1776; 11:593–98) and *Neue Hypothese über die Evangelisten* (1778; 11:495–514), where he puts forward the view that there were essential only "two gospels": first there was a "Gospel of the flesh,"

---

28. Brown, *Gesamtkunstwerk*, 92–98.

29. Bell, *Parsifal*, 133–34, 200, 267. The reference to Lessing's works given here and in the following is to the twelve-volume edition in his Dresden library.

30. He engages with Lessing's *Laocoon* (6:372–546) at the very beginning of Part II (*PW* 2:119–21; *GSD* 4:1–3). Note also the possible negative allusion to the *Hamburgische Dramaturgie* (7:1–460) in Part III (*PW* 2:329–30; *GSD* 4:184–85); see Borchmeyer, *Theatre*, 160–61.

31. Cosima's diary entry for 12 November 1878 tells how Richard "reads to me the conversation about John's will and two of the replies to Goeze; much pleasure in their acuity and elegance: 'What wit there is in such a brain!' says R." Note that the intolerant Patriarch in *Nathan* is modelled on Johann Melchior Goeze (1717–86), the head minister of Hamburg, known for his disputes with Lessing and others (Brown, *Jesus*, 7–8, 280 n. 37).

32. See his "Tagebuchaufzeichnung" for King Ludwig II, 15 September 1865 (*KB* 4:9), where he puts Lessing's name among those of Goethe, Schiller, Haydn, Mozart, Beethoven, and Kant.

33. E.g., *Ueber das Heldenbuch* (11:30–43), *Anmerkungen zu Winkelmann's Geschichte der Kunst* (11:114–25), *Zur Geschichte der deutschen Sprache und Literatur, von der Minnesänger bis auf Luther* (11:468–91).

34. Chadwick, *Lessing's Theological Writings*, 53.

a Hebrew or Aramaic gospel of the Nazarenes, which was used independently by each of the Synoptic evangelists; but then there was a "Gospel of the spirit," i.e., John, whose gospel was necessary so that Christianity was not to become a "mere Jewish sect" but to be an "independent religion."[35] Wagner would no doubt be attracted to the emphasis on love in John's Gospel and in the first letter of John[36] and this would further be reinforced by reading Lessing's *Das Testament Johannis*.[37]

A final possible influence on Wagner's Jesus of Nazareth sketches is the appendix in his copy of the New Testament, which discusses the circumstances in which the books of the New Testament arose.[38] The notable aspect of this "Nachweisung" is that there is no reference at all to any modern critical scholarship: traditional authorships are assumed, and for the Gospels there is no discussion of literary dependence, the views expressed having a resemblance to those of Irenaeus, *Adv. haer*. 3.1.1. Both Matthew and Mark are dated to 61–66 AD, Matthew having been originally composed in Jerusalem in the "syrisch-chaldäische Sprache" ("Syrian-Chaldean language") to show that Jesus fulfills the Old Testament.[39] Luke was probably composed in Rome in AD 64 (as was Acts) to show that Jesus was the saviour of all people, not just the Jews.[40] John (who also wrote Revelation) wrote his gospel in Ephesus after 80 AD.[41] None of this appendix is marked by Wagner and even had he read it I think it unlikely he would hold to such highly traditional views given any knowledge of Lessing.

Wagner's knowledge of the New Testament

Even before Wagner's reading through the New Testament to prepare for his *Jesus of Nazareth* opera, he most likely had a good knowledge of the New Testament. He had been baptized and confirmed in the Lutheran Church, had experienced and performed works based on New Testament texts,[42] and had composed six operas, all of

---

35. Chadwick, *Lessing's Theological Writings*, 80–81. Chadwick, in his introduction, points out that "[a]lthough Lessing's literary hypothesis lack a sound historical and critical basis, his work is the first of the long series of studies in the Gospels which have begun from his theological starting point in placing the fourth Gospel in a category by itself" (21).

36. He marked twenty-seven verses in 1 John.

37. Chadwick, *Lessing's Theological Writings*, 57–61. Lessing's dialogue concerns a passage in Jerome's commentary on Galatians that relates how John in old age in Ephesus said nothing more than a constant "Little children, love one another." When asked why he always repeated this, John replied: "Because it is the Lord's command; because this alone, if it is done, is enough, is sufficient and adequate." (cf. Chadwick, *Lessing's Theological Writings*, 61).

38. *Das neue Testament*, 303–20.

39. *Das neue Testament*, 303.

40. *Das neue Testament*, 304.

41. *Das neue Testament*, 305.

42. For example in 1843 he heard a performance of, and wrote some reflections on, Mendelssohn's oratorio *Saint Paul* (*PW* 8:279–80).

which display, to a greater or lesser extent, theological insight.[43] Of particular interest is his oratorio *Das Liebesmahl der Apostel* (*The Love Feast of the Apostles*), which was performed in the Frauenkirche in Dresden on 6 July 1843 with the massive forces of 1,200 male singers and 100 orchestral players. Wagner described the work as "eine biblische Szene" ("a biblical scene") and is essentially a free development of passages from Acts 1–4.[44] But when the composer read through the New Testament to prepare for his *Jesus of Nazareth* opera, he clearly worked through the text systematically; this is indicated by the fact that in section II.2 of the sketches, texts are quoted in canonical order for each of the five acts in turn, a quotation being anything from a single verse to more extended passages.[45] Sometimes he will name chapters or sections of chapters rather than quoting these extended sections and this is particularly the case with John, where, rather than the laconic sayings of Jesus in the Synoptic Gospels, there are extended discourses that would be rather laborious to quote. The number of verses quoted for each of the Gospels is Matthew (131), Mark (2), Luke (57), John (18). To some extent the pattern for the Synoptic Gospels can be explained by the fact that as he worked through the New Testament and quoted texts in their canonical order that once a text was quoted from Matthew he then felt it unnecessary to quote parallels in Mark or Luke.

His relative interests in the Gospels is better represented by the number of verses marked in his copy of the New Testament: Matthew (199), Mark (14), Luke (176), and John (222). This pattern of marking the Gospels could be explained by the simple fact that after marking Matthew he found in Mark little new material; one of his rare markings in Mark is at 2:27 where Jesus speaks of the Sabbath being made for humankind not humankind for the Sabbath, which was to be useful ammunition for the composer's criticism of "legal" religion.[46] When he came to Luke he found much new material, such as Luke 17:20–21 (the kingdom of God is within you), which again would support his theological interests. And, of course, when he came to John he found a whole new world of theological richness upon which he could draw.

---

43. Especially important are the three operas of what is considered the Wagnerian "canon," *Der fliegende Holländer* (1841), *Tannhäuser* (1845), and *Lohengrin* (1848), each offering theological insight together with biblical allusions.

44. The sketch can be found in *PW* 8:280–82; *SSD* 11:264–66. The full text is given in *SSD* 11:266–69. For a helpful discussion of the work see Kirsch, "Biblische Scene."

45. For examples of extended quotations see, e.g., Matt 15:2-6, 11–13 (Act I, *PW* 8:324–25; *DTB* 260); Matt 5:2–14 with gaps and 6:7–27 with gaps (Act II, *PW* 8:328–29; *DTB* 261–62); Acts 17:23b–29 (Act III, *PW* 8:335–36; *DTB* 264–65).

46. Note that the markings and quotations give a good but *approximate* idea of his interests in the texts. So in the dramatic outline we find clear allusions to New Testament texts which are neither marked in his New Testament nor quoted in II.2. A good example is the raising of the publican Levi's daughter. This is largely based on the raising of the daughter of the synagogue leaders, Jairus (Mark 5:21–24, 35–43; cf. the parallel in Matt 9:18–19, 23–26). There are also allusions to the Jesus' raising the widow's son at Nain since Levi's daughter is already being taken out on a bier (cf. Luke 7:14) for burial (cf. Luke 7:12). However, none of these texts are either marked or quoted.

One does wonder whether questions of source criticism interested him as he worked through the Synoptic Gospels. Did he realize, for example, that one of his rare markings in Mark just mentioned (2:27) was what was to be later understood as one of those significant "minor agreements," in this case where Matthew and Luke agree in "omitting" Markan material? The prevalent Synoptic hypothesis at the time was that of J. J. Griesbach, which was put forward in 1789 and dominated scholarship until H. J. Holtzmann placed the two-source hypothesis on a firmer footing in 1863.[47] This new hypothesis was first put forward by C. H. Weisse in 1838 and it was just six years earlier in the winter semester of 1831–32 that Wagner attended some his lectures on aesthetics at Leipzig University. On becoming personally acquainted with him at the home of his uncle, Adolf Wagner, he was "greatly attracted" by his "distracted air, manner of speaking rapidly but in fits and starts, and above all interesting and pensive physiognomy" as he spoke with his uncle on matters of "philosophy and philosophers."[48] But it seems unlikely that Wagner would have any clear idea of the work of Weisse (or Griesbach[49]) on source criticism when he worked his way through the Gospels and, as I suggested above, any first-hand knowledge of Gospel criticism would most likely come from Lessing.

Of the Gospels Wagner certainly had a special interest in John. Although in section II.2 only eighteen verses are actually quoted, he lists long passages from this gospel and the list for Act IV is especially striking: John 12:4ff ("Jesus' anointment and Judas") together with chapters 13–17 ("*Last Supper*").[50] Further in the dramatic outline (I) there are a number of distinctive Johannine features. First, in the Gethsemane scene Jesus passes over the brook Kidron (cf. John 18:1). Secondly, as in John at this point, there is no "agony" in the Garden.[51] Although John does write of Jesus' distress earlier (John 12:27; 13:21), the sense of desperation one finds in the Synoptic Gospels is lacking[52] and in Wagner's *Jesus* sketches the saviour approaches his death either with some confidence or with some stoicism.[53] Thirdly, when "Caia-

---

47. Griesbach, who introduced the name "Synoptics" for the first three gospels, put forward the hypothesis (sometimes called the two-gospel hypothesis) that Mark used both Matthew and Luke. The two-source hypothesis maintained that Mark was not the last of the Synoptic gospels but the first. Matthew and Luke were dependent on Mark and a source name "Q" ("Quelle").

48. *My Life* 54; *Mein Leben* 1:62.

49. The Griesbach hypothesis was held by Strauß, *Life of Jesus*, 71. As suggested above, Wagner may have had some second-hand knowledge of Strauß but, as Tuckett, "Griesbach Hypothesis," 19–20, argues, the Griesbach hypothesis, indeed any questions of Synoptic source criticism, were hardly central to Strauß's thinking.

50. *PW* 8:338; *DTB* 266. It would clearly be too much to write out this whole section of six chapters and this is presumably why he resorts simply to listing them.

51. *PW* 8:293; *DTB* 244.

52. See Hengel, *Die johanneische Frage*, 198–99, who argues that John 12:27 actually contradicts Mark 14:36.

53. The only sign of Jesus' vulnerability concerning his coming death is when he "demands (fordert) his disciples to follow him out of the city, to pass the night in open air" (*DTB* 244). Ellis

phas, Priests and Pharisees" come to Pilate's headquarters, they do not enter since they do not want to be defiled for the Passover.[54] So like John, Wagner places the trial (and crucifixion) before the Passover; but whereas John places it on Passover eve (John 19:14, 14th Nisan) Wagner actually places it three days before the Passover.[55] Fourthly, and this is the most significant parallel to John, it is stressed that the Spirit is given as a result of Jesus' death.[56]

This fourth point indicates that his interest in John is clearly driven by theological concerns, many of which relate to Hegel's understanding of Jesus' death.[57] Further, his preference for both John and Matthew, in addition to the literary dependence and canonical order discussed above, may to some extent be explained by the following. First, these gospels would likely have been seen as the most "antisemitic" of the Gospels. We do in fact find that texts that could be so understood are marked (e.g., Matt 21:43; John 8:42–52);[58] further, he clearly appreciates Jesus' denunciation of the Pharisees found in the special material of Matthew.[59] A second possible reason for his preference for Matthew and John is the fact that Bach's two great Passions are based on the passion narratives of these gospels.[60]

As far as the rest of the New Testament is concerned, Wagner draws on a number of key themes. He clearly treasures Romans and 1 Corinthians. Paul's ideas of freedom from law are strongly represented in the dramatic outline and especially in the commentary. Texts that deal with love are emphasized (e.g., 1 Cor 13:1, 3, 4–10)[61] and he takes the liberty of replacing "faith" with "love" in Rom 3:28.[62] A series of texts

---

translates "fordert" with "begs" (*PW* 8:292), but if this were Wagner's intention he would have used a verb such as "erbitten."

54. *PW* 8:294; *DTB* 245. Cf. John 18:28.

55. *PW* 8:294; *DTB* 245: "It is three days before the feast of the Passover, and in this sabbath-time their law forbids their entering the dwelling of an unbeliever." This reference to the priests and Pharisees not entering Pilate's dwelling is based on John 18:28: "Then they took Jesus from Caiaphas to Pilate's headquarters. It was early morning. They themselves did not enter the headquarters, so as to avoid ritual defilement and to be able to eat the Passover." It is not clear why Wagner wishes to place the death of Jesus on 12th Nisan. It is almost as though he wishes to avoid any Passover lamb symbolism for Jesus' death (no such symbolism in John's Gospel is taken up in the sketches). According to Casey, *Aramaic Sources*, 224, Passover lambs could be slaughtered on 13th or 14th Nisan (see *m. Zeb.* 1:3). Although Wagner changes the date he does not deny that Jesus' death occurred on the Friday.

56. Wagner explicitly points to this Johannine theme (*PW* 8:292; *DTB* 244), which will be discussed below.

57. See chapter 6 above and chapters 10 and 11 in volume 2.

58. Matt 21:43 is both heavily underlined in the New Testament and quoted. John 8:40–41, 42–52 is marked and "[t]he whole chapter from 31" is referred to in section II.2 (*PW* 8:335; *DTB* 264).

59. E.g., he marked Matt 23:1, 16b–28; but note he also marked the roughly parallel material in Luke 11:46–47, 52, which clearly chimed in with his dislike of "lawyers."

60. The *St Matthew Passion* was fairly well known after Mendelssohn revived the work in 1829; on Wagner's possible knowledge of the *St John Passion* see volume 2, chapter 11.

61. He also doubly marks 1 Cor 12:25–27 and writes "liebe" ("love") in the margin.

62. *PW* 8:336 (modified): "We reckon therefore that a person is justified, without the work of the

in James are marked (2:5–9, 14–16; 26; 4:2; 5:1–6, 12), which clearly appeal to the composer's socialist convictions and Rev 18 is heavily marked (he refers to the whole chapter in II.2[63]), which he no doubt saw as a prophecy of the fall of capitalism! The only books he neither marks nor quotes in the sketches are Philippians, Colossians, 1 Peter, 2 and 3 John, and Jude.

Jesus of Nazareth Sketches

The *Jesus of Nazareth* sketches, briefly discussed in chapter 2 above, were an important milestone in the development of the *Ring*. They were written shortly after the first version of *Siegfried's Tod* (*Erstschrift des Textbuches*)[64] and many themes from the sketches appear in the final *Ring* such as law and sexual ethics, the priority of love, death and immortality, and ultimate questions of God, sacrifice, and redemption. One of the key questions is how the various versions of the "Ring" relate to these sketches and how the sketches may be able to open up the theological concerns of the *Ring*. This question, together with an examination of the whole series of theological and ethical issues the *Ring* raises, will be addressed in volume 2.

---

law, through (love) alone"); *DTB* 265. Wagner follows Luther in using the singular "work" (the Greek has "works").

63. *PW* 8:337; *DTB* 265.
64. *TBRN1* 50–112.

Bibliography

Orchestral Scores of the *Ring*

Voss, Egon, ed. *Das Rheingold*. 2 vols. SW 10.I–II. Mainz: B. Schott's Söhne, 1988–89.
Jost, Christa, ed. *Die Walküre* 3 vols. SW 11.I–III. Mainz: Schott Musik International, 2002–5.
Döge, Klaus, Egon Voss, and Annette Oppermann, ed. *Siegfried*. 3 vols. SW 12.I–III. Mainz: Schott Music, 2006–14.
Fladt, Hartmut, ed. *Götterdämmerung*. 3 vols. SW 13.I–III. Mainz: B. Schott's Söhne, 1981–82.

Vocal Scores of the *Ring*

The Rhinegold. Complete Vocal Score by Otto Singer. English Translation by Ernest Newman. London: Breitkopf & Härtel, 1910.
Die Walküre. Vollständiger Klavierauszug von Karl Klindworth. English Translation by Frederick Jameson. Mainz: B. Schott, 1899.
Siegfried. Complete Vocal Score in a Facilitated Arrangement by Karl Klindworth. English Translation by Frederick Jameson. New York: Schirmer, 1904.
Götterdämmerung. Vollständiger Klavierauszug von Karl Klindworth. English Translation by Frederick Jameson. Mainz: B. Schott, 1899.

The Ring Poem

Wagner, Richard. *Der Ring des Nibelungen: Ein Bühnenfestspiel für drei Tage und einen Vorabend*. Privately published. 1853.
———. *Der Ring des Nibelungen: Ein Bühnenfestspiel fur drei Tage und einen Vorabend*. 2nd ed. Leipzig: J. J. Weber, 1873 (1st ed. 1863).

Secondary literature

Abbate, Carolyn. *Unsung Voices: Opera and Musical Narrative in the Nineteenth Century*. Princeton Studies in Opera. Princeton, NJ: Princeton University Press, 1991.
Adorno, Theodor. *In Search of Wagner*. Translated by Rodney Livingstone. London: Verso, 2005.

Afzelius, Arv. Aug. *Edda Sæmundar hinns Fróda*. Holmiæ: Typis Elmenianis, 1818.
Allen, Roger. *Richard Wagner's Beethoven*. Woodbridge, UK: Boydell, 2014.
———. "*Die Weihe des Hauses* (The Consecration of the House): Houston Stewart Chamberlain and the Early Reception of *Parsifal*." In *A Companion to Wagner's Parsifal*, edited by William Kinderman and Katherine R. Syer, 245–76. Rochester, NY: Camden House, 2005.
Anderson, Bernhard W. "Tradition and Scripture in the Community of Faith." *JBL* 10 (1981) 5–21.
Andersson, Theodore M. *The Legend of Brynhild*. Islandica 43. Ithaca, NY: Cornell University Press, 1980.
Apponyi, Albert. *The Memoirs of Count Apponyi*. London: Heinemann, 1935.
Arndt, Andreas. "Idealismus." In *Hegel-Lexikon*, edited by Paul Cobben, Paul Cruysberghs, Peter Jonkers, and Lu De Vos, 262–64. Darmstadt: Wissenschaftliche Buchgesellschaft, 2006.
Arnkiel, Trogillus. *Außführliche Eröffnung*. Hamburg: Thomas von Wierung, 1703 (in 4 Parts, the first being *Cimbrische Heyden-Religion* 1702).
Bakounine, Michel. *Considérations philosophiques sur le fantôme divin, le monde reel et l'homme*. Geneva: Entremonde, 2010.
Bakunin, Mikhail, *The Confession of Mikhael Bakunin with the Marginal Comments of Tsar Nicholas I*. Translated by Robert C. Howes. Introduction and notes by Lawrence D. Orton. Ithaca, NY: Cornell University Press, 1977.
Bailey, Robert. "Wagner's Musical Sketches for *Siegfrieds Tod*." In *Studies in Musical History: Essays for Oliver Strunk*, edited by Harold Powers, 459–94. Princeton, NJ. Princeton University Press, 1968.
Baillie, J. B., ed. *G. W. F. Hegel: The Phenomenology of Mind*. 2nd ed. London: Allen & Unwin, 1949.
Barth, Herbert, Dietrich Mack, and Egon Voss, eds. *Wagner: A Documentary Study*. Translated by P. R. J. Ford and Mary Whittall. London: Thames and Hudson, 1975.
Bartholin, Thomas. *Antiquitatum Danicarum de causis contemptae a Danis adhuc gentilibus mortis libri tres*. Copenhagen, 1689.
Bauer, Hans-Joachim, ed. *Richard Wagner: Briefe*. Stuttgart: Reclam, 1995.
Bauer, Oswald Georg. *Die Geschichte der Bayreuther Festspiele*. 2 vols. Deutscher Kunstverlag, 2016.
Bayer, Oswald. "Gegen Gott für die Menschen: Feuerbachs Lutherrezeption." In *Leibliches Wort: Reformation und Neuzeit im Konflikt*, 205–41. Tübingen: J. C. B. Mohr (Paul Siebeck), 1992.
Beach, Edward Allen. *The Potencies of God(s): Schelling's Philosophy of Mythology*. SUNY Series in Philosophy and SUNY Series in Hegelian Studies. Albany, NY: State University of New York Press, 1994.
Beiser, Frederick C., ed. *The Early Political Writings of The German Romantics*. CTHPT. 1996. Reprint. Cambridge: Cambridge University Press, 2005.
———. *Hegel*. London: Routledge, 2005.
———. "Introduction: Hegel and the Problem of Metaphysics." In *The Cambridge Companion to Hegel*, edited by Frederick C. Beiser, 1–24. Cambridge: Cambridge University Press, 1993.
Bell, Richard H. "Are Wagner's Views of 'Redemption' Relevant for the Twenty-first Century?" In *Das Kunstwerk der Zukunft: Perspektive der Wagnerrezeption im 21. Jahrhundert*,

edited by Sven Friedrich, 71–86. Wagner in der Diskussion 11. Würzburg: Königshausen & Neumann, 2014.

———. *The Irrevocable Call of God: An Inquiry into Paul's Theology of Israel*. WUNT 184. Tübingen: Mohr Siebeck, 2005.

———. *No one seeks for God: An Exegetical and Theological Study of Romans 1.18—3.20*. WUNT 106. Tübingen: Mohr Siebeck, 1998.

———. "Review of Marcel Hébert, *Religious Experience in the Work of Richard Wagner*." *CHR* 103 (2017) 599–600.

———. "Richard Wagner's Prose Sketches for Jesus of Nazareth: Historical and Theological Reflections on an Uncompleted Opera." *Journal for the Study of the Historical Jesus*. 15 (2017) 260–90.

———. "Teleology, Providence and the 'Death of God': A New Perspective on the *Ring* Cycle's Debt to G. W. F. Hegel." *The Wagner Journal* 11.1 (2017) 30–45.

———. *Wagner's Parsifal: An Appreciation in the Light of His Theological Journey*. Eugene, OR: Wipf & Stock, 2013.

———. "Wagner's Siegfried Act III Scene 1: A Study in 'Renunciation of the Will' and the 'Sublime.'" *The Wagner Journal* 10.2 (2016) 18–35.

Benders, Raymond J., et al. *Friedrich Nietzsche: Chronik in Bildern und Texten*. Munich: Hanser, 2000.

Benes, Tuska. "From Indo-Germans to Aryans: Philology and the Racialization of Salvationist National Rhetoric, 1806–30." In *The German Invention of Race*, edited by Sara Eigen and Mark Larrimore, 167–81. SUNY Series: Philosophy and Race. Albany, NY: State University of New York Press, 2006.

Bermbach, Udo. *Der Wahn des Gesamtkunstwerkes: Richard Wagners politisch-ästhetische Utopie*. 2nd ed. Stuttgart: J.B. Metzler, 2004.

Berry, Mark. "The Positive Influence of Wagner upon Nietzsche." *The Wagner Journal* 2.2 (2008) 11–28.

———. *Treacherous Bonds and Laughing Fire: Politics and Religion in Wagner's Ring*. Aldershot, UK: Ashgate, 2006.

Bielik-Robson, Agata. "The God of Luria, Hegel and Schelling: The Divine Contraction and the Modern Metaphysics of Finitude." In *Mystical Theology and Continental Philosophy: Interchange in the Wake of God*, edited by David Lewin, Simon Podmore, and Duan Williams, 32–50. Contemporary Theological Explorations in Christian Mysticism. London: Routledge, 2017.

Bigler-Marshall, Ingrid. "Wagner, (Wilhelm) Richard (Ps. Wilhelm Drach, K. Freigedank, Conto Spianato)." *DL-L³* 27:87–258.

Björnsson, Árni. *Wagner and the Volsungs: Icelandic Sources of Der Ring des Nibelungen*. University College London: Viking Society for Northern Research, 2003.

Blanc, L.G. "Review of Adolf Wagner, ed., *Il parnasso italiano*." *Allgemeine Literatur-Zeitung* 312–313 (1827) 857–64, 865–72.

Bloch, Ernst. *Subjekt-Objekt: Erläuterungen zu Hegel*. Frankfurt am Main: Suhrkamp, 1962.

Blok, Josine H. "Quest for a Scientific Mythology: F. Creuzer and K.O. Müller on History and Myth." *History and Theory* 33.4 (1994) 26–52.

Blumenbach, Johann Friedrich. *Handbuch der Naturgeschichte*. 2nd ed. Göttingen: Johann Christian Dietrich, 1782.

———. *The Institutions of Physiology*. Translated from the Latin of the Third and Last Edition by John Elliotson. 2nd ed. London: E. Cox, 1817.

———. *Ueber den Bildungstrieb*. 1781. 2nd ed. Göttingen: Johann Christian Dietrich, 1789.
Blumenberg, Hans. *Work on Myth*. Translated by R. M. Wallace. Cambridge: MIT, 1985.
Bockmühl, Klaus Erich. *Leiblichkeit und Gesellschaft: Studien zur Religionskritik und Anthropologie im Frühwerk von Ludwig Feuerbach und Karl Marx*. FSThR 7. Göttingen: Vandenhoeck & Ruprecht, 1961.
Bodmer, Johann Jakob. *Chriemhilden Rache, und die Klage: zwey Heldengedichte aus dem schwaebischen Zeitpuncte*. Zurich: Orell, 1757.
Böldl, Klaus. *Der Mythos der Edda: Nordische Mythologie zwischen europäischer Aufklärung und nationaler Romantik*. Tübingen: Franke, 2000.
Böhme, Jakob. *Optime de pietate & sapientia meriti oder Jacob Böhmens von alt Seidenburg Theosophische Schriften*. Amsterdam: Betkio, 1675 (Wahnfried).
———. *Sämtliche Werke*. Edited by K. W. Schieber. 7 vols. Leipzig: Barth, 1831–47 (Wahnfried).
Böttger, Adolf, ed. *Byron's sämmtliche Werke*. 12 vols. Leipzig: Otto Wigand, 1841 (DB 13).
Borchmeyer, Dieter. "Liszt und Wagner: Allianz in Goethes und Schillers Spuren." In *Wagnerspectrum: Wagner und Liszt*, 69–82. Würzburg: Königshausen & Neumann, 2011.
———. *Richard Wagner: Theory and Theatre*. Translated by Stewart Spencer. Oxford: Clarendon, 2002.
Boyle, Nicholas. *Goethe: The Poet and the Age*. 2 vols. Oxford: Oxford University Press, 1990–99.
Branscombe, Peter. "The Dramatic Texts." In *Wagner Handbook*, edited by Ulrich Müller, Peter Wapnewski, and John Deathridge, 269–86. Cambridge: Harvard University Press, 1992.
Braschowanoff, Georg. *Wagner und die Antike: Ein Beitrag zur kunstphilosophischen Weltanschauung Richard Wagners*. Leipzig: Xenien, 1910.
Breazeale, Daniel. "Editor's Introduction." In *Fichte: Early Philosophical Writings*, edited by Daniel Breazeale, 1–49. Ithaca, NY: Cornell University Press, 1988.
———. "The Spirit of the Wissenschaftslehre." In *The Reception of Kant's Critical Philosophy: Fichte, Schelling, and Hegel*, edited by Sally Sedgwick, 171–98. Cambridge: Cambridge University Press, 2000 (= *German Idealism: Critical Concepts in Philosophy, Volume III*, edited by Klaus Brinkmann, 89–115. London: Routledge, 2007).
Brinkmann, Reinhold. "'Drei der Fragen stell' ich mir frei': zur Wanderer-Szene im 1. Akt von Wagners 'Siegfried.'" *Jahrbuch des Staatlichen Instituts für Musikforschung, Preussischer Kulturbesitz* (1972) 120–62.
Brown, Colin. *Jesus in European Protestant Thought 1778–1860*. Grand Rapids: Baker, 1988.
Brown, Hilda M. *The Quest for the Gesamtkunstwerk and Richard Wagner*. Oxford: Oxford University Press, 2016.
———. "Richard Wagner and the Zurich Writings 1849–1851: From Revolution to 'Ring.'" *The Wagner Journal* 8.2 (2014), 28–42.
Brown, Raymond E. *The Gospel according to John*. 2 vols. London: Chapman, 1978.
Brown, Robert. *The Later Philosophy of Schelling: The Influence of Boehme on the Works of 1809–15*. Lewisburg, PA: Bucknell University Press, 1977.
Bubner, Rüdiger, ed. *German Idealist Philosophy*. London: Penguin, 1997.
Bujić, Bojan. *Music in European Thought 1851–1912*. Cambridge: Cambridge University Press, 1988.
Bultmann, Christoph. "Vatke, Wilhelm." *TRE* 34:552–55.

Bultmann, Rudolf. "New Testament and Mythology." In *Kerygma and Myth: A Theological Debate, Volume 1*, edited by Hans Werner Bartsch, 1–44. 2nd ed. Translated by Reginald H. Fuller. London: SPCK, 1964.

Bungay, Stephen. *Beauty and Truth: A Study in Hegel's Aesthetics*. Oxford: Oxford University Press, 1984.

Burian, Peter. "Myth into *Muthos*: The Shaping of Tragic Plot." In *The Cambridge Companion to Greek Tragedy*, edited by P. E. Easterling, 178–208. Cambridge: Cambridge University Press, 1997.

Büttner, Wolfgang. "Der andere Herwegh—über sein Verhältnis zu internationalen Arbeiterbewegung." In *Heine Jahrbuch 2003*, edited by J. A. Kruse, 124–39. Stuttgart: J. B. Metzler, 2003.

Byock, Jesse, ed. *The Prose Edda*. London: Penguin, 2005.

———, ed. *The Saga of the Volsungs: The Norse Epic of Sigurd the Dragon Slayer*. London: Penguin, 1990.

Caird, George B. *A Commentary on the Revelation of St John the Divine*. 1966. Reprint. London: Adam & Charles Black, 1977.

Carnegy, Patrick. *Wagner and the Art of the Theatre*. New Haven: Yale University Press, 2006.

Carr, E. H. *Michael Bakunin*. 1937. Reprint. Basingstoke, UK: Macmillan, 1975.

Cartwright, David E. *Schopenhauer: A Biography*. Cambridge: Cambridge University Press, 2010.

Casey, P. M. *Aramaic Sources of Mark's Gospel*. SNTSMS 102. Cambridge: Cambridge University Press, 1998.

Chadwick, Henry, ed. *Lessing's Theological Writings*. London: A. & C. Black, 1956.

Chamberlain, Houston Stewart. *Die Grundlagen des Neuzehnten Jahrhunderts*. 4th ed. 2 vols. Munich: F. Bruckmann, 1903.

———. "Richard Wagners Philosophie." *Münchener Allgemeine Zeitung* (25–28 February, 1899).

———. *Richard Wagner*. 10th ed. Munich: F. Bruckmann, 1940.

Clark, Robert T. *Herder: His Life and Thought*. Berkeley: University of California Press, 1955.

Cohen, G. A. *Karl Marx's Theory of History: A Defence*. Princeton, NJ: Princeton University Press, 2000.

Collinwood, R. G. *The Idea of History*. Oxford: Clarendon, 1946.

Conway, David. *Jewry in Music: Entry to the Profession from the Enlightenment to Richard Wagner*. Cambridge: Cambridge University Press, 2012.

Cooke, Deryck. *I Saw the World End: A Study of Wagner's Ring*. 1979. Reprint. Oxford: Clarendon, 2002.

Cooper, Barry. "Calendar of Beethoven's Life, Works and Related Events." In *The Beethoven Compendium: A Guide to Beethoven's Life and Music*, edited by Barry Cooper, 12–33. London: Thames and Hudson, 1991.

Corse, Sandra. *Wagner and the New Consciousness: Language and Love in the Ring*. Rutherford, NJ: Associated University Press, 1990.

Creuzer, Friedrich. *Symbolik und Mythologie der alten Völker, besonders der Griechen*. 4 vols. 2nd ed. Vols. 1–2. Leipzig/Darmstadt: Heyer und Leske, 1819–20. Vols. 3–4. Leipzig: Carl Wilhelm Leske, 1821 (Wahnfried).

Dahlhaus, Carl. *The Idea of Absolute Music*. Translated by Roger Lustig. Chicago: University of Chicago Press, 1991.

———. *Richard Wagner's Music Dramas*. Translated by Mary Whittall. Cambridge: Cambridge University Press, 1979.

Dante Alighieri. *Die göttliche Komôdie übersetzt und erläurtert von Karl Streckfuß*. 3 vols. Halle: Hemmende und Schwetschke, 1824–26 (DB 17).

———. *Dante Alighieri's Goettliche Comoedie, Metrisch übertragen und mit kritischen und historischen Erläuterungen versehen von Philalethes (König Johann von Sachsen)*. 3 vols. Dresden/Leipzig: Arnoldische Buchhandlung, 1839–49 (DB 18).

Dante et al. *Il parnasso italiano, ovveroi quattro opoeti celeberrimi italiani. La divina commedia di Dante Alighieri; Le rime di Francesco Petrarca; L'Orlando Furioso di Lodovico Ariosto; La Gerusalemme liberata di Torquato Tasso*. Leipzig: Ernest Fleischer, 1826 (DB 19).

Darcy, Warren. "*Creatio ex nihilo*: The Genesis, Structure, and Meaning of the *Rheingold* Prelude." *19th Century Music* 13 (1989) 79–100.

Daub, Adrian. "Herwegh, Georg Friedrich Rudolph Theodor." *CWE* 194.

Daverio, John. *Nineteenth-Century Music and the German Romantic Ideology*. New York: Schirmer, 1993.

Dawson-Bowling, Paul. *The Wagner Experience and Its Meaning to Us*. 2 vols. Brecon, UK: Old Street, 2013.

Daz ist der Nibelunge Liet. Leipzig: Wigand, 1840 (DB 98).

Deathridge, John. "The Beginnings of 'The Ring.'" In *Wagner: The Rhinegold*, 7–14. London: John Calder/New York: Riverrun, 1985.

———. "Cataloguing Wagner." In *The Richard Wagner Centenary in Australia*, edited by Peter Dennison, 185–99. Miscellanea musicologica 14. Adelaide: University of Adelaide Press, 1985.

———. "Reviews of A. D. Sessa, *Richard Wagner and the English*; J. L. DiGaetani (ed.), *Penetrating Wagner's Ring*; P. Burbidge and R. Sutton (eds.), *The Wagner Companion*; C. von Westernhagen, *Wagner: A Biography*." *19th Century Music* 5 (1981–82) 81–89.

———, ed. *Richard Wagner: The Ring of the Nibelung*. Translated and edited with an introduction by John Deathridge. London: Penguin, 2018.

———. "The Ring: An Introduction." Booklet accompanying *Das Rheingold* (Levine/Metropolitan Opera) 1989, 31–38.

———. *Wagner beyond Good and Evil*. Berkeley: University of California Press, 2008.

———. "Wagners Kompositionen zu Goethes 'Faust.'" *Jahrbuch der Bayerischen Staatsoper* (1982), 90–99.

———. "Wagner und sein erster Lehrmeister: Mit einem unveröffentlichen Brief Richard Wagners." In *Meistersinger Programmheft der Bayerischen Staatsoper*, edited by Klaus Schultz, 71–75. Munich, 1979.

———. "Wagner's Sketches for the 'Ring': Some Recent Studies." *Musical Times* 118.1611 (1977) 383–89.

De Boor, Helmut, ed. *Das Nibelungenlied, Zweisprachig*. 5th ed. Cologne: Parkland, 2003.

Devrient, Eduard. *Aus seinen Tagebüchern, Berlin/Dresden/Karlsruhe*. Edited by Rolf Kabel. 2 vols. Weimar: Böhlhaus, 1964.

Dinger, Hugo. *Richard Wagners geistige Entwickelung: Versuch einer Darstellung der Weltanschauung Richard Wagners, Band I; Die Weltanschauung Richard Wagners in den Grundzügen ihrer Entwickelung*. Leipzig: E. W. Fritsch, 1892.

Dischner, Gisela, ed. *Friedrich Schlegels Lucinde und Materialien zu einer Theorie des Müßiggangs*. Hildesheim: Gerstenberg, 1980.

Donner, J. J. C., ed. *Euripides.* 2 vols. Heidelberg: Akademische Verlagshandlung von C. F. Winter, 1841–45 (DB 29).

Donner, J. J. C., ed. *Sophocles.* 2 vols. Heidelberg: Akademische Verlagshandlung von C. F. Winter, 1842 (DB 134).

Dorion, Louis-André. "The Rise and Fall of the Socratic Problem." In *The Cambridge Companion to Socrates,* edited by Donald R. Morrison, 1–23. Cambridge: Cambridge University Press, 2011.

Drews, Arthur. *Der Ideengehalt von Richard Wagners dramatischen Dichtungen in Zusammenhange mit seinem Leben und seiner Weltanschauung.* Leipzig: Eduard Pfeiffer, 1931.

Dreyfus, Laurence. *Wagner and the Erotic Impulse.* Cambridge: Harvard University Press, 2010.

Dronke, Ursula. *The Poetic Edda, Volume I: Heroic Poems.* Oxford: Clarendon, 1969.

———. *The Poetic Edda, Volume II: Mythological Poems.* Oxford: Clarendon, 1997.

———. *The Poetic Edda, Volume III: Mythological Poems II.* Oxford: Clarendon, 2011.

Droysen, Johann Gustav. *Des Aischylos Werke.* 2 vols. Berlin: G. Finke, 1832 (DB 1).

———. *Aischylos.* 3rd ed. Berlin: Herz, 1868.

———. *Geschichte des Hellenismus. Erster Theil: Geschichte der Nachfolger Alexanders. Zweiter Theil: Geschichte der Bildung des hellenistischen Staatensystemes. Mit einem Anhang über die hellenistischen Städtegründungen.* 2 vols. Hamburg: Friedrich Perthes, 1836–43 (DB 26).

Drüner, Ulrich. *Richard Wagner: Die Inszenierung eines Lebens: Biografie.* Munich: Blessing, 2016.

Durrani, Osman. *Faust and the Bible: A Study of Goethe's Use of Scriptural Allusions and Christian Religious Motifs in Faust I and II.* Frankfurt am Main: Lang, 1977.

Easterling, P. E. "A Show for Dionysus." In *The Cambridge Companion to Greek Tragedy,* edited by P. E. Easterling, 36–53. Cambridge: Cambridge University Press, 1997.

Ehrismann, Otfrid. *Das Nibelungenlied in Deutschland: Studien zur Rezeption des Nibelungenlieds von der Mitte des 18. Jhrunderts bis zum Erste Weltkrieg.* Münchner Germanistische Beiträge 14. Munich: Fink, 1975.

Eichner, Barbara. *History in Mighty Sounds: Musical Constructions of German National Identity, 1848–1914.* Woodbridge, UK: Boydell, 2012.

Eichner, Hans. *Friedrich Schlegel.* New York: Twayne, 1970.

Einarsson, Sigurbjörn. "Island." *TRE* 16:358–68.

Ellis, William Ashton (Carl Friedrich Glasenapp). *Life of Richard Wagner.* 6 vols. London: Kegan Paul, Trench, Trübner & co, 1900–8.

Ellis Davidson, H. R. *Gods and Myths of Northern Europe.* 1964. Reprint. Harmondsworth, UK: Penguin, 1976.

Engels, Frederick. *Ludwig Feuerbach and the Outcome of Classical German Philosophy.* Edited by C. P. Dutt. Little Marx Library. 1941. Reprint. New York: International, 1970.

Ermatinger, Emil. *Gottfried Kellers Briefe und Tagebücher, 1830–1861.* Stuttgart: Cotta, 1916.

Ettmüller, Ludwig. *Altnordisches Lesebuch nebst kurzgefasster Formlehre und Wörterbuch.* Zurich: Meyer & Zeller, 1861 (Wahnfried).

———, ed. *Die Lieder der Edda von den Nibelungen: Stabreimende Verdeutschung.* Zurich: Drell, Füßli und Compagnie, 1837 (borrowed from Dresden Royal library).

———, ed. *Vaulu-spá: Das älteste Denkmal germanisch-nordischer Sprache, nebst einigen Gedanken über Nordens Wissen und Glauben und nordische Dichtkunst*. Leipzig: Weidmannsche Buchhandlung, 1830 (DB 149).

Ewans, Michael. *Wagner and Aeschylus: The Ring and the Oresteia*. London: Faber and Faber, 1982.

Faulkes, Anthony. *Snorri Sturluson: Edda*. Everyman Library. London: J.M. Dent, 1987.

———. *Two Versions of the Snorra Edda*. 2 vols. Reykjavík: Stofnun Árna Magnússonar, 1977–79.

Fazio, Domenico M. "Die 'Schopenhauer-Schule.'" In *Schopenhauer-Handbuch: Leben—Werk—Wirkung*, edited by Matthias Koßler and Daniel Schubbe, 270–75. Darmstadt: Wissenschaftliche Buchgesellschaft, 2014.

Feuerbach, Ludwig. *The Essence of Christianity*. Translated by George Eliot. Introductory essay by Karl Barth. Foreword by H. Richard Niebuhr. New York: Harper & Brothers, 1957.

———. *The Essence of Faith according to Luther*. Translated by Melvin Cherno. New York: Harper & Row, 1967.

———. *Lectures on the Essence of Religion*. Translated by Ralph Manheim. New York: Harper & Row, 1967.

———. *Principles of the Philosophy of the Future*. Translated by Manfred H. Vogel. Indianapolis: Bobbs-Merrill, 1966.

———. *Thoughts on Death and Immortality*. Translated, with introduction and notes, by James A. Massey. Berkeley: University of California Press, 1980.

———. *Vorlesungen über das Wesen der Religion nebst Zusätze und Anmerkungen*. Edited by Werner Schuffenhauer and Wolfgang Harich. Ludwig Feuerbach: Gesammelte Werke 6. Berlin: Akademie, 1967.

———. *Das Wesen des Christentums*. Edited by Werner Schuffenhauer and Wolfgang Harich. Ludwig Feuerbach: Gesammelte Werke 5. Berlin: Akademie, 1973.

Fichte, Johann Gottlieb. *Introductions to the Wissenschaftslehre and Other Writings (1797–1800)*. Edited and translated with an introduction and notes by Daniel Breazeale. Indianapolis, IN: Hackett, 1994.

———. *Foundations of Transcendental Philosophy (Wissenschaftslehre) nova methodo (1796/99)*. Edited and translated by Daniel Breazeale. Ithaca, NY: Cornell University Press, 1992.

———. *Reden an die deutsche Nation*. Edited by Immanuel Hermann Fichte. Tübingen: Laupp, 1859 (Wahnfried).

———. "Review of *Aenesidemus*." In *Fichte: Early Philosophical Writings*, edited by Daniel Breazeale, 59–77. Ithaca, NY: Cornell University Press, 1988.

———. *Science of Knowledge (Wissenschaftslehre) with the First and Second Introductions*. Edited and translated by Peer Heath and John Lachs. CPS. New York: Appleton-Century-Crofts, 1970.

Fifield, Christopher. *Hans Richter*. 2nd ed. Woodbridge, UK: Boydell, 2016.

Finch, R. G. *The Saga of the Volsungs*. Icelandic Texts. London: Thomas Nelson, 1965.

Finglass, P. J. *Sophocles: Oedipus the King, edited with Introduction, Translation and Commentary*. Cambridge: Cambridge University Press, 2018.

Finlay, Alison, and Anthony Faulkes, ed. *Snorri Sturluson, Heimskringla Volume I: The Beginnings to Óláfr Tryggvason*. University College London: Viking Society for Northern Research, 2011.

Firchow, Peter, ed. *Friedrich Schlegel's Lucinde and the Fragments*. Minneapolis, MN: University of Minnesota, 1971.

Fischer, Jens Malte, ed. *Richard Wagners Das Judentum in der Musik: Eine kritische Dokumentation als Beitrag zur Geschichte des Antisemitismus*. Wagner in der Discussion 15. Würzburg: Königshausen & Neumann, 2015.

Foster, Daniel H. *Wagner's Ring Cycle and the Greeks*. Cambridge: Cambridge University Press, 2010.

Fouqué, Friedrich Baron de la Motte. *Der Held des Nordens*. Berlin: Julius Eduard Hitzig, 1810.

———. *Sigurd der Schlangentödtner: ein Heldenspiel in sechs Abentheurer*. Berlin: Julius Eduard Hitzig, 1808.

Frantz, Gustav Adolph Constantin. *Schelling's positive Philosophie. Nach ihrem Inhalt wie nach ihrer Bedeutung für den allgemeinen Umschwung der bis jetzt noch herrschenden Denkweise, für gebildete Leser dargestellt*. 3 parts. Köthen: Paul Schettler, 1879–80.

Frauer, Ludwig. *Die Walkyrien der skandinavisch-germanischen Götter- und Heldensage*. Weimar, 1846 (DB: Minna).

Fricke, Richard. *Bayreuth vor Dreissig Jahren: Erinnerungen an Wahnfried und aus dem Festspielhaus*. Dresden: Richard Bertling, 1906.

Friedrich, Sven. *Das auratische Kunstwerk: Zur Ästhetik von Richard Wagners Musiktheater-Utopie*. Theatron 19. Tübingen; Max Niemeyer, 1996.

Fuchs, Ernst. "Das Sprachereignis in der Verkündigung Jesu, in der Theologie des Paulus und im Ostergeschehen." In *Zum hermeneutischen Problem in der Theologie: Die existentiale Interpretation*, 281–305. 2nd ed. Tübingen: Mohr (Siebeck), 1965.

Gardner, Sebastian. "Schopenhauer, Will, and the Unconscious." In *The Cambridge Companion to Schopenhauer*, edited by Christopher Janaway, 375–421. Cambridge: Cambridge University Press, 1999.

Geck, Martin. *Richard Wagner: A Life in Music*. Translated by Stewart Spencer. Chicago: University of Chicago Press, 2013.

Geibel, Emanuel. *Juniuslieder*. 3rd ed. Stuttgart: J. G. Cotta, 1848.

Gese, Hartmut. "Das biblische Schriftverständnis." In *Zur biblische Theologie: Alttestamentliche Vorträge*, 9–30. 3rd ed. Tübingen: Mohr (Siebeck), 1989.

Gfrörer, August Friedrich. *Geschichte des Urchristenthums*. 3 vols. Stuttgart: Schweizerbart, 1838.

Giessel, Matthew. "Richard Wagner's Jesus von Nazareth." MA dissertation, Virginia Commonwealth University, 2013.

Gillespie, George T. *A Catalogue of Persons Named in German Heroic Literature (700–1600) including Named Animals and Objects and Ethnic Names*. Oxford: Clarendon, 1973.

Glasenapp, Carl Fr. "Aus Schillers Briefen 'über die aesthetische Erziehung des Menschen 1795.'" *Bayreuther Blätter* 2 (March 1879) 79–81.

———. *Das Leben Richard Wagners in sechs Büchern*. 1905–11. Reprint. Liechtenstein: Sändig, 1977.

Godley, A. D., ed. *Herodotus I–IV*. LCL. 4 vols. London: William Heinemann, 1920–24.

Goethe, Johann Wolfgang. *Goethe's sämmtliche Werke in vierzig Bänden*. Stuttgart/Tübingen: J. G. Cotta'scher, 1840 (DB 38).

———. *Goethe's sämmtliche Werke in dreißig Bänden*. Stuttgart: J. G. Cotta'scher, 1857–58 (Wahnfried).

Goldhill, Simon. "The Language of Tragedy: Rhetoric and Communication." In *The Cambridge Companion to Greek Tragedy*, edited by P. E. Easterling, 127–50. Cambridge: Cambridge University Press, 1997.

Golther, Wolfgang, ed. *Richard Wagner an Mathilde Wesendonk: Tagebuchblätter und Briefe 1853–1871*. Berlin: Duncker, 1908.

———. *Die sagengeschichtlichen Grundlagen der Ringdichtung Richard Wagners*. Charlottenburg-Berlin: Verlag der "Allgemeine Musik-Zeitung," 1902.

———. *Studien zur germanischen sagengeschichte. I der valkyrjenmythus. II über das verhältniss der nordsichen und deutschen form der Nibelungensage*. Munich: G. Franz, 1888.

Göttling, Karl Wilhelm. *Nibelungen und Gibelinen*. Rudolstadt: Im Verlage der Hof- Buch- und Kunsthandlung, 1816.

———. *Ueber das Geschichtliche im Nibelungenliede*. Rudolstadt: Hof-Buch-Handlung, 1814.

Graap, Paul-Gerhard. *Richard Wagners dramatischer Entwurf 'Jesus von Nazareth': Entstehungsgeschichte und Versuch einer kurzen Würdigung*. Leipzig: Breitkopf & Härtel, 1921.

Gräße, Johann Georg Theodor. *Gesta Romanorum*. 2 vols. Dresden: Arnoldische Buchhandlung, 1842 (DB 35).

———. *Die Sage vom Ritter Tannhäuser, aus dem Munde des Volks erzählt*. Dresden: Arnoldische Buchhandlung, 1846.

Graf, Hans Gerhard, and Albert Leitzmann, ed. *Der Briefwechsel zwischen Schiller und Goethe*. 2 vols. Leipzig: Insel, 1912.

Graziosi, Barbara. *Inventing Homer: The Early Reception of the Epic*. Cambridge Classical Studies. Cambridge: Cambridge University Press, 2002.

Gregor-Dellin, Martin. *Richard Wagner: His Life, His Work, His Century*. Translated by J. Maxwell Brownjohn. San Diego: Harcourt Brace Jovanovich, 1983.

———. *Richard Wagner: Sein Leben—Sein Werk—Sein Jahrhundert*. 1980. Reprint. Munich: Piper, 2005.

———. *Wagner-Chronik: Daten zu Leben und Werk*. 2nd ed. Kassel: Bärenreiter, 1983.

Grey, Thomas S., ed. *Richard Wagner and his World*. Princeton, NJ: Princeton University Press, 2009.

———. *Wagner's Musical Prose: Texts and Contexts*. Cambridge: Cambridge University Press, 1995.

———. "Wagner Introduces Wagner (and Beethoven): Program Notes Written for Concert Performances by and of Richard Wagner, 1846–1880." In *Richard Wagner and His World*, edited by Thomas S. Grey, 479–90. Princeton, NJ: Princeton University Press, 2009.

Griffiths, Mark. *The Authenticity of "Prometheus Bound."* Cambridge Classical Studies. Cambridge: Cambridge University Press, 1977.

Grimm, Jacob. *Deutsche Mythologie*. 2 vols. 2nd ed. Göttingen: Dieterichsche Buchhandlung, 1844 (DB 44).

———. *Deutsche Mythologie*. 3 vols. 4th ed. (by Elard Hugo Meyer). Berlin: Ferd. Dümmler, 1875–78.

———. *Teutonic Mythology*. Translated from the fourth edition by James Steven Stallybrass, with notes and appendix. 4 vols. London: George Bell, 1882–88.

Grimm, Wilhelm, ed. *Die deutsche Heldensage*. Göttingen: Dieterichsche Buchhandlung, 1829 (DB 47).

———, ed. *Der Rosengarte*. Göttingen: Dieterichsche Buchhandlung, 1836 (DB 118).

Grimm, Jacob, and Wilhelm Grimm, eds. *Kinder- und Hausmärchen.* 2nd ed. 3 vols. Berlin: Reimer, 1819–22 (DB: Minna)

———, eds. *Lieder der alten Edda.* 2 vols. Berlin: Realschulbuchhandlung, 1815 (DB: Minna).

Hagen, Friedrich Heinrich von der, ed. *Der Helden Buch, Erster Band.* Berlin: Johann Friedrich Unger, 1811 (DB 58).

———, ed. *Lieder der älteren oder Sämundischen Edda: Zum erstenmal herausgegeben durch Friedrich Heinrich von der Hagen.* Berlin: Haude und Spener, 1812 (DB 27).

———, ed. *Das Nibelungenlied in der Ursprache.* Berlin: Julius Eduard Hitzig, 1810. 3rd ed. Breslau: Max, 1820.

———, ed. *Der Nibelungen Lied nebst Glossar.* Berlin: Julius Eduard Hitzig, 1807.

———, ed. *Der Nibelungen Noth.* 3rd ed. Breslau: Max, 1820.

———. *Die Nibelungen, ihre Bedeutung für die Gegenwart für immer.* Breslau: Max, 1819 (possibly borrowed from Dresden Royal library).

———, ed. *Völsunga Saga oder Sigurd der Fafnirstöter und die Niflungen: Nordische Heldenromane,* vol. 4. Breslau: Max, 1815 (borrowed from Dresden Royal library).

———, ed. *Wilkina- und Niflunga saga, oder Dietrich von Bern und die Nibelungen. Nordische Heldenromane,* vols. 1–3 Breslau: Max, 1814–15 (borrowed from Dresden Royal library).

Hall, Jonathan M. *Ethnic Identity in Greek Antiquity.* Cambridge: Cambridge University Press, 1997.

Halliwell, Stephen, et al. *Aristotle XXIII: Poetics; Longinus; On the Sublime; Demetrius: On Style.* LCL 199. Cambridge: Harvard University Press, 1994.

Hamann, Brigitte. *Winifred Wagner: A Life at the Heart of Hitler's Bayreuth.* Translated by Alan Bance. London: Granta, 2005.

Harnack, Adolf von. "Das Alte Testament in den paulinischen Briefen und in den paulinischen Gemeinden." *Sitzungsberichte der Preußischen Akademie der Wissenschaften.* Berlin (1928) 124–41.

Harris, H. S. *Hegel's Development: Toward the Sunlight, 1770–1801.* Oxford: Clarendon, 1972.

Hartenstein, Gustav, ed. *Immanuel Kant's Kritik der reinen Vernunft.* Leipzig: Voss, 1868 (Wahnfried).

Hartlich, Christian, and Walter Sachs. *Der Ursprung des Mythosbegriff in der modernen Bibelwissenschaft.* Tübingen: J. C. B. Mohr (Paul Siebeck), 1952.

Hartwich, Wolf-Daniel. *Die Sendung Moses: von der Aufklärung bis Thomas Mann.* Munich: Fink, 1997.

Harvey, Van A. *Feuerbach and the Interpretation of Religion.* Cambridge Studies in Religion and Critical Thought 1. Cambridge: Cambridge University Press, 1995.

Hausegger, Friedrich von. *Richard Wagner und Schopenhauer: Eine Darlegung der philosophischen Anschauungen R. Wagners an der Hand seiner Werke.* 2nd ed. Leipzig: Feodor Reinboth, 1892.

Hauer, Stanley R. "Wagner and the *Völospá.*" *19th Century Music* 15 (1991) 52–63.

Haymes, Edward R., ed. *The Saga of Thidrek of Bern.* Garland Library of Medieval Literature, Series B, 56. New York: Garland, 1988.

———. "Introduction." In *Das Nibelungenlied: Song of the Nibelungs,* edited by Burton Raffel, XIII–XXI. New Haven: Yale University Press, 2006.

———. *Wagner's Ring in 1848: New Translations of the Nibelung Myth and Siegfried's Death.* Rochester, NY: Camden House, 2010.

BIBLIOGRAPHY

Hébert, Marcel. *Religious Experience in the Work of Richard Wagner*. Edited by C. J. T. Talar. Translated by C. J. T. Talar and Elizabeth Emery. Foreword by Stephen Schloesser. Washington, DC: The Catholic University of America Press, 2015.

———. *Le Sentiment Religieux dans l'Œuvre de Richard Wagner*. Paris: Librairie Fischbacher, 1895.

Heer, Friedrich. *The Holy Roman Empire*. Translated by Janet Sondheimer. London: Weidenfeld & Nicholson, 1968.

Hegel, G. W. F. *Aesthetics: Lectures on Fine Art*. 2 vols. Translated by T. M. Knox. 1975. Reprint. Oxford: Clarendon, 2010.

———. *On Christianity: Early Theological Writings*. Translated by T. M. Knox. With an introduction, and fragments translated by Richard Kroner. Gloucester, MA: Smith, 1970.

———. *The Difference between Fichte's and Schelling's System of Philosophy*. Translated by H. S. Harris and Walter Cerf. Albany, NY: State University of New York Press, 1977.

———. *The Encyclopaedia Logic (with the Zusätze): Part I of the Encyclopaedia of the Philosophical Sciences with the Zusätze*. A new translation with introduction and notes by T. F. Geraets, W. A. Suchting, and H. S. Harris. Indianapolis, IN: Hackett, 1991.

———. *Encyclopedia of the Philosophical Sciences in Basic Outline, Part I: Science of Logic*. Translated and edited by Klaus Brinkmann and Daniel O. Dahlstrom. CHT. Cambridge: Cambridge University Press, 2010.

———. *Frühe Schriften*. Edited by Eva Moldenhauer and Karl Markus Michel. Werke 1. 3rd ed. Frankurt am Main: Suhrkamp, 1994.

———. *Das Leben Jesu: Harmonie der Evangelien nach eigener Übersetzung: Nach der ungedruckten Handscrift in ungekürzter Form*. Edited by Paul Roques. Jena: Diederichs, 1906.

———. *Lectures on the Philosophy of World History. Introduction: Reason in History*. Translated by H. B. Nisbet. Introduction by D. Forbes. Cambridge Studies in the History and Theory of Politics. Cambridge: Cambridge University Press, 1975.

———. *Lectures on the Philosophy of History*. Preface by Charles Hegel. Translated by J. Sibree. 1861. Reprint. Meneola, NY: Dover 1956.

———. *Lectures on the Philosophy of Religion*. Edited by Peter C. Hodgson. 3 vols. 2007. Reprint. Oxford: Oxford University Press, 2011–12.

———. *Lectures on the Proofs of the Existence of God*. Edited and translated by Peter C. Hodgson. Oxford: Clarendon, 2007.

———. *The Letters*. Translated by Clark Butler and Christiane Seiler, with a commentary by Clark Butler. Bloomington, IN: Indiana University Press, 1984.

———. *Outlines of the Philosophy of Right*. Edited by T. M. Knox and Stephen Houlgate. Oxford World's Classics. Oxford: Oxford University Press, 2008.

———. *Hegel's Philosophy of Mind*. Translated from the 1830 Edition, together with *Zusätze* by W. Wallace and A. V. Miller with Revisions and Commentary by M. J. Inwood. Oxford: Clarendon, 2007.

———. *Hegel's Science of Logic*. Translated by A. V. Miller. Foreword by J. N. Findlay. London: George Allen & Unwin, 1969.

———. *System of Ethical Life (1802/3) and First Philosophy of Spirit (Part III of System of Speculative Philosophy 1803/4)*. Edited and translated by H. S. Harris and T. M. Knox. Albany, NY: State University of New York Press, 1979.

---. *Three Essays, 1793–95: The Tübingen Essay, Berne Fragments, The Life of Jesus*. Edited and translated with introduction and note by Peter Fuss and John Dobbins. Notre Dame, IN: University of Notre Dame Press, 1984.

---. *Vorlesungen über Naturphilosophie: Berlin 1823/24*. Edited by G. Marmasse. Frankfurt am Main: Lang, 2000.

---. *Vorlesungen über die Philosophie der Geschichte*. Edited by Eva Moldenhauer and Karl Markus Michel. Werke 12. Frankurt am Main: Suhrkamp, 1986.

---. *Vorlesungen über die Philosophie der Geschichte*. Edited by Eduard Gans and Karl Hegel. Berlin: Duncker und Humblot, 1840 (DB 55).

---. *Vorlesungen über die Philosophie der Kunst: Berlin 1823. Nachgeschrieben von Heinrich Gustav Hotho*. Edited by Annemarie Gethmann-Siefert. G. W. F. Hegel Vorlesungen. Ausgewählte Nachschriften und Manuskripte 2. Hamburg: Felix Meiner, 1998.

---. *Vorlesungen über die Philosophie der Religion. Teil 1: Einleitung. Der Begriff der Religion*. Edited by Walter Jaeschke. Vorlesungen: Ausgewählte Nachschriften und Manuskripte 3. Hamburg: Felix Meiner, 1983.

---. *Vorlesungen über die Philosophie der Religion. Teil 3: Die vollendete Religion*. Edited by Walter Jaeschke. Vorlesungen: Ausgewählte Nachschriften und Manuskripte 5. Hamburg: Felix Meiner, 1984.

---. *Wissenschaft der Logik I: Die Objektive Logik, Das Sein (1812)*. Edited by Hans-Jürgen Gawoll and Friedrich Hogemann. Philosophische Bibliothek 375. Hamburg: Felix Meiner, 1999.

Heimskringla. Sagen der Könige Norwegens von Snorre Sturlason. Aus dem Isländischen von Gottlieb Mohnike. Erster Band. Mit einer Karte. Stralsund: C. Löfflersche Buchhandlung, 1837 (DB 133).

Heintz, Albert. "Richard Wagner in Zürich: Ein Gedenkblatt zum 13. Februar." *Allgemeine Musik-Zeitung* 23 (14 February 1896) 91–94.

Heinzle, Joachim. "The Manuscripts of the Nibelungenlied." In *A Companion to the Nibelungenlied*, edited by Winder McConnell, 105–26. Columbia, SC: Camden House, 1998.

Hengel, Martin. *Die johanneische Frage: Ein Lösungsversuch mit einem Beitrag zur Apokalypse von Jörg Frey*. WUNT 67. Tübingen: J. C. B. Mohr (Paul Siebeck), 1993.

Henrich, Dieter. "Fichte's Original Insight," In *Contemporary German Philosophy, Volume 1*, edited by D. E. Christensen et al., 15–53. University Park, PA: Pennsylvania State University Press, 1982.

Herder, Johann Gottfried von. *Ausgewählte Werke in Einem Bande*. Stuttgart/Tübingen: J. G. Cotta, 1844 (DB 61).

---. *Ideen zur Philosophie der Geschichte der Menschheit*. Edited by Martin Bollacher. Johann Gottfried Herder Werke 6. Frankurt am Main: Deutscher Klassiker, 1989.

---. *Philosophical Writings*. Edited by Michael N. Forster. CTHP. Cambridge: Cambridge University Press, 2002.

Hermann, Franz Rudolph *Die Nibelungen. In drei Theilen. 1. Der Nibelungen Hort. 2. Siegfried. 3. Chriemhildens Rache*. Leipzig: F. A. Brockhaus, 1819.

Herodot. *Die Geschichte des Herodotos übersetzt von Friedrich Lange*. 2 vols. 2nd ed. Breslau: Josef Max, 1824 (DB 62).

Hett, W. S., ed. *Aristotle VIII: One the Soul; Parva Naturalia; On Breath*. LCL 288. 1957. Reprint. Cambridge: Harvard University Press, 2000.

Hinsberg, J. von., ed. *Das Lied der Nibelungen*, 4th ed. Munich: J. Lindauer, 1838 (borrowed from Dresden Royal library).

Hodgson, Peter C. *Shapes of Freedom: Hegel's Philosophy of World History in Theological Perspective*. 2005. Reprint. Oxford: Oxford University Press, 2012.

———. *Hegel and Christian Theology: A Reading of the Lectures on the Philosophy of Religion*. Oxford: Oxford University Press, 2005.

Hoffmann, Ernst T. A. *E. T. A. Hoffmann's gesammelte Schriften*. 12 vols. Berlin: G. Reimer, 1857.

Hoffmann, Werner. "The Reception of the Nibelungenlied in the Twentieth Century." In *A Companion to the Nibelungenlied*, edited by Winder McConnell, 127–52. Columbia, SC: Camden House, 1998.

Hoffmeister, Johannes, ed. *Georg Wilhelm Friedrich Hegel: Phänomenologie des Geistes*. Der philosophische Bibliothek 114. 6th ed. Hamburg: Felix Meiner, 1952.

Hollander, Lee M., ed. *The Poetic Edda*. 2nd ed. Austin, TX: University of Austin Press, 1962.

Holloway, Robin. "Motif, Memory and Meaning in 'Twilight of the Gods.'" In *Twilight of the Gods/Götterdämmerung*, 13–38. Opera Guides 31. London: Calder, 1985.

Hornstein, Robert von. *Memoiren, herausgegeben von Ferdinand von Hornstein*. Munich: Süddeutsche Monatshefte, 1908.

Houlgate, Stephen. "Hegel's Theory of Tragedy." In *Hegel and the Arts*, edited by Stephen Houlgate, 146–78. Topics in Historical Philosophy. Evanston, IL: Northwestern University Press, 2007.

———. "G. W. F. Hegel: An Introduction to His Life and Thought." In *A Companion to Hegel*, edited by Stephen Houlgate and Michael Baur, 1–19. Blackwell Companions to Philosophy. Oxford: Wiley Blackwell, 2011.

———. "G. W. F. Hegel: The Phenomenology of Spirit." In *The Blackwell Guide to Continental Philosophy*, edited by Robert C. Solomon and David Sherman, 8–29. Blackwell Philosophy Guides 12. Oxford: Blackwell, 2003.

———. *Introduction to Hegel: Freedom, Truth and History*. 2nd ed. Oxford: Blackwell, 2005.

Hölderlin, Friedrich. *Sämtliche Werke*. Edited by Christoph Theodor Schwab. 2 vols. Stuttgart Tübingen: J. G. Cotta, 1846 (Wahnfried).

Huber, Herbert. "Nemo contra Deum, nisi Deus ipse: Das Wotan-Problem in Richard Wagners 'Ring des Nibelungen.'" *NZSyTh* 23 (1981) 272–96.

———. *Der Ring des Nibelungen: Vollständiger Text mit Kommentar*. Weinheim: VCH, 1988.

Hübner, Hans. *Erlösung bei Richard Wagner und im Neuen Testament*. Neukirchen-Vluyn: Neukirchener, 2008.

Hübscher, Arthur, ed. *Arthur Schopenhauer: Gesammelte Briefe*. Bonn: Bouvier Verlag Herbert Grundmann, 1978.

Huray, Pete le, and James Day. *Music and Aesthetics in Eighteenth and Early Nineteenth Centuries*. Cambridge: Cambridge University Press, 1981.

Hutton, M., et al. *Tacitus I: Agricola, Germania, Dialogus*. LCL 35. 1914. Reprint. Cambridge: Harvard University Press, 1992.

Hyppolite, Jean. "The Concept of Life and Consciousness of Life in Hegel's Jena Philosophy." In *Studies on Marx and Hegel*, 3–21. Translated, with an introduction, notes, and bibliography, by John O'Neill. London: Heinemann, 1969.

Insole, Christopher J. *Kant and the Creation of Freedom: A Theological Problem*. Oxford: Oxford University Press, 2013.

Inwood, Margaret. *The Influence of Shakespeare on Richard Wagner*. Lampeter, UK: Edwin Mellen, 1999.
Inwood, Michael J. *Hegel*. 1983. Reprint. London: Routledge, 1998.
———. *A Hegel Dictionary*. The Blackwell Philosopher Dictionaries. Oxford: Blackwell, 1992.
———. "Fichte, Johann Gottlieb." In *OCP* 277–79.
Irrlitz, Gerd. *Kant Handbuch: Leben und Werk*. Stuttgart Weimar: J. B. Metzler, 2002.
Istel, Edgar. "Wagner and Shakespeare." Translated by Theodore Baker. *Musical Quarterly* 8.4 (1922) 495–509.
Jesch, Judith. *The Viking Diaspora*. London: Routledge, 2015.
Jolley, Nicholas. *Leibniz*. London: Routledge, 2005.
Jones, William. "Third Anniversary Discourse: On the Hindus." In *The Works of Sir William Jones*, 1:19–34. 6 vols. London: G. G. and J. Robinson, 1799.
Josephus Flavius. *De antiquitatibus Iudaicis Libri XX*. Frankfurt, 1580 (Wahnfried).
Julian of Norwich. *Revelations of Divine Love*. Translated by Elizabeth Spearing with an introduction and notes by A. C. Spearing. London: Penguin, 1998.
Jüngel, Eberhard. *God as the Mystery of the World: On the Foundation of the Theology of the Crucified One in the Dispute between Theism and Atheism*. Translated by Darrell L. Guder. Edinburgh: T. & T. Clark, 1983.
———. *Gott als Geheimnis der Welt: Zur Begründung der Theologie des Gekreuzigten im Streit zwischen Theismus und Atheismus*. 5th ed. Tübingen: J. C. B. Mohr (Paul Siebeck), 1986.
Kalbeck, Max. "Richard Wagner's Nibelungen. Erste Aufführung vom 13. bis 17. August 1876 in Bayreuth." *Schlesische Zeitung* (Breslau) 1876.
Kamenka, Eugene. *The Philosophy of Ludwig Feuerbach*. London: Routledge & Kegan Paul, 1970.
Kapp, Julius. *Richard Wagner: Eine Biographie*. Mit 156 Bildern. New ed. Berlin: Max Hesses, 1929.
Kämper, Dietrich. "Über die Uraufführung von *Rheingold* und *Walküre*." In *Richard Wagner: Werk und Wirkung*, edited by Carl Dahlhaus, 65–74. Studien zur Musikgeschichte des 19. Jahrhunderts. Regensburg: Gustav Bosse, 1971.
Kant, Immanuel. *Critique of the Power of Judgment*. Edited by Paul Guyer. Translated by Paul Guyer and Eric Matthews. CEWIK. Cambridge: Cambridge University Press, 2000.
———. *Critique of Judgement*. Edited by James Creed Meredith and Nicholas Walker. Oxford World's Classics. Oxford: Oxford University Press, 2007.
———. *Critique of Pure Reason*. Translated by Norman Kemp Smith, with a new introduction by Howard Caygill. Basingstoke, UK: Palmgrave Macmillan, 2003.
———. *Religion within the Boundaries of Mere Reason and Other Writings*. Edited by Allen Wood and George di Giovanni. Introduction by Robert Merrihew Adams. CTHP. Cambridge: Cambridge University Press, 1998.
Kienzle, Ulrike. "Brünnhilde—das Wotanskind." In *"Alles ist nach seiner Art": Figuren in Richard Wagners "Der Ring des Nibelungen,"* edited by Udo Bermbach, 81–103. Stuttgart: Metzler, 2001.
———. *. . . daß wissend würde die Welt! Religion und Philosophie in Richard Wagners Musikdramen*. Wagner in der Diskussion 1. Würzburg: Königshausen & Neumann, 2005.

———. "*Parsifal* and Religion: A Christian Music Drama?" In *A Companion to Wagner's Parsifal*, edited by William Kinderman and Katherine R. Syer, 81–130. Rochester: Camden House, 2005.

Kirkpatrick, Robin, ed. *Dante Alighieri, The Divine Comedy I: Inferno*. London: Penguin, 2006.

———. "Introduction." In *Dante Alighieri, The Divine Comedy I: Inferno*, viii–cxiii. London: Penguin, 2006.

Kirsch, Winfried. "Richard Wagners Biblische Scene *Das Liebesmahl der Apostel*." In *Geistliche Musik: Studien zu ihrer Geschichte und Funktion im 18. und 19. Jahrhundert*, edited by Constantin Floros, Hans Joachim Marx, and Peter Petersen, 157–84. Laaber: Laaber, 1985.

Knatz, Lothar. *Geschichte—Kunst—Mythos: Schellings Philosophie und die Perspektive einer philosophischen Mythostheorie*. Würzburg: Königshausen & Neumann, 1999.

Knight, Douglas A. "Revelation through Tradition." In *Tradition and Theology in the Old Testament*, edited by Douglas A. Knight. Philadelphia: Fortress, 1977.

Koch, Ernst. *Richard Wagner's Bühnenfestspiel Der Ring des Nibelungen in seinem Verhältnis zur alten Sage wie zur modernen Nibelungendichtung betrachtet*. Leipzig: C. F. Kahnt, 1875.

Koch, Max. *Richard Wagner*. 3 vols. Berlin: Ernst Hofmann, 1907–18.

Kohls, Ernst-Wilhelm. *Luther oder Erasmus: Luthers Theologie in der Auseinandersetzung mit Erasmus*. 2 vols. Basel: Friedrich Reinhardt, 1972–78.

Koßler, Matthias, and Maurizio Morini. "Zur Entwicklung des Hauptwerkes." In *Schopenhauer-Handbuch: Leben—Werk—Wirkung*, edited by Matthias Koßler and Daniel Schubbe, 32–35. Darmstadt: Wissenschaftliche Buchgesellschaft, 2014.

Klaproth, Julius. *Asia Polyglotta*. Paris: J. M. Eberhart, 1823.

Köhler, Joachim. *Richard Wagner: The Last of the Titans*. Translated by Stewart Spencer. New Haven: Yale University Press, 2004.

Kreckel, Manfred. *Richard Wagner und die französischen Frühsozialisten: Die Bedeutung der Kunst und des Künstlers für eine neue Gesellschaft*. EH 3.284. Frankfurt am Main: Lang, 1986.

Krömmelbein, Thomas. "Jacob Schimmelmann und der Beginn der Snorra Edda Rezeption in Deutschland." In *Snorri Sturluson: Beiträge zu Werk und Rezeption*, edited by H. Fix, 109–30. ERGA 18. Berlin: Walter de Gruyter, 1998.

Kühnel, Jürgen. "The Prose Writings." In *Wagner Handbook*, edited by Ulrich Müller, Peter Wapnewski, and John Deathridge, 565–651. Cambridge: Harvard University Press, 1992.

Kümmel, Werner Georg. *The New Testament: The History of the Investigation of Its Problems*. Translated by S. McLean Gilmour and Howard C. Kee. London: SCM, 1972.

Lachmann, Karl, ed. *Der Nibelunge Not und die Klage nach der ältesten Überlieferung mit Bezeichnung des Unechten und mit den Abweichungen der gemeinen Lesart*. Berlin: G. Reimer, 1826, 2nd ed. 1841 (borrowed from Dresden Royal library).

———, ed. *Zu den Nibelungen und zur Klage*. Anmerkungen von Karl Lachmann. Wörterbuch von Wilhelm Wackernagel. Berlin: G. Reimer, 1836 (DB 78).

———. "De ordine narrationum in evangeliis synopticis." *ThStKr* 8 (1835) 570–90.

———. "Rechenschaft über seine Ausgabe des Neuen Testaments." *ThStKr* 3 (1830) 817–45.

Lachmann, Karl, and Philip Buttmann, ed. *Novum Testamentum Graece et Latine*. 2 vols. Berlin: G. Reimer, 1842–50.

Lamm, Julia A. "The Art of Interpreting Plato." In *The Cambridge Companion to Schleiermacher*, edited by Jacqueline Mariña, 91–108. Cambridge: Cambridge University Press, 2005.

Larrington, Carolyn, ed. *The Poetic Edda*. Oxford World's Classics. Rev. ed. Oxford: Oxford University Press, 2014.

Lassen, Annette, ed. *Hrafnagaldur Óðins (Forspjallsljóð)*. University College London: Viking Society for Northern Research, 2011.

Laughland, John. *Schelling versus Hegel: From German Idealism to Christian Metaphysics*. Aldershot, UK: Ashgate, 2007.

Laurence, Dan H., ed. *Shaw's Music: The Complete Musical Criticism of Bernard Shaw, Volume 3: 1893–1950*. London: The Bodley Head, 1989.

Lawing, Sean B. "The Place of Evil: Infant Abandonment in Old Norse Society." *Scandinavian Studies* 85.2 (2013) 133–50.

Lee, Christina. "A Useful Great-Grandmother: *Edda* Reception in Post-Medieval Germany." In *Germania Remembered, 1500–2009: Commemorating and Inventing a German Past*, edited by Christina Lee and Nicola McClelland, 99–119. MRTS 425. Tempe; ACMRS, 2012.

Legis, Gustav Thormod (Glückselig, Anton August). *Fundgruben des alten Nordens, erste Band: Die Runen und ihre Denkmäler*. Leipzig: Johann Ambrosius Barth, 1829.

———. *Fundgruben des alten Nordens, zweiter Band, erste Abtheilung: Edda, die Stammmutter der Poësie und der Weisheit des Nordens*. Leipzig: Wilhelm Nauck, 1829 (borrowed from Dresden Royal library).

Lehning, Arthur, ed. *Michael Bakunin: Selected Writings*. Translated by Steven Cox and Olive Stevens. London: Jonathan Cape, 1973.

Lessing, Gotthold Ephraim. *Sämtliche Schriften herausgegeben von Karl Lachmann: Neue rechtmäßige Ausgabe*. 12 vols. Berlin: Voß'sche Buchhandlung, 1838–40 (DB 81).

———. *Sämtliche Schriften herausgegeben von Karl Lachmann; auf's Neue durchgesehen u. verm. v. Wendelin von Maltzahn*. 12 vols. Berlin: Voß'sche Buchhandlung, 1853–57 (Wahnfried).

Lewes, George H. *Goethe's Leben and Schriften*. Translated by Julius Frese. 2 vols. 7th ed. Berlin; Duncker, 1866.

Lichtenberger, Henri. *Richard Wagner: Poète et penseur*. Bibliothéque de philosophie contemporaine. 4th ed. Paris: Félix Alcan, 1907.

Lindemann, Andreas. "Die biblische Toragebote und die paulinische Ethik." In *Studien zum Text und der Ethik des Neuen Testament: Festschrift zum 80. Geburtstag von Heinrich Greeven*, edited by Wolfgang Schrage, 242–65. Berlin: Walter de Gruyter, 1986.

Lionarons, Joyce Tally. "The Otherworld and Its Inhabitants." In *A Companion to the Nibelungenlied*, edited by Winder McConnell, 153–71. Columbia, SC: Camden House, 1998.

Liszt, Franz. *Eine Symphonie zu Dantes Divina Commedia für großes Orchester und Sopran- und Alt-Chor*. Franz Liszts Musikalische Werke 1.2.7. Leipzig: Breitkopf & Härtel, 1920.

Loader, William. "Reading Romans 1 on Homosexuality in the Light of Biblical/Jewish and Greco-Roman Perspectives of Its Time." *ZNW* 108.1 (2017) 119–49.

Loebell, Johann Wilhelm. *Gregor von Tours und seine Zeit vornehmlich aus seinen Werken geschildert*. Leipzig: F. A. Brockhaus, 1839 (DB 83; Wahnfried).

Lloyd-Jones, Hugh, ed. *Aeschylus: Oresteia*. 1979. Reprint. London: Duckworth, 2001.

———, ed. *Sophocles*. 2 vols. LCL 20–21. Cambridge: Harvard University Press, 1994.

———. "Wagner." In *Blood for the Ghosts: Classical Influences in the Nineteenth and Twentieth Centuries*, 126–42. London: Duckworth, 1982.
Look, Brandon C. "Blumenbach and Kant on Mechanism and Teleology in Nature: The Case of the Formative Drive." In *The Problem of Animal Generation in Early Modern Philosophy*, edited by Justin E. H. Smith, 355–72. Cambridge Studies in Philosophy and Biology. Cambridge: Cambridge University Press, 2006.
Ludwig, Ernst. "Stimmen aus der Vergangenheit: Aus 'Rameaus Neffe' von Diderot." *Bayreuther Blätter* 1882 (Januar/Februar Doppelstuck) 58–62.
Luke, David, editor and translator. *Goethe, Faust Part One*. Oxford World's Classics. 1987. Reprint. Oxford/New York: Oxford University Press, 1998.
———, editor and translator. *Goethe, Faust Part Two*. Oxford World's Classics. 1994. Reprint. Oxford/New York: Oxford University Press, 1998.
Luther, Martin. *Sermons of Martin Luther*. Edited and translated by John Nicholas Lenker. 8 vols. Grand Rapids, MI: Baker, 1995.
McCarney, Joseph. *Hegel on History*. Routledge Philosophical Guidebooks. London: Routledge, 2000.
McConnell, Winder. "Introduction." In *A Companion to the Nibelungenlied*, edited by Winder McConnell, 1–17. Columbia, SC: Camden House, 1998.
McLaughlin, Paul. *Mikhail Bakunin: The Philosophical Basis of His Theory of Anarchism*. New York: Algora, 2002.
McManus, Laurie. "Feminist Revolutionary Music Criticism and Wagner Reception: The Case of Louise Otto." *19th Century Music* 37.3 (2014) 161–87.
McTaggert, John McTaggert Ellis. *Studies in Hegelian Cosmology*. Cambridge: Cambridge University Press, 1918.
Magee, Bryan. *The Great Philosophers*. Oxford: Oxford University Press, 1987.
———. *The Philosophy of Schopenhauer*. 2nd ed. Oxford: Oxford University Press, 1997.
———. *Wagner and Philosophy*. London: Penguin, 2001.
Magee, Elizabeth. *Richard Wagner and the Nibelungs*. Oxford: Clarendon, 1990.
Magee, Glen Alexander. "Hegel and Mysticism." In *The Cambridge History to Hegel and Nineteenth-Century Philosophy*, edited by Frederick C. Beiser, 253–80. Cambridge: Cambridge University Press, 2008.
Majer, Friedrich, ed. *Mythologische Dichtungen und Lieder der Skandinavier*. Aus dem Isländlischen der jüngeren und älteren Edda übersetzt und mit einigen Anmerkungen begleitet von Friedrich Majer. Leipzig: Carl Cnobloch, 1818 (DB 28).
Mann, Thomas. "Richard Wagner and the *Ring*." In *Essays of Three Decades*, translated by H. T. Lowe-Porter, 353–71. London: Secker & Warburg, n.d.
Mattes, Mark C. "Hegel's Lutheran Claim." *Lutheran Quarterly* 19 (2000) 249–79.
Matthews, Denis. *Beethoven*. The Master Musicians. London/Melbourne: J. M. Dent, 1985.
Meiners, Christoph. *Grundriss der Geschichte der Menschheit*. Lemgo: Meyerschen, 1785.
Mertens, Völker. "Wagner's Middle Ages." In *Wagner Handbook*, edited by Ulrich Müller, Peter Wapnewski, and John Deathridge, 236–68. Cambridge: Harvard University Press, 1992.
Metzger, Bruce M. *The Text of the New Testament: Its Transmission, Corruption, and Restoration*. 3rd ed. Oxford: Oxford University Press, 1992.
Miller, A. V., ed. *Hegel's Phenomenology of Spirit with an Analysis of the Text and Foreword by J. N. Findlay*. Oxford: Oxford University Press, 1977.

Millington, Barry, ed. *The Wagner Compendium: A Guide to Wagner's Life and Music*. London: Thames and Hudson, 1992.

———. "All in It Together: The *Gesamtkunstwerk* Revisited." *The Wagner Journal* 11.1 (2017) 46–61.

———. "The Ring and Its Times: The Social and Political Background to the Tetralogy." In *Wagner's Ring and Its Icelandic Sources: A Symposium at the Reykjavík Arts Festival, 29 May 1994*, edited by Úlfar Bragason, 17–30. Reykjavík: Stofnun Sigurðar Nordals, 1995.

———. *Richard Wagner: The Sorcerer of Bayreuth*. London: Thames & Hudson, 2012.

Mone, Franz Joseph. *Untersuchungen zur Geschichte der teutschen Heldensage*. Bibliothek der gesammten deutschen National-Literatur von der ältesten bis auf die neuere Zeit. Zweite Abtheilung. Erste Band. Queblinburg/Leipzig: Gottfr. Basse, 1836 (DB 93; Wahnfried).

———. *Geschichte des nordischen Heidentums*. 2 vols. Leipzig: Heyer und Leske, 1822–23.

———. *Symbolik und Mythologie der alten Völker*. 2 vols. Leipzig: Carl Wilhelm Leske, 1822–23.

Montgomery, Ingun (with Svein Helge Birkeflet). "Norwegen." *TRE* 24:643–59.

Most, Glenn W., ed. *Hesiod I: Theogony, Works and Days, Testimonia*. LCL 57. Cambridge: Harvard University Press, 2006.

Müller, Hieronymus, ed. *Die Lustspiele des Aristophanes*. 3 vols. Leipzig: F. A. Brockhaus, 1843–46 (DB 5).

Müller, Karl Otfried. *Geschichten hellenischer Stämme und Städte*. 3 vols. Breslau: Josef Max, 1844 (DB 96; Wahnfried).

Müller, Carl Otfried. *History and Antiquities of the Doric Race*. Translated by Henry Tufnell and George Cornewall Lewis. 1830. Reprint. 2 vols. Cambridge: Cambridge University Press, 2010.

Müller, Franz Carl Friedrich. *Der Ring des Nibelungen: eine Studie zur Einführung in die gleichnamige Dichtung Richard Wagners*. Leipzig: G. Heinze, 1862.

Müller, Johann Wilhelm. *Chriemhilds Rache; Trauerspiel in drey Abteilungen, mit dem Chor*. Heidelberg: Groos, 1822.

Müller, Ulrich. "Wagner and Antiquity." In *Wagner Handbook*, edited by Ulrich Müller, Peter Wapnewski, and John Deathridge, 227–35. Cambridge: Harvard University Press, 1992.

Müller, Ulrich, and Oswald Panagl, eds. *Ring und Gral: Texte, Kommentare und Interpretationen zu Richard Wagners 'Der Ring des Nibelungen', 'Tristan und Isolde', "Die Meistersinger von Nürmberg" und "Parsifal*. Würzburg: Königshausen & Neumann, 2002.

Munz, Peter. *Frederick Barbarossa: A Study in Medieval Politics*. London: Eyre & Spottiswoode, 1969.

Murdoch, Brian. "Politics in the *Nibelungenlied*." In *A Companion to the Nibelungenlied*, edited by Winder McConnell, 229–50. Columbia, SC: Camden House, 1998.

Murphy, G. Ronald. *The Owl, the Raven, and the Dove: The Religious Meaning of the Grimms' Magic Fairy Tales*. Oxford: Oxford University Press, 2000.

Nattiez, Jean-Jacques. *Wagner Androgyne: A Study in Interpretation*. Translated by Stewart Spencer. Princeton, NJ: Princeton University Press, 1993.

Das Neue Testament, unseres Herrn und Heilandes Jesu Christi. Leipziger Jubelausgabe, nach der letzten Ausgabe Dr. Martin Luthers (vom Jahre 1545) revidiert von Hofrath Dr. (E. G.) Gersdorf und Dr. K. A. Espe. Leipzig: Möller, 1845.

Newman, Ernst. *The Life of Richard Wagner*, 4 vols. London: Cassell, 1933–47.

Nicolin, Friedhelm. "Unbekannte Aphorismen Hegels aus der Jenaer Periode." In *Hegel-Studien 4*, edited by Friedhelm Nicolin and Otto Pöggeler, 9–19. Hamburg: Felix Meiner, 1967.

Niecks, Frederick. *Frederick Chopin as a Man and Musician*. 2 vols. London: Novello, n.d.

Nietzsche, Friedrich. *The Anti-Christ, Ecce Homo, Twilight of the Idols and Other Writings*. CTHP. Edited by Aaron Ridley and Judith Norman. 2005. Reprint. Cambridge: Cambridge University Press, 2012.

———. *"On the Genealogy of Morality" and Other Writings*. Edited by Keith Ansell Pearson. Translated by Carol Diethe. CTHPT. 3rd ed. Cambridge: Cambridge University Press, 2017.

———. *Beyond Good and Evil*. Edited by Rolf-Peter Horstmann and Judith Norman. 2002. CTHP. Reprint. Cambridge: Cambridge University Press, 2018.

———. *Untimely Meditations*. Edited by Daniel Breazeale. Translated by R.J. Hollingdale. CTHP. 1997. Reprint. Cambridge: Cambridge University Press, 2001.

Nivala, Asko. *The Romantic Idea of the Golden Age in Friedrich Schlegel's Philosophy of History*. New York: Routledge, 2017.

Novalis. *Fichte Studies*. Edited by Jane Kneller. CTHP. Cambridge: Cambridge University Press, 2003.

Nussbaum, Martha C. *Luck and Ethics in Greek Tragedy and Philosophy*. Cambridge: Cambridge University Press, 1986.

Oergel, Maike. *Culture and Identity: Historicity in German Literature and Thought 1770–1815*. Berlin: Walter de Gruyter, 2006.

———. *The Return of King Arthur and the Nibelungen: National Myth in Nineteenth-Century English and German Literature*. European Cultures: Studies in Literature and the Arts 10. Berlin: Walter de Gruyter, 1998.

Orchard, Andy, ed. *The Elder Edda*. London: Penguin, 2011.

Otto, Louise. *Die Nibelungen: Text zu einer großen heroischen Oper in 5 Acten*. Gera: Hofmeister'schen Zeitungs-Expedition, 1852.

———. "Die Nibelungen als Oper." *Neue Zeitschrift für Musik* in volume 23 no. 13 (12 August 1845), 49ff, no 33 (21 October 1845), 129ff and no 43 (21 November 1845), 171f.

O'Regan, Cyril. *The Heterodox Hegel*. SUNY Series in Hegelian Studies. Albany, NY: State University of New York Press, 1994.

Otto, Werner. *Richard Wagner: Ein Lebens- und Charakterbild in Dokumenten und zeitgenössischen Darstellungen*. Berlin: Der Morgen, 1990.

Oxenford, John. "Contemporary Literature of Germany." *Westminster Review* 57, no. 112; New Series 2, no. 2 (1852) 677–97.

———. "Iconoclasm in German Philosophy." *Westminster Review* 59 no. 116; New Series 3, no. 2 (1853) 388–407.

Panzer, Friedrich. *Das Nibelungenlied: Entstehung und Gestalt*. Stuttgart: W. Kohlhammer, 1955.

Pecht, Friedrich. *Aus meiner Zeit*. 2 vols. Munich: Kunst und Wissenschaft, 1894.

Perschmann, Wolfgang. *Die optimistische Tragödie: Sinndeutende Darsstellung*. Graz: Österreicher Richard-Wagner-Society, 1986.

Petsch, Robert. "*Der Ring des Nibelungen* in seinen Beziehungen zur griechischen Tragödie und zur zeitgenössischen Philosophie." In *Richard-Wagner Jahrbuch* 2, edited by Ludwig Frankenstein, 284–330. Berlin: Hausbücher, 1907.

Pfizer, Gustav. *Der Nibelungen Noth*. Stuttgart: J. G. Cotta, 1843 (DB 100).

Pinkard, Terry. *Hegel: A Biography*. Cambridge: Cambridge University Press, 2000.

———. "Hegel: A Life." In *The Cambridge History to Hegel and Nineteenth-Century Philosophy*, edited by Frederick C. Beiser, 15–51. Cambridge: Cambridge University Press, 2008.

Pippin, Robert. "Fichte's Alleged Subjective, Psychological, One-Sided Idealism." In *The Reception of Kant's Critical Philosophy: Fichte, Schelling, and Hegel*, edited by Sally Sedgwick, 147–70. Cambridge: Cambridge University Press, 2000.

Platon Werke. Translated by F. Schleiermacher. 6 vols. 1.1; Berlin: Realschulbuchhandlung, 1817^2; 1.2: Berlin: Realschulbuchhandlung, 1818^2; 2.1: Berlin: Realschulbuchhandlung, Berlin: Realschulbuchhandlung 1818^2; 2.2: Berlin: G. Reimer, 1824^2; 2.3: Berlin: G. Reimer, 1824^2; 3.1 Berlin: G. Reimer, 1824^2 (DB 108).

Porges, Heinrich. *Wagner Rehearsing the 'Ring': An Eye-Witness Account of the Stage Rehearsals of the First Bayreuth Festival*. Translated by Robert L. Jacobs. Cambridge: Cambridge University Press, 1983.

Pretzsch, Paul. *Cosima Wagner und Houston Stewart Chamberlain im Briefwechsel, 1888–1908*. Leipzig: Philipp Reclam jun., 1934.

Quinn, Judy. "Editing the Edda—The Case of *Völuspá*." *Scripta Islandica* 51 (2001) 69–92.

Raffel, Burton, ed. *Das Nibelungenlied: Song of the Nibelungs*. Foreword by Michael Dirda. Introduction by Edward R. Haymes. New Haven: Yale University Press, 2006.

Rask, Rasmus. *Snorra-Edda*. Stockholm, 1818.

Rasmussen, Joel D. S. "The Transformation of Metaphysics." In *The Oxford Handbook of Nineteenth-Century Christian Thought*, edited by Joel Rasmussen, Judith Wolfe, and Johannes Zachhuber, 12–34. Oxford: Oxford University Press, 2017.

Raumer, Friedrich von. *Geschichte der Hohenstaufen und ihrer Zeit*. 2nd ed. 6 vols. Leipzig: F. A. Brockhaus, 1840–41. Wagner possessed vols 1 (1840); 2 (1841); 4: (1841) (DB 112).

Raupach, Ernst. *Der Nibelungen-Hort: Tragödie in fünf Auszügen, mit einem Vorspiel*. Hamburg: Hoffmann und Campe, 1834.

Rawidowicz, S. *Ludwig Feuerbachs Philosophie: Ursprung und Schicksal*. 2nd ed. Berlin: Walter de Gruyter, 1964.

Requadt, P. "Grimm, Jacob." RGG^3 2:1876–77.

Resen, Peder (Resenius), Stephan Olafsen, and Gudmundur Andreae. *Edda Islandorum*. Copenhagen, 1665.

Reuß, Roland, ed. *"Lieder [. . .] die nicht seyn sind." Der Briefwechsel zwischen Jacob Grimm, Wilhelm Grimm, Achim v. Arnim und Friedrich Carl v. Savigny aus dem Jahre 1811 und das Problem der Edition. Einführung und Faksimile-Edition mit diplomatischer Umschrift*. Frankfurt am Main: Stroemfeld, 2002.

Robertson, Ritchie. "German Literature and Thought from 1810 to 1890." In *The Oxford Handbook of Modern German History*, edited by Helmut Walser Smith, 260–77. Oxford: Oxford University Press, 2011.

———. *Goethe: A Very Short Introduction*. Oxford: Oxford University Press, 2016.

———. *The 'Jewish Question' in German Literature 1749–1939: Emancipation and Its Discontents*. Oxford: Oxford University Press, 1999.

Rogerson, John. *Myth in Old Testament Interpretation*. Berlin: Walter de Gruyter, 1974.

Rosenkranz, Karl, and Friedrich W. Schubert, ed. *Immanuel Kant's sämmtliche Werke*. 12 vols. Leipzig: Voss, 1838–40 (Wahnfried).

Rosner, Brian S. *Paul, Scripture and Ethics: A Study of 1 Corinthians 5–7*. AGJU 22. Leiden: E. J. Brill, 1994.

Ross, G. MacDonald. *Leibniz*. Past Masters. Oxford: Oxford University Press, 1984.

Rousseau, Jean Jacques. "A Dissertation on the Origin and Foundation of the Inequality of Mankind." In *The Social Contract and Discourses by Jean Jacques Rousseau*, translated with introduction by G. D. H. Cole, 160–229. 1913. Reprint. Everyman's Library 660. New York: Dutton, 1947.

Ruffell, Ian A. *Aeschylus: Prometheus Bound*. Companions to Greek and Roman Tragedy. Bristol: Bristol Classical, 2012.

Rühs, Friedrich. *Die Edda nebst einer Einleitung über nordische Poesie und Mythologie und einem Anhang über die historische Literatur der Isländer*. Berlin: Realschulbuchhandlung, 1812 (DB 119).

Russell, Bertrand. *History of Western Philosophy and its Connection with Political and Social Circumstances from the Earliest Times to the Present Day*. 2nd ed. London: Allen & Unwin, 1961.

Rußwurm, C. *Nordische Sagen der deutschen Jugend*. Leipzig: Friedrich Fleischer, 1842 (DB 121).

Sabor, Rudolph. *Richard Wagner: Die Walküre*. London: Phaidon, 1997.

Sagaenbibliothek des Skandinavischen Alterthums in Auszügen mit litterarischen Nachweisungen von Peter Erasmus Müller. Translated by Karl Lachmann. Berlin: Realschulbuchhandlung, 1816. *Die Saga von Fridthjof dem Starken*. Translated by G. C. F. Mohnike. Stralsund: Wilhelm Trinius, 1830 (DB 123).

Saine, Thomas P., and Jeffrey L. Sammons, eds. *From My Life: Poetry and Truth (Parts One to Three)*. Goethe's Collected Works vol. 4. Princeton, NJ: Princeton University Press, 1987.

Salis, Ludwig Rudolf von. *Leges Burgundionum*. Monumenta Germaniae Historia I.II.I Hannover: privately published, 1892.

Sans, Edouard. *Richard Wagner et la pensée schopenhauerienne*. Paris: Klincksieck, 1969.

Sansone, David. "Wagner, Droysen and the Greek Satyr-Play." *Antike und Abendland* 61.1 (2015) 1–9.

Sass, H. M. "Feuerbach statt Marx. Zur Verfasserschaft des Aufsatzes 'Luther als Schiedsrichter zwischen Strauß und Feuerbach.'" *International Review of Social History* 12 (1967) 108–19.

Saxo Grammaticus. *Gesta Danorum. The History of the Danes*. 2 vols. Oxford Medieval Texts. Edited by Karsten Friis-Jensen. Translated by Peter Fisher. Oxford: Clarendon, 2015.

———. *Saxonis Grammatici Historia Danica. Recensuit et commentariis illustravit Petrus Erasmus Müller. Opus morte Mülleri interruptum absolvit Joannes Matthias Velschow*. 2 vols. Havniae [Copenhagen]: Gyldendal, 1839 (DB 125).

Schadewaldt, Wolfgang. "Richard Wagner und die Griechen." In *Hellas und Hesperien: Gesammelte Schriften zur Antike und zur neueren Literatur in zwei Bänden*, 341–405. Zurich: Artemis, 1970.

Schaefer, Georg Theodor. "Aischylos' Prometheus und Wagners Loge." In *Festschrift der 45. Versammlung deutscher Philologen und Schulmänner: dargeboten von der öffentlichen höheren Lehranstalten Bremens*, 1–94. Bremen: G. Winter, 1899.

Schaff, Philip, and David Schaff, ed. *The Creeds of Christendom. With a History and Critical Notes*. 3 vols. 1931,. Reprint. Grand Rapids: Baker, 1983.

Schelling, Friedrich Wilhelm Joseph von. *Briefe 1: Briefwechsel 1786–1799*. Edited by Irmgard Möller and Walter Schieche. Historisch-kritische Ausgabe III.1. Stuttgart: Frommann-Holzboog, 2001.

———. *Ideas for a Philosophy of Nature*. Texts in German Philosophy. Translated by Errol E. Harris and Peter Hearth, with an introduction by Robert Stern. Cambridge: Cambridge University Press, 1988.

———. *Philosophical Investigations into the Essence of Human Freedom*. Translated and with an introduction by Jeff Love and Johannes Schmidt. SUNY Series in Contemporary Continental Philosophy. Albany, NY: State University of New York Press, 2006.

———. *The Philosophy of Art*. Edited, translated and introduced by Douglas W. Scott. Foreword by David Simpson. Theory and History of Literature 58. Minneapolis: University of Minnesota Press, 1989.

———. *System of Transcendental Idealism (1800)*. Translated by Peter Heath with an introduction by Michael Vater. Charlottesville: University Press of Virginia, 1978.

Schiller, Friedrich. *Sämtliche Werke*. 12 vols. Stuttgart: J. G. Cotta, 1838 (DB 126).

Schiller, Friedrich, and Johann Wolfgang Goethe. *Briefwechsel zwischen Schiller und Goethe in den Jahren 1794–1805*. 6 vols. Stuttgart: J. G. Cotta, 1828–29 (DB 127).

Schiller, Friedrich, and Johann Wolfgang Goethe. *Briefwechsel zwischen Schiller und Goethe in den Jahren 1794–1805*. 2nd ed. 2 vols. Stuttgart: J. G. Cotta, 1856 (Wahnfried).

Schlegel, A. W. "Aus einer noch ungedruckten historischen Untersuchung über das Lied der Nibelungen." In Friedrich Schlegel, ed., *Deutsches Museum*, vol. 1, 9–36. Vienna: Gamesianische Buchhandlung, 1812–13.

———. *Kritische Schriften*, 2 vols. Berlin: G. Reimer, 1828 (Wahnfried).

———. *Kritische Schriften und Briefe*. Edited by Edgar Lohner. 7 vols. Stuttgart: W. Kohlhammer, 1962–74.

———. "De l'Origine des Hindous." In *Essais littéraires et historiques*, 439–518. Bonn: Eduard Weber, 1842.

———. *Vorlesungen über dramatische Kunst und Litteratur*, edited by Eduard Böcking. 3 vols. Leipzig: Weidmann, 1846 (Wahnfried).

———. *Vorlesungen über dramatische Kunst und Literatur*. Kritische Ausgabe. Eingeleitet und mit Anmerkungen von Giovanni Vittorio Amoretti. Vols. 1–2 in 1. Bonn/Leipzig: Kurt Schröder, 1923.

Schlegel, Friedrich. "Geschichte der alten und neuen Literatur." *KFSA* 1.6:5–420.

———. "Über die Sprache und Weisheit der Indier: Ein Beitrag zur Begründung der Alterthumskunde." *KFSA* 1.8:105–433 (Heidelberg: Mohr und Zimmer, 1808 (Wahnfried)).

———. "Über den Anfang unserer Geschichte und die letzte Revolution der Erde, als wahrscheinliche Wirkung eines Kometen. Von J.G. Rhode." *KFSA* 1.8:474–528 (*Jahrbücher der Literatur*, 8 (1819) 413–68).

———. "Vorlesungen über Universalgeschichte." *KFSA* 2.14:1–256.

Schneider, Hermann. "Richard Wagner und das germanische Altertum." In *Kleinere Schriften: Zur germanischen Heldensage und Literatur des Mittelalters*, edited by Kurt Herbert Halbach and Wolfgang Mohr, 107–24. Berlin: Walter de Gruyter, 1962 (= *Philosophie und Geschichte: Eine Sammlung von Vorträgen und Schriften aus dem Gebiet der Philosophie und Geschichte*, Heft 66. Tübingen: J. C. B. Mohr (Paul Siebeck), 1939).

Schoof, Wilhelm, ed. *Briefe der Brüder Grimm an Savigny*. Veröffentlichungen der historischen Kommission für Hessen und Waldeck XXIII.1. Berlin: Erich Schmidt, 1953.

Schopenhauer, Arthur. *On the Fourfold Root of the Principle of Sufficient Reason*. Translated by E.F.J. Payne. Introduction by Richard Taylor. La Salle IL: Open Court, 1974.

———. *Parerga und Paralipomena*. 2 vols. Berlin: Hayn, 1851 (Wahnfried).

———. *Die Welt als Wille und Vorstellung*. 1st ed. Leipzig: F. A. Brockhaus, 1819.

———. *Die Welt als Wille und Vorstellung*. 2 vols. 2nd ed. Leipzig: F. A. Brockhaus, 1844.

———. *Die Welt als Wille und Vorstellung*. 2 vols. 3rd ed. Leipzig: F. A. Brockhaus, 1859 (Wahnfried).

———. *World as Will and Representation*. 2 vols. 1958. Reprint. Translated by E. F. J. Payne. New York: Dover, 1966.

Schrage, Wolfgang. *Der erste Brief an die Korinther: 1. Teilband (1 Kor 1,1–6,11)*. EKK VII/1. Zurich: Neukirchener, 1991.

Schuler, John. *The Language of Richard Wagner's Ring des Nibelungen*. Lancaster, PA: Steinman & Foltz, 1909.

Schulze, Wilhelm A. "Zum Verständnis der Stuttgarter Privatvorlesungen Schellings." *Zeitschrift für philosophische Forschung* 11 (1957) 575–93.

Scott, Walter. *Waverley Novels*. 25 vols. Edinburgh: Black, 1871 (Wahnfried).

Scruton, Roger. *The Ring of Truth: The Wisdom of Wagner's Ring of the Nibelung*. Milton Keynes, UK: Allen Lane, 2016.

Seaford, Richard A. S. "Thespis" *OCD*[3] 1510.

Seidel, George J. *Fichte's Wissenschaftslehre of 1794: A Commentary on Part 1*. Purdue University Research Foundation. West Lafayette, IN: Purdue University Press, 1993.

Seidel, Siegfried, ed. *Briefwechsel zwischen Schiller und Goethe, Erster Band: Briefe der Jahre 1794–1797*. Munich: C. H. Beck, 1984.

Seydlitz, Reinhard von. "Erinnerungen an Richard Wagner." *Völkischer Beobachter* 44.350–355 (16, 17, 18, 19, 20/21 December 1931).

Shakespeare, William. *Shakespeare's dramatische Werke übersetzt von August Wilhelm von Schlegel und Ludwig Tieck*. 12 vols. Berlin: G. Reimer, 1851–52 ("DB 128").

———. *Shakespeare's dramatische Werke nach der Uebersetzung von August Wilhelm Schlegel und Ludwig Tieck*. Revised by H. Ulrici. 12 vols. Berlin: Georg Reimer, 1867–71 (Wahnfried).

———. *Quellen des Shakespeare in Novellen, Märchen, und Sagen*. Edited by Theodor Echtermeyer, Ludwig Henschel, and Karl Simrock. 3 vols. Berlin: Finkesche Buchhandlung, 1831 (DB 130).

Shklar, Judith N. *Freedom and Independence: A Study of the Political Ideas of Hegel's Phenomenology of Mind*. Cambridge: Cambridge University Press, 1976.

Silk, M. S., and J. P. Stern. *Nietzsche on Tragedy*. Cambridge: Cambridge University Press, 1981.

Simrock, Karl, ed. *Die Edda: die ältere und jüngere nebst den mythischen Erzählungen der Skalda*. Stuttgart: J. G. Cotta, 1851.

———, ed. *Das Amelungenlied*. 3 vols. Das Heldenbuch, vols 4–6. Stuttgart: J. G. Cotta, 1843–49 (DB 3).

———, ed. *Das kleine Heldenbuch*. Das Heldenbuch, vol 3. Stuttgart: J. G. Cotta, 1844 (DB 59).

———, ed. *Nibelungenlied*. 3rd ed. Das Heldenbuch, vol. 2. Stuttgart: J. G. Cotta, 1843 (DB 101).

———, ed. *Das Nibelungenlied, Mittelhochdeutsch und Neuhochdeutsch. Auf Grund der Übersetzung von Karl Simrock bearbeitet von Prof. Dr. Andreas Heusler*. Die Tempel – Klassiker. Wiesbaden: Vollmer, n.d.

Sisson, C. H., ed. *Dante Alighieri: The Divine Comedy*. Translated by C. H. Sisson. With an introduction and notes by David H. Higgins. Oxford World's Classics. Oxford: Oxford University Press, 1998.

Smith, Henry Preserved. *The Books of Samuel*. ICC. 1899. Reprint. Edinburgh: T. & T. Clark, 1969.

Smith, Joseph P. *St. Irenaeus: Proof of the Apostolic Preaching*. Ancient Christian Writers. The Works of the Fathers in Translation. Westminster, MD: Newman, 1952.

Smith, William, ed. *The Popular Works of Johann Gottlieb Fichte. Translated from the German*. 2 vols. London: John Chapman, 1848-49.

Snorre Sturluson's Weltkreis (Heimskringla) übersetzt und erläutet von Ferdinand Wachter. 2 vols. Leipzig: Breitkopf und Härtel, 1835-36 (DB 132).

Sommerstein, Alan, ed. *Aeschylus*. 2 vols. LCL 145-46. Cambridge: Harvard University Press, 2008.

Spinoza, Benedict de. *Ethics*. Edited and translated by Edwin Curley with an introduction by Stuart Hampshire. London: Penguin, 1996.

Spotts, Frederic. *Bayreuth: A History of the Wagner Festival*. New Haven: Yale University Press, 1994.

Spencer, Stewart, and Barry Millington. *Wagner's Ring of the Nibelung: A Companion*. London: Thames & Hudson, 2010.

Spencer, Stewart. "The 'Romantic operas' and the turn to myth." In *The Cambridge Companion to Wagner*, edited by Thomas S. Grey, 67-73. Cambridge: Cambridge University Press, 2008.

———. "'Or Strike at Me Now as I Strangle thy Knee': A note on the text and translation." In *Wagner's Ring of the Nibelung: A Companion*, edited by Stewart Spencer and Barry Millington, 11-13. London: Thames & Hudson, 2010.

———. "Engi má við sköpum vinna: Wagner's Use of his Icelandic Sources." In *Wagner's Ring and Its Icelandic sources: a symposium at the Reykjavík Arts Festival, 29 May 1994*, edited by Úlfar Bragason, 55-76. Reykjavík: Stofnun Sigurðar Nordals, 1995.

———. *Wagner Remembered*. London/New York: Faber and Faber, 2000.

Stadtwald, Kurt. *Roman Popes and German Patriots: Antipapalism in the Politics of the German Humanist Movement from Gregor Heimbarg to Martin Luther*. Geneva: Libraire Droz, 1996.

Stederoth, Dirk. "Wille." In *Hegel-Lexikon*, edited by Paul Cobben, Paul Cruysberghs, Peter Jonkers, and Lu De Vos, 494-96. Darmstadt: Wissenschaftliche Buchgesellschaft, 2006.

Stein, Heinrich von. "Ueber Werke und Wirkungen Rousseau's." *Bayreuther Blätter* 4 (Dezember Zwölftes Stück 1881) 345-56.

Steinacker, Peter. *Richard Wagner und die Religion*. Darmstadt: Wissenschaftliche Buchgesellschaft, 2008.

Steiner, George. *The Death of Tragedy*. London: Faber and Faber, 1961.

Stern, Robert. *Hegel and the Phenomenology of Spirit*. Routledge Philosophy Guidebook. London/New York: Routledge, 2002.

Stoeßl, F. "Stasimon," In *Der Kleine Pauly, Band 5*, edited by Konrat Ziegler, Walther Sontheimer, and Hans Gärtner, 342-43. Munich: Deutscher Taschenbuch, 1979.

Stone, Jon R., ed. *The Essential Max Müller: On Language, Mythology, and Religion*. New York: Palgrave Macmillan, 2002.

Strauß, David Friedrich. *Das Leben Jesu*. Tübingen: C. F. Osiander, 1835.

———. *Das Leben Jesu kritisch bearbeitet (mit einer Einleitung von Werner Zager)*. 2 vols. Darmstadt: Wissenschaftliche Buchgesellschaft, 2012.

———. *Das Leben Jesu für das deutsche Volk bearbeitet*. Leipzig: F. A. Brockhaus, 1864 (Wahnfried).

———. *The Life of Jesus Critically Examined*. Translated by George Eliot. London: SCM, 1973.

Strobel, Otto. *Richard Wagner: Skizzen und Entwürfe zur Ring-Dichtung: Mit der Dichtung "Der junge Siegfried."* Munich: F. Bruckmann, 1930.

———. "Zur Entstehungsgeschichte der Götterdämmerung: Unbekannt Dokumente aus Wagners Dichterwerkstatt." *Die Musik* 35 (1933) 336–41.

Studach, J.L., ed. *Sämund's Edda des Weisen oder die ältesten norräniaschen Lieder. Als reine Quellen über Glauben und Wissen des Germanogothischen vorchristlichen Norden*. Nuremberg: Johann Leonhard Schrag, 1829 (borrowed from Dresden Royal library).

Sturluson, Snorri. *Heimskringla: History of the Kings of Norway*. Translated with introduction and notes by Lee M. Hollander. 1964. Austin, TX: University of Texas Press, 1999.

Sturma, Dieter. "Politics and the New Mythology." In *The Cambridge Companion to German Idealism*, edited by Karl Ameriks, 314–35. 2nd ed. Cambridge: Cambridge University Press, 2017.

Swales, Martin. "Goethe's Prose Fiction." In *The Cambridge Companion to Goethe*, edited by Lesley Sharpe, 129–46. Cambridge: Cambridge University Press, 2002.

Tacitus. *Des Cajus Cornelius Tacitus sämmtliche Werke, übersetzt von Wilhelm Bötticher*. 4 vols. Berlin: Theod. Christ. Friedr. Enslin, 1831–34 (DB 137).

Tappert, Theodore G. *The Book of Concord: The Confessions of the Evangelical Lutheran Church*. Philadelphia: Fortress, 1959.

Taylor, Charles. *Hegel*. Cambridge: Cambridge University Press, 1975.

Taylor, Ronald. *Richard Wagner: His Life, Art, and Thought*. London: Elek, 1979.

Tuckett, Christopher M. "The Griesbach Hypothesis in the Nineteenth Century." In *New Testament Interpretation and Methods: A Sheffield Reader*, edited by Stanley E. Porter and Craig A. Evans, 15–43. Sheffield, UK: Sheffield Academic, 1997.

Uhland, Ludwig. *Gedichte*. Stuttgart: J. G. Cotta, 1842 (DB 145).

———. *Uhlands Schriften zur Geschichte der Dichtung und Sage*. Edited by W. L. Holland. 8 vols. Stuttgart: J. G. Cotta, 1865–73 (Wahnfried).

Vatke, Wilhelm. *Die Biblische Theologie wissenschaftlich dargestellt I: Die Religion des Alten Testaments nach den kanonichen Büchern entwickelt*. Berlin: Bethage, 1835.

Vischer, Friedrich. "Der alte und neue Glaube. Ein Bekenntnis von D. Fr. Strauß." In *Kritische Gänge: Band 2* (Neue Folge), 203–27. Tübingen: Ludwig Friedrich Fues, 1873.

———. "Vorschlag zu einer Oper." In *Kritische Gänge: Band 2*, 397–436. Tübingen: Ludwig Friedrich Fues, 1844.

Vollmer, A. J., ed. *Der Nibelunge Nôt und diu Klage*. Dichtungen des deutschen Mittelalters 1. Leipzig: G. J. Göschen'sche, 1843 (DB 99).

Voltaire, Francois M. *Oeuvres de Voltaire*. 7 vols. Paris: Bacquenois, 1836–38 (Wahnfried).

Voss, Egon, ed. *Richard Wagner: Klavierlieder*. SW 17. Mainz: Schott's Söhne, 1976.

———. *Richard Wagner: Eine Faust-Ouvertüre*. Meisterwerk der Musik, Werkmonographien zur Musikgeschichte 31. Munich: Fink, 1982.

Voss, Johann Heinrich, ed. *Homer: Ilias*. Stuttgart: J. G. Cotta, 1842 (DB: Minna).

———, ed. *Homers Odyssee*. Leipzig: Immanuel Müller, 1843 (DB 64).

———, ed. *Homers Werke. In Einem Bande*. Stuttgart: J. G. Cotta, 1840 (DB 65).

Wagner, Gottlob Heinrich Adolf. *Theater und Publikum: Eine Didaskalie*. Leipzig: Weygand, 1826.

———. *Zwei Epochen der modernen Poesie, dargestellt in Dante, Petrarca, Boccaccio, Goethe, Schiller and Wieland*. Leipzig: Breitkopf und Härtel, 1806.

Walker, Alan. *Franz Liszt*. 3 vols. London: Faber and Faber, 1983–1996.

———. *Hans von Bülow: A Life and Times*. Oxford: Oxford University Press, 2010.

Wallmann, Johannes. "Ludwig Feuerbach und die theologische Tradition." *ZThK* 67 (1970) 56–86.

Walton, Chris. *Richard Wagner's Zurich: The Muse of Place*. Studies in German Literature, Linguistics, and Culture. Rochester, NY: Camden House, 2007.

Warner, Emma. "The Artwork of the Future." *The Wagner Journal*, Special Issue (2013).

Way, A. S., ed. *Euripides I: Iphigeneia at Aulis, Rhesus, Hecuba, Daughters of Troy, Helen*. LCL 9. 1912. Reprint. Cambridge: Harvard University Press, 1988.

Weinhold, Karl. "Die Sagen von Loki." *Zeitschrift für deutsches Alterthum* 7 (1849) 1–94.

Weischedel, Wilhelm, ed. *Immanuel Kant. Werke in Zehn Bänden*. 1956–64. Reprint. Darmstadt: Wissenschaftliche Buchgesellschaft, 1983.

Weisse, Christian Hermann. *Die evangelische Geschichte kritisch und philosophisch bearbeitet*. 2 vols. Leipzig: Breitkopf und Härtel, 1838.

———. *System der Ästhetik*. Edited by Rudolf Seydel. Leipzig: J. G. Findel, 1872.

Welch, Claude. *Protestant Thought in the Nineteenth Century*. 2 vols. New Haven: Yale University Press, 1972–85.

Westernhagen, Curt von. *Die Entstehung des "Ring": Dargestellt an den Kompositionsskizzen Richard Wagners*. Zurich/Freiburg im Breisgau Atlantis, 1973.

———. *The Forging of the "Ring": Richard Wagner's Composition Sketches for Der Ring des Nibelungen*. Translated by Arnold and Mary Whittall. Cambridge: Cambridge University Press, 1976.

———. *Richard Wagners Dresdener Bibliothek 1842 bis 1849*. Wiesbaden: F. A. Brockhaus, 1966.

———. *Richard Wagner: Sein Werk, sein Wesen, seine Welt*. Zürich: Atlantis, 1956.

———. *Wagner: A Biography*. Translated by Mary Whittall. 2 vols. Cambridge: Cambridge University Press, 1978.

———. *Wagner*. 2nd ed. Zurich: Atlantis, 1979.

Westernhagen, Dörte von. "Und was haben Sie vor 1945 gemacht? Der Wagner-Forscher Curt von Westernhagen." In *Wagnerspectrum: Wagner und Liszt*, 83–99. Würzburg: Königshausen & Neumann, 2011.

Weston, Jessie L. *The Legends of the Wagner Dramas: Studies in Mythology and Romance*. London: David Nutt, 1896.

Whaley, Joachim. *Germany and the Holy Roman Empire, Volume 1: Maximilian I to the Peace of Westphalia, 1493–1648*. Oxford: Oxford University Press, 2012.

Wille, Eliza. *Erinnerungen an Richard Wagner. Mit 15 Briefen Richard Wagners*. Zurich: Atlantis, 1982.

Williams, Robert R. *Tragedy, Recognition, and the Death of God: Studies in Hegel and Nietzsche*. Oxford: Oxford University Press, 2012.

Williamson, George S. "Gods, Titans, and Monsters: Philhellenism, Race, and Religion in Early-Nineteenth-Century Mythology." In *The German Invention of Race*. Edited by Sara Eigen and Mark Larrimore, 147–65. Suny series, Philosophy and Race. Albany, NY: State University of New York Press, 2006.

Wilson, Pearl Cleveland. *Wagner's Dramas and Greek Tragedy*. New York: Columbia University Press, 1919.

Wimmer, Ludwig F. *Altnordische Grammatik*. Translated from the Danish by Eduard Sievers. Halle: Buchhandlung des Waisenhauses, 1871 (Wahnfried).

Windell, George G. "Hegel, Feuerbach, and Wagner's Ring." *Central European History* 9.1 (1976) 27–57.

Winiger, Josef. *Ludwig Feuerbach: Denker der Menschlichkeit*. Darmstadt: Wissenschaftliche Buchgesellschaft, 2011.

Weitling, Wilhelm. *The Poor Sinner's Gospel*. Translated by Dinah Livingston. London/Sydney: Sheed and Ward, 1969.

Wilberg, Petra-Hildegard. *Richard Wagners mythische Welt: Versuche wider den Historismus*. Rombach Wissenschaft, Reihe Musicae 1. Freiburg im Breisgau: Rombach, 1996.

Wilkinson, Elizabeth M, and L.A. Willoughby, ed. *Friedrich Schiller: On the Aesthetic Education of Man*. 1967. Reprint. Oxford: Clarendon, 1982

Wittenburg, A. "I Dori di K.O. Müller." *ASNSP* 14 (1984) 1031–44.

Wittke, Carl. *The Utopian Communist: A Biography of Wilhelm Weitling, Nineteenth-Century Reformer*. Baton Rouge: Louisiana State University Press, 1950.

Wolzogen, Hans von. *Führer durch die Musik zu Richard Wagner's Festspiel Der Ring des Nibelungen: Ein thematischer Leifaden*. Neue wohlfeile Ausgabe. Leipzig: Feodor Reinboth, n.d.

Wurm, Christian. *Die Nibelungen: Siegfrieds Tod. Eine romantische Tragodie in funf Akten*. Erlangen: Palm, 1839.

Young, Julian. *The Philosophies of Richard Wagner*. Lanham, MD: Lexington, 2014.

———. *Schopenhauer*. Routledge Philosophers. London: Routledge, 2005.

Yovel, Yirmiyahu. Nietzsche and the Jews: The Structure of an Ambivalence." In *Nietzsche and Jewish Culture*, edited by Jacob Golomb, 117–34. London: Routledge, 1997.

———. "'Nietzsche contra Wagner' und die Juden." In *Richard Wagner und die Juden*, edited by Dieter Borchmeyer, Ami Maayani, and Susamme Vill, 123–43. Stuttgart: J. B. Metzler, 2000.

Zachhuber, Johannes. "The Historical Turn." In *The Oxford Handbook of Nineteenth-Century Christian Thought*, edited by Joel Ramussen, Judith Wolfe, and Johannes Zachhuber, 53–71. Oxford: Oxford University Press, 2017.

Zu den Nibelungen und zur Klage. Anmerkungen von Karl Lachmann. Wörterbuch von Wilhelm Wackernagel. Berlin: G. Reimer, 1836 (DB 78).

Index of Authors

Abbate, Carolyn, 112
Adorno, Theodor, 38
Aeschylus, *see Index of Subjects and Names*
Afzelius, Arv. Aug., 60, 74
Allen, Roger, 9, 135, 149–50, 156, 162–63, 168, 171, 173, 193, 202, 220
Anderson, Bernhard W., 10
Andersson, Theodore M., 55
Apel, Friedmar, xiii
Apponyi, Albert, 45, 247–48
Aristo, Ludovico, 110, 131–32
Aristophanes, *see Index of Subjects and Names*
Aristotle, *see Index of Subjects and Names*
Arndt, Andreas, 194
Arnkiel, Trogillus, 61, 67, 97

Baader, Franz von, 181–82, 187, 198
Bakunin, Mikhail (Bakounine, Michel), 35, 141, 174, 176–77, 180, 184, 189, 204, 237, 254–55
Bailey, Robert, 37
Baillie, J.B., 209, 213
Balzac, Honoré de, 171–72
Barth, Herbert, xv
Barth, Karl, 10
Bartholin, Thomas, 74
Barton, John, xiv
Bauer, Hans-Joachim, xiv, 9
Bauer, Oswald Georg, 148
Bayer, Oswald, 217, 228, 235
Beach, Edward Allen, 181–82, 187–88, 190
Behler, Ernst, xiii
Beiser, Frederick C., 163, 175, 180, 187, 193–200, 202–3, 208, 213–15, 217
Bell, Richard H., 2–5, 8, 33, 53, 128, 143, 165, 179, 198, 216, 235, 248, 254, 256
Benders, Raymond J., 249
Benes, Tuska, 166
Bergfeld, Joachim, xi
Bermbach, Udo, 141

Berry, Mark, 249
Bielik-Robson, Agata 198
Bigler-Marshall, Ingrid, 265
Birkeflet, Svein Helge, 281
Björnsson, Árni, 46, 49, 58–59, 64, 78, 89–90, 96
Bloch, Ernst, 190
Blok, Josine H., 101
Blumenbach, Johann Friedrich, 19
Blumenberg, Hans, 123
Bockmühl, Klaus Erich, 227
Bodmer, Johann Jakob, 50
Böldl, Klaus, 48, 97
Böhme, Jakob, 174, 182, 198
Böttger, Adolf, 136
Borchmeyer, Dieter, xiv, 117, 125, 142, 145, 152, 171–72, 255–56
Bowden, John, xiii
Boyle, Nicholas 146, 159
Branscombe, Peter, xv, 92–93
Braschowanoff, Georg, 116
Breazeale, Daniel, 178, 193
Breig, Werner, xii, xv
Breitinger, J.J., 50
Brinkmann, Reinhold, 10
Brown, Colin, 253–54, 256
Brown, Hilda M., 109, 189, 256
Brown, Raymond E., 10
Brown, Robert, 182
Bubner, Rüdiger, 173
Bujić, Bojan, 192–93
Bultmann, Christoph, 4
Bultmann, Rudolf, 2
Bungay, Stephen, 120
Burian, Peter, 119, 122
Burmeister, Klaus, xiv
Büttner, Wolfgang, 237
Buttmann, Philip, 179
Byock, Jesse, 65–69, 78
Byron (George Gordon), 136

INDEX OF AUTHORS

Caird, George B., 76
Carnegy, Patrick, 45
Carr, E.H., 35, 176–77, 184, 204, 237, 255
Cartwright, David E., 239–40, 243
Casey, P.M., 260
Chadwick, Henry, 256–57
Chamberlain, Houston Stewart, *see also Index of Subjects and Names*, 167–68, 190, 219–20, 241–42
Clark, Robert T., 143
Cohen, G.A., 200, 207
Colli, Giorgio, xii–xiii
Collinwood, R.G., 203
Conway, David, 38
Cooke, Deryck, 1, 14, 49, 60–61, 76, 79
Cooper, Barry, 59
Corse, Sandra, 192, 213
Creuzer, Friedrich, 64, 101, 188
Curley, Edwin, 173, 193, 195

Dahlhaus, Carl, 96, 148
Dante Alighieri, *see also Index of Subjects and Names*, 108, 110, 131–34
Darcy, Warren, 10
Daub, Adrian, 237
Daverio, John, 163
Dawson-Bowling, Paul, 1
Day, James, 192
Deathridge, John, xv, 1, 10–11, 14–16, 38, 40, 43, 54, 61, 119, 127, 129–30, 154–55, 207, 212
De Boor, Helmut, 268
Descartes, René, 186
Devrient, Eduard, 11, 15, 17, 26, 31–32
Dinger, Hugo, 35–36, 254
Dischner, Gisela, 164
Döge, Klaus, 263
Donner, J.J.C., 103, 126
Dorion, Louis-André, 107
Drews, Arthur, 59, 116, 124
Dreyfus, Laurence, 29–30, 190, 232
Dronke, Ursula, 23, 69, 73–75, 98, 112, 230
Droysen, Johann Gustav, 86, 103, 105–6, 109, 115–120, 123–24, 203
Drüner, Ulrich, 44,
Dürrer, Martin, xiv–xv
Durrani, Osman, 155, 159, 160

Easterling, Patricia E., 118
Echtermeyer, Theodor, 136
Edwards, Cyril, xiii
Ehrismann, Otfrid, 50
Eichner, Barbara, 52
Eichner, Hans, 19, 164

Einarsson, Sigurbjör, 65
Eliot George (Mary Anne Evans), *see Index of Subjects and Names*
Ellis Davidson, H.R., 87, 98
Ellis, William Ashton, xi, xiv, 30, 33–34, 78, 96, 151, 202, 206, 233, 254, 259–60
Engels, Friedrich (Frederick), 35, 236–37
Ermatinger, Emil, 218
Espe, K.A., 281
Ettmüller, Ludwig, 4, 47–48, 64, 70, 73–75, 77, 90–92, 94, 247
Ewans, Michael, 105, 116, 122–24

Faulkes, Anthony, 22, 62, 66–69, 74, 79–80, 86, 99, 230
Fazio, Domenico M., 243
Feuerbach, Ludwig, *see Index of Subjects and Names*
Fichte, Immanuel Hermann, xii, 177
Fichte, Johann Gottlieb, *see Index of Subjects and Names*
Fifield, Christopher, 44
Finch, R.G., 78–84
Findlay, J.N., 192
Finglass, P.J., 121
Finlay, Alison, 86
Firchow, Peter, 164
Fischer, Jens Malte, 176
Fladt, Hartmut, xii, 263
Forner, Johannes, xiv
Forster, Michael N., 142
Foster, Daniel H., 57, 104–6, 109–11, 116, 192
Fouqué, Friedrich Baron de la Motte, 57–59, 90
Frantz, Gustav Adolph Constantin, 184–85
Frauer, Ludwig, 86
Fricke, Gerhard, xii
Fricke, Richard, 44–45
Friedrich, Sven, xvi, 20
Fuchs, Ernst, 235

Gans, Eduard, 203
Gardner, Sebastian, 248
Gawoll, Hans-Jürgen, 208
Gebhardt, Hans, xiv
Geck, Martin, xv, 212
Geibel, Emanuel, 179
Geraets, T.F., 194, 196, 208, 216
Gersdorf, E.G., 281
Gese, Hartmut, 3
Gfrörer, August Friedrich, 8
Giessel, Matthew, 254
Gillespie, George T., 51
Glasenapp, Carl Fr., 35–36, 101, 133, 151–52, 165, 168, 184, 190–91, 241–42

INDEX OF AUTHORS

Godley, A.D., 271
Göpfert, Herbert G., xii
Goethe, Johann Wolfgang, *see Index of Subjects and Names*
Goldhill, Simon, 118
Golther, Wolfgang, 49, 61, 77, 86, 88, 242, 248
Göttling, Karl Wilhelm, 20, 25, 51, 107
Graap, Paul-Gerhard, 255
Gräße, Johann Georg Theodor, 47
Graf, Hans Gerhard, 272
Gray, Andrew, xiii
Graziosi, Barbara, 111
Gregor-Dellin, Martin, xii–xiii, 26, 34, 36, 43–44, 77, 107, 164, 201
Grey, Thomas S., 155, 202
Griffiths, Mark, 124
Grimm, Jacob, *see also Index of Subjects and Names*, 15, 18, 22, 29, 34, 46, 48, 50, 59–63, 70, 82, 87, 92, 97, 115, 252, 255
Grimm, Wilhelm, 46, 48–49, 59–60, 63, 70, 78, 82, 89, 92, 255
Guyer, Paul, xiv, 19, 186, 196

Hagen, Friedrich Heinrich von der, *see also Index of Subjects and Names*, 46–50, 58, 62–64, 66, 69–70, 78–79, 85, 88–89, 91–92
Hall, Jonathan M., 104–5
Halliwell, Stephen, 117–18, 121–22
Hamann, Brigitte, 243
Harich, Wolfgang, 270
Harnack, Adolf von, 6
Harris, H.S., 81, 193–96, 198, 208, 210, 216
Hartenstein, Gustav, 176
Hartlich, Christian, 254
Hartwich, Wolf-Daniel, 146
Harvey, Van A., 224, 226, 229–31
Hauer, Stanley R., 64, 73, 90–91
Hausegger, Friedrich von., 242
Haymes, Edward R., 4, 28–31, 37–38, 52, 85, 90, 92, 125, 229
Hébert, Marcel, 242
Heer, Friedrich, 20
Hegel, G.W.F., *see Index of Subjects and Names*
Hegel, Karl (Charles), 203
Heintz, Albert, 240–42
Heinzle, Joachim, 50
Hengel, Martin. 259
Henrich, Dieter, 178
Henschel, Ludwig, 136
Herder, Johann Gottfried von, *see Index of Subjects and Names*
Hermann, Franz Rudolph, 57
Herodotus, *see Index of Subjects and Names*
Hesiod, *see Index of Subjects and Names*

Hett, W.S., 186
Hinsberg, J. von., 47
Hodgson, Peter C. 203
Hölderlin, Friedrich, 169–70, 175, 182, 193, 195, 198, 215
Hoffmann, E.T.A., *see Index of Subjects and Names*
Hoffmann, Franz, xii
Hoffmann, Werner, 53
Hoffmeister, Johannes, 203
Hogemann, Friedrich, 208
Hollander, Lee M., 86, 230
Holloway, Robin, 4
Honderich, Ted, xiv
Hornblower, Simon, xiv
Hornstein, Robert von, 235
Houlgate, Stephen, 120, 193, 196, 198, 200–201, 206–8, 214–15
Huber, Herbert, 95
Hübner, Hans, 238
Humberger, Julius, xii
Huray, Pete le, 192
Hyppolite, Jean, 199

Insole, Christopher J., 176
Inwood, Margaret, 138
Inwood, Michael J., 204, 223
Irrlitz, Gerd, 19
Istel, Edgar, 137

Jameson, Frederick, 263
Jesch, Judith, 60, 65, 80, 171
Jestremski, Marget, xiv
Jolley, Nicholas, 186
Jones, William, 19, 165
Jost, Christa, 263
Julian of Norwich, 251
Jüngel, Eberhard, 178–79, 209–11, 236

Kamenka, Eugene, 219, 222, 238
Kämper, Dietrich, 44
Kant, Immanuel, *see Index of Subjects and Names*
Kapp, Julius, 37
Kienzle, Ulrike, 34, 210
Kirkpatrick, Robin, 132
Kirsch, Winfried, 258
Kirschbaum, Engelbert, xiii
Klaproth, Julius, 165–66
Klindworth, Karl, 263
Knatz, Lothar, 187
Knaupp, Michael, xii
Knight, Douglas A., 3
Knox, T.M., 200, 208
Koch, Ernst, 40, 49

INDEX OF AUTHORS

Koch, Max, 242
Köhler, Joachim, 20, 24, 26, 191, 220, 239
Kohls, Ernst-Wilhelm, 162
Koßler, Matthias, 242
Kraft, Isabel, xvi
Kreckel, Manfred, 34
Krömmelbein, Thomas, 67
Kropfinger, Klaus, xvi
Kühnel, Jürgen, 245
Kümmel, Werner Georg, 252–53

Lachmann, Karl, 18, 46–48, 50, 62, 89–90, 136, 252–53, 255
Lamm, Julia A., 107
Larrington, Carolyn, 60, 67, 73–74, 92, 230
Lassen, Annette, 77
Laughland, John, 180–81, 187
Laurence, Dan H., 35
Lawing, Sean B., 65
Lee, Christina, 61, 63, 67
Legis, Gustav Thormod (Glückselig, Anton August), 48, 70, 92
Lehning, Arthur, 177, 254
Lessing, Gotthold Ephraim, see Index of Subjects and Names
Lewes, George H., 153, 243
Leibniz, Gottfried Wilhelm, see Index of Subjects and Names
Lehmann, H.T., xv
Leitzmann, Albert, 272
Lichtenberger, Henri, 220
Lindemann, Andreas, 6
Lionarons, Joyce Tally, 56
Loader, William, 6
Loebell, Johann Wilhelm, 21, 51–52
Lloyd-Jones, Hugh, 102, 111, 116–17, 119, 121–22, 125, 127
Löhneysen, Wolfgang Frhr. von, xi
Look, Brandon C., 19
Ludwig, Ernst, 143
Luke, David, 11, 100, 128, 154–63, 252
Luther, Martin, see Index of Subjects and Names

McCarney, Joseph, 203, 216–17
McConnell, Winder, 50, 57
McLaughlin, Paul, 254
McManus, Laurie, 14
McTaggert, John McTaggert Ellis, 216
Mack, Dietrich, xii, xv
Magee, Bryan, 35, 192, 246
Magee, Elizabeth, 20, 22, 46–51, 57–59, 62, 64, 70, 77–78, 86–90, 190
Magee, Glen Alexander, 198

Majer, Friedrich, 48, 67–68, 70
Maltzahn, Wendelin von, 255
Mann, Thomas, 130
Manser, Martin H., xiv
Matthews, Denis, 59
Matthews, Eric, 19, 186, 196
Mattes, Mark C., 212
Medicus, Fritz, xiii
Meiners, Christoph 18
Meredith, James, Creed, 198
Mertens, Völker, 90
Metzger, Bruce M., xiv, 252
Meyer, Gabriele E., xv
Michel, Karl Markus, 203
Mielke, Andreas, xiv–xv
Miller, A.V., 181, 192, 209, 212–13, 215–16
Millington, Barry, xiv–xv, 35, 43, 142, 150, 189, 243
Mohnike, G.C.F., 46, 49, 86
Moldenhauer, Eva, 203
Mone, Franz Joseph, 18, 46, 50, 62–64
Montgomery, Ingun, 65
Montinari, Mazzino, xii–xiii
Morini, Maurizio, 242
Müller, Christoph Heinrich, 50
Müller, Franz Carl Friedrich, 11, 46, 49, 63
Müller, Hieronymus, 110, 117
Müller, Johann Wilhelm, 57
Müller, Julius, 223
Müller, Karl (Carl) Otfried, 101, 104–5, 112
Müller, Max, 10
Müller, Ulrich, 46, 116, 118
Munz, Peter, 20
Murdoch, Brian, 52
Murphy, G. Ronald, 82

Nattiez, Jean-Jacques, 9, 36, 190
Newman, Ernst, 12, 36, 42, 77, 90, 220, 235, 263
Nicolin, Friedhelm, 211
Niecks, Frederick, 59
Nietzsche, Friedrich, see Index of Subjects and Names
Nisbet, H.B., 194, 197, 203
Nivala, Asko, 163
Novalis (Hardenberg, Georg Philipp Friedrich Freiherr von), 62, 131, 164, 175, 180, 198
Nussbaum, Martha C., 120

Oergel, Maike, 14, 50, 144, 168–69, 179
Oppermann, Annette, 263
Orchard, Andy, 55, 63, 69–70, 76–77, 80–83, 97–99, 230
O'Regan, Cyril, 213, 215

INDEX OF AUTHORS

Otto, Louise, 12–14
Otto, Werner, 192
Oxenford, John, 240, 243–44

Panagl, Oswald, 46
Panzer, Friedrich, 57
Payne, E.F.J., xiv, xv
Pecht, Friedrich, 192
Pelikan, J., xiii
Perschmann, Wolfgang, 201
Petersen, Julius, xv
Petsch, Robert, 116, 124
Pfizer, Gustav, 47
Philalethes (König Johann von Sachsen), 132
Pinkard, Terry, 169, 180–81, 195, 198
Pippin, Robert, 178
Plato, *see Index of Subjects and Names*
Porges, Heinrich, 11, 126
Pretzsch, Paul, 220

Quinn, Judy, 69, 72

Raffel, Burton, xvi, 50
Rask, Rasmus, 60, 91
Rasmussen, Joel D.S., 185
Raumer, Friedrich von, 15
Raupach, Ernst, 57
Rawidowicz, S., 220
Requadt, P., 62
Resen, Peder (Resenius), 73–74
Reuß, Roland, 62
Richardson, Alan, xii–xiii
Richter, Jean (Johann) Paul, 59, 144
Robertson, Ritchie, 146, 218
Rogerson, John, 21
Rosenkranz, Karl, 176
Rosner, Brian S., 6
Ross, G. MacDonald, 95, 187
Rousseau, Jean Jacques, 141–42, 152
Rückert, Friedrich, 90
Rühs, Friedrich, 48, 67–68, 91
Ruffell, Ian A., 125
Russell, Bertrand, 178
Rußwurm, C., 29

Sabor, Rudolph, 8, 79
Sachs, Walter, 254
Saine, Thomas P., 153
Salaquada, Jörg, xiv
Salis, Ludwig Rudolf von, 51
Salter, Lionel, xv
Sammons, Jeffrey L., 153
Sans, Edouard, 240–42, 245

Sansone, David, 119
Sass, H.M., 217, 223
Saxo Grammaticus, 65, 87
Schadewaldt, Wolfgang, 102, 108, 111, 116, 121, 124–25, 127
Schaefer, Georg Theodor, 124
Schaff, David S., 212
Schaff, Philip, xiv, 212
Schelling, Friedrich Wilhelm Joseph von, *see Index of Subjects and Names*
Schiller, Johann Christoph Friedrich von, *see Index of Subjects and Names*
Schimmelmann, Jacob, 67
Schlegel, A.W., *see Index of Subjects and Names*
Schlegel, Friedrich, *see Index of Subjects and Names*
Schleiermacher, Friedrich Daniel Ernst, 107, 163, 235
Schneider, Hermann, 62
Schoof, Wilhelm, 63
Schopenhauer, Arthur, *see Index of Subjects and Names*
Schrage, Wolfgang, 6
Schröter, Manfred, xv, 188
Schubert, Friedrich W., 176
Schuffenhauer, Werner, 222–24
Schuler, John, 93, 183
Schulze, Wilhelm A., 182
Scott, Walter, 110, 131, 171–72
Scruton, Roger, 190
Seaford, Richard A.S., 110
Seidel, Siegfried, 146, 178
Seydlitz, Reinhard von, 45
Shakespeare, William, *see Index of Subjects and Names*
Shaw, George Bernard, 35, 190
Shklar, Judith N., 192
Sibree, J., 203–5, 229
Simrock, Karl, 12, 37, 46–49, 66–70, 76–77, 87–89, 92, 97, 136
Singer, Otto, 263
Singer, Peter, 192
Sisson, C.H., 133–34
Smith, Henry Preserved, 82
Smith, Norman Kemp, 175–76
Smith, William, 179–80
Sommerstein, Alan, 121, 124–25
Spawforth, Antony, xiv
Spencer, Stewart, xi, xiv–xv, 18, 44–45, 90, 94, 102, 168, 243
Spinoza, Benedict de (Baruch), *see Index of Subjects and Names*
Spotts, Frederic, 116

INDEX OF AUTHORS

Stallybrass, James Steven, 60
Stein, Heinrich von, 141, 168
Steinsiek, Angela, xiv
Stederoth, Dirk, 204
Steiner, George, 119, 155
Stern, Robert, 190
Stoeßl, F., 117–18
Stone, Jon R., 19
Strauß (Strauss), David Friedrich, *see Index of Subjects and Names*
Streckfuß, Karl, 132
Strobel, Gertrud, xiv
Strobel, Otto, xiii, xiv, 28, 30–32, 38–39, 46, 69, 116, 230, 246–47
Studach, J.L., 48, 70, 91–92
Sturluson, Snorri, 66, 72, 85, 87, 98
Sturma, Dieter, 152
Suchting, W.A., 194, 196, 208, 216
Swales, Martin, 171

Tacitus, Cornelius, *see Index of Subjects and Names*
Tappert, T.G., 143, 182–83
Taylor, Charles, 143, 182–83
Taylor, Ronald, 44
Thieck, Ludwig, *see Index of Subjects and Names*
Thies, Erich, xiii
Tuckett, Christopher M., 259

Uhland, Ludwig, 95, 170–71
Ulrici, H., 136

Vazsonyi, Nicholas, xii
Vatke, Wilhelm, 4
Vetter, Isolde, xii
Vischer, Friedrich, 12–15, 182
Vollmer, A.J., 46–47
Voltaire, François-Marie Arouet de, 147
Voss, Egon, xii, xv, 154, 160, 263
Voss, Johann Heinrich, 101, 108

Wachter, Ferdinand, 46, 49, 86
Wackernagel, Wilhelm, 48, 136
Wagner, Adolf, *see Index of Subjects and Names*

Wagner, Cosima, *see Index of Subjects and Names*
Wagner, Richard, *see Index of Wagner's Works and Index of Subjects and Names*
Walker, Alan, 59, 133, 157, 242
Walker, Nicholas, 198
Wallmann, Johannes, 217–18, 223, 227
Walton, Chris, 92, 128, 218
Warner, Emma, 109, 112
Way, A.S., 126
Weinhold, Karl, 29, 178
Weischedel, Wilhelm, 175–76, 196, 198
Weisse, Christian Hermann, *see Index of Subjects and Names*
Welch, Claude, 142
Westernhagen, Curt von, 8, 14–15, 37, 43–44, 47, 59, 64, 86–87, 103, 106, 108, 126, 135–36, 144, 153, 190, 220, 239, 247
Westernhagen, Dörte von, 190, 220
Weston, Jessie L., 49, 64
Whaley, Joachim, 25
Whittall, Mary, xiii
Wille, Eliza, 90, 240–42, 246–47
Williams, Robert R., 197
Williamson, George S., 101
Wilson, Pearl Cleveland, 116
Wimmer, Ludwig F., 64
Windell, George G., 218–20, 229–30, 237
Winiger, Josef., 223, 237
Weitling, Wilhelm, 255
Wilberg, Petra-Hildegard, 16, 26
Wilkinson, Elizabeth M, 151–53
Willoughby, L.A., 151–53
Wittenburg, A., 104
Wittke, Carl, 255
Wolf, Werner, xvi, 153–54
Wolzogen, Hans von, xi, 5, 154, 212
Wood, Allen W., xii
Wurm, Christian, 57

Young, Julian, 190, 248
Young, Thomas, 165
Yovel, Yirmiyahu, 249

Zachhuber, Johannes, 185

Index of Biblical Texts

I Old Testament

Genesis

1:1—3:24	21

Leviticus

18:22	6
20:13	6

Deuteronomy

32:15–27	75
32:22	75
32:24b	75

Job

1:1—42:17	153, 155

1 Samuel

8:1–22	82
9:1–10:16	82
10:17–25	82

Psalms

49:1–20	3
73:1–28	3
82:6	226
88:1–18	3

Proverbs

1:1—31:31	153

Song of Solomon

1:1—8:14	153

Zechariah

3:1–5	161

II New Testament

Matthew

1:1—28:20	252, 257–59
5:2–14	258
5:12	216
5:29–30	217
6:7–27	258
6:25–26	217
9:18–19	258
9:23–26	258
15:2–6	258
15:11–13	258
19:21	217
19:28	138
21:43	260
22:15–22	34
23:1	260
23:16b–28	260
24:6–7	75
24:10	75
24:12	75
24:29	75

Mark

1:1—16:20	252, 257–59
2:27	259
5:21–34	258
5:35–43	258
12:13–17	34
14:32–42	207
14:36	259

Luke

1:1—24:53	252, 257–59
7:12	258
7:14	258
7:36	162
11:46–47	260
11:52	260
17:20–21	258
20:20–26	34
22:39–46	207

John

1:1—21:25	10, 127, 179–80, 208, 254, 256–60
1:1	21, 155, 159–60
1:11	137
4:1–42	162
7:39	210
8:40–41	260
8:42–52	260
12:4ff	259
12:27	259
13:1—17:26	259
13:21	259
18:1	207, 259
18:28	260
19:14	260
19:30	156, 210

Acts of the Apostles

1:1—28:31	257
1:1—4:37	258
9:3–19	238
17:22–31	127
17:23b–29	258
22:6–16	238
26:12–18	238
26:14	158

Romans

1:1—16:27	260
1:26–27	6
1:32	6
3:28	260
5:15–21	234
5:17–18	234
8:16–17	234
8:18	216
8:29	234
8:32	6
13:8–10	6

1 Corinthians

1:1—16:24	260
5:1—7:40	6
5:1—6:20	6
6:9	6
6:15–17	6
9:1	238
9:9	6
12:25–27	260
13:1	260
13:3	260
13:4–10	260
14:11	151
14:34–35	6
15:8	238

2 Corinthians

4:6	238
6:14	8

Galatians

1:15–16	238

Ephesians

6:2	6

Philippians

1:1—4:20	261

Colossians

1:1—4:18	261

INDEX OF BIBLICAL TEXTS

1 Timothy

2:4	216

Titus

3:5	138

Philemon

15–16	7

James

2:5–9	261
2:14–16	261
2:26	261
4:2	261
5:1–6	261
5:12	261

1 Peter

1:1—5:14	261
1:3	138
1:23	138

Jude

1–25	261

1 John

1:1—5:21	257
4:8	209

2 John

1–13	261

3 John

1–15	261

Jude

1–25	261

Revelation

1:1—22:21	257
6:2	75
6:4	75
6:12–14	75
12:3–17	76
12:9	76
12:10	161
13:2	76
13:3	76
13:4	76
13:11	76
16:13	76
18:1–24	255, 261
18:3	255
18:5–21	255
18:23–24	255
20:2	76, 98

Index of Wagner's Works

I Der Ring des Nibelungen

Ring des Nibelungen, Der, see also *Siegfried's Tod (1848); Rheingold; Walküre; Siegfried; Götterdämmerung*
    Angelo Neumann's Berlin production of, 167
    first Bayreuth (1876) performance of, 44
    libretto completed, 40
Nibelungen-Mythus, Der, 11, 17, 28–31, 38, 78, 249
Siegfried's Tod (1848), 4, 11, 14, 22, 28, 31–32, 76–78, 88, 261
    Brünnhilde enters Valhalla in, 229
    choir of vassals in, 14
    deus absconditus in, 228–29
    Devrient's suggested improvements for, 31–32
    influence of *Prometheus Bound* on, 125
    influence of Rousseau on, 142
    Nibelungenlied in, 53–57
    poetry of, 90–94
    redemption of Nibelungs in, 54
    Siegfried enters Valhalla in, 229
    Wagner's dissatisfaction with, 110
Rheingold, Das, see also Index of Subjects and Names (Alberich; Loge; Mime; Wotan)
    and *Geist,* 201
    and *Iliad,* 108, 123
    and Satyr play, 119
    as *Der Raub,* 124
    Eddic material in, 77
    Fafner in, 30
    Fasolt in, 30, 89
    first (Munich) performances (1869–70) of, 40, 43–44
    first Bayreuth performance (1876) of, 44
    Fricka in, 108, 123
    Loge in, 58
    Marxism in, 237
    Mime in, 58
    musical composition of, 37, 41, 202
    Prelude to, 1
    prose sketches for, 39–40
    "Rheingold" motif in, 4
    Stabreim in, 94–95
    Wotan in, 58, 108, 122–23
Walküre, Die, see also Index of Subjects and Names (Brünnhilde; Hunding; Sieglinde; Siegmund; Wotan)
    and *Iliad,* 108, 123
    and *Iphigeneia auf Aulis,* 126
    and Uhland, 170
    and *Völsunga Saga,* 78–79
    "annunciation of death" in, 7, 86
    death of Siegmund in, 4, 39
    Eddic material in, 77
    eroticism in, 29, 233
    first (Munich) performances (1870) of, 43–44
    "glorification of Brünnhilde" in, 212
    "incarnation" in, 209
    influence of *Prometheus Bound* on, 124
    law/love opposition in, 7
    musical composition of, 41, 239, 241
    prose sketches for, 39–40
    Sieglinde carrying sins in, 161
    Sieglinde's love for Siegmund in, 7, 39, 119–20
    Siegmund as "the other" in, 39
    Siegmund's love for Sieglinde in, 7, 39, 119–20
    Siegmund's rejection of immortality in, 7–8, 217, 227, 232
    Stabreim in, 5, 96
Siegfried/Der junge Siegfried, see also Index of Subjects and Names (Brünnhilde; Mime; Siegfried; Wanderer), 2, 4, 7, 10, 37–39, 110, 112, 124–25, 229–30
    and *Judaism in Music,* 38

Siegfried/Der junge Siegfried (continued)
   and Oedipus myth, 125
   and Simrock's *Edda*, 77
   and *Thidrek's Saga*, 85
   as Aryan work, 167
   break in musical composition of, 41–42
   completion of libretto of, 40
   Eddic material in, 76
   eroticism in, 29–30
   first performance delayed, 44
   Mime in, 38–39
   prose sketches for, 30, 38–39, 69
   renaming (1856) of, 11, 68
   Schopenhauer's influence on, 244–47
   score completed, 43
   Rousseau's influence on, 142
   Siegfried and Brünnhilde like "animals" in, 167
   Siegfried as "comic" in, 85
   Siegfried destroys Wotan's spear in, 7
   Siegfried's disdain for riches in, 56
   Wagner resumes musical composition of, 42–43
   Wanderer/Erda (Act III) in, 244–47
Götterdämmerung/Siegfried's Tod, see also *Siegfried's Tod (1848)*; Index of Subjects and Names (Brünnhilde; Gunther; Gutrune; Hagen; Siegfried; Wotan), 39–40, 110, 116, 119
   and *Ragnarök*, 230
   and *Völsunga saga*, 83–84
   blood-brotherhood in, 27, 89–90
   Brünnhilde as free in, 200, 207, 211
   Brünnhilde as love personified in, 213
   Brünnhilde as redeemer in, 210
   Brünnhilde's transfiguration in, 209–10
   choir of vassals in, 14
   death of Brünnhilde in, 2
   "death of God" in, 209
   death of gods in, 230
   death of Siegfried in, 2, 98, 117, 207
   devastation of nature in, 2
   Feuerbach ending of, 232–33
   "glorification of Brünnhilde" in, 212
   Hagen in, 56–57
   influence of *Prometheus Bound* on, 124
   musical sketches for (1850), 37–38
   musical composition of, 43
   Nibelungenlied in, 53–57
   Norns in, 32, 37, 54, 59, 111–12
   renaming of (1856), 4, 11, 68
   "Rheingold" motif in, 4
   Rhinemaidens in, 57, 138
   Rousseau's influence on, 142
   Schopenhauer ending of, 175, 247, 251
   sacrifice of Brünnhilde in, 98, 126, 207, 210
   sacrifice of Siegfried in, 126
   score completed, 43
   Siegfried's disdain for riches in, 56
   Siegfried's Funeral March in, 117–18
   song of Siegfried (Act III), 112
   Stabreim introduced into, 5, 92–93
   tragic character of, 119, 121, 126–27
   Wotan "put to rest" in, 209

II Other Musical and Stage works (including sketches)

Achilles, 32, 106–7
Alexander, 106
Faust-Ouvertüre, Eine, 8, 137, 154–55
Fliegende Holländer, Der, 111, 130, 243–44
   theological insight of, 258
Friedrich I, 11, 15–18, 26, 106, 240
   as Grand Opera, 16
   as spoken drama, 16
Iphigeneia auf Aulis (Gluck arrangement), 102, 126
Jesus von Nazareth
   as tragedy, 17
   Barabbas in, 33–34
   death of Jesus in, 210
   Holy Spirit in, 33, 210
   Jesus as redeemer in, 34, 261
   Jesus' sacrifice in, 261
   Judas in, 259
   Peter in, 33, 210
   Pharisees in, 33–34, 260
   Pilate in, 33, 260
   Trinitarian theology in, 24
Kompositionen zu Goethe's Faust, 154–55
Liebesmahl der Apostel, Das
   performance of, 258
Liebesverbot, Das, 137
Leubald und Adelaïde, 129, 134, 137
Lohengrin
   and incarnation, 119
   and *Nibelungenlied*, 54
   as tragedy, 126
   Christian character of, 258
   composition of, 11, 16, 63
   Elsa in, 54, 94, 119
   first performance under Liszt, 37, 156
   Gottfried in, 126
   grail in, 24, 27
   grail narration (Act III) in, 111
   libretto of, 4

Lohengrin in, 119
  music of, 148
  Ortrud in, 54
  redemption (not) in, 119
  relation to *Ring*, 27
  Telramund in, 119
  theological insight of, 258
Meistersinger von Nürnberg, Die, 41
  and enemies of German people, 109
  and Schopenhauer, 251
  Uhland's influence on, 170
Parsifal, 2, 236, 241, 251
  Amfortas in, 120
  and Gfrörer, 8
  and Oedipus myth, 125
  and Schopenhauer, 251
  Christian symbolism in, 3
  compassion (*Mitleid*) in, ix
  death of Jesus in, 180, 216
  grail in, 327
  Kundry (as Sphinx) in, 125
  relationship to *Ring*, 27
  Titurel in, 24, 137
Rienzi, der Letzte der Tribunen, 17
Schäferoper, 153
Tannhäuser und der Sängerkrieg auf Wartburg
  Rome narration (Act III) in, 111
  theological insight of, 258
Tribschen (Siegfried) Idyll, 137
Tristan und Isolde, see also Index of Names and Subjects (Tristan; Isolde), 42, 103, 120, 137, 167, 251
  and F. Schlegel's *Lucinde*, 164
  and Schopenhauer, 251
  and yearning, 164
  as "half caste affair", 167
  as tragedy, 126
  Berlioz' influence on, 137
  king Marke in, 120, 126
  musical composition of, 42
  Nietzsche on, 251
  transfiguration in, 126
Wieland der Schmied, 36–37

III Writings

Annals, 9, 15–17, 32, 63, 106–7, 203, 206, 239–40, 242, 244, 253
Art and Climate, 221, 234
Art and Revolution, 36, 116, 127, 219
  and Feuerbach, 219–20, 233–34
  and the Greeks, 100, 109, 145
  Jesus and Apollo in, 127
  on Greek tragedy, 116
Artwork of the Future
  and Feuerbach, 219, 232–33, 235
  and Greeks, 109, 112, 117, 145
  and Schelling, 189
  on dance, tone, and poetry, 117
  on fall, 188
  on Greek tragedy, 116
  on purely human artwork (*das rein menschliche Kunstwerk*), 112
  on *Stabreim*, 4, 93
  Wieland der Schmied in, 36–37
Autobiographical Sketch, 34, 134, 183
Beethoven, see also Index of Subjects and Names, 162, 171, 173, 193, 201
  and Goethe's *Faust*, 162–63, 171
  and Hegel, 201–2
  and Schiller, 149
  and Shakespeare, 135
Beethoven's Choral Symphony at Dresden, 1846, 155
Brown Book, 16–18, 32, 63, 106–7, 115, 137, 171–72, 192, 203–4, 239, 253
Communication to my Friends, A, 36
  and *Nibelungenlied*, 54
  and *Wieland der Schmied*, 36
  on end-rhyme, 93–94
  on *Friedrich I (Barbarossa)*, 11, 15–17
  on *Lohengrin*, 119
  on "Siegfried", 11, 16–17
  on *Stabreim*, 93–94
  on Wagner as poet, 130
  origins of *Ring* in, 11, 16–17
Destiny of Opera, The (Über die Bestimmung der Oper), 127–28
Epilogue to the "Nibelung's Ring", 77, 202
Fatherland Society (Vaterlandsverein) Speech, 34–35, 152
Foreword to the 1850 planned publication of the poem Siegfried's Death, 94
Freischütz, Der, 176
German Art and German Policy, 136, 145, 162, 172
Happy Evening, A, 245
Heroism and Christianity
  on Aryans, 166–67
  on race, 167–68
How Do Republican Endeavours Stand in Relation to the Monarchy? 35
Judaism in Music, 36, 38, 176
  and *Siegfried/Der junge Siegfried*, 38
  Mendelssohn in, 38

Letter to Heinrich von Stein, 135
My Life, 15–17, 31–33, 35–36, 38, 59–60, 64, 77–78, 87, 101–4, 107–8, 126–27, 120–30, 133–35, 141, 144–45, 153–54, 157, 183–84, 191–92, 194, 204, 218–19, 235, 239–40, 244, 259
Music of the Future, 145
On Poetry and Composition, 108–9, 111, 131
On the Name Musikdrama, 160, 201
Open Letter to Friedrich Nietzsche, 102
Opera and Drama, 36
    and Feuerbach, 219, 234
    Antigone in, 120, 125,
    Creon in, 120
    Jocasta in, 125
    Oedipus in, 125
    on Aristotle, 107
    on Beethoven/Schiller, 149,
    on Christian myth, 127, 254
    on dance-gesture (*Tanzgebärde*), 140
    on dance, tone, and poetry, 6
    on dogma, 134
    on drama, 57
    on end-rhyme, 97
    on epic, 57, 109
    on eternal womanly, 162
    on feeling (*Gefühl*), 138
    on Goethe, 137
    on Greek tragedy, 116, 118, 127
    on historical romance, 171
    on Lessing, 256
    on love and state, 125
    on lyric, 113, 115
    on music, drama, and dance, 6
    on orchestra as chorus, 118
    on orchestra as dance-gesture (*Tanzgebärde*), 140
    on reason (*Vernunft*), 138
    on Shakespeare, 141
    on song, 143
    on *Stabreim*, 93, 130
    on total work of art (*Gesamtkunstwerk*), 5
    on understanding (*Verstand*), 138
Pilgrimage to Beethoven, 148
Poetry and Composition, 108–9, 111, 131
Prologue to a Reading of Götterdämmerung, 118, 145
Public and Popularity, 137, 146
Public in Time and Space, 133
Religion and Art, vii
    and Jesus' non-Jewish descent, 180
    Dante's *Comedia* in, 134
    denial of will in, 248
    Eucharist/Communion in, 128
    Indo-German hypothesis in, 19
    mythic allegories in, 189
    Schiller in, 150
Rendering of Beethoven's Ninth Symphony, The, 148
Revolution, 36
Rote Brieftasche, Die, 153
Shall we hope? 134, 150–51
Toast on the Tercentenary of the Royal Kapelle at Dresden, 205–6
What is German? 137
What Use Is This Knowledge? 159, 176
Wibelungen, Die
    Christ in, 18, 23, 26
    dragon in, 22
    Friedrich Barbarossa in, 18, 20, 25–27
    grail in, 24–25, 27
    hoard in, 25
    myth and history in, 18, 21
    Lohengrin in, 24
    Siegfried in, 16, 18–19, 21–23, 26, 105

Index of Subjects and Names

absolute, the
    as substance, 195
    freedom of, 181
    Hegel on, 194–95, 197, 199, 214, 222
    Schelling on, 181, 185, 194–95, 199
    Wagner on, 194, 201, 204
absolute Spirit
    Brünnhilde personified as, 213
    Golgotha of, 213
    inwardizing of, 213
Achilles, 103, 106–7, 126
Adam (Genesis 1–3), 19, 67, 76, 212
Aeschylus
    Oresteia, 103, 105, 111, 116–17, 119, 121, 123, 138
    Agamemnon, 103, 111, 121, 123–24
    Libation-Bearers (Choephoroi), 103, 123
    Eumenides, 103, 127
    Prometheus Bound, 124–25
    Suppliants, 103
    as "indispensable", 103
Æsir, 22, 65–68, 86
Alberich (*Ring*), 28–30, 56, 95, 123, 245, 249
Albrich (*Nibelungenlied*), 54, 56
Alexander the Great, 105–6, 203
allegory, 4, 21, 45, 101, 163, 189
Alphart (Simrock), 89
Alpharts Tod (von der Hagen), 89
Alvíssmál, 71, 76
Amelungenlied, 49, 87–88
Amfortas (Wagner's *Parsifal*), 120
Anaxagoras, 197
androgyny
    and Wagner, 36, 164, 182, 188
    von Baader on, 182
    Schelling on, 188
    F. Schlegel on, 164
Andvari, 56, 81
Antigone, 120, 125

animals, *see also dragon; midgard serpent; serpent; Sleipnir; Wurm*, 75, 86, 108, 141, 167, 186, 204, 23
anti-Judaism
    definition of, 7
    in New Testament, 260
    of Schiller, 144, 146
    of Wagner, 7
antisemitism
    definition of, 7
    in Gospels, 260
    in *Siegfried*, 38
    Nietzsche on, 249–50
    of Fichte, 179–80
    of Schiller, 144, 146
    of Wagner, 38, 180, 249–50
Apollo, 21, 109, 127
    and Dorians, 104–5
    as Sun-god, 26, 105, 144
appearances (*Erscheinungen*), *see phenomenal world*
Ariosto, Ludovico, 110, 131–32
Aristophanes, 110
    the clouds, 117
Aristotle, 108, 116, 173, 191, 217
    Poetics, 107, 117, 121–22, 173
    on organic worldview, 107, 186, 196–97, 202
    on tragedy, 121–22, 173
Arnim, Achim von, 62
Arnkiel, Trogillus, 61, 67, 97
art, *see also "dance", tone, and poetry; Gesamtkunstwerk; music; Index of Wagner's Works (Art and Climate; Art and Revolution; Artwork of the Future; German Art and German Policy, Opera and Drama; Religion and Art)*
    and philosophy, 153, 193
    and religion, 153, 193
Artemis, 126

305

INDEX OF SUBJECTS AND NAMES

Asher, David, 143
atheism
    and Feuerbach, 221–22
    and Fichte, 178
    and Wagner, 221
Atlakvida, 72
Atlamál in grœnlenzku, 72
Attila the Hun, *see also Etzel*, 51, 79, 85
Augustine of Hippo, 215, 244

Baader, Franz von, 181–82, 187, 198
Bach, Johann Sebastian, 137
Bakunin, Mikhail, 35, 141, 174, 176–77, 180, 184, 189, 204, 237, 254–55
Baldr, 74, 87
    death of, 73, 76, 98
    sacrifice of, 98
Baldrs draumar (Baldr's dreams; Vegtamskvida), 72, 76
Balzac, Honoré de, 171–72
baptism
    in *Jesus of Nazareth*, 33, 210
    Luther on, 212
    of Jesus, 33
    of Wagner, 239, 257
Baumgartner, Wilhelm, 218
Bayreuther Blätter, xi, 5, 141, 148, 150–51, 159
Bayreuth Festival Theatre, *see Festspielhaus*
Beck, C.D., 191
Becker, Johann August, 243
Beethoven, Ludwig van, *see also Index to Wagner's Works (Beethoven, etc)*, 59, 148, 191, 256
    Coriolanus Overture, 154
    Symphony no. 9, 13, 35, 148, 154–55
    and creator God, 150
    and Schiller, 148–50, 156
    as counterpart to Shakespeare, 135
Berlioz, Hector, 37, 154
    Grande symphonie funèbre et triomphale, 154
    Harold en Italie, 154
    Roméo et Juliette, 137, 154
    Symphonie fantastique, 154
    Wagner's debt to, 8, 244
Berthold, Wilhelm, 36
Betz, Franz, 44
Bloch, Ernst, 190, 212
blood, 119
    and communion, 199–200, 215
    and family ties, 27, 120, 234
    and hoard, 26
    of Christ, 120
    of Fafner/Fafnir, 27, 52, 56, 81
    of Hagen, 27
    of Siegfried, 27
blood-brotherhood, 27, 89–90
Blumenbach, Johann Friedrich, 19
Böhme, Jakob, 174, 182, 198
Brahmanism, 167
Brahms, Johannes, 43
Brandt, Carl, 44
Brandt, Fritz, 45
Brockhaus, F.A. (publisher), 156, 239, 242
Brockhaus, Friedrich Arnold, 239
Brockhaus, Friedrich, 239
Brockhaus, Heinrich, 135–36, 150, 239
Brockhaus, Hermann, 239, 248
Brockhaus, Luise, 153, 239
Brockhaus, Ottilie, 239, 248
Brot af Sigurdarkvidu, 55, 69–71
Bruckner, Anton, 44
Brünnhilde (*Ring*)
    as absolute spirit personified, 213
    as Athene, 123
    as "divine virgin", 31
    as love personified, 213
    as redeemer, 4, 210
    glorification of, 212
    incarnation of, 209, 228–29
    "redemption of", 251
    sacrifice of, 6, 98, 126, 207, 210
    transfiguration of, 209–10
Brunichild, 21, 51–52
Brynhild (Norse mythology), 3, 55, 70–71, 82–84, 98–99
Bülow, Cosima von, *see Wagner, Cosima*
Bülow, Hans von, 44, 239, 242
Bürger, Gottfried August, 90

Calderón de la Barca, Pedro, 131, 168, 240
Calvin, John
    on accommodation, 21
    on sin, 244
capitalism, 2, 35, 237, 261
Catholicism, 85, 165, 228
cause (causation)
    efficient, 194
    final, 194, 196
    formal, 196
    formal-final, 196–97, 202
Cervantes, Miguel de, 110, 131
Chamberlain, Houston Stewart, 190, 241–42
    on Feuerbach, 219–20
    on race, 167–68
Chilperich, 51–52
chorus (Greek tragedy), 111, 121, 124–25, 172
    as orchestra, 115, 117–18, 145
    stasimon, 117–18

INDEX OF SUBJECTS AND NAMES

Chrétien de Troyes
    Jacob Grimm's criticism of, 61
Christianity, *see also Catholicism; Protestantism*
    Bakunin on, 254
    conversion to, 61–62, 64–65, 70, 97
    degeneration (*Ausartung*) of, 179
    Feuerbach on, 217, 221–34
    Fichte on, 179–80
    Hegel on, 199–200, 207–8, 215
    Nietzsche on, 249–50
    Schelling on, 185
    F. Schlegel on, 165
    Schiller on, 146
    supercedes Judaism, 146–47
Church
    dogma of, 134, 159
    in Germany, 4
    in Iceland, 65
    in *Nibelungenlied*, 54
    moral debates in, 6–8
    music in, 4, 97
    of England, 7–8
Church, Roman Catholic, *see Catholicism*
civilization, 134, 149–50, 172
Communion, Holy
    Luther on, 128
    Zwingli on, 128
compassion (*Mitleid*)
    in Wagner's *Parsifal*, ix
Cornelius, Peter, 42, 244
creation
    of artworks, 1, 3, 135, 247
    of world, 5, 67, 73, 76, 213
    realm of, 7, 21
creator God
    and conflict with science, 147
    Fichte on, 180
    Schiller on, 150
    Wagner on, 147, 150
cross of Christ, 62, 97–98, 211, 216, 249

"dance", tone, and poetry, *see also Wagner, on dance*, 6, 8, 117, 189
Dante Alighieri, 108, 110, 131, 170
    Divine Comedy, 132–34
    La vita nuova, 132
Daub, Karl, 217
death
    and egoism, 230, 232
    and immortality, x, 4–5, 218, 221, 230, 232, 261
    and love, 2
    life after, 3
    of Agamemnon, 123
    of Baldr, 73, 76, 98
    of Brünnhilde, 2, 54, 210, 212
    of Brynhild, 84
    of Christ, 23, 33, 98, 180, 206, 210–11, 215–16, 234, 236, 254, 259–60
    of Fáfnir, 76, 81
    of Faust, 154
    of God, 191, 207, 209, 211, 236, 254
    of gods, 2, 69, 73, 230,
    of Siegfried, 2, 22–23, 98, 117, 207
    of Siegmund, 4, 8, 39, 86, 120
    of Sigurd, 85
    of Sinfjotli, 80
    of Sivrit, 51–53
degeneration, 19, 165, 179
Descartes, René, 186
deus absconditus (hidden God), 225, 228–29
deus revelatus (revealed God), 228
Devrient, Eduard, 11, 15, 17, 26, 31–32
Dietrich von Bern, 49, 85, 89
Dinter, Artur, 180
Dionysus, 170, 188, 215
dogma, *see Church, dogma of*
Donar (Norse mythology), 61–62
Dorguth, Friedrich Ludwig Andreas, 243
Dorians, 104–5, 112
Dorn, Heinrich Ludwig Egmont (*Die Nibelungen*), 58
Doß, Adam Ludwig von, 243
dragon, 26, 30
    heir of, 22
    killed by Siegfried, 21–22, 31, 58
    killed by Sigurd, 81–82
    killed by Sivrit, 52, 56
    of book of *Revelation*, 76
Dráp Niflunga, 69, 72
Dresden
    Frauenkirche, 258
    Kreuzkirche, 36, 107
    Kreuzschule, 101, 184
    library of Wagner in, 8, 12, 15, 21–22, 29, 37, 46–49, 51, 59, 63, 85–87, 89, 91, 101–8, 110, 132, 135–36, 141–42, 144, 153, 164, 170, 177, 184, 192, 220, 252, 255–56
    Royal library, 4, 47, 58, 70, 78, 85, 91
    uprising in, 35–36
Duparc, Henri, 43

Ecken Ausfahrt (von der Hagen), 89
Eckhart, Meister, 198
Edda, *see Elder Edda, Prose Edda*
Egils Saga
    King Eiríkr Blood-Axe in, 89
    Queen Gunnhildr in, 89

307

INDEX OF SUBJECTS AND NAMES

Eiser, Otto, 244
Elder Edda, *see also Völuspá; Hávamál; Vafthrúdnismál; Grímnismál; För Skírnis; Hárbardsljöd; Hymiskvida; Lokasenna; Thrymskvida; Völundarkvida; Alvíssmál; Helgakvida Hundingsbana in fyrri; Helgakvida Hjörvardssonar; Helgakvida Hundingsbana önnur; Frá dauda Sinfjötla; Grípisspá; Reginsmál; Fáfnismál; Sigrdrífumál; Brot af Sigurdarkvidu; Gudrúnarkvida in fyrsta; Sigurdarkvida in skamma; Helreid Brynhildar; Dráp Niflunga; Gudrúnarkvida in forna; Gudrúnarkvida in thridja; Oddrúnargrátr; Atlakvida; Atlamál in grænlenzku; Gudrúnarhvöt; Hamdismál; Rígsthula; Baldrs draumar; Hyndluljód; Grottasöngr*
    date of, 69
    Wagner's editions of, 48, 70–72
Eliot, George (Mary Anne Evans), 153
    and *Westminster Review*, 243
    translator of Feuerbach, 223
Elliot, T.S., 190
Ellis, William Ashton, xiii, xvi, 30, 33–34, 78, 96, 151, 202, 206, 233, 254, 259–60
Elsa (*Lohengrin*), 54, 94
    as Semele, 119
    needing redemption, 119
emotionalizing of the intellect (*Gefühlswerdung des Verstandes*), 192
Engels, Friedrich (Frederick), 35, 236–37
epic, *see Greek epic; Nibelungenlied; Virgil*
Erda, 29–30, 123–24, 209, 247
erotic love, *see also love, erotic; Schopenhauer, on erotic love; Wagner, on erotic love*, 29–30, 232–33
    redemption from, 248
    redemption through, 127, 248
Eschenbach, Wolfram von, 53, 252,
eternal womanly/feminine (*das ewig Weibliche*), 162–63
    love as, 210
    music as, 163
    Virgin Mary as, 134, 162
ethics
    categorial imperative, 176, 238
    Fichte on, 199
    Hegel on, 199
    Kant on, 176, 238
    Paul on, 6
    Schopenhauer on, 176, 238
    sexual, viii, 2, 5, 261
    situation, 7
    Wagner on, 6–7

Etzel (*Nibelungenlied*), 51, 53, 85, 88
Etzels Hofhaltung (von der Hagen), 89
Eucharist, *see Communion, Holy*
Eugel, 38, 58
Euripides, 102–3, 110, 123, 126
    Alcestis, 102
    Bacchae, 103
    Iphigeneia at Aulis, 103, 110–11, 126
    Phoenisseae, 103
evolution of natural order, 2, 115
existential displacement/change, 235
Eyvindr skáldaspillir, 86

Fafner (*Ring*), 27, 30, 58
Fafnir (Norse mythology), 52, 76, 80–81, 83
Fáfnismál, 71, 76, 81
faith, Christian
    and reason, 175–76, 179, 208
    and self-love, 226–27
    Feuerbach on, 226–27, 231
    Fichte on, 179
    Hegel on, 208
    justification by, 6
    Kant on, 176, 179
    Luther on, 226
faith, "heathen", 61
fall
    and *O felix culpa*, 181–82
    von Baader on, 181–82, 187
    of Alberich, 30
    of humankind, 2, 58, 76, 142, 165, 181
    of state, 120
    Schelling on, 181–82, 187–89
Fasolt (*Rheingold*), 30, 89
Faust (Goethe's *Faust*),
    death of, 154
    translates John 1:1, 41, 159
feeling (*Gefühl*), 113–14, 139–40, 149, 152
Festspiel (Bayreuth 1876), 44–45, 249–50
Festspielhaus (Bayreuth)
    double proscenium of, 118
    "mystic abyss" of, 118
    ideas for, 40–41
Feuerbach, Ludwig
    Essence of Christianity, 217–19, 221–24, 226–30, 233
    Essence of Faith according to Luther, 218, 224–27
    Essence of Religion, 218, 230, 235
    Principles of the Philosophy of the Future, 218–19, 223, 227–28, 231
    Thoughts on Death and Immortality, 218, 221, 230, 232
    and *Art and Revolution*, 219–20, 233–34

INDEX OF SUBJECTS AND NAMES

and *Artwork of the Future*, 219, 232–33, 235
and death of God, 236
and Luther, 217–18, 223–29, 231, 235–36
and *Ring*, 227–38
atheism of, 222
influence on *Jesus of Nazareth*, 220–21, 226–27, 231
on Christianity as absolute religion, 223, 229
on humanization of God, 223–24, 227–28, 238
on immortality, 218, 230, 232
on species, 185, 233–34
on Trinity, 222, 231
Ring's Feuerbach ending, 232–33
Wagner's rejection of, 235–36
Fichte, Johann Gottlieb, 59, 175–76, 180–81, 184, 191, 226, 238
  Critique of all Revelation, 193, 207
  Guide to a Blessed Life, 177, 180
  Wissenschaftslehre, 177–78, 180
  admirer of John's Gospel, 179–80
  and freedom, 176, 193–94
  antisemitism of, 179–80
  as subjective idealist, 178
  attacked by Schopenhauer, 177
  criticised by Wagner, 177
  influence on Adolf Wagner, 177
  influence on Bakunin, 177
  influence on Richard Wagner, 174, 177
  misrepresentation of, 177–78
  on Christianity, 179–80
  on freedom, 193
  on God, 178–80, 207,
  on morality, 199
  on myth, 179
  on noumenal/phenomenal distinction, 238
  on self-consciousness, 178, 193
  on subjectivity, 178
  original insight of, 178
Fischer, Wilhelm, 78
Flatt, J.F., 210
Flatt, Karl Christian, 210
fornyrdislag, 91–92
För Skírnis, 71
Frá dauda Sinfjötla, 69, 71
Frantz, Gustav Adolph Constantin, 184–85
Frauenkirche (Dresden), 258
Frauenstädt, Julius, 243
Fredegunda, 52
Frederick I (*Friedrich Barbarossa (Rotbart)*), 11, 15–18, 20, 25–27, 106, 171
freedom, 109
  and fate, 2
  and necessity, viii, 5, 183, 185

Fichte on, 193
from law, 34, 260
Hegel on, 193–94, 200, 207, 211, 215
Jesus on, 254
Kant on, 175–76
of Brünnhilde, 200, 207, 211
Paul on, 260
Schelling on, 181–83, 185, 187–88
Schiller on, 152, 183
Wagner on, 185, 194, 207, 254, 260
Freia/Holda (*Ring*), 29, 31, 123
Freyja, 65, 73
  identified as "Third", 67
Freyr, 65
Fricka/Frikka (*Ring*), 7, 39, 87, 108, 121, 123
Fricke, Richard, 44–45
Frigg (Norse mythology), 65, 76, 87

Gade, Niels, 13
Gautier (-Mendès), Judith, 43–44
Gefühl, see feeling
Genelli, Bonaventura, 108
Gernot (*Nibelungenlied*), 51–52
Gesamtkunstwerk, 6, 117, 163, 189
Geyer, Ludwig (step-father), 129
Gibica, 51
Gibich (*Nibelungenlied*; *Götterdämmerung/Siegfried's Tod*), 51
Gibichungs (*Nibelungen-Mythus*; *Götterdämmerung/Siegfried's Tod*), 29, 142
Giselher (*Nibelungenlied*), 51–52
Gísla Saga, 89–90
Gluck, Christoph Willibald,
  Alceste, 14
  Iphigénie en Aulide, 14, 102, 106, 126, 128
Gobineau, Joseph-Arthur de, 167–68
God, *see also creator God; deus absconditus; deus revelatus; Jesus Christ*
  abstract views of, 194
  as creator, 147, 150, 180
  as Father, 24
  as Holy Spirit, 24
  as love, 209, 226, 228–29
  as Son, 24
  death of, 191, 207, 209–13, 236
  Feuerbach on, 222–24, 227–28, 231, 238
  Fichte on, 178–80, 207
  Goethe on, 159
  Hegel on, 194, 197, 206–7, 209–16, 236
  humanity of, 223, 225
  Jewish view of, 147
  kingdom of, 165, 2216, 258
  providence of, 179, 191, 206–7, 216

God *(continued)*
    Schiller on, 150
    self-knowledge of, 214
    self-knowledge in, 214
    suffering of, 133, 211
    Wagner's conception of, 147–48, 150, 159, 224
gods
    death of, 2, 69, 73, 230
    end of, 31, 245–47
    guilt of, 31
    ruling of, 31
Göring, Hermann, 53
Goethe, Johann Wolfgang, *see also Goethe, Faust I; Goethe Faust II*, 10, 134, 146, 152, 168, 235, 256
    Dichtung und Wahrheit, 153
    Götz von Berlechingen, 134, 137
    Iphigenie auf Tauris, 14, 145
    Laune des Verliebten, Die, 153
    Torquato Tasso, 156
    Wilhelm Meisters Lehrjahre, 171
    Wilhelm Meisters Wanderjahre, 171
    Xenien von Schiller und Goethe, 145
    and Adolf Wagner, 131–32
    and Diderot's *Rameau's Nephew*, 143
    and German idealism, 175
    and Greeks, 100, 153, 158
    and Luther, 159–61
    as theologian, 252
    Christology of, 159
    letters to Schiller, 144, 153
    marriage of Greeks and German, 100, 131, 158
    on nature, 198
    on theatre, 157
    on Trinity, 159
    use of alliteration, 90
    Wagner's editions of, 153
    Wagner's knowledge of, 3, 153–54
Goethe, *Faust I*, *see also Gretchen*
    Prolog im Himmel, 128
    Nacht, 156
    Studierzimmer I, 156, 159
    Studierzimmer II, 81, 156
    Auerbachs Keller, 156
    compared to *Ring*, 157–58
    performance of, 11–2, 158
    translation of John 1:1 in, 41, 159
Goethe, *Faust II*, *see also Gretchen*, 11–12, 156, 163
    Klassische Walpurgisnacht, 100, 158
    Chorus Mysticus in, 157, 162, 182
    compared to *Ring*, 157–58
    not intended for performance, 12, 158
Goethestiftung, 156

Good Friday, 210–11
    speculative, 209, 211
Gospel of John, *see also Index of Biblical Texts*
    as tragedy, 127
    evolution of, 10
    Fichte on, 179–180
    Holy Spirit in, 210
    in *Jesus of Nazareth*, 254
    Lessing on, 256–57
    on love, 208, 257
Gospels, Synoptic
    agony in Gethsemane, 207
    Griesbach on, 259
    Lachmann on, 252
    Lessing on, 256–57
    C.H. Weisse on, 253, 259
grail (myths/legends of)
    as transfigured Nibelung hoard, 25
    in *Lohengrin*, 24, 27, 111
    in *Parsifal*, 3, 27
    in *Wibelungen*, 24–25, 27
Grand Opera, 16, 58
Green, Roger Lancelyn, 97
Greek epic, 14, 50, 57, 101, 108–115, 139–40
Greek history, *see Alexander the Great; Dorians; Herodotus*
Greek mythology, *see also Apollo, Artemis; Dionysus; Hera; Heracles; Hermes; Zeus etc.*, 111
    and epic, 57, 109–11, 113–14, 139–40
    elucidating Norse mythology, 122–23
    in *Ring*, 121–23
    Oedipus in, 111, 121–22, 125, 138
    Wagner's interest in, 3, 101
Greek philosophy, *see Anaxagoras; Aristotle; Plato*
Greek tragedy, *see tragedy, Greek*
Gregory of Tours, 51, 55
Gretchen (Goethe's *Faust*)
    as redeemer, 162
    as Una Poenitentia, 162
    guilt of, 154, 160–61
    in Liszt's *Faust Symphony*, 157
Grieg, Edvard, 44
Grimhild (Norse mythology), 15, 83, 85
Grimhild (historical), 51
Grimm, Jacob, *see also Index of Authors*,
    on Norse/Germanic mythology, 58–62
    on "paganism", 60–62
    criticism of Chrétien de Troyes, 61
Grimm, Wilhelm, *see Index of Authors*,
Grímnismál, 75, 77, 98
Grípisspá, 71, 80–81
Grottasöngr, 70, 72

INDEX OF SUBJECTS AND NAMES

Gudrun, 15, 51, 55, 83–84
Gudrun, 49, 87
Gudrúnarkvida in fyrsta, 72
Gudrúnarkvida in forna, 72
Gudrúnarkvida in thridja, 72
Gudrúnarhvöt, 72
Gundaharius, 51
Gunnar (Norse mythology), 51, 55, 76, 83–84
Gunnars Harfenschlag (*Gunnar's harp-playing*), 72
Gunther (*Götterdämmerung/Siegfried's Tod*), 14, 27, 55
Gunther (*Nibelungenlied*), 51–53, 55, 57
Gutrune/Gudrune (*Götterdämmerung/Siegfried's Tod*), 14, 52, 55, 84
Gylfaginning, see also *Prose Edda*, 22, 48, 67–68, 72
Gylfi, 67–68

Habeneck, François, 154
Hagen (*Götterdämmerung/Siegfried's Tod*), 14, 22, 27–28, 56–57, 90, 98, 120
Hagen (*Nibelungenlied*), 22, 26, 52–54, 56–57
Hagen, Friedrich von der, *see also Heldenbuch; Index of Authors*
    Edda, 48, 63–64, 69–70, 91–92
    Heldenbuch, 49, 66, 88–89
    Nibelungen, Die, 58
    Nibelungenlied, 58
    Wilkina- und Niflungen saga, 49
    criticism of, 63
Hahn, Johann Michael, 182
Hahn, Philipp Matthäus, 182
Hákonarmál, 86, 98
Hamdismál, 72
Hans Sachs, 50
Hárbardsljöd, 71
Hattatal, 69
Hávamál, 23, 71, 74
Haydn, Franz Joseph, 256
Hegel, Georg Wilhelm Friedrich, *see also Index of Authors*
    Differenzschrift, 180, 195–96
    Encyclopaedia I (*Logic*), 194, 196, 216
    Encyclopaedia III (*Philosophy of Mind*), 214
    Lectures on the Philosophy of History, 18, 23, 64, 115, 192, 194, 197, 200–1, 203–7, 210, 216
    Lectures on the Philosophy of Religion, 174, 197, 215–16
    Life of Jesus (*Leben Jesu*), 208
    Love, 199
    Phenomenology of Spirit, 181, 190, 192, 195, 198, 207, 209, 211–13, 215–16
    Philosophy of Right, 101, 200, 208
    Reason in History (*Vernunft in der Geschichte*), 197, 203
    Science of Logic, 197, 208, 213–14
    Spirit of Christianity, 199–200
    absolute idealism of, 191, 194–97
    and Kant, 193
    and Luther, 212
    and Spinoza, 193–94
    as objective idealist, 197
    as Spinozist, 195
    attacked by Schopenhauer, 177
    heterodoxy of, 213–17
    influence on Adolf Wagner, 191
    influence on C.H. Weisse, 183, 191
    on absolute knowing, 212–13
    on categories, 193
    on Christianity as absolute religion, 207, 215
    on death of God, 191, 207, 209–13, 236
    on Dionysus, 215
    on ethics, 199
    on Fichte, 93
    on finite/infinite, 213–14
    on freedom, 193–94, 200, 207, 211, 215
    on God, 194, 197, 206–7, 209–16, 236
    on history, 18, 23, 64, 115, 192, 194, 197, 200–201, 203–7, 210, 216
    on human agency, 194
    on idea, 197, 200–202
    on immortality, 213, 216–17
    on incarnation, 207, 209, 214–15
    on love, 191, 194, 197–200, 208
    on mind, 199, 213
    on *Nibelungenlied*, 57
    on noumenal/phenomenal distinction, 238
    on providence, 57, 179, 191, 206–7, 216
    on reason, 192, 196–97, 201, 203, 206–7, 211, 214
    on reconciliation (*Versöhnung*), 210, 212, 215–16, 229
    on redemption (*Erlösung*), 210, 215
    on religion, absolute, 207–13
    on salvation, 214–16
    on self-consciousness, 197, 199, 205, 214–15
    on spirit (*Geist*), 198–200
    on subjectivity, 197, 209, 211, 214, 216
    on substance, 195–97, 214
    on suffering, 204
    on the absolute, 194–95, 197, 199, 214, 222
    on thing-in-itself, 197, 216
    on tragedy, 115–16, 120
    on Trinity, 207, 214
    on unhappy consciousness, 212, 215

Hegel, Georg Wilhelm Friedrich *(continued)*
   organic worldview of, 198
   Wagner's knowledge of, 191–93
Heimskringla, 46, 49, 65, 85–86
Heldenbuch, see also Gudrun; Nibelungenlied;
   kleine Heldenbuch, Das; Amelungenlied;
   Hörnen Siegfried; Etzels Hofhaltung;
   Rosengarten Lied, Das; Alpharts Tod;
   Ecken Ausfahrt; Riese Siegenot, 63, 169,
   256
   of Simrock, 37, 47, 49, 66, 87–88
   of von der Hagen, 46, 66, 89
Helgakvida Hundingsbana in fyrri, 71
Helgakvida Hjörvardssonar, 71, 76–77, 98
Helgakvida Hundingsbana önnur, 71, 98
Helreid Brynhildar, 72, 83
Helmholtz, Hermann, 44, 107
Hera, 108, 119, 123
Heracles, 123, 125, 167
Herder, Johann Gottfried von, 19, 21, 48, 61, 104,
   142–44, 165, 203, 252
Hermes, *see also Mercury*, 61
Herodotus, 104
Herwegh, Georg
   as revolutionary, 237, 255
   interest in Feuerbach, 219, 235
   introduces Wagner to Schopenhauer, 239–40,
   242, 244
Hesiod, 101, 124
Hildebrandtslied, Das (Siegfried), 89
history
   and myth, 5, 16, 18, 21, 68, 179, 226
   bare (*nackte Geschichte*), 20
   Hegel on, 18, 23, 64, 115, 192, 194, 197,
   200–201, 203–7, 210, 216
   Kant on, 203
   of religion and saga, 20
   reason in, 197, 203, 206
Hjördis, 80–81
Höd, 74, 98
Hölderlin, Friedrich, 169–70, 175, 182, 193, 195,
   198, 215
Hörnen Siegfried (von der Hagen), 89
hörnene Siegfried, Der (Simrock), 89
Hoffmann, E.T.A., 59, 131
   Fantasiestücke, 144
Hohenstaufens, *see also Frederick I (Friedrich*
   Barbarossa), 15, 20–21, 27
Holda/Freia (*Ring*), 29, 31, 123
Holy Spirit, *see also Hegel, on spirit*
   in Gospel of John, 210
   in *Jesus of Nazareth*, 33, 210
   Wagner on, 24

Homer, 101, 111, 116, 127, 132
   Iliad, 50, 57, 101, 108–9
   Odyssey, 50, 101, 108, 111
   as "indispensable", 108
   translation of Voss, 108, 168
homosexuality, 6
Hrafnagaldr Odhins (Odin's raven-magic), 72, 77
human, purely (*rein menschlich*), 26, 96, 112
Hürnen Seyfrid, Das Lied von, 50, 58
Hürnen Seufrid (Hans Sachs), 50
Hunding (*Nibelungen-Mythus*), 31
Hunding (*Norse mythology*), 71, 79–81
Hunding (*Walküre*), 7, 89, 121
Hymiskvida, 71
Hyndluljód, 72

idealism
   absolute, 191, 194–97
   objective, 175, 197
   subjective, 175, 178
immortality
   Feuerbach on, 218, 230, 232
   Hegel on, 213 216–17
   Kant on, 175
   of soul, 216
   Siegmund's rejection of, 7–8, 217, 227, 232
incarnation, viii
   Feuerbach on, 228–29
   Hegel on, 207, 209, 214–15
   of Brünnhilde, 209, 228–29
   of Christ, 209, 229
   Wagner on, 209, 214
Irenaeus, 257
Isaiah, book of, 10
Isolde, *see also Index of Wagner's Works (Tristan*
   und Isolde), 251
   transfiguration of, 126

Jacobi, Friedrich Heinrich, 195, 208
James, letter of, *see also Index of Biblical Texts*,
   and Wagner's socialism, 261
   in *Jesus of Nazareth*, 261
Jean (Johann) Paul Richter, 59, 144
Jerome, St (Hieronymus), 257
Jesus Christ/Jesus of Nazareth
   as preacher of love, 208
   as redeemer, 4, 25, 34, 147, 225
   as representative, 234
   as savior, 147, 224, 257, 259
   as Son, 23–24
   as (spiritual) father of all, 23
   as non-Jew, 179–80
   baptism of, 33, 210
   birth of, 33, 254

INDEX OF SUBJECTS AND NAMES

blood of, 120
crucifixion of, 33, 210, 213, 228, 236, 260
death of, 23, 33, 98, 180, 206, 210–11, 215–16, 234, 236, 254, 259–60
divinity of, 188, 224, 226
incarnation of, 209, 229
kingdom of, 34
miracles of, 254
on freedom, 254
presence in his followers, 254
resurrection of, 254
sacrifice of, 3, 6, 98, 180, 188, 207, 215–16, 261
second coming of, 147–48
suffering of, 216, 236
Jewish people, 7, 23, 257
as "enemy within", 109
Feuerbach on, 230
in music, 38
Nietzsche on, 249–50
Schiller on, 146
Joachim, Joseph, 43
John, Gospel of, *see Gospel of John*
Judaism, *see also* anti-Judaism; Index of Wagner's Works (*Judaism in Music*)
Nietzsche on, 249–51
F. Schlegel on, 165
Schiller on, 144, 146
superceded by Christianity, 146–47
Wagner on, 7
Judas Iscariot, 98, 259
Judgement of world, 74, 76, 165
Jupiter (god), 22, 61

Kabbala, Jewish, 182
Kant, Immanuel, *see also* Index of Authors, 19, 143, 175, 177, 184, 191, 195, 207–8, 223, 235, 248
Critique of Pure Reason, 174–76, 193, 238
Critique of Practical Reason, 193
Critique of the Power of Judgement, 186
as subjective idealist, 197
influence on Schiller, 144
influence on Schopenhauer, 174, 238
influence on Wagner, 174–76
on categories, 176
on concept (*Begriff*), 196
on faith, 179
on freedom, 176
on history, 203
on immortality, 175
on noumenal/phenomenal distinction, 195, 238
on practical reason, 176
on pure reason, 174, 175–76, 193, 238
on space and time, 176
on teleology, 198
Wagner's admiration for, 173, 176, 243, 256
Karl the Great (Charlemagne), 22–23, 25, 27
Keller, Gottfried, 218
Kellermann, Berthold, 44–45
kingdom of God, 34, 165, 211, 216, 258
Klaproth, Julius, 165–66
kleine Heldenbuch, Das (Simrock), *see also Walther und Hildegunde*; *Alphart*; *hörnene Siegfried, Der*; *Rosengarten, Der*; *Hildebrandtslied, Das*; *Ortnit*, 49, 87, 89
Klemm, Gustav, 12
Klindworth, Karl, 263
knowing
absolute, 212–13
science of, 213
Kriemhilt (*Nibelungenlied*), 52–57
Krüger, Eduard, 192
Kundry (as Sphinx), 125

Lachner, Franz, 253
Lagarde, Paul Anton de, 39
law of Moses, *see also* Index of Biblical Texts
and Paul of Tarsus, 6, 260
condemning function of, 6
on homosexuality, 6
law, primeval (*Urgesetz*), 249
Lehrs, Franz Siegfried (born Levi, Samuel), 102, 218
Leibniz, Gottfried Wilhelm
on monads, 186–87
on organic worldview, 186–87, 198
Leipzig
Nikolaischule, 101–2
Thomaskirche, 239
Thomasschule, 102
leitmotifs
as melodic moments/impulses, 202
as teleological, 202
"glorification of Brünnhilde", 212
"nature" motifs, 4
"Rheingold", 4
"Siegfried", 118, 210
"Siegmund's rebellion", 8
"Volsung", 118
von Wolzogen on, 212
Lessing, Gotthold Ephraim, 131, 252, 255–57
Anti-Goeze, 256
Eine Duplik, 256
Hamburgische Dramaturgie, 256
Laokoon (*Laocoon*), 109, 256
Nathan der Weise, 256

Lessing, Gotthold Ephraim *(continued)*
   Neue Hypothese über die Evangelisten, 256
   Testament Johannis, Das, 256–57
   Theses aus der Kirchengeschichte, 256
   Ueber den Beweis des Geistes und der Kraft, 256
   and Reimarus, 254, 256
   on God, 195
   on gospels, 256–57
   on historical Jesus, 254, 256
   on Winkelmann, 256
   Wagner's praise of, 131
Lewes, G.H., 153
Lewis, C.S., 97
Linder, Ernst Otto, 243
Lippmann, Edmund von, 212
Lippmann, Eduard von, 212
Liszt, Franz, 33, 59
   Dante Symphony, 132–33
   Faust Symphony, 156–57
   Tasso, 156
   and *Wieland der Schmied*, 37
   attends *Walküre* (1870), 43
   attends *Ring* (1876), 44
   conducts Dorn's *Die Nibelungen*, 58
   conducts *Lohengrin*, 156
   in Weimar, 156
   supports *Goethestiftung*, 156
   Wagner's gratitude to, 45
   Wagner's letters to, 2, 37, 39, 41, 43, 110–11, 132, 134, 155, 176, 190, 239, 242–45, 247
ljodahattr, 91–92, 96
Loge, 28–29, 58, 209
   as Hephaestus, 125
   as Prometheus, 123
Lohengrin (*Lohengrin*)
   as failed redeemer, 119
Lohengrin (*Die Wibelungen*), 24
Lokasenna (*Oegisdrecka*), 71, 77
Loki, 28, 49, 68, 75, 78, 81,
   as Judas Iscariot, 98
love, *see also* erotic love
   replaces Hegel's "spirit", 213
   and death, 2
   and hoard, 26
   and power, viii, 5
   and spirit (Hegel), 198–200
   and state, 125
   as eternal feminine, 210
   as redeemer, 221
   cognitive nature of, 234
   conflicts with "faith", 7–8, 226
   erotic, 29, 232–33
   Feuerbach on, 221, 225–27

   free love, 25, 251
   God as, 209, 226, 228–29
   Hegel on, 191, 194, 197–200, 208
   in Dante's *Comedia*, 133
   in *Jesus* sketches, 231–32, 261
   in John's gospel, 208, 257
   in 1 John, 209, 257
   in Schlegel's *Lucinde*, 164
   in *Testament of John*, 257
   Luther on, 225–26
   music expressing love itself, 245
   of Agamemnon, 126
   of Antigone, 120
   of Brünnhilde, 92–93, 124
   of Fasold/Fasolt, 89
   of Jesus Christ, 211, 226–27, 234
   of God, 197, 209, 227–28
   of Prometheus, 124
   of Sieglinde, 7, 39, 119–20
   of Siegmund, 7, 39, 119–20
   of Sigurd, 83
   of Sivrit, 53, 55
   of Wotan, 39
   opposed to egoism, 230
   opposed to faith, 226
   opposed to law, 7, 221
   Paul on, 6
   potion, 15
   redemption from erotic love, 248
   redemption through (erotic) love, 30, 127, 212, 248
   replaces "faith" (Rom 3:28), 260
   self-love, 227, 230–31
   sexual, 231
   suffering of, 247
   Wagner's New Testament markings on, 260
   within Trinity, 24
Ludwig II
   and 1869 performance of *Rheingold*, 43–44
   and 1870 performances of *Rheingold* and *Walküre*, 43–44
   "rescues" Wagner, 8, 41–42
   Wagner's letters to, 106, 167, 256
Luria, Isaac, 198
Luther, Martin, *see also* Communion, 143
   On the Bondage of the Will, 228–29
   Shorter Catechism, 212
   and death of God, 210
   and Feuerbach, 217–18, 223–29, 231, 235–36
   and Goethe's *Faust*, 159–61
   "anger against Pope" of, 149
   as German nationalist, 145
   bible translation of, 33, 108, 138, 149, 151, 156, 159, 256, 261

deus absconditus/revelatus, 225, 228–29
   on baptism, 212
   on Communion, 128, 147
   on faith, 226
   on God, 224
   on music, 128
   on reality, 21
   on sin, 142, 144
   on word of God, 21
   Wagner's admiration for, 6, 161–62, 127
Lutheranism
   Formula of Concord, 210, 223–24
   and Feuerbach, 227, 238
   and Kurfürst Moritz of Saxony, 205
   and Wagner, 127, 238
   pessimism of, 127

Mars (god), 22
Marx, A.B., 192
Marx, Karl, 217, 222–23, 236–37
   Wagner's knowledge of, 35, 174, 237
   on Wagner, 237
Medieval mythology, 169
Mendelssohn, Felix Bartholdy, 13, 38, 102
   Die Märchen von der schönen Melusine, 8–9
   Saint Paul, 257
   and Bach's *St Matthew Passion*, 260
   and Wagner's antisemitism, 38
   Wagner's debt to, 8–9, 244
Mendelssohn, Moses, 195
Mendès, Catulle, 43
Mercury, 22, 61
Meyerbeer, Giacomo,
   Les Huguenots (Die Welfen und Ghibellinen), 20
Meysenbug, Malwide von, 169
Michel, Oskar, 180
Midgard serpent (Norse mythology), 62, 75
Mime (*Ring*), 38, 58, 76, 82, 129
   as master in technology, 38–39
   as synagogue singer, 38
Mone, Franz Joseph, 18, 46, 50, 62–64
monism
   of Hegel, 196
   of Spinoza, 195, 197
Moses, *see also* law of Moses
   Schiller on, 146
Mozart, Wolfgang Amadeus, 256
   Don Giovanni, 128
Müller, Christian Gottlieb, 130, 183
Müller, Franz Carl Friedrich, 11, 46, 49, 63
music, *see also* Gesamtkunstwerk
   absolute, 148–49
   and Hegel, 201
   and Jewish people, 38
   and lyric, 112
   as feminine, 1
   as idea itself, 201, 208
   as objectification of the will, 201
   as "Word of God", 235
   Church, 4, 97
   enables existential change, 235
   eternal feminine as, 163
   expressing love itself, 245
   in Church, 4, 97
   Luther on, 128
   "married" to poet/poetry, 1
   origins of, 141
   rationality for development of spirit, 202
   Schopenhauer on, 245
   Zwingli on, 128
music drama, 16, 127, 148
mysticism, *see also* Böhme, Jakob; Luria, Isaac; Tauler, Johannes
   and Feuerbach, 223
   and Hegel, 198
   and von Baader, 181
   Jewish, 198
myth, *see also* Greek mythology; Medieval mythology; Norse/Germanic mythology
   and allegory, 4, 21, 188–89
   and epic, 57–58, 109–11, 113–14, 139–40
   and history, 5, 16–18, 21, 68, 179, 226
   R. Bultmann on, 2
   Christian, 58, 254
   dramatic, 138–40
   Feuerbach on, 238
   Fichte on, 179
   Germanic, 2–3, 47, 63, 122
   Greek, 3, 101, 111, 113–14, 121–23
   Herder on, 21
   mixes human and divine, 122
   Norse, 2–3, 63, 97–98
   of Adam and Eve, 67, 76
   of grail, 3, 24–25, 27, 111
   of Melusine, 9
   of Nibelungs, 21–22, 26, 28
   of Oedipus, 111, 121–22, 125, 138
   ontology of, 21
   Schelling on, 187–90
   D.F. Strauß on, 254
   Wagner as myth-maker, 3, 94, 110, 113–14, 122–23, 139–40, 190, 226
   "work on", 123
mythology, *see* Greek mythology; Medieval mythology; Norse/Germanic mythology

nationalism
  and *Nibelungenlied*, 50
  Nietzsche on, 249
  of Droysen, 105, 109, 123
  of Fichte, 177
  of Hegel, 109
  of Schiller, 145
  of Wagner, 177, 249–50
Nepos, Cornelius, 129
Neumann, Angelo
  Ring production in Berlin of, 167
Nibelunc, (*Nibelungenlied*), 54, 56
Nibelungenlied, *see also* Albrich, Etzel, Gernot, Gibich, Giselher, Gunther, Hagen, Kriemhilt, Nibelunc, Prünhilt, Rü[e]deger, Schilbunc, Sivrit, Uote
  as tragedy, 52–53
  authorship, 50
  Christianity in, 54
  compared to Homer, 50, 57, 109
  dating, 50
  discovery of, 50
  Hegel on, 57
  historical sources of, 51–52
  nationalism and, 50
  A.W. Schlegel on, 50, 169
  F. Schlegel on, 50
  Wagner's editions of, 47–49, 57–58
  Wagner's criticism of, 57
  Wagner's praise of, 57
Nibelungs
  "doom of", 52–53
  myth of, 21–22, 26, 28
  Nibelungen-Mythus, Der, 11, 17, 28–31, 38, 78, 249
  redemption of, 28, 54
Nietzsche, Friedrich
  Beyond Good and Evil, 249–50
  Birth of Tragedy, 102, 127, 188
  The Case of Wagner, 201
  David Strauss the Confessor and the Writer, 253
  Ecce homo, 250
  Genealogy of Morals, 250
  Nietzsche contra Wagner, 249–50
  and tragedy, 127–28
  attacks Wagner, 249–51
  first meeting with Wagner, 148–49
  on antisemitism, 249–50
  on Brünnhilde, 251
  on Christianity, 251
  on Hegel, 201
  on Judaism, 249–51
  on Schelling, 201
  on Schopenhauer, 248, 251
  on *Tristan und Isolde*, 251
Niord, 65
Norns (*Nibelungen-Mythus*), 4, 29–30
Norns (*Ring*), 32, 37, 54, 59, 111–12
Norns (*Völsunga Saga*), 80
Norse/Germanic mythology, *see also* Elder Edda; Prose Edda
  and Christian theology, 97–99
  as deception, 67–68
  J. Grimm on, 58–62
  von der Hagen on, 63
  Mone on, 63–64
noumenal-phenomenal distinction, *see also* thing-in-itself, 193, 238
Novalis (Hardenberg, Georg Philipp Friedrich Freiherr von), 62, 131, 164, 175, 180, 198

Odin, 65, 73, 76, 79, 80–82, 86–88
  and white horse (Rev 6:2), 75
  as nature-god, 22
  crucifixion of, 23
  identified as "Just-as-high", 67
Oddrúnargrátr, 72
Oedipus, *see also* Antigone; myth, of Oedipus; Sophocles, Antigone
  and *Parsifal* Act II, 125
  and *Siegfried* Act III, 125
Oetinger, Friedrich Christoph, 182, 198
Old Testament, *see also* law of Moses
  and tradition history, 10
  contradictions in, 82
  fall in, 165
  idea of kingship, 27
  in Prose Edda, 67
  law in, 6
  Nietzsche on, 249–50
  relation to the New Testament, 97, 257
  Ring likened to, vii
  Schiller on, 146
  sea monsters in, 76
orchestra
  as chorus, 115, 117–18, 145
  as dance-gesture (*Tanzgebärde*), 140
  invisible, 40
  of *Ring*, 1
  omnipresent, 172
original sin
  Luther on, 142
  Schopenhauer on, 142, 244–45
  Wagner on, 142, 244–45
Ortnit (Simrock), 89
Otto von Freisingen, 20

INDEX OF SUBJECTS AND NAMES

"paganism", 97
    Arnkiel on, 97
    Creuzer on, 101
    Fichte on, 180
    Hegel on, 57
    Jacob Grimm on, 60–62
    Wagner on, 8
pantheism, 232
Paul of Tarsus/St Paul, *see also Index of Biblical Texts*
    as former Pharisee, 6
    Christ as representative in, 234
    conversion of, 238
    Fichte on, 180
    on freedom from law, 260
    on homosexuality, 6
    on law, 6, 260
    on love, 260
    on redemption, 6
Pecht, Friedrich, 192
Paulus, H.E.G., 217
Pentateuch, 10
Phantasie/phantasy, 113–14, 139–41
Pharisees
    in *Festspielhaus*, 251
    in *Jesus of Nazareth*, 33–34, 260
    in New Testament, 34, 260
    Paul as former, 6,
phenomenal world, 195, 238
Pilate, Pontius
    in *Jesus of Nazareth*, 33, 260
Planer, Minna, *see Wagner, Minna*
Plato, 116, 163, 173–74, 196
    Critias, 107
    Laws, 107
    Symposium, 107
    Timaeus, 107
    Schleiermacher's translation of, 107, 163
    Schopenhauer's admiration for, 173
    Wagner's admiration for, 107, 173
poetic intent (*dichterische Absicht*), 115, 149
poetry, *see also Goethe; Hölderlin; Rückert; Schiller; Schlegel, Friedrich; Uhland*
    Eddic, 66, 91–93
    end-rhyme, 4, 94, 97
    French, 146
    lyric, 112–15
    Stabreim, 4–5, 59, 77, 90–97, 130
    "universal", 163
Porges, Heinrich, 11, 126
power, 2
    and love, viii, 5
    of Agamemnon, 126
    of Alberich, 29–30
    of Wotan, 31, 142, 245
    will to power, 230, 249
property
    in *Ring*, 27
    Jesus on (according to Weitling), 255
    Proudhon on, 334
    Wagner on, 25–26, 36
Prose Edda, see also Gylfaginning, Skaldskaparmal, Hattatal
    authorship of, 66
    date of, 66
    Prologue of, 66–67
    Wagner's editions of, 48, 68
Protestantism, 127, 223–24, 228
Proudhon, Pierre Joseph, 34–35, 237
providence
    Hegel on, 57, 179, 191, 206–7, 216
Prünhilt (*Nibelungenlied*), 3, 53–56, 99
Puccini, Giacomo (*Tosca*), 130
purely human, *see human, purely*

race
    Aryan, 166–67
    Chamberlain on, 167–68
    Gobineau on, 167–68
    F. Schlegel on, 166–67
    A.W. Schlegel on, 168
    semitic, 167
    Wagner on, 166–68
Racine, Jean-Baptiste, 103, 141
Ragnarök, 62, 67–68, 73, 230
Raphael (*Sistine Madonna*), 147
Raupach, Ernst (*Der Nibelungen-Hort*)
    Eugel in, 57
    Siegfried in, 57
reason (*Vernunft*)
    desire and, 211
    faith and, 175–76, 179, 208
    Feuerbach on, 222, 231
    Hegel on, 192, 196–97, 201, 203, 206–7, 211, 214
    in history, 197, 203, 206
    infinite of, 214
    Lessing on, 256
    practical, 176
    pure, 174, 175–76, 193, 213, 238
    Schopenhauer on, 248
    Wagner on, 113–14, 138–40
reconciliation
    Hegel on 210, 212, 215–16, 229
    in Greek tragedy, 105, 119–20
redeemer
    Brünnhilde as, 4, 210
    Christ as, 25, 34, 47

redeemer *(continued)*
   God as, 225
   Gretchen as, 162
   Lohengrin as (failed), 119
   love as, 221
   Siegfried as, 210
redemption, viii, 5, 76, 138, 147, 156, 165, 168, 232, 261
   and eternal womanly, 162–63
   central to Wagner, 127, 216
   from erotic love (Schopenhauer), 248
   Hegel on, 210, 215
   in Goethe's *Faust*, 162–63
   of Brünnhilde, 251
   of Nibelungs, 28, 54
   of the world, 138
   through love, 30, 127, 212, 248
   through sacrifice, 6, 98, 210
Regin, 38, 71, 76, 80–82
Reginsmál, 70–71, 77
reincarnation, 138, 247
Reimarus, Hermann Samuel, 254, 256
   Von dem Zwecke Jesu und seiner Jünger, 254
religion, *see also* Catholicism; Christianity; faith, Christian; Judaism; Protestantism; Index of Wagner's Works (Religion and Art)
   absolute, 207–13, 215, 223, 229
   aesthetic, 146
   as dream of mind, 222
   as oppressive, 160–61, 254
   Creuzer on, 101
   dogma-free, 134
   Dorian, 112
   Feuerbach on, 221–222
   in Greek tragedy, 117, 121–23
   legal, 258
   of Iceland, 64–65
   pagan/heathen, 8, 57, 60–62, 68, 97, 101, 180
   Pelasgian, 101, 109, 112
Renan, Ernst, 167
renunciation
   of divinity, 229
   of the will, 247
   of the world, 240, 243
repentance
   Amfortas' inability for, 120
   Luther on, 212
resurrection
   Feuerbach on, 226
   Hegel on, 211, 215
   Lessing on, 256
   Luther on, 212
   Strauß on, 254
   Wagner on, 254

Woolston on, 254
revelation, *see also* myth
   abstract, 3
   and Shakespeare, 135
   Feuerbach on, 229
   Fichte on, 184, 193, 207
   in tradition history, 3
   "original", 165
   Schelling on, 84–85
   Wagner on, 147, 221
Rhinemaidens (*Götterdämmerung*), 57, 138
Richter, Hans, 44
Richter, Jean (Johann) Paul, 59, 144
Rígsthula, 72
ring (Andvaranaut), 81, 83
ring (in *Wieland*), 36
ring (of Nibelung), 28–31, 37, 55, 138
Rist, Johann, 211–12
Röckel, August, 37, 41
   as revolutionary, 35
   Völksblätter, 220
   Wagner's letters to, 3, 39, 177, 190, 207, 210, 219, 231, 235
Romans, 22, 33, 51, 109
Rosengarten, Der (Simrock), 89
Rosengarten Lied, Das (von de Hagen), 89
Rosenberg, Alfred, 140
Rousseau, Jean Jacques, 141–42, 152
Rousseau, Johann Baptist, 141
Rückert, Friedrich, 90
Rü[e]deger (*Nibelungenlied*), 57

sacrifice, *see also* Jesus Christ, sacrifice of; redemption
   in Old Testament, 3
   of Baldr, 98
   of Brünnhilde, 6, 98, 126, 207, 210
   of Dionysus, 188
   of God, 211
   of Iphigenia, 126
   of Jesus, 3, 6, 98, 180, 188, 207, 215–16, 261
   of Siegfried, 6, 126, 210
Saga of Ynglings, 86
Saint-Saëns, Camille, 43–44
salvation, *see also* redemption
   Feuerbach on, 224, 226–27
   Hegel on, 214–16
   Wagner on, 6
satyr play, 118–19
savior, *see Jesus Christ*
Schelling, Friedrich Wilhelm Joseph von, 19, 169, 181–90, 238
   Bruno, 199
   Essence of Human Freedom, 187

INDEX OF SUBJECTS AND NAMES

Ideas for a Philosophy of Nature, 185, 187
On the World Soul, 187, 198
System of Transcendental Idealism, 181–85, 187–89
and Hegel, 191, 193–95, 199
attacked by Schopenhauer, 177, 181
influence on Adolf Wagner, 184
influence on Richard Wagner, 174, 182–89
interest in romanticism, 175
Naturphilosophie of, 180, 186, 195,
on the absolute, 194–95, 199
on art, 189
on Dionysus, 170, 188
on fall, 181–82, 187–89
on freedom, 176
on *Gesamtkunstwerk*, 189
on myth/mythology, 101, 187–90
on nature, 185–87
on noumenal/phenomenal distinction, 238
on organic worldview, 108, 186–87, 199
on teleology, 179
Wagner's criticism of, 184–85
Wagner's knowledge of, 182–89
Schilbunc (*Nibelungenlied*), 54, 56
Schiller, Johann Christoph Friedrich von
An die Freude (Ode to Joy), 148–50
Deutsche Genius, 145
Die Braut von Messina, 40, 128, 145
Die Freundschaft, 213
Die Jungfrau von Orleans, 146, 148
Don Carlos, 150, 167
Über die ästhetische Erziehung, 151–53
Über naïve und sentimentalische Dichtung, 152
Xenien von Schiller und Goethe, 145
Wallenstein, 150
letters to Goethe, 14, 146, 178
nationalism of, 145
on God, 150
on Judaism, 144, 146
on Moses, 146
on theatre and state, 150–52
Wagner's edition of, 144
Schimmelmann, Jacob, 67
Schleiermacher, Friedrich Daniel Ernst, 107, 163, 235
Schlegel, A.W., see also Index of Authors, 252
De l'Origine des Hindous, 168
Kritische Schriften, 168–69
Vorlesungen über dramatische Kunst und Literatur, 120, 168–69
on *Antigone*, 120
on Greeks, 100, 168–69
on Indology, 168
on *Nibelungenlied*, 50, 169
translation of Shakespeare, 135–38, 168
Schlegel, Friedrich, see also Index of Authors
Athenæm Fragments, 163, 180
Geschichte der Poësie der Griechen und Römer, 112
Geschichten der alten and neuen Literatur, 163
Lucinde, 164, 171
Über den Anfang unserer Geschichte, 19, 166
Über die Sprache und Weisheit der Indier, 19, 26, 104, 163–66
Vorlesungen über Universalgeschichte, 19, 165
and German idealism, 175
as theologian, 252
Indo-German hypothesis, 19, 24, 164–68
on Aryans, 166
on Fichte, 180
on *Gesamtkunstwerk*, 163, 189
on Judaism, 165
on love and sex, 164
on *Nibelungenlied*, 50
on organic worldview, 198
on *Universalpoesie*, 163
suggested translation of Plato, 107
Schlesier, Gustav, 101, 184
Schlesinger, Maurice (Moritz), 184
Schopenhauer, Arthur, see also *sufficient reason, principle of*, xiv
admires Kant, 107, 173
admires Plato, 107, 173
and Beethoven, 201
and Oxenford, 240, 243–44
and *Siegfried* Act III, 246–47
and *Walküre* Act II, 245–46
as Kant's "continuator", 176, 238
as subjective idealist, 175, 197
attacks Fichte, 177
attacks Hegel, 177, 206
attacks Schelling, 177
dating Wagner's "discovery" of, 240–45
German disciples of, 143
Herwegh's introduction, 239–41
influence on *Parsifal*, vii
influence on *Ring*, vii, 174, 190, 245–48
interest in romanticism, 175
Nietzsche admires, 248
Nietzsche criticizes, 251
on concept (*Begriff*), 248
on denial of the will, 243, 246–48
on erotic love, 248
on music, 245
on noumenal/phenomenal distinction, 238
on original sin, 142

Schopenhauer, Arthur *(continued)*
   on thought and language, 143
   on reason, 248
   on renunciation, 240, 243, 247
   on subject-object, 186, 248
   on will, 187
   opposes categorical imperative, 176, 238
   parroted by Wagner, 200–201.
   problems of, 248
   receives *Ring* libretto, 41
   Ring's Schopenhauer ending, 247
   Wagner on, 238–47
Schumann, Robert, 13, 169, 192
Scott, Walter, 110, 131, 171–72
self-consciousness
   Fichte on, 178, 193
   Hegel on, 197, 199, 205, 214–15
   Wagner on, 197, 205
serpent (killed by Sigurd), *see Fáfnir*
serpent (Nidhauggr), 74–76
serpent (Rev 20:2), 62, 76
Seydlitz, Reinhardt von, 45
sexual desire, *see erotic love*
Shaw, George Bernard, 35, 190
Shakespeare, William
   Hamlet, 134, 137
   Henry IV Part I, 135, 137
   King Lear, 134, 137–38
   Macbeth, 116, 134, 137–38
   Measure for Measure, 137
   Othello, 131, 136
   Richard III, 135
   Romeo and Juliet, 137
   as counterpart to Beethoven, 135
   as tragedian, 134, 138
   Cassio, 131
   Hamlet, 121
   Henry IV, 135
   Lear, 121
   Othello, 121
   Schlegel-Tieck translation, 131, 135–38, 168
   superior dramatist to Goethe, 137–38
   Wagner's admiration for, 103, 134, 157
Siegbert (Austrasier), 107
Siegfried (*Nibelungen-Mythus*), 29–31
Siegfried (*Ring*), *see also sacrifice; Index of Wagner's Works (Siegfried)*, 3–4, 14–15, 30, 52, 55, 59, 82, 85, 88, 119, 123, 125, 130, 209
   and Nietzsche's *Übermensch*, 249
   as "archetypal revolutionary", 251
   as Bakunin, 35
   as free hero (Rousseau), 142
   as Greek tragic hero, 138
   as Heracles, 123, 125, 167
   as redeemer, 210
   betrays Brünnhilde, 120, 207
   compared to Oedipus, 121, 138
   consciousness of, 197
   death of, 2, 98, 117, 207
   destroys Wotan's spear, 7
   like an animal with Brünnhilde, 167
   Nietzsche on, 251
   sacrifice of, 6, 126, 210
   song of (*Götterdämmerung* III), 112
   Wagner compared to, 45, 129, 183, 244
Siegfried (*Siegfried's Tod* (1848)), 32, 54
Siegfried (*Die Wibelungen*), 18–19, 21, 26
   as Apollo, 105
   as Barbarossa, 16, 18
   as Christ, 23, 26
   as Nibelung, 19, 22
   as Sun-god, 19
   blood of, 21
   death of, 21
   slays dragon, 22
Siegfried's Funeral March, 117–18
Sieglinde (*Nibelungen-Mythus*), 29, 31
Sieglinde (*Walküre*), 8, 96, 125, 212
   carries sins, 161
   love for Siegmund of, 7, 39, 119–20
   praise for Brünnhilde of, 21
Siegmund (*Nibelungen-Mythus*), 29, 31
Siegmund (*Völsunga Saga*), 79
Siegmund (*Walküre*), 5, 43, 79, 89, 117, 121, 170, 234
   as "the other", 39
   death of, 4, 39
   love for Sieglinde of, 7, 39, 119–20
   rejects immortality, 7–8, 217, 227, 232
Sigibert, 21, 51–52
Sigismund, 51
Sigrdrífa (Norse mythology), 82–83, 98–99
Sigrdrífumál, 69, 71, 77, 82–83, 98
Sigrun (Norse mythology), 98–99
Sigurd (Norse mythology), 48–49, 52–55, 58–59, 69, 71–72, 76, 78, 80, 82–85, 99
Sigurdarkvida in skamma, 72
Sillig, Julius, 101–2
Simrock, Karl, *see also Heldenbuch; Index of Authors*
   Amelungenlied, 49, 87–88
   Edda, 48, 67–68, 70, 76–77, 92
   Heldenbuch, 49, 66, 87–88
   kleine Heldenbuch, Das, 49, 87, 89
   Nibelungenlied, xiv, 47, 87
sin, original, *see original sin*
Sinfjotli (*Völsunga Saga*), 79–80

INDEX OF SUBJECTS AND NAMES

Sivrit (*Nibelungenlied*), 51–56
Skaldskaparmal, 48, 68, 80
Sleipnir, 80
Sophocles
    Antigone, 102, 116, 120, 125, 170
    Oedipus Tyrannus/Rex, 102, 111, 116, 125, 170
    Oedipus at Colonus, 116, 122
    as "indispensable", 103
soul
    immortality of, 216
    migration of, 247
species, 19, 185, 233–34
Spinoza, Benedict de (Baruch), 181, 195, 197
    on determinism, 193–94
    on nature, 173
    on substance, 173, 194–95
    Wagner on, 173
Spirit (*Geist*)
    absolute, 213
    Hegel on, 198–200
    Holy, 24, 33, 210
Stabreim, *see poetry, Stabreim*
stasimon, 117–18
state
    and theatre, 150–52
    fall of, 120
    love in relation to, 125
    personified in Creon, 120
Strauß, David Friedrich, 182, 190
    Leben Jesu, 234, 253–54
    Old Faith and New Faith, 12
    and Griesbach hypothesis, 259
    Bakunin's knowledge of, 254
    influence on Wagner, 255
    Nietzsche on, 253
    on myth, 254
    on resurrection, 254
    Wagner's sonnet for, 253
    C.H. Weisse on, 253
Sturluson, Snorri, 66, 72, 85, 87, 98
subject-object correlation (Schopenhauer), 186, 248
subjectivity
    and Fichte, 178
    and Schiller, 146
    Hegel on, 197, 209, 211, 214, 216
    Schelling on, 182–83
substance
    Hegel on, 195–97, 214
    Spinoza on, 173, 194–95
suffering
    Hegel on, 204
    of Brünnhilde, 210, 247
    of Christ, 216, 236
    of God, 133, 211
    of Gretchen, 161
    of love, 247
    of the world, 216
sufficient reason, principle of
    according to, 248
    independent of, 248
Sváva (Norse mythology), 98–99
Svipdagsmál, 72, 76–77
Swedenborg, Emanuel, 198

Tacitus, Cornelius, 22
    Germania, 22
Tauler, Johannes, 198
Tausig, Aloys, 182
Tausig, Carl, 182
Tchaikovsky, Pyotr Ilyich, 44
Theodoric the Ostrogoth, 85
Thidrek, 85
Thidrek's Saga, 64–65, 85, 88
thing-in-itself (Ding an sich) *see also noumenal-phenomenal distinction*, 197, 216
Thor (Norse mythology), 62, 65, 67–68, 76, 87
    identified as "High", 67
    opponent of Christ, 97
    parallel to Christ, 97
Thrymskvida, 71
Tieck, Ludwig, 135–38, 164
Titurel (Wagner's *Parsifal*), 24, 137
Tolkein, J.R.R. 97
tragedy, Germanic and Norse
    death of Brynhild (*Völsunga Saga*) as, 84
    death of Sigurd (*Thidrek's Saga*) as, 85
    death of Sivrit (*Nibelungenlied*) as, 53
    "Doom of the Nibelungs", 52–53
    Hürnen Seufrid (Hans Sachs) as, 50
tragedy, Greek, *see also* Aeschylus; Euripides; Sophocles; chorus (Greek tragedy), 14
    Aristotle on, 107, 121–22, 173
    "baptized" by Wagner, 127
    chorus in, 111, 115, 117–18, 121, 124–25, 145, 172
    Droysen on, 105, 115
    Hegel on, 115–16, 120
    Jesus of Nazareth as, 17
    John's Gospel as, 127
    pessimism of, 127
    reconciliation in, 105, 119–20
    Ring as, 2, 45, 118–28, 148–49
    Schiller on, 144–45
    stasimon, 117–18
    Wagner's interest in, 101–3, 110, 112–28

tragedy, Shakespearean
    and *Leubald und Adelaïde*, 134–35
    and *Ring*, 138
transfiguration
    of Brünnhilde, 209–10
    of death, 212
    of Isolde, 126
    of Nibelung hoard, 25
    through death, 254
Trinity
    Feuerbach on, 222, 231
    Goethe on, 159
    Hegel on, 207, 214
    Wagner on, 24, 159
trombone choir (*Posaunenchor*), 4
Tryggvason, King Olaf, 65, 86
Tübinger Stift, 12, 169, 181–82, 198

Uhland, Ludwig, 95, 170–71
Uhlig, Theodor, 13
    Wagner's diagram for, 113–14, 138–40, 149
    Wagner's letters to, 37–38, 77–78, 94, 110, 113, 155, 219, 237, 247
understanding (*Verstand*), 113–15, 138–40, 196, 224
    infinite of, 214
Uote, Queen (*Nibelungenlied*), 52

Vafthrúdnismál, 67, 70–71, 76
Valhalla
    in Norse mythology, 67, 86
    in Wagner's *Ring*, 2, 7–8, 29, 209, 229, 246
Valkyries
    in Norse mythology, 15, 67, 76, 83, 86–87, 98–99,
    in Wagner's *Ring*, 37, 39, 54, 59, 76, 98, 125, 229
Vanir, 65, 86
Vatke, Wilhelm, 4
Vernunft, see reason
Verstand, see understanding
Villiers de l'Isle-Adam, Philippe-Auguste, 43
Virgil
    Aeneid, 109, 111
    as Dante's guide, 133
Virgin Mary
    as eternal womanly, 162
    as *Mater dolorosa*, 162
    as *Mater gloriosa*, 157, 162
    assumption of, 126
    Sistine Madonna, 147
Vogelweide, Walther von der, 252
Volsung (*Völsunga Saga*), 79,
Völsunga Saga, 51, 64–65, 78–85

death of Brynhild in, 84
    Norns in, 80
    Siegmund in, 79
    Sinfjotli in, 79–80
    Volsung in, 79
Völund, 63
Völundarkvida, 63, 71
Völuspá, 71–76, 91, 112, 230
    Christian additions to, 73–74
    Christian theology in, 73–76, 98
Voltaire, François-Marie Arouet de, 147

Wagner, Adolf (uncle)
    and Fichte, 177
    and Hegel, 191
    and Schelling, 184
    and Schiller, 144
    and F. Schlegel's *Lucinde*, 164
    and C.H. Weisse, 259
    on Greek literature, 102
    on Italian literature, 131–32
    on Norse mythology, 58–59
Wagner, Cosima, xiv, 9, 43–44, 57, 65, 101–6, 117, 131, 134, 137–38, 143, 145–46, 150, 153, 157, 162–63, 167, 169, 171, 173, 183–84, 200–201, 212, 220, 235, 241, 246
Wagner, Luise (sister), *see* Brockhaus, Luise
Wagner, Minna (née Planer)
    and Dresden library, 47–48, 86, 108, 135
    Richard Wagner's letters to, 32, 34, 182
Wagner, Ottilie (sister), *see* Brockhaus, Ottilie
Wagner, Richard, *see also* Redemption
    admires Luther, 6, 161–62, 127
    and Angelo Neumann, 167
    anti-Judaism of, 7
    antisemitism of, 38, 180, 249–50
    as "atheist", 221
    as poet, 111, 130
    as seer, 111
    baptism of, 239, 257
    Christian faith of, 213, 251
    confirmation of, 257
    "discovery" of Schopenhauer, 238–45
    Dresden library of, 8, 12, 15, 21–22, 29, 37, 46–49, 51, 59, 63, 85–87, 89, 91, 101–8, 110, 132, 135–36, 141–42, 144, 153, 164, 170, 177, 184, 192, 220, 252, 255–56
    humor of, 218
    influenced by Luther, 142
    knowledge of Greek of, 101–2
    love for animals of, 141, 204
    New Testament edition of, 258–61
    on the absolute, 194, 201, 204
    on androgyny, 36, 164, 182, 188

on Aryans, 167
on atonement, 180
on creator God, 147, 150
on "dance", 6, 8, 117, 140
on "denial of the will",
on erotic love, 127, 232–33, 248
on eternal feminine, 163, 210
on eternity, 163
on ethics, 6–7
on Feuerbach, 235–36
on Fichte, 177
on freedom, 185, 194, 254, 260
on free will, 31
on Hegel, 200–201
on Holy Spirit, 24
on incarnation, 209, 214
on Kant, 173, 176, 243, 256
on original sin, 142, 244–45
on paganism, 8
on property, 25–26, 36
on race, 166–68
on Raphael, 147
on reason, 113–14, 138–40
on redemption, *see* redemption
on resurrection, 254
on revelation, 147, 221
on salvation, 6
on Schelling, 183–85
on Schopenhauer, 238–47
on second coming of Jesus, 147–48
on self-consciousness, 197, 205
on Shakespeare, 103, 134, 157
on species, 185, 233–34
on Spinoza, 173
on Trinity, 24, 159
pessimism of, 127, 172, 247
relation of God to world in, 163
Wahnfried library of, 8, 64, 101–3, 105, 107–8, 136, 141, 144, 147, 153, 165, 168, 171, 176–77, 182, 184–85, 201, 220, 242, 253, 255
Wagner, Rosalie (sister), 154, 245–46
Wagner, Wieland, 116, 124
Weber, Carl Maria von
  Overture to Freischütz, 129, 154, 160, 176
Weinlig, Christian Theodor, 183
Weimar (of Goethe and Schiller), 146, 152
Weisse, Christian Hermann,
  and Adolf Wagner, 191
  and Aristotle, 108, 191
  and Hegel, 183, 191

and Schelling, 174, 183, 189
on aesthetics, 183, 191, 253
on eschatology, 253
on gospels, 252–53, 259
on the resurrection,
Wesendonck (Wesendonk), Mathilde, 132–33, 153, 240–41, 248
Wiesand, Wilhelm, 239
Wigand, Otto, 219
Wilamowitz-Möllendorf, Ulrich von, 102
Wille, Eliza, 90, 240–42, 246–47
Wille, François, 240
Wittgenstein, Carolyne von Sayn, 33, 133, 244
Wolzogen, Hans von
  as editor of *Bayreuther Blätter*, xi, 5
  author of *Work and Mission*, 154
  writing on leitmotifs, 212
Woolston, Thomas, 254
World Ash Tree, *see* Yggdrasil
Wotan (Wodan, Wuotan), 3, 8, 29–31, 58, 76, 79, 93, 105, 108, 112, 121–23, 142
  and self-consciousness, 197
  as Agamemnon, 126
  as All-Father (*Allvater*), 29, 31, 229
  as god of Aryans, 167
  as Shakespearean tragic hero, 138
  death of, 209
  "denies will", 246
  devastates nature, 2
  humanity of, 39, 228–30
  identified with Christ, 18, 23, 26
  identified with Friedrich I, 18
  promotes "situation ethics", 7
  sung by Franz Betz, 44
  sung by Hans Hotter, 116
  will to power of, 249
Wüllner, Franz, 44
Wurm, 75, 81

Yahweh/Jehovah, *see also* creator God; *deus absconditus*, 147
Yggdrasil, 75–76
Ynglinga Saga, 86
Young, Thomas, 165

Zelter, Carl Friedrich, 11
Zeus, 108, 119, 123
Zwingli
  on communion, 128, 147
  on music, 128